CULTURES OF THE UNITED STATES

Second Edition

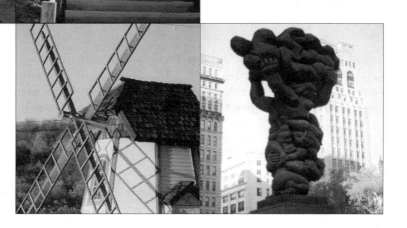

Lauren Arenson, Ph.D.
Jennifer Miller-Thayer, A.B.D.

D1279142

Printed in the United States of America

10 9 8 7 6 5 4 3 2 1

ISBN 978-0-7380-2701-2

Hayden-McNeil Publishing
14903 Pilot Drive
Plymouth, MI 48170
www.hmpublishing.com

Arenson 2701-2 F08

Table of Contents

CULTURES OF THE UNITED STATES

TABLE OF CONTENTS

CULTURES OF THE UNITED STATES

TABLE OF CONTENTS

CULTURES OF THE UNITED STATES

INTRODUCTION TO AMERICAN CULTURE

In researching for this book, we attempted to collect and categorize accounts of diverse practices exhibited by individuals living throughout the United States. The considerable amount of variation in behavioral patterns is broken down by factors which include wealth, region, ethnic background, language, gender, foods, politics, sexual preferences, religions, and actions, just to mention a few categories. While there is certainly great diversity with respect to personal and individual lifestyles, there remains a great deal of uniformity and conformity with regard to public life.

To begin our investigation of American culture, we must identify the varying patterns of learned and shared behaviors. It must also be understood that culture is transmitted socially, from one individual to the next, down through the generations. Culture consists of what we do (behavioral patterns), what we think (ideas, values, and attitudes), and what we make (material objects).

Moreover, cultural anthropology teaches us about other peoples, and in doing so, it teaches us about ourselves. Anthropological methods of investigation are different from those of other social sciences, in that it consists of translating other peoples' cultural beliefs and practices into something we all can comprehend. Anthropologists also help us to appreciate differing customs and beliefs by revealing the social context in which such actions occur. Finally, the focus of cultural anthropology is the explanation of various life ways, comparing such behavioral patterns between cultures and across generations.

L E T ' S   P O N D E R . . .

 **Let's Ponder...**

PART ONE—AN EXERCISE IN COLLECTING DATA, MAKING ASSUMPTIONS, AND VERIFYING ASSUMPTIONS

Take an object out of your book bag which reveals something about yourself. Find a partner and exchange artifacts. Do not talk to your partner during this activity.

A. Look at the object. Touch it; pick it up; turn it around. How big is it? How does it feel in your hand? What is it made of? Describe the texture, color, weight. Is it old or new? Handmade or manufactured?

B. Now, think more deeply about the artifact. Write down adjectives that come to your mind as you interact with it. Think about the artifact and the person who gave it to you. What connections can you make between the person and the artifact? Why do you think that person chose it as a representation of himself or herself? What does the artifact tell you about the person?

C. You have spent time thinking about the artifact—objectively and poetically. What is your strongest impression? Try to narrow your thoughts and express your feelings in ONE sentence—a BIG IDEA.

INTRODUCTION TO AMERICAN CULTURE

PART TWO—STORYTELLING
Spend a few minutes thinking about a story that somehow relates to your artifact. It might be about the person who gave the artifact to you, the place where you bought it, or a funny or sad story related to it. Get together with your partner and exchange stories. As you tell your story, your partner will take notes. Then, switch roles.

After hearing your partner's story, do you want to change your big idea?

PART THREE—THE INTERVIEW
After you finish telling each other a story that is somehow related to your artifact, interview each other. One person asks questions based on the cues below and takes notes based on the answers. Then, switch roles.
1. Name—What…?

2. Age and date of birth—How old…? When…?

3. Place of birth—Where…?

4. Native language—What…?

5. Length of time in the U.S.—How long…?

6. Length of time studying English—How long…?

7. Length of time in school—How long…?

8. Education: major, future plans—What…?

9. Family: single/married, siblings, children, etc.—Are you…? Do you…?

10. Interests: sports, hobbies, special talents—What…?

11. Other information to share: travel, accomplishments, goals—What…?

After the interview, do you want to change your big idea?

LET'S PONDER...

PART FOUR—THE COMPOSITION

Based on the information that you have collected, introduce your classmate. Focus your ideas. Come up with a BIG IDEA—what do you want to tell the class about this person?

WRITING ESSAYS FOR THIS CLASS

The **introduction** will include the big idea. In the **body**, include specific information that supports your big idea. Decide what is important to mention. Once again, be selective, and focus on examples that relate to the big idea. Be sure to describe the anthropological technique(s) used to first collect data, then to make assumptions, and finally, to reach accurate conclusions.

Finally, in your **conclusion**, provide some final thoughts about the subject matter being addressed.

"Let's Ponder" exercises reprinted by permission of Professor Brock Klein, Pasadena City College.

INTRODUCTION TO AMERICAN CULTURE

1 SCIENCE OF CULTURAL ANTHROPOLOGY

Cultural anthropology is the study of specific contemporary cultures and the more general underlying patterns of human behavior derived through cross-cultural comparison. Before anthropologists can examine cultural similarities and differences, they must first describe observed behaviors in detail. These detailed descriptions are the result of extensive field studies in which the researcher observes, talks to, and lives with the people he or she is studying. Thus, engaging in fieldwork is an essential practice to the cultural anthropologist. Today, anthropologists have studied a multitude of cultures, including their own, in order to gain the **anthropological perspective** (the investigation of cross-cultural comparisons.)

A distinguishing feature of the discipline is its **holistic** approach to the study of human groups. In essence, cultural anthropologists study the totality of the human experience. If you look at each chapter of this book, you will notice that each focuses on a distinct subject matter. Yet anthropologists must recognize the interconnections between all of the aspects of our lives, including family structure, marital regulations, means of making a living, conflict resolution, social organization, religious beliefs, and language, in order to understand the depth and richness within each of our lives. Comprehensively, all of these aspects (and many more) comprise the holistic approach to the investigation of culture.

Cultural anthropologists begin their research by collecting data while in the field. Over time, the raw data are transformed into a written document, or **ethnography**. An ethnography is comprised of the writings of the anthropologist, detailing the life ways of a particular culture, investigated by means of direct fieldwork. The anthropologist thus reports on how the culture being investigated views the world—from an **emic** (native's) perspective. Additionally, scientific means of analysis are utilized to grasp the objective view, or the **etic** (outsider's), perspective.

Barbara Myerhoff, in her ethnography entitled *Number Our Days*, analyzed the lives of the elderly Jewish population in Venice Beach, California. She describes anthropological research techniques in the following way:

> The anthropologist engages in peculiar work. He or she tries to understand a different culture to the point of finding it to be intelligible, regardless of how strange it seems in comparison with one's own background. This is accomplished by attempting to experience the new culture from within, living in it for a time as a member, all the while maintaining sufficient detachment to observe and analyze it with some objectivity. This peculiar posture—being inside and outside at

the same time—is called participant-observation. It is a fruitful paradox, one that has allowed anthropologists to find sense and purpose within a society's seemingly illogical and arbitrary customs and beliefs. This assumption of the native's viewpoint, so to speak, is a means of knowing others through oneself, a professional technique that can be mastered fairly easily in the study of different peoples. Working with one's own society, and more specifically, those of one's own ethnic and familiar heritage, is perilous, and much more difficult. Yet it has a certain level of validity and value not available in other circumstances. Identifying with the "Other"—Indians, Chicanos, if one is Anglo, blacks if one is white, males if one is female—is an act of imagination, a means of discovering what one is not and will never be. Identifying with what one is now and will be someday is quite a different process. (Myerhoff 1978:18)

Why do we conduct field research? That question has various answers depending on the objectives of the individual fieldworker. Some conduct cultural research in order to interpret one culture for persons in another culture. Some researchers engage in cultural research purely for scientific interest. For example, perhaps a fieldworker will seek to understand which gender role differences can be observed universally. Others engage in cultural research for pragmatic reasons. **Applied anthropologists** utilize cross-cultural studies to help others in need. For instance, as police officers work in increasingly diverse communities, their academies are emphasizing recognition of traditional ethnic practices. Applied anthropologists heighten public awareness and educate people about the various behaviors accepted in differing cultures.

Let's consider an actual case. Police arrive at a hospital to find an Asian child with bruises on his back and chest. The doctors at the hospital had phoned the police to notify them of potential child abuse. Fortunately, the police officers were led through diversity training and learned about the ancient Asian method for treating a fever, the practice of coining. The practice of lightly rubbing hot coins over the surface of the child's body is believed to have a medicinal purpose. Yet, to the outsider, attention will be focused on the severity of the lesions that may appear on the child's body for up to two days. One officer stated that without knowing about this cultural practice, he would have taken the parents to jail for felony child endangerment.

When thirty police officers were initially polled in a diversity training class as to what they would do if faced with such a situation, two-thirds agreed that they would arrest the parents and hold them accountable for child endangerment. After learning about coining as an acceptable Asian practice, some officers still believed that the parents' actions were not legal. What would you do?

We must ask the following question: As members of a society, are there times when we feel we must judge the actions of others as wrong or as jeopardizing the human rights of another, even if such behaviors are accepted in other cultures?

There are some cultural practices that are simply unaccepted in the United States. For instance, immigrants have been arrested for female circumcision, a ritual practiced in a variety of cultures, yet illegal in the United States. One such case occurred in Massachusetts, where a couple was indicted in June, 1999 on charges of mutilating the genitals of their 3-year-old daughter. However, the couple was practicing their cultural tradition.

In Laos, the Hmong tribal tradition of "marriage by capture" is considered to be an acceptable form of elopement. Yet, in the United States, it is considered kidnapping and rape. The tradition dictates that the Hmong girl feign resistance. If the prospective groom does not transport her to his home and consummate the union, he is considered too weak to be a husband.

In another example, a man was shot and killed by a Thai performer during amateur night in a nightclub in Hollywood, California for putting his shoe on the table. It was later explained to the police that pointing the sole of your foot at someone is a serious insult in Thai culture. The motive was then explained and it became much easier to find the suspect.

How are anthropologists to view such actions? Should anthropologists criticize members of a particular culture for violating basic human rights or accept the behavior as a cultural practice? Should Americans accept that different cultures have varying practices, and thus, should we remain accepting of such actions within our society? (See Chapter 11 for more on Applied Anthropology.)

Cultural anthropologists investigate the variation in such behavioral patterns and participate in the culture being investigated, in order to gather accurate facts for scientific analysis. This is referred to as **participant-observation**. Anthropologists often spend a tremendous amount of time participating with the members of the culture being investigated in order to gather first-hand knowledge and experience in how the culture operates. Anthropologists ideally strive to obtain an **emic** perspective: gaining an understanding and relevance of the worldview as seen by a member of the culture under investigation. This perspective offers a subjective viewpoint of the meaning of the concepts and categories presented to members of this culture. Yet, the anthropologist, as a social scientist, must remain objective. The **etic** perspective uses the concepts and categories designated by the researcher in order to accurately describe observations of behavioral patterns associated with a particular culture, without judgment or bias.

Studies of American culture seem to reveal a considerable consensus on a particular point. Alex Inkeles sampled American adults in the 1970s–1980s and discovered that Americans view themselves as individuals. In his book, entitled *National Character Revisited*, it was demonstrated that Americans perceive themselves as unique individuals, in a sense, "rebels without a cause." While our media depicts us as remaining true to ourselves, especially when placed in uncooperative settings, does this accurately reflect American culture? Should others correctly label American behavioral patterns as selfish, compassionless, or simply rude? Do Americans label themselves as cooperative and caring? In any case, we must be aware of the dangers associated with "labels" or **stereotyping** behavioral patterns for members of any group. Labels can lead to misrepresentations and negative social actions toward others.

It is true that American culture can be broken down into sub-groupings or **sub-cultures**. These sub-sets reflect diversity in our taste of music, religion, politics, food, and economics, to name a few. Sub-cultures reflect personal choices and decisions. For instance, a cultural anthropologist may investigate the cultural practices associated with funk music. Not only would the researcher need to investigate music choices and entertainment clubs, but the anthropologist should also investigate clothing styles, body

ornamentation, age groupings, dialect, geographical locations, social stratification, etc. We all belong to numerous sub-cultures, reflecting the diversity of values and beliefs represented in the United States.

As you will see throughout this book, one of America's greatest strengths is its diverse population. We hope that you view this book as a journey into culture. The goal is to learn about the great diversity in cultures that surround each of us, while simultaneously learning more about ourselves. This book will hopefully answer questions as to why you act, think or use objects the way you do. Most important, this book offers a variety of cultural perspectives from which each of us can choose—creating an individual lifestyle, comfortable yet harmonious for all.

Cultural Event Papers
Assignment

- Cultural similarities and differences take many forms, such as styles and forms of language, food, dress, manners, music, family, and ritual symbols. To increase your awareness and knowledge of these similarities and differences, each student **will attend a public cultural event** relating to an ethnic group, nationality, or other kind of social group with which you are not yet very knowledgeable. The group you choose should be basically different from your own main group.

- One of the purposes of this exercise is to give you some experience of doing cross-cultural fieldwork and participant-observation. This exercise will introduce you to the practice of observation, a fundamental part of doing anthropology. You will be asked to observe people, take notes on what you observe, and prepare **a short paper** describing what you observed from an anthropological perspective. You will need to use anthropological concepts and keywords in your paper. You can and should participate in activities that occur at this site and discuss your observations in your paper.

- Examples of appropriate cultural events include: a live cultural event, festival, street fair, or swap meet, visiting a museum or cultural center connected to a specific cultural group, visiting public art/murals, going to an ethnic restaurant, going to a location that has different ethnic music, etc.

A **short written proposal** for your project which includes (1) the event you are going to attend, and (2) the anthropological concepts and keywords you plan to use *prior* to you attending your event is required.

After attending your cultural event, you need to write a short paper. As you do your participant observation at the cultural event, you will need to take notes on what you observe. Include any information that will help you answer the questions listed below for your paper. **Attach your notes** from your observations to your paper.

Each paper should include the following information about the event (in no particular order):

- Describe the cultural event you attend.
- Where and when they are held and/or located?
- Who attended the event? (In general, note ages, sexes, ethnicities, etc.)
- What happened at the event?
- What culture(s) is represented at the event?
- How is the culture(s) represented (art, video, dance, song, speech, decorations, clothing, costumes, music, food, etc.)?
- What is the purpose of the event?
- What is its "message" (if it has one)?
- Who is presenting/organizing the event? Why?
- How is the site perceived from an emic perspective?
- How is the site perceived from an etic perspective?
- How does this event compare to events in your own culture (similarities and differences)?
- What did you learn about the culture(s) while attending this event? (You can also include what you already knew and how this event compared with that knowledge.)
- How does this event tie in with cultural anthropology? (Use relevant terms and definitions.)
- Any additional interesting observations you had while attending the event.

Format of the Paper
4–5 pages in length, one-inch margins, double spaced, 12 point font, notes attached.

Spell and grammar check!

Reference appropriately in your paper and include a references cited page if necessary.

Use the **ethnographic present**—writing in the present tense as though your audience is actually witnessing events as they unfold.

One Hundred Per Cent American—
Ralph Linton

Our solid American citizen awakens in a bed built on a pattern that originated in the Near East—but that was modified in Northern Europe before it was transmitted to America. He throws back covers made from cotton, domesticated in India, or linen, domesticated in the Near East, or wool from sheep, also domesticated in the Near East, or silk, the use of which was discovered in China. All of these materials have been spun and woven by processes invented in the Near East. He slips into his moccasins, invented by the Indians of the Eastern woodlands, and goes to the bathroom, whose fixtures are a mixture of European and American inventions, both of recent date. He takes off his pajamas, a garment invented in India, and washes with soap, invented by the ancients Gauls. He then shaves—a masochistic rite that seems to have been derived from either Sumer or ancient Egypt.

Returning to the bedroom, he removes his clothes from a chair of southern European type and proceeds to dress. He puts on garments whose form originally derived from the skin clothing of the nomads of the Asiatic steppes, puts on shoes made from skins tanned by a process invented in ancient Egypt and cut to a pattern derived from the classical civilizations of the Mediterranean, and ties around his neck a strip of bright-colored cloth that is a vestigial survival of the shoulder shawls worn by the seventeenth-century Croatians. Before going out for breakfast, he glances through the window, made of glass invented in Egypt, and, if it is raining, puts on overshoes made of rubber discovered by the Central American Indians and takes an umbrella, invented in Southeastern Asia. Upon his head he puts a hat made of felt, a material invented in the Asiatic steppes.

On his way to breakfast, he stops to buy a paper, paying for it with coins, an ancient Lydian invention. At the restaurant, a whole new series of borrowed elements confronts him. His plate is made of a form of pottery invented in China. His knife is of steel, an alloy first made in southern India; his fork, a medieval Italian invention; and his spoon, a derivative of a Roman original. He begins breakfast with an orange from the eastern Mediterranean, a cantaloupe from Persia, or perhaps a piece of African watermelon. With this he has coffee, an Abyssinian plant, with cream and sugar. Both the domestication of cows and the idea of milking them originated in the Near East, while sugar was first made in India. After his fruit and first coffee, he goes on to waffles, cakes made by a Scandinavian techniques from wheat domesticated in Asia Minor. Over these he pours maple syrup, invented by the Indians of the Eastern woodlands. As a side dish, he may have the egg of a species of bird domesticated in Indochina, or thin strips of the flesh of an animal domesticated in Eastern Asia that have been salted and smoked by a process developed in Northern Europe.

When our friend has finished eating, he settles back to smoke, an American Indian habit, consuming a plant domesticated in Brazil in either a pipe, derived from the Indians of Virginia, or a cigarette, derived from Mexico. If he is hardy enough, he may even attempt a cigar, transmitted to us from the Antilles by way of Spain. While smoking, he reads the news of the day, imprinted in characters written by the ancient Semites upon a material invented in China by a process invented in Germany. As he absorbs the accounts of foreign troubles, he will, if he is a good, conservative citizen, thank a Hebrew deity in an Indo-European language that he is 100 per cent American.

SCIENCE OF CULTURAL ANTHROPOLOGY

E X E R C I S E

Name _____

Section _____

Date _____

EXERCISE 1.1: PROUD TO BE YOU AND ME: BUT WHAT DOES IT MEAN WHEN WE SAY WE ARE AMERICAN?

Using your own words, explain what is meant by the term "American."

What physical and cultural traits would you use to differentiate Americans from other people living around the globe?

Review the Table of Contents of this book. How do the chapters presented in your text fit into your definition of an American?

Various authors have written about what they believe it means to be American. Read through the excerpt written by Ralph Linton in 1935. Linton is describing the typical morning of an American. How does this fit in with your daily routines? After reading "One Hundred Per Cent American," explain if this excerpt strengthens or weakens your personal definition of what it means to be American.

Culture Shock

When people relocate or travel for extensive periods of time, they experience **culture shock**; the change or adjustment period of becoming socialized into a new culture with its own life ways. If culture shock is not understood, it can lead to feelings of fear, confusion, and depression. Even if you are aware of this phenomenon, it still occurs. It is simply the adjustment period to a culture with behavioral patterns, beliefs, and policies different from those with which you are accustomed.

Culture shock occurs in four phases. The length of each phase will differ from person to person, and people may jump backwards in the phases before reaching final resolution. The four stages are as follows:

1. **Honeymoon Period:** characterized by excitement about the new environment and cultural ways.
2. **Disenchantment Phase:** loneliness and frustration develop as a result of living in a society with a different set of rules, beliefs, and customs.
3. **Beginning Resolution Phase:** the individual starts to learn new patterns of behavior appropriate to the new setting.
4. **Effective Function Phase:** marked by a comfort level in the new society that is equivalent to that of the original culture.

THE ADJUSTMENT PROCESS

"...when an individual enters a strange culture...he or she is like fish out of water." Newcomers feel at times that they do not belong and consequently may feel alien-ated from the native members of the culture. When this happens, visitors may want to reject everything about the new environment and may glorify and exaggerate the positive aspects of their own culture. Conversely, visitors may scorn their native country by rejecting its values and instead choosing to identify with (if only temporarily) the values of the new country. This may occur as an attempt to over-identify with the new culture in order to be accepted by the people in it.

Reactions to a new culture vary, but experience and research have shown that there are distinct stages in the adjustment process of foreign visitors. When leaving the comfortably secure environment of home, a person will naturally experience some stress and anxiety. The severity of culture shock depends on visitors' personalities, language ability, emotional support, and duration of stay. It is also influenced by the extent of differences, either actual or perceived, between the two cultures.

Visitors coming for short periods of time do not always experience the same intense emotions as visitors who live in foreign countries for longer terms. The adjustment stages during prolonged stays may last several months to several years. The following "W" shaped diagram illustrates periods of adjustment in a second culture and might apply to a one-year stay in a foreign culture. Although the stages in the cycle do not always occur in the same order and some stages may be skipped, the following pattern is a common one:

The Adjustment Process in a New Culture

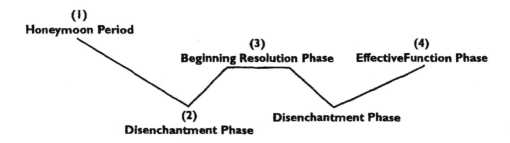

"The Adjustment Process in a New Culture," p. 41 from *Beyond Language: Cross Cultural Communication*. 2nd ed., by Deena R. Levine and Mara B. Adelman. Copyright © 1993 by Prentice-Hall, Inc. Reprinted by permission of Pearson Education, Inc.

SCIENCE OF CULTURAL ANTHROPOLOGY

Each stage in the process is characterized by "*symptoms*" or *outward* signs *typifying* certain kinds of behavior:

1. **Honeymoon Period.** Initially many people are fascinated and excited by everything new. The visitor is elated to be in a new culture.

2. **Disenchantment Phase.** The individual is immersed in new problems: housing, transportation, shopping, and language. Mental fatigue results from continuously straining to comprehend the foreign language. Individuals have been away from their family and good friends for a long period of time and may feel lonely. Many still feel they cannot express themselves as well as they can in their native language. Frustration and sometimes a loss of self-confidence result. Some individuals remain at this stage.

3. **Beginning Resolution Phase.** Initial adjustment. Everyday activities such as housing and shopping are no longer major problems. Although the visitor may not yet be fluent in the language spoken, basic ideas and feelings in the second language can be expressed.

4. **Effective Function Phase.** A routine (e.g., work, business, or school) has been established. The visitor has accepted the habits, customs, foods, and characteristics of the people in the new culture. The visitor feels comfortable with friends, associates, and the language of the country.

Anthropologists state that once an individual fits in and is functioning well in the new culture, he or she is acculturated. The term **acculturation** means to take on the culture of another group. It is not essential to drop one's original cultural practices—we can become acculturated into a number of societies. Thus, we may act as natives in multiple cultural settings—actively participating in the life ways represented in different societies.

The process of acculturation is very different from **assimilation**, a term often used in our society today. Assimilation refers to a person who has given up the ways of their original culture, exclusively taking on the life ways of the new culture. Do you believe that most immigrants to the U.S. are assimilated? What is the reasoning behind your conclusion?

_____

Term Project Ideas

Cultural anthropology reviews the principles of diversity in human beliefs, customs, and behaviors and how such values impact the natural environment. Essential methods of anthropological data collection include in-depth field research as well as techniques to draw comparisons between different societies and observed patterns of behavior.

The anthropological perspective is based upon cross-cultural comparisons. The goal of this assignment is to learn more about a specific place or area that exists around you. Next, compare your observations with those discussed in this text. What similarities and differences should be noted across groups?

Students are required to complete ONE of the following projects, either the ethnographic study or the visits to various cultural centers. Each project is broken down into three sections. Papers should be typed, 3–5 pages, double-spaced, 12 point type, with one-inch margins.

ETHNOGRAPHIC STUDY

1. **Mapping exercise:** Record the physical layout of a specific city block or market place. (Choose an area you enjoy, since you will be spending time at the site throughout the school term!) Begin by diagramming your site and learning more about how it fits in with the surrounding area. Obtain census data and/or city records to learn more about the people who live in this general location.

    In your paper, diagram the site and discuss its importance within the community. Discuss how the site is used relating to the economic, social, political, and cultural events that take place at this location, and how the site is perceived from an emic perspective. Participate in activities that occur at the site and discuss your observations in this paper.

2. **Ethnographic research techniques:** Conduct a minimum of two interviews and gather additional literature concerning one sub-culture connected to the site described in the first paper. Utilize both qualitative and quantitative methods of investigation to assess the importance of the location to its community.

3. **Cross-cultural analysis:** Define important cultural practices as perceived by the community members you are investigating. Describe how the actions that you have documented compare or contrast to other cultural practices described in this book.

-OR-

VISIT THREE CULTURAL MUSEUMS/FESTIVALS

Participate in a minimum of three events/exhibitions representing cultural practices that differ from your own. (One paper per each museum visit for a total of three papers.) Highlight in each paper the methods of inquiry and means of data collection in each exhibition installation, interviews with museum staff, statements of authenticity from other visitors, and interpretive accuracy from an etic perspective. Discuss how you enjoy the activity and what could be accomplished to improve the visit.

Your professor will offer more details about the assignment. Typed papers are due on the following dates:

Paper 1:

Paper 2:

Paper 3:

When approaching assignments in this book, you may wish to first select an ethnography to serve as a model for research techniques and strategies. Such a model can lead you to investigate areas of the culture that you may not have considered before, as well as to provide direction for your research.

Be sure to begin recording observations immediately. When it comes time to write each paper, concentrate your observations and analysis toward someone with a "working" knowledge of the community under investigation. Be sure to utilize anthropological terms and concepts when analyzing your field data.

Lastly, be sure to make use of the **ethnographic present**— writing in the present tense as though your audience is actually witnessing events as they unfold. This writing style simplifies life for the anthropologist, and it also allows the reader to feel as though he/she is participating in the culture, and witnessing the people first-hand.

E X E R C I S E

Name _____

Section _____

Date _____

EXERCISE 1.2: INTERVIEWING

Interview a fellow classmate or family member about their experiences in another country. Focus your attention on one cultural practice that is accepted in the culture of origin, but not in the United States and visa versa (accepted in the U.S. but not in another country). Write a brief essay defining how such actions are viewed in each culture. Next, interpret the behavior from an emic and etic perspective. (Be sure to review the guidelines for conducting an interview, listed on the following page.)

SCIENCE OF CULTURAL ANTHROPOLOGY

Interviewing Techniques

When conducting an interview, be sure to follow basic guidelines:

1. Engage in "small talk" with your informant before beginning the formal interview. Be sure to introduce yourself formally, to explain the purpose of this interview and how you plan to utilize the information being shared. If you wish to tape record the conversation, ask for permission in advance.

2. Avoid asking yes and no questions only. These questions, known as "closed-ended questions," do not necessarily lead to any depth or motive for the informant's behaviors or decisions. "Open-ended questions" lead to further explanation—like why they choose to take this trip (or to relocate), how the experience transpired, and what those around them thought of their decision.

3. Be sure that you repeat any of your interpretations of their original statements. Be sure that your interpretations are correct and valid. True representation of the informant and the conversation is of utmost importance. Also, be respectful of their wishes. If the subject indicates that a statement is not for public disclosure, respect such a desire.

4. Ask for more details and examples. To be a good interviewer, you must never be afraid to admit that you do not understand. Ask for another explanation.

5. If the informant strays from the original topic, gently steer him or her back on track.

6. Pay attention to non-verbal behavioral cues. Note their body language and tone. Is the informant uncomfortable discussing particular topics? Does he/she appear to be describing what you want to hear instead of an accurate depiction of events? Be sure that whenever possible, you have chosen an informant that experienced the event first-hand, not a person who is passing down information that may be subject to interpretation or lack accuracy.

Body Ritual Among the Nacirema—
Horace Miner

The anthropologist has become so familiar with the diversity of ways in which different peoples behave in similar situations that he is not apt to be surprised by even the most exotic customs. In fact, if all of the logically possible combinations of behavior have not been found somewhere in the world, he is apt to suspect that they must be present in some yet undescribed tribe. This point has, in fact, been expressed with respect to clan organization by Murdock (1949:71). In this light, the magical beliefs and practices of the Nacirema present such unusual aspects that it seems desirable to describe them as an example of the extremes to which human behavior can go.

Professor Linton first brought the ritual of the Nacirema to the attention of anthropologists twenty years ago (1936:326), but the culture of this people is still very poorly understood. They are a North American group living in the territory between the Canadian Cree, the Yaqui and Tarahumare of Mexico, and the Carib and Arawak of the Antilles. Little is known of their origin, though tradition states that they came from the east. According to Nacirema mythology, their nation was originated by a culture hero, Notgnishaw, who is otherwise known for two great feats of strength—the throwing of a piece of wampum across the river Pa-To-Mac and the chopping down of a cherry tree in which the Spirit of Truth resided.

Nacirema culture is characterized by a highly developed market economy which has evolved in a rich natural habitat. While much of the people's time is devoted to economic pursuits, a large part of the fruits of these labors and a considerable portion of the day are spent in ritual activity. The focus of this activity is the human body, the appearance and health of which loom as a dominant concern in the ethos of the people. While such a concern is certainly not unusual, its ceremonial aspects and associated philosophy are unique.

The fundamental belief underlying the whole system appears to be that the human body is ugly and that its natural tendency is to debility and disease. Incarcerated in such a body, man's only hope is to avert these characteristics through the use of the powerful influences of ritual and ceremony. Every household has one or more shrines devoted to this purpose. The more powerful individuals in the society have several shrines in their houses and, in fact, the opulence of a house is often referred to in terms of the number of such ritual centers it possesses. Most houses are of wattle and daub construction, but the shrine rooms of the more wealthy are walled with stone. Poorer families imitate the rich by applying pottery plaques to their shrine walls.

While each family has at least one such shrine, the rituals associated with it are not family ceremonies but are private and secret. The rites are normally only discussed with children, and then only during the period when they are being initiated into these mysteries. I was able, however, to establish sufficient rapport with the natives to examine these shrines and to have the rituals described to me.

The focal point of the shrine is a box or chest which is built into the wall. In this chest are kept the many charms and magical potions without which no native believes he could live. These preparations are secured from a variety of specialized practitioners. The most powerful of these are the medicine men, whose assistance must be rewarded with substantial gifts. However, the medicine men do not provide the curative potions for their clients, but decide what the ingredients should be and then write them down in an ancient and secret language. This writing is understood only by the medicine men and by the herbalists who, for another gift, provide the required charm.

The charm is not disposed of after it has served its purpose, but is placed in the charm-box of the household shrine. As these magical materials are specific for certain ills, and the real or imagined maladies of the people are many, the charm-box is usually full to overflowing. The magical packets are so numerous that people forget what their purposes were and fear to use them again. While the natives are very vague on this point, we can only assume that the idea in retaining all the old magical materials is that their presence in the charm-box, before which the body rituals are conducted, will in some way protect the worshipper.

Beneath the charm-box is a small font. Each day every member of the family, in succession, enters the shrine room, bows his head before the charm-box, mingles different sorts of holy water in the font, and proceeds with a brief rite of ablution. The holy waters are secured from the Water Temple of the community, where the priests conduct elaborate ceremonies to make the liquid ritually pure.

In the hierarchy of magical practitioners, and below the medicine men in prestige, are specialists whose designation is best translated "holy-mouth-men." The Nacirema have an almost pathological horror and fascination with the mouth, the condition of which is believed to have a supernatural influence on all social relationships. Were it not for the rituals of the mouth, they believe that their teeth would fall out, their gums bleed, their jaws shrink, their friends desert them, and their lovers reject them. (They also believe that a strong relationship exists between oral and moral characteristics. For example, there is a ritual ablution of the mouth for children which is supposed to improve their moral fiber.)

The daily body ritual performed by everyone includes a mouth-rite. Despite the fact that these people are so punctilious about care of the mouth, this rite involves a practice which strikes the uninitiated stranger as revolting. It was reported to me that the ritual consists of inserting a small bundle of hog hairs into the mouth, along with certain magical powders, and then moving the bundle in a highly formalized series of gestures.

In addition to the private mouth-rite, the people seek out a holy-mouth-man once or twice a year. These practitioners have an impressive set of paraphernalia, consisting of a variety of augers, awls, probes, and prods. The use of these objects in the exorcism of the evils of the mouth involves almost unbelievable ritual of the client. The holy-mouth-man opens the client's mouth and, using the above mentioned tools, enlarges any holes which decay may have created in the teeth. Magical materials are put into these holes. If there are no naturally occurring holes in the teeth, large sections of one or more teeth are gouged out so that the supernatural substance can be applied. In the client's view, the purpose of these ministrations is to arrest decay and to draw friends. The extremely sacred and traditional character of the rite is evident in the fact that the natives return to the holy-mouth-men year after year, despite the fact that their teeth continue to decay.

It is to be hoped that, when a thorough study of the Nacirema is made, there will be a careful inquiry into the personality structure of these people. One has but to watch the gleam in the eye of a holy-mouth-man, as he jabs an awl into an exposed nerve, to suspect that a certain amount of sadism is involved. If this can be established, a very interesting pattern emerges, for most of the population shows definite masochistic tendencies. It was to these that Professor Linton referred in discussing a distinctive part of the daily body ritual which is performed only by men. This part of the rite involves scraping and lacerating the surface of the face with a sharp instrument. Special women's rites are performed only four times during each lunar month, but what they lack in frequency is made up in barbarity. As part of this ceremony, women bake their heads in small ovens for about an hour. The theoretically interesting point is that what seems to be a preponderantly masochistic people have developed sadistic specialists.

The medicine men have an imposing temple, or *latipso*, in every community of any size. The more elaborate ceremonies required to treat very sick patients can only be performed at this temple. These ceremonies involve not only the thaumaturge but a permanent group of vestal maidens who move sedately about the temple chambers in distinctive costume and headdress.

The *latipso* ceremonies are so harsh that it is phenomenal that a fair proportion of the really sick natives who enter the temple ever recover. Small children whose indoctrination is still incomplete have been known to resist attempts to take them to the temple because "that is where you go to die." Despite this fact, sick adults are not only willing but eager to undergo the protracted ritual purification, if they can afford to do so. No matter how ill the supplicant or how grave the emergency, the guardians of many temples will not admit a client if he cannot give a rich gift to the custodian. Even after one has gained admission and survived the ceremonies, the guardians will not permit the neophyte to leave until he makes still another gift.

The supplicant entering the temple is first stripped of all his or her clothes. In everyday life the Nacirema avoids exposure of his body and its natural functions. Bathing and excretory acts are performed only in the secrecy of the household shrine, where they are ritualized as part of the body-rites. Psychological shock results from the fact that body secrecy is suddenly lost upon entry into the *latipso*. A man, whose own wife has never seen him in an excretory act, suddenly finds himself naked and assisted by a vestal maiden while he performs his natural functions into a sacred vessel. This sort of ceremonial treatment is necessitated by the fact that the excreta are used by a diviner to ascertain the course and nature of the client's sickness. Female clients, on the other hand, find their naked bodies are subjected to the scrutiny, manipulation and prodding of the medicine men.

Few supplicants in the temple are well enough to do anything but lie on their hard beds. The daily ceremonies, like the rites of the holy-mouth-men, involve discomfort and torture. With ritual precision, the vestals awaken their miserable charges each dawn and roll them about on their beds of pain while performing ablutions, in the formal movements of which the maidens are highly trained. At other times they insert magic wands in the supplicant's mouth or force him to eat substances which are supposed to be healing. From time to time the medicine men come to their clients and jab magically treated needles into their flesh. The fact that these temple ceremonies may not cure, and may even kill the neophyte, in no way decreases the people's faith in the medicine men.

There remains one other kind of practitioner, known as a "listener." This witch-doctor has the power to exorcise the devils that lodge in the heads of people who have been bewitched. The Nacirema believe that parents bewitch their own children. Mothers are particularly suspected of putting a curse on children while teaching them the secret body rituals. The counter-magic of the witch-doctor is unusual in its lack of ritual. The patient simply tells the "listener" all his troubles and fears, beginning with the earliest difficulties he can remember. The memory displayed by the Nacirema in these exorcism sessions is truly remarkable. It is not uncommon for the patient to bemoan the rejection he felt upon being weaned as a babe, and a few individuals even see their troubles going back to the traumatic effects of their own birth.

In conclusion, mention must be made of certain practices which have their base in native aesthetics but which depend upon the pervasive aversion to the natural body and its functions. There are ritual fasts to make fat people thin and ceremonial feasts to make thin people fat. Still other rites are used to make women's breasts large if they are small, and smaller if they are large. General dissatisfaction with breast shape is symbolized in the fact that the ideal form is virtually outside the range of human variation. A few women afflicted with almost inhuman hypermammary development are so idolized that they make a handsome living by simply going from village to village and permitting the natives to stare at them for a fee.

Reference has already been made to the fact that excretory functions are ritualized, routinized, and relegated to secrecy. Natural reproductive functions are similarly distorted. Intercourse is taboo as a topic and scheduled as an act. Efforts are made to avoid pregnancy by the use of magical materials or by limiting intercourse to certain phases of the moon. Conception is actually very infrequent. When pregnant, women dress so as to hide their condition. Parturition takes place in secret, without friends or relatives to assist, and the majority of women do not nurse their infants.

Our review of the ritual life of the Nacirema has certainly shown them to be a magic-ridden people. It is hard to understand how they have managed to exist so long under the burdens which they have imposed upon themselves. But even such exotic customs as these take on real meaning when they are viewed with the insight provided by Malinowski when he wrote (1948:70):

> Looking from far and above, from our high places of safety in the developed civilization, it is easy to see all the crudity and irrelevance of magic. But without its power and guidance early man could not have mastered his practical difficulties as he has done, nor could man have advanced to the higher stages of civilization.

REFERENCES

Linton, Ralph. 1936. *The Study of Man*. New York, D. Appleton-Century Co.

Malinowski, Bronislaw. 1948. *Magic, Science, and Religion*. Glencoe, The First Press.

Murdock, George P. 1949. *Social Structure*. New York, The Macmillan Co.

Horace Miner 1956, "Body Ritual of the Nacirema," *American Anthropologist*, June 1956, pp. 503–507.

SCIENCE OF CULTURAL ANTHROPOLOGY

E X E R C I S E

Name _____

Section _____

Date _____

EXERCISE 1.3: NACIREMA

Read through the article entitled "Body Ritual Among the Nacirema" to see if the author offers any hints to the investigation of American culture. In what ways are your daily routines similar to or different from the culture being described in this article?

Even though this article was published some time ago, it seems to describe the culture in great detail. Would you assume that the Nacirema act the same way today as described in the article? If we look at written documents as a "picture in time," what does this teach us about the readers understanding of current cultural practices?

SCIENCE OF CULTURAL ANTHROPOLOGY

KEY TERMS

Name _____

Section _____

Date _____

Acculturation:

American:

Anthropological perspective:

Applied anthropology:

Assimilation:

Cultural anthropology:

Culture:

Culture shock (and phases):

Emic:

Ethnographic present:

SCIENCE OF CULTURAL ANTHROPOLOGY

Ethnography:

Etic:

Holistic perspective (holism) or approach:

Nacirema:

Participant observation:

Stereotyping:

Sub-cultures:

2 FIELD RESEARCH

Cultural anthropologists conduct in-depth field analysis in order to grasp a richer understanding of the culture under investigation. While studying the patterns of behavior, material objects, and ideas found in each contemporary culture, anthropologists also seek to obtain an understanding of the more general underlying patterns of human behavior derived through **cross-cultural comparison**. The study of **ethnology** is the analysis of various ethnographies, or the detailed descriptions produced by researchers as a result of extensive fieldwork, conducted through **participant-observation**.

The Beginnings of Ethnographic Fieldwork—
Paul Bohannan and Dirk van der Elst

It often amazes people how long it took humanity to discover or accept ideas which to us, today, are self-evident. One thing this demonstrates, far better than changes in technology can, is that culture channels and determines human thought and perception. Until the 1800s, for example, everybody "knew" that men had more teeth than women. Ancient Greek philosophers had logically deduced that "fact," and what arrogance would induce one to argue with those Authorities-of-Reference-for-all-Western-Thought? So until the advent of science, nobody thought to check mouths and count teeth. And when it came to the customs and motives of people in faraway places with strange-sounding names, conventional wisdom—a misnomer if ever there was one—clung tenaciously to the idea that you could treat them as if they were different animals, as was the custom in medieval "bestiaries." It is easy to laugh now, but even today you can still encounter the odd individual who professes absolute certainty that men must have fewer ribs than women. Because of Adam—that earliest ancestor who traded his rib for a wife in the book of Genesis—many people, it seems, would rather believe than know.

But not scientists. The idea that you can go and ask about custom and culture took shape in England and the United States at about the same time—and, with a somewhat different philosophical base, also in Germany—but started from rather different assumptions in these countries.

In Britain the process began in what were called Discoverers' Clubs. The first "real" effort was to send an expedition to the Torres Strait Islands, which lie between Papua New Guinea and the Cape York Peninsula of Australia. That expedition (which included medical doctors, psychologists, and anthropologists who taught primarily about human origins) set out to study what they called "native" societies. They wanted to collect the "facts" themselves, in the belief that they themselves would get it "right," and they would never have to trust travelers again.

FIELD RESEARCH

These researchers all had independent incomes, so expense was not a major consideration. A lot of information about Pacific Islanders, indigenous Australians, and tribal peoples of India was collected during this period.

During that same period, the British were developing a book of questions that they called *Notes and Queries in Anthropology*, whose last edition was published in the late 1940s.

The book had questions and blank spaces where you could fill in the answers. You could, it was said, take it anywhere you went, ask the questions, fill in the blanks, and make a contribution to ethnography.

Actually, little worthwhile information was ever gathered on the basis of *Notes and Queries*. The reason is simple: a major part of training people to collect ethnographies lies in teaching them to discern whether a question is in fact understood by the person being questioned. You need to know enough about your **informant** (the person you are asking) to be able to tell whether he or she thinks it is a sensible question. Only then can you begin to see how the answers fit together. *Notes and Queries in Anthropology* essentially denied any need for understanding what you heard: just fill in the blanks; after all, "those people" all have the same mental framework for their ideas and words.

Today we know that there can never be a complete "list of cultural elements" whose blanks you just fill in. In the first place, all of the people's own perceptions of their culture is lost in such a method. Translation problems are not even considered. Unless you understand the ideas and are very careful about how they are translated into English (or French, or whatever), the result is not merely lifeless but useless. Then too, every ethnographer must go beyond questioning into careful observation and description, because even when the question is perfectly understood and honestly answered, that answer may contradict actual behavior.

In the United States some of the same mistakes were made, as well as other, home-grown ones. The Bureau of American Ethnology (BAE) was organized in association with the Indian Service (then in the Department of War, later moved to the Department of the Interior) and with the Smithsonian Institution. The people who worked at the BAE were interested in what the Native Americans had been like before the destructive waves of White immigrants descended on them. This was in the days before the dynamics of culture and its constantly changing nature were understood—a point we will examine later.

The American ethnographic tradition actually derives from Germany rather than England. Its founder, **Franz Boas** (1858–1942), had earned his doctorate at the University of Kiel in 1881. In 1883 he began a year-long scientific expedition to Baffin Island. There, intrigued with the Eskimos, he began to study their language, writing it down as they spoke. He even trained some of them to dictate it to him. This experience converted him to the study of anthropology. The main body of his ethnographic work was on the Kwakiutl of Vancouver Island in British Columbia.

Franz Boas became the undisputed father of cultural anthropology in the United States. He championed the idea of "texts" as devices by which one could simultaneously study language and culture, and advocated "total recovery" of ethnographic data before any generalization was attempted. Unlike the so-called "unilinear evolutionists" who focused on the similarities among cultures, Boas stressed cultural differences and ascribed them to the diverging and ultimately unique historical development of evolving societies.

During his many years at Columbia University he trained almost all the important North American anthropologists in the first half of the twentieth century, imbuing them with his own *holistic* approach to fieldwork and a sense that the discipline was grounded in the four fields of archaeological, cultural, linguistic, and physical anthropology. The Boasian school enshrined *culture* as the key concept in North American anthropology and brought us two ideas which are debated to this day: *cultural relativism* and *cultural determinism*.

Boas established the *International Journal of American Linguistics*, and was a founder of the American Anthropological Association. He made it a tenet of the anthropological worldview that all human ethnicities have an equal capacity to develop culture, and that all behavioral differences among populations result from cultural, not racial or genetic, causes.

In establishing culture as the key concept of anthropology, and stressing that the uniqueness of each culture results from its specific and singular historical development, Boasian thought marks North American anthropology to this day. We owe Boas something else: anthropological societies had admitted women since the nineteenth century; Matilda Cox Stevenson studied Native Americans in the southwestern United States and in Mexico before Boas got to Columbia. But Boas actively encouraged women (including Ruth Benedict and Margaret Mead) to enter the field. In the 1980s, anthropology became the first traditional discipline to award more doctoral degrees to women than to men.

Franz Boas is often referred to as the father of American Anthropology. The definition of the term "cultures" was first stated by Boas at the beginning of the 20th century and is still used today. According to Boas, **cultures** are made up of learned and shared patterns of behavior. The notion of this definition of the term promotes an **egalitarian** view of all societies, with no one way of life being superior to any other. Thus, all cultural practices are to be accepted as equal in importance and value.

Yet, to understand Boas' complete impact upon American anthropology, one must learn about the zeitgeist in which his actions took place. The German term **zeitgeist** refers to the spirit of the time: what is it that most people in society hold as true or right. These beliefs do not need to be based upon facts—but rather, what collectively most Americans hold as truths.

Boas was a product of his upbringing, just as we all are. Humans are social beings: during youth we are **enculturated**, or learn the processes of our culture from those around us. Through **socialization**, the passing down of cultural traditions from one generation to the next, we are capable of keeping our traditions and culture alive.

Boas believed in the importance of **cultural determinism**, that there are no biological differences between the races that make one superior to another. At the same time, he promoted the concept of **cultural relativism**, which emphasizes the unique aspects of each culture, without passing judgments on ways of life that differ from his own.

Anthropologists today continue to promote the understanding of culture within the environment in which it occurs. Also, certain aspects of any culture, even those components that do not seem of great importance to us (for instance, our daily routines) may be of great value when studying behavioral patterns from a holistic perspective.

American Album—
Stephanie Simon
For this, they pay him?

Tom Fricke, long blond hair clipped back in a ponytail, is hanging out. He's hanging out with farmers, with a high school principal, with a manufacturing executive. He orders the 13-ounce prime rib when they do. He matches them, scoop for scoop, at the ice cream counter. He zips about town in his mini-sport-utility vehicle, gabbing with the locals every chance he gets. And yes—although even his parents don't believe it—all this hanging out is work.

Fricke, a professor at the University of Michigan, is on the vanguard of a new trend in academia: an intense, anthropological study of us.

That is, of average, hard-working, middle-class Americans. Folks who wake up, grumbling, to an alarm clock each morning, who juggle job and family, who try to give their kids the best. "We're interested in the extraordinariness of everyday life," said Charles Darrah, an anthropologist at San Jose State University.

SHADOWING SUBJECTS IN SEARCH OF INSIGHTS
Darrah focuses on Silicon Valley professionals. Fricke, on rural North Dakotans. Other anthropologists are examining suburbanites in Philadelphia, African Americans in New York, and stressed-out families in Atlanta. Using what they call an "ethnographic" approach—which basically means shadowing their subjects at home, at work, and at play—they watch our humdrum lives up close in an effort to figure out how we're all coping.

"It's not exactly that we're voyeurs," Fricke starts to say. Then he thinks about it and backtracks. "If we are voyeurs," he amends, sounding pretty sure the description fits, "at least we have degrees."

He chuckles. "We're credentialed voyeurs."

Fricke's work is funded by a $2.8-million grant from the Alfred P. Sloan Foundation in New York, which has set aside $20 million over four years for just such prosaic studies. The foundation has supported research centers at UC Berkeley, the University of Chicago and Cornell University, along with Fricke's Center for the Ethnography of Everyday Life.

"We are in the midst of profound changes in society, but people are not aware of them because we're so caught up in living them," said Kathleen Christensen, a Sloan Foundation program director. "Just as a fish doesn't understand the water, I don't know that we fully understand what day-to-day life is like."

By tailing actual people through typical days, anthropologists—who have traditionally focused on exotic foreign cultures—hope to help us understand ourselves.

"When I shadow a 3-year-old around, on the surface, that wouldn't seem to be an encapsulation of our culture," said Jan English-Leuck, who works in the Silicon Valley. "But when that 3-year-old turns to his little sister and says: 'Don't bother me, I'm working,' well, that's something you wouldn't hear in a small village in Suriname. That [illustrates] part of American culture: our view of the primacy of work."

Hanging out in this snug little town of 626, set amid the broad vistas and lumpy hay bales of western North Dakota, Fricke seeks another perspective on everyday life: the view from a rural land that's swiftly emptying out as young people leave for better jobs or smoother lives.

So far, Fricke has discovered that this exodus of the young has forced the parents they leave behind to adjust their definition of family. North Dakotans have typically viewed family as an overflowing clan of extended relatives who all got together every Sunday for supper. Now, those left in Richardton are forced to adjust to their kids' priorities, which involve moving out of state for work or for school.

It's been a painful wrench into the realities of modern, middle-class life, where jobs often take top billing over family.

"There's tension and friction there," Fricke says.

Fricke hopes, after another year of study here, to turn his insights into a book on the peculiar stresses of life in a fading rural community. The Silicon Valley anthropologists, meanwhile, are working on a text of their own, about a very different culture—one where parents network, cell phones at the ready, even as they pace the sidelines of their children's soccer games.

Disparate themes, to be sure, but with a common goal: exposing the tensions and tradeoffs in everyday life that everyone seems aware of, if only in a vague, unsettling sense.

"The feeling that there is a problem is pervasive. It's absolutely pervasive," said Bradd Shores, an anthropologist studying family rituals in Atlanta.

"Maybe the more we know ourselves, the more capable we'll be of improving," suggested Kenneth Kreitinger, a Richardton executive who has been cooperating with Fricke.

But anthropologists readily admit their methods have some drawbacks.

For one, it's hard to get representative samples.

Anthropologists can't just pick random people and follow them around all day. They need their subjects' cooperation. And there always will be plenty of folks like the waitress in the coffee shop here who snapped: "I'm not worthy of study. I got too much work to do." Or the elderly lady nibbling her fries who huffed: "It's a bunch of baloney. What good's going to come of it? I don't need anybody seeing how I live."

Plus, by their very presence, researchers may affect the choices their subjects make—or at least make them feel self-conscious. "Everyone wants to be the fly on the wall, but you can't be," said John L. Jackson Jr., an anthropologist doing doctoral work in Harlem.

WORKING HARD TO GET DIVERGENT VIEWS

Because of these limitations, "it's very difficult to make policy on the basis of anthropological studies," said sociologist Barbara Schneider of the University of Chicago. "*Ethnographies* offer rich detail and texture but require randomized, controlled surveys to back up their anecdotal points," Schneider said.

Aware of the problem, anthropologists say they work hard to get divergent views. But they naturally spend the most time with the friendliest people.

Fricke, for instance, has been hanging out with farmers Callen and Julie Hoff and their teenage son, Casey. The Hoffs invited Fricke to dinner the first time they met. Now, they keep urging him to stay in their spare bedroom. They cheerfully acknowledge they're not quite sure just what he's studying. ("The other night," Julie Hoff recounted, "I looked at Cal and asked, 'What does an anthropologist do, anyway?' So we got out the World Book and looked it up.")

Still, they willingly talk into his tape recorder.

"We kind of like to talk about ourselves," Julie Hoff said.

"If someone's willing to listen, we'll ramble on and on," her husband added. "It's human nature."

FIELD RESEARCH

E X E R C I S E

Name _____

Section _____

Date _____

EXERCISE 2.1: PARTICIPANT-OBSERVATION

Try These Techniques Associated with Participant-Observation:

One of the most important techniques or methods used by cultural anthropologists is participant-observation. For this exercise you will get a chance to experience what it is like to practice this method. (See example on back.)

1. The first step is to pick a question that you can answer easily by observing behavior, taking good field notes and analyzing your results. This will be your **hypothesis**. Write your question below:

2. The next step is to figure out how you will collect data to answer your question. Your **method** will be participant-observation, but you will need to figure out where you will conduct your research, what you need to observe and how to control for any unnecessary information. Write this information below:

3. Make a table of your data to show what you collected and when. These are your **data results**. Attach it to this page. (See sample on back.)

4. The final step is to **analyze** your data. What did you find out? What was the answer to your question, and how do you know? What are your **conclusions**? Write your answers below:

FIELD RESEARCH

See example below to help you.

Example:

1. Do women or men tip more?

2. I observed whether or not men tipped more than women did at Big Bopper Restaurant [pseudonym] in Los Angeles, California. The observations took place during eight shifts between 3 p.m. and 10 p.m., May 18, 2006–May 30, 2006. The only people observed were all male or all female tables consisting of two or more people.

3. This is my data table for my observations:

MEN			WOMEN	
Amount of check	Amount of tip		Amount of check	Amount of tip
$1.75	$.25		$4.25	$1.00
$2.25	$.50		$15.17	$2.00
$3.50	$.50		$21.59	$3.00
$1.75	$.25		$27.35	$4.50
$39.05	$3.00		$26.86	$3.15
$22.36	$2.00		$20.92	$4.00
$18.61	$2.39		$13.50	$3.50
$27.30	$5.00		$13.50	$3.50
$13.50	$1.50		$13.50	$1.50
$29.97	$5.00		$20.00	$2.50
Totals:				
$160.04	$20.39		$176.64	$28.65
	13% tips			16% tips

4. According to my observations of ten all-male and ten all-female tables at the dates and times stated above, the men tipped 3% less than the women. One factor that could account for this difference is that more of the male sales were lower totals so the amount they tipped could have represented the 'change' left over. Another possible influence could be that women have a higher likelihood of working as a waitress and might view it as hard work and have a more sympathetic attitude toward waitresses and thus tip more than males. These conclusions would need further testing to see if they are valid or not.

Rites of Passage

Humans depend upon the social transmission of knowledge for survival. Group living provides the basic context in which we learn from others about ourselves and about what is expected within a given culture. Each culture (and sub-culture) may have different means of celebrating **rites of passage**, marking the transitions within one's lifetime—from childhood to death. A rite of passage is defined as a ceremony to celebrate the transition of a person from one social status to another. The five rites of passage most commonly recognized include birth, puberty, marriage, child bearing, and death. The socialization process assures that cultural practices are maintained throughout the generations, thus keeping traditions alive from one generation to the next.

Most cultures have ritualized ceremonies associated with rites of passage, yet not all cultures participate in initiation rites. **Initiation rites** mark the transition from one phase to another with education about what is to come; for instance, from childhood to adulthood. Oftentimes the youth are separated from the group, at which time they are trained to become responsible adults. When the youth return to the group to participate in the ceremonial rites of passage, they are then viewed by society as adults.

During the initiation, the child learns what is necessary to become a capable, functional adult, with a clear understanding of the roles and responsibilities expected from a mature member of society. During the initiation, the child may learn about tribal folklore, or be asked to demonstrate his/her ability to care for the group as an adult. The process whereby youth learn what is expected of them throughout the stages of their lives occurs through the process of **enculturation**.

Rites of passage, coupled with initiation rites, maintain solidarity in the group, offer effective means by which to educate and transmit social responsibilities across the generations, and stress the importance of organization in social life. What if you live in a society where such rites are not stressed or even encouraged? How do you learn to be a productive adult member of society? How do you learn the folklore and tales of your people? How do you learn about the process of maturation?

This lack of rites of passage, initiation rites, or both, occurs in many countries, most notably the United States. Moffatt studied American college students to see how they learned what was expected of them upon graduation and entrance into the work world. In his book entitled *Coming of Age*, Moffatt notes that most Americans never participate in initiation rites. Some students interviewed by Moffatt suggested that their graduation from college marks their transition to adulthood. Yet, what if you decided to postpone your college studies or forsake them entirely? Does that mean that you will never be a mature member of society? Of course not. In societies like our own, there is variation in when and how we learn to be productive adults. We may turn to religious practices to assist us in learning about our heritage. Specific ethnic groups may also have ritualized rites of passage to mark important transitions throughout one's lifetime.

The rite of passage marking the transition from one stage of life to another in the Hasidic population of the United States occurs when a boy turns thirteen years of age. The Hasidic Jews, most of whom arrived in the United States after World War II, have resisted assimilation by drawing cultural boundaries between themselves and American society in general. Hasadim (meaning "pious ones") adhere to a strict dress code, speak Yiddish (the language of Eastern and Central European Jews), and resist the anglicization of their names. They follow the words of their Holy Scripture, the Torah, literally.

Age thirteen denotes an important rite of passage for the males. The celebration, known as a *bar mitzvah*, signals the end of childhood and the beginning of manhood. After the *bar mitzvah*, a boy becomes a man of Israel, with all expectations associated with a man of that status. Minor violations of Jewish law are no longer accepted. Serious *davening* (prayer) and strict adherence to Torah and scholarship are expected of an adult male. At this celebration, the boy is given his *tifillin*—two leather cases, containing verses from the Books of Exodus and Deuteronomy which are strapped to his left arm and forehead each morning during prayer. For the Hasadim, this rite of passage and the reading of the Torah are reserved for males only. Traditionally, these celebrations are small, intimate gatherings.

FIELD RESEARCH

E X E R C I S E

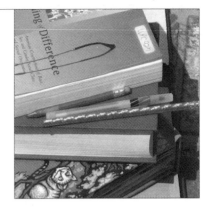

Name _____

Section _____

Date _____

EXERCISE 2.2: CULTURAL VALUES

Answer the following questions concerning your cultural values toward dress, accessories, and food selection.

Describe, in your own words, your style of dress. How do you vary your style according to different situations (such as work, school, job interview, church/temple)? What do these varying styles symbolize? What does your fashion sense mean in terms of cultural values and beliefs?

Describe, in your own words, what is meant by accessorizing. Do you include jewelry, change in hair color, tattoos, body piercing? How does your interpretation fit with American standards? How would a visitor to the United States respond to your definition?

List foods you enjoy eating. What is the country of origin for each of these foods? Do you prepare the foods as originally prepared in the country of origin? What utensils do you use to eat these foods? How does your answer fit in with American standards of behavioral practices?

(continued on the next page)

FIELD RESEARCH

Is there such a thing as "typical" American standards, beliefs, and values?

List and describe five characteristics associated with "typical" Americans.

"Cultural Values" exercise, by Sue Saul. Reprinted by permission.

Parents or Pop Culture? Children's Heroes and Role Models—
Kristin J. Anderson and Donna Cavallaro

What kind of heroes a culture promotes reveals a great deal about that culture's values and desires.

One of the most important features of childhood and adolescence is the development of an identity. As children shape their behavior and values, they may look to heroes and role models for guidance. They may identify the role models they wish to emulate based on possession of certain skills or attributes. While the child may not want to be exactly like the person, he or she may see *possibilities* in that person. For instance, while Supreme Court Justice Ruth Bader Ginsberg may not necessarily directly influence girls and young women to become lawyers, her presence on the Supreme Court may alter beliefs about who is capable of being a lawyer or judge (Gibson & Cordova, 1999).

Parents and other family members are important role models for children, particularly early on. Other influences may be institutional, such as schools, or cultural, such as the mass media. What kind of heroes a culture promotes reveals a great deal about the culture's values and desires. Educators not only can model important behaviors themselves, but also can teach about values, events, and people that a culture holds dear.

Television, movies, computer games, and other forms of media expose children to an endless variety of cultural messages. Which ones do children heed the most? Whom do children want to be like? Do their role models vary according to children's ethnicity and gender? Finally, what role can educators play in teaching children about role models they may never have considered?

This article examines the impact of the mass media on children's choices of heroes and role models. The authors address the questions posed above in light of results from a survey and focus groups conducted with children ages 8 to 13.

THE MENU OF POP CULTURE CHOICES
Television and Film for Children

Male characters—cartoon or otherwise—continue to be more prevalent in children's television and film than female characters. Gender-stereotyped behaviors continue to be the norm. For instance, male characters are more commonly portrayed as independent, assertive, athletic, important, attractive, technical, and responsible than female characters. They show more ingenuity, anger, leadership, bravery, and aggression, and they brag, interrupt, make threats, and even laugh more than female characters do. In fact, since male characters appear so much more frequently than female characters, they do more of almost *everything* than female characters. Also, while the behavior of female characters is somewhat less stereotypical than it was 20 years ago, in some ways male characters behave *more* stereotypically than 20 years ago (for instance, males are now in more leadership roles, are more bossy, and are more intelligent) (Thompson & Zerbinos, 1995). These gender-stereotyped images, and the inflexibility of male characters' roles, make for a restricted range of role models.

Parents, educators, and policymakers are also concerned about the aggressive and violent content in children's programs. Gerbner (1993) studied the violent content of children's programs and observed that "despite all the mayhem, only 3.2% of Saturday morning characters suffer any injury"; thus, children do not learn about the likely consequences of aggressive action. In children's shows, bad characters are punished 59 percent of the time. Even more telling, good characters who engage in violence are punished only 18 percent of the time. The characters that might be the most appealing to kids—the heroes and protagonists—rarely feel remorse, nor are they reprimanded or impeded when they engage in violence (National Television Violence Study, 1998). The authors found that 77 percent of the children surveyed watch television every day. Thus, many children may be learning to use violence as a problem-solving tool.

Characters in animated films also tend to follow stereotypes. While some positive changes in the portrayal of ethnic minority and female characters can be noted, both groups often remain narrowly defined in children's animated films. In his discussion of Disney films, Henry Giroux (1997) notes how the villains in the film *Aladdin* are racially stereotyped. The main character, Aladdin, the hero of the film, is drawn with very light skin, European features, and no accent. Yet the villains in the story appear as Middle Eastern caricatures: they have beards, large noses, sinister eyes, heavy accents, and swords. Pocahontas, who in real life was a young Native American girl, was portrayed by Disney as a brown-skinned, Barbie-like supermodel with an hourglass figure (Giroux, 1997). Consequently, animated characters, even those based on historical record, are either stereotyped or stripped of any meaningful sign of ethnicity. Fortunately, educators have the power to counter such unrealistic images with more accurate representations of historical characters.

Real-Life Television Characters

While some progress can be seen in the representation of ethnic minorities on television, the late 1990s actually brought a decrease in the number of people of color on prime time programming. In 1998, only 19 percent of Screen Actors Guild roles went to people of color. Roles for African Americans, Latinos, and Native Americans decreased from 1997 to 1998 (Screen Actors Guild [SAG], 1999). Women make up fewer than 40 percent of the characters in prime time. Female characters tend to be younger than male characters, conveying the message to viewers that women's youthfulness is more highly valued than other qualities. In terms of work roles, however, female characters' occupations are now less stereotyped, while male characters' occupations continue to be stereotyped (Signorielli & Bacue, 1999). This research suggests that girls' potential role models are somewhat less gender-stereotyped than before, while boy's potential role models are as narrowly defined as ever.

From Comic Book to Playground

Superheroes are the larger-than-life symbols of American values and "maleness." Perhaps the medium in which superheroes are most classically represented is comic books, which date back to the 1930s. The role of the hero is central to the traditional comic book. While female superheroes can be found in comics today (e.g., Marvel Girl, Phoenix, Shadow Cat, Psylocke), they represent only a small proportion—about 24 percent of Marvel Universe superhero trading cards (Young, 1993). Moreover, women and people of color do not fare well in superhero comics. To the extent that female characters exist, they often appear as victims and nuisances. People of color are marginalized

as well. African American and Native American characters are more likely to be portrayed as villains, victims, or simply incompetent than as powerful and intelligent (Pecora, 1992).

One indirect way to gauge the impact of role models on children is to examine the nature of superhero play. Superhero play involving imitation of media characters with superhuman powers is more prevalent among boys than girls (Bell & Crosbie, 1996). This might be a function of the mostly male presence of superhero characters in comics and on television, or it may be due to girls receiving more sanctions from parents and teachers against playing aggressively. Children's imitations of superheroes in play concerns many classroom teachers, because it usually involves chasing, wrestling, kicking, and mock battles. Some researchers argue that superhero play may serve an important developmental function by offering children a sense of power in a world dominated by adults, thus giving children a means of coping with their frustrations. Superhero play also may allow children to grapple with ideas of good and evil and encourage them to work through their own anxieties about safety. Such play also may help children safely express anger and aggression (Boyd, 1997).

Other researchers and educators express concern that superhero play may legitimize aggression, endanger participants, and encourage stereotypical male dominance (Bell & Crosbie, 1996). One researcher observed children's superhero play in a school setting and found that boys created more superhero stories than girls did, and that girls often were excluded from such play. When girls were included they were given stereotypical parts, such as helpers or victims waiting to be saved. Even powerful female X-Men characters were made powerless in the boys' adaptations (Dyson, 1994). Thus, without teacher intervention or an abundance of female superheroes, superhero play may only serve to reinforce gender stereotypes.

One way to gauge popular culture's influence on superhero play is to compare the kind of play children engaged in before and after the arrival of television. In one retrospective study (French & Pena, 1991), adults between the ages of 17 and 83 provided information about their favorite childhood play themes, their heroes, and the qualities of those heroes. While certain methodological pitfalls common to retrospective studies were unavoidable, the findings are nevertheless intriguing. People who grew up before television reported engaging in less fantasy hero play and playing more realistically than kids who grew up with television. While media was the main source of heroes for kids who grew up with television, the previous generations found their heroes not only from the media, but also from direct experience, friends/siblings, and parents' occupations (French & Pena, 1991).

Recent Media Forms: Music Television and Video Games

Video games and music television videos are relatively recent forms of media. In a recent poll, girls and boys from various ethnic backgrounds reported that television and music were their favorite forms of media (Children Now, 1999). What messages about race/ethnicity and gender emerge from music videos—the seemingly perfect merger of children's favorite two media? Seidman (1999) found that the majority of characters were white (63 percent) and a majority were male (63 percent). When people of color, especially women of color, appeared in a video, their characters were much less likely to hold white collar jobs. In fact, their occupations were more gender-stereotyped than in real life. Gender role behavior overall was stereotypical. Thus, music television is yet another domain that perpetuates racial and gender stereotypes.

In the survey described below, the authors found that nearly half (48 percent) of the children surveyed played video and computer games every day or almost every day. Boys, however, were much more likely than girls to play these games. Of those who play computer/video games every day or almost every day, 76 percent are boys and only 24 percent are girls. Consequently, girls and boys might be differentially influenced by the images represented in video and computer games.

What *are* the images presented in video and computer games? Dietz's (1998) content analysis of popular video and computer games found that 79 percent of the games included aggression or violence. Only 15 percent of the games showed women as heroes or action characters. Indeed, girls and women generally were *not* portrayed—30 percent of the videos did not include girls or women at all. When female characters were included, 21 percent of the time they were the damsel in distress. Other female characters were portrayed as evil or as obstacles. This research points to at least two implications of these games. First, girls may not be interested in playing these video and computer games, because the implicit message is that girls are not welcome as players, and that girls and women can only hope to be saved, destroyed, or pushed aside (see also Signorielli, 2001). Second, these images of girls and women found in video and computer games may influence boys' perceptions of gender.

In the past few years, a growing number of computer and video games geared toward girls have been made available by companies such as Purple Moon and Girl Games. These games have adventurous content without the violence typical of games geared toward boys. Two of the best-selling computer games for girls, however, have been *Cosmopolitan Virtual Makeover* and *Barbie Fashion Designer*. While these games may encourage creativity, ultimately their focus is on beauty. One columnist addresses the dilemma of creating games that will appeal to girls while fostering creativity and ingenuity:

> A girl given a doll is being told, "Girls play with dolls just like mommies take care of babies." A boy given a computer game is being told, "Boys play with computers just like daddies use them for work." A girl given *Barbie Fashion Designer* is being told, "Girls play with computers just like girls play with dolls." A lucky few might get the message that, as some girls exchange dolls for real babies, others might progress from *Barbie Fashion Designer* to real-life fashion designer, or engineering systems designer, or software designer. But there's a good chance that many will not (Ivinski, 1997, p. 28).

As more and more educators begin using the Internet, CD-ROMS, and videos as teaching tools (Risko, 1999), they will be faced with the challenge of finding materials that fairly represent a wide range of characters, people, and behavior. Paradoxically, the use of "new" technology, such as CD-ROMs and computer games, implies that a student is going to enjoy a progressive, cutting-edge experience. However, educators must be vigilant about the content, as they should be with any textbook or film. The cutting-edge format of these new technologies does not guarantee nonstereotyped material.

FIELD RESEARCH

A SURVEY OF CHILDREN'S ROLE MODELS AND HEROES

Whom do children actually choose as role models, and why? The authors surveyed children about their heroes and role models, both people they know and famous people or imaginary characters. Survey questions also addressed children's interaction with television, film, computer/ video games, books, and comic books. The children talked about their answers in small groups. One hundred and seventy-nine children, ages 8 to 13, were surveyed from five day camp sites in central and southern California. The ethnic breakdown of the survey sample was as follows: 24 African Americans, 31 Asian Americans, 74 Latinos, 1 Middle Eastern American, 2 Native Americans, 45 whites, and 2 "other." Ninety-five girls and 84 boys participated. The samples of ethnic and gender categories were then weighted so that each of these demographic groups, when analyzed, reflects their actual contribution to the total population of children in the United States.

Do Children Admire People They Know or Famous People?

The survey began with the following: "We would like to know whom you look up to and admire. These might be people you know, or they might be famous people or characters. You may want to be like them or you might just think they are cool." More respondents described a person they knew (65 percent) rather than a person they did not know, such as a person or character in the media (35 percent). When asked in focus groups why they picked people they knew instead of famous people, one 10-year-old white girl said, "I didn't put down people I don't know because when nobody's paying attention, they do something bad." Another student said, "Some [media figures] are just not nice. Some famous people act good on TV but they're really horrible." Thus, some children employed a level of skepticism when judging the worthiness of a role model.

Figure 1 represents the percentages of role models the children knew versus media heroes they identified. Similar to the overall sample, 70 percent of the African American and 64 percent of the white children chose people they knew as heroes. In contrast, only 35 percent of the Asian American kids and 49 percent of the Latino kids named people they knew. This latter finding seems paradoxical;

Asian American and Latino children would seem more likely to choose people they know as role models because their ethnic groups are represented less frequently in mass media than are African Americans and whites. Perhaps Asian American and Latino children have internalized a message that they should not look up to fellow Asian Americans or Latinos as role models, or it may be a by-product of assimilation. Obviously, further work in this area is needed.

On average, responses from girls and boys differed. While both girls and boys named people they knew as their heroes, 67 percent of the girls did so as compared with only 58 percent of the boys. Since boys and men are seen more frequently as sports stars, actors, and musicians, girls may have a smaller pool of potential role models from which to choose. Another factor might be that the girls in this study reported watching less television than the boys did, and so they may have known fewer characters. Sixty-seven percent of the girls reported watching television one hour a day or more, while 87 percent of the boys reported watching television this amount.

Do Children Choose Role Models Who Are Similar to Themselves?

One feature of role modeling is that children tend to choose role models whom they find relevant and with whom they can compare themselves (Lockwood & Kunda, 2000). Children who do not "see themselves" in the media may have fewer opportunities to select realistic role models. Two ways to assess similarity is to consider the ethnicity and gender of children's chosen role models. Do children tend to select heroes who are of their same ethnic background? Because data was not available on the ethnic background of the reported role models whom the children knew personally, the authors examined only the heroes from the media, whose backgrounds were known, to explore this question (see Figure 2). African American and white children were more likely to have media heroes of their same ethnicity (67 percent for each). In contrast, Asian American and Latino children chose more white media heroes than other categories (40 percent and 56 percent, respectively). Only 35 percent of the Asian-American respondents, and 28 percent of the Latino respondents, chose media heroes of their own ethnicity.

Figure 1. Percentages of Known Role Models and Media Role Models

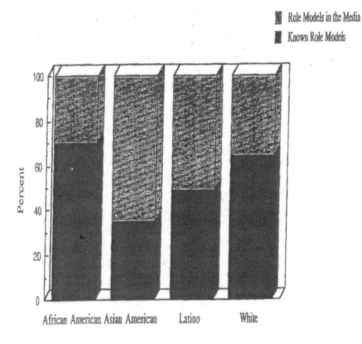

Figure 2. Ethnicity of Media Heroes

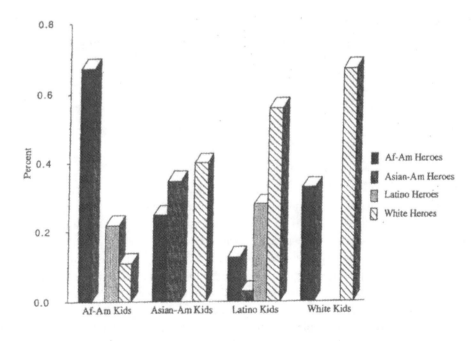

How can we explain the fact that African American and white children are more likely to have media heroes of their same ethnicity, compared to Asian American and Latino children? There is no shortage of white characters for white children to identify with in television and film, and African Americans now make up about 14 percent of television and theatrical characters (SAG, 2000). While African American characters are represented less frequently than white characters, their representation on television, film, and music television is much higher than for Asian American and Latino characters (e.g., Asians represent 2.2 percent, and Latinos represent 4.4 percent, of television and film characters) (SAG, 2000). Also, fewer famous athletes are Asian American or Latino, compared to African American or white.

Also of interest was whether children choose role models of the same, or other, gender. Overall, children in this study more often chose a same-gender person as someone they look up to and admire. This pattern is consistent across all four ethnic groups, and stronger for boys than girls. Only 6 percent of the boys chose a girl or woman, while 24 percent of the girls named a boy or man. Asian American boys actually picked male heroes exclusively. Asian American girls chose the fewest female role models (55 percent) compared to the other girls (see Figure 3). These findings associated with Asian American children present a particular challenge for educators. Asian Americans, and particularly Asian American women, are seldom presented as heroes in textbooks. This is all the more reason for schools to provide a broader and more diverse range of potential role models.

At the same time, it has been reported that boys will tend to imitate those who are powerful (Gibson & Cordova, 1999). Thus, while boys tend to emulate same-gender models more than girls do, boys may emulate a woman if she is high in social power. Therefore, boys may be especially likely to have boys and men as role models because they are more likely to be portrayed in positions of power. It also has been noted that college-age women select men *and* women role models with the same frequency, whereas college-age men still tend to avoid women role models. The fact that young women choose both genders as role models might be a result of the relative scarcity of women in powerful positions to serve as role models (Gibson & Cordova, 1999).

WHO *ARE* CHILDREN'S ROLE MODELS AND HEROES?

Overall, children most frequently (34 percent) named their parents as role models and heroes. The next highest category (20 percent) was entertainers; in descending order, the other categories were friends (14 percent), professional athletes (11 percent), and acquaintances (8 percent). Authors and historical figures were each chosen by only 1 percent of the children.

Patterns were somewhat different when ethnicity was taken into account. African American and white children chose a parent more frequently (30 percent and 33 percent, respectively). In contrast, Asian Americans and Latinos chose entertainers (musicians, actors, and television personalities) most frequently (39 percent for Asian Americans and 47 percent for Latinos), with parents coming in second place. When gender was taken into account, both girls and boys most frequently mentioned a parent (girls 29 percent, boys 34 percent), while entertainers came in second place. Figure 4 illustrates these patterns.

When taking both ethnicity and gender into account, the researchers found that Asian American and Latina girls most frequently picked entertainers (50 percent of the Asian American girls and 41 percent of the Latinas), while African American and white girls chose parents (33 percent and 29 percent, respectively). Asian American boys most frequently named a professional athlete (36 percent), African American boys most frequently picked a parent (30 percent), Latino boys most frequently chose entertainers (54 percent), and white boys picked parents (38 percent).

What Qualities about Their Role Models and Heroes Do Children Admire?

When asked why they admired their heroes and role models, the children most commonly replied that the person was nice, helpful, and understanding (38 percent). Parents were appreciated for their generosity, their understanding, and for "being there." For instance, an 11-year-old African American girl who named her mother as her hero told us, "I like that she helps people when they're in a time of need." Parents were also praised for the lessons they teach their kids. A 9-year-old Asian American boy told us, "I like my dad because he is always nice and he teaches me."

Figure 3. Children Who Have Same-Gender Role Models

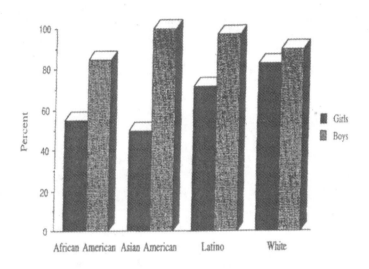

Figure 4. Most Frequently Chosen Role Models by Ethnicity

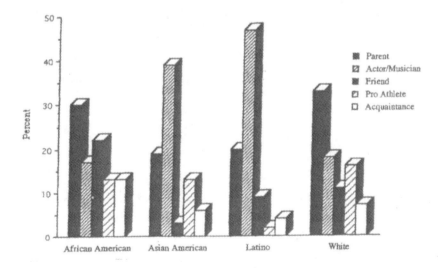

The second most admired feature of kids' role models was skill (27 percent). The skills of athletes and entertainers were most often mentioned. One 12-year-old white boy said he admires Kobe Bryant because "he's a good basketball player and because he makes a good amount of money." A 10-year-old Asian American girl chose Tara Lipinski because "she has a lot of courage and is a great skater." A 9-year-old Latino boy picked Captain America and said, "What I like about Captain America is his cool shield and how he fights the evil red skull." The third most frequently mentioned characteristic was a sense of humor (9 percent), which was most often attributed to entertainers. For instance, a 10-year-old Latino boy picked Will Smith "because he's funny. He makes jokes and he dances funny."

These findings held true for children in all four ethnic groups and across the genders, with two exceptions: boys were more likely than girls to name athletes for their skill, and entertainers for their humor. Given the media attention to the U.S. women's soccer team victory in the World Cup in 1999, and the success of the WNBA (the women's professional basketball league), the researchers expected girls to name women professional athletes as their heroes. However, only four girls in the study did so. Despite recent strides in the visibility of women's sports, the media continue to construct men's sports as the norm and women's sports as marginal (e.g., references to men's athletics as "sports" and women's athletics as "women's sports").

Summary and Implications

Whether the children in this study had heroes they knew in real life, or whether they chose famous people or fictional characters, depended, to some extent, on the respondents' ethnicity and gender. Overall, however, the most frequently named role model for kids was a parent. This is good news for parents, who must wonder, given the omnipresence of the media, whether they have an impact at all on their children. Popular culture was a significant source of heroes for children as well. Entertainers were the second most frequently named role models for the children, and the number increases significantly if you add professional athletes to that category. The attributes that children valued depended on whom they chose. For instance, children who named parents named them because they are helpful and understanding. Media characters were chosen because of their skills. When children's heroes

were media characters, African American and white children were more likely to name media heroes of their same ethnicity. In contrast, Asian American and Latino children tended to name media heroes who were not of their same ethnicity. Children kept to their own gender when choosing a hero; boys were especially reluctant to choose girls and women as their heroes.

The frequency with which boys in this study named athletes as their role models is noteworthy. Only four girls in the study did the same. The implications of this gender difference are important, because many studies find that girls' participation in sports is associated with a number of positive attributes, such as high self-esteem and self-efficacy (Richman & Shaffer, 2000). Therefore, school and community support of girls' athletic programs and recognition of professional women athletes would go a long way to encourage girls' participation in sports, as well as boys' appreciation of women athletes as potential role models.

The mass media are hindered by a narrow view of gender, and by limited, stereotyped representations of ethnic minorities. Parents and educators must take pains to expose children to a wider variety of potential role models than popular culture does. Historical figures and authors constituted a tiny minority of heroes named by the children surveyed. Educators can play a significant role by exposing students to a wide range of such historical heroes, including people from various professions, people of color, and women of all races.

Finally, educators could capitalize on children's need for guidance to expose them to a greater variety of role models. Doing so affirms for the children that their race and gender are worthy of representation. A variety of potential heroes and role models allows children to appreciate themselves and the diversity in others.

REFERENCES

Bell, R., & Crosbie, C. (1996, November 13). Superhero play of 3–5-year-old children. Available: http://labyrinth.net.au/~cccav/sept97/superhero.html.

Boyd, B. J. (1997). Teacher response to superhero play: To ban or not to ban. *Childhood Education, 74*, 23–28.

Children Now. (1999, September). *Boys to men: Messages about masculinity*. Oakland, CA: Author.

Dietz, T. L. (1998). An examination of violence and gender role portrayals in video games: Implications for gender socialization. *Sex Roles, 38*, 425–433.

Dyson, A. H. (1994). The ninjas, the X-men, and the ladies: Playing with power and identity in an urban primary school. *Teachers College Record, 96*, 219–239.

French, J., & Pena, S. (1991). Children's hero play of the 20th century: Changes resulting from television's influence. *Child Study Journal, 21*, 79–94.

Gerbner, C. (1993). *Women and minorities on television: A study in casting and fate.* A report to the Screen Actors Guild and the American Federation of Radio and Television Artists, Philadelphia: The Annenberg School of Communication, University of Pennsylvania.

Gibson, D. E., & Cordova, D. I. (1999). Women's and men's role models: The importance of exemplars. In A. J. Murrell, F. J. Crosby, & R. J. Ely (Eds.), *Mentoring dilemmas: Developmental relationships within multicultural organizations* (pp. 121–141). Mahwah, NJ: Lawrence Erlbaum Associates.

Giroux, H. A. (1997). Are Disney movies good for your kids? In S. R. Steinberg & J. L. Kincheloe (Eds.), *Kinderculture: The corporate construction of childhood* (pp. 53–67). Boulder, CO: Westview Press.

Ivinski, P. (1997). Game girls: Girl market in computer games and educational software. *Print, 51*, 24–29.

Lockwood, P., & Kunda, Z. (2000). Outstanding role models: Do they inspire or demoralize us? In A. Tesser, R. B. Felson, et al. (Eds.), *Psychological perspectives on self and identity* (pp. 147–171). Washington, DC: American Psychological Association.

National Television Violence Study. Vol. 3. (1998). Thousand Oaks, CA: Sage.

Pecora, N. (1992). Superman/superboys/supermen: The comic book hero as socializing agent. In S. Craig (Ed.), *Men, masculinity, and the media* (pp. 61–77). Newbury Park, CA: Sage.

Richman, E. L., & Shaffer, D. R. (2000). "If you let me play sports": How might sport participation influence the self-esteem of adolescent females? *Psychology of Women Quarterly, 24*, 189–199.

Risko, V. J. (1999). The power and possibilities of video technology and intermediality. In L. Sernali & A. Watts Pailliotet (Eds.), *Intermediality: The teachers' handbook of critical media literacy* (pp. 129–140). Boulder, CO: Westview Press.

Screen Actors Guild. (1999, May 3). *New Screen Actors Guild employment figures reveal a decline in roles for Latinos, African American and Native American Indian performers.* Press Release. Available: www.sag.org.

Screen Actors Guild. (2000, December 20). *Screen Actors Guild employment statistics reveal percentage increases in available roles for African Americans and Latinos, but total number of roles to minorities decrease in 1999.* Press Release. Available: www.sag.org.

Seidman, S. A. (1999). Revisiting sex-role stereotyping in MTV videos. *International Journal of Instructional Media, 26*, 11.

Signorielli, N. (2001). Television's gender role images and contribution to stereotyping: Past, present, future. In D. G. Singer & J. L. Singer (Eds.), *Handbook of children and the media* (pp. 341–358). Thousand Oaks, CA: Sage.

Signorielli, N., & Bacue, A. (1999). Recognition and respect: A content analysis of prime-time television characters across three decades. *Sex Roles, 40*, 527–544.

Thompson, T. L., & Zerbinos, E. (1995). Gender roles in animated cartoons: Has the picture changed in 20 years? *Sex Roles, 32*, 651–673.

Young, T. J. (1993). Women as comic book superheroes: The "weaker sex" in the Marvel universe. *Psychology: A Journal of Human Behavior, 30*, 49–50.

AUTHORS' NOTES

This project was conducted in conjunction with Mediascope not-for-profit media education organization. The terms "hero" and "role model" tend to be used interchangeably in the literature. When a distinction between the terms is made, role models are defined as known persons (e.g., parents, teachers) and heroes are defined as figures who may be less attainable, or larger than life. Both kinds of persons and figures are of interest here; therefore, the terms are used interchangeably, and we specify whether known people or famous figures are being discussed.

From Kristin J. Anderson and Donna Cavallaro, "Parents or Pop Culture? Children's Heroes and Role Models," *Childhood Education*, Spring 2002, pp. 161–168. Reprinted by permission.

FIELD RESEARCH

Epistemology: How You Know What You Know—
Kenneth L. Feder

KNOWING THINGS

The word **epistemology** means the study of knowledge—how you know what you know. Think about it. How does anybody know anything to be actual, truthful, or real? How do we differentiate the reasonable from the unreasonable, the meaningful from the meaningless—in archaeology or in any other field of knowledge? Everybody knows things, but how do we really know these things?

I know that there is a mountain in a place called Tibet. I know that the mountain is called Everest, and I know that it is the tallest land mountain in the world (there are some a bit taller under the ocean). I even know that it is precisely 29,028 feet high. But I have never measured it; I've never even been to Tibet. Beyond this, I have not measured all of the other mountains in the world to compare them to Everest. Yet I am quite confident that Everest is the world's tallest peak. But how do I know that?

On the subject of mountains, there is a run-down stone monument on the top of Bear Mountain in the northwestern corner of Connecticut. The monument was built toward the end of the nineteenth century and marks the "highest ground" in Connecticut. When the monument was built to memorialize this most lofty and auspicious of peaks—the mountain is all of 2,316 feet high—people knew that it was the highest point in the state and wanted to recognize this fact with the monument.

There is only one problem. In recent times, with more accurate, sophisticated measuring equipment, it has been determined that Bear Mountain is not the highest point in Connecticut. The slope of Frissell Mountain, which actually peaks in Massachusetts, reaches a height of 2,380 feet on the Connecticut side of the border, eclipsing Bear Mountain by about 64 feet.

So, people in the late 1800s and early 1900s "knew" that Bear Mountain was the highest point in Connecticut. Today we *know* that they really did not "know" that, because it really was not true—even though they thought it was and built a monument saying so.

Now, suppose that I read in a newspaper, hear on the radio, or see on television a claim that another mountain has been found that is actually ten (or fifty or ten thousand) feet higher than Mount Everest. Indeed, recently, new satellite data convinced a few, just for a while, that a peak neighboring Everest was, in actuality, slightly higher. You and I have never been to Tibet. How do we know if these reports are true? What criteria can we use to decide if the information is not? It all comes back to **epistemology**. How indeed do we know what we think we "know"?

Collecting Information: Seeing Isn't Necessarily Believing

In general, people collect information in two ways:

1. Directly through their own experiences.

2. Indirectly through specific information sources like friends, teachers, parents, books, TV, etc.

People tend to think that number 1—obtaining firsthand information, the stuff they see or experience themselves—is always the best way. This is unfortunately a false assumption because most people are poor observers.

For example, the list of animals alleged to have been observed by people that turn out to be figments of their imaginations is staggering. It is fascinating to read Pliny, a first-century thinker, or Topsell, who wrote in the seventeenth century, and see detailed accounts of the nature and habits of dragons, griffins, unicorns, mermaids, and so on (Byrne 1979). People claimed to have seen these animals, gave detailed descriptions, and even drew pictures of them. Many folks read their books and believed them.

Some of the first European explorers of Africa, Asia, and the New World could not decide if some of the native people they encountered were human beings or animals. They sometimes depicted them with hair all over their bodies and even as having tails.

Neither are untrained observers very good at identifying known, living animals. A red or "lesser" panda escaped from the zoo in Rotterdam, Holland, in December 1978. Red pandas are very rare animals and are indigenous to India, not Holland. They are distinctive in appearance and cannot be readily mistaken for any other sort of animal.

The zoo informed the press that the panda was missing, hoping the publicity would alert people in the area of the zoo and aid in its return. Just when the newspapers came out with the panda story, it was found, quite dead, along some railroad tracks adjacent to the zoo. Nevertheless, over one hundred sightings of the panda *alive* were reported to the zoo from all over the Netherlands *after* the animal was obviously already dead. These reports did not stop until several days after the newspapers announced the discovery of the dead panda (van Kampen 1979). So much for the absolute reliability of firsthand observation.

Collecting Information: Relying on Others

When we explore the problems of secondhand information, we run into even more complications. Now we are not in place to observe something firsthand; we are forced to rely on someone else's observations, interpretations, and reports—as with the question of the height of Mount Everest. How do we know what to believe? This is a crucial question that all rational people must ask themselves, whether talking about medicine, religion, archaeology, or anything else. Again, it comes back around to epistemology; how do we know what we think we know, and how do we know what or whom to believe?

Science: Playing by the Rules

There are ways to knowledge that are both dependable and reliable. We might not be able to get to absolute truths about the meaning of existence, but we figure out quite a bit about our world—about chemistry and biology, psychology and sociology, physics and history, and even prehistory. The techniques we are talking about to get at knowledge that we can feel confident in—knowledge that is reliable, truthful, and factual—are referred to as *science*.

In large part, science is a series of techniques used to *maximize* the probability that what we think we know really reflects the way things are, were, or will be. Science makes no claim to have all the answers or even to be right all of the time. On the contrary, during the process of the growth of knowledge and understanding, science is often wrong. The only claim that we do make in science is that if we honestly, consistently, and vigorously pursue knowledge using some basic techniques and principles, the truth will eventually surface and we can truly know things about the nature of the world in which we find ourselves.

The question then is, "What exactly is science?" If you believe Hollywood, science is a mysterious enterprise where in old, white-haired, rather eccentric bearded gentlemen labor feverishly in white lab coats, mix assorted chemicals, invent mysterious compounds, and attempt to reanimate dead tissue. So much for Hollywood. Scientists don't have to look like anything in particular. We are just people trying to arrive at some truths about how the world and universe work. While the application of science can be a slow, frustrating, all-consuming enterprise, the basic assumptions we scientists hold are really very simple. Whether we are physicists, biologists, or archaeologists, we all work under four underlying principles. These principles are quite straightforward, but equally quite crucial.

1. There is a real and knowable universe.

2. The universe (which includes stars, planets, animals, and rocks, as well as people, their cultures, and their histories) operates according to certain understandable rules or laws.

3. These laws are immutable—that means they do not, in general, change depending on where you are or "when" you are.

4. These laws can be discerned, studied, and understood by people through careful observation, experimentation, and research.

Let's look at these assumptions one at a time.

There Is a Real and Knowable Universe

In science we have to agree that there is a real universe out there for us to study—a universe full of stars, animals, human history, and prehistory that exists whether we are happy with that reality or not.

The Universe Operates According to Understandable Laws

In essence, what this means is that there are rules by which the universe works: stars produce heat and light according to the laws of nuclear physics; nothing can go faster than the speed of light; all matter in the universe is attracted to all other matter (the law of gravity).

Even human history is not random but can be seen as following certain patterns of human cultural evolution. For example, the development of complex civilizations in Egypt, China, India/Pakistan, Mesopotamia, Mexico, and Peru was not based on random processes (Lamberg-Karlovsky and Sabloff 1979; Haas 1982). Their evolution seems to reflect similar general patterns. This is not to say that all of these civilizations were identical, any more than we say that all stars are identical. On the contrary, they existed in different physical and cultural environments, and so we should expect that they would be different. However, in each case the rise to civilization was preceded by the development of an agricultural economy. In each case, civilization was also preceded by some degree of overall population increase as well as increased population density in some areas (in other words, the development of cities). Again, in each case we find monumental works (pyramids, temples), evidence of long-distance trade, and the development of mathematics, astronomy, and methods of record keeping (usually, but not always, in the form of writing). The cultures in which civilization developed, though some were unrelated and independent, shared these factors because of the non-random patterns of cultural evolution.

The point is that everything operates according to rules. In science we believe that, by understanding these rules or laws, we can understand stars, organisms, and even ourselves.

THE LAWS ARE IMMUTABLE

That the laws do not change under ordinary conditions is a crucial concept in science. A law that works here, works there. A law that worked in the past will work today and will work in the future.

For example, if I go to the top of the Leaning Tower of Pisa today and simultaneously drop two balls of unequal mass, they will fall at the same rate and reach the ground at the same time, just as they did when Galileo performed a similar experiment in the seventeenth century. If I do it today, they will. Tomorrow, the same. If I perform the same experiment countless times, the same thing will occur because the laws of the universe (in this case, the law of gravity) do not change through time. They also do not change depending on where you are. Go anywhere on the earth and perform the same experiment—you will get the same results (try not to hit any pedestrians or you will see some other "laws" in operation). This experiment was even performed by U.S. astronauts on the moon. A hammer and a feather were dropped from the same height, and they hit the surface at precisely the same time (the only reason this will not work on earth is because the feather is caught by the air and the hammer, obviously, is not). We have no reason to believe that the results would be different anywhere, or "any-when" else.

If this assumption of science, that the laws do not change through time, were false, many of the so-called historical sciences, including prehistoric archaeology, could not exist.

For example, a major principle in the field of historical geology is that of *uniformitarianism*. It can be summarized in the phrase, "the present is the key to the past." Historical geologists are interested in knowing how the various landforms we see today came into being. They recognize that they cannot go back in time to see how the Grand Canyon was formed. However, since the laws of geology that governed the development of the Grand Canyon have not changed through time, and since these laws are still in operation, they do not need to. Historical geologists can study the formation of geological features today and apply what they learn to the past. The same laws they can directly study operating in the present were operating in the past when geological features that interested them first formed.

The present that we can observe is indeed the "key" to the past that we cannot. This is true because the laws or rules that govern the universe are constant—those that operate today operated in the past. This is why science does not limit itself to the present, but makes inferences about the past and even predictions about the future (just listen to the weather report for an example of this). We can do so because we can study modern, ongoing phenomena that work under the same laws that existed in the past and will exist in the future.

This is where science and theology are often forced to part company and respectfully disagree. Remember, science depends on the constancy of the laws that we can discern. On the other hand, advocates of many religions, though they might believe that there are laws that govern things (and which, according to them, were established by a Creator), usually (but not always) believe that these laws can be changed at any time by their God. In other words, if God does not want the apple to fall to the ground, but instead, to hover, violating the law of gravity, that is precisely what will happen. As a more concrete example, scientists know that the heat and light given off by a fire results from the transformation of mass (of the wood) to energy. Physical laws control this process. A theologian, however, might agree with this ordinarily, but feels that if God wants to create a fire that does not consume any mass (like the "burning bush" of the Old Testament), then this is exactly what will occur. Most scientists simply do not accept this assertion. The rules are the rules. They do not change, even though we might sometimes wish that they would.

The Laws Can Be Understood

This may be the single most important principle in science. The universe is knowable. It may be complicated, and it may take years and years to understand even apparently simple phenomena. However, little by little, bit by bit, we expand our knowledge. Through careful observation and objective research and experimentation, we can indeed know things.

So, our assumptions are simple enough. We accept the existence of a reality independent of our own minds, and we accept that this reality works according to a series of unchanging laws or rules. We also claim that we can recognize and understand these laws or at least recognize the patterns that result from these universal rules. The question remains then: how do we do science—how do we explore the nature of the universe, whether our interest is planets, stars, atoms, or human prehistory?

THE WORKINGS OF SCIENCE

We can know things by employing the rules of logic and rational thought. Scientists—archaeologists or otherwise—usually work through a combination of the logical processes known as **induction** and **deduction**. The dictionary definition of induction is "arguing from specifics to generalities," while deduction is defined as the reverse, arguing from generalities to specifics.

What is essential to good science is objective, unbiased observations—of planets, molecules, rock formations, archaeological sites, and so on. Often, on the basis of these specific observations, we induce explanations called *hypotheses* for how these things work.

For example, we may study the planets Mercury, Venus, Earth, and Mars (each one presents specific bits of information). We then induce general rules about how we think these inner planets in our solar system were formed. Or, we might study a whole series of different kinds of molecules and then induce general rules about how all molecules interact chemically. We may study different rock formations and make general conclusions about their origin. We can study a number of specific prehistoric sites and make generalizations about how cultures evolved.

Notice that we cannot directly observe planets forming, the rules of molecular interaction, rocks being made, or prehistoric cultures evolving. Instead, we are inducing general conclusions and principles concerning our data that seem to follow logically from what we have been able to observe.

This process of induction, though crucial to science, is not enough. We need to go beyond our induced hypotheses by testing them. If our induced hypotheses are indeed valid—that is, if they really represent the actual rules according to which some aspect of the universe (planets, molecules, rocks, ancient societies) works—they should be able to hold up under the rigors of scientific hypothesis testing.

Observation and suggestion of hypotheses, therefore, are only the first steps in a scientific investigation. In science we always need to go beyond observation and hypothesizing. We need to set up a series of "if…then" statements; "if" our hypothesis is true "then" the following deduced "facts" will also be true. Our results are not always precise and clear–cut, especially in a science like archaeology, but this much should be clear—scientists are not just out there collecting a bunch of interesting facts. Facts are always collected within the context of trying to explain something or in trying to test a hypothesis.

As an example of this logical process, consider the health effects of smoking. How can scientists be sure that smoking is bad for you? After all, it's pretty rare that someone takes a puff on a cigarette and immediately drops dead. The certainty comes from a combination of induction and deduction. Observers have noticed for about three hundred years that people who smoked seemed to be more likely than people who did not to get certain diseases. As long ago as the seventeenth century, people noticed that habitual pipe smokers were subject to tumor growths on their lips and in their mouths. From such observations we can reasonably, though tentatively, induce a hypothesis of the unhealthfulness of smoking, but we still need to test such a hypothesis. We need to set up "if... then" statements. If, in fact, smoking is a hazard to your health (the hypothesis we have induced based on our observations), then we should be able to deduce some predictions that must also be true. Sure enough, when we test specific, deduced predictions like

1. Smokers will have a higher incidence than nonsmokers of lung cancer

2. Smokers will have a higher incidence of emphysema

3. Smokers will take more sick days from work

4. Smokers will get more upper respiratory infections

5. Smokers will have diminished lung capacity

6. Smokers will have a shorter life expectancy

we see that our original, induced hypothesis—cigarette smoking is hazardous to your health—is upheld.

That was easy, but also obvious. How about an example with more mystery to it, one in which scientists acting in the way of detectives had to solve a puzzle in order to save lives? Carl Hempel (1966), a philosopher of science, provided the following example in his book *The Philosophy of Natural Science*.

THE CASE OF CHILDBED FEVER

In the 1840s things were not going well at the Vienna General Hospital, particularly in Ward 1 of the Maternity Division. In Ward 1 more than one in ten of the women brought in to give birth died soon after of a terrible disease called "childbed fever." This was a high death rate even for the 1840s. In one year 11.4 percent of the women who gave birth in Ward 1 died of this disease. It was a horrible situation and truly mystifying when you consider the fact that in Ward 2, another maternity division in the *same* hospital at the same time, only about one in fifty of the women (2 percent) died from this disease.

Plenty of people had tried their hand at inducing some possible explanations or hypotheses to explain these facts. It was suggested that more women were dying in Ward 1 due to "atmospheric disturbances," or perhaps it was "cosmic forces." However, no one had really sat down and considered the deductive implications of the various hypotheses—those things that would necessarily have been true if the proposed, induced explanations were in fact true. No one, that is, until a Hungarian doctor, Ignaz Semmelweis, attacked the problem in 1848.

Semmelweis made some observations in the maternity wards at the hospital. He noted some differences between Wards 1 and 2 and induced a series of possible explanations for the drastic difference in the mortality rates. Semmelweis suggested:

1. Ward 1 tended to be more crowded than Ward 2. The overcrowding in Ward 1 was the cause of the higher mortality rate there.

2. Women in Ward 1 were from a lower socioeconomic class and tended to give birth lying on their backs, while in Ward 2 the predominate position was on the side. Birth position was the cause of the higher mortality rate.

3. There was a psychological factor involved; the hospital priest had to walk through Ward 1 to administer the last rites to dying patients in other wards. This sight so upset some women already weakened by the ordeal of childbirth that it contributed to their deaths.

4. There were more student doctors in Ward 1. Students were rougher than experienced physicians in their treatment of the women, unintentionally harming them and contributing to their deaths.

These induced hypotheses all sounded good. Each marked a genuine difference between Wards 1 and 2 that might have caused the difference in the death rate. Semmelweis was doing what most scientists do in such a situation; he was relying on creativity and imagination in seeking out an explanation.

Creativity and imagination are just as important to science as good observation. But being creative and imaginative was not enough. It did not help the women who were still dying at an alarming rate. Semmelweis had to go beyond producing possible explanations; he had to test each one of them. So, he deduced the necessary implications of each:

1. If hypothesis 1 were correct, then cutting down the crowding in Ward 1 should cut down the mortality rate. Semmelweis tried precisely that. The result: no change. So the first hypothesis was rejected. It had failed the scientific test; it simply could not be correct.

2. Semmelweis went on to test hypothesis 2 by changing the birth positions of the women in Ward 1 to match those of the women in Ward 2. Again, there was no change, and another hypothesis was rejected.

3. Next, to test hypothesis 3, Semmelweis rerouted the priest. Again, women in Ward 1 continued to die of childbed fever at about five times the rate of those in Ward 2.

4. Finally, to test hypothesis 4, Semmelweis made a special effort to get the student doctors to be more gentle in their birth assistance to the women in Ward 1. The result was the same; 10 or 11 percent of the women in Ward 1 died compared to about 2 percent in Ward 2.

Then, as so often happens in science, Semmelweis had a stroke of luck. A doctor friend of his died, and the way he died provided Semmelweis with another possible explanation for the problem in Ward 1. Though Semmelweis's friend was not a woman who had recently given birth, he did have precisely the same symptoms as did the women who were dying of childbed fever. Most importantly, this doctor had died of a disease just like childbed fever soon after accidentally cutting himself during an autopsy.

Viruses and bacteria were unknown in the 1840s. Surgical instruments were not sterilized, no special effort was made to clean the hands, and doctors did not wear gloves during operations and autopsies. Semmelweis had another hypothesis; perhaps the greater number of medical students in Ward 1 was at the root of the mystery, but not because of their inexperience. Instead, these students, as part of their training, were much more likely than experienced doctors to be performing autopsies. Supposing that there was something bad in dead bodies and this something had entered Semmelweis's friend's system through his wound—could the same bad "stuff" (Semmelweis called it "cadaveric material") get onto the hands of the student doctors, who then might, without washing, go on to help a woman give birth? Then, if this "cadaveric material" were transmitted into the woman's body during the birth of her baby, this material might lead to her death. It was a simple enough hypothesis to test. Semmelweis simply had the student doctors carefully wash their hands after performing autopsies. The women stopped dying in Ward 1. Semmelweis had solved the mystery.

SCIENCE AND NONSCIENCE: THE ESSENTIAL DIFFERENCES

Through objective observation and analysis, a scientist, whether a physicist, chemist, biologist, psychologist, or archaeologist, sees things that need explaining. Through creativity and imagination, the scientist suggests possible hypotheses to explain these "mysteries." The scientist then sets up a rigorous method through experimentation or subsequent research to deductively test the validity of a given hypothesis. If the implications of a hypothesis are shown not to be true, the hypothesis must be rejected and then it's back to the drawing board. If the implications are found to be true, we can uphold or support our hypothesis.

A number of other points should be made here. The first is that in order for a hypothesis, whether it turns out to be upheld or not, to be scientific in the first place, it must be testable. In other words, there must be clear, deduced implications that can be drawn from the hypothesis and then tested. Remember the hypotheses of "cosmic influences" and "atmospheric disturbances"? How can you test these? What are the necessary implications that can be deduced from the hypothesis, "More women died in Ward 1 due to atmospheric disturbances"? There really aren't any, and therefore such a hypothesis is not scientific—it cannot be tested. Remember, in the methodology of science, we ordinarily need to:

1. Observe

2. Induce general hypotheses or possible explanations for what we have observed

3. Deduce specific things that must also be true if our hypothesis is true

4. Test the hypothesis by checking out the deduced implications

If there are no specific implications of a hypothesis that can then be analyzed as a test of the validity or usefulness of that hypothesis, then you simply are not doing and cannot do "science."

For example, suppose you observe a person who appears to be able to "guess" the value of a playing card picked from a deck. Next, assume that someone hypothesizes that "psychic" ability is involved. Finally, suppose the claim is made that the "psychic" ability goes away as soon as you try to test it (actually named the "shyness effect" by some researchers of the paranormal). Such a claim is not itself testable and therefore not scientific.

Beyond the issue of testability, another lesson is involved in determining whether an approach to a problem is scientific. Semmelweis induced four different hypotheses to explain the difference in mortality rates between Wards 1 and 2. These "competing" explanations are called *multiple working hypotheses*. Notice that Semmelweis did not simply proceed by a process of elimination. He did not, for example, test the first three hypotheses and—after finding them invalid—declare that the fourth was necessarily correct since it was the only one left that he had thought of.

Some people try to work that way. A light is seen in the sky. Someone hypothesizes it was a meteor. We find out that it was not. Someone else hypothesizes that it was a military rocket. Again this turns out to be incorrect. Someone else suggests that it was the Goodyear Blimp, but that turns out to have been somewhere else. Finally, someone suggests that it was the spacecraft of people from another planet. Some will say that this must be correct, since none of the other explanations panned out. This is nonsense. There

are plenty of other possible explanations. Eliminating all of the explanations *we* have been able to think of except one (which, perhaps, has no testable implications) in no way allows us to uphold that final hypothesis…

It's like seeing a card trick. You are mystified by it. You have a few possible explanations: the magician did it with mirrors, there was a helper in the audience, the cards were marked. But when you approach the magician and ask which it was, he assures you that none of your hypotheses are correct. Do you then decide that what you saw was an example of genuine, supernatural magic? Of course not! Simply because you or I cannot come up with the right explanation does not mean that the trick has a supernatural explanation. We simply admit that we do not have the expertise to suggest a more reasonable hypothesis.

Finally, there is another rule to hypothesis ranking and testing. It is called *Occam's Razor* or *Occam's Rule*. In essence it says that when a number of hypotheses are proposed through induction to explain a given set of observations, the simplest hypothesis is probably the best.

Take this actual example. During the eighteenth and nineteenth centuries, huge, buried, fossilized bones were found throughout North America and Europe. One hypothesis, the simplest, was that the bones were the remains of animals that no longer existed. This hypothesis simply relied on the assumption that bones do not come into existence by themselves, but always serve as the skeletons of animals. Therefore, when you find bones, there must have been animals who used those bones. However, another hypothesis was suggested: the bones were deposited by the Devil to fool us into thinking that such animals existed (Howard 1975). This hypothesis demanded many more assumptions about the universe than did the first: there is a Devil, that Devil is interested in human affairs, he wants to fool us, he has the ability to make bones of animals that never existed, and he has the ability to hide them under the ground and inside solid rock. That is quite a number of unproven (and largely untestable) claims to swallow. Thus, Occam's Razor says the simpler hypothesis, that these great bones are evidence of the existence of animals that no longer exist—in other words, dinosaurs—is better. The other one simply raises more questions than it answers.

FIELD RESEARCH

THE ART OF SCIENCE

Don't get the impression that science is a mechanical enterprise. Science is at least partially an art. It is much more than just observing the results of experiments.

It takes great creativity to recognize a "mystery" in the first place. In the apocryphal story, countless apples had fallen from countless trees and undoubtedly conked the noggins of multitudes of stunned individuals who never thought much about it. It took a fabulously creative individual, Isaac Newton, to even recognize that herein lay a mystery. Why did the apple fall? No one had ever articulated the possibility that the apple could have hovered in midair. It could have moved off in any of the cardinal directions. It could have gone straight up and out of sight. But it did not. It fell to the ground as it always had, in all places, and as it always would. It took great imagination to recognize that in this simple observation (and in a bump on the head) rested the eloquence of a fundamental law of the universe.

Further, it takes great skill and imagination to invent a hypothesis in this attempt to understand why things seem to work the way they do. Remember, Ward 1 at the Vienna General Hospital did not have written over its doors, OVERCROWDED WARD or WARD WITH STUDENT DOCTORS WHO DON'T WASH THEIR HANDS AFTER AUTOPSIES. It took imagination first to recognize that there were differences between the wards and, quite importantly, that some of the differences might logically be at the root of the mystery. After all, there were in all likelihood many, many differences between the wards: their compass orientations, the names of the nurses, the precise alignment of the windows, the astrological signs of the doctors who worked in the wards, and so on. If a scientist were to attempt to test all of these differences as hypothetical causes of a mystery, nothing would ever be solved. Occam's Razor must be applied. We need to focus our intellectual energies on those possible explanations that require few other assumptions. Only after all of these have been eliminated, can we legitimately consider others. As summarized by that great fictional detective, Sherlock Holmes:

> It is of the highest importance in the art of detection to be able to recognize, out of a number of facts, which are incidental and which are vital. Otherwise, your energy and attention must be dissipated instead of being concentrated.

Semmelweis concentrated his attention on first four, then a fifth possible explanation. Like all good scientists he had to use some amount of what we can call "intuition" to sort out the potentially vital from the probably incidental. Even in the initial sorting we may be wrong. Overcrowding seemed a very plausible explanation to Semmelweis, but it was wrong nonetheless.

Finally, it takes skill and inventiveness to suggest ways for testing the hypothesis in question. We must, out of our own heads, be able to invent the "then" part of our "if…then" statements. We need to be able to suggest those things that must be true if our hypothesis is to be supported. There really is an art to that. Anyone can claim there was a Lost Continent of Atlantis, but often it takes a truly inventive mind to suggest precisely what archaeologists must find if the hypothesis of its existence were indeed to be valid.

Semmelweis tested his hypotheses and solved the mystery of childbed fever by changing conditions in Ward 1 to see if the death rate would change. In essence, the testing of each hypothesis was an experiment. In archaeology, the testing of hypotheses often must be done in a different manner. There is a branch of archaeology called, appropriately enough, "experimental archaeology" that involves the experimental replication and utilization of prehistoric artifacts in an attempt to figure out how they were made and used. In general, however, archaeology is largely not an experimental science. Archaeologists more often need to create "models" of some aspect of cultural adaptation and change. These models are simplified, manipulable versions of cultural phenomena.

For example, James Mosimann and Paul Martin (1975) created a computer program that simulated or modeled the first human migration into America some 12,000 years ago. By varying the size of the initial human population and their rate of growth and expansion, as well as the size of the big-game animal herds in the New World, Mosimann and Martin were able to test their hypothesis that these human settlers caused the extinction of many species of game animals. The implications of their mathematical modeling can be tested against actual archaeological and paleontological data.

Ultimately, whether a science is experimentally based or not makes little logical difference in the testing of hypotheses. Instead of predicting what the results of a given experiment must be if our induced hypothesis is useful or valid, we predict what new data we must be able to find if a given hypothesis is correct.

For instance, we may hypothesize that long-distance trade is a key element in the development of civilization based upon our analysis of the ancient Maya. We deduce that if this is correct—if this is, in fact, a general rule of cultural evolution—we must find large quantities of trade items in other parts of the world where civilization also developed. We might further deduce that these items should be found in contexts that denote their value and importance to the society (for example, in the burials of leaders). We must then determine the validity of our predictions and, indirectly, our hypothesis by going out and conducting more research. We need to excavate sites belonging to other ancient civilizations and see if they followed the same pattern as seen for the Maya relative to the importance of trade.

Testing a hypothesis certainly is not easy. Sometimes errors in testing can lead to incorrectly validating or rejecting a hypothesis. Some of you may have already caught a potential problem in Semmelweis's application of the scientific method. Remember hypothesis 4? It was initially suggested that the student doctors were at the root of the higher death rate in Ward 1, because they were not as gentle in assisting in birthing as were the more experienced doctors. This hypothesis was not borne out by testing. Retraining the students had no effect on the mortality rate in Ward 1. But suppose that Semmelweis had tested this hypothesis instead by removing the students altogether prior to their retraining. From what we now know, the death rate would have indeed declined, and Semmelweis would have concluded incorrectly that the hypothesis was correct. We can assume that once the retrained students were returned to the ward (gentler, perhaps, but with their hands still dirty) the death rate would have jumped up again since the students were indeed at the heart of the matter, but not because of their presumed rough handling of the maternity patients.

This should point out that our testing of hypotheses takes a great deal of thought and that we can be wrong. We must remember we have a hypothesis, we have the deduced implications, and we have the test. We can make errors at any place within this process—the hypothesis may be

incorrect, the implications may be wrong, or the way we test them may be incorrect. Certainty in science is a scarce commodity. There are always new hypotheses, alternative explanations, and more deductive implications to test. Nothing is ever finished, nothing is set in concrete, nothing is ever defined or raised to the level of religious truth.

Beyond this, it must be admitted that scientists are, after all, ordinary human beings. They are not isolated from the cultures and times in which they live. They share many of the same prejudices and biases of other members of their societies. Scientists learn from mentors at universities and often inherit their perspectives. It often is quite difficult to go against the scientific grain, to question accumulated wisdom, and to suggest a new approach or perspective.

For example, when German meteorologist Alfred Wegener hypothesized in 1912 that the present configuration of the continents resulted from the breakup of a single inclusive landmass and that the separate continents had "drifted" into their current positions (a process called *continental drift*), most rejected the suggestion outright. Yet today, Wegener's general perspective is accepted and incorporated into the general theory of *plate tectonics*.

Philosopher of science Thomas Kuhn (1970) has suggested that the growth of scientific knowledge is not neatly linear, with knowledge simply building on knowledge. He maintains that science remains relatively static for periods and that most thinkers work under the same set of assumptions—the same *paradigm*. New ideas or perspectives, like those of Wegener or Einstein, that challenge the existing orthodoxy, are usually initially rejected. Only once scientists get over the shock of the new ideas and start testing the new frameworks suggested by these new paradigms are great jumps in knowledge made.

That is why in science we propose, test, tentatively accept, but never prove a hypothesis. We keep only those hypotheses that cannot be disproved. As long as a hypothesis holds up under the scrutiny of additional testing through experiment and/or is not contradicted by new data, we accept it as the best explanation so far. Some hypotheses sound good, pass the rigors of initial testing, but are later shown to be inadequate or invalid. Others—for example, the hypothesis of biological evolution—have held up so well (all new data either were or could have been deduced from it) that they will probably always be upheld. We usually call these very well supported hypotheses *theories*. However, it is in the nature of science that no matter how well an explanation of some aspect of reality has held up, we must always be prepared to consider new tests and better explanations.

We are interested in knowledge and explanations of the universe that work. As long as these explanations work, we keep them. As soon as they cease being effective because new data and tests show them to be incomplete or misguided, we discard them and seek new ones. In one sense, Semmelweis was wrong after all, though his explanation worked at the time—he did save lives through its application. We now know that there is nothing inherently bad in "cadaveric material." Dead bodies are not the cause of childbed fever. Today we realize that it is a bacteria that can grow in the flesh of a dead body that can get on a doctor's hands, infect a pregnant woman, and cause her death. Semmelweis worked in a time before the existence of such things was known. Science in this way always grows, expands, and evolves.

Kenneth L. Feder, 1990, "Epistemology: How You Know What You Know," *Frauds, Myths, and Mysteries*, Chapter 2, pp. 9–26. Copyright © 1990 The McGraw-Hill Companies. Reproduced with permission of The McGraw-Hill Companies.

Does Ethnography Falsify Reality?—
Paul Bohannan and Dirk van der Elst

In North America, ethnography began with studies of those who peopled the New World before Westerners arrived. The context of early observations included a painful awareness that the indigenous tribes had been knocked askew by movements of European immigrants, freed slaves of African descent, and the American Indians themselves. The first Americans were still being decimated by alien diseases and the policies of various national governments, and the survivors were turned into encapsulated minorities.

The early ethnographers set out to learn and describe what pre-contact cultures had been like before they were hit by the Euro-American juggernaut. Unfortunately they had, especially in the beginning, a terribly simplistic view of culture: they assumed all non-Western lifeways were

necessarily stable until "disturbed." At that early date, no one yet realized that *all* societies are *always* in a state of change. Sometimes the pace of change is fast, sometimes slow, but as long as people die and are replaced, and as long as they keep having ideas, culture will change (**culture change**).

To "recover" that imaginary static state, early ethnographers interviewed old men (and, less often, old women) who remembered "the good old days"—overlooking the fact that the attitudes and memories of the elderly, like everybody else's, are influenced by everything that has happened to them since the events in question occurred.

The memories of old people are, of course, immensely valuable to understanding any culture—if we remember that culture is an ongoing process and that they are telling you what they *now* think happened *then*. Memories reflect our views of the present and the past, and they certainly affect our views of the future. Myths and legends often contain references to events that archaeology or history can substantiate. But to assume that memories can provide a factually accurate picture of the past is naive at best—here we run into the eyewitness problem again. Early ethnographers did indeed leave us much valuable information, but their basic assumptions about culture history do not stand up.

Culture is *not a thing*. As it goes on—in a constantly progressing Present that links a Past with a Future—it is a set of complicated processes.

Moreover, every person who uses "the same" culture knows and operates a slightly different aspect of it. Your America—or Europe or Asia—is not the same as your neighbor's, or ours. As an ethnographer you must consider just who it was that told you what—the personal history of that person, and what the person had to gain or lose by reporting it. Furthermore, you must always remember that people have different kinds of experiences and will therefore have different opinions about the same issue.

There is an ever deeper problem. When people's words and works are recorded, they become static. **Ethnography**, like a snapshot, freezes a moment. Every photograph is indeed a glimpse of truth, but the full truth comes out only when you remember that there was a before and an after for each photograph. Real life is *never* static, but written or photographed ethnography *always* is. Life goes on after ethnography, just as it does after the snapshot is taken. Moving pictures don't alter that snapshot quality; ethnographic reporting has included movies ever since film was invented.

Succeeding scholars provide more such photographs. When there are several ethnographers, we are offered snapshots taken at different times, with different cameras, from different angles or perspectives. Sometimes they may seem to contradict one another; usually that indicates nothing more than that we haven't hooked the photographs together in a sensible historical sequence; occasionally it indicates that different ethnographers focused on different details. But it can happen that two ethnographers actually disagree on the meaning of what they saw.

Because of these difficulties, some anthropologists have gone so far as to call all written ethnography "fiction." It isn't, of course. Any ethnographer like any photographer, can be second guessed: Why did you record this but not that; why did you start here and stop there? The point is that a record exists, and we can examine it. When we consider what any fieldworker wrote, we must remember that *all* ethnographers are limited by their own culture—including whatever anthropological culture they have learned. We are all limited by our particular abilities and convictions, by the perceptions and values instilled into us.

Thus, no **ethnography** is ever a "true" and "complete" picture of "the" culture. It is wrong-headed to assume that the static quality in a published report reflects some static quality in the culture itself. Cultures change, all the time. They change when we are not present, they change while we are there. They even change just because we are there! I vividly remember walking down a path in Tivland in Africa one bright morning and hearing somebody whistle the opening bars of Brahms's Fourth Symphony. Startled, I went to check it out. It turned out to be a man I knew. "Where did you learn that?" I asked him. His answer surprised me again but in a different way:

"From you!"

It is not disagreement among ethnographers working at different times that ought to make us suspicious, but their total consensus. *That* would indicate collusion or censorship!

As late as the 1940s, efforts were still being made to record traditional Native American culture "before it disappears." It was easy to ignore the fact that Indians were necessarily adapting and changing before the arrival of European and African immigrants. But they were, because every population uses in its daily lives some combination of old and new ideas to produce ever-newer ones. There never has been a stable "before" to which you can compare the present: every culture is always undergoing drift and change, at times very slow, at times very fast.

Recovering past culture is a worthy pursuit—*if* you remember the traps that await you. Those traps become evident when you think about what we humans have physically inherited from ancestors as close to us as the people who lived by hunting and gathering. The biology of our digestion today comes from those forebears' adjustment to *their* environment. They ate lots of vegetable fiber, very little in the way of fats and even less in the way of sugars. The bodies we inherit from them evolved, over eons, to make us like the taste of scarce fats and sweets. Today, when both are ubiquitous and cheap, we need to make a conscious adjustment to curb our Paleolithic appetites. Many of us find that isn't easy.

It is debatable whether there are any hunters and gatherers left who can be meaningfully compared to those ancestors, but their cultural inheritance still affects us. Native Alaskans, for example, are by law allotted special hunting and fishing rights beyond the privileges of other citizens of that state. The Alaskan legislature and its Department of Fish and Game agree that Native Alaskans have what they call "subsistence rights" because it is "their culture." Although historically the ancestors of today's Native Alaskans did indeed subsist as hunters and gatherers, and although many of them still fish and hunt some meat and gather some plants, what the law actually does is set them apart from Alaska's other citizens. It dictates that some people have rights that others would also like but do not have. Native Alaskan culture today includes (in addition to the right to fish and hunt out of season) government-supported schools, modern corporations into which tribal members have organized themselves, and salaried work for oil companies. It also includes snowmobiles and canned foods, kerosene and television, Guns-and-Roses T-shirts, and a lot of other stuff that they share with the other North Americans living all around them. Many Native Alaskans buy expensive fishing boats and sell their catch in Seattle.

FIELD RESEARCH

Their situation is far from unique; native peoples in British Columbia and other Canadian provinces undergo similar acculturative experiences. So, with local variations, do the peoples who live on reservations in the western United States. Their **political** *apartheid*—a special legal position based on the myth of their historical culture—helps them maintain an identity that they value. Please note that we did *not* say that they shouldn't have it.

But we have just introduced another problem—again a problem with definition, not with the "facts." The classification "hunters and gatherers" or "food collectors" was created by anthropologists. Like every other diagnostic category, it has limitations and therefore raises questions. What portion of a people's diet must come from a food-collecting economy before we can classify that people as hunters and gatherers? In the 1960s, some Caucasian northern Minnesotans got well over half their calories from food they hunted and gathered. They butchered the animals they hunted (mainly deer) and put them into their freezers. In the summer they prepared, blanched, and froze the vegetables and berries they gathered. Were these Euro-Americans "hunters and gatherers?"

How they lived is not in doubt, but the category "hunter and gatherer" must be. Do I belong in it because I pick blackberries and gather wild morel mushrooms? Categories, like straightjackets, are useful and necessary only under specific conditions. What people do can be stated with some certainty, but *any* classification of behavior is necessarily limiting and full of holes and exceptions. We do indeed need categories—but we also need to beware of them, for they can trick us into not seeing what is in front of us.

This brings us back once again to asking, what is "a culture" in our mixed-up world? There are no natural borders between cultures. Ethnic groups can usually define which people are "Us" and which are not. But they always share some—usually many, even most—elements of their culture with neighbors who belong to another ethnic group.

What does learning about all this tell you then about facing your own day-to-day problems? That the more you know about the changes and the activities of other cultures, the better you will be able to understand and adapt to and benefit from your own.

We do indeed live in unique times—everybody always has. We live in an environment just a little different from that which our parents grew up in, one that is a great deal different from our grandparents' and increasingly different from our more distant ancestors'. Change is the only certainty. If you do not adapt, if you let yourself grow static, you perish.

If you limit yourself too strictly to what you already know—or, worse, to what your grandparents knew—you cripple your capacity to adapt, and you will find yourself in deep trouble. What some call "the eternal verities" may be useful as goals, but you have to remember that even timeless truths are expressed in ever–changing idioms. Eternal verities, expressed in varied and manifold ways, enrich your world—and each may show you a different facet of eternal truth.

Life expects you to adapt (read "change") when the environment changes. Your adaptation creates additional change in your environment. You have to keep your eye on your physical needs and limitations. It helps if you understand that there are *many* more ways to be an OK human being than the ones you have been taught. No one way is more human than any other, although some may be technologically more efficient or promote more comfortable and effective social interactions.

You have to make choices, everyday. What you choose may be fatal—unless, of course, you allow yourself to change your mind and learn something, saving yourself in the process.

Ethnographers, being human, have to learn these same lessons. At the simplest level, ethnography is about what specific people do—or did, the day the data were gathered. But at another level, of course, all ethnography is about all of us.

Let's Talk About Sex, Baby

Contrary to common belief, the terms sex and gender are not the same. In fact, the terms represent two very different concepts.

The term **sex** refers to a person's anatomy, that of either male, female, or intersexed. How an individual acts, or their expected roles within society in terms of masculine or feminine behaviors, refers to **gender**.

While the notion of sex has obviously remained constant, the idea of gender stereotyping has changed in the United States over the past 50 years. For instance, Americans, at one time, believed that the cowboy was the sign of masculinity. This image demonstrated strength, power and prestige. It depicted men and their ability to conquer all that stands in their way—including nature. On the other hand, women were perceived as being the nurturers, staying at home and caring for issues relating to the family.

Different societies perceive the traditional roles of males and females in different ways. How would you describe the traditional gender roles in our society today?

Learning to Be Male or Female—
Richard H. Robbins

American parents teach male children that it is "masculine" to endure pain, to be strong and tough. Male children are discouraged from expressing discomfort and encouraged when they can withstand it. Female children, on the other hand, are comforted when they hurt themselves. Traditionally, American male children are encouraged to be aggressive and competitive; they learn to compete in games and play with toys that require aggressive behavior. Females are taught to be caring and helpful; they are given toys such as dolls that encourage "feminine" behavior.

Anthropologist Margaret Mead pioneered the idea that gender is a matter of culture. She illustrates her point by comparing three New Guinea societies: the **Arapesh**, the **Mundugumor**, and the **Tchambuli**. Among the Arapesh, both male and female children are discouraged from fighting or other acts of aggression, and they are never

taught to accept discomfort. Children are fed when they are hungry, and they are taught to share. The Arapesh do not believe that sex is a powerful driving force in defining one's identity. As a consequence, Mead says, both males and females are gentle, cooperative, and responsive to others. Unlike the Arapesh, both Mundugumor men and women are expected to be ruthless and aggressive, much like American males, says Mead. Among the Tchambuli, gender definitions are the reverse of those in American society. Women are taught to be dominant and controlling, while men were expected to be emotionally dependent. On the basis of these findings, Mead concludes that culture defines and creates gender differences in personality, values, and behavior.

The number of gender categories recognized in societies also differs. For example, many Native American societies traditionally recognized a third gender, that of *berdache* among the Cheyenne and Lakota, and the *nadle* among the Navajo. The *berdache* or *nadle* is a biological male who does not fill a standard male role. Such individuals are not seen as men, nor are they defined as women. They occupy a third role, one that is culturally defined, accepted, and in some cases, revered. Male children in the Navajo, Lakota, Cheyenne, and other groups thus could choose from two gender categories. Among the Lakota, male children learned that if they desired, they could adopt the dress and work roles of women, and have sex with men, although the *berdache* role did not necessarily involve sexual behavior. The *berdache* or *nadle* did not play only women's roles, however; some were noted for their hunting skills and exploits in war. In American society, in contrast, persons who do not assume the gender roles associated with their anatomy are defined as deviant, abnormal, or nonconformist.

From *Cultural Anthropology*, 2nd edition, by Richard Robbins. Copyright © 1997 Wadsworth, a part of Cengage Learning, Inc. Reproduced by permission. www.cengage.com/permissions.

The Princess Paradox—
James Poniewozik

Hollywood's newest Cinderella stories seek to inject some feminist messages into the age-old fantasy. But can you really wear your tiara while spurning it too?

It's the recurring nightmare of high-minded modern parents of daughters. You ask your relatives to lay off the pink pinafores at the baby shower. You give your daughter Legos and soccer balls, not Barbies. You encourage her to play fire fighter and immerse her in *Dora the Explorer* videos. Then one Halloween rolls around, and your empowered, self-confident budding Marie Curie tells you that she wants to be…a princess.

Call it nature or nurture, harmless fantasy or insidious indoctrination, but Hollywood is discovering that it still pays not to fight the royal urge. Following 2001's $108 million-grossing *The Princess Diaries*, Hollywood has waved its wand and conjured a set of Cinderella stories for girls, including next month's *The Prince & Me* and *Ella Enchanted*, as well as *A Cinderella Story* in July and a *Princess Diaries* sequel in August. That's not to mention other fairy-tale projects (*Shrek 2*) and transformational stories like *13 Going On 30*, in which a gawky teen is magically morphed into a fashion-plate magazine editor played by the perpetually miniskirted Jennifer Garner.

We've come a long way, it seems, from the girls-kick-ass culture of just a few years ago (*Charlie's Angels; Crouching Tiger, Hidden Dragon*) in which a 360° flying-roundhouse kick was a girl's best friend. (On the proto girl-power cartoon, *Powerpuff Girls*, one of the heroines' worst enemies was a spoiled brat named Princess Morbucks.) But brush off the fairy dust, and you find a new kind of Cinderella, one who would rather save Prince Charming, thank you, and who has learned the lessons of feminism—or at least learned to pay lip service to them. You can have the girly dream of glass slippers and true love, these films say, as well as the womanly ideal of self-determination and independence—and any contradictions between them are no match for the movies' magic.

Ella Enchanted, for instance, is a spoof of *Cinderella* in which the title character (*Diaries'* Anne Hathaway, Hollywood's queen of princesses) spends her free time protesting the discriminatory anti-elf and -giant policies of the family of Prince Charmont (Hugh Dancy). What she wants at first is not love but to free herself of a fairy's curse that forces her to be obedient. In *The Prince & Me* (what, *The Prince & I* would have been too egghead-y?), Paige Morgan (Julia Stiles) is a workaholic soon-to-be medical student who rolls her eyes at friends rushing to get their M.R.S. degrees. When she falls for Eddie (Luke Mably), a rakish-but-sweet exchange student who turns out to be Danish Crown Prince Edvard, the prospect of becoming queen upsets her dreams of working for Doctors Without Borders. (Stiles, who played Ophelia in the 2000 film *Hamlet*, should know that dating the prince of Denmark can be a pain.) "The Cinderella story has always frustrated me," Stiles says. "What I like about *The Prince & Me* is that my character is a lot more active and is ready to live a life by herself and be independent."

SPOILER ALERT: Skip this paragraph if you don't want to know how these movies end. O.K., here's the shocker—they end happily. What is surprising, however, is that, in the original ending of *The Prince & Me*, Paige broke up with Edvard to go to med school (in the final version, she gets to have both the guy and the career). And what's down right shocking is that Paramount approved the first, decidedly non-fairy-tale ending. "But when I saw it," says director Martha Coolidge, "I knew it was wrong. What was wrong about it was not what we thought—whether she got together with him or not. The real issue was about him making a compromise and the monarchy making a compromise."

Reinventing fairy tales has been a favorite project of feminist authors from Angela Carter (*The Bloody Chamber*) to Marlo Thomas (*Free to Be… You and Me*), who understood that wish-fulfillment stories are about teaching people what they should wish for. Among an earlier generation of women, the wish was to be able to do everything men could. For the modern Cinderellas' audience, which takes that freedom as a given, the wish is to also be able—unashamedly—to fall in love and go to the ball. Indeed, in *Prince*, Paige realizes that she needs to be "rescued" from her disciplined but single-minded careerism as much as she needs to assert her independence. Girls asserting their right to choose the fairy-tale ending is not a bad thing, says Thomas, since now the movies are balanced by varied depictions of young women in films from *Whale Rider* to *Blue Crush*. "What women have tried to achieve for other women," she says, "is choice in every step of their lives."

But to succeed on both the feminist and the fantasy level, the new Cinderella has developed rules and conventions as strict as a Joseph Campbell template. She should be pretty, but in a class-president way, not a head-cheerleader way. She should be able to stand up for herself (recall the *Crouching Tiger* moves of *Shrek's* Princess Fiona). She must be socially conscious—a result, says Meg Cabot, author of the *Princess Diaries* books, of Princess Diana's charitable work. And she should above all not want to be a princess—at least until she changes her mind. In *Diaries*, *Prince*, and *Ella*, it's not the girl who must prove herself worthy of princesshood; princesshood must prove itself worthy of the girl.

There's something a little have-your-tiara-and-disdain-it-too about making your protagonists ambivalent about the very fantasy that people paid $9 to see them live out. But that may make the fantasy more palatable to parents and filmmakers: men and, especially, women who are educated professionals. "I don't want to sound like an archfeminist," says Sherry Lansing, chairman of Paramount, which produced *Prince*, "but it really is important that it imparts contemporary values. It's a good love that allows both people to remain whole in it." Still, the fantasy couple that this earnestness yields in *Prince* is more yuppie than romantic: she, committing to years of med school; he, giving up his love of car racing to strap on a necktie and negotiate labor disputes. Goodbye, Chuck and Di; hello, Abbey and Jed Bartlet.

But it's easy for someone who has been through college to say a diploma and career are not cure-alls. The movies' audience of young girls makes the filmmakers much more message conscious—at least as far as the girls are concerned. The princes in these stories have fewer options than their Cinderellas. Edvard and Charmont are both reluctant to be come king, but they learn, through the love of a good woman, to mature into the role and use it for good. The girls fight to control their destiny; the boys good-naturedly learn to accept theirs. Of course, they're not the target audience. "It's nice to have something that's not toxic or repellent to men," says Nina Jacobson, a top executive at Disney (*Diaries*' studio). "But we know we don't need guys to make a movie like that successful." You just need a feisty girl, a prophylactic dose of skepticism and a fabulous ball gown—about which no ambivalence is necessary.

James Poniewozik, 2004, "The Princess Paradox," *TIME*, April 5, 2004, pages 72–74. Copyright © 2004 Time, Inc. Reprinted by permission.

FIELD RESEARCH

E X E R C I S E

Name _____

Section _____

Date _____

EXERCISE 2.4: GENDER AND ADVERTISING

Anthropologists often rely on the printed word in order to learn more about a particular society, how its members interact with one another, and the environment in which they live. Pick up a copy of your favorite magazine. Clip out three advertisements that include images of males and three advertisements with photos of females. Next, put these images together on one sheet.

Based upon the images collected, what assumptions can you make about gender differentiation? How do these assumptions depict the perceived roles of American males and females? Utilizing your first-hand knowledge of this culture, determine if there is any truth in how the media depicts masculinity and femininity.

FIELD RESEARCH

From Uretics to Uremics: A Contribution Toward the Ethnography of Peeing— *Elliott Oring*

Here is an amusing article, yet it is so only in part because the author is a funny person. Humor is also derived from the choice of a subject that many people discuss only with difficulty. The action is so common that it would seem to require little discussion, yet discussion is needed. In this essay, we are given the opportunity to explore such different levels of culture as the "explicit" and "implicit." Just as the grammar of language is learned informally and at an implicit level, so is proper bathroom behavior. A number of students, having read this article, have gone home and quizzed their young male offspring and have found that even at an early age these young have become practitioners of the described behavior. It seems that children are not formally instructed in the area of what proper options remain if, for example, urinal two is occupied, yet there is conformity through adherence to unspoken rules. We are also given the opportunity to examine situations where individuals, made to feel uncomfortable, believe that their discomfort is idiosyncratic when in fact most people feel the same way. We can see that what people perceive as personal anxiety is really shared anxiety. This duality is also present in other areas of cultural behavior and may have special importance with reference to attitudes concerning health as well as to the nature of services provided. Readers interested in other uses of and attitudes toward human exudations might read Theodor Rosebury's Life on Man *(1969), especially Chapters 9 through 12.*

Other than the concern with toilet training practices inspired by psychoanalytic theory, elimination behavior has excited little anthropological interest to date. There has been a tendency to keep one's ethnographic mind above one's middle, and although social scientists have devoted full sessions at their annual meetings to the study of foodways, the investigation of the inevitable consequences of foodways, elimination patterns, is a veritable wasteland.

It is not surprising that elimination behavior has merited so little attention given the negative attitude our culture holds towards bodily exuviae and exudations. Feces, urine, sperm, ear wax, mucus, spittle, sweat, and dandruff are all regarded as dirty and defiling. Only tears are exempt. Otherwise we tend to avoid these substances when produced by others and conceal those of our own making. The colloquial terms for such substances are regularly employed in speech to connote negative properties and attributes.

"*Shithead*! Go and *piss* away your life with those *scum* you call friends, and take that *snot* of a brother with you," may serve as a synoptic if untypical example. The proverbial "shit, piss, and corruption" perhaps states the American attitude most succinctly.

This paper will focus on only one small aspect of elimination behavior in our culture, urination patterns in public men's rooms, but it hopes to suggest the fertility of the entire field. A typical peeing pattern commences, not with the physiological process itself, but rather with the withdrawal from the social group. Such withdrawal may require some explanation, and one must choose the appropriate terminology from the various language levels available to describe the intended activity.

The *formal language* includes such terms as "urine," "urination," and "micturition." They are rarely employed in casual social situations and tend to be restricted to doctor's offices, laboratories, lectures, and educational films and pamphlets. "To piss," "to take a wicked piss," and possibly "to take a leak," are examples of what might be called the *vulgar language* and though employed with some regularity, their use significantly depends upon the social composition of the group from which one is withdrawing. If *baby language* is used, by adults, women tend to employ it more than men. Its use implies that there is something cute, childish or humorous about the intended activity. "I've got to go do number one," "go tinkle," "go wee wee," "go pee," "make sissy," or "go potty" are typical examples. *Euphemistic language* is most commonly employed. It usually refers to the place rather than the activity to be performed, for example: "I've got to go to the bathroom," "to the john," "to the head," "to the men's room," or "to the can." However, more hyperbolic euphemisms describe activity rather than setting: "I've got to see a man about a horse," "I'm going to walk the dog," "I'm going to use the sandbox," "I'm going to powder my nose" (female), or "I'm going to wash up." (See Sagarin, 1962:44–78; also Ellis, 1951:117–125.)

Bathrooms serve as loci for social activity only when such activities are otherwise prohibited by particular circumstances. Thus soldiers may gather in the john after lights-out or junior high school students may hang out in the bathroom while classes are in session, but in most situations entering a public men's room implies you have come with the purpose of using one of the facilities: stalls, urinals, basins, mirror or paper supplies. When your activity is completed you are expected to depart.

Peeing is the activity primarily intended by the majority of males entering a men's room. As the facilities in a men's room are spatially separated, the committed pee-er must approach the urinals and select one of several, arranged usually in a line along the wall. Though the situation most often noted by this observer involved a series of five adjacent wall urinals, many of the principles governing behavior seem applicable to a variety of other arrangements.

THE PRINCIPLE OF PERSONAL PEEING SPACE

One's personal space during urination extends one urinal to the left and right of the pee-er and therefore a minimum one-urinal distance between oneself and fellow pee-ers should be maintained whenever possible. Thus if urinal 1 is occupied, theoretically, urinals 3, 4, and 5 are available. If 3 is occupied, 1 and 5 are available. Of course, if the only unoccupied urinals are adjacent to other pee-ers, they may be selected. But if there are any isolated urinals, they must be filled before urinals adjacent to other pee-ers can be used. There are some individuals who will not violate peeing space even when the only urinals available are adjacent to other pee-ers and will wash their hands or comb their hair until the distribution of people changes sufficiently to allow them their personal space. Others will simply use the stalls when they feel their personal space cannot be guaranteed (See Hall, 1969).

THE PRINCIPLE OF EXCESSIVE DISSOCIATION

Despite the need for spacing during urination beyond that permitted by bathroom design, excessive spacing is avoided. There is a unidirectional maximum distance which should not be exceeded in the selection of a urinal. Thus, if urinal 1 is occupied, urinal 3 or 4 is subsequently selected, rather than 5. As soon as urinal 3 is occupied, however, urinal 5 becomes the necessary choice. This spacing is unidirectional with respect to the bathroom entrance. If urinal 5 is initially occupied, urinal 1 nevertheless remains a viable choice.

When all the urinals are unoccupied all urinals are theoretically available, yet only urinals 1, 2, 3, and 4 are serious considerations and then urinals 1 or 3 are selected twice as frequently as urinals 2 or 4. A possible explanation of this pattern of initial selection is that strategy-minded individuals will realize that selection of an odd numbered urinal allows for the accommodation of *two* more individuals with personal peeing space, should they enter the room, whereas the initial selection of an even numbered urinal limits further accommodation to only *one*.

The state of a particular urinal will also affect selection. A "clean" urinal is preferred to one that is unflushed or covered with occasional pubic hairs. But unless the state of the urinal is so extreme as to be regarded by all individuals as "unusable," and thus alter his perception of urinals available, it will only govern choice within a range of urinals that will not lead to a violation of the principle of personal peeing space. Thus, if urinal 1 is occupied, the state of the urinal may determine whether 3 or 4 is selected. All other urinals would have to be regarded as "unusable" before urinal 2 would be chosen.

The violation of the principle of personal peeing space regularly occurs in only one situation. One may stand adjacent to another pee-er, with other urinals available, only when that person is known. Conversation invariably develops between these individuals. Such conversation is often phatic and serves to demonstrate the existence of a prior social relationship rather than to convey specific information. All conversations in men's rooms are loud and can be heard by all present. There is no attempt at whispered or surreptitious communication.

During the act of peeing itself, eyes are front. One may look up, straight ahead, or slightly down (but only slightly). Looking to either side at fellow pee-ers, even though they may be more than one urinal's distance away, may be regarded as a violation of peeing space. Staring, of course, is absolutely forbidden.

The hands play a rather limited part for most pee-ers. They unzip or unbutton the fly and extract the member from its bondage within the underclothing. From that point on the hands are of little use. They are not used to hold the penis but are placed at the sides, behind the back, on the hips, in the pockets, or are rested on the flushing mechanism above the urinal. Peeing into the bowl in a stall or private bathroom requires a greater use of the hands to assure direction of the stream into the bowl rather than onto the floor. Wall urinals, however, do not require marksmanship, and thus free the hands. The hands become active again in shaking behavior and in putting the penis back. However, all this may be more a matter of individual style than adherence to a rigid set of rules.

Shaking behavior is common among most male pee-ers. It involves shaking the penis up and down several times in order to extract the last drop of urine remaining in the urethra by centrifugal force before reinserting it in one's clothing. Of course, every male knows that it is impossible to extract all the urine in this manner, and that inevitably the final drops emerge only after the penis is safely back in the pants. Nevertheless, the fact that shaking behavior is only partly successful is rarely acknowledged by individual pee-ers, though the problem is common enough and causes sufficient anxiety to produce various pieces of scatological folklore: "No matter how hard you jiggle and squeeze, the last drop always goes down to your knees," (Kira, 1966:75n62), as well as a rather excellent joke about a fellow who is sufficiently bothered by the condition to go to a physician to find out whether it can be surgically corrected.

Despite the fact that most intended pee-ers select a urinal with the best of intentions for action, the road to hell is paved with good intentions. It is not that peeing is not always what it seems to be, but rather that what it seems to be is not always peeing.

When you go in you really have to go. You don't go in just to be screwin' around. You have to go. And when you're there and all of a sudden you can't, you say, "Aw, it'll come any second now." Two seconds go by, three seconds... If all else fails you can fake it. You can flush the little goodie and split and no one will ever know the difference.

The fact that one is not actually urinating does not override the rules and patterns of peeing behavior. If anything, they are followed more conscientiously.

Upon leaving the men's room an ablution at the wash basin is usual though not required. The washing is often perfunctory, indicating that its value is symbolic rather than medical. It serves to signal that elimination behavior

has concluded, and that the individual is now prepared to resume his previously planned activities.

These singular patterns associated with peeing in public men's rooms may be explained as the behavioral consequences of three interrelated American values: privacy, masculinity, and cool.

Since American culture regards urine and other excretions as dirty, its members are encouraged to eliminate in private from early childhood. The bathroom thus develops as the one truly private room. It is the only room which comes with a lock already on the door. The bathroom is to the home as the home is to the rest of society. It is our sanctum sanctorum, our ultimate refuge. For a brief period of time, in the inviolate privacy of the bathroom, we are suspended from the requirements of sociable behavior. Here we may perform our most private and most asocial acts. We may urinate, defecate, masturbate, shoot heroin, and commit suicide without criticism or interruption.

When urination is performed in the semipublic environment of the men's room, behavioral patterns attempt to maintain an illusion of privacy. Thus a sense of personal peeing space develops and is rigorously observed. This peeing space is considerably reinforced by the American male abhorrence of unmasculine behavior. Thus males must display no interest in other men, spatially or visually, particularly at a time when they have bared the organ of their sex. One must stand beyond touching distance and keep the eyes averted. To do otherwise would be to invite the suspicion of homosexual interest.

In our culture we do not entirely dissociate excretory and sexual functions. Because the penis serves double duty for elimination and sex, male urination is likely regarded as a sexual performance. Should the inadequate privacy of the men's room inhibit urination, the inability to perform is regarded as a challenge to masculinity. Rather than acknowledge excretory impotence, the would-be pee-er "fakes it" and departs with his public image intact.

The masculine image is also very much involved with particular discomfort and anxiety created by the last few drops that invariably leak out after shaking behavior is completed. Though urine itself is regarded as a defiling substance it is not the sense of pollution that is primary:

There are always a few drops that leak out after you get it back in. It always happens. You can't avoid it. You just hope that the wet spot is on the inside rather than on your pants. No one can see it there.

The fear is not that you have contaminated yourself, but that others will notice. The last few drops challenge an important aspect of the masculine image or feeling of control. A man is supposed to control his situation, his women, and his emotions. It goes without saying that he should also be able to control his own bodily functions. With those last few drops a man has once again become a child; he has as in days long past "peed in his pants." He is no longer a man, and this knowledge he attempts to conceal for, other than effeminacy, childishness is the most severe accusation that can be directed against an American male. It is perhaps no accident that the term "sissy" connotes unmanliness but is also a reference to urine.

The last significant value affecting public peeing patterns is cool. Cool is related to the masculine image, and it dictates that the myriad of anxieties created by urinating in public are not to be acknowledged. Despite the fact that privacy is desired, if urinal 1 is occupied one does not go to 5. The principle of excessive dissociation is a function of cool. To choose urinal 5 would be to acknowledge that the individual is really uptight about his privacy or that he maximizes his peeing space because he has an inordinate fear of homosexuals or of being considered homosexual. Cool is the value that attempts to publicly deny that privacy and masculinity are bathroom issues. Because of cool, most individuals will choose a urinal adjacent to another pee-er, when no others are available, rather than opt for the privacy of a stall. Because of cool, conversations develop between pee-ers who know each other, for to remain silent is to acknowledge that special principles operate in the bathroom. To avoid conversing with people you know, you must pretend not to notice them. In many cases they will be more than happy to comply.

Basically, this paper hopes to suggest that elimination patterns are intimately linked with a culture's system of values, and that their careful investigation will prove a worthwhile effort. Needless to say, the field of ethnoelimination is wide open and will undoubtedly provide many a student with a wealth of subject matter for serious perusal. Those ethnologists who bemoan the disappearance of the field need only remember it is as near as their own bathrooms.

Elliot Oring, 1975, "From Uretics to Uremics: A Contribution Toward the Ethnography of Peeing," *California Anthropologist*, Vol. 4, pp. 1–5. Reprinted by permission.

E X E R C I S E

Name

Section

Date

EXERCISE 2.5: URANTICS

1. What are the "rules" for male restroom behavior? (List them below.)

2. What do you think of the peeing "rules"? If you are male, do they reflect your experiences? If you are female, do you think that they represent "true" bathroom behavior for males?

3. If someone asked you what the rules were, could you have told them in this type of detail? Or is much of this taken-for-granted knowledge for most of us?

4. What about the rules for women? Do women have similar rules for public restroom behavior? If so, what are the "rules"?

(continued on the next page)

5. How do we learn these rules? From whom?

6. In what way(s) was the researcher implementing the practice of participant-observation when producing this ethnography?

KEY TERMS

Name

Section

Date

Cross-cultural comparisons:

Cultural determinism:

Cultural relativism:

Culture:

Culture change:

Deduction:

Egalitarian:

Enculturation:

Epistomology:

Ethnography:

FIELD RESEARCH

Field Research:

Franz Boas:

Gender:

Hypothesis:

Induction:

Initiation rites:

Participant-observation:

Political apartheid:

Rites of passage:

Science:

Sex:

Socialization:

Zeitgeist:

3 RESPONSIBILITIES OF THE FIELD RESEARCHER

Cultural anthropologists promote the understanding and appreciation of unique patterns of behavior and thoughts; however, they sometimes find it difficult to put the principle of cultural relativism into practice. **Cultural relativism** means the acceptance of a behavior as practiced in a particular culture.

A good example has to do with what is known in the United States as **female genital mutilation** (FGM), or termed **female circumcision** in countries where it is practiced. While the tradition is often described as an African, Egyptian, and Sudanese puberty rite, in 1996 it was estimated that 100 million women have undergone some form of traditional genital mutilation, and each year at least 2 million more girls living throughout the world undergo the procedure. Nawal Saadawy, the Egyptian feminist who describes her experience with genital mutilation in her book entitled *The Hidden Face of Eve*, estimates that about 40,000 of these cases occur annually in the United States. While it is viewed as unethical, and justification for a physician to lose his/her license to practice medicine, the procedure is believed to occur in non-sterile locations, outside of hospital settings.

The procedure, it is argued, eliminates or severely reduces any genital sexual sensation for the woman. Clitoridectomy, or the removal of the clitoris, is less drastic than infibulation, which involves the removal of all of the female's external genitalia and sewing the wound shut until she is married, leaving only a small hole for urination and the passing of blood during monthly menstruation. Each year, many females subjected to this procedure suffer from infections, and some, even death. While the practice is not found in any holy scriptures, it continues today as a means of cultural identity. We must ask ourselves why this practice continues and why the cultural anthropologist should be expected to accept this behavior simply because it can be explained in terms of its social context.

Ethnocentrism

The antithesis of cultural relativism is known as **ethnocentrism**. Ethnocentrism is the belief that your culture's way of doing things is right or natural, while other practices, beliefs, or ideas are inferior by comparison. Even though the tendency toward ethnocentrism seems to exist in virtually all cultures, and has existed throughout recorded history, it is important to understand that the act of judging others according to one's worldview is not biologically inherited. Ethnocentrism is a learned response having to do with intolerance to diversity. In Nancy Gallagher's book entitled *Breeding Better Vermonters* (1999), she states that early in the 20th century, social reformers sought to improve conditions for the poor. They tackled issues concerning inadequate housing, health care, and poor work conditions. These same reformers also explored **eugenics**, using genetics to improve inherited qualities.

RESPONSIBILITIES OF THE FIELD RESEARCHER

In the 1920s and 1930s, a project called Vermont Eugenics Survey was used to distinguish so-called "good-families" from "bad-families." This survey project, originally funded by a professor at the University of Vermont, sought to sterilize members of these so-called "bad-families." This effort later became official state policy when Vermont legislators passed a law in 1931 that allowed for sterilization of the handicapped and feebleminded. With time, poor, teenage, and unwed mothers were targeted for sterilization. Ultimately, the Abnaki Indian families were also scrutinized for their level of poverty and acceptance of traditional life ways, such as continuing to live off the land. Native Americans were then listed as prime candidates for sterilization under the guidelines of the survey project.

The belief was that if, for instance, handicapped people who have hereditary handicaps were not capable of reproducing, then maybe this would relieve the nation and the state of all burdens concerning future health care. Gallagher discusses in her book that the insidiousness of this is that some people are denied having children, whereas other people are encouraged to have more. The author continues on to say that this is a really disturbing part of the survey project: that the founders wanted future Vermonters to come from certain types of people.

The author acknowledges that Vermont was not the only state to practice eugenics, and typically those seeking to restrict the reproduction of people who are considered by some to be unsuitable parents was closely immersed in social welfare reforms, reforms affecting children, special education initiatives and other reforms associated with the progressive era. It is important to note that there are various degrees to which ethnocentrism can occur within any given society. Examples of genocide and eugenics are extreme cases.

EXERCISE

Name _____

Section _____

Date _____

EXERCISE 3.1: HOW TO MOVE FROM ETHNOCENTRISM TO CULTURAL RELATIVITY
Questions to Ask Yourself

As people, we all categorize items, other people, ideas, etc. When you see something that you would categorize as "weird," "strange," "unacceptable," "stupid," etc., stop and analyze your reaction and ask yourself the following questions:

"Why do I think that?"

"What if I am wrong about that?"

"What other alternative explanations could there be for that?"

"Are there benefits to doing something in a different way than I would normally expect?"

"If so, what are those?"

Look at a practice from another culture and ask yourself these questions. Do they help you move away from ethnocentrism and toward cultural relativity? Explain.

RESPONSIBILITIES OF THE FIELD RESEARCHER

E X E R C I S E

Name _____

Section _____

Date _____

EXERCISE 3.2: REAL LIFE

Describe a personal example of ethnocentrism that you have witnessed or learned about. How did this situation make you feel? In thinking back upon the situation, what could you have done to change the final outcome?

RESPONSIBILITIES OF THE FIELD RESEARCHER

Cultural Relativism and Universal Rights—
Carolyn Fluehr-Lobban

Cultural relativism, long a key concept in anthropology, asserts that since each culture has its own values and practices, anthropologists should not make value judgments about cultural differences. As a result, anthropological pedagogy has stressed that the study of customs and norms should be value-free, and that the appropriate role of the anthropologist is that of observer and recorder.

Today, however, this view is being challenged by critics inside and outside the discipline, especially those who want anthropologists to take a stand on key human-rights issues. I agree that the time has come for anthropologists to become more actively engaged in safeguarding the rights of people whose lives and cultures they study.

Historically, anthropology as a discipline has declined to participate in the dialogue that produced international conventions regarding human rights. For example, in 1947, when the executive board of the American Anthropological Association withdrew from discussions that led to the "Universal Declaration of Human Rights," it did so in the belief that no such declaration would be applicable to all human beings. But the world and anthropology have changed. Because their research involved extended interaction with people at the grassroots, anthropologists are in a unique position to lend knowledge and expertise to the international debate regarding human rights.

Doing so does not represent a complete break with the traditions of our field. After all, in the past, anthropologists did not hesitate to speak out against such reprehensible practices as Nazi **genocide** and South African **apartheid**. And they have testified in U.S. courts against government rules that impinge on the religious traditions or sacred lands of Native Americans, decrying government policies that treat groups of people unjustly.

However, other practices that violate individual rights or oppress particular groups have not been denounced. Anthropologists generally have not spoken out, for example, against the practice in many cultures of **female circumcision**, which critics call a mutilation of women. They have been unwilling to pass judgment on such forms of culturally based homicide as the killing of infants or the aged. Some have withheld judgment on acts of communal

violence, such as clashes between Hindus and Muslims in India or Tutsis and Hutus in Rwanda, perhaps because the animosities between those groups are of long standing.

Moreover, as a practical matter, organized anthropology's refusal to participate in drafting the 1947 human-rights declaration has meant that anthropologists have not had much of a role in drafting later human-rights statements, such as the United Nations' "Convention on the Elimination of All Forms of Discrimination Against Women," approved in 1979. In many international forums discussing women's rights, participants have specifically rejected using cultural relativism as a barrier to improving women's lives.

The issue of violence against women throws the perils of cultural relativism into stark relief. Following the lead of human-rights advocates, a growing number of anthropologists and others are coming to recognize that violence against women should be acknowledged as a violation of a basic human right to be free from harm. They believe that such violence cannot be excused or justified on cultural grounds.

Let me refer to my own experience. For nearly 25 years, I have conducted research in the Sudan, of the African countries where the practice of female circumcision is widespread, affecting the vast majority of females in the northern Sudan. Chronic infections are a common result, and sexual intercourse and childbirth are rendered difficult and painful. However, cultural ideology in the Sudan holds that an uncircumcised woman is not respectable, and few families would risk their daughter's chances of marrying by not having her circumcised. British colonial officials outlawed the practice in 1946, but this served only to make it surreptitious and thus more dangerous. Women found it harder to get treatment for mistakes or for side effects of the illegal surgery.

For a long time I felt between, on one side, my anthropologist's understanding of the custom and of the sensitivities about it among the people with whom I was working, and on the other, the largely feminist campaign in the West to eradicate what critics see as a "barbaric" custom. To ally myself with Western feminists and condemn female circumcision seemed to me to be a betrayal of the value system and culture of the Sudan, which I had come to understand. But as I was asked over the years to comment on female circumcision because of my expertise in the Sudan, I came to realize how deeply I felt that the practice was harmful and wrong.

In 1993, female circumcision was one of the practices deemed harmful by delegates at the International Human Rights Conference in Vienna. During their discussions, they came to view circumcision as a violation of the rights of children as well as of the women who suffer its consequences throughout life. Those discussions made me realize that there was a moral agenda larger than myself, larger than Western culture or the culture of the northern Sudan or my discipline. I decided to join colleagues from other disciplines and cultures in speaking out against the practice.

Some cultures are beginning to change, although cause and effect are difficult to determine. Women's associations in the Ivory Coast are calling for an end to female circumcision. In Egypt, the Cairo Institute of Human Rights has reported the first publicly acknowledged marriage of an uncircumcised woman. In the United States, a Nigerian woman recently was granted asylum on the grounds that her returning to her country would result in the forcible circumcision of her daughter, which was deemed a violation of the girl's human rights.

To be sure, it is not easy to achieve consensus concerning the point at which cultural practices cross the line and become violations of human rights. But it is important that scholars and human-rights activists discuss the issue. Some examples of when the line is crossed may be clearer than others. The action of a Japanese wife who feels honor-bound to commit suicide because of the shame of her husband's infidelity can be explained and perhaps justified by the traditional code of honor in Japanese society. However, when she decides to take the lives of her children as well, she is committing murder, which may be easier to condemn than suicide.

What about **"honor" killings** of sisters and daughters accused of sexual misconduct in some Middle Eastern and Mediterranean societies? Some anthropologists have explained this practice in culturally relativist terms, saying that severe disruptions of the moral order occur when sexual impropriety is alleged or takes place. To restore the social equilibrium and avoid feuds, the local culture

required the shedding of blood to wash away the shame of sexual dishonor. The practice of honor killings, which victimizes mainly women, has been defended in some local courts as less serious than premeditated murder, because it stems from long standing cultural traditions. While some judges have agreed, anthropologists should see a different picture: a pattern of cultural discrimination against women.

As the issue of domestic violence shows, we need to explore the ways that we balance individual and cultural rights. The "right" of a man to discipline, slap, hit, or beat his wife (and often, by extension, his children) is widely recognized across many cultures in which male dominance is an accepted fact of life. Indeed, the issue of domestic violence has only recently been added to the international human-rights agenda, with the addition of women's rights to the list of basic human rights at the Vienna conference.

The fact that domestic violence is being openly discussed and challenged in some societies (the United States is among the leaders) helps to encourage dialogue in societies in which domestic violence has been a taboo subject. This dialogue is relatively new, and no clear principles have emerged. But anthropologists could inform and enrich the discussion, using their knowledge of family and community life in different cultures.

Cases of genocide may allow the clearest insight into where the line between local culture and universal morality lies. Many anthropologists have urged the Brazilian and Venezuelan governments to stop gold miners from slaughtering the Yanomami people, who are battling the encroachment of miners on their rain forests. Other practices that harm individuals or categories of people (such as the elderly, women, and enslaved or formerly enslaved people) may not represent genocide *per se*, and thus may present somewhat harder questions about the morality of traditional practices. We need to focus on the harm done, however, and not on the scale of the abuse. We need to be sensitive to cultural differences but not allow them to override widely recognized human rights.

The exchange of ideas across cultures is already fostering a growing acceptance of the universal nature of some human rights, regardless of cultural differences. The right of individuals to be free from harm or the threat of harm, and the right of cultural minorities to exist freely within states, are just two examples of rights that are beginning to be universally recognized—although not universally applied.

Fortunately, organized anthropology is beginning to change its attitude toward cultural relativism and human rights. The theme of the 1994 convention of the American Anthropological Association was human rights. At the sessions organized around the topic, many anthropologists said they no longer were absolutely committed to cultural relativism. The association has responded to the changing attitude among its members by forming a Commission for Human Rights, charged with developing a specifically anthropological perspective on those rights, and with challenging violations and promoting education about them.

Nevertheless, many anthropologists continue to express strong support for cultural relativism. One of the most contentious issues arises from the fundamental question: What authority do we Westerners have to impose our own concept of universal rights on the rest of humanity? It is true that Western ideas of human rights have so far dominated international discourse. On the other hand, the cultural relativists' argument is often used by repressive governments to deflect international criticism of their abuse of their citizens. At the very least, anthropologists need to condemn such misuse of cultural relativism, even if it means that they may be denied permission to do research in the country in question.

Personally, I would go further: I believe that we should not let the concept of relativism stop us from using national and international forums to examine ways to protect the lives and dignity of people in every culture. Because of our involvement in local societies, anthropologists could provide early warnings of abuses—for example, by reporting data to international human-rights organizations, and by joining the dialogue at international conferences. When there is a choice between defending human rights and defending cultural relativism, anthropologists should choose to protect and promote human rights. We cannot just be bystanders.

Carolyn Fluehr-Lobban, 1995, "Cultural Relativism and Universal Rights," *Chronicle of Higher Education*, June 9, 1995. Reprinted by permission.

Circumcision, Pluralism, and Dilemmas of Cultural Relativism—
Corinne A. Kratz

One of the things about studying anthropology is that we encounter cultural ideas and practices that are very alien to our own. Encountering the "other" can be a challenge in two ways. On an intellectual level, it can be a challenge to understand vastly different cultures and customs—why do people do/believe that? How does it fit within the wider context of their lives? The second of these challenges can be on a personal level, because the beliefs and practices of others might offend our own notions of morality and propriety. Studying and living in other cultures sometimes brings up our own ugly ethnocentrism.

At the same time, it is fair to ask, are there limits to cultural relativism? Looking cross-culturally, anthropologists can identify some universal (or at least extremely common) elements in cultural codes about proper personal conduct. All societies follow the ethnocentric line of thought that *their own traditions* are correct and right, but at the same time there are gigantic areas of controversy. In a complex society, the laws that are recognized and enforced often reflect the interests of the dominant social group.

The topic of this selection, female circumcision, really bothers some students; they can hardly believe that such cultural practices exist in the twenty-first century. In Africa, female circumcision has been a controversial topic for nearly a century, and there have been repeated international efforts to "eradicate" the custom, as if it were a disease. But this is not simply a medical issue, and to oversimplify the complex issue misses the point.

It is important to recognize that the single term FGM (*female genital modification* or *mutilation*) refers to a wide variety of surgeries with different levels of invasiveness. It is also important to remember that the symbolic and ritual meanings of this practice also vary among cultures. Finally, as students of anthropology, we need to recognize that there are at least two different views of what is at stake here, and, as in many other arenas of public controversy, there is real value to a sympathetic understanding of both sides.

This selection has two parts. The first provides a description of female circumcision in Africa—reporting the "facts" almost as it might be reported in a reference book. The second part discusses the author's strategies for *teaching* about the female circumcision controversy in the college classroom context. This controversy is both local and global—it involves traditional cultures, immigrants, and international nongovernmental organizations (NGOs). Understanding the different dimensions of the argument is an important educational goal; hopefully, it will also challenge you to come to your own well-informed opinion.

As you read this selection, ask yourself the following questions:

- For the women in the societies that practice it, FGM is related to beliefs about aesthetics of the body. Can you think of traditions in your own culture that transform or modify the body for purposes of beauty or identity? (Try relating this to Miner's description of body ritual among the Nacirema in Selection 1.)
- What are the potential health complications of female circumcision? What are the possible social complications of not being circumcised?
- What are the human rights issues involved? Is this a question where local societies should debate it themselves, or is international intervention necessary?
- Why does this tradition persist even when it is made against the law? Why would loving parents have this done to their daughters?
- Is the analogy to male circumcision in the West appropriate?

Differences of social and cultural practice have been a source of both puzzlement and edification around the world and throughout human history, interpreted and treated in vastly different ways in different circumstances.[1] They have been perennial resources through which people form their own identities, defining themselves through contrasts with other cultures. Distinctions in dress, cuisine, language, music, and ritual are particularly common as such markers of identity and difference. When ethnic or religious groups and minorities are reviled, differences in cultural practice have been used to help justify derogatory attitudes and discrimination. In other settings, cultural difference and diversity have been celebrated through various forms of multiculturalism.

With such remarkable diversity in the world, however, situations inevitably arise where incompatible social and cultural values, practices, and aesthetics produce conflict or controversy. How should they be dealt with? Cultural relativism would suggest that each set of practices and understandings is valid within its own circumstances and way of life. Yet plural societies combine and blend different beliefs and practices within the same social settings. Further, certain practices seem to challenge the nonjudgmental tolerance that cultural relativism implies (Shweder 2002) and raise serious questions about how to define human rights and who should define them. To many Americans, for instance, religious practices of discipline and self-mortification might seem extreme when they include self-flagellation, or political martyrdom might be taken as a sign of fanaticism. To people in other parts of the world, on the other hand, certain American economic practices might seem exploitative and certain modes of American dress might be seen as indecent or immoral.

Anthropologists seek to understand cultural production, i.e., how cultural meanings and social worlds continually take shape and change through daily interaction, communication, and exchange, through interpretations of personal and community histories and negotiations of political economic differences. They seek to understand the range of experience, meanings, and values produced by the world's diverse societies and cultures, examining how people perceive and make sense of lives and circumstances as different as those of African pastoralists caught in a long civil war, Chinese women working in a silk factory, men in an urban homeless shelter in the United States, contemporary Australians maintaining complex ritual traditions and fighting for land and mining claims, or radical political activists in Europe (Hutchinson 1996; Rofel 1999; Desjarlais 1997; Dussart 2000; Holmes 2000). In doing so, anthropologists may move beyond simple relativism to develop knowledge and judgments based on pluralism. Philosopher and social theorist Isaiah Berlin describes the distinction between relativism and pluralism (1991:10–11):

"I prefer coffee, you prefer champagne. We have different tastes. There is no more to be said." That is relativism.... [Pluralism is] the conception that there are many different ends that men [sic] may seek and still be fully rational, fully men [sic], capable of understanding each other and sympathising and deriving light from each other, as we derive it from reading Plato or the novels of medieval Japan—worlds, outlooks, very remote from our own.

Members of one culture can, by the force of imaginative insight, understand…the values, the ideals, the forms of life of another culture or society, even those remote in time or space. They may find these values unacceptable, but if they open their minds sufficiently they can grasp how one might be a full human being, with whom one could communicate, and at the same time live in the light of values widely different from one's own, but which nevertheless one can see to be values, ends of life, by the realisation of which men [sic] could be fulfilled.

Anthropological research may not be able to resolve conflicts and controversies that emerge from social and cultural difference, but the knowledge produced can provide the foundation of understanding needed for engagement and debate grounded in pluralism. It can help to identify the basic value contradictions and issues at stake as well as the different positions and interests in play. It is also important to pay attention to such controversies and debates themselves as cultural phenomena, analyzing their rhetorics, weighing competing arguments, and placing them within their own social and historical contexts. These analytical skills are important in understanding debates concerning issues of social justice, abortion rights, defining human rights, or controversial practices such as *sati* in India, and they are critical to effective political action related to any of these issues.

This essay considers a widespread cultural practice that has many different forms and meanings throughout the world and a long history of sparking debate and controversy at different times and places: forms of genital modification commonly called circumcision. Vehement debates have swirled around male and female circumcision alike, but the essay focuses particularly on practices of female genital modification because they currently receive the greatest attention and are at the center of recent contention. After outlining the varied practices of female genital modification and some of the meanings associated with them, the essay will turn to controversies and debates about these cultural practices.

THE VARIED PRACTICES AND MEANINGS OF FEMALE GENITAL MODIFICATION

Female circumcision is a term commonly used to refer to surgical operations performed in over thirty African, Middle Eastern, and Southeast Asian countries, by im-

migrants from those communities living elsewhere, and for roughly a century (about 1850 to 1950) by physicians in Europe and the United States. As this geographic and historical span suggests, the operations are embedded in a wide range of cultural and historical contexts and can be quite different in definition, meaning, and effect. All involve surgical modification of female genitals in some way, though this ranges from relatively minor marking for symbolic purposes to the most radical operation, infibulation.[2]

The general term **female circumcision** includes at least three clinically distinct kinds of surgery. Clitoridectomy removes all or part of the clitoris and the hood, or prepuce, covering it.[3] The second type, excision, includes clitoridectomy but also removes some or all of the labia minora; all or part of the labia majora might also be cut. The most extreme form of circumcision, infibulation, goes beyond excision.[4] After removing the labia, the sides of the vulva are joined so that scar tissue forms over the vaginal opening, leaving a small gap for urination and menstruation. Infibulated women often require surgical opening to allow first intercourse and birthing; in many cases women are reinfibulated after each childbirth, In addition to these three well-recognized types of female circumcision, a fourth is sometimes included. The mildest form, this involves a symbolic pricking or slight nicking of the clitoris or prepuce. Excision and infibulation are the most widely practiced types of female genital modification. In Africa, infibulation is common primarily in the Horn of Africa (Somalia, Sudan, Djibouti, Ethiopia).

Whether and how circumcision practices affect women's sexuality is much debated. It is important to distinguish sexual desire, sexual activity, and sexual pleasure when considering this question. Sexual desire and sexual activity may not diminish with female genital operations. Evidence about sexual feeling and pleasure is variable, difficult to define or measure, and hard to come by.[5] Euro-American opponents of the practices assert that circumcised women feel no sexual pleasure, but a number of African women disagree with these assertions. Studies suggest that the effect varies widely with type of operation, with prior sexual experience, and other circumstances as well. Some African activists also suggest that the stress on sexual pleasure in anti-circumcision campaigns reflects a recent, primarily Western concept of sexuality.[6]

The operations have also been said to carry a number of health risks. While the range of possible health problems is well known, there has been little epidemiological research to determine how widespread each problem might be in different areas. Immediate risks include infection, shock, excessive bleeding, and urinary retention, risks that are related to hygienic conditions and care during and after the operations. Longer term health problems are most common with infibulation but can be associated with excision as well. Most of these problems are related to heavy scarring and to covering over of vaginal and urinary openings after infibulation: keloid scars, vulvar cysts, retention of urine or menses, painful menstruation, difficulty urinating, and chronic pelvic infections. Clinical studies on the relation between these health problems and genital modification are contradictory, however, and a recent study in Gambia found that many negative consequences commonly cited for the operations were not significantly more common in women who had been cut (Morison et al. 2001).[7]

In many places where female circumcision is practiced, the physical operation is but one moment in an elaborate ceremony that contains many other events. For Okiek people in Kenya, for instance, initiation into adulthood includes circumcision for boys and excision for girls, but the full initiation process continues for several months and includes much more as well: moral teaching, family and community engagement, the negotiation of new social relationships, and important cultural meanings and values. While the operations are a central initiation trial and create a permanent physical mark of adulthood, initiation cannot be reduced to circumcision or excision alone. In many other societies, initiation does not involve circumcision at all.

In every case the purposes and meanings of female genital modification are related to specific cultural understandings of identity, personhood, morality, adulthood, gender, bodily aesthetics, and other important issues. In the Sudan, for instance, it is seen as enhancing a woman's purity, cleanliness, and beauty. For the Kikuyu people of Kenya, circumcision was the foundation of moral self-mastery for women and men alike, performed as part of initiation into adulthood. The age of those circumcised varies widely according to these cultural understandings. In much of Mali and the Sudan, for instance, girls are circumcised at six to eight years, while various communities in Kenya

and Sierra Leone perform the operation in the early teens. Yoruba people in Nigeria often circumcise their children at just a few days old, much like male circumcision in the United States and Europe. Circumcision and excision are not connected with initiation for the Yoruba people, but they do relate the operations to moral concepts associated with shame and fertility. Circumcision is not regularly performed after puberty in Africa, where the operation is usually seen as related to a person's social and moral development.[8] The history of female circumcision in Europe and the United States contrasts with most of the world with regard to circumcision age. For roughly a century beginning in the 1850s, clitoridectomy was prescribed for adult women in Europe and the United States as medical treatment for insomnia, sterility, and masturbation (which was defined as an ailment at that time).

Many societies practice male but not female circumcision, but the reverse is rare. Where both are practiced, they can only be understood fully when considered together, in relation to one another. In many societies, cultural meanings and patterns link the two and equate them. A single word refers to both operations in many African languages, and this correspondence is often central to the way their practitioners understand them. The English translation, "female circumcision," maintains this parallel between male and female genital operations, though anti-circumcision activists have criticized the term for being misleading (as discussed below).

DEBATES AND CONTROVERSIES ABOUT CIRCUMCISION

Both male and female genital operations have engendered long histories of debate and opposition; these have often involved cross-cultural disagreements about the meaning and worth of the practices. The value of Jewish male circumcision, for instance, was debated in Rome during the first century A.D., and male circumcision has become a topic of heated opposition in the United States again today. The most wide spread and vociferous opposition currently centers on female genital modification, but these practices have been the subject of international political controversies and abolition campaigns since at least the 1910s.[9] Contemporary campaigns continue the tradition and rhetoric of colonial and missionary opposition and also build on decades of Africa-based activism. Health consequences have consistently been part of the debate, particularly in relation to infibulation, but the issues have also been defined at times in terms of colonialism, neocolonialism, feminism, sexuality, and human rights.

Controversies can be confusing. Heated arguments based on strong convictions are rarely presented in ways that make clear the different assumptions, perspectives, and interests fueling contention. When controversies cross cultural and national boundaries, they can be very complicated indeed. To begin to understand circumcision debates, it is important to first identify the grounds of controversy: Who is involved, what is it about, and what is at issue. Circumcision controversies concern a wide variety of actors and cross a number of social and legal arenas, from family and household relations to international tribunals. This renders it impossible to characterize the debates in simple terms. It is inaccurate and misleading to describe them merely as contests of women versus men or Africans versus outsiders.

To understand today's debates, it is helpful to think about them in relation to several contexts. Most central are the sociocultural contexts of the varied practices at issue and the history and contexts of the current controversies themselves. An effective way to highlight the issues and perspectives involved is to consider these contexts comparatively, to relate different situations and practices, or to explore similarities and differences between several controversies (e.g., debates about male and female genital operations, debates that occur at different historical periods, or debates that might concern different practices but are presented in similar ways (such as *sati* in India[10]). Examining cultural practices in context also means identifying the different actors, perspectives, and meanings involved (see below). It is important to recognize that trying to understand unfamiliar practices does not necessarily mean supporting them. However, to oppose or help alter practices that some might consider problematic, it is essential to work *with* the people involved, as equal peers. Such understanding is critical to effective engagement.

One of the best-documented historical examples of circumcision controversy took place in central Kenya during the colonial era. Colonial missionaries and administrators there made judgments about which local customs violated Christian behavior and sought to discourage them. Campaigns to abolish female circumcision in central Kenya

were among these efforts. When the Church of Scotland Mission and segments of the Church Missionary Society tried to prohibit the practice in the 1910s and 1920s, Kikuyu female circumcision became connected with the anticolonial movement and defense of cultural tradition (Murray 1974, 1976). Jomo Kenyatta, later president of Kenya, was a prominent opponent of colonial attempts to alter Kikuyu custom. These local protests against abolishing female circumcision provided an impetus for starting independent schools and churches in central Kenya.

Arenas encompassed in this debate, then, included British politics (with pressure from feminist parliamentarians and anticolonial activists), rivalries between Christian denominations with missions in Kenya, the colonial administration in Kenya, and local Kenyan communities. In addition to anticolonial movements and defense of cultural tradition, the debate also became connected with relations of authority between men and women and between women of different generations, and even the introduction of maternity clinics.[11] Since 1979, the Kenyan government has conducted several anti-circumcision campaigns that were tinged with Christian and colonial overtones, banning female circumcision in 1982, but with little effect. In 1996, a national organization proposed an alternative initiation ceremony as a substitute. Like Kenya, each country has its own such history of circumcision debates and policies.

To place contemporary controversies in context, we should also consider their own history and the different arenas where debates occur. The debates have been related to feminist movements in various times and places, to colonial administration and missionary campaigns, to Islamic religious movements, and a number of other issues. Arenas of debate shift as different parties become involved. Several decades after the Kenyan controversy, in the late 1950s, international efforts to have the World Health Organization (WHO) address female circumcision were not effective. Later, in the 1970s, a number of publicizing efforts and publications converged to galvanize international attention. These included articles in African publications in the mid 1970s, a press conference held in Switzerland before the WHO assembly in 1977 and publications by Fran Hosken (1979) and Mary Daly (1990) in the United States. The Inter-African Committee on Traditional Practices affecting the Health of Women and Children was formed in Geneva in 1977. A 1979 WHO seminar in

Khartoum helped to begin regular discussion of female genital operations by international bodies and at regular conferences. The resurgence of anti-circumcision activity in the 1970s was also buoyed by the United Nations Decade of Women (1975–1985).

Since the early 1990s, international debates about female genital modification have again become increasingly heated and highly politicized. Greater media coverage in the 1990s and publicity over legal cases concerning African immigrants in France and the United States brought the debates to a wider public than previously.[12] In the United States, involvement by such well-known figures as novelist Alice Walker also helped to publicize and polarize the debate. A number of African scholars and activists based in the United States (such as Seble Dawit, Salem Mekuria, and Micere Mugo) have been highly critical of the way Walker and others have represented female circumcision in Africa.[13] They argue that Walker and others are engaged in neocolonial depictions that demonize African practitioners, distort the social meanings and contexts involved, portray African women only as victims, ignore decades of activism in Africa, and isolate female circumcision from other issues of women's health, economic status, and education.

Both practices of female genital modification and the arenas of debate have shifted over the years as other circumstances changed and different constituencies became involved. Public health education about the potential risks of the operations has increased in most countries where they are practiced. Similarly, an increasing number of female genital modifications are being performed either by specialists who have received some hygienic training or in health clinics and hospitals. As noted above, alternative rituals have also been proposed in some countries, though it is not clear whether they will be widely adopted. Shifts in practice also include adoption of genital modification by non-circumcising communities (Leonard 1999) and modification of long-standing rituals toward what I call "circumcision by pronouncement" or "performative circumcision," i.e., substituting a verbal formula for actual cutting (Abusharaf 1999:7; Hernlund 1999). There are intense debates among African activists about whether a medicalized, minor form of female genital modification should be promoted as an interim substitute for more severe operations (Obiora 1997; Shell-Duncan 2001).

African immigrant communities in Europe and the United States often continue traditional practices in new ways in their new homes. Their preservation of the practices has brought all these debates to the fore in those countries as immigrant communities and their children have grown in recent decades. Sweden, Switzerland, the United Kingdom, and several other European countries passed laws restricting the operations in the 1980s and early 1990s. The United States followed suit in 1997.

CONTEXTS FOR UNDERSTANDING THE DEBATES AND ISSUES

These examples illustrate how many different parties and perspectives can become involved in these controversies. In tracing the shape of today's debates, it is useful to distinguish the following three interacting arenas. The social, cultural, and historical contexts of debates about female and male genital operations can be examined for each:

1. *Home countries* are countries in Africa, the Middle East, and Southeast Asia where circumcising practices have traditional standing. There may be a variety of traditions and practices that include genital modification within each home country and a number of different positions within each community, if the practices are debated.

2. The *United States* and *Europe* are the second arena to consider. These countries also have a history of genital operations for both boys and girls. The histories are related to changing understandings of health, class, ethnicity, gender, and sexuality. In the U.K., for instance, male circumcision had become a middle-class fashion by the 1920s (Lonsdale 1992:388). In Nazi Germany, it was taken as a mark of Jewish identity. In the United States today, white men are more likely to be circumcised than African Americans or Hispanics; higher education levels are also related to higher circumcision rates (Laumann et al. 1997:1053–1054). Clitoridectomy was a recognized medical treatment for women in these countries for decades, as noted above. Concern about female genital operations within these countries is now related particularly to immigrants from home countries.

3. The third arena is that of *international campaigns*. Though obviously related to the other two, it is useful to consider how international campaigns differ from

debates within the other arenas, how international bodies and action groups establish their legitimacy to intervene in other countries, and how the international arena redefines issues central to particular communities and nations.[14]

In addition to identifying the complex social geographies and range of actors involved, it is equally important to pay attention to the ways that language and rhetoric shape the presentation of issues and convey particular values and judgments. For instance, the growing intensity of the debates became encapsulated in the very terms used for female genital operations between the 1970s and 1990s, illustrating the political divisions and rhetorics involved. *Female circumcision* was the most common term for decades, the English phrase ordinarily used in the debates about British colonial attempts to outlaw female genital operations in Kenya in the 1920s–30s. In the 1970s, anti-circumcision activists increasingly criticized the term *female circumcision*, claiming that it condoned a brutal custom by creating what they considered false similarities between male and female circumcision.[15] A more partisan alternative was coined and eventually popularized: *female genital mutilation*.[16] The new term did not attempt impartial description, but condemned the practices through a label that defined them all as intentional mistreatment and disfigurement. Promotion of the new "mutilation" term was part of an escalating anti-circumcision campaign that used more sensationalism and gory images.[17] As this term became more common, it was shortened to an acronym, "FGM." Others reject this term as misrepresenting the intentions of African families, criminalizing parents and relatives, and judging them through Euroamerican cultural values.

The increasingly heated and polarized nature of the debate thus became embedded in its very terms. Attempting to find an appropriate phrase, *New York Times* reporter Celia Duggers used the term *genital cutting* in her late 1996 articles, a term she adopted from demographic and health surveys.[18] A number of other alternative terms also came into use in the mid-1990s, seeking more neutral ground: genital surgery, genital operations, genital modification, and body modification. This last term acknowledges broad similarities among such practices as male and female genital surgeries, genital/body piercing, and other cosmetic surgery. Female circumcision, genital cutting, and FGM remain the most common terms in English, though the acronym FGM has now also been redefined as "female genital *modification*" in efforts to use less polarizing, descriptive language.

Whatever terms are used, the topic at the center of controversy is a generalized category defined and shaped by that very debate. The category is created by extracting and combining fragments from many different cultural practices found in dozens of countries, a variety of practice described above. The fragments all concern genital modification but may share little else. Taken out of their social and cultural contexts, they combine to form a new, abstract category (e.g., "female circumcision"). Scientific, medical language is an important tool in this process. The clinical emphasis makes the general category seem like an objective and universal way to talk about women's bodies, but it also narrows the range of information defined as relevant to the debate. For instance, the physically different operations described above are combined and treated as the same thing, though they vary considerably in extent and effects. The rest of the ceremonies in which the physical operations may be embedded are often ignored.

The terms used in circumcision controversies convey different impressions of the people involved as well. A number of African women and others have objected to the word *mutilation*, for instance, because it misrepresents parents and families. It suggests that they intend harm to their children, likening to child abuse what they themselves might see as a cultural triumph, "carried out for the noblest of reasons, the best of intentions, and in good faith" (Iweriebor 1996). Accounts often demonize women who perform the operations as well. In recent French legal cases, for instance, they were portrayed as avaricious and predatory and received the harshest rulings.

A prominent example concerns the way African or "Third World" women in general are represented as a single, unified group, as seen across a range of sources: news media, informational publicity material produced by action groups, scholarly writing, or novels.[19] This stereotyped concept of "African women" is usually formed by homogenizing divergent circumstances; it assumes women to be a pre-existent, coherent group with shared interests and desires. This requires removing the concept of "woman" from any specific cultural context and isolating it from related notions that help form understandings of gender. How are differences based on nationality, class, ethnicity, religion, education, or age accommodated in this generalized figure and how might these variations affect the debates? The "average" Third World woman that emerges is set in contrast to elite women, though the contrast is often implicit. Elite women are presented as self-conscious, active, choice-making agents. They are not exclusively Western, but also include women born in the Third World who have joined the campaign against female genital modification. Yet African activists consistently protest that their work is rarely recognized when controversies are described. The rhetoric and structure of these controversies might be examined further by looking at how different kinds of men are portrayed, or by considering parallel cases in contemporary campaigns against male genital operations, abortion, or welfare.[20]

These different portrayals of Third World women and other actors in circumcision controversies are often bound up with notions of "progress" and other values as they have been defined in Euroamerican contexts. But conflicting values are the very crux of controversy. Diverse social and political positions inform the perspectives of those involved, but they are also grounded in different cultural frameworks, competing definitions of the practices at issue, and what seem to be irreconcilable values. In seeking to understand circumcision debates, it can be helpful to identify the various positions on each issue, along with the priorities and cultural values associated with each. Issues at stake would include the following:

Human Rights Circumcision debates presented in human rights terms often emphasize the integrity and inviolability of the human body, sometimes using analogies with torture and child abuse. As noted above, this falsely attributes evil intent to parents and relatives. "Human rights" as a concept is itself under considerable debate. Should social and economic rights be included? Whose values will be enshrined as universal when there are fundamental disagreements (An-Na'im 1992; An-Na'im and Deng 1990)? How might the language of human rights accommodate the diverse people, practices, and circumstances involved?

Self-Determination The human rights approach does not fit easily with another common way that circumcision debates are framed, in terms of self-determination.[21] However, self-determination can be defined in relation to individuals, families, or communities, each with rather different implications. Upholding family autonomy, community values, or religious freedom would seem to support continuing traditional practices understood as central to personal and community identity. Does this include male and female initiation ceremonies? How does individual self-determination apply in the intricate contexts of family and community relations? How do questions of self-determination apply to children of different ages?

Health Issues and Sexuality These were discussed earlier in this essay. Both have been central to debates about female genital modification. Questions of sexuality have also figured in opponents' efforts to explain the operations. They commonly assert that male desire to control female sexuality is the origin and reason for all such practices. This universal conspiracy theory, however, does not correspond to what is known about circumcising practices. There is no evidence or discussion of when or how this might have happened in so many places, how this explanation would account for the variety of circumcising practices, why women also staunchly defend them, or how the theory relates to explanations offered by practitioners.[22]

Yet even when the issues and stances in circumcision controversies are delineated, the fact remains that the debates involve fundamentally different perceptions and lived understandings of aesthetics, morality, society, and personhood that come together with questions of authority, class, power, gender, and history.[23] There are no simple, single answers to the issues they raise. They pinpoint a nexus whose very opaqueness of understanding illustrates recalcitrant problems and issues of cultural translation. In this respect, recent circumcision controversies draw attention to the limits and dilemmas of cultural relativism and moral judgments. How are such judgments, choices, and even laws to be made in plural societies (which ultimately means all societies)? Can incommensurable values be accommodated? As Sir Isaiah Berlin noted, "A certain humility in these matters is very necessary" (1991:18).

CULTURAL AND MORAL VALUES: DILEMMAS OF RELATIVISM

Many people would agree that cultural difference and diversity should be recognized, respected, and accommodated. Cultural relativism has fairly wide currency in the United States as a general way to approach cultural difference, though it coexists with popular notions of cultural evolution and civilizational hierarchy. The relativist view that each society's practices and values are valid and understandable in the particular context of their lives may be easiest to hold, however, when applied to distant people or to practices that seem strange but harmless. What happens when people with incompatible practices and values live closely together, when culturally justified practices seem to be physically harmful, or when an overarching national legal system must deal with radically different values? Does cultural relativism imply moral relativism as well?

The controversies over genital operations present such dilemmas and flashpoints. Usually associated with ceremonial performances, the songs, dances, costumes, and other beliefs that give meaning to the ceremonies are readily accepted as part of "tradition," as markers of particular forms of ethnic or religious identity. Scarification or tattooing might also be recognized and appreciated as part of a different aesthetic or religion, so what is different about genital operations? Why are they seen as an exception that raises this moral dilemma? What other practices pose similar dilemmas?

In the last decade, legal cases dealing with African immigrants in the United States and Europe have raised these issues in particularly clear and urgent ways. Examining these cases—particularly court procedure and sections of testimony—provides a way to again consider the different actors and interests involved, this time in situations even closer to home (Kratz 2002). Among the many questions that these cases raise are the following:

- Legislation is written in general terms, intended as applicable to the broadest range of cases. However, laws are interpreted through individual cases and precedents. Should a case about, for instance, Somali immigrants (who practice infibulation for young girls) serve as precedent for families from Sierra Leone (where initiated individuals are older, the operation is less severe, and family relations are quite different)?

- Whose legal rights should be protected and when? Parents' rights to raise their children in accordance with their beliefs and traditions? What if parents disagree? The rights of the girls affected? What if they *choose* to undergo the operation? What if they are minors legally?

- When female genital operations are outlawed, who is legally responsible and liable for prosecution? At different times and places, the accused have included fathers, mothers, initiates, and surgeons. What constructions of actors, intentions, and meanings are involved in each of these scenarios?

- When court proceedings involve immigrants, how are issues of adequate translation and adequate legal representation handled? These were important problems in the way French cases in the 1990s were handled.

- Are judges, juries, lawyers, and those concerned with civil liberties informed about the communities and cultural values involved? For instance, a lawyer in one case argued that the girls affected would have psychological problems when they realized they were not like other women, but the "other women" assumed in this statement were not women of the immigrant community. In fact, most women in their own ethnic community had had the operation, making the argument one that would more appropriately support the operation (cf. Matias 1996:4).

- How do gendered differences in immigrant experiences influence knowledge about relevant laws and services and the ways people participate in legal proceedings?

These questions raise some of the difficult practical implications of general issues of cultural translation and the moral dilemmas involved. They provide another way to ground the circumcision debates in specific questions and situations. Such groundings provide useful ways to understand and engage with controversies that are puzzling and sometimes troubling in their passions and complexities.

NOTES

1. This paper includes portions of Kratz (1999a) and (1999b) that have been combined, revised, and updated for inclusion here.

2. Wide variation in female genital modification can be found on the African continent alone, where it is practiced across a band of the continent that includes parts of Mauritania, Senegal, Gambia, Guinea-Bissau, Sierra Leone, Liberia, Mali, Burkina Faso, Côte

d'Ivoire, Ghana, Togo, Benin, Niger, Nigeria, Chad, Cameroon, Central African Republic, Democratic Republic of the Congo (formerly Zaire), Sudan, Egypt, Eritrea, Ethiopia, Djibouti, Somalia, Kenya, Tanzania, and Uganda. The percentage of women circumcised in each country varies considerably (e.g., 5–10% in Uganda, 25–30% in Ghana, 80% in the Sudan), as does the kind of operation practiced, its cultural and personal significance, and its history. Female circumcision is not practiced at all in some communities within this broad area, but it is commonplace in others. Regional, ethnic, and religious variation in practice is considerable. Christians, Muslims, and followers of traditional religions all might practice forms of female circumcision. Communities have adopted, abandoned, and modified the practices in various ways over the centuries, in keeping with the complex histories of political and religious influence and interaction among societies on the African continent.

3. This is sometimes called *sunna circumcision*, though *sunna circumcision* might also refer to preputial cutting alone. The name *sunna* relates the practice to Islamic traditions, though most Muslim scholars and theologians deny Koranic justification for female circumcision.

4. Infibulation is also called *pharaonic circumcision*, a name originating in beliefs that the practice was part of ancient Egyptian life.

5. See Apena (1996:8); Kratz (1994:345–346); Lyons (1981:507, 510); Obiora (1997:298). Matias (1996:3) and Ogbu (1997:414–415) cite examples where they are seen as enhancing sexuality. Again, the type of operation is critical. Infibulation is more often discussed as reducing desire (Boddy 1989:54), though Obiora (1997:310) cites another study in the Sudan to opposite effect. As for sexual pleasure, according to Gruenbaum (also writing about the Sudan), some infibulated women do have orgasms, perhaps because "many midwives, fearing hemorrhage, leave much of the clitoral (erectile) tissue intact beneath the infibulation when they perform the surgeries" (1996:462). She notes, though, that other infibulated women report finding sex unsatisfying. See also Parker (1995:514);

Obiora (1997:308–310); Koso-Thomas (1987:37–42). Several of these sources note that reports of sexual pleasure are related to sexual experience before circumcision as well as other factors.

6. Even in Europe and the United States, the pleasure-oriented definition of sexuality became prominent in recent decades. In this view, recent international debates about female genital operations have taken a form that resonates particularly with recent Western concerns and anxieties (Parker 1995). The paradoxical nature of questions of sexuality can be brought into relief through comparison. Historically, classical theologians and philosophers made parallel claims about men; they promoted male circumcision because it reduces male sexual passion (Boyarin 1992:486–487; Lyons 1981:503–504). Though circumcised men today might not agree, similar assumptions still inform medical research. A study publicized on National Public Radio in 1997 found that circumcised men are more "sexually adventurous," but explained this as compensation for loss of sexual feeling (Laumann et al. 1997). "Adventurousness" was defined through behavioral range and frequencies, suggesting that sexual interest, desire, and activity were actually greater with circumcision. Considering such gender reversals can raise critical questions about all these claims and show that understandings of sexuality are neither universal nor unchanging.

7. Obiora (1997:292) cites studies that show no obstetric or gynecological complication when infibulation is performed at an early age. Parker (1995:514–516) notes that findings in some studies of health risks from other forms of genital operations are not clear, though it is generally accepted that some complications can occur.

8. See Shell-Duncan and Hernlund (2000) for a collection of case studies on female genital modification in various parts of Africa.

9. Far earlier, in the 1820s, circumcising practices were also at the center of debates in the Sudan (Abusharaf 1999).

10. In the Hindu practice of *sati*, a widow immolates herself on her husband's funeral pyre. *Sati* became the subject of considerable debate in India during British colonial rule, leading to abolition in 1829. The *sati* controversy, like debates about female genital operations, involves a wide range of perspectives and has been framed at various times in terms of women's status, issues of tradition, authority, religious rights, personal autonomy, and humanitarianism. Outlawing *sati* did not make it disappear entirely. "Through the 1970s and 1980s...[the same time when circumcision controversies were heating up], either incidents of *sati* increased or greater scrutiny was brought to bear on the issue, primarily by women's organizations" (Courtright 1994:47). In September 1987, the case of Roop Kanwar, a young Hindu woman who burned in Rajasthan, galvanized national debate. Nandy (1988) and Mani (1990b) have noted continuities of language and argument between contemporary Indian positions and earlier colonial debates, parallels similar to those in circumcision controversies. Both debates involve "instabilities of perspective, of meaning, of judgment," and provide avenues for considering the "social history of moral imagination" (Geertz 1983:42). See also Mani (1990a), Nandy (1975), and Teltscher (1995:37–72).

11. Different aspects of this debate are described in Murray (1974; 1976), Pederson (1991), and Lonsdale (1992:388–397). Descriptions of Kikuyu initiation and contemporary women's attitudes can be found in Davison et al. (1989). Thomas discusses debates in nearby Meru, Kenya, and their connections with many other domains of life (1996; 1997).

12. For instance, several 1990s immigration cases and asylum claims in the United States have been based on arguments about the persecution of women through genital operations. Lydia Oluloro, a Nigerian woman, fought deportation on the grounds that she was protecting her daughters from the procedure. Her case was profiled in newspapers and on television in a segment of *Sixty Minutes* in 1994. A woman from Togo, Fauziya Kassindja, was also granted asylum in 1996, and a woman calling herself "Adelaide Abankwah" received asylum in the United States in 1999. Highly publicized cases in France in the 1990s prosecuted

immigrant parents and ritual surgeons who continued the practice in their new country (Verdier 1992; Winter 1994). Kratz (2002) analyzes several asylum cases heard in the United States.

13. See for example Dawit (1997).

14. Actors and institutions involved in each arena might include the following. (1) *In each home country*: National governments and politicians' local NGOs and national action groups; international action groups; churches; religious and ethnic communities whose circumcising practice may differ and whose histories of education and involvement with government also differ. Within each circumcising community, differences of age, gender, education, religion, and wealth also influence positions. For instance, a Christian mother, her non-Christian husband, his educated brother, and their school-child daughter might disagree about whether the girl should participate with her friends in initiation ceremonies during a school holiday. Peters (1997:484–486) discusses the different positions within the Togolese family and community in the asylum case of Fauziya Kassindja as an actual example. See Gruenbaum (1996:463–470) and the film *Bintou in Paris* for other examples. (2) *In the United States and Europe*: Female genital modification was historically recognized as a viable medical procedure in these countries, "cosmetic" labial surgery on women is currently performed, and male circumcision is also widely practiced. Current female genital operations within their borders are usually debated in relation to immigrant families and communities from various "home countries." Some families and communities have lived outside their home countries for quite a while, with some children born and raised in the United States and Europe. Actors involved in these debates include immigrants themselves (again with differences of gender, religion, ethnicity, education, length of residence, etc.); their community organizations and spokespersons; national, state, and municipal governments, judiciaries, and agencies dealing with immigrants (e.g., Immigration and Naturalization Service, Health and Human Services, child welfare services, etc.); national action groups and organizations concerned with women and children; and international action groups. (3) *In international campaigns*:

These actors may also be engaged with those in "home countries" and in the United States or Europe, but they reach beyond national boundaries as well. They include international action groups based in various countries; the United Nations, World Health Organization, and related international agencies and NGOs; journalists; religious officials; national governments and politicians who seek conditionality clauses for foreign policy and provision of aid.

15. In many contexts, however, ritual meanings and patterns unite the two for practitioners, who often use a single word for both operations in local languages.

16. Fran Hosken may have coined the term, though I could not verify this. She certainly played a key role in popularizing it through the Women's International Network (WIN) newsletter she wrote. By the time she wrote the Hosken Report in 1979, *female genital mutilation* had become her standard term. Before 1975, she vacillated between that term and *female circumcision*. Mary Daly also used "genital mutilations" in her 1978 book. In the British parliamentary debates about Kenya, the word *mutilation* was used at times to distinguish between two different types of genital operations (infibulation was not at issue in this controversy), but it did not become the primary term of reference (Pederson 1991:666). The Church of Scotland Mission, however, did begin to use the term *sexual mutilation* (Pederson 1991:671).

17. There are striking parallels between these shifts in rhetoric and tactics and the rhetoric of radical anti-abortion organizations such as Operation Rescue.

18. Duggers eschewed the automatic condemnation of "mutilation," the medical implications of "surgery," and what she considered the "mildness" of "female circumcision" (Moses 1997:4).

19. A number of scholarly papers discuss the problems with these generalized images and show how they are constructed; Mohanty (1988) and Stephens (1989) are a good starting place. Alice Walker's books, *Possessing the Secret of Joy* and *Warrior Marks*, are commonly used as novelistic examples. Walker's representations of African women have also been discussed by a number

of scholars; Obiora (1997:323–328) and Mugo (1997) are examples focused on their relation to controversies about female genital modification.

20. Information about campaigns against male genital operations is available from NOCIRC (National Organization of Circumcision Information Resource Centers) or NOHARMM (National Organization to Halt the Abuse and Routine Mutilation of Males). Both can be found through web searches.

21. Examples of different body modifications illustrate the different kinds and contexts of "choice" involved in self-determination. Operations for breast reduction or enhancement, multiple ear piercings, and body piercings (including genital piercings) are modifications often presented by their American or European practitioners as ways to take control of one's body. These self-definitions are very much like local definitions of female genital operations in initiation, also seen as a sign of self-control, maturity, and both social and personal change. In both cases, the practices are linked to understandings of the body, aesthetics, sexuality, and gender relations, but the understandings are rather different, as are their social and institutional settings.

22. See Gruenbaum (1996:460–463) for further discussion of so-called false consciousness and the costs and benefits of female genital operations for various segments of Sudanese communities.

23. I have talked with many people in the United States who seek a "logical" explanation or rationale for traditions of female genital modification. When I summarize what Okiek in Kenya might say in response—e.g., that initiation is necessary for children to become adults—Americans have a hard time understanding and accepting these as "reasons." What for Okiek are logically satisfying, deeply felt, and natural understandings do not have for Americans the same intuitive sense and resonance. It is equally hard to answer Okiek questions about Americans, whom they sometimes encounter as tourists: Why do the women paint their mouths to look like they drink blood? Why do they walk about without clothing (e.g., in bathing suits)? Don't they feel shame? Why aren't girls initiated—how can they live their entire lives as children?

REFERENCES

Abusharaf, Rogaia Mustafa. 1999. Beyond "The External Messiah Syndrome": What Are Sudanese People Doing to End Ritualized Genital Surgeries? Paper presented at the Annual Meetings of the American Anthropological Association, Chicago. Session on Female Genital Cutting: Local Dynamics of a Global Debate.

An-Na'im, Abdullahi, ed. 1992. *Human Rights in Cross-Cultural Perspectives: A Quest for Consensus.* Philadephia: University of Pennsylvania Press.

An-Na'im, Abdullahi, and Francis Deng, eds. 1990. *Human Rights in Africa: Cross-Cultural Perspectives.* Washington, DC: The Brookings Institution.

Apena, Adeline. 1996. Female Circumcision in Africa and the Problem of Cross-Cultural Perspectives. *Africa Update* 3(2):7–8 (see below for web version).

Berlin, Isaiah. 1991. *The Crooked Timber of Humanity.* New York: Alfred A. Knopf.

Boddy, Janice. 1989. *Wombs and Alien Spirits.* Madison: University of Wisconsin Press.

Boyarin, Daniel. 1992. "This We Know to Be Carnal Israel": Circumcision and the Erotic Life of God and Israel. *Critical Inquiry* 18(3):474–505.

Courtright, Paul. 1994. The Iconographies of Sati. In *Sati, the Blessing and the Curse.* Ed. John S. Hawley. New York: Oxford University Press.

Daly, Mary. 1990. African Genital Mutilation: The Unspeakable Atrocities. In *Gynecology.* Boston: Beacon Press (originally 1978).

Davison, Jean, with the women of Mutira. 1989. *Voices from Mutira: Lives of Rural Gikuyu Women.* Boulder: Lynn Rienner.

Dawit, Seble. 1997. Letter from a Female Circumcision Activist. *Colloquium: The On-line Magazine of the Case Western Reserve Law Review.* November 1997: lawwww.cwru.edu/cwrulaw/publications/colloquium/dawitfea.html.

Desjarlais, Robert. 1997. *Shelter Blues: Sanity and Selfhood Among the Homeless.* Philadelphia: University of Pennsylvania Press.

Dussart, Françoise. 2000. *The Politics of Ritual in an Aboriginal Settlement: Kinship, Gender and the Currency of Knowledge.* Washington, DC: Smithsonian Institution Press.

Geertz, Clifford. 1983. Found in Translation: On the Social History of Moral Imagination. In *Local Knowledge.* New York: Basic Books.

Gruenbaum, Ellen. 1996. The Cultural Debate over Female Circumcision: The Sudanese Are Arguing This One Out for Themselves. *Medical Anthropology Quarterly* 10(4):455–475.

Hernlund, Ylva. 1999. Ritual Negotiations and Cultural Compromise: An Alternative Initiation in the Gambia. Paper presented at the Annual Meetings of the American Anthropological Association, session on Female Genital Cutting: Local Dynamics of a Global Debate.

Holmes, Douglas R. 2000. *Integral Europe: Fast-Capitalism, Multiculturalism, Neofascism.* Princeton, NJ: Princeton University Press.

Hosken, Fran. 1979. *The Hosken Report.* Lexington, MA: Women's International Network News.

Hutchinson, Sharon. 1996. *Nuer Dilemmas.* Berkeley: Univerity of California Press.

Iweriebor, Ifeyinwa. 1996. Brief Reflections on Clitoridectomy. *Africa Update* 3(2):2 (see below for Web version).

Koso-Thomas, Olayinka. 1987. *The Circumcision of Women: A Strategy for Eradication.* London: Zed Books.

Kratz, Corinne. 1994. *Affecting Performance: Meaning, Movement, and Experience in Okiek Women's Initiation.* Washington, DC: Smithsonian Institution Press.

—. 1999a. Contexts, Controversies, Dilemmas: Teaching Circumcision." In *Great Ideas for Teaching About Africa.* Eds. Misty Bastian and Jane Parpart. Boulder: Lynne Rienner, pp. 103–118.

—. 1999b. Female Circumcision in Africa. In *Africana: Encyclopedia of the African and African American Experience.* Eds. Kwame Anthony Appiah and Henry Louis Gates, Jr. New York: Perseus Publishing. Copublished with CD-ROM version by Microsoft.

—. 2002. Circumcision Debates and Asylum Cases: Intersecting Arenas, Contested Values, and Tangled Webs. In *Engaging Cultural Differences: The Multicultural Challenge in Liberal Democracies.* Eds. Richard A. Shweder, Hazel R. Markus, and Martha Minow. New York: Russell Sage Foundation.

Laumann, E. O., C. M. Masi, and E. W. Zuckerman. 1997. Circumcision in the United States: Prevalence, Prophylactic Effects, and Sexual Practice. *Journal of the American Medical Association* 277(13):1052–1057.

Leonard, Lori. 1999. "We Did It for Pleasure Only": Hearing Alternative Tales of Female Circumcision. Paper presented at the Annual Meetings of the American Anthropological Association, session on Female Genital Cutting: Local Dynamics of a Global Debate.

Lonsdale, John. 1992. Wealth, Poverty, and Civic Virtue in Kikuyu Political Thought. In B. Berman and J. Lonsdale, *Unhappy Valley: Conflict in Kenya and Africa*. London: James Currey.

Lyons, Harriet. 1981. Anthropologists, Moralities, and Relativities: The Problem of Genital Mutilations. *Canadian Review of Sociology and Anthropology* 18(4):499–518.

Mani, Lata. 1990a. Contentious Traditions: The Debate on *Sati* in Colonial India. In *The Nature and Context of Minority Discourse*. Eds. A. JanMohamed and D. Lloyd. Oxford: Oxford University Press.

—. 1990b. Multiple Mediations: Feminist Scholarship in the Age of Multinational Reception. *Feminist Review* 35:24–40.

Matias, Aisha Samad. 1996, Female Circumcision in Africa. *Africa Update* 3(2):3–6.

Mohanty, Chandra. 1988. Under Western Eyes: Feminist Scholarship and Colonial Discourses. *Feminist Review* 30:61–88.

Morison, Linda, Caroline Scherf, Gloria Ekpo, et. al. 2001. The Long-term Reproductive Health Consequences of Female Genital Cutting in Rural Gambia: A Community-Based Survey. *Tropical Medicine and International Health* 6(8):643–653.

Moses, Meredith. 1997. Watching the Watchdog: Female Circumcision in *The New York Times*. Student paper, Emory University.

Mugo, Micere. 1997. Elitist Anti-Circumcision Discourse as Mutilating and Anti-Feminist. *Case Western Reserve Law Review* 47(2):461–80.

Murray, Jocelyn. 1974. The Kikuyu Female Circumcision Controversy, with Special Reference to the Church Missionary Society's "Sphere of Influence." Ph.D. dissertation, University of California, Los Angeles.

—. 1976. The Church Missionary Society and the "Female Circumcision" Issue in Kenya, 1929–1932. *Journal of Religion in Africa* 8(2):92–104.

Nandy, Ashis. 1975. *Sati*: A Nineteenth Century Tale of Women, Violence, and Protest. In *Rammohun Roy and the Process of Modernization in India*. Ed. V. C. Joshi. Delhi: Vikas Publishing House.

—. 1988. The Human Factor. *The Illustrated Weekly of India*, 17 January, pp. 20–23.

Obiora, L. Amede. 1997. Bridges and Barricades: Rethinking Polemics and Intransigence in the Campaign Against Female Circumcision. *Case Western Reserve Law Review* 47(2):275–378.

Ogbu, M. A. 1997. Comment on Obiora's "Bridges and Barricades." *Case Western Reserve Law Review* 47(2):411–422.

Parker, Melissa. 1995. Rethinking Female Circumcision. *Africa* 65(4):506–524.

Pederson, Susan. 1991. National Bodies, Unspeakable Acts: The Sexual Politics of Colonial Policymaking. *Journal of Modern History* 63:647–680.

Peters, Pauline. 1997. Another Bridge to Cross: Between "Outside" and "Inside." *Case Western Reserve Law Review* 47(2):481–490.

Rofel, Lisa. 1999. *Other Modernities: Gendered Yearnings in China After Socialism*. Berkeley: University of California Press.

Shell-Duncan, Bettina. 2001. The Medicalization of Female "Circumcision": Harm Reduction or Promotion of a Dangerous Practice? *Social Science and Medicine* 52: 1013–1028.

Shell-Duncan, Bettina, and Ylva Hernlund, eds. 2000. *Female "Circumcision" in Africa: Culture, Controversy and Change*. Boulder, CO: Lynne Rienner.

Shweder, Richard. 2002. What About Female Genital Mutilation? And Why Understanding Culture Matters in the First Place. In *Engaging Cultural Differences: The Multicultural Challenge in Liberal Democracies*. Eds. Richard A. Shweder, Hazel R. Markus, and Martha Minow. New York: Russell Sage Foundation.

Stephens, Julie. 1989. Feminist Fictions: A Critique of the Category "Non-Western Woman" in Feminist Writings on India. In *Subaltern Studies VI*. Ed. R. Guha. New York: Oxford University Press.

Teltscher, Kate. 1995. *India Inscribed: European and British Writing on India, 1600–1800*. Oxford: Oxford University Press.

Thomas, Lynn. 1996. "Ngaitana (I will circumcise myself)": The Gender and Generational Politics of the 1956 Ban on Clitoridectomy in Meru, Kenya. *Gender and History* 8(3):338–363.

—. 1997. Imperial Concerns and "Women's Affairs": State Efforts to Regulate Clitoridectomy and Eradicate Abortion in Meru, Kenya, c. 1920–1950. *Journal of African History*.

Verdier, Raymond. 1992. The *Exiseuse* in Criminal Court: the Trial of Soko Aramata Keita. *Passages* 3:1–3 (originally in *Droit et Cultures: Revue semestrielle d'anthropologie et d'histoire*, 1991).

Winter, Bronwyn. 1994. Women, the Law, and Cultural Relativism in France: The Case of Excision. *Signs* 19(4):939–974.

The United Nations on the Rights of Women

Article 1—Discrimination against women, denying or limiting as it does their equality of rights with men, is fundamentally unjust and constitutes an offense against human dignity.

Article 2—All appropriate measures shall be taken to abolish existing laws, customs, regulations, and practices which are discriminatory against women, and to establish adequate legal protection for equal rights of men and women...

Article 3—All appropriate measures shall be taken to educate public opinion and to direct national aspirations towards the eradication of prejudice and the abolition of customary and all other practices which are based on the idea of the inferiority of women.

Article 4—All appropriate measures shall be taken to ensure to women on equal terms with men, without any discrimination:

a. The right to vote in all elections and be eligible for election to all publicly elected bodies;

b. The right to vote in all public referenda;

c. The right to hold public office and to exercise life, all public functions. Such rights shall be guaranteed by legislation.

Article 5—Women shall have the same rights as men to acquire, change or retain their nationality. Marriage to an alien shall not automatically affect the nationality of the wife either by rendering her stateless or by forcing upon her the nationality of her husband.

Article 6—
1. Without prejudice to the safeguarding of the unity and the harmony of the family, which remains the basic unit of any society, all appropriate measures, particularly legislative measures, shall be taken to ensure to women, married or unmarried, equal rights with men in the field of civil law...

2. All appropriate measures shall be taken to ensure the principle of equality of status of the husband and wife, and in particular:

a. Women shall have the same right as men as to free choice of a spouse and to enter into marriage rights with men during marriage and at its dissolution. In all cases the interest of the children shall be paramount...

b. Parents shall have equal rights and duties in matters relating to their children. In all cases the interest of the children shall be paramount.

3. Child marriage and the betrothal of young girls before puberty shall be prohibited, and effective action, including legislation, shall be taken to specify a minimum age for marriage and to make the registration of marriages in an official registry compulsory.

Article 7—All provisions of penal codes which constitute discrimination against women shall be repealed.

Article 8—All appropriate measures, including legislation, shall be taken to combat all forms of traffic in women and exploitation of prostitution of women.

Article 9—All appropriate measures shall be taken to ensure to girls and women, married or unmarried, any discrimination equal rights with men in education at all levels...

Article 10—All appropriate measures shall be taken to ensure to women, married or unmarried, equal rights with men in the field of economic and social life...

1. In order to prevent discrimination against women on account of marriage or maternity and to ensure their effective right to work, measures shall be taken to prevent their dismissal in the event of marriage or maternity and to provide paid maternity leave, with the guarantee of returning to former employment, and to provide the necessary social services, including child-care facilities.

2. Measures taken to protect women in certain types of work, for reasons inherent in their physical nature, shall not be regarded as discriminatory.

Article 11—

1. The principle of equality of rights of men and women demands implementation in all States in accordance with the principles of the Charter of the United Nations and of the Universal Declaration of Human Rights.

2. Governments, non-governmental organizations and individuals are urged, therefore, to do all in their power to promote the implementation of the principles contained in this Declaration.

"The United Nations on the Rights of Women," excerpted from *United Nations Declaration on the Rights of Women*, adopted November 7, 1967. Reprinted by permission of the United Nations.

E X E R C I S E

Name _____

Section _____

Date _____

EXERCISE 3.3: FEMALE CIRCUMCISION

List five reasons in favor of female circumcision.

1.

2.

3.

4.

5.

List five reasons against the act of female circumcision.

1.

2.

3.

4.

5.

Describe what you would do if you witnessed such an act while conducting field research.

RESPONSIBILITIES OF THE FIELD RESEARCHER

Army's New Troops Are Anthropologists— *David Rohde*

Military: Their understanding of local cultures has won the praise of officers.

SHABAK VALLEY, AFGHANISTAN—In this isolated Taliban stronghold in eastern Afghanistan, American paratroopers are fielding what they consider a crucial new weapon in counterinsurgency operations here: a soft-spoken civilian anthropologist named Tracy.

Tracy, who asked that her surname not be used for security reasons, is a member of the first Human Terrain Team, an experimental Pentagon program that assigns anthropologists and other social scientists to U.S. combat units in Afghanistan and Iraq.

Her team's ability to understand subtle points of tribal relations—in one case spotting a land dispute that allowed the Taliban to bully parts of a major tribe—has won the praise of officers who say they are seeing concrete results.

Col. Martin Schweitzer, commander of the 82nd Airborne Division unit working with the anthropologists in the Shabak Valley, said that the unit's combat operations had been reduced by 60 percent since the social scientists arrived in February, and that the soldiers were now able to focus more on improving security, health care and education for the population.

"We're looking at this from a human perspective, from a social scientist's perspective," he said. "We're not focused on the enemy. We're focused on bringing governance down to the people."

UNCLE SAM WANTS SCHOLARS
In September, Defense Secretary Robert Gates authorized a $40 million expansion of the program, which will assign teams of anthropologists and social scientists to each of the 26 U.S. combat brigades in Iraq and Afghanistan.

As a result, military officials are scrambling to find more scholars willing to deploy to the front lines. Since early September, five new teams have been deployed in the Baghdad area, bringing the total to six.

Yet criticism is emerging in academia. Citing past misuse of social sciences in counterinsurgency campaigns, including in Vietnam and Latin America, some denounce the program as "mercenary anthropology" that exploits social science for political gain.

Opponents fear that, whatever their intention, the scholars who work with the military could inadvertently cause all anthropologists to be viewed as intelligence gatherers for the American military.

SCIENTISTS URGE BOYCOTT
Hugh Gusterson, an anthropology professor at George Mason University, and 10 other anthropologists are circulating an online pledge calling for anthropologists to boycott the teams, particularly in Iraq.

"While often presented by its proponents as work that builds a more secure world," the pledge says, "at base, it contributes instead to a brutal war of occupation which has entailed massive casualties."

In Afghanistan, the anthropologists arrived along with 6,000 troops, which doubled the U.S. military's strength in the area it patrols, the country's east.

The troop buildup, a smaller version of the Bush administration's troop increase in Iraq, has allowed American units to carry out the counterinsurgency strategy in Afghanistan, where U.S. forces generally face less resistance and are better able to take risks.

Since Gen. David Petraeus, the overall U.S. commander in Iraq, oversaw the drafting of the Army's new counterinsurgency manual last year, the strategy has become the new mantra of the military. A recent U.S. military operation in Afghanistan offered a window into how efforts to apply the new approach are playing out on the ground in counterintuitive ways.

In interviews, U.S. officers lavishly praised the anthropology program, saying that the social scientists' advice has proved to be "brilliant," helping them see the situation from an Afghan perspective and allowing them to cut back on combat operations.

The eventual aim, they say, is to improve the performance of local government officials, persuade local tribesmen to join the police, ease poverty and protect villagers from the Taliban and criminals.

Afghans and Western civilian officials, too, praised the anthropologists and the new U.S. military approach but were cautious about predicting long-term success. Many of the economic and political problems fueling instability can be solved only by large numbers of Afghan and American civilian experts.

"My feeling is that the military are going through an enormous change right now where they recognize they won't succeed militarily," said Tom Gregg, the chief U.N. official in southeastern Afghanistan. "But they don't yet have the skill sets to implement" a coherent nonmilitary strategy, he added.

Deploying small groups of U.S. soldiers into remote areas, Schweitzer's paratroopers organized *jirgas*, or local councils, to resolve tribal disputes that have simmered for decades.

Officers shrugged off questions about whether the military was comfortable with what David Kilcullen, an Australian anthropologist and an architect of the new strategy, calls "armed social work."

'YOU HAVE TO EVOLVE'
"Who else is going to do it?" asked Lt. Col. David Woods, commander of the Fourth Squadron, 73rd Cavalry. "You have to evolve. Otherwise you're useless."

The anthropology team in the Shabak Valley also played a major role in what the military called Operation Khyber. That was a 15-day drive late this summer in which 500 Afghan and 500 U.S. soldiers tried to clear an estimated 200 to 250 Taliban insurgents out of much of Paktia Province, secure southeastern Afghanistan's most important road and halt a string of suicide attacks on U.S. troops and local governors.

In one of the first districts the team entered, Tracy identified an unusually high concentration of widows in one village, Woods said.

The widows' lack of income created financial pressure on their sons to provide for their families, she determined, a burden that could drive the young men to join well-paid insurgents. Citing Tracy's advice, U.S. officers decided to develop a job training program for the widows as a step toward easing their financial burdens.

In another district, the anthropologist interpreted the beheading of a local tribal elder as more than a random act of intimidation: the Taliban's goal, she said, was to divide and weaken the Zadran, one of southeastern Afghanistan's largest tribes. If Afghan and U.S. officials could unite the Zadran, she said, the tribe could block the Taliban from operating in the area.

"Call it what you want, it works," said Woods, a native of Denbo, Pa. "It works in helping you define the problems, not just the symptoms."

Creation of the teams began in late 2003, after U.S. officers in Iraq complained that they had little to no information about the local population. Pentagon officials contacted Montgomery McFate, a Yale-educated cultural anthropologist working for the Navy who advocated using social science to improve military operations and strategy.

McFate helped develop a computer database in 2005 that provided commanders with detailed information on the local population. The next year, Steve Fondacaro, a retired Special Operations colonel, joined the program and advocated embedding social scientists with U.S. combat units.

McFate, the program's senior social science adviser and an author of the military's new counterinsurgency manual, dismissed criticism of scholars working with the military.

"I'm frequently accused of militarizing anthropology," she said. "But we're really anthropologizing the military."

Roberto J. González, an anthropology professor at San Jose State University, called participants in the program naïve and unethical. He said that the military and the CIA had consistently misused anthropology in counterinsurgency and propaganda campaigns and that military contractors were now hiring anthropologists for their local expertise as well.

"Those serving the short-term interests of military and intelligence agencies and contractors," he wrote in the June issue of *Anthropology Today*, an academic journal, "will end up harming the entire discipline in the long run."

Arguing that her critics misunderstand the program and the military, McFate said other anthropologists were joining the teams. She said their goal was to help the military decrease conflict instead of provoking it, and she vehemently denied that the anthropologists collected intelligence for the military.

In eastern Afghanistan, Tracy said her goal was to reduce the use of heavy-handed military operations focused solely on killing insurgents, which she said alienated the population and created more insurgents.

"Army's New Troops Are Anthropologists," by David Rohde, *The New York Times*, October 5, 2007. Copyright © 2007 by The New York Times Co. Reprinted with permission.

RESPONSIBILITIES OF THE FIELD RESEARCHER

KEY TERMS

Name _____

Section _____

Date _____

Apartheid:

Cultural relativism:

Ethnocentrism:

Eugenics:

Female circumcision (or female genital mutilation/modification):

Genocide:

Honor killings:

Human rights:

War

RESPONSIBILITIES OF THE FIELD RESEARCHER

4 RACE AND ETHNICITY

Can't We Just Get Along?

In addition to anthropologists being interested in the investigation of physical and cultural differences between peoples of the world, it is also of interest to the people themselves. To one degree or another, societies differentiate between their members. Humans often categorize themselves on the basis of distinctive physical characteristics or learned cultural traits. Those sharing similar cultural characteristics are said to belong to the same **ethnic group,** not race.

An **ethnic group** is a population of individuals that identify with one another, generally based upon common ancestry, language, history, geography, behavioral patterns or religious practices. This term is different from **nationality** which refers to citizenship with regard to a given country. Since many countries are made up of a multitude of ethnic groups these two terms are not the same.

Race refers to ethnic groups assumed to have a distinct biological basis. Therefore, this term is not the same as **ethnicity**. The "races" which we hear about everyday, and which appear as a means of classification on the United States Census Bureau, are more correctly called "*social races*," meaning that they differentiate cultural or social distinctions rather than biological categories.

Many Americans mistakenly assume skin color, eye shape, or hair texture to be biological distinctions and that physical traits can determine discrete races. This cannot be farther from the truth. We all belong to one race, the human race. Other forms of racial classification have led to confusion between the terms ethnicity and race.

More important, historically, confusion between the terms ethnicity and race have led to discrimination, violent confrontation, and even death.

RACE AND ETHNICITY

Identifying Race and Ethnicity

Historically, the decennial census has included questions on race and ethnicity. The growing racial and ethnic diversity of the American population, changing attitudes about race and ethnicity, and the increasing use of census data now make census questions on race and ethnicity a controversial topic.

U.S. Census Categories 1870–1980

(Federal budget HJ2051/A595)

1870

White
Colored (Negro)
Chinese, Japanese, and Civilized Indians

1880

White
Colored (Negro)
Asiatic (Chinese, Japanese, East Indians)
Other Indians—tribal and reservation
"American Indians and halfbreeds not included"

1890

White (foreign, native, and nativity of parents: native, foreign, mixed)
Colored (Negro descent, Chinese, Japanese, and Civilized Indians)

1900

White
Colored (persons of Negro descent, Chinese, Japanese, Indians)
Negro [subset of colored]

1910

White (foreign, native, and nativity of parents: native, foreign, mixed)
Negro
Other colored (Indian, Chinese, Japanese, and other)

1920

White (pure-blooded: foreign, native, and nativity of parents: native, foreign, mixed)
Negro
Indian
Chinese
Japanese
Filipino
Hindu
Korean
Hawaiian
Part Hawaiian
Other Polynesian
*Puerto Rico (white, Negro [black, mulatto])
*Phillippine Islands (Filipino)

1930

White (foreign, native, and nativity of parents: native, foreign, mixed)
Negro
Other races (Mexican [new category in 1930], Indian, Chinese, Japanese)
*Country of origin of foreign-born listed

1940

White (foreign + country of birth, native, and nativity of parents: native, foreign, mixed)
Negro
"Persons of Mexican birth or ancestry were designated Mexican in 1930 (but not prior censuses) were returned to white in 1940 if not definitely Indian or of other non-white race"
Other races (Indian, Chinese, Japanese, Filipino, Hindu, other)

1950

White/nonwhite
Nonwhite (Negro, Indian, Japanese, Chinese, other)

1960

White
Negro
American Indian
Japanese
Filipino
Hawaiian
Aleut

1970

White
Negro
Indian
Japanese
Chinese
Filipino
Korean
Hawaiian
"Persons of Spanish heritage"

1980

White
Black
Spanish origin
American Indian
Japanese
Chinese
Filipino
Korean
Vietnamese
Hawaiian
Guamanian

After the 1990 census, public pressure became more intense for revising and expanding race and ethnic classifications in the census, given the nation's diversity. At the same time, people recognized the ambiguity of racial and ethnic identities, especially because survey respondents were allowed to "self-identify" their race and ethnicity. At the direction of the Office of Management and Budget (OMB), the 1990 census included a race question that asked people to identify themselves as white, black or Negro, American Indian, Eskimo, Aleut, Asian or Pacific Islander, or other. American Indians were asked to provide a specific tribal affiliation. Asians and Pacific Islanders were asked to select from a list of nationality groups.

Separate from the race question, respondents were asked if they were of Spanish or Hispanic origin or descent and, if so, to choose Mexican, Puerto Rican, Cuban, or other. Write-in items in the 1990 census elicited more than 300 race responses, approximately 600 American Indian tribes, 70 different Hispanic origin groups, and more than 600 ancestry groups. Almost 10 million people wrote in their race after selecting "other race." Many of the write-in responses were from individuals with two or more racial and Hispanic origins.

At the direction of OMB, the 2000 census includes race and Hispanic items similar to those in 1990, but respondents will have the opportunity to check more than one race group. Unlike previous censuses when people of multiple racial backgrounds needed to check "other" and then write in a response, the 2000 census will collect direct information on the specific backgrounds for people of multiple racial ancestry.

2000 Census: 63 Racial Categories— U.S. Census Bureau

CURRENT CATEGORIES

White alone

Black or African American alone

American Indian or Alaska Native

Asian

Native Hawaiian or Other Pacific Islander

Some other race

Two or more races

    White and Black or African American

    White and American Indian and Alaska Native

    White and Asian

    White and Native Hawaiian and Other Pacific Islander

    White and Some other race

    Black and American Indian and Alaska Native

    Black and Asian

    Black and Native Hawaiian and Other Pacific Islander

RACE AND ETHNICITY

Black and Some other race

American Indian and Alaska Native and Asian

American Indian and Alaska Native and Native Hawaiian or Other Pacific Islander

American Indian and Alaska Native and Some other race

Asian and Native Hawaiian and Other Pacific Islander

Asian and Some other race

Native Hawaiian and Other Pacific Islander and Some other race

White, Black, and American Indian and Alaska Native

White, Black, and Asian

White, Black, and Native Hawaiian and Other Pacific Islander

White, Black, and Some other race

White, American Indian and Alaska Native, and Asian

White, American Indian and Alaska Native, and Native Hawaiian and Other Pacific Islander

White, American Indian and Alaska Native, and Some other race

White, Asian, and Native Hawaiian and Other Pacific Islander

White, Asian, and Some other race

White, Native Hawaiian and Other Pacific Islander, and Some other race

Black, American Indian and Alaska Native, and Asian

Black, American Indian and Alaska Native, and Native Hawaiian and Other Pacific Islander

Black, American Indian and Alaska Native, and Some other race

Black, Asian, and Native Hawaiian and Other Pacific Islander

Black, Asian, and Some other race

Black, Native Hawaiian and Other Pacific Islander, and Some other race

American Indian and Alaska Native, Asian, and Native Hawaiian and Other Pacific Islander

American Indian and Alaska Native, Asian, and Some other race

American Indian and Alaska Native, Native Hawaiian and Other Pacific Islander, and Some other race

Asian, Native Hawaiian and Other Pacific Islander, and Some other race

White, Black, American Indian and Alaska Native, and Asian

White, Black, American Indian and Alaska Native, and Native Hawaiian and Other Pacific Islander

White, Black, American Indian and Alaska Native, and Some other race

White, Black, Asian and Native Hawaiian and Other Pacific Islander

White, Black, Asian and Some other race

White, Black, Native Hawaiian and Other Pacific Islander and Some other race

White, American Indian and Alaska Native, Asian and Native Hawaiian and Other Pacific Islander

White, American Indian and Alaska Native, Asian and Some other race

White, American Indian and Alaska Native, Native Hawaiian and Other Pacific Islander and Some other race

White, Asian, Native Hawaiian and Other Pacific Islander and Some other race

Black, American Indian and Alaska Native, Asian and Native Hawaiian and Other Pacific Islander

Black, American Indian and Alaska Native, Asian and Some other race

Black, American Indian and Alaska Native, Native Hawaiian and Other Pacific Islander and Some other race

Black, Asian, Native Hawaiian and Other Pacific Islander and Some other race

American Indian and Alaska Native, Asian, Native Hawaiian and Other Pacific Islander and Some other race

White, Black, American Indian and Alaska Native, Asian and Native Hawaiian and Other Pacific Islander

White, Black, American Indian and Alaska Native, Asian and Some other race

White, Black, American Indian and Alaska Native, Native Hawaiian and Other Pacific Islander and Some other race

White, Black, Asian, Native Hawaiian and Other Pacific Islander and Some other race

White, American Indian and Alaska Native, Asian, Native Hawaiian and Other Pacific Islander and Some other race

Black, American Indian and Alaska Native, Asian, Native Hawaiian and Other Pacific Islander and Some other race

White, Black, American Indian and Alaska Native, Asian, Native Hawaiian and Other Pacific Islander and Some other race

"63 Racial Categories," U.S. Census Bureau.

Five BIG Reasons Why You Should Fill Out Your Census Form—
U.S. Census Bureau

1. **Help Your Community Thrive.** Does your neighborhood have a lot of traffic congestion, elderly people living alone or over-crowded schools? Census numbers can help your community work out public improvement strategies.

   Non-profit organizations use census numbers to estimate the number of potential volunteers in communities across the nation.

2. **Get Help in Times of Need.** Many 911 emergency systems are based on maps developed for the last census. Census information helps health providers predict the spread of disease through communities with children or elderly people. When floods, tornadoes or earthquakes hit, the census tells rescuers how many people will need their help.

When Hurricane Andrew hit South Florida in 1991, census information aided the rescue effort by providing estimates of the number of people in each block.

3. **Make Government Work for You.** It's a good way to tell our leaders who we are and what we need. The numbers are used to help determine the distribution of over $100 billion in federal funds and even more in state funds. We're talking hospitals, highways, stadiums and school lunch programs.

   Using census numbers to support their request for a new community center, senior citizens in one New England community successfully argued their case before county commissioners.

4. **Reduce Risk for American Business.** Because census numbers help industry reduce financial risk and locate potential markets, businesses are able to produce the products you want.

   "All the Basic Facts You Need to Know to Start a New Business," a publication of the Massachusetts Department of Commerce, shows small businesses how to use census numbers to determine the marketability of new products.

5. **Help Yourself and Your Family**. Individual records are held confidential for 72 years, but you can request a certificate from past censuses that can be used as proof to establish your age, residence or relationship, information that could help you qualify for a pension, establish citizenship or obtain an inheritance. In 2072, your great-grandchildren may want to use census information to research family history. Right now, your children may be using census information to do their homework.

   Because we've had a census every 10 years since 1790, we know how far America has come.

"5 Big Reasons Why You Should Fill Out Your Census Form," U.S. Census Bureau.

Fifty Ways to Use Census 2000—
U.S. Census Bureau

- Decision-making at all levels of government
- Reapportionment of seats in the U.S. House of Representatives
- Drawing federal, state and local legislative districts
- Drawing school district boundaries
- Budget planning for government at all levels
- The distribution of over $100 billion in federal funds and even more in state funds
- Spotting trends in the economic well-being of the nation
- Forecasting future transportation needs for all segments of the population
- Planning for public transportation services
- Planning for hospitals, nursing homes, clinics and the location of other health services
- Planning health and educational services for people with disabilities
- Forecasting future housing needs for all segments of the population
- Establishing fair market rents and enforcing fair lending practices
- Directing funds for services for people in poverty
- Directing services to children and adults with limited English language proficiency
- Designing public safety strategies
- Urban planning
- Rural development
- Land use planning
- Analyzing local trends
- Understanding labor supply
- Estimating the numbers of people displaced by natural disasters
- Assessing the potential for spread of communicable diseases
- Developing assistance programs for low-income families
- Analyzing military potential
- Creating maps to speed emergency services to households in need of assistance
- Making business decisions
- Delivering goods and services to local markets
- Understanding consumer needs
- Designing facilities for people with disabilities, the elderly or children
- Planning for congregations

- Product planning
- Locating factory sites and distribution centers
- Investment planning and evaluation of financial risk
- Setting community goals
- Publication of economic and statistical reports about the United States and its people
- Standard for creating both public- and private-sector surveys
- Scientific research
- Comparing progress between different geographic areas
- Developing "intelligent" maps for government and business
- Genealogical research (after 2072)
- Proof of age, relationship or residence (certificates provided by the Census Bureau)
- School projects
- Medical research
- Developing adult education programs
- Media planning and research, back up for news stories
- Historical research
- Evidence in litigation involving land use, voting rights and equal opportunity
- Determining areas eligible for housing assistance and rehabilitation loans
- Attracting new businesses to state and local areas

"Fifty Ways to Use Census 2000," U.S. Census Bureau.

E X E R C I S E

Name _____

Section _____

Date _____

EXERCISE 4.1: AMERICA AT WORK

Every ten years, Congress directs an investigation of the American public, conducted by the United States Census Bureau. The form is to be filled out by one member of every household in America. Congress is interested in learning more about family income, ethnicity, and unmet needs in our communities. Yet many people refuse to complete the census forms, risking a $1,000.00 fine for not complying with government regulations.

How do you feel about the government asking personal questions concerning your family? List five reasons in favor of completing the form.

How could you and your family benefit by completing the survey?

Why do you suppose that some people fear sharing this information with government officials?

RACE AND ETHNICITY

Let's Ponder...

It is not uncommon for each of us to note behavioral patterns that differ from our own. Franz Boas attempted to explain why we judge others who act or believe differently than ourselves. Ethnocentrism, Boas stated, exists when a human (or a culture) comes into contact with others and evaluates the others' practices based upon standards having to do with their own cultural assumptions and behaviors.

There has been a long-standing debate in the social sciences over the importance of **nature versus nurture** in impacting human behavior. Nature refers to our biological or genetic make-up influencing our actions. Nurture refers to the notion that our environment, culture, and experiences impact how we behave. While most researchers today seem to believe that human behavior is comprised of an interaction of nature AND nurture (rather than the two being mutually exclusive) geneticists are often quantifying the importance of one over the other. For instance, it has been stated that aggressive tendencies are a result of 60% biology and 40% environmental influences, meaning that such actions are a result of a genetic make-up that makes one prone to such behaviors. What do you think about quantifying such reactions? As a cultural anthropologist, how does this impact your studies?

RACE AND ETHNICITY

ETHNICITY AND CULTURE

The issue of race in American society is very ambiguous. In fact, we often utilize the terms race and ethnicity interchangeably. However, this is not correct.

The American Association of Anthropologists has issued the following statement on race.

American Anthropological Association Statement on "Race"—
Audrey Smedley

The following statement was adopted by the Executive Board of the American Anthropological Association, acting on a draft prepared by a committee of representative American anthropologists. It does not reflect a consensus of all members of the AAA, as individuals vary in their approaches to the study of "race." We believe that it represents generally the contemporary thinking and scholarly positions of a majority of anthropologists.

In the United States both scholars and the general public have been conditioned to viewing **human races** as natural and separate divisions within the human species based on visible physical differences. With the vast expansion of scientific knowledge in this century, however, it has become clear that human populations are not unambiguous, clearly demarcated, biologically distinct groups. Evidence from the analysis of genetics (e.g., DNA) indicates that most physical variation, about 94%, lies within so-called racial groups. Conventional geographic "racial" groupings differ from one another only in about 6% of their genes. This means that there is greater variation within "racial" groups than between them. In neighboring populations there is much overlapping of genes and their phenotypic (physical) expressions. Throughout history whenever different groups have come into contact, they have interbred. The continued sharing of genetic materials has maintained all of humankind as a single species.

Physical variations in any given trait tend to occur gradually rather than abruptly over geographic areas. And because physical traits are inherited independently of one another, knowing the range of one trait does not predict the presence of others. For example, skin color varies largely from light in the temperate areas in the north to dark in the tropical areas in the south; its intensity is not related to nose shape or hair texture. Dark skin may be associated with frizzy or kinky hair or curly or wavy or straight hair, all of which are found among different indigenous peoples in tropical regions. These facts render any attempt to establish lines of division among biological populations both arbitrary and subjective.

Historical research has shown that the idea of "race" has always carried more meanings than mere physical differences; indeed, physical variations in the human species have no meaning except the social ones that humans put on them. Today scholars in many fields argue that "race" as it is understood in the United States of America was a social mechanism invented during the 18th century to refer to those populations brought together in colonial America: the English and other European settlers, the conquered Indian peoples, and those peoples of Africa brought in to provide slave labor.

From its inception, this modern concept of "race" was modeled after an ancient theorem of the Great Chain of Being, which posited natural categories on a hierarchy established by God or nature. Thus "race" was a mode of classification linked specifically to peoples in the colonial situation. It subsumed a growing ideology of **inequality** devised to rationalize European attitudes and treatment of the conquered and enslaved peoples. Proponents of slavery in particular during the 19th century used "race" to justify the retention of slavery. The ideology magnified the differences among Europeans, Africans, and Indians, established a rigid hierarchy of socially exclusive categories, underscored and bolstered unequal rank and status differences, and provided the rationalization that the inequality was natural or God-given. The different physical traits of African-Americans and Indians became markers or symbols of their status differences.

As they were constructing U.S. society, leaders among European-Americans fabricated the cultural/behavioral characteristics associated with each "race," linking superior traits with Europeans and negative and inferior ones to blacks and Indians. Numerous arbitrary and fictitious beliefs about the different peoples were institutionalized and deeply embedded in American thought.

RACE AND ETHNICITY

Early in the 19th century the growing fields of science began to reflect the public consciousness about human differences. Differences among the "racial" categories were projected to their greatest extreme when the argument was posed that Africans, Indians, and Europeans were separate species, with Africans the least human and closer taxonomically to apes.

Ultimately "race" as an ideology about human differences was subsequently spread to other areas of the world. It became a strategy for dividing, ranking, and controlling colonized people used by colonial powers everywhere. But it was not limited to the colonial situation. In the latter part of the 19th century it was employed by Europeans to rank one another and to justify social, economic, and political inequalities among their peoples. During World War II, the Nazis under Adolf Hitler enjoined the expanded ideology of "race" and "racial" differences and took them to a logical end: the extermination of 11 million people of "inferior races" (e.g., Jews, Gypsies, Africans, homosexuals, and so forth) and other unspeakable brutalities of the Holocaust.

"Race" thus evolved as a worldview, a body of prejudgments that distorts our ideas about human differences and group behavior. Racial beliefs constitute myths about the diversity in the human species and about the abilities and behavior of people homogenized into "racial" categories. The myths fused behavior and physical features together in the public mind, impeding our comprehension of both biological variations and cultural behavior, implying that both are genetically determined. *Racial myths bear no relationship to the reality of human capabilities or behavior*. Scientists today find that reliance on such folk beliefs about human differences in research has led to countless errors.

At the end of the 20th century, we now understand that human cultural behavior is learned, conditioned into infants beginning at birth, and always subject to modification. No human is born with a built-in culture or language. Our temperaments, dispositions, and personalities, regardless of genetic propensities, are developed within sets of meanings and values that we call "culture." Studies of infant and early childhood learning and behavior attest to the reality of our cultures in forming who we are.

It is a basic tenet of anthropological knowledge that all normal human beings have the capacity to learn any cultural behavior. The American experience with immigrants from hundreds of different language and cultural backgrounds who have acquired some version of American culture traits and behavior is the clearest evidence of this fact. Moreover, people of all physical variations have learned different cultural behaviors and continue to do so as modern transportation moves millions of immigrants around the world.

How people have been accepted and treated within the context of a given society or culture has a direct impact on how they perform in that society. The "racial" worldview was invented to assign some groups to perpetual low status, while others were permitted access to privilege, power, and wealth. The tragedy in the United States has been that the policies and practices stemming from this worldview succeeded all too well in constructing unequal populations among Europeans, Native Americans, and peoples of African descent. Given what we know about the capacity of normal humans to achieve and function within any culture, we conclude that present day inequalities between so-called "racial" groups are not consequences of their biological inheritance but products of historical and contemporary social, economic, educational, and political circumstances.

Audrey Smedley, "Statement on Race," American Anthropological Association. Reprinted by permission.

E X E R C I S E

Name

Section

Date

EXERCISE 4.2: ERASING AN ILLUSION

After reading the American Anthropological Association's (AAA) statement on race go to the companion web page for the series "Race: The Power of an Illusion" at the following web address and do the activity and analysis sections below:

http://www.pbs.org/race/000_General/000_00-Home.htm

Activity

Choose one of the following options and then answer the questions below once you have completed the activity:

1. Click on "Background Readings" and select one of the readings from the "science," "history," and "social" sections for a total of three readings (except for the first two as they are summaries). Summarize their main points and list three things that you learned about race that you did not know before.

2. Click on the "Learn More" button to the right. Go through the six options on the right side (beginning with the first page "What is Race?" and ending with "Where Race Lives") and do the activities (reading, sorting, etc.). For more, you can click on the "go deeper" option.

Analysis

Does the information from the activity above change your views on race? Why or why not?

How would you answer the question "what race are you?" Is this different from how you would have answered it before? Explain.

For more information go to the American Anthropological Association's (AAA) website on race at:

http://www.aaanet.org/resources/A-Public-Education-Program.cfm

RACE AND ETHNICITY

Media Blackface: "Racial Profiling" in News Reporting—
Mikal Muharrar

Racial profiling—the discriminatory practice by police of treating blackness (or brownness) as an indication of possible criminality—has lately been the focus of frequent legal or legislative action, resulting in a significant amount of coverage in the mainstream news media (e.g., *New York Times*, 5/8/98, 5/10/98; *Nightline*, 5/31/98; *Time*, 6/15/98).

The coverage of police racial profiling has been fairly accurate and balanced. Yet while the mainstream media continues to cover *police* racial profiling, they have generally failed to acknowledge their *own* practice of *media* racial profiling. And when it has, the result has been more cover-up than coverage.

ISSUES IN BLACKFACE

There is need for a broader understanding of "racial profiling." As a general concept and not just a specific police policy, racial profiling may best be understood as the politically acceptable and very American practice of defining a social problem in "blackface"—i.e., in racial terms—through indirect association. Once portrayed in blackface, the "blackness" of the problem encourages suspicion, polarizing antagonism, and typically leads to the targeting of the racial group for punitive (public policy) action.

The link between the stereotypical profile and public policy is key. In police racial profiling it is direct: Individual officers act on racial stereotypes against racial minorities, especially African-Americans. But when it comes to the news media, the racial profiles projected are indirectly related to punitive public policies, thus giving the mainstream news media the "out" of deniability. When the news media over-represents the number of black people in the category that is at issue, the issue becomes "black," stigmatized, linked to some form of always-justified politically punishing behavior, and, in turn, further racialized.

Examples of issues defined in blackface and subjected to a racial profile include the black drug abuser and drug dealer, the threatening and invasive black criminal, the black welfare cheat and queen, and the undeserving black affirmative action recipient. The punitive actions associated with drugs, crime, welfare and affirmative action policy are self-evident, and involve punitive action disproportionately affecting African-American people.

The brilliance of racial profiling as an instrument of modern, deniable racism is that the issue—be it crime, welfare, drug abuse or what have you—is seen by many as a real issue that is only *coincidentally* about race. The trait of blackness associated with the problem is viewed as nothing more than an unfortunate reality that is secondary to the public hostility and the punitive measures. So it's not really racist, is it?

By looking at the ways in which the mainstream news media has covered (or failed to cover) several recent studies/stories involving the news media and race, we can begin to get a better understanding of this practice of racial profiling as it relates to the news media.

RACIAL PROFILING AS THE MISSING LINK

In March 1998, two studies on U.S. drug policy were released by two prominent groups of physicians within a day of each other. The first study was issued by Physician Leadership on National Drug Policy (PLNDP), a high-profile group of doctors composed, in part, of high-ranking health officials from the Reagan, Bush and Clinton administrations. The voluminous and exhaustively documented PLNDP study concluded that drug treatment for drug addiction was not only an effective health measure but that it was much more cost-effective than the criminalizing policies of the current "drug war."

One section of the study showed how, contrary to popular perception, drug addicts are *not* primarily members of minority racial and ethnic groups. "The research we are releasing today," the PLNDP announced at its press conference, "shows, conclusively, that drug addiction is very treatable and that it reaches across all strata of society, with affluent, educated Caucasians being the most likely drug users, and the most likely to be addicted." Looking at adult drug users, the PLNDP study found that more than half of those who admitted using heroin last year are white and 60 percent of monthly cocaine users are white. (Also, 77 percent of regular marijuana users are white, while one in six is African-American.) Youth drug use followed similar patterns.

Paralleling this point about the public misperception of drug use were the results of a survey of 50 years of public opinion called the "The Public and the War on Illicit Drugs," which was featured in the *Journal of the American Medical Association (JAMA)* (3/11/98). The study found that although Americans did not think the so-called "War on Drugs" was succeeding, they did not want to abandon the criminalization approach pushed by the government. The study also found that there was weak support for increasing funding for drug treatment.

One of its key conclusions was that public opinion polls indicated the overwhelming majority of Americans had "relatively little firsthand experience with the extent of the problems associated with drug use," and that "the majority of Americans report getting most of their information about the seriousness of the illicit drug problems from the news media, mainly television." In fact, the PLNDP presented the *JAMA* study at its press conference to emphasize how public opinion and the judgment of seasoned physicians were at odds with each other, and how the news media was playing a leading role in misinforming the public about the health and financial issues at the heart of "Drug War" policy.

The powerful findings of these two reports were not covered by any of the three major newsweeklies (*Time, US. News & World Report, Newsweek*), nor were they covered by the *New York Times* or *Washington Post*. When the story was covered, moreover, the dominant media focused on the disconnect between the views of the public and the research of the physicians—but said nothing about the role of the news media in fostering the stereotypes fueling the bad drug policy (*CNN Today*, 3/1 7/98; *Associated Press*, 3/17/98; *USA Today*, 3/18/98).

The role of the news media in promoting racial stereotypes was the missing link between the two studies. Even when *Nightline* (3/18/98) began its coverage of the story with the acknowledgment that, when it came to the issue of drug addiction and drug policy in the U.S., "most Americans get their information from the media/news, the show glossed over the central problem of news media misinformation. Nor did *Nightline* host Ted Koppel refrain from reinforcing the very misconceptions his show could have been debunking: Koppel's repeated emphasis on how "society does not want to spend money on rehabilitation"—when a

main point of the PLNDP report was that treatment saves money—amounted to a brief for the very media-enforced ignorance the doctors' groups sought to dispel.

Almost alone in its coverage of this story was an article by Raja Mishra written for the *Knight Ridder News Service* and appearing in the *Denver Post* (3/19/98). Mishra went to the heart of the story when reporting how "the doctors said the public had been misled by media accounts." The role of the news media in promoting racial stereotypes was the missing link between the two studies. Given the nature of the studies, an obvious conclusion. But it was all but obvious to the mainstream press.

NO SURPRISE

Another study, "Crime in Black and White: The Violent, Scary World of Local News" appeared in the academic journal *Press Politics* at the end of 1996 (Spring/96). Although appearing in a scholarly journal on journalism, this study received almost no attention in the media, except for its coverage in the *Washington Post* (4/28/97) by its media correspondent, Howard Kurtz.

Done by UCLA professors Franklin Gilliam and Shanto Iyengar, "Crime in Black and White" found through a content analysis of local television station *KABC* in Los Angeles that featured two important cues: "crime is violent and criminals are nonwhite." The real revelation, however, was that television viewers were so accustomed to seeing African-American crime suspects on the local news that even when the race of a suspect was not specified, viewers tended to remember seeing a black suspect. Moreover, when researchers used digital technology to change the race of certain suspects as they appeared on the screen, a little over a half of those who saw the "white" perpetrator recalled his race, but two-thirds did when the criminal was depicted as black. "Ninety percent of the false recognitions involved African-Americans and Hispanics," Gilliam said.

To his credit, Kurtz acknowledged the public policy implications of the study when he stated that "support for punitive law-enforcement policies was highest when the stories featured black suspects or provided no information about race and was lowest when the suspects were white." But his response to the "riveting" findings was fatalistic:

"This is not the first complaint about coverage of minorities and crime, and most local stations have not seen fit to change their approach," he wrote. And when he said that the study placed a "surprisingly harsh light on television and racial attitudes," one might ask: To whom should this be surprising?

When, a few months later, Kurtz addressed another study of racism in the news media, he again expressed surprise. The study by Yale University professor Martin Gilens, entitled "Race and Poverty in America: Public Misperceptions and the American News Media," was published in *Public Opinion Quarterly* (vol. 6, 1996) and found that while African-Americans make up 29 percent of the nation's poor, they constitute 62 percent of the images of the poor in the leading news magazines, and 65 percent of the images of the poor on the leading network television news programs. Not only were the poor disproportionately portrayed as black, but they were also portrayed in the most unsympathetic fashion. The most sympathetic groups of the poor—i.e., the elderly and the working poor—were under-represented and the least sympathetic group—unemployed working-age adults—was over-represented.

Kurtz, who did not discuss these findings in the *Washington Post*, was part of a discussion of the study on the *CNN* "media watch" program *Reliable Sources* (8/24/97). "Who Put the Black Face on Poverty," the show asked. Well, the mainstream media "whiteout" of the story provides a clue. Gilens' study specifically looked at the coverage of *Time, Newsweek, U.S. News & World Report* and *ABC, NBC* and *CBS* news. Unsurprisingly, none of these big media outlets covered the release of the study results. Neither did the *New York Times. USA Today* (8/9/97) and the *Washington Post* (5/15/97) covered it in a mere paragraph or two.

It was left to the *Associated Press* (8/18/97) and *CNN's Reliable Sources* (8/24/97) to really cover the story. *AP's* coverage stood out because it addressed Gilen's point about the news media perpetuating racist misperceptions of the poor that are associated with greater opposition to welfare policy among whites.

But in "Who Put the Black Face on Poverty," *CNN's Reliable Sources* succeeded in avoiding this point altogether—and in denying that racism was the reason the "black face" was on poverty in the first place. The problem, according

to Kurtz, was one of "video wallpaper"—"the pictures that automatically get thrown up" when big city media outlets use photos from, well, big cities with inner cities populated by high concentrations of poor black people.

The fact that Gilens explicitly addressed and refuted this claim in his study never came up. Also unmentioned was Gilen's point about how "apparently well-meaning, racially liberal news professionals generate images of the social world that consistently misrepresent both black Americans and poor people in destructive ways." Surprised?

SPOOKING THE PUBLIC
Given the prevalence of racial profiling documented here and elsewhere, it only makes sense that a recent survey of young people found that they not only recognized that racial stereotyping was rampant on television, but that TV news was a worse perpetrator of racial stereotyping than TV's entertainment programming.

The poll, sponsored by the child advocacy group Children Now, interviewed 1,200 boys and girls aged 10–17, with 300 children coming from each of the four largest racial groups. White and African-American children said they see people of their own race on television, while Latino and Asian children were much less likely to see their race represented.

Across all races, children are more likely to associate positive characteristics with white characters and negative characteristics with minority characters. "A Different World: Children's Perceptions of Race and Class in the Media" reported that "children of all races agree that the news media tend to portray African-American and Latino people more negatively than white and Asian people, particularly when the news is about young people. In addition, "large majorities of African-American (71 percent), Latino (63 percent) and Asian (51 percent) children feel there should be more people of their race as newscasters, while most white children feel there are enough white newscasters (76 percent)."

Again, there was a virtually complete news media white-out of this critical finding. All *CNN Newsnight* (5/7/98) could say was that the study found that children were "influenced by television news." The *Associated Press* (5/6/98) did no better.

RACE AND ETHNICITY

On a *Nightline* (5/6/98) program about the study, guests complained of disproportionately negative images of people of color. The children said they wanted to see television reflect the "realities of their lives," to "feature more teenagers," to be "real," and most importantly, to show more people of all races interacting with each other. The *Nightline* guests echoed this sense. In response, *Nightline* host Ted Koppel asked if it was the function of the media to present things "as it is or as we think it should be?"

The children's perception that the news media were the worse perpetrator of racial stereotyping was indeed mentioned but was never really addressed in the show. Clearly, then, news media are not presenting things as they are—but rather as racial fears project them to be. And a racialized policy agenda is being served up and served. The news media's practice of racial profiling gives the news consumer no real choice: Too often, we don't get the reality of what really is, or the dream of what should be, but an imaginary nightmare in blackface.

From Mikal Muharrar, "Media Blackface: Racial Profiling in News Reporting," *Extra!*, Fairness and Accuracy in Reporting, September/October 1998. Reprinted by permission.

EXERCISE

Name _____

Section _____

Date _____

EXERCISE 4.3: DEFINING YOURSELF

1. Based on your readings, are the definitions for the terms race and ethnicity, as listed in the 1990 census, correct? Be sure to substantiate your opinion.

2. Look through the list of "racial categories" on the previous pages. Which of these categories of race best fits you, and why? Which of these categories best fits your ethnicity, and why?

RACE AND ETHNICITY

Race Without Color—
Jared Diamond

Basing race on body chemistry makes no more sense than basing race on appearance—but at least you get to move the membership around.

Science often violates simple common sense. Our eyes tell us that the Earth is flat, that the sun revolves around the Earth, and that we humans are not animals. But we now ignore that evidence of our senses. We have learned that our planet is in fact round and revolves around the sun, and that humans are slightly modified chimpanzees. The reality of human races is another commonsense "truth" destined to follow the flat Earth into oblivion. The commonsense view of races goes somewhat as follows. All native Swedes differ from all native Nigerians in appearance: there is no Swede whom you would mistake for a Nigerian, and vice versa. Swedes have lighter skin than Nigerians do. They also generally have blond or light brown hair, while Nigerians have very dark hair. Nigerians usually have more tightly coiled hair than Swedes do, dark eyes as opposed to eyes that are blue or gray, and fuller lips and broader noses.

In addition, other Europeans look much more like Swedes than like Nigerians, while other peoples of sub-Saharan Africa—except perhaps the Khoisan peoples of southern Africa—look much more like Nigerians than like Swedes. Yes, skin color does get darker in Europe toward the Mediterranean, but it is still lighter than the skin of sub-Saharan Africans. In Europe, very dark or curly hair becomes more common outside Scandinavia, but European hair is still not as tightly coiled as in Africa. Since it's easy then to distinguish almost any native European from any native sub-Saharan African, we recognize Europeans and sub-Saharan Africans as distinct races, which we name for their skin colors: whites and blacks, respectively.

What could be more objective?

As it turns out, this seemingly unassailable reasoning is not objective. There are many different, equally valid procedures for defining races, and those different procedures yield very different classifications. One such procedure would group Italians and Greeks with most African blacks. It would classify Xhosas—the South African "black" group to which President Nelson Mandela belongs—with Swedes

rather than Nigerians. Another equally valid procedure would place Swedes with Fulani (a Nigerian "black" group) and not with Italians who would again be grouped with most other African blacks. Still another procedure would keep Swedes and Italians separate from all African blacks but would throw the Swedes and Italians into the same race as New Guineans and American Indians. Faced with such differing classifications, many anthropologists today conclude that one cannot recognize any human races at all.

If we were just arguing about races of nonhuman animals, essentially the same uncertainties of classification would arise. But the debates would remain polite and would never attract attention outside the halls of academia. Classification of humans is different "only" in that it shapes our views of other peoples, fosters our subconscious differentiation between "us" and "them," and is invoked to justify political and socioeconomic discrimination. On this basis, many anthropologists therefore argue that even if one *could* classify humans into races, one should not.

To understand how such uncertainties in classification arise let's steer clear of humans for a moment and instead focus on warblers and lions, about which we can easily remain dispassionate. Biologists begin by classifying living creatures into species. A **species** is a group of populations whose individual members would, if given the opportunity, interbreed with individuals of other populations of that group. But they would not interbreed with individuals of other species that are similarly defined. Thus all human populations, no matter how different they look, belong to the same species because they do interbreed and have interbred whenever they have encountered each other. Gorillas and humans, however, belong to two different species because—to the best of our knowledge—they have never interbred despite their coexisting in close proximity for millions of years.

We know that different populations classified together in the human species are visibly different. The same proves true for most other animal and plant species as well, whenever biologists look carefully. For example, consider one of the most familiar species of bird in North America, the yellow-rumped warbler. Breeding males of eastern and western North America can be distinguished at a glance by their throat color, white in the east, yellow in the west. Hence they are classified into two different races, or subspecies (alternative words with identical meanings), termed the myrtle and Audubon races, respectively. The white throated eastern birds differ from the yellow-throated western birds in other characteristics as well, such as in voice and habitat preference. But where the two races meet, in western Canada, white-throated birds do indeed interbreed with yellow-throated birds. That's why we consider myrtle warblers and Audubon warblers as races of the same species rather than different species.

Racial classification of these birds is easy. Throat color, voice and habitat preference all vary geographically in yellow-rumped warblers, but the variation of those three traits is "concordant"—that is, voice differences or habitat differences lead to the same racial classification as differences in throat color because the same populations that differ in throat color also differ in voice and habitat.

Racial classification of many other species, though, presents problems of concordance. For instance, a Pacific island bird species called the golden whistler varies from one island to the next. Some populations consist of big birds, some of small birds; some have black-winged males, others green-winged males; some have yellow-breasted females, others gray-breasted females; many other characteristics vary as well. But, unfortunately for humans like me who study these birds, those characteristics don't vary concordantly. Islands with green-winged males can have either yellow-breasted or gray-breasted females, and green-winged males are big on some islands but small on other islands. As a result if you classified golden whistlers into races based on single traits, you would set entirely different classifications depending on which trait you chose.

Classification of these birds also presents problems of "hierarchy." Some of the golden whistler races recognized by ornithologists are wildly different from all the other races, but some are very similar to one another. They can therefore be grouped into a hierarchy of distinctness. You start by establishing the most distinct population as a race separate from all other populations. You then separate the most distinct of the remaining populations. You continue by grouping similar populations, and separating distinct populations or groups of populations as races or groups of races. The problem is that the extent to which you continue the racial classification is arbitrary, and it's a decision about which taxonomists disagree passionately. Some taxonomists, the "splitters," like to recognize many different races, partly for the egotistical motive of getting

credit for having named a race. Other taxonomists, the "lumpers," prefer to recognize few races. Which type of taxonomist you are is a matter of personal preference.

How does that variability of traits by which we classify races come about in the first place? Some traits vary because of natural selection: that is, one form of the trait is advantageous for survival in one area, another form in a different area. For example, northern hares and weasels develop white fur in the winter, but southern ones retain brown fur year-round. The white winter fur is selected in the north for camouflage against the snow, while any animal unfortunate enough to turn white in the snowless southern states would stand out from afar against the brown ground and would be picked off by predators.

Other traits vary geographically because of sexual selection, meaning that those traits serve as arbitrary signals by which individuals of one sex attract mates of the opposite sex while intimidating rivals. Adult male lions, for instance, have a mane, but lionesses and young males don't. The adult male's mane signals to lionesses that he is sexually mature, and signals to young male rivals that he is a dangerous and experienced adversary. The length and color of a lion's mane vary among populations, being shorter and blacker in Indian lions than in African lions. Indian lions and lionesses evidently find short black manes sexy or intimidating; African lions don't.

Finally, some geographically variable traits have no known effect on survival and are invisible to rivals and to prospective sex partners. They merely reflect mutations that happened to arise and spread in one area. They could equally well have arisen and spread elsewhere—they just didn't.

RACE BY RESISTANCE

Traditionally we divide ourselves into races by the twin criteria of geographic location and visible physical characteristics. But we could make an equally reasonable and arbitrary division by the presence or absence of a gene, such as the sickle-cell gene, that confers resistance to malaria. By this reckoning we'd place Yemenites, Greeks, New Guineans, Thai, and Dinkas in one "race," Norwegians and several black African peoples in another.

Nothing that I've said about geographic variation in animals is likely to get me branded a racist. We don't attribute higher IQ or social status to black-winged whistlers than to green-winged whistlers. But now let's consider geographic variation in humans. We'll start with invisible traits, about which it's easy to remain dispassionate.

Many geographically variable human traits evolved by natural selection to adapt humans to particular climates or environments—just as the winter color of a hare or weasel did. Good examples are the mutations that people in tropical parts of the Old World evolved to help them survive malaria, the leading infectious disease of the old-world tropics. One such mutation is the sickle-cell gene, so called because the red blood cells of people with that mutation tend to assume a sickle shape. People bearing the gene are more resistant to malaria than people without it. Not surprisingly, the gene is absent from northern Europe, where malaria is nonexistent, but it's common in tropical Africa, where malaria is widespread. Up to 40 percent of Africans in such areas carry the sickle-cell gene. It's also common in the malaria-ridden Arabian Peninsula and southern India, and rare or absent in the southernmost parts of South Africa, among the Xhosas who live mostly beyond the tropical geographic range of malaria.

The geographic range of human malaria is much wider than the range of the sickle-cell gene. As it happens, other antimalarial genes take over the protective function of the sickle-cell gene in malarial Southeast Asia and New Guinea and in Italy, Greece, and other warm parts of the Mediterranean basin. Thus human races, if defined by antimalarial genes, would be very different from human races as traditionally defined by traits such as skin color. As classified by antimalarial genes (or their absence), Swedes are grouped with Xhosas but not with Italians or Greeks. Most other peoples usually viewed as African blacks are grouped with Arabia's "whites" and are kept separate from the "black" Xhosas.

RACE BY DIGESTION

We could define a race by any geographically variable trait—for example, the retention in adulthood of the enzyme lactase, which allows us to digest milk. Using this as our divisive criterion, we can place northern and central Europeans with Arabians and such West African peoples as the Fulani; in a "lactase-negative race," we can group most other African blacks with east Asians, American Indians, southern Europeans, and Australian aborigines.

Antimalarial genes exemplify the many features of our body chemistry that vary geographically under the influence of natural selection. Another such feature is the enzyme lactase, which enables us to digest the milk-sugar lactose. Infant humans, like infants of almost all other mammal species, possess lactase and drink milk. Until about 6,000 years ago most humans, like all other mammal species, lost the lactase enzyme on reaching the age of weaning. The obvious reason is that it was unnecessary—no human or other mammal drank milk as an adult. Beginning around 4000 B.C., however, fresh milk obtained from domestic mammals became a major food for adults of a few human populations. Natural selection caused individuals in these populations to retain lactase into adulthood. Among such peoples are northern and central Europeans, Arabians, north Indians, and several milk-drinking black African peoples, such as the Fulani of West Africa. Adult lactase is much less common in southern European populations and in most other African black populations, as well as in all populations of east Asians, aboriginal Australians, and American Indians.

Once again races defined by body chemistry don't match races defined by skin color. Swedes belong with Fulani in the "lactase-positive race," while most African "blacks," Japanese, and American Indians belong in the "lactase-negative race."

Not all the effects of natural selection are as invisible as lactase and sickle cells. Environmental pressures have also produced more noticeable differences among peoples, particularly in body shapes. Among the tallest and most long-limbed peoples in the world are the Nilotic peoples, such as the Dinkas, who live in the hot, dry areas of East Africa. At the opposite extreme in body shape are the Inuit, or Eskimo, who have compact bodies and relatively short arms and legs. The reasons have to do with heat loss. The greater the surface area of a warm body, the more body heat that's lost, since heat loss is directly proportional to surface area. For people of a given weight, a long-limbed, tall shape maximizes surface area, while a compact, short-limbed shape minimizes it. Dinkas and Inuit have opposite problems of heat balance: the former usually need desperately to get rid of body heat, while the latter need desperately to conserve it. Thus natural selection molded their body shapes oppositely, based on their contrasting climates.

RACE AND ETHNICITY

(In modern times, such considerations of body shape have become important to athletic performance as well as to heat loss. Tall basketball players, for example, have an obvious advantage over short ones, and slender, long-limbed tall players have an advantage over stout, short-limbed tall players. In the United States, it's a familiar observation that African Americans are disproportionately represented among professional basketball players. Of course, a contributing reason has to do with their lack of socioeconomic opportunities. But part of the reason probably has to do with the prevalent body shapes of some black African groups as well. However, this example also illustrates the dangers in facile racial stereotyping. One can't make the sweeping generalization that "whites can't jump," or that "blacks' anatomy makes them better basketball players." Only certain African peoples are notably tall and long-limbed; even those exceptional peoples are tall and long-limbed only on the average and vary individually.)

Other visible traits that vary geographically among humans evolved by means of sexual selection. We all know that we find some individuals of the opposite sex more attractive than other individuals. We also know that in sizing up sex appeal, we pay more attention to certain parts of a prospective sex partner's body than to other parts. Men tend to be inordinately interested in women's breasts and much less concerned with women's toenails. Women, in turn, tend to be turned on by the shape of a man's buttocks or the details of a man's beard and body hair, if any, but not by the size of his feet.

But all those determinants of sex appeal vary geographically. Khoisan and Andaman Island women tend to have much larger buttocks than most other women. Nipple color and breast shape and size also vary geographically among women. European men are rather hairy by world standards, while Southeast Asian men tend to have very sparse beards and body hair.

What's the function of these traits that differ so markedly between men and women? They certainly don't aid survival: it's not the case that orange nipples help Khoisan women escape lions, while darker nipples help European women survive cold winters. Instead, these varying traits play a crucial role in sexual selection. Women with very large buttocks are a turn-on, or at least acceptable, to Khoisan and Andaman men but look freakish to many men from other parts of the world. Bearded and hairy men readily find mates in Europe but fare worse in Southeast Asia. The geographic variation of these traits, however, is as arbitrary as the geographic variation in the color of a lion's mane.

RACE BY FINGERPRINTS

Probably the most trivial division of humans we could manage would be based on fingerprint patterns. As it turns out, the prevalence of certain basic features varies predictably among peoples: in the "Loops" race we could group together most Europeans, black Africans, and east Asians. Among the "Whorls" we could place Mongolians and Australian aborigines. Finally, in an "Arches" race, we could group Khoisans and some central Europeans.

There is a third possible explanation for the function of geographically variable human traits, besides survival or sexual selection—namely, no function at all. A good example is provided by fingerprints, whose complex pattern of arches, loops, and whorls is determined genetically. Fingerprints also vary geographically: for example, Europeans' fingerprints tend to have many loops, while aboriginal Australians' fingerprints tend to have many whorls.

If we classify human populations by their fingerprints, most Europeans and black Africans would sort out together in one race, Jews and some Indonesians in another, and aboriginal Australians in still another. But those geographic variations in fingerprint patterns possess no known function whatsoever. They play no role in survival: whorls aren't especially suitable for grabbing kangaroos, nor do loops help bar mitzvah candidates hold on to the pointer for the Torah. They also play no role in sexual selection: while you've undoubtedly noticed whether your mate is bearded or has brown nipples, you surely haven't the faintest idea whether his or her fingerprints have more loops than whorls. Instead it's purely a matter of chance that whorls became common in aboriginal Australians, and among Jews. Our rhesus factor blood groups and numerous other human traits fall into the same category of genetic characteristics whose geographic variation serves no function.

Arches

Loops

Whorls

RACE BY GENES

One method that seems to offer a way out of arbitrariness is to classify people's degree of genetic distinctness. By this standard the Khoisans of southern Africa would be in a race by themselves. African blacks would form several other distinct races. All the rest of the world's peoples—Norwegians, Navajo, Greeks, Japanese, Australian aborigines, and so on—would, despite their greatly differing external appearance, belong to a single race.

You've probably been wondering when I was going to get back to skin color, eye color, and hair color and form. After all, those are the traits by which all of us members of the lay public, as well as traditional anthropologists, classify races. Does geographic variation in those traits function in survival, in sexual selection, or in nothing?

The usual view is that skin color varies geographically to enhance survival. Supposedly, people in sunny, tropical climates around the world have generally dark skin, which is supposedly analogous to the temporary skin darkening of European whites in the summer. The supposed function of dark skin in sunny climates is for protection against skin cancer. Variations in eye color and hair form and color are also supposed to enhance survival under particular conditions, though no one has ever proposed a plausible hypothesis for how those variations might actually enhance survival.

Alas, the evidence for natural selection of skin color dissolves under scrutiny. Among tropical peoples, anthropologists love to stress the dark skins of African blacks, people of the southern Indian peninsula, and New Guineans and love to forget the pale skins of Amazonian Indians and Southeast Asians living at the same latitudes. To wriggle

out of those paradoxes, anthropologists then plead the excuse that Amazonian Indians and Southeast Asians may not have been living in their present locations long enough to evolve dark skins. However, the ancestors of fair-skinned Swedes arrived even more recently in Scandinavia, and aboriginal Tasmanians were black-skinned despite their ancestors' having lived for at least the last 10,000 years at the latitude of Vladivostok.

Besides, when one takes into account cloud cover, peoples of equatorial West Africa and the New Guinea mountains actually receive no more ultraviolet radiation or hours of sunshine each year than do the Swiss. Compared with infectious diseases and other selective agents, skin cancer has been utterly trivial as a cause of death in human history, even for modern white settlers in the tropics. This objection is so obvious to believers in natural selection of skin color that they have proposed at least seven other supposed survival functions of skin color, without reaching agreement. Those other supposed functions include protection against rickets, frostbite, folic acid deficiency, beryllium poisoning, overheating, and overcooling. The diversity of these contradictory theories makes clear how far we are from understanding the survival value (if any) of skin color.

It wouldn't surprise me if dark skins do eventually prove to offer some advantage in tropical climates, but I expect the advantage to turn out to be a slight one that is easily overridden. But there's an overwhelming importance to skin, eye, and hair color that is obvious to all of us— sexual selection. Before we can reach a condition of intimacy permitting us to assess the beauty of a prospective sex partner's hidden physical attractions, we first have to pass muster for skin, eyes, and hair.

RACE AND ETHNICITY

We all know how those highly visible "beauty traits" guide our choice of sex partners. Even the briefest personal ad in a newspaper mentions the advertiser's skin color, and the color of skin that he or she seeks in a partner. Skin color, of course, is also of overwhelming importance in our social prejudices. If you're a black African American trying to raise your children in white U.S. society, rickets and overheating are the least of the problems that might be solved by your skin color. Eye color and hair form and color, while not so overwhelmingly important as skin color, also play an obvious role in our sexual and social preferences. Just ask yourself why hair dyes, hair curlers, and hair straighteners enjoy such wide sales. You can bet that it's not to improve our chances of surviving grizzly bear attacks and other risks endemic to the North American continent.

Nearly 125 years ago Charles Darwin himself, the discoverer of natural selection, dismissed its role as an explanation of geographic variation in human beauty traits. Everything that we have learned since then only reinforces Darwin's view.

We can now return to our original questions: Are human racial classifications that are based on different traits concordant with one another? What is the hierarchical relation among recognized races? What is the function of racially variable traits? What, really, are the traditional human races?

Regarding concordance, we *could* have classified races based on any number of geographically variable traits. The resulting classifications would not be at all concordant. Depending on whether we classified ourselves by antimalarial genes, lactase, fingerprints, or skin color, we could place Swedes in the same race as either Xhosas, Fulani, the Ainu of Japan, or Italians.

Regarding hierarchy, traditional classifications that emphasize skin color face unresolvable ambiguities. Anthropology textbooks often recognize five major races: "whites," " African blacks," "Mongoloids," "aboriginal Australians," and "Khoisans," each in turn divided into various numbers of sub-races. But there is no agreement on the number and delineation of the sub-races, or even of the major races. Are all five of the major races equally distinctive? Are Nigerians really less different from Xhosas than aboriginal Australians are from both? Should we recognize 3 or 15 sub-races of Mongoloids? These questions have remained unresolved because skin color and other traditional racial criteria are difficult to formulate mathematically.

A method that could in principle overcome these problems is to base racial classification on a combination of as many geographically variable genes as possible. Within the past decade, some biologists have shown renewed interest in developing a hierarchical classification of human populations—hierarchical not in the sense that it identifies superior and inferior races but in the sense of grouping and separating populations based on mathematical measures of genetic distinctness. While the biologists still haven't reached agreement, some of their studies suggest that human genetic diversity may be greatest in Africa. If so, the primary races of humanity may consist of several African races, plus one race to encompass all peoples of all other continents. Swedes, New Guineans, Japanese, and Navajo would then belong to the same primary race; the Khoisans of southern Africa would constitute another primary race by themselves; and African "blacks" and Pygmies would be divided among several other primary races.

As regards the function of all those traits that are useful for classifying human races, some serve to enhance survival, some to enhance sexual selection, while some serve no function at all. The traits we traditionally use are ones subject to sexual selection, which is not really surprising. These traits are not only visible at a distance but also highly variable; that's why they became the ones used throughout recorded history to make quick judgments about people. Racial classification didn't come from science but from the body's signals for differentiating attractive from unattractive sex partners, and for differentiating friend from foe.

Such snap judgments didn't threaten our existence back when people were armed only with spears and surrounded by others who looked mostly like themselves. In the modern world, though, we are armed with guns and plutonium, and we live our lives surrounded by people who are much more varied in appearance. The last thing we need now is to continue codifying all those different appearances into an arbitrary system of racial classification.

From Jared Diamond, "Race Without Color," *Discover*, November 1994, Vol. 15. Reprinted by permission.

Black, White, Other—
Jonathan Marks

RACIAL CATEGORIES ARE CULTURAL CONSTRUCTS MASQUERADING AS BIOLOGY

While reading the Sunday edition of the *New York Times* one morning last February, my attention was drawn by an editorial inconsistency. The article I was reading was written by attorney Guinier. (Guinier, you may remember, had been President Clinton's nominee to head the civil rights division at the Department of Justice in 1993. Her name was hastily withdrawn amid a blast of criticism over her views on political representation of minorities.) What had distracted me from the main point of the story was a photo caption that described Guinier as being "half-black." In the text of the article, Guinier had described herself simply as "black."

How can a person be black and half-black at the same time? In algebraic terms, this would seem to describe a situation where $x = 1/2x$, to which the only solution is $x = 0$.

The inconsistency in the *Times* was trivial, but revealing. It encapsulated a longstanding problem in our use of racial categories—namely, a confusion between biological and cultural heredity. When Guinier is described as "half-black," that is a statement of biological ancestry, for one of her two parents is black. And when Guinier describes herself as black, she is using a cultural category, according to which one can either be black or white, but not both.

Race—as the term is commonly used—is inherited, although not in a strictly biological fashion. It is passed down according to a system of folk heredity, an all-or-nothing system that is different from the quantifiable heredity of biology. But the incompatibility of the two notions of race is sometimes starkly evident—as when the state decides that racial differences are so important that interracial marriages must be regulated or outlawed entirely. Miscegenation laws in this country (which stayed on the books in many states through the 1960s) obliged the legal system to define who belonged in what category. The resulting formula stated that anyone with one-eighth or more black ancestry was a "negro." (A similar formula, defining Jews, was promulgated by the Germans in the Nuremberg Laws of the 1930s.)

Applying such formulas led to the biological absurdity that having one black great-grandparent was sufficient to define a person as black, but having seven white great-grandparents was insufficient to define a person as white. Here, race and biology are demonstrably at odds. And the problem is not semantic but conceptual, for race is presented as a category of nature.

Human beings come in a wide variety of sizes, shapes, colors, and forms—or, because we are visually-oriented primates, it certainly seems that way. We also come in larger packages called populations; and we are said to belong to even larger and more confusing units, which have long been known as races. The history of the study of human variation is to a large extent the pursuit of those human races—the attempt to identify the small number of fundamentally distinct kinds of people on earth.

This scientific goal stretches back two centuries, to Linnaeus, the father of biological systematics, who radically established *Homo sapiens* as one species within a group of animals he called Primates. Linnaeus's system of naming groups within groups logically implied further breakdown. He consequently sought to establish a number of subspecies within *Homo sapiens*. He identified five: four geographical species (from Europe, Asia, Africa, and America) and one grab-bag subspecies called *monstrosus*. This category was dropped by subsequent researchers (as was Linnaeus's use of criteria such as personality and dress to define his subspecies).

While Linnaeus was not the first to divide humans on the basis of the continents on which they lived, he had given the division a scientific stamp. But in attempting to determine the proper number of subspecies, the heirs of Linnaeus always seemed to find different answers, depending upon the criteria they applied. By the mid-twentieth century, scores of anthropologists—led by Harvard's Earnest Hooton—had expended enormous energy on the problem. But these scholars could not convince one another about the precise nature of the fundamental divisions of our species.

Part of the problem—as with the *Times*' identification of Lani Guinier—was that we humans have two constantly intersecting ways of thinking about the divisions among us.

RACE AND ETHNICITY

On the one hand, we like to think of "race"—as Linnaeus did—as an objective, biological category. In this sense, being a member of a race is supposed to be the equivalent of being a member of a species or of a phylum—except that race, on the analogy of subspecies, is an even narrower (and presumably more exclusive and precise) biological category.

The other kind of category into which we humans allocate ourselves—when we say "Serb" or "Hutu" or "Jew" or "Chicano" or "Republican" or "Red Sox fan"—is cultural. The label refers to little or nothing in the natural attributes of its members. These members may not live in the same region and may not even know many others like themselves. What they share is neither strictly nature nor strictly community. The groupings are constructions of human social history.

Membership in these *un*biological groupings may mean the difference between life and death, for they are the categories that allow us to be identified (and accepted or vilified) socially. While membership in (or allegiance to) these categories may be assigned or adopted from birth, the differentia that mark members from nonmembers are symbolic and abstract; they serve to distinguish people who cannot be readily distinguished by nature. So important are these symbolic distinctions that some of the strongest animosities are often expressed between very similar-looking peoples. Obvious examples are Bosnian Serbs and Muslims, Irish and English, Huron and Iroquois.

Obvious natural variation is rarely so important as cultural difference. One simply does not hear of a slaughter of the short people at the hands of the tall, the glabrous at the hands of the hairy, the red-haired at the hands of the brown-haired. When we do encounter genocidal violence between different looking peoples, the two groups are invariably socially or culturally distinct as well. Indeed, the tragic frequency of hatred and genocidal violence between biologically indistinguishable peoples implies that biological differences such as skin color are not motivations but, rather, excuses. They allow nature to be invoked to reinforce group identities and antagonisms that would exist without these physical distinctions. But are there any truly "racial" biological distinctions to be found in our species?

Obviously, if you compare two people from different parts of the world (or whose ancestors came from different parts of the world), they will differ physically, but one cannot therefore define three or four or five basically different kinds of people, as a biological notion of race would imply. The anatomical properties that distinguish people—such as pigmentation, eye form, body build—are not clumped in discrete groups, but distributed along geographical gradients, as are nearly all the genetically determined variants detectable in the human gene pool.

These gradients are produced by three forces. Natural selection adapts populations to local circumstances (like climate) and thereby differentiates them from other populations. Genetic drift (random fluctuations in a gene pool) also differentiates populations from one another, but in non-adaptive ways. And gene flow (via intermarriage and other child-producing unions) acts to homogenize neighboring populations.

In practice, the operations of these forces are difficult to discern. A few features, such as body build and the graduated distribution of the sickle-cell anemia gene in populations from western Africa, southern Asia, and the Mediterranean can be plausibly related to the effects of selection. Others, such as the graduated distribution of a small deletion in the mitochondrial DNA of some East Asian, Oceanic, and Native American peoples, or the degree of flatness of the face, seem unlikely to be the result of selection and are probably the results of random bio-historical factors. The cause of the distribution of most features, from nose breadth to blood group, is simply unclear.

The overall result of these forces is evident, however. As Johann Friedrich Blumenbach noted in 1775, "you see that all do so run into one another, and that one variety of mankind does so sensibly pass into the other, that you cannot mark out the limits between them." (Posturing as an heir to Linnaeus, he nonetheless attempted to do so.) But from humanity's gradations in appearance, no defined groupings resembling races readily emerge. The racial categories with which we have become so familiar are the result of our imposing arbitrary cultural boundaries in order to partition gradual biological variation.

Unlike graduated biological distinctions, culturally constructed categories are ultrasharp. One can be French or German, but not both; Tutsi or Hum, but not both; Jew or Catholic, but not both; Bosnian Muslim or Serb, but not both; black or white, but not both. Traditionally, people of "mixed race" have been obliged to choose one and thereby identify themselves unambiguously to census takers and administrative bookkeepers—a practice that is now being widely called into question.

A scientific definition of race would require considerable homogeneity within each group, and reasonably discrete differences between groups, but three kinds of data militate against this view: First, the groups traditionally described as races are not at all homogeneous. Africans and Europeans, for instance, are each a collection of biologically diverse populations. Anthropologists of the 1920s widely recognized *three* European races: Nordic, Alpine, and Mediterranean. This implied that races could exist within races. American anthropologist Carleton Coon identified *ten* European races in 1939. With such protean use, the term race came to have little value in describing actual biological entities within *Homo sapiens*. The scholars were not only grappling with a broad north-south gradient in human appearance across Europe, they were trying to bring the data into line with their belief in profound and fundamental constitutional differences between groups of people.

But there simply isn't one European race to contrast with an African race, nor three, nor ten: the question (as scientists long posed it) fails to recognize the actual patterning of diversity in the human species. Fieldwork revealed, and genetics later quantified, the existence of far more biological diversity within any group than between groups. Fatter and thinner people exist everywhere, as do people with type 0 and type A blood. What generally varies from one population to the next is the *proportion* of people in these groups expressing the trait or gene. Hair color varies strikingly among Europeans and native Australians, but little among other peoples. To focus on discovering differences between presumptive races, when the vast majority of detectable variants do not help differentiate them, was thus to define a very narrow—if not largely illusory—problem in human biology. (The fact that Africans are biologically more diverse than Europeans, but have rarely been split into so many races, attests to the cultural basis of these categorizations.)

Second, differences between human groups are only evident when contrasting geographical extremes. Noting these extremes, biologists of an earlier era sought to identify representatives of "pure," primordial races presumably located in Norway, Senegal, and Thailand. At no time, however, was our species composed of a few populations within which everyone looked pretty much the same. Ever since some of our ancestors left Africa to spread out through the Old World, we humans have always lived in the "in-between" places. And human populations have also always been in genetic contact with one another. Indeed, for tens of thousands of years, humans have had trade networks; and where goods flow, so do genes. Consequently, we have no basis for considering *extreme* human forms the most pure, or most representative, of some ancient primordial populations. Instead, they represent populations adapted to the most disparate environments.

And third, between each presumptive "major" race are unclassifiable populations and people. Some populations of India, for example, are darkly pigmented (or "black"), have Europeanlike ("Caucasoid") facial features, but inhabit the continent of Asia (which should make them "Asian"). Americans might tend to ignore these "exceptions" to the racial categories, since immigrants to the United States from West Africa, Southeast Asia, and northwest Europe far outnumber those from India. The very existence of unclassifiable peoples undermines the idea that there are just three human biological groups in the Old World. Yet acknowledging the biological distinctiveness of such groups leads to a rapid proliferation of categories. What about Australians? Polynesians? The Ainu of Japan?

Categorizing people is important to any society. It is, at some basic psychological level, probably necessary to have group identity about who and what you are, in contrast to who and what you are not. The concept of race, however, specifically involves the recruitment of biology to validate those categories of self-identity.

Mice don't have to worry about that the way humans do. Consequently, classifying them into subspecies entails less of a responsibility for a scientist than classifying humans into sub-species does. And by the 1960s, most anthropologists realized they could not defend any classification of *Homo sapiens* into biological subspecies or races that could be considered reasonably objective. They therefore stopped doing it, and stopped identifying the endeavor as a central goal of the field. It was a biologically intractable problem—the old square-peg-in-a round-hole enterprise; and people's lives, or welfares, could well depend on the ostensibly scientific pronouncement. Reflecting on the social history of the twentieth century, that was a burden anthropologists would no longer bear.

This conceptual divorce in anthropology—of cultural from biological phenomena—was one of the most fundamental scientific revolutions of our time. And since it affected assumptions so rooted in our everyday experience, and resulted in conclusions so counterintuitive—like the idea that the earth goes around the sun, and not vice-versa—it has been widely underappreciated.

Kurt Vonnegut, in *Slaughterhouse Five*, describes what he remembered being taught about human variation: "At that time, they were teaching that there was absolutely no difference between anybody. They may be teaching that still." Of course there are biological differences between people, and between populations. The question is: How are those differences patterned? And the answer seems to be: Not racially. Populations are the only readily identifiable units of humans, and even they are fairly fluid, biologically similar to populations nearby, and biologically different from populations far away.

In other words, the message of contemporary anthropology is: You may group humans into a small number of races if you want to, but you are denied biology as a support for it.

Culture, Not Race, Explains Human Diversity—
Mark Nathan Cohen

We are not likely to convince students that racist views are wrong if we teach them only about biology and ignore culture. The basic facts about the broad patterns of human biological variation and "race" are fairly clear and well established: Individual human beings undeniably differ in myriad ways, and each specific difference may be important. Variation in skin color, for example, affects susceptibility to sunburn, skin cancer, and rickets. Variations in body build affect the ability to keep warm or cool; variations in the shape of the nose affect its ability in warm and moisten the air inhaled. Unseen genetic variations protect some people from (and predispose other people to) diseases ranging from malaria and smallpox to diabetes and cancer.

However, "races" as imagined by the public do not actually exist. Any definition of "race" that we attempt produces more exceptions than sound classifications. No matter what system we use, most people don't fit.

As almost every introductory textbook in physical anthropology explains, the distinctions among human populations are generally graded, not abrupt. In other words, skin color comes in a spectrum from dark to light, not just in black or white; noses come in a range of shapes, not just broad or narrow. Furthermore, the various physical traits such as skin color and nose shape (plus the enormous number of invisible traits) come in an infinite number of combinations; one cannot predict other traits by knowing one trait that a person possesses. A person with dark skin can have any blood type and can have a broad nose (a combination common in West Africa), a narrow nose (as many East Africans do), or even blond hair (a combination seen in Australia and New Guinea).

Of the 50,000 to 100,000 pairs of genes needed to make a human being, perhaps 35,000 to 75,000 are the same in all people, and 15,000 to 25,000 may take different forms in different people, thus accounting for human variation. But only a tiny number of these genes affect what many people might consider to be racial traits. For example, geneticists believe that skin color is based on no more than 4 to 10 pairs of genes. The genes of black and white Americans probably are 99.9 percent alike.

In addition, studies of the human family tree based on detailed genetic analysis suggest that traits such as skin color are not even good indicators of who is related to whom, because the traits occur independently in several branches of the human family. When we consider the pairs of genes that may differ among humans, we see that, beyond the genes determining skin color, black people from Africa, Australia, and the south of India are not particularly closely related to each other genetically.

We...have to stop teaching or accepting the idea that humans are divided into three races—Caucasian, Negroid, and Mongoloid—an idea that is at least 50 years out of date.

All of this means that variations among "races" cannot possibly explain the differences in behavior or intelligence that people think they see. Although black Americans on average receive lower scores on standardized tests than do white Americans, neither "race" is actually a biological group. Skin color alone cannot account for the differences in group averages. Although we know a great deal about the role of many of our genes—for instance, which ones cause sickle-cell anemia—no genes are known to control differences in specific behavior or in intelligence among human groups. Even if someone discovered such genes, we have no reason to assume that they would correlate with skin color any more than most other genes do.

Anthropologists and other academics must do a better job of communicating these facts to our students and to the public at large. But even if we make sure that everyone understands these facts, racism will persist—unless we convince people that a different explanation for variations in behavior makes more sense. The alternative that we need to emphasize is the concept of culture—but a concept of culture far deeper and more sophisticated than that taught by many multiculturalists.

The anthropological concept of culture can be explained best by an analogy with language. Just as language is more than vocabulary, culture is more than, say, art and music. Language has rules of grammar and sound that limit and give structure to communication, usually without conscious thought. In English, for example, we use word order to convey the relationship among the words in a sentence. Latin uses suffixes to show relationships; Swahili uses prefixes. Even languages as similar as French, Spanish, and Italian use different subsets of the many sounds the human mouth can make.

Equally, culture structures our behavior, thoughts, perceptions values, goals, morals, and cognitive processes—also usually without conscious thought. Just as each language is a set of arbitrary conventions shared by those who speak the language, so each culture is made up of its own arbitrary conventions. Many languages work perfectly well; many cultures do, too.

Just as familiarity with the language of one's childhood makes it harder to learn the sounds and grammar of another language, so one's culture tends to blind one to alternatives. All of us—Americans as well as members of remote Amazonian tribes—are governed by culture. Our choices in life are circumscribed largely by arbitrary rules, and we have a hard time seeing the value of other people's choices and the shortcomings of our own. For example, many societies exchange goods not for profit, but to foster social relationships, as most Americans do within their own families. Some peoples prefer to maintain their surrounding environment rather than to seek "progress." Other groups have a very different sense than we do of the balance between individual freedom and responsibility to one's community.

Besides teaching our students about the importance of culture, we need to revive the anthropological concept of **cultural relativism**—perhaps the most important concept that liberal education can teach. The enemies of relativism have claimed that the concept means that everything is equal—that no moral judgments are possible, that Americans must accept whatever other people do. But this is not what relativism means.

What it does mean is that we must look carefully at what other people are doing and try to understand their behavior in context before we judge it. It means that other people may not share our desires or our perceptions. It also means that we have to recognize the arbitrary nature of our own choices and be willing to reexamine them by learning about the choices that other people have made. In medicine, for example, many cultures have long tried to treat the whole

RACE AND ETHNICITY

patient, mind and body together, which some of our doctors are just beginning to focus on, having been trained instead to concentrate on treating a particular disease.

The key point is that what we see as "racial" differences in behavior may reflect the fact that people have different values, make different choices, operate within different cultural "grammars," and categorize things (and therefore think) in different ways. Over the years, we have learned that culture shapes many things we once thought were determined by biology, including sexuality, aggression, perception, and susceptibility to disease. But many people still confuse the effects of biology and those of culture.

Many scholars of colonialism have described how members of oppressed minorities create a sense of community by choosing to ignore their colonizers' culture.

For example, we still use analogy problems to test students' skill in logic, which we then define as innate, genetically driven intelligence, which, some argue, differs by "race." But solving the problems depends on putting items into categories, and the categories we use are cultural, not universal. Giving the correct answer depends less on inherent intelligence than it does on knowing the classification rules used by those who created the test. Most U.S. students would flunk analogy problems put to them by Mesoamerican peasants, who divide things into "hot" and "cold"—categories that, in their usage, go far beyond physical temperature.

To communicate the importance of culture to students, we have to make some adjustments in our teaching. First, we have to stop teaching world and American history in ways that deny the contributions of others and prevent thoughtful analysis of our own actions. Teaching along these lines has improved, but it can be better yet. For instance, how many students are taught that George Washington and Benjamin Franklin were speculators who wanted to enrich themselves with land on the Western frontier—land the British had intended to reserve for Native American use?

We also have to stop teaching or accepting the idea that humans are divided into three races—Caucasian, Negroid, and Mongoloid—an idea that is at least 50 years out of

date. I constantly face students who have been taught the concept of three races in the 1990s by high school and college teachers in other social sciences.

In addition, psychologists, in particular, must stop assuming that only one pattern exists for human cognition, perception, formation of categories, and so forth. All too many psychologists believe that standardized I.Q. test are equally valid for assessing individuals from different cultural backgrounds. Operating from that mistaken assumption, they teach a narrow view of "correct" human behavior, which promotes racism.

We must realize that students from some minority groups are likely to do badly on I.Q. tests for a variety of reasons beyond the poor health, nutrition, and education that many of them have experienced because of poverty. The content of the tests is biased toward students in the mainstream, both in terms of the subject matter of the questions and in more subtle ways, such as expectations about what is important in a problem.

Cultural relativism is the only road to tolerance and real freedom of thought, because it lets us get outside the blinders imposed by our own culture.

And some minority students see no reason to try to do well on I.Q. tests. They may not expect to go to college. Their sense of self-worth may depend on their lack of interest in the mainstream culture, which they feel has rejected them. Many scholars of colonialism have described how members of oppressed minorities create a sense of community by choosing to ignore their colonizers' culture. John Ogbu, an anthropologist at the University of California at Berkeley, has shown that the same phenomenon occurs in U.S. schools.

Thus, scores on I.Q. tests depend not only on how "smart" one is, but also on familiarity with middle-class, white American culture. Different cultural groups are likely to pay more attention to different parts of test questions, not even noticing what someone from another group would consider crucial. A student who did not grow up in the middle-class might well believe that to appear smart, one should give a slow, thoughtful answer—not a snap answer or sound bite. Such a student will probably be put off by the idea of competitiveness and individual ranking, and thus by the whole experience of the I.Q. test.

Anthropologists must do a better job of communicating these and other important facts about human biological and cultural variation to their students and to the public at large. Rather than revel in the details of obscure populations, our courses in cultural anthropology should focus on interpretations of significant contemporary events. We have to demonstrate to students that not all events outside—and even within—the United States can be understood from the single cultural perspective that other social sciences tend to teach.

We can be more outspoken in the media about alternative perspectives on international events, seeking opportunities to explain cultural practices and conventions in other countries that may lead to their different decisions or priorities. Indeed, anthropologists have to be more confident about the significance of their discipline and more willing to assert the importance of their knowledge. We need to find ways to work both with faculty members in other disciplines and with policy makers to convey our awareness that, in virtually every contemporary problem, different participants not only speak differently but also think differently.

For example, we could attempt to understand the behavior of Iranians in the United States 20-year-old confrontation with Iran by looking objectively at their culture and history, and at ours. One of the most obvious points is that traditional Iranian leadership involves a blend of religious and secular power that is foreign to Americans. The result is that leaders of the two countries have very different agendas. And many Iranians have a different sense of the proper balance among business, profit, family, community, and spirituality.

We must show our students that they, just as much as our adversaries or "primitive peoples" in isolated cultures, are bound by the arbitrary rules of their own culture. If we don't teach these points, we are failing to show that racist assumptions about why people behave as they do are not legitimate.

We also have to stop focusing on details of the human fossil record in our introductory physical anthropology courses. Basic courses should deal instead with human variation in a variety of populations, by looking at such issues as fertility, mortality, growth, nutrition, adaptation to the environment, and disease. It would be productive to teach, for example, that hypertension and diabetes are not simply natural results of individual genetic endowment or the aging process but, in fact, rarely occur among people whose food does not go through the commercial processing that is customary in the West.

Finally, administrators and professors across the disciplines need to recognize that it is crucial for all students to understand the concepts of culture and cultural relativism—not the inaccurate caricatures of these concepts that have been bandied about in the culture wars, but the sophisticated, carefully defined and nuanced versions that anthropologists have evolved over decades of work. Cultural relativism is the only road to tolerance and real freedom of thought, because it lets us get outside the blinders imposed by our own culture. It must be built into courses taught in core curricula—not taught only as an elective frill if a student happens to sign up for an anthropology course.

From Mark Nathan Cohen, "Culture, Not Race, Explains Human Diversity," *Chronicle of Higher Education*, April 17, 1998, pp. B4–B5. Reprinted by permission.

RACE AND ETHNICITY

E X E R C I S E

Name _____

Section _____

Date _____

EXERCISE 4.4: RACE AND ETHNICITY

In your own words, define what is meant by the term "ethnicity" and differentiate this concept from "race."
Explain three ways in which confusion of these terms can hinder one's acceptance of others.

RACE AND ETHNICITY

KEY TERMS

Name

Section

Date

Cultural constructs:

Cultural prejudice:

Ethnicity/Ethnic group:

Inequality:

Nationality:

Nature vs. nurture:

Prejudice:

Race:

Racial Profiling:

RACE AND ETHNICITY

Racism:

Species:

United States Census Bureau:

5 LANGUAGE

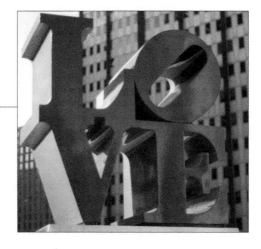

Say It, Don't Spray It

Sociolinguists are interested in studying how people use verbal and non-verbal communication when conversing with others, depending upon the social situation or context in which they are operating. Cultures influence language to the extent that the vocabulary in any language tends to emphasize those words that are adaptively important in the environment in which the society exists.

As important as language is in human communication, the majority of our messages are sent and received without using words. Non-verbal communication is said to be so important to human survival that human infants are capable of reading facial expressions, such as a smile, at the time of birth. In addition to facial expressions, **non-verbal cues** include gestures, eye contact, touching, posturing, and use of personal space.

LANGUAGE

Let's Ponder...

SAY IT FROM A DISTANCE

Each culture has its own set of rules for deciding the use of personal space. If you have ever felt someone invading your "turf" during a conversation, you are aware of how essential that empty space is between ourselves and our neighbors. Complete the chart on the following page based upon observable behaviors between individuals in the United States. Be sure to observe and record the non-verbal messages being sent by each person involved. Also, note if the distance between people is different for males than for females. Compare your answers with those found on the following page.

"Let's Ponder" exercises reprinted by permission of Professor Brock Klein, Pasadena City College.

LANGUAGE

Situation	Distance People Sit or Stand from Each Other	Type of Body Language People Use
1. Riding on a bus with people you don't know.	People try to sit at least one seat from another person and avoid touching. They stand as far apart as possible.	Looking away or out the window, reading, crossing arms, clutching packages.
2. Waiting in a doctor's office.		
3. Waiting in line.		
4. Eating lunch in a restaurant or café.		
5. Talking to one's boss or teacher.		
6. Talking to friends in a group.		
7. Talking to a friend about something personal.		
8. Talking to a stranger.		
9. Talking to a child.		

Typical Responses in the United States

2. At least one seat apart if possible.
3. At least 2 feet apart or more if possible. People do not touch or shove.
4. At least one seat apart if possible. People generally do not speak to other people in a restaurant unless they know them.
5. 3 to 4 feet
6. 2 to 3 feet
7. As close as 18 inches (1 1/2 feet)
8. 3 to 4 feet
9. 3 to 4 feet unless you know the child well. People do not touch or kiss unless they are members of the family.

Question:

These responses reflect Americans' need for personal space. In fact, the average amount of space between speakers in the United States is 18 inches. How is this similar to or different from other cultures?

Sociolinguists on Verbal and Non-verbal Cues

Language is the primary tool by which children acquire cultural knowledge. **Language** is the medium of socialization and the means by which children acquire the meanings, beliefs, and worldviews which characterize their culture. Enculturation and language acquisition are interactive processes, since it is by means of interaction that the child comes to internalize cultural and linguistic norms and acquires the ability to perform appropriately in the various contexts of his or her culture. In short, as children acquire language, they also are acquiring knowledge of the statuses and roles which comprise the social order of their society.

Every healthy child is born with the ability to learn language, since that is part of every human being's genetic make-up. It is an aspect of the cognitive structure which all humans have inherited from their distant ancestors. To researchers such as Noam Chomsky (in his text entitled *Language and Mind*) and others, the knowledge of language is acquired through an innate faculty, which is activated as a consequence of the experiences of the maturing infant. The output of the cognitive structure is language. Thus, the interactions and early experiences of a child, linguistic and otherwise, are needed for the development of language. Chomsky's underlying premises are that there is a universal mental scheme and that all languages have a series of fundamental properties, or **linguistic invariants**, in common. These linguistic invariants are another way of talking about language universals. The following articles focus on the importance of the spoken word.

Learning the World's Languages...Before They Vanish—
Bernice Wuethrich

Pat Gabori loves to talk, and when he does, linguists listen. Gabori, who estimates his age at about 80, is the last native-born male speaker of Kayardild, an aboriginal language spoken only on Bentinck Island off north Australia. Once a skilled dugong hunter, now blind, Gabori has relayed a wealth of stories—and the grammar of his language—to linguist Nick Evans of the University of Melbourne in Victoria. Evans found Kayardild full of grammatical rarities. For example, whereas most languages change only the verb to indicate past or future tense, Kayardild marks tense on other words too, including nouns. Thus Gabori might say "The boy spear-ed the fish-ed." Or rather, he would probably say "Speared fish-ed the boy," as Kayardild also allows speakers to explode the traditional structure of phrases.

Whatever the word order, only one other known language marks nouns with tense—a sister language to Kayardild called Lardil that has only one fully competent speaker. "If you didn't know about these two languages, you would say this phenomenon is impossible," Evans says. And if every known language followed the rule that only verbs express tense, you might conclude, following the famous theory proposed by linguist Noam Chomsky almost 50 years ago, that the rule is an innate part of language, genetically programmed into the brain of every child. But to Evans and a vocal minority of other linguists, the possibilities seen in languages like Kayardild challenge the "universal" rules of grammar, and suggest that far more of grammar is learned and culturally viable.

Even the handful of linguists who study Kayardild and Lardil disagree on the significance of their idiosyncrasies, however. To Ken Hale of the Massachusetts Institute of Technology (MIT), who has studied Lardil for 30 years, the languages, far from undermining Chomsky's theory, actually subtly reinforce many of the "universals" of grammar. "Linguists rarely find things that challenge universals," he says.

Although linguists spar about the deeper meaning of Kayardild grammar, they agree on one thing: The data they need to settle linguistic arguments are fast disappearing. In Australia alone, aboriginal people spoke about 260 languages at the time of European contact in the late 1700s; today about 160 of those tongues are extinct, and only about 20 have a reasonable number of speakers. The world's 6 billion people speak approximately 6000 to 7000 languages, and most experts expect that at least half—and perhaps up to 90%—will disappear in the 21st century. War or scattering can demolish a linguistic community in a generation or two, so that even a language with thousands of speakers today may be at risk tomorrow; most linguists consider a language "endangered" when fewer and fewer children learn it.

LANGUAGE

The loss of languages is not only a crisis for many communities, but also presents a major challenge for researchers intent on analyzing the structure of languages and how they convey meaning. Just as biologists study species to understand evolution, so linguists scrutinize grammars and vocabularies to understand what aspects of language are innate and what are learned. "We're losing our natural laboratory of variation, our Galapagos," says Steve Levinson of the Max Planck Institute for Psycholinguistics in Nijmegen, the Netherlands.

The causes of this global loss are many: wars, diasporas, education that emphasizes national languages, and assimilation into dominant cultures. To date, with less than 1000 fully described languages, "every language lost is a loss of clues as to how the human language faculty works," says Jerry Sadock, a linguist at the University of Chicago. This realization is prompting a small community of linguists to increase their fieldwork, compiling grammars and lexicons and putting spoken languages into writing, helping to preserve some languages as they learn more about them. But the work is slow going. "Describing a language is a 10- to 15-year job," says Evans, who wrote a 600-page grammar of Kayardild.

Linguists argue passionately that each language is precious. The particulars of a language "encapsulate a long history of people in an ecology, a way of living and a way of thinking," Levinson says. Different languages reflect peoples' perception of the world, capture their prehistory, and may subtly shape thought itself. "When these languages die, we'll lose these glimpses into the capacities of the human mind," says linguist Marianne Mithun of the University of California, Santa Barbara.

UNIVERSAL QUESTIONS
Whether grammar—the structure of language—is innate or learned is the longest running battle in modern linguistics. It was fired up by Chomsky back in the 1950s and hasn't calmed down since. He proposed that universal grammar is a manifestation of linguistic ability that is hard-wired into the human brain, a genetic endowment that allows every child to master language with ease and also dramatically restricts the types of language that are possible. Ever since, linguists have sought to test his ideas in the world's languages. Today, most researchers agree that at least some grammar, such as rules for how questions may be framed, is universal and therefore probably innate. But they clash fiercely over just how extensive this "universal grammar" is.

For example, one of the most basic aspects of grammar concerns sentence structure—the order in which the subject (S), verb (V), and object (O) appear. Most languages are either SVO (like English), SOV (like Japanese), or VSO (like Irish Gaelic). Linguists had thought that other orders were prohibited. But OVS does occur—in fewer than 1% of the world's languages, all of them endangered, notes Norvin Richards of MIT. One such language is Hixkaryana, spoken by some 300 people on a tributary of the Amazon River in Brazil. "If linguists had waited another couple of decades, languages with this construction would all be dead, and we would say it is not possible," says Richards.

Another recently appreciated realm of variability concerns affixes such as prefixes and suffixes. Affixes added to the beginning or the end of a word typically change its meaning in particular ways, such as prenatal or sturdiness. Some linguists have thought that all languages share a set of affix meanings that are part of universal grammar, and that there is always a clear distinction between stem words and affixes. But the Yup'ik language, spoken by about 10,000 people in Alaska, breaks with that presumption, according to work published by Mithun last year.

Mithun points out that Yup'ik has suffixes with meanings like "eat" and "hunt" that in English would seem like stems rather than add-ons. When speakers add the suffix "hunt" to the word for seal, it means "seal hunt," added to "egg," it means "egg hunt." But in addition to a suffix for hunt, Yup'ik also has a stem for hunt, so that there are different ways to say "seal hunt," each with its own shade of meaning. "These kinds of differences offer speakers tremendous rhetorical alternatives," she says.

Whereas some Yup'ik suffixes relate to subsistence or the environment, others refer to ways of being or behavior. There are suffixes that mean "willfully" and "secretively." One suffix means "to be inept at." Added to the verb "sleep," it yields "to have insomnia." Another suffix means, "finally, after desiring to do so, but being prevented by circumstance," and can be added to verbs such as "go." Not only does this complex suffix system challenge the idea that affixes play a restricted role in carrying meaning, it preserves a record of the cultural transmission that creates grammars, says Mithun.

Another linchpin of universal grammar is the distinction between nouns, verbs, and adjectives. Some languages have thousands of verbs and some less than a dozen, but few wholly dispense with that distinction. But David Gil, a linguist at the Max Planck Institute for Evolutionary Anthropology in Leipzig, Germany, says that Riau, a dialect of Indonesian, does just that, allowing nearly any word to function as a verb, a noun, or an adjective, depending on the context. The same word can be used to mean "eat" or "food," and any word can appear anywhere in the sentence. "The key to meaning lies in the larger context of the sentence," explains Bernard Comrie, director of the Institute's linguistics department.

A Sampling of Endangered Languages

Language	Where Spoken	# of Ethnic Group/# of Speakers	Scientific Interest
Ahlon	Southwest Togo, West Africa	2000–3000/ unknown	May reveal clues to West African migration; unusual grammar
Cambap	Cameroon, Central Africa	250/30	Evidence of the region's history
Harsusi	South-central Oman	600/600	Clues to the relationship between classical and modern Semitic languages
Kayardild	Two islands off northern Australia	About 1 50/4–6	Rare features challenge universal grammar
Leco	Andes Mountains in Bolivia	80/20	Clues to ancient contact between Amazonian and mountain-dwelling people
Mohawk	New York, Quebec, and Toronto	Tens of thousands/ 1000–2000	Complex word constructions add insights into universal grammar
Yup'ik	Southwestern Alaska	20,000/10,000	Unusual grammar challenges universal rules
Yélî dnye	Rossel Island, Papua New Guinea	4000/4000	Unique sounds; vocabulary that upsets universal color terminology

Other languages retain nouns and verbs, but bend the grammatical structures thought to govern their use, says Sadock. For example, in most languages the verb agrees with the subject. But in Aleut—now spoken by only about 100 people in the Aleutian Islands off the coast of Alaska and heard in daily conversation in just a single village, Atka—the verb can agree not only with the subject or the object, but also with the possessor of the subject or object. Thus instead of saying, "Their house is big," an Aleut speaker says, "Their house are big"—something Sadock calls "virtually unprecedented." Yet, he adds, "the fact that Aleut is so seriously endangered means that we might never know its true genius."

Sadock, who chairs the Committee on Endangered Languages and Their Preservation for the Linguistic Society of America, says that such "wild differences" in grammar as seen in Aleut and Yup' ik "challenge our notions about what kind of language the human mind can construct." He thinks that the realm of universal grammar has been exaggerated and that many grammatical rules are culturally variable. "Most grammar arises out of human cognition and interaction with people and objects, rather than being an innate hard-wired system that has nothing to do with daily life," agrees Dan Slobin, a psycholinguist at the University of California, Berkeley.

But others argue that although various languages may be unusual, the differences are superficial. For instance, Hale and MIT colleague Richards think that Lardil and Kayardild actually conform to universal grammar rather than breaking the rules. Although these languages allow speakers to jumble the words of a sentence, the words inside a phrase are first modified by tense markers, notes Richards. Thus, he argues, traces of the phrase structure remain.

To take an even more basic example, linguist Mark Baker of Rutgers University in New Brunswick, New Jersey, makes the case that many languages reported to lack distinctions between parts of speech such as nouns and adjectives do indeed make such distinctions—if you know where to look. "I can show that even those languages have adjectives," he says. For example, Nunggubuyu, an endangered aboriginal language in Australia, has been described as using nouns and adjectives interchangeably. But Baker reports in a monograph to be published by Cambridge University

Press that the elusive distinction between these parts of speech becomes apparent in a particular way of forming compound words called noun incorporation.

Nunggubuyu speakers can say, "I bought meat" or "I meat bought," incorporating the noun into the verb. They can also say "I bought big" (akin to "I bought the big one"), but they cannot say "I big bought," incorporating the adjective into the verb.

"If big had the same status as meat, it should be able to incorporate the same way," Baker says, arguing that this is indeed a distinction between the two word categories.

Baker recently applied this kind of analysis to a range of extremely different languages all thought to lack distinctions in parts of speech, including Mohawk and Salish, two endangered Native American languages; Edo, spoken in Nigeria; and Chichewa, spoken in Malawi. His results show that all these languages have noun, verb, and adjective categories, although they may be subtly expressed. "In any language where we can frame these questions precisely enough to measure, we can find a lot that's universal," Baker says.

As the argument continues, both sides realize that their evidence is vanishing. "In a few years everyone will speak English, Mandarin, and Spanish, and the similarities among languages will exist by accident, not because they reflect limits of human cognition," says Baker. Adds Mithun: "Without the variability, proposals about universals have been and will be hopelessly naïve."

FROM WORDS TO THOUGHTS
In addition to adding much-needed data to the question of universal grammar, the diversity of languages also offers insight into the relationship between language and thought—how speakers perceive and understand the world. "Put bluntly, does the language you speak affect the way you think?" Levinson asks.

He has approached this by studying how unwritten, often endangered languages express spatial concepts. Many cognitive scientists have presumed that all languages express spatial concepts in similar ways, because thinking spatially is a necessity for higher animals and therefore is likely to be hard-wired into the human brain. "This is the very last area in which we would expect to find significant cultural variation," Levinson says. But find it he did.

Many languages, including English, express spatial concepts using relative coordinates established through the planes of the body, such as left-right and front-back. But Levinson found languages that use very different systems. Guugu Yimithirr, an endangered Australian language spoken by fewer than 800 people, uses a fixed environmental system of four named directions that resemble north, south, east, and west. Speakers modify the four words to yield some 50 terms that indicate such things as motion toward or away from a direction. They use the same terminology to describe both landscape and small-scale space, for example: "The school is to the west of the river" and "There's an ant on your eastern leg."

The Guugu Yimithirr terminology reflects an entirely different way of conceptualizing a scene, says Levinson. It requires laying out all memories in terms of the four directions and continually running a mental compass and a positioning system.

Levinson has now investigated a similar phenomenon in the Mayan language Tzeltal, in work in press and co-authored with Penelope Brown, also of the Max Planck Institute for Psycholinguistics. Brown gathered 600 hours of videotape of 15 Tzeltal-speaking children performing various tasks and found that children as young as four years old have mastered the positioning system. Children were asked to describe the arrangement of toys on a table, then turn 180 degrees and describe an identical arrangement arrayed in front of them. English-speaking children rotate their coordinate system as they turn—left becomes right. But for Tzeltal-speaking children, north was always north and south remained south.

Levinson concludes that even spatial thinking is learned, not innate. Rather than starting from a biologically set concept of space, children quickly learn the system used in their culture. Concurs psycholinguist Slobin: "The results show flexibility for how we can organize spatial concepts for talking and probably thinking."

THE ART OF LANGUAGE
As linguists uncover such cultural differences, many find themselves fascinated with the diverse linguistic systems that humans are capable of creating. Each language preserves a society's history, culture, and knowledge and is itself something akin to art, they say. "Language is one of the most intimate parts of culture," says Mithun.

Peering Into the Past, With Words

Prehistorians typically rely on stones, bones, and DNA to piece together the past, but linguists argue that words preserve history too. Two new studies, both based on endangered languages, offer new insights into the identity of mysterious ancient peoples, from the first farmers to early inhabitants of the British Isles.

Archaeologists have long known that some 10,000 years ago, ancient people in Mesopotamia discovered farming, raising sheep, cattle, wheat, and barley. And researchers knew that by 8000 years ago agriculture had spread north to the Caucasus Mountains. But they had little inkling of whether traces of this first farming culture lived on in any particular culture today. People have migrated extensively through the region over the millennia, and there's no continuous archaeological record of any single culture. Linguistically, most languages in the region and in the Fertile Crescent itself are relatively recent arrivals from elsewhere.

Now, however, linguist Johanna Nichols of the University of California, Berkeley, has used language to connect modern people of the Caucasus region to the ancient farmers of the Fertile Crescent. She analyzed the Nakh-Daghestanian linguistic family, which today includes Chechen, Ingush, and Batsbi on the Nakh side and some 24 languages on the Daghestanian side; all are spoken in parts of Russia (such as Chechnya), Georgia, and Azerbaijan.

Nichols had previously established the family tree of Nakh-Daghestanian by analyzing similarities in the related languages much the way biologists create a phylogeny of species. She found that three languages converge at the very base of the tree. Today, speakers of all three live side by side in the southeastern foothills of the Caucasus Mountains, suggesting that this was the homeland of the ancestral language—on the very fringes of the Fertile Crescent. To get a rough estimate of when the language arose, Nichols used a linguistic method that assumes a semi-regular rate of vocabulary loss per 1000 years, and she dated the ancestral language to about 8000 years ago.

Nichols also found that the ancestral language contains a host of words for farming. The Chechen words mug (barley), stu (bull), and tkha (wool), for example, all have closely related forms in the earliest branches of Daghestanian, as do words for pear, apple, dairy product, and oxen yoke—all elements of the farming package developed in the Fertile Crescent. Thus, location, time, and vocabulary all suggest that the farmers of the region were proto-Nakh-Daghestanians. "The Nakh-Daghestanian languages are the closest thing we have to a direct continuation of the cultural and linguistic community that gave rise to Western civilization." Nichols says.

Population geneticist Henry Harpending of the University of Utah, Salt Lake City, has just begun the job of unraveling the genetic ancestry of Daghestanian speakers and is impressed with Nichols's work. "For years I wished linguists would get in the game. Nichols sure is."

Nichols is now reconstructing the ancestral language, hoping for more clues to the culture of these early farmers. But she has to work fast, for the three Nakh languages are vanishing. Although there are still about 900,000 Chechen speakers left, the other two tongues have fewer speakers, and all three are being eroded by war, economic chaos, and Russian educational practices, Nichols says.

More than 3200 kilometers away, another linguist is mining Celtic languages—which are also considered endangered—for clues to the inhabitants of the early British Isles. Artifacts show that the islands were occupied long before Celts from the European continent made landfall about 700 B.C. But mysteries remain as to their identity.

So Orin Gensler of the Max Planck Institute for Evolutionary Anthropology in Leipzig, Germany, analyzed Celtic languages, including Irish Gaelic, Scottish Gaelic, Welsh, and Breton. Once prevalent throughout Europe, these languages are now spoken only in the British Isles and Brittany in France. Linguists have noted surprising grammatical differences between Celtic languages and related languages such as French, while at the same time seeing striking resemblances between Celtic and Afro-Asiatic languages spoken for millennia across a swath of coastal Northern Africa and the Near East.

In a forthcoming monograph, Gensler studied 20 grammatical features found in both Celtic and Afro-Asiatic languages. He sought these linguistic traits in 85 unrelated languages from around the world, reasoning that if the features were widespread, their appearance in both Celtic and Afro-Asiatic languages might be mere coincidence. But if the shared features are rare, coincidence is unlikely. Overall, Gensler found that about half the shared features are rare elsewhere. "I think the case against coincidence is about as good as it could be," he says.

A closer look at a number of features, including word order, offers a provocative theory for just how the Celtic islanders acquired these linguistic traits. In Gaelic and Welsh—and many Afro-Asiatic languages—the standard sentence structure is verb-subject-object. But Celtic languages spoken in Continental Europe in antiquity have the verb in the final or middle position. The best explanation for the shift to verb-initial order, says Gensler, is that when Celtic speakers made landfall on the British Isles, Afro-Asiatic speakers were already there. As these people learned Celtic, they perpetuated aspects of their own grammar into the new language.

Although others are interested in Gensler's idea, so far "there is no significant northwest African genetic signature... in Celtic populations," says Peter Underhill, a molecular geneticist at Stanford University in California. But in this instance, he adds, the linguists may be ahead of the geneticists, for researchers need more genetic markers before they can confirm or refute Gensler's idea.

Languages can gracefully encapsulate society's values, for example. Mayali has a special set of words that simultaneously indicates the relationship of both the speaker and the hearer to the person being discussed. A speaker uses a different term for mother when speaking to her grandmother, her brother, or her husband. The terms, which are so complicated that Mayali speakers don't learn them until adulthood, "represent the ability to simultaneously take two points of view. Using them forces you to pay attention to where everyone fits into the kinship system and to make incredibly complex calculations," Evans says.

Mayali culture values proper use of the kinship terms, which indicate consideration for others by subtly factoring in their point of view. But this feature is being lost as younger speakers either adopt English or speak a simplified form of Mayali.

Although linguists delight in such examples, all this richness means that the task of understanding and preserving languages is huge. "Most of the currently receding languages will disappear without even being recorded," says Matthias Brenzinger of the University of Cologne in Germany. Last February, he convened linguistics experts from all regions of the world to begin the difficult task of rating the degree of danger faced by the world's languages, to help linguists focus their efforts. Dozens of researchers are already working with native speakers to preserve languages. Hale and Richards compiled a dictionary with Lardil speakers, for example, and Richards plans to put together readers for teaching.

Such efforts can be successful: Back in the early 1970s, Mithun worked with the Mohawk community in Quebec, Canada, to codify Mohawk spelling conventions. That text and others later became part of a public school curriculum, and now a Quebec elementary school teaches Mohawk to hundreds of students; older students can even study Mohawk linguistics at McGill University.

Success stories are hard won, however. And as researchers contemplate the impending loss of the world's linguistic diversity, they see their opportunities for gaining insights into human linguistic development slipping away. "If you understand what the constraints of a possible language are," says Levinson, "you would understand a fundamental part of what it is to be human."

From Bernice Wuethrich, "Learning the World's Languages—Before They Vanish," *Science*, Vol. 288, No. 5469, p. 1158. Reprinted with permission from the American Association for the Advancement of Science.

A Cultural Approach to Male-Female Miscommunication—
Daniel N. Maltz and Ruth A. Borker

This article presents what we believe to be a useful new framework for examining differences in the speaking patterns of American men and women. It is based not on new data, but on a reexamination of a wide variety of material already available in the scholarly literature. Our starting problem is the nature of the different roles of male and female speakers in informal cross-sex conversations in American English. Our attempts to think about this problem have taken us to preliminary examination of a wide variety of fields often on or beyond the margins of our present competencies: children's speech, children's play, styles and patterns of friendship, conversational turn-taking, discourse analysis, and interethnic communication. The research which most influenced the development of our present model includes John Gumperz's work on problems in interethnic communication (1982) and Marjorie Goodwin's study of the linguistic aspects of play among black children in Philadelphia (1978, 1980a, 1980b).

Our major argument is that the general approach recently developed for the study of difficulties in cross-ethnic communication can be applied to cross-sex communication as well. We prefer to think of the difficulties in both cross-

sex and cross-ethnic communication as two examples of the same larger phenomenon: cultural difference and miscommunication.

THE PROBLEM OF CROSS-SEX CONVERSATION

Study after study has shown that when men and women attempt to interact as equals in friendly cross-sex conversations they do not play the same role in interaction, even when there is no apparent element of flirting. We hope to explore some of these differences, examine the explanations that have been offered, and provide an alternative explanation for them.

The primary data on cross-sex conversations come from two general sources: social psychology studies from the 1950s such as Soskin and John's (1963) research on two young married couples and Strodbeck and Mann's (1956) research on jury deliberations, and more recent sociolinguistic studies from the University of California at Santa Barbara and the University of Pennsylvania by Candace West (Zimmerman and West 1975; West and Zimmerman 1977; West 1979), Pamela Fishman (1978), and Lynette Hirschman (1973).

WOMEN'S FEATURES

Several striking differences in male and female contributions to cross-sex conversation have been noticed in these studies.

First, women display a greater tendency to ask questions. Fishman (1978:400) comments that "at times I felt that all women did was ask questions," and Hirschman (1973:10) notes that "several of the female-male conversations fell into a question-answer pattern with the females asking the males questions."

Fishman (1978:408) sees this question-asking tendency as an example of a second, more general characteristic of women's speech, doing more of the routine "shitwork" involved in maintaining routine social interaction, doing more to facilitate the flow of conversation (Hirschman 1973:3). Women are more likely than men to make utterances that demand or encourage responses from their fellow speakers and are therefore, in Fishman's words, "more actively engaged in ensuring interaction than the men" (1978:404). In the earlier social psychology studies,

LANGUAGE

these features have been coded under the general category of "positive reactions" including solidarity tension release, and agreeing (Strodbeck and Mann 1956).

Third, women show a greater tendency to make use of positive minimal responses, especially "mm hmm" (Hirschman 1973:8), and are more likely to insert "such comments throughout streams of talk rather than [simply] at the end" (Fishman 1978:402).

Fourth, women are more likely to adopt a strategy of "silent protest" after they have been interrupted or have received a delayed minimal response (Zimmerman and West 1975; West and Zimmerman 1977:524).

Fifth, women show a greater tendency to use the pronouns "you" and "we," which explicitly acknowledge the existence of the other speaker (Hirschman 1973:6).

MEN'S FEATURES
Contrasting contributions to cross-sex conversations have been observed and described for men.

First, men are more likely to interrupt the speech of their conversational partners, that is, to interrupt the speech of women (Zimmerman and West 1975; West and Zimmerman 1977; West 1979).

Second, they are more likely to challenge or dispute their partners' utterances (Hirschman 1973:11).

Third, they are more likely to ignore the comments of the other speaker, that is, to offer no response or acknowledgment at all (Hirschman 1973:11), to respond slowly in what has been described as a "delayed minimal response" (Zimmerman and West 1975:118), or to respond unenthusiastically (Fishman 1978).

Fourth, men use more mechanisms for controlling the topic of conversation, including both topic development and the introduction of new topics, than do women (Zimmerman and West 1975).

Finally, men make more direct declarations of fact or opinion than do women (Fishman 1978:402), including suggestions, opinions, and "statements of orientation" as

Strodbeck and Mann (1956) describe them, or "statements of focus and directives" as they are described by Soskin and John (1963).

EXPLANATIONS OFFERED
Most explanations for these features have focused on differences in the social power or in the personalities of men and women. One variant of the social power argument, presented by West (Zimmerman and West 1975; West and Zimmerman 1977), is that men's dominance in conversation parallels their dominance in society. Men enjoy power in society and also in conversation. The two levels are seen as part of a single social-political system. West sees interruptions and topic control as male displays of power—a power based in the larger social order but reinforced and expressed in face-to-face interaction with women. A second variant of this argument, stated by Fishman (1978), is that while the differential power of men and women is crucial, the specific mechanism through which it enters conversation is sex-role definition. Sex roles serve to obscure the issue of power for participants, but the fact is, Fishman argues, that norms of appropriate behavior for women and men serve to give power and interactional control to men while keeping it from women. To be socially acceptable as women, women cannot exert control and must actually support men in their control. In this casting of the social power argument, men are not necessarily seen to be consciously flaunting power, but simply reaping the rewards given them by the social system. In both variants, the link between macro and micro levels of social life is seen as direct and unproblematic, and the focus of explanation is the general social order.

Sex roles have also been central in psychological explanations. The primary advocate of the psychological position has been Robin Lakoff (1975). Basically, Lakoff asserts that, having been taught to speak and act like "ladies," women become as unassertive and insecure as they have been made to sound. The impossible task of trying to be both women and adults, which Lakoff sees as culturally incompatible, saps women of confidence and strength. As a result, they come to produce the speech they do, not just because it is how women are supposed to speak, but because it fits with the personalities they develop as a consequence of sex-role requirements.

The problem with these explanations is that they do not provide a means of explaining why these specific features appear as opposed to any number of others, nor do they allow us to differentiate between various types of male-female interaction. They do not really tell us why and how these specific interactional phenomena are linked to the general fact that men dominate within our social system.

AN ALTERNATIVE EXPLANATION: SOCIOLINGUISTIC SUBCULTURES

Our approach to cross-sex communication patterns is somewhat different from those that have been previously proposed. We place the stress not on psychological differences or power differentials, although these may make some contribution, but rather on a notion of cultural differences between men and women in their conceptions of friendly conversation, their rules for engaging in it, and, probably most important, their rules for interpreting it. We argue that American men and women come from different **sociolinguistic subcultures** having learned to do different things with words in a conversation, so that when they attempt to carry on conversations with one another, even if both parties are attempting to treat one another as equals, cultural miscommunication results.

The idea of distinct male and female subcultures is not a new one for anthropology. It has been persuasively argued again and again for those parts of the world such as the Middle East and southern Europe in which men and women spend most of their lives spatially and interactionally segregated. The strongest case for sociolinguistic subcultures has been made by Susan Harding from her research in rural Spain (1975).

The major premise on which Harding builds her argument is that speech is a means for dealing with social and psychological situations. When men and women have different experiences and operate in different social contexts, they tend to develop different genres of speech and different skills for doing things with words. In the Spanish village in which she worked, the sexual division of labor was strong, with men involved in agricultural tasks and public politics while women were involved in a series of networks of personal relations with their children, their husbands, and their female neighbors. While men developed their verbal skills in economic negotiations and public political argument, women became more verbally adept at

a quite different mode of interactional manipulation with words: gossip, social analysis, subtle information gathering through a carefully developed technique of verbal prying, and a kind of second-guessing the thoughts of others (commonly known as "women's intuition") through a skillful monitoring of the speech of others. The different social needs of men and women, she argues, have led them to sexually differentiated communicative cultures, with each sex learning a different set of skills for manipulating words effectively.

The question that Harding does not ask, however, is, if men and women possess different subcultural rules for speaking, what happens if and when they try to interact with each other? It is here that we turn to the research on interethnic miscommunication.

INTERETHNIC COMMUNICATION

Recent research (Gumperz 1977, 1978a, 1978b, 1979; Gumperz and Tannen 1978) has shown that systematic problems develop in communication when speakers of different speech cultures interact and that these problems are the result of differences in systems of conversational inference and the cues for signalling speech acts and speaker's intent. Conversation is a negotiated activity. It progresses in large part because of shared assumptions about what is going on.

Examining interactions between English-English and Indian-English speakers in Britain (Gumperz 1977, 1978a, 1979; Gumperz et al. 1977), Gumperz found that differences in cues resulted in systematic miscommunication over whether a question was being asked, whether an argument was being made, whether a person was being rude or polite, whether a speaker was relinquishing the floor or interrupting, whether and what a speaker was emphasizing, whether interactants were angry, concerned, or indifferent. Rather than being seen as problems in communication, the frustrating encounters that resulted were usually chalked up as personality clashes or interpreted in the light of racial stereotypes which tended to exacerbate already bad relations.

To take a simple case, Gumperz (1977) reports that Indian women working at a cafeteria, when offering food, used a falling intonation, e.g., "gravy," which to them indicated a question, something like "do you want gravy?" Both Indian

LANGUAGE

and English workers saw a question as an appropriate polite form, but to English-English speakers a falling intonation signalled not a question, which for them is signalled by a rising intonation such as "gravy," but a declarative statement, which was both inappropriate and extremely rude.

A major advantage of Gumperz's framework is that it does not assume that problems are the result of bad faith, but rather sees them as the result of individuals wrongly interpreting cues according to their own rules.

THE INTERPRETATION OF MINIMAL RESPONSES

How might Gumperz's approach to the study of conflicting rules for interpreting conversation be applied to the communication between men and women? A simple example will illustrate our basic approach: the case of positive minimal responses. Minimal responses such as nods and comments like "yes" and "mm hmm" are common features of conversational interaction. Our claim, based on our attempts to understand personal experience, is that these minimal responses have significantly different meanings for men and women, leading to occasionally serious miscommunication.

We hypothesize that for women a minimal response of this type means simply something like "I'm listening to you; please continue," and that for men it has a somewhat stronger meaning such as "I agree with you" or at least "I follow your argument so far." The fact that women use these responses more often than men is in part simply that women are listening more often than men are agreeing.

But our hypothesis explains more than simple differential frequency of usage. Different rules can lead to repeated misunderstandings. Imagine a male speaker who is receiving repeated nods or "mm hmm"s from the woman he is speaking to. She is merely indicating that she is listening, but he thinks she is agreeing with everything he says. Now imagine a female speaker who is receiving only occasional nods and "mm hmm"s from the man she is speaking to. He is indicating that he doesn't always agree; she thinks he isn't always listening.

What is appealing about this short example is that it seems to explain two of the most common complaints in male-female interaction: (1) men who think that women are always agreeing with them and then conclude that it's impossible to tell what a woman really thinks, and (2) women who get upset with men who never seem to be listening. What we think we have here are two separate rules for conversational maintenance which come into conflict and cause massive miscommunication.

SOURCES OF DIFFERENT CULTURES

A probable objection that many people will have to our discussion so far is that American men and women interact with one another far too often to possess different subcultures. What we need to explain is how it is that men and women can come to possess different cultural assumptions about friendly conversation.

Our explanation is really quite simple. It is based on the idea that by the time we have become adults we possess a wide variety of rules for interacting in different situations. Different sets of these rules were learned at different times and in different contexts. We have rules for dealing with people in dominant or subordinate social positions, rules which we first learned as young children interacting with our parents and teachers. We have rules for flirting and other sexual encounters which we probably started learning at or near adolescence. We have rules for dealing with service personnel and bureaucrats, rules we began learning when we first ventured into the public domain. Finally, we have rules for friendly interaction, for carrying on friendly conversation. What is striking about these last rules is that they were learned not from adults but from peers, and that they were learned during precisely that time period, approximately age 5 to 15, when boys and girls interact socially primarily with members of their own sex.

The idea that girls and boys in contemporary America learn different ways of speaking by the age of five or earlier has been postulated by Robin Lakoff (1975), demonstrated by Andrea Meditch (1975), and more fully explored by Adelaide Haas (1979). Haas's research on school-age children shows the early appearance of important male-female differences in patterns of language use, including a male tendency toward direct requests and information giving and a female tendency toward compliance (1979:107).

But the process of acquiring gender-specific speech and behavior patterns by school-age children is more complex than the simple copying of adult "genderlects" by preschoolers. Psychologists Brooks-Gunn and Matthews

158

(1979) have labelled this process the "consolidation of sex roles"; we call it learning of gender-specific "cultures."

Among school-age children, patterns of friendly social interaction are learned not so much from adults as from members of one's peer group, and a major feature of most middle-childhood peer groups is homogeneity; "they are either all-boy or all-girl" (Brooks-Gunn and Matthews 1979). Members of each sex are learning self-consciously to differentiate their behavior from that of the other sex and to exaggerate these differences. The process can be profitably compared to accent divergence in which members of two groups that wish to become clearly distinguished from one another socially acquire increasingly divergent ways of speaking.[1]

Because they learn these gender-specific cultures from their age-mates, children tend to develop stereotypes and extreme versions of adult behavior patterns. For a boy learning to behave in a masculine way, for example, Ruth Hartley (1959, quoted in Brooks-Gunn and Matthews 1979:203) argues that:

> both the information and the practice he gets are distorted. Since his peers have no better sources of information than he has, all they can do is pool the impressions and anxieties they derived from their early training. Thus, the picture they draw is oversimplified and overemphasized. It is a picture drawn in black and white, with little or no modulation and it is incomplete, including a few of the many elements that go to make up the role of the mature male.

What we hope to argue is that boys and girls learn to use language in different ways because of the very different social contexts in which they learn how to carry on friendly conversation. Almost anyone who remembers being a child, has worked with school-age children, or has had an opportunity to observe school-age children can vouch for the fact that groups of girls and groups of boys interact and play in different ways. Systematic observations of children's play have tended to confirm these well-known differences in the ways girls and boys learn to interact with their friends.

In a major study of sex differences in the play of school-age children, for example, sociologist Janet Lever (1976) observed the following six differences between the play of boys and that of girls: (1) girls more often play indoors; (2) boys tend to play in larger groups; (3) boys' play groups tend to include a wider age range of participants; (4) girls play in predominantly male games more often than vice versa; (5) boys more often play competitive games, and (6) girls' games tend to last a shorter period of time than boys' games.

It is by examining these differences in the social organization of play and the accompanying differences in the patterns of social interaction they entail, we argue, that we can learn about the sources of male-female differences in patterns of language use. And it is these same patterns, learned in childhood and carried over into adulthood as the bases for patterns of single-sex friendship relations, we contend, that are potential sources of miscommunication in cross-sex interaction.

THE WORLD OF GIRLS

Our own experience and studies such as Goodwin's (1980b) of black children and Lever's (1976, 1978) of white children suggest a complex of features of girls' play and the speech within it. Girls play in small groups, most often in pairs (Lever 1976; Eder and Hallinan 1978; Brooks-Gunn and Matthews 1979), and their play groups tend to be remarkably homogeneous in terms of age. Their play is often in private or semi-private settings that require participants be invited in. Play is cooperative and activities are usually organized in noncompetitive ways (Lever 1976; Goodwin 1980b). Differentiation between girls is not made in terms of power, but relative closeness. Friendship is seen by girls as involving intimacy, equality, mutual commitment, and loyalty. The idea of "best friend" is central for girls. Relationships between girls are to some extent in opposition to one another, and new relationships are often formed at the expense of old ones. As Brooks-Gunn and Matthews (1979:280) observe, "friendships tend to be exclusive, with a few girls being exceptionally close to one another. Because of this breakups tend to be highly emotional," and Goodwin (1980a:172) notes that "the non-hierarchical framework of the girls provides a fertile ground for rather intricate processes of alliance formation between equals against some other party."

LANGUAGE

There is a basic contradiction in the structure of girls' social relationships. Friends are supposed to be equal and everyone is supposed to get along, but in fact they don't always. Conflict must be resolved, but a girl cannot assert social power or superiority as an individual to resolve it. Lever (1976), studying fifth-graders, found that girls simply could not deal with quarrels and that when conflict arose they made no attempt to settle it; the group just broke up. What girls learn to do with speech is cope with the contradiction created by an ideology of equality and cooperation and a social reality that includes differences and conflict. As they grow up they learn increasingly subtle ways of balancing the conflicting pressures created by a female social world and a female friendship ideology.

Basically girls learn to do three things with words: (1) to create and maintain relationships of closeness and equality, (2) to criticize others in acceptable ways, and (3) to interpret accurately the speech of other girls.

To a large extent friendships among girls are formed through talk. Girls need to learn to give support, to recognize the speech rights of others, to let others speak, and to acknowledge what they say in order to establish and maintain relationships of equality and closeness. In activities they need to learn to create cooperation through speech. Goodwin (1980a) found that inclusive forms such as "let's," "we gonna," "we could," and "we gotta" predominated in task-oriented activities. Furthermore, she found that most girls in the group she studied made suggestions and that the other girls usually agreed to them. But girls also learn to exchange information and confidences to create and maintain relationships of closeness. The exchange of personal thoughts not only expresses closeness but mutual commitment as well. Brooks-Gunn and Matthews (1979:280) note of adolescent girls:

> much time is spent talking, reflecting, and sharing intimate thought. Loyalty is of central concern to the 12- to 14-year-old girl, presumably because, if innermost secrets are shared, the friend may have "dangerous knowledge" at her disposal.

Friendships are not only formed through particular types of talk, but are ended through talk as well. As Lever (1976:4) says of "best friends," "sharing secrets binds the union together, and 'telling' the secrets to outsiders is symbolic of the 'break-up.' "

Secondly, girls learn to criticize and argue with other girls without seeming overly aggressive, without being perceived as either "bossy" or "mean," terms girls use to evaluate one another's speech and actions. Bossiness, ordering others around, is not legitimate because it denies equality. Goodwin (1980a) points out that girls talked very negatively about the use of commands to equals, seeing it as appropriate only in role play or in unequal relationships such as those with younger siblings. Girls learn to direct things without seeming bossy, or they learn not to direct. While disputes are common, girls learn to phrase their arguments in terms of group needs and situational requirements rather than personal power or desire (Goodwin 1980a). Meanness is used by girls to describe nonlegitimate acts of exclusion, turning on someone, or withholding friendship. Excluding is a frequent occurrence (Eder and Hallinan 1978), but girls learn over time to discourage or even drive away other girls in ways that don't seem to be just personal whim. Cutting someone is justified in terms of the target's failure to meet group norms and a girl often rejects another using speech that is seemingly supportive on the surface. Conflict and criticism are risky in the world of girls because they can both rebound against the critic and can threaten social relationships. Girls learn to hide the source of criticism; they present it as coming from someone else or make it indirectly through a third party (Goodwin 1980a, 1980b).

Finally, girls must learn to decipher the degree of closeness being offered by other girls, to recognize what is being withheld, and to recognize criticism. Girls who don't actually read these cues run the risk of public censure or ridicule (Goodwin 1980a). Since the currency of closeness is the exchange of secrets which can be used against a girl, she must learn to read the intent and loyalty of others and to do so continuously, given the system of shifting alliances and indirect expressions of conflict. Girls must become increasingly sophisticated in reading the motives of others, in determining when closeness is real, when conventional, and when false, and to respond appropriately. They must learn who to confide in, what to confide, and who not to approach. Given the indirect expression of conflict, girls must learn to read relationships and situations sensitively. Learning to get things right is a fundamental skill for social success, if not just social survival.

THE WORLD OF BOYS

Boys play in larger, more hierarchically organized groups than do girls. Relative status in this ever-fluctuating hierarchy is the main thing that boys learn to manipulate in their interactions with their peers. Nondominant boys are rarely excluded from play but are made to feel the inferiority of their status positions in no uncertain terms. And since hierarchies fluctuate over time and over situation, every boy gets his chance to be victimized and must learn to take it. The social world of boys is one of posturing and counterposturing. In this world, speech is used in three major ways: (1) to assert one's position of dominance, (2) to attract and maintain an audience, and (3) to assert oneself when other speakers have the floor.

The use of speech for the expression of dominance is the most straightforward and probably the best-documented sociolinguistic pattern in boys' peer groups. Even ethological studies of human dominance patterns have made extensive use of various speech behaviors as indices of dominance. Richard Savin-Williams (1976), for example, in his study of dominance patterns among boys in a summer camp uses the following speech interactions as measures of dominance: (1) giving of verbal commands or orders, such as "Get up," "Give it to me," or "You go over there"; (2) name calling and other forms of verbal ridicule, such as "You're a dolt"; (3) verbal threats or boasts of authority such as "If you don't shut up, I'm gonna come over and bust your teeth in"; (4) refusals to obey orders; and (5) winning a verbal argument as in the sequence: "I was here first"/"Tough," or in more elaborate forms of verbal duelling such as the "dozens."[2]

The same patterns of verbally asserting one's dominance and challenging the dominance claims of others form the central element in Goodwin's (1980a) observations of boys' play in Philadelphia. What is easy to forget in thinking about this use of words as weapons, however, is that the most successful boy in such interaction is not the one who is most aggressive and uses the most power-wielding forms of speech, but the boy who uses these forms most successfully. The simple use of assertiveness and aggression in boys' play is the sign not of a leader but of a bully. The skillful speaker in a boys' group is considerably more likeable and better liked by his peers than is a simple bully. Social success among boys is based on knowing both how and when to use words to express power as well as knowing

when not to use them. A successful leader will use speech to put challengers in their place and to remind followers periodically of their nondominant position, but will not browbeat unnecessarily and will therefore gain the respect rather than the fear of less dominant boys.

A second sociolinguistic aspect of friendly interaction between boys is using words to gain and maintain an audience. Storytelling, joke telling, and other narrative performance events are common features of the social interaction of boys. But actual transcripts of such storytelling events collected by Harvey Sacks (Sacks 1974; Jefferson 1978) and Goodwin (1980a), as opposed to stories told directly to interviewers, reveal a suggestive feature of storytelling activities among boys: audience behavior is not overtly supportive. The storyteller is frequently faced with mockery challenges and side comments on his story. A major sociolinguistic skill which a boy must apparently learn in interacting with his peers is to ride out this series of challenges, maintain his audience, and successfully get to the end of his story. In Sacks' account (1974) of some teenage boys involved in the telling of a dirty joke, for example, the narrator is challenged for his taste in jokes (an implication that he doesn't know a dirty joke from a non-dirty one) and for the potential ambiguity of his opening line "Three brothers married three sisters," not, as Sacks seems to imply, because audience members are really confused, but just to hassle the speaker. Through catches,[3] put-downs, the building of suspense, or other interest-grabbing devices, the speaker learns to control his audience. He also learns to continue when he gets no encouragement whatever, pausing slightly at various points for possible audience response but going on if there is nothing but silence.

A final sociolinguistic skill which boys must learn from interacting with other boys is how to act as audience members in the types of storytelling situations just discussed. As audience member as well as storyteller, a boy must learn to assert himself and his opinions. Boys seem to respond to the storytelling of other boys not so much with questions on deeper implications or with minimal-response encouragement as with side comments and challenges. These are not meant primarily to interrupt, to change topic, or to change the direction of the narrative itself, but to assert the identity of the individual audience member.

LANGUAGE

WOMEN'S SPEECH

The structures and strategies in women's conversation show a marked continuity with the talk of girls. The key logic suggested by Kalcik's (1975) study of women's rap groups, Hirschman's (1973) study of students and Abrahams's (1975) work on black women is that women's conversation is interactional. In friendly talk, women are negotiating and expressing a relationship, one that should be in the form of support and closeness, but which may also involve criticism and distance. Women orient themselves to the person they are talking to and expect such orientation in return. As interaction, conversation requires participation from those involved and back-and-forth movement between participants. Getting the floor is not seen as particularly problematic; that should come about automatically. What is problematic is getting people engaged and keeping them engaged—maintaining the conversation and the interaction.

This conception of conversation leads to a number of characteristic speech strategies and gives a particular dynamic to women's talk. First, women tend to use personal and inclusive pronouns, such as "you" and "we" (Hirschman 1973). Second, women give off and look for signs of engagement such as nods and minimal response (Kalcik 1975; Hirschman 1973). Third, women give more extended signs of interest and attention, such as interjecting comments or questions during a speaker's discourse. These sometimes take the form of interruptions. In fact, both Hirschman (1973) and Kalcik (1975) found that interruptions were extremely common, despite women's concern with politeness and decorum (Kalcik 1975). Kalcik (1975) comments that women often asked permission to speak but were concerned that each speaker be allowed to finish and that all present got a chance to speak. These interruptions were clearly not seen as attempts to grab the floor but as calls for elaboration and development, and were taken as signs of support and interest. Fourth, women at the beginning of their utterances explicitly acknowledge and respond to what has been said by others. Fifth, women attempt to link their utterance to the one preceding it by building on the previous utterance or talking about something parallel or related to it. Kalcik (1975) talks about strategies of tying together, filling in, and serializing as signs of women's desire to create continuity in conversation, and Hirschman (1973) describes elaboration as a key dynamic of women's talk.

While the idiom of much of women's friendly talk is that of support, the elements of criticism, competition, and conflict do occur in it. But as with girls, these tend to take forms that fit the friendship idiom. Abrahams (1975) points out that while "talking smart" is clearly one way women talk to women as well as to men, between women it tends to take a more playful form, to be more indirect and metaphoric in its phrasing and less prolonged than similar talk between men. Smartness, as he points out, puts distance in a relationship (Abrahams 1975). The target of criticism, whether present or not, is made out to be the one violating group norms and values (Abrahams 1975). Overt competitiveness is also disguised. As Kalcik (1975) points out, some stories that build on preceding ones are attempts to cap the original speaker, but they tend to have a form similar to supportive ones. It is the intent more than the form that differs. Intent is a central element in the concept of "bitchiness," one of women's terms for evaluating their talk, and it relates to this contradiction between form and intent, whether putting negative messages in overtly positive forms or acting supportive face to face while not being so elsewhere.

These strategies and the interactional orientation of women's talk give their conversation a particular dynamic. While there is often an unfinished quality to particular utterances (Kalcik 1975), there is a progressive development to the overall conversation. The conversation grows out of the interaction of its participants, rather than being directed by a single individual or series of individuals. In her very stimulating discussion, Kalcik (1975) argues that this is true as well for many of the narratives women tell in conversation. She shows how narrative "kernels" serve as conversational resources for individual women and the group as a whole. How and if a "kernel story" is developed by the narrator and/or audience on a particular occasion is a function of the conversational context from which it emerges (Kalcik 1975:8), and it takes very different forms at different tellings. Not only is the dynamic of women's conversation one of elaboration and continuity, but the idiom of support can give it a distinctive tone as well. Hannerz (1969:96), for example, contrasts the "tone of relaxed sweetness, sometimes bordering on the saccharine," that characterizes approving talk between women, to the heated argument found among men. Kalcik (1975:6) even goes so far as to suggest that there is an "underlying aesthetic or organizing principle" of "harmony" being expressed in women's friendly talk.

MEN'S SPEECH

The speaking patterns of men, and of women for that matter, vary greatly from one North American subculture to another. As Gerry Philipsen (1975:13) summarizes it, "talk is not everywhere valued equally; nor is it anywhere valued equally in all social contexts." There are striking cultural variations between subcultures in whether men consider certain modes of speech appropriate for dealing with women, children, authority figures, or strangers; there are differences in performance rules for storytelling and joke telling; there are differences in the context of men's speech; and there are differences in the rules for distinguishing aggressive joking from true aggression.

But more surprising than these differences are the apparent similarities across subcultures in the patterns of friendly interaction between men and the resemblances between these patterns and those observed for boys. Research reports on the speaking patterns of men among urban blacks (Abrahams 1976; Hannerz 1969), rural Newfoundlanders (Faris 1966; Bauman 1972), and urban blue-collar whites (Philipsen 1975; LeMasters 1975) point again and again to the same three features: storytelling, arguing and verbal posturing.

Narratives such as jokes and stories are highly valued, especially when they are well performed for an audience. In Newfoundland, for example, Fans (1966: 242) comments that "the reason 'news' is rarely passed between two men meeting in the road—it is simply not to one's advantage to relay information to such a small audience." Loud and aggressive argument is a second common feature of male-male speech. Such arguments, which may include shouting, wagering, name-calling, and verbal threats (Faris 1966:245), are often, as Hannerz (1969:86) describes them, "debates over minor questions of little direct import to anyone," enjoyed for their own sake and not taken as signs of real conflict. Practical jokes, challenges, put-downs, insults, and other forms of verbal aggression are a third feature of men's speech, accepted as normal among friends. LeMasters (1975:140), for example, describes life in a working-class tavern in the Midwest as follows:

> It seems clear that status at the Oasis is related to the ability to "dish it out" in the rapid-fire exchange called "joshing": you have to have a quick retort, and preferably one that puts you "one up" on your opponent. People who can't compete in the game lose status.

Thus challenges rather than statements of support are a typical way for men to respond to the speech of other men.

WHAT IS HAPPENING IN CROSS-SEX CONVERSATION

What we are suggesting is that women and men have different cultural rules for friendly conversation and that these rules come into conflict when women and men attempt to talk to each other as friends and equals in casual conversation. We can think of at least five areas, in addition to that of minimal responses already discussed, in which men and women probably possess different conversational rules, so that miscommunication is likely to occur in cross-sex interaction.

1. There are two interpretations of the meaning of questions. Women seem to see questions as a part of conversational maintenance, while men seem to view them primarily as requests for information.

2. There are two conventions for beginning an utterance and linking it to the preceding utterance. Women's rules seem to call for an explicit acknowledgment of what has been said and making a connection to it. Men seem to have no such rule and in fact some male strategies call for ignoring the preceding comments.

3. There are different interpretations of displays of verbal aggressiveness. Women seem to interpret overt aggressiveness as personally directed, negative, and disruptive. Men seem to view it as one conventional organizing structure for conversational flow.

4. There are two understandings of topic flow and topic shift. The literature on storytelling in particular seems to indicate that men operate with a system in which topic is fairly narrowly defined and adhered to until finished and in which shifts between topics are abrupt, while women have a system in which topic is developed progressively and shifts gradually. These two systems imply very different rules for and interpretations of side comments, with major potential for miscommunication.[4]

5. There appear to be two different attitudes towards problem sharing and advice giving. Women tend to discuss problems with one another, sharing experiences and offering reassurances. Men, in contrast,

tend to hear women, and other men, who present them with problems as making explicit requests for solutions. They respond by giving advice, by acting as experts, lecturing to their audiences.

CONCLUSIONS

Our purpose in this paper has been to present a framework for thinking about and tying together a number of strands in the analysis of differences between male and female conversational styles. We hope to prove the intellectual value of this framework by demonstrating its ability to do two things: to serve as a model both of and for sociolinguistic research.

As a model *of* past research findings, the power of our approach lies in its ability to suggest new explanations of previous findings on cross-sex communication while linking these findings to a wide range of other fields, including the study of language acquisition, of play, of friendship, of storytelling, of cross-cultural miscommunication, and of discourse analysis. Differences in the social interaction patterns of boys and girls appear to be widely known but rarely utilized in examinations of sociolinguistic acquisition or in explanations of observed gender differences in patterns of adult speech. Our proposed framework should serve to link together these and other known facts in new ways.

As a model *for* future research, we hope our framework will be even more promising. It suggests to us a number of potential research problems which remain to be investigated. Sociolinguistic studies of school-age children, especially studies of the use of speech in informal peer interaction, appear to be much rarer than studies of young children, although such studies may be of greater relevance for the understanding of adult patterns, particularly those related to gender. Our framework also suggests the need for many more studies of single-sex conversations among adults, trying to make more explicit some of the differences in conversational rules suggested by present research. Finally, the argument we have been making suggests a number of specific problems that appear to be highly promising lines for future research:

1. A study of the sociolinguistic socialization of "tomboys" to see how they combine male and female patterns of speech and interaction;

2. An examination of the conversational patterns of lesbians and gay men to see how these relate to the sex-related patterns of the dominant culture;

3. An examination of the conversational patterns of the elderly to see to what extent speech differences persist after power differences have become insignificant;

4. A study of children's cultural concepts for talking about speech and the ways these shape the acquisition of speech styles (for example, how does the concept of "bossiness" define a form of behavior which little girls must learn to recognize, then censure, and finally avoid?);

5. An examination of "assertiveness training" programs for women to see whether they are really teaching women the speaking skills that politically skillful men learn in boyhood or are merely teaching women how to act like bossy little girls or bullying little boys and not feel guilty about it.

We conclude this paper by reemphasizing three of the major ways in which we feel that an anthropological perspective on culture and social organization can prove useful for further research on differences between men's and women's speech.

First, an anthropological approach to culture and cultural rules forces us to reexamine the way we interpret what is going on in conversations. The rules for interpreting conversations are, after all, culturally determined. There may be more than one way of understanding what is happening in a particular conversation and we must be careful about the rules we use for interpreting cross-sex conversations, in which the two participants may not fully share their rules of conversational inference.

Second, a concern with the relation between cultural rules and their social contexts leads us to think seriously about differences in different kinds of talk, ways of categorizing interactional situations, and ways in which conversational patterns may function as strategies for dealing with specific aspects of one's social world. Different types of interaction lead to different ways of speaking. The rules for friendly conversation between equals are different from those for service encounters, for flirting, for teaching, or for polite formal interaction. And even within the apparently uniform domain of friendly interaction, we argue that there are systematic differences between men and women in the way friendship is defined and thus in the conversational strategies that result.

Third and finally, our analysis suggests a different way of thinking about the connection between the gender-related behavior of children and that of adults. Most discussions of sex-role socialization have been based on the premise that gender differences are greatest for adults and that these adult differences are learned gradually throughout childhood. Our analysis, on the other hand, would suggest that at least some aspects of behavior are most strongly gender- differentiated during childhood and that adult patterns of friendly interaction, for example, involve learning to overcome at least partially some of the gender-specific cultural patterns typical of childhood.

NOTES

1. The analogy between the sociolinguistic processes of dialect divergence and genderlect divergence was pointed out to us by Ron Macaulay.

2. In the strict sense of the term, "dozens" refers to a culturally specific form of stylized argument through the exchange of insults that has been extensively documented by a variety of students of American black culture and is most frequently practiced by boys in their teens and pre-teens. Recently folklorist Simon Bronner (1978) has made a convincing case for the existence of a highly similar but independently derived form of insult exchange known as "ranking," "mocks," or "cutting" among white American adolescents. What we find striking and worthy of note is the tendency for both black and white versions of the dozens to be practiced primarily by boys.

3. "Catches" are a form of verbal play in which the main speaker ends up tricking a member of his or her audience into a vulnerable or ridiculous position. In an article on the folklore of black children in South Philadelphia, Roger Abrahams (1963) distinguishes between catches which are purely verbal and tricks in which the second player is forced into a position of being not only verbally but also physically abused, as in the following example of a catch which is also a trick:

A. Adam and Eve and Pinch-Me-Tight
Went up the hill to spend the night.
Adam and Eve came down the hill.
Who was left?

B. Pinch-Me-Tight

[A pinches B]

What is significant about both catches and tricks is that they allow for the expression of playful aggression and that they produce a temporary hierarchical relation between a winner and loser, but invite the loser to attempt to get revenge by responding with a counter-trick.

4. We thank Kitty Julien for first pointing out to us the tendency of male friends to give advice to women who are not necessarily seeking it and Niyi Akinnaso for pointing out that the sex difference among Yoruba speakers in Nigeria in the way people respond verbally to the problems of others is similar to that among English speakers in the United States.

REFERENCES

Abrahams, R. D. 1963. The "Catch" in Negro Philadelphia. Keystone Folklore Quarterly 8(3):107–116.

Abrahams, R. D. 1975. Negotiating respect: patterns of presentation among black women. In *Women in Folklore*. C. R. Farrat, ed. Austin: University of Texas Press.

Abrahams, R. D. 1976. *Talking Black*. Rowley, Mass.: Newbury House.

Bauman, R. 1972. The La Have Island General Store: Sociability and verbal art in a Nova Scotia community. *Journal of American Folklore* 85:330–43.

Bronner, S. J. 1978. A Re-examining of white dozens. *Western Folklore* 37(2):118–28.

Brooks-Gunn, J. and Matthews, W. S. 1979. *He and She: How Children Develop Their Sex-Role Identity*. Englewood Cliffs, NJ: Prentice Hall.

Eder, D. and Hallinan, M. T. 1978. Sex differences in children's friendships. *American Sociological Review* 43: 237–50.

LANGUAGE

Faris, J. C. 1966. The dynamics of verbal exchange: A Newfoundland example. *Anthropologica* (Ottawa) 8(2): 235–48.

Fishman, P. M. 1978. Interaction: The work women do. *Social Problems* 25(4):397–406.

Goodwin, M. 1978. Conversational practices in a peer group of urban black children. Doctoral dissertation. University of Pennsylvania, Philadelphia.

Goodwin, M. 1980a. Directive-response speech sequences in girls' and boys' task activities. In *Women and Language in Literature and Society*. S. McConneil-Ginet, R. Borker, and N. Furman, eds. New York: Praeger.

Goodwin, M. 1980b. He-said-she-said: Formal cultural procedures for the construction of a gossip dispute activity. *American Ethnologist* 7(4): 674–95.

Gumperz, J. J. 1977. Sociocultural knowledge in conversational inference. In *Linguistics and Anthropology*. M. Savifie-Troike, ed. Washington DC: Georgetown University Press (Georgetown University Round Table on Languages and Linguistics), 1977.

Gumperz, J. J. 1978a. The conversational analysis of interethnic communication. In *Interethnic Communication*. E. Lamar Ross, ed. Athens, Ga.: University of Georgia Press.

Gumperz, J. J. 1978b. Dialect and conversational inference in urban communication. *Language in Society* 7(3):393–409.

Gumperz, J. J. 1979. The sociolinguistic basis of speech act theory. In *Speech Act Ten Years After*. J. Boyd and S. Fertara, eds. Milan: Versus.

Gumperz, J. J. 1982. *Discourse Strategies*. Cambridge: Cambridge University Press.

Gumperz, J. J., Agrawal, A., and Aulakh, G. 1977. Prosody, paralinguistics and contextualization in Indian English. Language Behavior Research Laboratory, typescript. University of California, Berkeley.

Gumperz, J. J. and Tannen, D. 1978. Individual and social differences in language use. *In Individual Differences in Language Ability and Language Behavior*. W. Wang and C. Fillmore, eds. New York: Academic Press.

Haas, A. 1979. The acquisition of genederlect. In *Language, Sex and Gender: Does La Différence Make a Difference?* J. Orasnu, M. Slater, and L. Adler, eds. *Annals of the New York Academy of Sciences* 327:101–13.

Hannerz, U. 1969. *Soulside*. New York: Columbia University Press.

Harding, S. 1975. Women and words in a Spanish village. In *Towards an Anthropology of Women*. R. Reiter, ed. New York: Monthly Review Press.

Hirschman, L. 1973. Female-male differences in conversational interaction. Paper presented at Linguistic Society of America, San Diego.

Jefferson, G. 1978. Sequential aspects of storytelling in conversation. In *Studies in the Organization of Conversation Interaction*. J. Schenker, ed. New York: Academic Press.

Kalcik S. 1975. "... Like Anne's gynecologist or the time I was almost raped": Personal narratives in women's rap groups. In *Women and Folklore*. C. R. Farrar, ed. Austin:University of Texas Press.

Lakoff, R. 1975. *Language and Women's Place*. New York: Harper and Row.

LeMasters, E. E. 1975. *Blue Collar Aristocrats: Life-Styles at a Working-Class Tavern*. Madison: University of Wisconsin Press.

Lever, J. 1976. Sex differences in the games children play. *Social Problems* 23:478–83.

Lever, J. 1978. Sex differences in the complexity of children's play and games. *American Sociological Review* 43:471–83.

Meditch, A. 1975. The development of sex-specific speech patterns in young children. *Anthropological Linguistics* 17:421–33.

Philipsen, G. 1975. Speaking "like a man" in Teamsterville: Cultural patterns of role enactment in an urban neighborhood. *Quarterly Journal of Speech* 61:13–22.

Sacks, H. 1974. An analysis of the course of a joke's telling in conversation. In *Explorations in the Ethnography of Speaking*. R. Bauman and J. Scherzer, eds. Cambridge: Cambridge University Press.

Savin-Williams, R C. 1976. The ethological study of dominance formation and maintenance in a group of human adolescents. *Child Development* 47:972–79.

Soskin, W. F and John, V. P. 1963. The study of spontaneous talk. In *The Stream of Behavior*. R. G. Barker, ed. New York: Appleton-Century-Croft.

Strodbeck, F L. and Mann, R. D. 1956. Sex role differentiation in jury deliberations. *Sociometry* 19:3–11.

West, C. 1979. Against our will: Male interruptions of females in cross-sex conversation. In *Language, Sex and Gender: Does La Différence Make a Difference?* J. Oran zanu, M. Slater and L. Adler, eds. *Annals of the New York Academy of Sciences* 327:81–100.

West, C. and Zimmerman, D. H. 1977. Women's place in everyday talk: Reflections on parent-child interaction. *Social Problems* 24(5):521–9.

Zimmerman, D. H. and West, C. 1975. Sex roles, interruptions, and silences in conversation. In *Language and Sex: Differences and Dominance*. B. Thorne and N. Henley, eds. Rowley, Mass.: Newbury House.

Daniel Maltz and Ruth Borker, 1982, "A Cultural Approach to Male-Female Miscommunication," in *Language and Social Identity*, John L. Gumperz, ed., pp. 196–216. New York: Cambridge University Press. Reprinted with the permission of Cambridge University Press.

LANGUAGE

E X E R C I S E

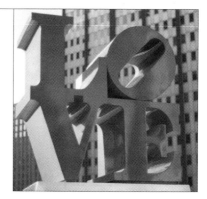

Name _____

Section _____

Date _____

EXERCISE 5.1: PLAYING TELEPHONE
To What Degree Are Oral Traditions Passed Down Intact?

Anthropologists conducting research must interact with the people they are studying, both participating in their practices and observing them from the outside. When an ethnographer studies people, she is faced with, among other challenges, an issue of trust. How much of what her informers tell her about their history is accurate? How might she resolve inaccuracies such that she does justice to the ethnographic record?

As you play the following game as a class and answer the questions afterward, think about how this exercise applies by analogy to the passage and mutation of oral histories through the generations:

1. Divide the class into two roughly equal groups.

2. The instructor creates a sentence, and writes it down on a piece of paper.

3. The instructor then shows the piece of paper to one person from each of the two groups.

4. Each person then whispers the sentence to the next person in their group. Members of opposite groups are not supposed to talk to each other.

5. The sentence continues to be passed down swiftly until the last person in each group receives the sentence and, without saying it out loud, writes it down on separate pieces of paper.

6. When both groups are done, compare each group's written sentence with the original one created by the instructor.

Some Tips
1. The more participants in this exercise, the better.

2. The instructor should create a sentence that is not overly long, but unusual enough so that students cannot guess what the sentence is and must rely solely on what they hear the person next to them whisper.

3. Aside from the whispering of the sentence from person to person, everyone should remain quiet while the game is being played.

4. The game should be played FAST! The faster the better.

(continued on the next page)

5. Nobody is allowed to ask for repetition or clarification of the sentence that they heard.

6. Try your best to listen closely and faithfully repeat what you hear to the next person.

Questions for Analysis and Food for Thought

1. Were the sentences that were recorded by the last member of each of the groups identical to the sentence created by the instructor? Why?

2. Do oral histories transcend generations unchanged? Why?

3. No matter how unusual the starting sentence, why couldn't it be heard and repeated perfectly for an infinite number of generations?

4. Were the resulting sentences the same for both groups? How could this be explained?

5. What, if anything, does this game tell us about human nature?

6. If oral histories change as they are passed down over time, to what degree can anthropologists trust the accuracy of what an informant tells them? Would we be better off conducting anthropology as "armchair anthropologists" who theorize but need not rely much on informants?

7. What tips or guidelines should anthropologists follow to make sure that their ethnographies are both realistic and accurate?

8. How might DNA be used to verify the accuracy of an oral history?

A Real-life Example

The Lemba of southern Africa are a group of black Jews, and are thought by some to be one of the "lost tribes" of Israel. They are an excellent example of how cultural and physical anthropology intersect. The Lemba case study illustrates how anthropologists can seek to verify the oral tradition of a group of people, in this case, through the use of DNA. As you follow the links below to information about the Lemba, think about some of the terms ("Sena," "Pusela," "Hadramut") of the Lemba's oral tradition, and whether or not their oral history has changed as it was passed down through the ages.

The Lemba Example:

On the Lemba, Y-Chromosome Genetic Markers, and Researcher Tudor Parfitt:

http://en.wikipedia.org/wiki/Lemba
http://www.pbs.org/wgbh/nova/israel/parfitt.html
http://www.soas.ac.uk/staff/staffinfo.cfm?contactid=184
http://www.home.nc.rr.com/arnbiient/site/ychromo.htm
http://www.pbs.org/wgbh/nova/israel/family.html
http://www.pbs.org/wgbh/nova/israel/familywave.html

"The Passing Down of Oral Traditions" exercise by Mark Gordon. Reprinted by permission.

Medical Vocabulary Knowledge Among Hospital Patients—
Julian Samora, Lyle Saunders, Richard F. Larson

"When I use a word," Humpty Dumpty said, "it means just what I choose it to mean, neither more nor less."
—Lewis Carroll

Some years ago, several nurses provided me with a list of expressions representing what patients either thought they heard staff say or conditions which they thought they themselves had. A selection from that list includes: "fireballs in the useless" (fibroids in the uterus), "smiling mighty Jesus" (spinal meningitis), "slipped-a-pippus" (slipped epiphysis), and a "strangulated unicorn" (?). Though in some ways humorous, these serve to illustrate misunderstanding between professionals and clients. The following very brief selection demonstrates how people speaking basically the same language may fail to communicate. While the patient appears to understand such words as *paraphernalia* and *catheterization*, her vocabulary is selective (as is everyone's). Communication fails. There is a tendency to emphasize communication problems between people who speak mutually unintelligible languages and to believe that such problems will disappear if people speak the same language. This naïve view of communication does not take into consideration the variety of differences that can exist within cultures.

I'll tell you something, a good one on me. When my first child was born the doctor—like I told you I think it would be nice if they would reduce the language to where a person with hardly no education could understand these people; but me, I'm so frank myself that I tell them, "Look, let's knock this thing down and let's speak English to me because I don't know what the devil you're talking about." And they always have; the doctors I've went to and those that seen my children have always been very nice about it. In other words, they knock it down to where it is just plain English to me. But this doctor kept coming in every day and asking, "Have you voided?" So I'd say, "No." So in comes the nurse with some paraphernalia that was scary. So I said, "What the devil are you going to do?" And she said, "I'm going to catheterize you, you haven't voided." Well of course I knew what catheterization was. I said, "You are going to play hell. I've peed every day since I've

been here." I said, "Is that what he said?" And she said, "Of course, Rusty, didn't you know?" And I said, "Well, of course why didn't he just ask me if I'd peed? I'd have told him."

Julian Samora, Lyle Saunders, and Richard F. Larson, 1961, "Medical Vocabulary Knowledge Among Patients," *Journal of Health and Human Behavior*, Vol. 2, p. 83.

Suite for Ebony and Phonics—
John R. Rickford

To James Baldwin, writing in 1979, it was "this passion, this skill…this incredible music." Toni Morrison, two years later, was impressed by its "five present tenses" and felt that "the worst of all possible things that could happen would be to lose that language." What these novelists were talking about was Ebonics, the informal speech of many African Americans, which rocketed to public attention a year ago this month [1996] after the Oakland School Board approved a resolution recognizing it as the primary language of African American students.

The reaction of most people across the country—in the media, at holiday gatherings, and on electronic bulletin boards—was overwhelmingly negative. In the flash flood of e-mail on America Online, Ebonics was described as "lazy English," "bastardized English," "poor grammar," and "fractured slang." Oakland's decision to recognize Ebonics and use it to facilitate mastery of Standard English also elicited superlatives of negativity: "ridiculous, ludicrous," "VERY, VERY STUPID," "a terrible mistake."

However, linguists—who study the sounds, words, and grammars of languages and dialects—though less rhapsodic about Ebonics than the novelists, were much more positive than the general public. Last January, at the annual meeting of the Linguistic Society of America, my colleagues and I unanimously approved a resolution describing Ebonics as "systematic and rule-governed like all natural speech varieties." Moreover, we agreed that the Oakland resolution was "linguistically and pedagogically sound."

Why do we linguists see the issue so differently from most other people? A founding principle of our science is that we describe *how* people talk; we don't judge how language should or should not be used. A second principle is that all languages, if they have enough speakers, have **dialects**— regional or social varieties that develop when people are separated by geographic or social barriers. And a third principle, vital for understanding linguists' reactions to the Ebonics controversy, is that all languages and dialects are systematic and rule-governed. Every human language and dialect that we have studied to date—and we have studied thousands—obeys distinct rules of grammar and pronunciation.

What this means, first of all, is that Ebonics is not slang. **Slang** refers just to a small set of new and usually short-lived words in the vocabulary of a dialect or language. Although Ebonics certainly has slang words—such as *chillin* ("relaxing") or *homey* ("close friend"), to pick two that have found wide dissemination by the media—its linguistic identity is described by distinctive patterns of pronunciation and grammar.

But is Ebonics a different language from English or a different dialect of English? Linguists tend to sidestep such questions, noting that the answers can depend on historical and political considerations. For instance, spoken Cantonese and Mandarin are mutually unintelligible, but they are usually regarded as "dialects" of Chinese because their speakers use the same writing system and see themselves as part of a common Chinese tradition. By contrast, although Norwegian and Swedish are so similar that their speakers can generally understand each other, they are usually regarded as different languages because their speakers are citizens of different countries. As for Ebonics, most linguists agree that Ebonics is more of a dialect of English than a separate language, because it shares many words and other features with other informal varieties of American English. And its speakers can easily communicate with speakers of other American English dialects.

Yet Ebonics is one of the most distinctive varieties of American English, differing from Standard English—the educated standard—in several ways. Consider, for instance, its verb tenses and aspects. ("Tense" refers to *when* an event occurs, "aspect" to *how* it occurs, whether habitual or on-going.) When Toni Morrison referred to the "five present tenses" of Ebonics, she probably had usages like these— each one different from Standard English—in mind:

1. He runnin. ("He is running.")

2. He be runnin. ("He is usually running.")

3. He be steady runnin. ("He is usually running in an intensive, sustained manner.")

4. He bin runnin. ("He has been running.")

5. He BIN runnin. ("He has been running for a long time and still is.")

In Standard English, the distinction between habitual or nonhabitual events can be expressed only with adverbs like "usually." Of course, there are also simple present tense forms, such as "he runs," for habitual events, but they do not carry the meaning of an ongoing action, because they lack the "-ing" suffix. Note too that "bin" in example 4 is unstressed while "BIN" in example 5 is stressed. The former can usually be understood by non-Ebonics speakers as equivalent to "has been" with the "has" deleted, but the stressed BIN form can be badly misunderstood. Years ago, I presented the Ebonics sentence "She BIN married" to 25 whites and 25 African Americans from various parts of the United States and asked them if they understood the speaker to be still married or not. While 23 of the African Americans said yes, only 8 of the whites gave the correct answer. (In real life a misunderstanding like this could be disastrous!)

Word pronunciation is another distinctive aspect of dialects, and the regularity of these differences can be very subtle. Most of the "rules" we follow when speaking Standard English are obeyed unconsciously. Take for instance English plurals. Although grammar books tell us that we add "s" to a word to form a regular English plural, as in "cats" and "dogs," that's true only for writing. In speech, what we actually add in the case of "cat" is an s sound; in the case of "dog" we add z. The difference is that s is voiceless, with the vocal cords spread apart, while z is voiced, with the vocal cords held closely together and noisily vibrating.

Now, how do you know whether to add s or z to form a plural when you're speaking? Easy. If the word ends in a voiceless consonant, like "t," add voiceless s. If the word ends in a voiced consonant, like "g," add voiced z. Since all vowels are voiced, if the word ends in a vowel, like "tree," add z. Because we spell both plural endings with "s," we're not aware that English speakers make this systematic difference every day, and I'll bet your English teacher never told you about voiced and voiceless plurals. But you follow the "rules" for using them anyway, and anyone who doesn't—for instance, someone who says "bookz"—strikes an English speaker as sounding funny.

One reason people might regard Ebonics as "lazy English" is its tendency to omit consonants at the ends of words—especially if they come after another consonant, as in "tes(t)" and "han(d)." But if one were just being lazy or cussed or both, why not also leave out the final consonant in a word like "pant"? This is not permitted in Ebonics; the "rules" of the dialect do not allow the deletion of the second consonant at the end of a word unless both consonants are either voiceless as with "st," or voiced, as with "nd." In the case of "pant," the final "t" is voiceless, but the preceding "n" is voiced, so the consonants are both spoken. In short, the manner in which Ebonics differs from Standard English is highly ordered; it is no more lazy English than Italian is lazy Latin. Only by carefully analyzing each dialect can we appreciate the complex rules that native speakers follow effortlessly and unconsciously in their daily lives.

Who speaks Ebonics? If we made a list of all the ways in which the pronunciation and grammar of Ebonics differ from Standard English, we probably couldn't find anyone who always uses all of them. While its features are found most commonly among African Americans (*Ebonics* is itself derived from "ebony" and "phonics," meaning "black sounds"), not all African Americans speak it. The features of Ebonics, especially the distinctive tenses, are more common among working-class than among middle-class speakers, among adolescents than among the middle-aged, and in informal contexts (a conversation on the street) rather than formal ones (a sermon at church) or writing.

The genesis of Ebonics lies in the distinctive cultural background and relative isolation of African Americans, which originated in the slaveholding South. But contemporary social networks, too, influence who uses Ebonics. For example, lawyers and doctors and their families are more likely to have more contact with Standard English

speakers—in schools, work, and neighborhoods—than do blue-collar workers and the unemployed. Language can also be used to reinforce a sense of community. Working-class speakers, and adolescents in particular often embrace Ebonics features as markers of African American identity, while middle-class speakers (in public at least) tend to eschew them.

Some Ebonics features are shared with other vernacular varieties of English, especially Southern white dialects, many of which have been influenced by the heavy concentration of African Americans in the South. And a lot of African American slang has "crossed over" to white and other ethnic groups. Expressions like "givin five" ("slapping palms in agreement or congratulation") and "Whassup?" are so widespread in American culture that many people don't realize they originated in the African American community. Older, nonslang words have also originated in imported African words. *Tote*, for example, comes from the Kikongo word for "carry," *tota*, and *hip* comes from the Wolof word *hipi*, to "be aware." However, some of the distinctive verb forms in Ebonics—he run, he be runnin, he BIN runnin—are rarer or non-existent in white vernaculars.

How did Ebonics arise? The Oakland School Board's proposal alluded to the Niger-Congo roots of Ebonics, but the extent of that contribution is not at all clear. What we do know is that the ancestors of most African Americans came to this country as slaves. They first arrived in Jamestown in 1619, and a steady stream continued to arrive until at least 1808, when the slave trade ended, at least officially. Like the forebears of many other Americans, these waves of African "immigrants" spoke languages other than English. Their languages were from the Niger-Congo language family, especially the West Atlantic, Mande, and Kwa subgroups spoken from Senegal and Gambia to the Cameroons, and the Bantu subgroup spoken farther south. Arriving in an American milieu in which English was dominant, the slaves learned English. But how quickly and completely they did so and with how much influence from their African languages are matters of dispute among linguists.

The Afrocentric view is that most of the distinctive features of Ebonics represent imports from Africa. As West African slaves acquired English, they restructured it according to the patterns of Niger-Congo languages. In this view,

LANGUAGE

Ebonics simplifies consonant clusters at the ends of words and doesn't use linking verbs like "is" and "are"—as in, for example, "he happy"—because these features are generally absent from Niger-Congo languages. Verbal forms like habitual "be" and BIN referring to a remote past, it is argued, crop up in Ebonics because these kinds of tenses occur in Niger-Congo languages.

Most Afrocentrists, however, don't cite a particular West African language source. Languages in the Niger-Congo family vary enormously, and some historically significant Niger-Congo languages don't show these forms. For instance, while Yoruba, a major language for many West Africans sold into slavery, does indeed lack a linking verb like "is" for some adjectival constructions, it has another linking verb for other adjectives. And it has *six* other linking verbs for nonadjectival constructions, where English would use "is" or "are." Moreover, features like dropping final consonants can be found in some vernaculars in England that had little or no West African influence. Although many linguists acknowledge continuing African influences in some Ebonics and American English words, they want more proof of its influence on Ebonics pronunciation and grammar.

A second view, the Eurocentric—or dialectologist—view, is that African slaves learned English from white settlers, and that they did so relatively quickly and successfully, retaining little trace of their African linguistic heritage. Vernacular, or non-Standard features of Ebonics, including omitting final consonants and habitual "be," are seen as imports from dialects spoken by colonial English, Irish, or Scotch-Irish settlers, many of whom were indentured servants. Or they may be features that emerged in the twentieth century after African Americans became more isolated in urban ghettos. (Use of habitual "be," for example, is more common in urban than in rural areas.) However, as with Afrocentric arguments, we still don't have enough historical details to settle the question. Crucial Ebonics features, such as the absence of linking "is," appear to be rare or nonexistent in these early settler dialects, so they're unlikely to have been the source. Furthermore, although the scenario posited by this view is possible, it seems unlikely. Yes, African American slaves and whites sometimes worked alongside each other in households and fields. And yes the number of African slaves was so low, especially in the early colonial period, that distinctive African American dialects may not have formed. But the assumption that slaves rapidly and successfully acquired the dialects of the whites around them requires a rosier view of their relationship than the historical record and contemporary evidence suggest.

A third view, the creolist view, is that many African slaves, in acquiring English, developed a pidgin language—a simplified fusion of English and African languages—from which Ebonics evolved. Native to none of its speakers, a **pidgin** is a mixed language, incorporating elements of its users' native languages but with less complex grammar and fewer words than either parent language. A pidgin language emerges to facilitate communication between speakers who do not share a language; it becomes a creole language when it takes root and becomes the primary tongue among its users. This often occurs among the children of pidgin speakers—the vocabulary of the language expands, and the simple grammar is fleshed out. But the creole still remains simpler in some aspects than the original languages. Most Creoles, for instance, don't use suffixes to mark tense ("he walk*ed*") plurals ("boys"), or possession ("John's house").

Creole languages are particularly common on the islands of the Caribbean and the Pacific, where large plantations brought together huge groups of slaves or indentured laborers. The native languages of these workers were radically different from the native tongues of the small groups of European colonizers and settlers, and under such conditions, with minimal access to European speakers, new, restructured varieties like Haitian Creole French and Jamaican Creole English arose. These languages do show African influence, as the Afrocentric theory would predict, but their speakers may have simplified existing patterns in African languages by eliminating more complex alternatives; like the seven linking verbs of Yoruba I mentioned earlier.

Within the United States African Americans speak one well-established English creole, Gullah. It is spoken on the Sea Islands off the coast of South Carolina and Georgia, where African Americans at one time constituted 80 to 90 percent of the local population in places. When I researched one of the South Carolina Sea Islands some years ago, I recorded the following creole sentences. They sound much like Caribbean Creole English today:

1. E. M. run an gone to Suzie house. ("E. M. went running to Suzie's house.")

2. But I does go to see people when they sick. ("But I usually go to see people when they are sick.")

3. De mill bin to Bluffton dem time. ("The mill was in Bluffton in those days.") Note the creole traits: the first sentence lacks the past tense and the possessive form; the second sentence lacks the linking verb "are" and includes the habitual "does"; the last sentence uses unstressed "bin" for past tense and "dem time" to refer to a plural without using an *s*.

What about creole origins for Ebonics? Creole speech might have been introduced to the American colonies through the large numbers of slaves imported from the colonies of Jamaica and Barbados, where Creoles were common. In these regions the percentage of Africans ran from 65 to 90 percent. And some slaves who came directly from Africa may have brought with them pidgins or creoles that developed around West African trading forts. It's also possible that some creole varieties—apart from well-known cases like Gullah—might have developed on American soil.

This would have been less likely in the northern colonies, where blacks were a very small percentage of the population. But blacks were much more concentrated in the South, making up 61 percent of the population in South Carolina and 40 percent overall in the South. Observations by travelers and commentators in the eighteenth and nineteenth centuries record creole-like features in African American speech. Even today, certain features of Ebonics, like the absence of the linking verbs "is" and "are," are widespread in Gullah and Caribbean English creoles but rare or nonexistent in British dialects.

My own view is that the creolist hypothesis incorporates the strengths of the other hypotheses and avoids their weaknesses. But we linguists may never be able to settle that particular issue one way or another. What we can settle on is the unique identity of Ebonics as an English dialect.

So what does all this scholarship have to do with the Oakland School Board's proposal? Some readers might be fuming that it's one thing to identify Ebonics as a dialect and quite another to promote its usage. Don't linguists realize that nonstandard dialects are stigmatized in the larger society, and that Ebonics speakers who cannot shift to Standard English are less likely to do well in school and on the job front? Well, yes. The resolution we put forward last January in fact stated that "there are benefits in acquiring Standard English." But there is experimental evidence both from the United States and Europe that mastering the standard language might be easier if the differences in the student vernacular and Standard English were made explicit rather than entirely ignored.

To give only one example: At Aurora University, outside Chicago, inner-city African American students were taught by an approach that contrasted Standard English and Ebonics features through explicit instruction and drills. After eleven weeks, this group showed a 59 percent reduction in their use of Ebonics features in their Standard English writing. But a control group taught by conventional methods showed an 8.5 percent increase in such features.

This is the technique the Oakland School Board was promoting in its resolution last December. The approach is not new; it is part of the 16-year-old Standard English Proficiency Program, which is being used in some 300 California schools. Since the media uproar over its original proposal, the Oakland School Board has clarified its intent: the point is not to teach Ebonics as a distinct language but to use it as a tool to increase mastery of Standard English among Ebonics speakers. The support of linguists for this approach may strike nonlinguists as unorthodox, but that is where our principles—and the evidence—lead us.

From John R. Rickford, "Suite for Ebony and Phonics," *Discover*, December 1997, Vol. 18. Reprinted by permission.

LANGUAGE

Sociolinguistics

The branch of linguistic anthropology that investigates how language and culture are related and how language is used in different social contexts is referred to as **sociolinguistics**. Sociolinguists concentrate on variations in language use, depending upon the relationship between language and social structure. We can tell about the social relationships between two people based upon the language they use to communicate thoughts. The analysis of terms of address can be particularly useful for explanation purposes. Professor Arenson, for example, could be addressed as Dr. Arenson, Ma'am, Lauren, Doc, Professor, Kobe's mom, Marshall's wife, or "hey you"—depending on who is doing the addressing. We expect that the term of address chosen would reflect the relative social status of the two parties. That is, in American society, the reciprocal use of first names indicates an informal relationship between equals, where the reciprocal use of last names is reserved for more formal situations. The nonreciprocal use of first name and titles is used among people of unequal status. ("Hey you" is not a polite way to call for anyone!)

Sociocultural linguists have made an important contribution in developing new methods for teaching children to read in the United States. In 1979, a federal court in Ann Arbor, Michigan, concluded that black students from a public elementary school were being denied their civil rights because they were not being taught to read, write, and speak Standard English as an alternative to their dialect of **Black English Vernacular** (BEV). The judge presiding over the case ruled that because the school system failed to recognize and use BEV as the basis for teaching Standard English, these children were put at a disadvantage for succeeding in school and, consequently, in life.

This decision rested strongly on establishing the basic premise that BEV actually exists as a bona fide language. While BEV was popularly held, and was implicitly built into the reading curriculum in Ann Arbor public schools, the language of African-American students was regarded as nothing more than slang, street talk, or a pathological form of Standard English. But as William Labov, the sociolinguist from the University of Pennsylvania, was able to establish to the satisfaction of the court, BEV is a linguistic system with its own grammatical rules, phonology (sounds), and semantics. Thus, Labov's testimony demonstrated that the differences that exist between BEV and Standard English are governed by linguistic rules rather than being the result of errors in Standard English. Labov stressed this point by demonstrating that BEV was not merely spoken in this region of the country, but the same as spoken by African-American children in New York, Washington, Chicago, and Los Angeles.

On the basis of Labov's testimony, the federal court concluded that language is a vital link between the child and the education that he/she receives. Children who speak the same language as the language of instruction, learn more effectively than those who speak a nonstandard version of the language of instruction. It should be pointed out that the court did not rule that children had to be taught in BEV. Rather, the court ordered that the local schools were to acknowledge the fact that language used at home and in the community can pose a barrier to student learning when teachers fail to recognize it, understand it, and incorporate it into their instructional methods. (A basic tenet held in favor by bilingual educators.)

In short, the judge's ruling ordered the Ann Arbor schools to develop strategies to inform teachers how best to teach Standard English to students who enter school speaking BEV.

Here, then, is a situation in which the data and testimony from a linguistic anthropologist made important contributions to both civil rights litigation and classroom instruction.

The spoken word can be of importance in determining who we are and in labeling ourselves as different from others. Again, the label of **ethnicity** exemplifies this point.

País de mis sueños: Reflections on Ethnic Labels, Dichotomies, and Ritual Interactions—
Gisela Ernst

Ethnic categorization and labeling are questioned as abstractions of either reality or accurate features of the persons or groups to which these labels are attached. The author explores the polarizing and negative applications of English language qualifiers relating to "race" and ethnicity, viewing them as system-maintaining devices in service to the hierarchical structure of American society. The essay concludes with some of Ernst's impressions of American friendliness viewed as ritual.

Gisela Ernst grew up in Lima, Peru, coming to the United States in the 1980s to study sociolinguistics and anthropology at the University of Florida. She is an assistant professor in the College of Education, Department of Teaching and Learning at Washington State University.

Some of the most interesting questions are raised by the study of words whose job it is to make things fuzzier or less fuzzy. (Lakoff 1972:195)

Like Saint Paul, I have seen the light. It happened while I was finishing my master's degree, when I was introduced to sociolinguistics; what I learned about language, language use, and culture literally changed the direction of my career. I had found an area of study that allowed me to grapple with the interplay of linguistic, social, and cultural factors in human communication. During my doctoral program at the University of Florida, I had the opportunity to think more deeply about why people use language the way they use it and why language can be clear and precise. At the same time, language often can be characterized by vagueness, ambiguity, and imprecision.

Perhaps nowhere is the interplay of language and culture more "fuzzy" (to use Lakoff's term) than in the labels we use to define ourselves and others. In this chapter I will share some of my experiences, and my subsequent reflections upon those experiences, with the use of labels and terms used to refer to a person's ethnic, cultural, and racial background. Within this context I will share my feelings about, and explore the connotations of, the made-in-the-U.S.A. label "Hispanic." Then I will explore the use of dichotomies and negative constructions in English. These

structures will be better understood by contrasting them to Spanish. This comparison will illustrate that the existence in English of extreme dichotomies can often influence how native English speakers voice and manage their relations with others. Finally, I would like to illustrate how some of us "foreigners" can often be taken in by the friendliness of people in the United States.

ETHNIC LABELS: "I CAME AS A PERUVIAN AND IMMEDIATELY BECAME A HISPANIC"

I was a fortunate child who grew up in Lima, Peru. I was brought up in an upper-middle class environment, attended private schools, lived in a handsome neighborhood, and was surrounded by a protected haven of mostly well-educated friends and acquaintances. Like many others in Peru, I was a mestiza, the daughter of an Austrian father and a Peruvian mother, the product of an encounter of two continents, of two races. Like many others, I had European names and Peruvian looks, spoke more than one language, and was proud to be a Peruvian who also had knowledge about and appreciation for her father's homeland.

In spite of my good fortune, I also encountered my share of problems, sorrow, and broken dreams. This is why, like many others who leave their familiar lands in search of better lives, I too left mine in search of *el país de mis sueños* (the land of my dreams). I had little money but lots of hope, confidence, and a clear sense of national identity as a Peruvian woman. Therefore I set off happily, in June of 1985, unaware of the need for "clear" labels to identify my ethnicity, race, and culture. Soon after my arrival in Florida, I did what many other foreign students have to do if they want to get into graduate school in the United States: fill out multiple forms. Throughout this process I discovered two things: first, the momentousness of the written word in this society, and second, the importance of race and ethnicity as forms of social classification in the United States. It quickly dawned on me that my avowed national identity was of little relevance to the society at large. I realized that I was seldom considered a Peruvian but was most often either "Hispanic," "legal alien," "Latino," "Spanish-speaking," "South American," "Spanish," or, what is worse, "Other"! Within the context of official forms, institutionalized inquiries, and government requirements, I was faced with having to find the appropriate label to describe my nationality, culture, and background. The following question about ethnic origin will help illustrate my feeling of dubiousness, doubtfulness, and diffidence as I attempted to answer what, for some, might be just another question on a form.

Ethnic Origin (mark one)

___White (not Hispanic origin)
___Asian or Pacific Islanders
___Black (not Hispanic origin)
___American Indian or Alaskan Native
___Hispanic
___Other

Not only did I find the emphasis on racial categorizations in the United States perplexing, but I felt that the selection offered was limited and problematic. I felt that I had to summarize my nationality, ethnicity, upbringing, language, culture—in sum, my whole existence—in one fixed and unappealing label. I was not only appalled but also confused. For example, given the categories mentioned above, I could have marked the first option since I appeared "white" in both of my passports (Peruvian and Austrian). Yet, at the same time, that option would be incorrect since I am also what could be called "Hispanic."

I thought about marking "American Indian" or "Alaskan Native" since, in fact, I was born in (South) America and there is some Indian blood in my mother's ancestry (even though she might not want to admit to it). But these labels did not reflect all my other influences: my mother's descent from Spain, my father's Austrian and German blood, the fact that I do not speak the languages nor share the cultures of Peruvian Indians. Because I had to use my European passport, on which I appeared as "white" (it included my visa and my "alien" number), I felt that no available categories encompassed my national and cultural identity.

My confusion grew as the smorgasbord of categories changed—from form to form and from institution to institution, and I often found myself spending considerable time trying to select the most appropriate label. After several months and many more forms, I opted to leave the question unmarked (when possible) or to mark "Other" (if there was such an option). On some occasions, depending on my mood, when the question asked for "race," I would write "Cocker Spaniel," "German Shepherd," or "un-

known" on the blank line next to "Other." Because there often was an indication that this information was optional, I did not feel any remorse for perhaps skewing some demographic data. On the contrary, this simple act provided me with an opportunity to show my dissent toward questions that limited my individuality to a generic label.

Do the classifications recognized by the U.S. Census Bureau offer us a useful way of understanding our national and cultural experiences? Do terms such as *black*, *Asian American*, *Hispanic* have any real substance to them, or are they the creation of media czars and political impresarios? Let's examine the official definition of Hispanic (according to the 1990 U.S. census):

> A person is of Spanish/Hispanic origin if the person's origin (ancestry) is Mexican, Mexican-American, Chicano, Puerto Rican, Dominican, Ecuadorian, Guatemalan, Honduran, Nicaraguan, Peruvian, Salvadoran; from other Spanish-speaking countries of the Caribbean or Central or South America; or from Spain.

The ethnic label "Hispanic" began to be used heavily by state agencies in the early 1970s to refer to all people in this country whose ancestry is predominantly from one or more Spanish-speaking countries. As a result, millions of people of a variety of national and cultural backgrounds are put into a single arbitrary category. No allowances are made for our varied racial, linguistic, and national experiences, nor for whether we are recent immigrants, long-time residents, or belong to an associated territory. Furthermore, using "Hispanic" to refer to those who are of Spanish-speaking origin can be problematic in that it excludes a considerable sector of the population in Latin America for whom Spanish is not a first language. Many "Hispanic" immigrants come from regions that are not necessarily predominantly Spanish. This is the case of those who speak Nahuatl and Tiwa in Indian villages in Mexico; Kanjobal and Jacaltec in the southern part of Guatemala; Quechua and Aymara in the highlands of Peru and Bolivia; Guarani, Chulupi, and Mascoi in the Chaco region of Paraguay; Tukano and Tuyukaf in the swamps of Venezuela and Colombia; and others from predominantly non-Spanish-speaking regions. Thus, given that their native language may not be Spanish, it is inaccurate to call these people of "Spanish-speaking origin."

Furthermore, as Berkeley social scientist Carlos Muñoz writes, the term Hispanic is derived from *Hispania*, which was the name the Romans gave to the Iberian peninsula, most of which became Spain, and "implicitly emphasizes the white European culture of Spain at the expense of the non-white cultures that have profoundly shaped the experience of all Latin Americans" through its refusal to acknowledge "the non-white indigenous cultures of the Americas, Africa, and Asia, which historically have produced multicultural and multiracial peoples in Latin America and the United States" (1989: 11). It is a term that ignores the complexities within and throughout these various groups.

DICHOTOMIES AND NEGATIVE CONSTRUCTIONS: "I DIDN'T REALIZE I WAS A MINORITY UNTIL I CAME TO THE UNITED STATES."

As mentioned earlier, I always felt special and different among my fellow Peruvians. However, it was only until I came to this country that a label for being different was assigned to me: I became a **minority**! I must say that being labeled as such has not always been that bad; on occasion I have received some special treatment just because I fit the category of minority. However, the term *minority* has heavy connotations, especially when we realize that it signifies differences from those who make up the majority in this county. In other words, my status was assigned to me because I am not part of the majority, so therefore I should be part of the minority. The term minority, like other terms used to identify people's racial, ethnic, and cultural backgrounds, is defined in opposition to another term.

The same can be said about the term *Hispanic*. In contemporary discourse the term *Hispanic* has come to be used as a nonwhite racial designation. It is not unusual to read or hear people use the terms *whites*, *blacks*, and *Hispanics* as if they were mutually exclusive when, in fact, the 1990 census states that 52 percent of Hispanics identify themselves as white, 3 percent as black, and 43 percent as "other race."

The English language is constructed as a system of differences organized as extreme dichotomies—white/black, majority/minority, good/bad, dark/fair, and so on. The existence of this polarization influences how English speakers manage their relations with others. Consider the case of qualifiers or adjectives. The heavy emphasis on opposites often compels speakers of English to use one of two opposite adjectives when formulating questions. As a result,

people in the United States commonly use evaluative terms in questions and descriptions, and find it easier to be critical rather than positive or neutral. For example, let's compare pairs of adjectives in English and in Spanish:

English		*Spanish*	
old	young	viejo	joven
long	short	largo	corto
far	near	cerca	lejos

At first, it may seem as if both the English and Spanish pairs contain words that are opposite in meaning but equal in their power to describe a point on a continuum. However, this is not the case. Consider how the English adjectives are used in asking questions: "How old is he?" "How long is that ruler?" and "How far do we have to go?" Questions are not phrased using the secondary term, as in "How young is he?" (unless in reference to a baby or small child), "How short is that ruler?" and "How near do we have to go?" In all of these questions one of the terms is designated as the defining term—for age, *old*; for size, *long*; for distance, *far*.

To the Spanish speaker, these same dichotomies do not have the same dependent hierarchy; rather, these pairs enjoy symmetry. This weaker polarization of Spanish pairs is evident in the way questions are phrased. In Spanish, "How old is he?" becomes "*Qué edad tiene él?*" which can be literally translated as "What is his age?" The question "How long is that ruler?" becomes "*Cuanto mide esa regla?*"—that is, "What's the measurement of that ruler?"—and so on. In Spanish, the emphasis is placed on the middle ground of the continuum rather than on one of its ends.

Thus, one important aspect of opposing adjectives in English is that the primary term appears as the defining term or the norm of cultural meaning, while the secondary term is much more specific or derives its meaning from its relation to the first one. Examples of the "good-bad" dichotomy help to illustrate this point. If you ask a friend to help you with a new software program, you will probably say, "How good are you with MacMisha 5.1?" rather than "How bad are you with MacMisha 5.1?" That is, the use of the term good reflects a more general qualifier, while the use of the term bad already suggests that something is not good; thus, this latter term is more specific (in a negative sense).

This same polarity can be applied to some of the qualifiers used in discussing issues of race and ethnicity. For example, in the case of pairs of labels, as in white/black, majority/minority, resident/nonresident, white/colored, American/other, the defining term of the norm is given by the primary term; the secondary term represents what is different, alien, or abnormal.

The negative precision of English qualifiers yields a linguistic base for qualifying as negative whatever appears to be different. Thus, the labels and distinctions made among different ethnic and racial groups perpetuate a hierarchical system where some groups are the norm while the others, by default, do not fit the norm.

RITUAL INTERACTIONS: "PEOPLE ARE INCREDIBLY FRIENDLY!"

My brother, who recently visited me from Peru, shared with me his thoughts about American friendliness after spending two days wandering around a large northwestern city. He was taken aback by the Pacific Northwest because he found people to be "incredibly friendly." He went on to say that during his three-week stay in this part of the country, a number of people on the street, on the road, and in the parks had smiled or said "hello" to him. He found it "kind of strange because you just don't see that in Lima, New York, Vienna, or Paris." I was a bit taken aback myself when I heard the story, thinking to myself, "Is the difference tangible?" After pondering a moment, I answered my own questions, "Absolutely!" There's a unique, friendly spirit you find throughout the Pacific Northwest. I think we sometimes lose sight of that fact. When you live something every day, there's a chance you'll start taking it for granted. My brother's comments were somewhat of a wake-up call for me and reminded me of my first months in the United States.

Although at that time I was in northern Florida, I can recall having similar feelings about this unusual kind of friendliness. I clearly remember feeling incredibly special when someone would welcome me to the town, ask me how I was feeling, and wish me a pleasant day. Furthermore, I still remember how shocked I was when an auto mechanic spent almost two hours trying to install a tiny plastic hook in the door of my 1966 VW bug and charged me only $1.50 for the part. And, in perhaps the most startling demonstration of American "friendliness," I vividly recall how, just two months after my arrival in this country, a smiling police

officer said, "Welcome to America" after she gave me two (undeserved, I must add) traffic tickets.

Instances like these remind me of an incident recounted by British-born journalist Henry Fairlie in an article entitled "Why I Love America":

> One spring day, shortly after my arrival, I was walking down the long, broad street of a suburb, with its sweeping front lawns (all that space), its tall trees (all that sky), and its clumps of azaleas (all that color). The only other person on the street was a small boy on a tricycle. As I passed him, he said "Hi"— like that. No four-year-old boy had ever addressed me without an introduction before. Yet here was this one, with his cheerful "Hi!" Recovering from the culture shock, I tried to look down stonily at his flaxen head, but instead, involuntarily, I found myself saying in return: "Well—hi!" He pedaled off, apparently satisfied. He had begun my Americanization. (1983:12)

For Fairlie the word "Hi!" had an important meaning:

> (I come from a country where one can tell someone's class by how they say "Hallo!" or "Hello!" or "Hullo," or whether they say it at all.) But [in America] anyone can say "Hi!" Anyone does.

Like my brother and Henry Fairlie, I was also very impressed with the friendliness of people in this part of the globe, in particular the friendliness and concern of store clerks and waiters, who would often introduce themselves by their first names and treat me in a casual, friendly manner, even asking how I was feeling today. I was really taken by this caring manner. I remember thinking, How can you not feel special in this great nation if everyone is always trying to see if you are okay? In Lima, where everyone is in a hurry (and sometimes trying to take advantage of others), store clerks and waiters barely say "thank you," if they speak to you at all. And of course, as a customer, you would not spend time chatting or exchanging greetings with those who are in such unsuccessful positions.

One day, however, I was struck by a somewhat sad discovery: What I thought was true concern and friendliness was just a ritual interaction. On that day, I had just learned that Max, my roommate's Golden Retriever, was at a veterinary hospital; he had been run over by a car. On my way home, I stopped by the grocery store to get some milk. As on other days, a friendly clerk checked my groceries, and when she asked me, "How are you?" I responded, "A bit sad." To my surprise, the friendly clerk said, "Great! Have a nice day." After a few seconds of puzzlement, I grabbed my paper sack and left the store. Later, my roommate, a native Floridian, explained that this type of greeting was routine and that stores often require their employees to display "extreme friendliness" with customers. It was only after this explanation that I realized that the caring tone used by clerks and others working with the public was routine chat, part of a ritual exchange.

Ritual exchanges such as "How are you?" "I'm fine, thank you," "Nice meeting you," "Hope you have a nice day," and other similar phrases are, like any ritual exchange, more about form than substance. In other words, questions and answers are (or should be) the same, regardless of the participants in the interactions and their feelings. In the above incident, even though I responded candidly with an unscripted answer to the customary "How are you" questions, I got a conventional short and scripted answer.

The brevity and formulaic aspects of these ritual exchanges, I believe, have little to do with whether people are friendly or not. Rather, this behavior might be related to an informal, egalitarian approach to others characteristic of American culture. It might also have to do with the brevity, informality, and practicality that characterizes the American style of communication (which, by the way, reminds me of the typical monosyllabic answers that I receive from my students when I ask even complex questions: "Sure," "OK," or "Nope").

Ritual interactions, like many other aspects of language and communication, vary from culture to culture and from country to country. This becomes evident when contrasting the little and often impersonal ritual exchanges of Americans with the long and personal ritual interactions of Peruvians. In Peru, ritual exchanges like those mentioned above are not as common as in the United States. When they do occur, however, one generally asks about family members' health. On these occasions, one needs to be accurate in one's questioning and attentive in one's listening, not only in terms of asking about the appropriate family members (for instance, not asking a widow about her husband's health), but also in relation to the substance of the answer (for example, showing some empathy when someone mentions an illness in the family).

SOME FINAL THOUGHTS

The study of communication and miscommunication across cultures is a relatively new area of research and one that holds much promise in terms of what it can teach us about language and intercultural communication. In this piece I have shared my experiences and reflections about the powerful role played by some terms and ethnic labels in the construction of people's social identity. In addition, I have also discussed some aspects of face-to-face interaction that vary from culture to culture and, as in the case of ritual interactions, provide fertile ground for miscommunication. My intent has been not only to illustrate how individual misunderstandings emerge but also to signal how these interactional processes reproduce and reinforce larger patterns within a society.

All in all, my years in the United States have for the most part unfolded like a dream. Sure, I encountered some problems, misunderstandings, and barriers, and often I had to adjust my expectations and appeal to my flexibility in order to keep going. But then, that is life. I am still learning about how to survive in this, my new home, and in the process I am trying to figure out why we use language the way we use it and why language can make things fuzzier and or less fuzzy.

ACKNOWLEDGMENTS

I am grateful to Professors Cynthia Wallat at Florida State and Ginger Weade and Allan Bums at the University of Florida, who introduced me to the study of sociolinguistics. Appreciation is also due to Kern Richard, David Slavit, and Elsa Statzner for feedback on drafts of this essay.

NOTE

1. Ethnic labels, like all names, are constructs, abstractions of a reality. In this respect, social scientist Suzanne Oboler (1995) argues that perhaps the inevitable use of ethnic labels includes singling out particular socially constructed attributes, whether related to race, gender, class, or language. The attributes are assigned to be common to the group's members and used to homogenize the group-regardless of whether this designation corresponds to the reality of the group to whom the label is attached.

LANGUAGE

REFERENCES

Fairlie, H. 1983. Why I Love America. *The New Republic*, July 4, 1983, p. 12.

Lakoff, C. 1972. Hedges: A Study in Meaning Criteria and the Logic of Fuzzy Concepts. In *Chicago Linguistic Society Papers*. Chicago: Chicago Linguistic Society.

Muñoz, C. 1989. *Youth, Identity, Power*. London: Verso.

Oboler, S. 1995. *Ethnic Labels, Latino Lives: Identity and the Politics of (Re)presentation in the United States*. Minneapolis: University of Minnesota Press.

From Gisela Ernst-Slavit, 1998, "País de mis sueños: Reflections of Ethnic Labels, Dichotomies, and Racial Interactions," *Distant Mirrors: America as a Foreign Culture*, 2nd ed., by Philip R. DeVita and James D. Armstrong, pp. 102–109. Wadsworth Publishing. Reprinted by permission.

Nonverbal Communication

While the spoken word is of great significance to the cultural anthropologist, we also learn a tremendous amount of information through nonverbal cues. **Nonverbal communication** is important because it helps us to interpret linguistic messages and often carries messages of its own. It has been hypothesized that approximately 70 percent of all messages sent and received by humans are nonverbal in nature.

Like the spoken language, nonverbal forms of communication are learned and vary from one culture to the next. To illustrate, the hand gesture of making a circle with a thumb and forefinger, which means OK in the United States, signifies "money" in Japan, indicates "worthlessness" or "zero" in France, and can be construed as a sexual insult in parts of South America. Thus, cross-cultural misunderstandings can occur when the same nonverbal cue has different meanings.

Humans (as do other primate species) communicate without words in a number of important ways, including hand gestures, facial expressions, eye contact, touching (grooming), space usage, scents, gait and stance. We, as humans, often look to photographs in order to study the meaning of beauty in other cultures and to learn about acceptable ideals in societies other than our own. The cultural meaning of beauty, social status, acceptable behaviors, and ceremonial acts can often be visually cued through photographs.

The anthropologist Richard Scaglion is fond of telling the story of his friend, a member of the Abelam tribe of Papua New Guinea, who was looking through an issue of *Sports Illustrated* magazine. The friend, dressed in full ceremonial regalia with a feather in his nose, was laughing uncontrollably at a photo of a woman shown in a liquor advertisement. When he managed to stop laughing long enough to explain what he thought was so funny, he said, "This white woman has made holes in her ears and stuck things in them." When Scaglion pointed out that his friend had an ornament in his nose, he replied, "That's different. That's for beauty and has ceremonial significance. But I didn't know that white people mutilated themselves."

As stated in the old proverb, "different strokes for different folks." Nevertheless, nonverbal cues can lead to miscommunication, as well as misconceptions of others.

Wallbangin': Graffiti and Gangs in L.A.— *Susan Phillips*

THE CULTURE OF GRAFFITI

Technological innovations like television, automobiles, and computers have changed the ways in which we relate to one another. Shifts in our world structure have fundamentally altered the way we view ourselves and others around us. Instead of bringing us into a "one-world" type of global melting pot (as many have envisioned to be our inevitable future), we have instead Balkanized, fragmenting further the closer we become. These events have radically changed the way that anthropologists must approach the study of culture.

Traditionally, anthropologists would go "to the field"—to locations distant and unknown, where exotic peoples and places awaited discovery by Western eyes. Groups were bounded by subsistence, isolation, and history, making them more easily distinguishable from one another. With most groups now integrated into the global processes of capitalism, anthropologists can no longer rely on subsistence-based and isolationist notions of culture. How do we define culture in a globally linked world, where Westernized consumerism is spreading like wildfire through our sagebrush mountainsides? One way is to look at the mechanisms people use to distinguish themselves from one another.

All individuals manipulate material goods to balance, distinguish, and unify multiple layers of identity. Our relationships to spatial and material things allow different communities of people to develop within the same spaces. People create the ways in which they use things, and their use in turn defines their culture. Historian Benedict Anderson (1983) has argued that people rarely know all the other people in their community. Their connections are "imagined" and vicarious, he says—they come from people's interactions with the things around them, like mass media, newspapers, television, and so on. Material indicators of membership in ethnic, religious, or national groups like those that Anderson describes are some of our most powerful methods of sharing culture.

Through behavior, speech, and material creation, humans make their cultures into vibrant, vital entities. These are the realms through which people engage in forms of social "practice": how they act out their lives and their culture. Material productions like graffiti, therefore, become vehicles through which people define themselves and others.

Most **symbolic media** of communication, like speech or dress, exist in conjunction with a human element; their users are what give them life. But adding material to speech or behavior can extend their efficiency (Goody 1977; Miller 1987). The concrete nature of material objects allows them to take on a life of their own: they can exist beyond the scope of their makers and influence the world in unanticipated ways. Material objects are thus able to link people together without those people being present or ever even having to meet.

Sociologist Anthony Giddens (1979) recognized that the actions of humans may have both intentional and unintentional consequences. Material agents like graffiti suggest a similar dilemma. People create things to act for them in certain ways (just as a street sign, for example, tells you

the name of a street). But because people lose control of the objects they create and can rarely control the perceptions of others, creations may have additional unintended consequences (for example, when a monument designed to represent the greatness of an empire becomes instead the symbol of its oppressiveness).

Graffiti allows people to create identity, share cultural values, redefine spaces, and manufacture inclusive or exclusive relationships. But because of its illegal aspect, graffiti both creates and reflects alienation. Oftentimes, this is secondary to the graffiti writer's primary objective, which is communication to his or her own group. James Scott (1985, 1990) has written extensively about forms of resistance, ways of indirectly confronting the dominating class. Graffiti can also act like what Scott calls a "transcript" (hidden or open), which, with a little prodding in the right areas, can reveal the power relations at its base.

Graffiti has traditionally been viewed as the product of people who have little representation within traditional mass media. To look back on graffiti is to hear voices that otherwise would have remained silent. People in a number of different segments of the population use graffiti as a communicative alternative—but they sometimes use it in markedly different ways. Thus, the examination of graffiti requires its division into a few major genres.

GRAFFITI AS ART AND LANGUAGE

The diversity of graffiti research and approaches indicates its depth as a topic for study. I take certain comfort in the definitional problems that graffiti has incurred—they signify to me that the subject is indeed an important one. Like "culture," "ideology," or "community," "graffiti" is one of those words whose exact definition will always (and pleasantly) be just beyond our reach.

As a medium of communication, graffiti lies somewhere between art and language. Words become signifiers, solutions, and slogans; that is, they cease to be individual words but become symbols and images, which communicate at a variety of levels. These word images are laden with the visual modifiers of style, color, placement, and form. As much as the content of the writings, these modifiers may radically change the meaning, presentation, and effectiveness of any message.

LANGUAGE

Certain circumstances may influence the primacy of linguistic or artistic elements of graffiti. For example, with hip-hop, the content of graffiti is subsumed by its own artistic elaboration—one can hardly read the names of hip-hop writers for all the arrows, colors, and cryptic styles. Similarly, although content is important in Chicano gang graffiti, gigantic and cleanly rendered images of the gang name communicate power and prestige that enhances a gang's reputation. Among African American Bloods and Crips, writers instead engage in intriguing wordplays by manipulating the content of graffiti rather than being overly preoccupied by its style. Writers of political graffiti have always needed to prioritize a clear, straightforward presentation because of the didactic nature of many of their messages. In all these cases, graffiti writers combine elements of language and art to create variable impacts in a variety of circumstances.

Even within graffiti genres, people may manipulate the shape and position of their messages depending on their needs. Sociologist Lyman Chaffee makes this point in an article in which he distinguishes between traditions of political graffiti and wall painting in Buenos Aires. He writes that graffiti are most often spontaneous efforts with aerosol cans on an unprepared surface, while murals are created carefully with paint and brush on prepared backgrounds. Most intriguing is his analysis that, during authoritarian regimes, there is usually an increase in the percentage of graffiti—easily produced, instantaneous, covert—due to heightened surveillance and punishment. During periods of democracy, on the other hand, writers prefer the more elaborate and time-consuming wall painting because of "its larger size, its creative application, its refinement, and its visual domination" (1989, 39). Chaffee notes that "Political messages are therefore communicated through the medium most appropriate for groups in relation to the political structure of the system and the forces in control" (39–40). The technicalities of such distinctions are telling and sometimes difficult to formulate. But political variables in the Argentinian case help us to understand what is important about those messages from the writers' points of view—the common denominator of a visual mode of communication for political concerns.

Popularly, murals are considered more "legitimate" than graffiti, regardless of their legality. For one thing, they bear more direct similarity to pictorial art traditions in general. For another, mural productions may be part of city-endorsed neighborhood pride and graffiti abatement programs. Marcos Sanchez-Tranquilino (1995) notes that in the context of Los Angeles barrios, graffiti are viewed as vandalism and murals as art, though his work bridges the divisions between the two, emphasizing instead how they can both be used to achieve common goals.

Low literacy rates preclude the use of the written word as a main communicative method, be it in advertising, promoting religious ideology, or furthering political struggles. For example, pictures of "the Whale and the Crossbones" on inn signs in England informed nonliterate travelers that they had arrived at their destinations, just as stained glass windows in churches taught medieval people stories from the Bible. Throughout South Central Los Angeles, storefronts advertise their wares with drawings of large bottles of bleach, slabs of meat, cows or chickens, and cold beer. Muralism is not so different from this—drawings of political ideology and community identity, playing off one another through multiple layers of symbolism.

Sometimes it helps to define something (like graffiti) by considering what it's not (like a mural). The difference between graffiti and murals helps to explain the nature of graffiti as a particular mode of visual communication when we recognize that muralism is fundamentally image based, rooted in those nonliterate pictorial traditions.

Graffiti is fundamentally word based. It has its roots in literacy. It implies the presence of a written language. As a medium that combines language and art, graffiti is indeed an art of the word. Its etymology relates to writing: "graph" refers to pencil and writing media and is based on the Greek *graphein*, meaning "to write." Even the Italian graffio, "hook," has particular metaphorical implications apart from the scratchings to which it relates directly: the hook upon which an identity is hung; upon which a movement rests. All these things are related to words, to literacy, to writing. As John Bushnell points out in his *Moscow Graffiti*: "I was much slower than I ought to have been to realize that the graffiti functioned as a language—not just as a generic sign system, but as a real language…" (1990, xi).

This is easy to understand when we see the graffiti slogans of communist struggle: "!Cuba si, Yanqui no!" We can imagine people at a demonstration yelling these words or picture such slogans in leaflets strewn across city streets.

This type of graffiti is closely correlated to words as they exist both in speech and in formalized writing. Similarly, through graffiti, scholars of the ancient world have studied shifts in language use to chart the educational levels of writers. Greek soldiers in Egypt are known to have been basically literate because of the marks they left behind. The so-called graffiti on the bottoms of vases or on coins and signatures in churches and on walls have been used to examine shifts in language—like Pritchard's studies (1967) of medieval crusaders.

In graffiti are not only the intricacies of language development but all the implications of social and political change through the ages. Marks on today's L.A. walls show the development of alternative written systems that exist outside of well-established realms of traditional literacy. For example, Herbert Kohl described the nontraditional literacy of one of his main informants: "Yet none of this knowledge did him any good in school. Many of the words he could read were even prohibited in the classroom. I only managed to discover his reading vocabulary by talking with him about his life on the streets..." (1972, 17).

Literate aspects of graffiti are more difficult to pin down when one attempts to interpret a jumble of letters and numbers and pictures on a wall. Indeed, "ES43GC" means little to the everyday passerby. Even deciphered, the proclamation "East Side Foe Tray Gangster Crips" hardly seems to relate to common sentences or speech patterns as we know them. Some writings in fact seem to have no correlates in speech at all (crossing out enemies is one example).

In The Legacies of Literacy, Harvey Graff reasons that literacy "is above all *a technology or set of techniques for communications and for decoding and reproducing written or printed materials.* Writing *alone* is not an 'agent of change'; its impact is determined by the manner in which human agency exploits it in a specific setting" (1987,4; Graff's italics). As a technology, Graff argues that literacy is an "acquired skill." Graffiti as art and language similarly represents its own form of living literacy; it shifts and changes with its makers and settings. One must become literate in the symbols of its culture in order to read graffiti. One must read beyond the names to see what tagging and graffiti art are all about. One must learn the language of communism to follow wall-written references to communist struggles worldwide. As a system of writing, people learn to read

and write graffiti in much the same way that they learn to read and write standard language. Once they have acquired rudimentary skills, they may exploit the powers of this medium to change circumstances, to represent positions, and to negotiate relationships.

Currently significant in the United States is how alternative literacies become more marked as populations grow intertwined but construct self-imposed boundaries—especially now that rates of traditional literacy are shaky at best. While graffiti around the world are increasingly written in the language of America, specialized forms of writing on the wall within the United States have begun to affect traditional written languages as well. On the decorated envelopes gang members send from jail and in the letters they write, the shape and detail of words mirror gang graffiti on the wall. Punctuation in wall-written gang languages—decorative dots, dashes, and quote marks that separate words on walls—sometimes become the only punctuation present in their sentences. Further, since the advent of hip-hop, teachers in art classes rarely can get kids to work on elaborating anything but their names in their artwork. As Norman Mailer (1974) says, it is the name that is the faith of graffiti. What has happened to the *name* at different places and at different times is the history of graffiti.

Does graffiti function as "a real language," as Bushnell indicates? It does and it doesn't. Like writing, some types of graffiti correlate more closely to spoken words than other types. Also like writing, sometimes graffiti involves letters based on traditional alphabets, but they may also involve symbols or pictures. Graffiti writers combine both words and images, which are sometimes analogous to speech and sometimes analogous only to what they stand for—then again, sometimes only to themselves.

Inscriptions on rocks and on walls have long been made by humankind. They represent a need not only to live within our environments, but to place ourselves very indelibly into them. Rock art itself is arguably the root of written language around the world—this has been shown to be true in both the Middle East and China. Out of pictures come alphabets; out of alphabets come written systems. In writing, the power of the image becomes harnessed in shorthand, tamed for our use. It defines terms whose meanings are elusive; they are themselves imaginary.

For gangs, writing has become important because it has allowed gang members to rigidify their systems, to concretize symbolic and territorial boundaries, and to maintain connections over distances without actual contact. Far from imaginary concerns, these. For gang members living in hostile environments, it is as Jack Goody suggests, that "writing represents not only a method of communication at a distance, but a means of distancing oneself from communication" (1986, 50). In Goody's terms, gang expression represents gang members' separation from one another and from the society at large, both physically and metaphorically. As a boundary-maintaining device and a form of intracultural connection, graffiti is an important tool through which gang members materialize their concerns. They achieve this in writing by breaking down their system and locating themselves very specifically within it, as if to say, "This is where I belong among many like myself." In the process, they separate themselves from the need to be present to communicate those concerns. Only through this written form is it possible for entities like Bloods and Crips to blanket themselves across the nation while maintaining the classification and social order characteristic of their system.

Graffiti works because it presents these things visually. The messages themselves may come from language, but the artistic elements are what enable graffiti to communicate that language effectively. Much time and energy is lost arguing about whether graffiti is art. Such arguments only detract from other types of issues that might be useful to explore on a more practical level. Arguments about graffiti as art usually degenerate into protracted lectures on illegality. If something is illegal, then it cannot be art. So the Michelangelo question inevitably comes up. If Michelangelo were to have painted the ceiling of the Sistine Chapel on your garage without your permission, would it be art? Illegality and art are separate issues. Ultimately, such debates give people an excuse not to understand what graffiti is and why or how people are using it.

Susan Philips, 1999, *Wallbangin': Graffiti and Gangs in L.A.* Chicago: University of Chicago Press. Reprinted by permission.

Body Art as Visual Language—
Enid Schildkrout

Body art is not just the latest fashion. In fact, if the impulse to create art is one of the defining signs of humanity, the body may well have been the first canvas. Alongside paintings on cave walls created by early humans over 30,000 years ago, we find handprints and ochre deposits suggesting body painting. Some of the earliest mummies known—like the "Ice Man" from the Italian-Austrian Alps, known as Otzi, and others from central Asia, the Andes, Egypt and Europe—date back to 5000 years. People were buried with ornaments that would have been worn through body piercings, and remains of others show intentionally elongated or flattened skulls. Head shaping was practiced 5000 years ago in Chile and until the 18th century in France. Stone and ceramic figurines found in ancient graves depict people with every kind of body art known today. People have always marked their bodies with signs of individuality, social status, and cultural identity.

THE LANGUAGE OF BODY ART

There is no culture in which people do not, or did not paint, pierce, tattoo, reshape, or simply adorn their bodies. Fashions change and forms of body art come and go, but people everywhere do something or other to "package" their appearance. No sane or civilized person goes out in the raw; everyone grooms, dresses, or adorns some part of their body to present to the world. Body art communicates a person's status in society; displays accomplishments; and encodes memories, desires, and life histories.

Body art is a visual language. To understand it one needs to know the vocabulary, including the shared symbols, myths, and social values that are written on the body. From tattoos to top hats, body art makes a statement about the person who wears it. But body art is often misunderstood and misinterpreted because its messages do not necessarily translate across cultures. Elaborately pictorial Japanese tattooing started among men in certain occupational groups and depicts the exploits of a gangster hero drawn from a Chinese epic. The tattoos have more meaning to those who know the stories underlying the images than they do to people unfamiliar with the tales. Traditional Polynesian tattooing is mainly geometric and denotes rank and political status but more recently has been used to define ethnic identity within Pacific Island societies.

In an increasingly global world, designs, motifs, even techniques of body modification move across cultural boundaries, but in the process their original meanings are often lost. An animal crest worn as a tattoo, carved into a totem pole, or woven into a blanket may signify membership in a particular clan among Indians on the Northwest Coast of North America, but when worn by people outside these cultures, the designs may simply refer to the wearer's identification with an alternative way of life. Polynesian or Indonesian tattoo designs worn by Westerners are admired for the beauty of their graphic qualities, but their original cultural meanings are rarely understood. A tattoo from Borneo was once worn to light the path of a person's soul after death, but in New York or Berlin it becomes a sign of rebellion from "coat and tie" culture.

Because body art is such an obvious way of signaling cultural differences, people often use it to identify, exoticize, and ostracize others. Tattoos, scarification, or head shaping may be a sign of high status in one culture and low status in another, but to a total outsider these practices may appear to be simply "mutilation." From the earliest voyages of discovery to contemporary tourism, travelers of all sorts—explorers and missionaries, soldiers and sailors, traders and tourists—have brought back images of the people they meet. These depictions sometimes reveal as much about the people looking at the body art as about the people making and wearing it. Some early images of Europeans and Americans by non-Westerners emphasized elaborate clothing and facial hair. Alternatively, Western images of Africans, Polynesians and Native Americans focused on the absence of clothes and the presence of tattoos, body paint and patterns of scars. Representations of body art in engravings, paintings, photographs and film are powerful visual metaphors that have been used both to record cultural differences and to proclaim one group's supposed superiority over another.

BODY ART: PERMANENT AND EPHEMERAL

Most people think that permanent modification of the skin, muscles, and bones is what body art is all about. If one looks at body art as a form of communication, there is no logical reason to separate permanent forms of body art like tattoos, scarification, piercing, or plastic surgery from temporary forms, such as makeup, clothing, or hairstyles. Punks and side-show artists may have what appears to

be extreme body art, but everyone does it in one way or another. All of these modifications convey information about a person's identity.

Nonetheless, some forms of body art are more permanent than others. The decision to display a tattoo is obviously different from the decision to change color of one's lipstick or dye one's hair. Tattooing, piercing, and scarification are more likely to be ways of signaling one's place in society, or an irreversible life passage like the change from childhood to adulthood. Temporary forms of body art, like clothing, ornaments, and painting more often mark a moment or simply follow a fashion. But these dichotomies don't stand up to close scrutiny across cultures: tattoos and scarification marks are often done to celebrate an event and dying or cutting one's hair, while temporary, may signal a life-changing event, such as a wedding or a funeral.

CULTURAL IDEALS OF BEAUTY

Ideas of beauty vary from one culture to another. Some anthropologists and psychologists believe that babies in all cultures respond positively to certain kinds of faces. The beautiful body is often associated with the healthy body and non-threatening facial expressions and gestures. But this does not mean that beauty is defined the same way in all cultures. People's ideas about the way a healthy person should look are not the same in all cultures: some see fat as an indication of health and wealth while others feel quite the opposite. People in some cultures admire and respect signs of aging, while others do all they can to hide gray hair and wrinkles.

Notwithstanding the fact that parents often make decisions for their children, like whether or not to pierce the ears of infants, in general I would maintain that to be considered art and not just a marking, body art has to have some measure of freedom and intentionality in its creation. The brands put on enslaved people, or the numbers tattooed on concentration camp victims, or the scars left from an unwanted injury are body markings not body art.

CULTURAL SIGNIFICANCE OF BODY ART

Body art takes on specific meanings in different cultures. It can serve as a link with ancestors, deities, or spirits. Besides being decorative, tattoos, paint, and scars can mediate the relationships between people and the supernatural world.

The decorated body can serve as a shield to repel evil or as a means of attracting good fortune. Tattoos in central Borneo had the same designs as objects of everyday use and shielded people from dangerous spirits. Selk'nam men in Tierra del Fuego painted their bodies to transform themselves into spirits for initiation ceremonies. Australian Aborigines painted similar designs on cave walls and their bodies to indicate the location of sacred places revealed in dreams.

Transitions in status and identity, for example the transition between childhood and adulthood, are often seen as times of danger. Body art protects a vulnerable person, whether an initiate, a bride, or a deceased person, in this transitional phase. To ensure her good fortune, an Indian bride's hands and feet are covered in henna designs that also emphasize her beauty. For protection during initiation, a central African Chokwe girl's body is covered in white kaolin. In many societies, both the dead and those who mourn them are covered with paints and powders for decoration and protection.

Worldwide travel, large-scale migrations, and increasing access to global networks of communication mean that body art today is a kaleidoscopic mix of traditional practices and new inventions. Materials, designs, and practices move from one cultural context to another. Traditional body art practices are given new meanings as they move across cultural and social boundaries.

Body art is always changing, and in some form or another always engaging: it allows people to reinvent themselves—to rebel, to follow fashion, or to play and experiment with new identities. Like performance artists and actors, people in everyday life use body art to cross boundaries of gender, national identity, and cultural stereotypes.

Body art can be an expression of individuality, but it can also be an expression of group identity. Body art is about conformity and rebellion, freedom and authority. Its messages and meanings only make sense in the context of culture, but because it is such a personal art form, it continually challenges cultural assumptions about the ideal, the desirable, and the appropriately presented body.

BODY ART TECHNIQUES
Body Painting

Body painting, the most ephemeral and flexible of all body art, has the greatest potential for transforming a person into something else—a spirit, a work of art, another gender, even a map to a sacred place including the afterlife. It can be simply a way of emphasizing a person's visual appeal, a serious statement of allegiance, or a protective and empowering coating.

Natural clays and pigments made from a great variety of plants and minerals are often mixed with vegetable oils and animal fat to make body paint. These include red and yellow ochre (iron rich clay), red cam wood, cinnabar, gold dust, many roots, fruits and flowers, cedar bark, white kaolin, chalk, and temporary skin dyes made from indigo and henna leaves. People all over the world adorn the living and also treat the dead with body paint.

The colors of body paint often have symbolic significance, varying from culture to culture. Some clays and body paints are felt to have protective and auspicious properties, making them ideal for use in initiation rituals, for weddings, and for funerals—all occasions of transition from one life stage to another.

Historically, body paints and dyes have been important trade items. Indians of North America exchanged many valuable items for vermilion, which is mercuric sulphide (an artificial equivalent of the natural dye made from cinnabar). Mixed with red lead by European traders, it could cause or sometimes caused mercury poisoning in the wearer.

Makeup

Makeup consists of removable substances—paint, powders, and dyes—applied to enhance or transform appearance. Commonly part of regular grooming, makeup varies according to changing definitions of beauty. For vanity and social acceptance, or for medicinal or ritual purposes, people regularly transform every visible part of their body. They have tanned or whitened skin; changed the color of their lips, eyes, teeth, and hair; and added or removed "beauty" spots.

From the 10th to the 19th century, Japanese married women and courtesans blackened their teeth with a paste made from a mixture of tea and sake soaked in iron scraps; black teeth were considered beautiful and sexually appealing.

Makeup can accentuate the contrast between men and women, camouflage perceived imperfections or signify a special occasion or ritual state. Makeup, like clothing and hairstyles, allows people to reinvent themselves in everyday life.

Rituals and ceremonies often require people to wear certain kinds of makeup, clothing, or hairstyles to indicate that a person is taking on a new identity (representing an ancestor or a spirit in a masquerade, for example) or transforming his or her social identity as in an initiation ceremony, wedding, graduation or naming ceremony. Male Japanese actors in Kabuki theater represent women by using strictly codified paints and motifs, and the designs and motifs of Chinese theatrical makeup indicate the identity of a character.

Hair

Hair is one the easiest and most obvious parts of the body subject to change, and combing and washing hair is part of everyday grooming in most cultures. Styles of combing, braiding, parting, and wrapping hair can signify status and gender, age and ritual status, or membership in a certain group.

Hair often has powerful symbolic significance. Covering the head can be a sign of piety and respect, whether in a place of worship or all the time. Orthodox Jewish women shave their heads but also cover them with wigs or scarves. Muslim women in many parts of the world cover their heads, and sometimes cover their faces too, with scarves or veils. Sikh men in India never cut their hair and cover their heads with turbans. And the Queen of England is rarely seen without a hat.

Cutting hair is a ritual act in some cultures and heads are often shaved during rituals that signify the passage from one life stage to another. Hair itself, once cut, can be used as a symbol substance. Being part, and yet not part, of a person, living or dead, hair can take on the symbolic power of the person. Some Native Americans formerly attached hair from enemies to war shirts, while warriors in Borneo formerly attached hair from captured enemies to war shields.

Reversing the normal treatment of hair, whatever that is in a particular culture, can be a sign of rebellion or of special status. Adopting the uncombed hair of the Rastafarians can be a sign of rebellion among some people, while for Rastafarians it is a sign of membership in a particular religious group. In many cultures people in mourning deliberately do not comb or wash their hair for a period of time, thereby showing that they are temporarily not part of normal everyday life.

What we do with our hair is a way of expressing our identity, and it is easy to look around and see how hair color, cut, style, and its very presence or absence, tells others much about how we want to be seen.

Body Shaping

The shape of the human body changes throughout life, but in many cultures people have found ways to permanently or temporarily sculpt the body. To conform to culturally defined ideals of male and female beauty, people have bound the soft bones of babies' skulls or children's feet, stretched their necks with rings, removed ribs to achieve tiny waists, and most commonly today, sculpted the body through plastic surgery.

Becoming fat is a sign of health, wealth and fertility in some societies, and fattening is sometimes part of a girl's coming of age ceremony. Tiny waists, small feet, and large or small breasts and buttocks have been prized or scorned as ideals of female beauty. Less common are ways of shaping men's bodies but developing muscles, shaping the head, or gaining weight are ways in which cultural ideals of male beauty and power have been expressed.

Head shaping is still done in parts of South America. For the Inka of South America and the Maya of Central America and Mexico, a specially shaped head once signified nobility. Because the skull bones of infants and children are not completely fused, the application of pressure with pads, boards, bindings, or massage results in a gently shaped head that can be a mark of high status or local identity.

LANGUAGE

While Western plastic surgery developed first as a way of correcting the injuries of war, particularly after WWII today people use plastic surgery to smooth their skin, remove unwanted fat, and reshape parts of their bodies.

Scarification

Permanent patterns of scars on the skin, inscribed onto the body through scarification, can be signs of beauty and indicators of status. In some cultures, a smooth, unmarked skin represents an ideal of beauty, but people in many other cultures see smooth skin as a naked, unattractive surface. Scarification, also called cicatrization, alters skin texture by cutting the skin and controlling the body's healing process. The cuts are treated to prevent infection and to enhance the scars' visibility. Deep cuts leave visible incisions after the skin heals, while inserting substances like clay or ash in the cuts results in permanently raised wheals or bumps, known as keloids. Substances inserted into the wounds may result in changes in skin color, creating marks similar to tattoos. Cutting elaborate and extensive decorative patterns into the skin usually indicates a permanent change in a person's status. Because scarification is painful, the richly scarred person is often honored for endurance and courage. Branding is a form of scarification that creates a scar after the surface of the skin has been burned. Branding was done in some societies as a part of a rite of passage, but in western Europe and elsewhere branding, as well as some forms of tattoo, were widely used to mark captives, enslaved peoples, and criminals. Recently, some individuals and members of fraternities on U.S. college campuses have adopted branding as a radical form of decoration and self-identification.

Tattooing

Tattoo is the insertion of ink or some other pigment through the outer covering of the body, the epidermis, into the dermis, the second layer of skin. Tattooists use a sharp implement to puncture the skin and thus make an indelible mark, design, or picture on the body. The resulting patterns or figures vary according to the purpose of the tattoo and the materials available for its coloration.

Different groups and cultures have used a variety of techniques in this process. Traditional Polynesian tattooists punctured the skin by tapping a needle with a small hammer. The Japanese work by hand but with bundles of needles set in wooden handles. Since the late 19th century, the electric tattoo machine and related technological advances in equipment have revolutionized tattoo in the West, expanding the range of possible designs, the colors available, and the ease with which a tattoo can be applied to the body. Prisoners have used materials as disparate as guitar strings and reconstructed electric shavers to create tattoos. Tattoos are usually intended as permanent markings, and it is only recently through the use of expensive laser techniques that they can be removed.

While often decorative, tattoos send important cultural messages. The "text" on the skin can be read as a commitment to some group, an emblem of a rite of passage, a personal or a fashion statement. In fact, cosmetic tattooing of eyebrows and eyeliner is one of the fastest growing of all tattoo enterprises. Tattoos can also signify bravery and commitment to a long, painful process—as is the case with Japanese full body tattooing or Ma ori body and facial patterns. Though there have been numerous religious and social injunctions against tattooing, marking the body in this way has been one of the most persistent and universal forms of body art.

Piercing

Body piercing, which allows ornaments to be worn in the body, has been a widespread practice since ancient times. Piercing involves long-term insertion of an object through the skin in a way that permits healing around the opening. Most commonly pierced are the soft tissues of the face, but many peoples, past and present, have also pierced the genitals and the chest. Ear, nose and lip ornaments, as well as pierced figurines, have been found in ancient burials of the Inka and Moche of Peru, the Aztecs and Maya of ancient Mexico, and in graves of central Asian, European and Mediterranean peoples.

The act of piercing is often part of a ritual change of status. Bleeding that occurs during piercing is sometimes thought of as an offering to gods, spirits or ancestors. Particular ornaments may be restricted to certain groups—men or women, rulers or priests—or may be inserted as part of a ceremony marking a change in status. Because ornaments can be made of precious and rare materials, they may signal privilege and wealth.

Enid Schildkrout, "Body Art as a Visual Language," *Anthro Notes*, Winter 2001, pp. 108. Reprinted by permission.

People Illustrated: In Antiquity Tattoos Could Beautify, Shock, or Humiliate— *Adrienne Mayor*

I will tattoo you with pictures of the terrible punishments suffered by the most notorious sinners in Hades! I will tattoo you with the white-tusked boar!

Violent imagery promising gruesome harm to rivals or faithless lovers is common in Hellenistic curses, but the above poem stands out because it threatens revenge by tattoo. The author of this curse, on Egyptian papyrus fragments discovered in 1962 and 1991, is unknown, but a strong candidate is the poetess Moiro of Byzantium, who lived ca. 300 B.C. A like punishment turns up about the same time in a scene by the Greek playwright Herodas. In *The Jealous Woman*, the scorned Bitinna summons Kosis, a professional tattooer of slaves, criminals, and prisoners of war, to bring his needles to punish her unfaithful slave-lover.

While today tattoos are primarily decorative, in antiquity they also had punitive, magical, and medical functions. In Greece, the use of penal tattoos was probably introduced from Persia in the sixth century B.C. According to the historian Herodotus, the Persian king Xerxes, on his way to invade Greece (480 B.C.), was so infuriated when the sea swept away his bridge at the Hellespont that he ordered his soldiers to enslave the disobedient body of water by tossing iron fetters into the sea. Then he had men flog it with 300 lashes. "I even heard," writes an amused Herodotus, "that Xerxes commanded his royal tattooers to tattoo the water!"

Another Herodotean tale tells us that about 500 B.C., the Ionian tyrant Histiaeus of Miletus was imprisoned by the Persian king Darius. In an effort to inspire his son-in-law Aristagoras to revolt, Histiaeus secretly shaved the head of his most trusted slave and pricked his scalp with pin and ink. "Histiaeus to Aristagoras," the message read, "incite Ionia to revolt!" In a few weeks the slave's hair grew over the tattoo, and Histiaeus dispatched his living letter. On reaching his destination, the slave shaved. Aristogoras read the instructions written on the man's scalp and launched an ill-conceived revolt that ended in the Persian invasion of Greece.

Tattooing captives was common in wartime. After defeating the wealthy Aegean island of Samos in the fifth century B.C., the Athenians tattooed the foreheads of prisoners of war with an owl, Athens' emblem. When Samos in turn defeated the Athenians, the Samians tattooed their prisoners with the image of a Samian warship. The historian Plutarch was appalled by the "unthinkable indignity" inflicted on 7,000 Athenians and their allies captured at Syracuse in 413 B.C., their foreheads tattooed with a horse (the Syracusan insignia) before they were sold as slaves to work the quarries.

A legal inscription from Ephesus indicates that during the early Roman Empire all slaves exported to Asia were tattooed with the words "tax paid." Acronyms, words, sentences, and even doggerel were gouged on foreheads, necks, arms, and legs of slaves and convicts, either as routine identification marks or as punishment. "Stop me, I'm a runaway" was a standard motto etched on the brows of Roman slaves. The practice dehumanized social inferiors by turning their bodies into texts that forever recorded their captivity, servitude, or guilt.

The Greek philosopher Bion of Borysthenes (ca. 300 B.C.) described the brutally tattooed face of his father, a former slave, as "a narrative of his master's harshness." That some cruel slave owners tattooed their chattels without cause is suggested by a fragmentary Greek legal code of the third century B.C. that allowed masters to tattoo "bad" slaves, but forbade the tattooing of "good" ones. In Rome, Caligula (A.D. 38–41) "defaced many people of the better sort" with tattoos and condemned them to slavery, according to his biographer Suetonius. Gladiators were tattooed as public property, and in the later empire soldiers were tattooed to discourage desertion. Roman authorities also punished early Christians with forehead tattoos that condemned them to the mines, according to new research by Calvin College historian Mark Gustafson. In A.D. 300, the first Christian emperor, Constantine, banned the practice of tattooing the faces of convicts, gladiators, and soldiers. Because the human face reflected "the image of divine beauty," he said, "it should not be defiled."

Punitive tattoos were not carefully or artistically applied. Ink was poured into crude letters carved into a captive's flesh with iron needles; three needles bound together made a thicker line. Copious bleeding was common and the procedure was sometimes fatal. "Without hygiene, tattooing must always have been dangerous [which] contributed to its value as a form of punishment," writes Harvard's Christopher Jones. Marco Polo's vivid description of the ordeal of willing victims in thirteenth-century Central Asia gives a sense of traditional methods. To tattoo elaborate dragons, lions, and birds on the skin, an individual was "tied hand and foot and held down by others, while the master craftsman pricked out the images with five needles." The "victim suffered what might well pass for the pains of Purgatory!"

Roman doctors developed techniques for removing tattoos, but the methods were painful and risky. A typical procedure from the medical writer Aetius reads, "Clean the tattoo with niter, smear with resin of terebinth, and bandage for five days." On day six "prick out the tattoo with a sharp pin, sponge away the blood, and cover with salt. After strenuous running to work up a sweat, apply a caustic poultice; the tattoo should disappear in 20 days." Caustic preparations worked by ulcerating the skin, thereby obliterating the tattoo. A safer expedient, mentioned by other writers, was to hide shameful tattoos under long bangs or a bandanna.

The demeaning use of tattoos in their own cultures made it difficult for Greeks and Romans to understand why the Thracians, Scythians, Dacians, Gauls, Picts, Celts, and Britons willingly tattooed themselves. In Thrace, according to Herodotus, plain skin signaled a lack of identity and men and women with tattoos were much admired. One third-century account of the Scythian defeat of the Thracians notes that the victors incised symbols of defeat upon the losers, but that the Thracian women hit on the idea of embellishing the rest of their bodies with tattoos as a way off turning "the stamp of violence and shame into beautiful ornaments." Similarly, early Christians tattooed themselves with religious symbols to counteract those inscribed on them by their Roman persecutors. Among the Mossynoikoi of the Black Sea in the fifth century B.C., the historian Xenophon observed that "the chubby children of the best families were entirely tattooed back and front with flowers in many colors." For many ancient people, tattoos signaled bravery, ensured magical protection, and impressed enemies.

The Romans were amazed by warrior cultures that seemed to gather psychological strength from tattoos. The historian Herodian records the first encounters with the wildly illustrated natives of the British Isles about A.D. 200, "ferocious fighters [who] tatoo their bodies with myriad patterns and all sorts of animals." The historian Claudian (ca. A.D. 400) described a skirmish with the natives of Scotland. The Roman soldiers, themselves tattooed against their will by the state, lingered after the battle to stare at "the strange devices on the faces of the dying Picts."

Despite their misgivings about the practice, the Greeks were fascinated by the idea of tattoos as exotic beauty marks. In the fifth and fourth centuries B.C., a series of popular vase paintings illustrated the murder of the musician Orpheus by tattooed Thracian maenads wielding spears, daggers, and axes. Hanns Ebensten, a sociologist who studies tattoos, has found that "bold, audacious" designs are often used to accentuate musculature and motion. On these vases, the geometric and animal tattoos on the women's bodies draw attention to athletic strength and flexing muscles. On a red-figure column krater, two maenads running barefoot display fully tattooed arms and legs. One of the women has designs from ankle to knee: parallel lines, zigzags, a sunburst, and a deer. Other vases show women with chevrons, circles, vines, ladders, spirals, and animals.

The most technically and artistically brilliant tattoos from antiquity are preserved on three bodies discovered near Pazyryk, southern Siberia (see *Archaeology*, September/October 1994, p. 27, and January/February 1996, p. 33). The region was home to the nomadic horse people known to the Greeks as the Scythians. There, in 1948, Soviet archaeologist Sergei Rudenko discovered a fifth-century B.C. tattooed warrior preserved in permafrost. Imaginary and real creatures swirled across the man's body, the sophisticated compositions conforming to his anatomy.

How were the Scythian tattoos made? Rudenko speculated that a sure-handed artist had "stitched" the skin with a very fine needle and thread using soot as the coloring agent. Scythian grave goods included exceptionally fine bone needles and thin sinews for thread, but modern tattoo artists doubt that such intricate and deep tattoos could be achieved by this method. Nonetheless, freeze-dried Inuit mummies found at Qilakitsoq, Greenland, and examined by the Danish National Museum in 1978 provide evidence that the Scythian tattoos may have been stitched. Tattoos decorated six women who had died in the late 1400s. Scientists determined that the designs had been made by drawing a thread through the skin with a bone needle. Chemical analysis revealed ink made from soot, ash, and plant juices.

Rudenko was intrigued by 14 dots along the Scythian warrior's spine and six on his ankle. He knew that present-day Siberians believe such tattoos alleviate pain. Therapeutic tattooing is still practiced among Tibetans and peoples of the Arctic and Middle East. Like cauterization or acupuncture, such tattoos are thought to stimulate nerves or release toxins. This folk remedy is ancient: blue marks on the Eleventh Dynasty mummy of Lady Ament (ca. 2400 B.C.), for example, have been interpreted by French archaeologists as a therapy for chronic kidney disease.

A second tatooed body was found at Pazyryk in 1993 by Natalya Polosmak of the Russian Institute of Archaeology and Ethnography. The woman was wrapped in fur and buried with six horses, all perfectly preserved in solid ice. She was about 25 at the time of her death some 2,400 years ago. On her wrist and shoulder were exquisite tattoos of deer with fantastic antlers, recalling the deer tattoos of the Thracian maenads on ancient Greek vases. A third tattooed mummy was found in 1995. This young horseman wore his hair in braids and was buried with his horse around 500 B.C. A large tattoo of an elk in the distinctive Scythian style spans his chest, shoulder, and back. The animals on these three nomads may have had magical meanings, or they may have recorded important personal experiences such as hunting successes, vision quests, and perilous adventures.

Otzi the Iceman, who died in an Alpine blizzard some 5,000 years ago, has several tattoos: parallel lines on the right foot and ankle, bars along the lower spine, lines on the left calf, and crosses inside the right knee and left ankle. Noticing that they were concentrated at joints, and recalling Rudenko's medical interpretation of the dots on the Pazyryk warrior, Konrad Spindler of the University of Innsbruck ordered X-rays of Otzi. Sure enough, they revealed chronic degeneration of bone and cartilage in the spine and arthritic wear and tear of the knees and ankles. The "precise draftsmanship" indicates that an experienced tattooist scored the marks with a sharp point; the bone awl found in the Iceman's pouch "would have been ideal for the task," wrote Spindler in *The Man in the Ice.*

History shows that humans have had themselves tattooed for myriad reasons—for magical protection, to relieve pain, for vengeance, or to declare victory over an enemy. Tattoos could beautify, shock, or humiliate. They proclaimed valor, religious belief, group solidarity, or personal independence. Their messages could be hidden or in plain sight. Tattoos have always been complex and mutable. What other lifestyle decision could draw into the same circle such diverse people across the millennia as Otzi, Eurasian nomads, ancient slaves and prisoners of war, Roman gladiators, Egyptian priestesses, murderous Thracian maenads, and tattoo enthusiasts of our own era?

From Adrienne Mayor, 1999, "People Illustrated: In Antiquity Tattoos Could Beautify, Shock, or Humiliate," *Archaeology Magazine*, Vol. 52, No. 2. Reprinted by permission.

In Your Faith—
Jordan Elgrably

Many Jewish Gen-Xers are embracing their religious and cultural icons with defiance and bold irony. But are the piercings and tattoos a fad or spiritual expression?

With her purple mohawk and pierced eyebrows, nose and lip, Marina Vainshtein is not, at first glance, your average young Jewish woman. But look further and you'll find evidence of Marina's obsession with the history of her people: a star of David tattooed on her inner left arm, a tattooed armband in Hebrew on her right wrist that reads, "And now we are the last of many." And these are only the first signs that Marina, a 22-year-old Los Angeles photographer, is defining her Judaism in unconventional ways.

Much of Marina's body is tattooed with vivid scenes of the Holocaust: a hovering angel of death in a gas mask; a row of naked bodies hanging from the gallows; and, on her left arm and shoulder, gruesome images of the Nazi medical experiments performed on children.

Jewish law, or halachah, bans tattoos as a desecration of the body; only Holocaust survivors are the exception to the rule that you cannot be buried in a Jewish cemetery if tattooed. But now there are members of a generation of young Jews in their 20s and 30s who, like Vainshtein, are observing their Judaism in unorthodox—not to say radical—ways.

Even as the Jewish community has seen a renewed interest in the exploration of Jewish spirituality, there is a discernible movement among some younger Jews to explore their Jewish identity with in-your-face defiance and bold irony. This smaller movement is claiming Jewish ethnicity and cultural icons much the way blacks, Latinos and Asians did before them.

Ironically, Art Spiegelman, considered by some the god-father of this movement for his unusual exploration of Jewish identity in the satirical comic book series "Maus," expresses dismay at the idea that Jews are jumping on the multicultural bandwagon.

"This is the problem with an America that has gone crazy, that's just gone into ethnic madness," Spiegelman says. "I think what you're seeing is a response to the Balkanization of America, where Jews who felt themselves too embraced in America's assimilationist arms have now started to desperately backpedal. It seems to me that America has entered into an age of competing victimhoods, and that the left has become sapped by the rise of multiculturalism. The energy that used to go into trying to create a generally more just society has been rerouted into competing claims of ethnic rights."

Still, young Jews like Vainshtein remain unapologetic. "I love tattoos," she says, "I think they're beautiful. If they're done right they can be art." Yet Vainshtein hasn't unveiled her tattoos to her parents. She's afraid they'll have a conniption.

When Vainshtein was in high school, a woman who had survived seven concentration camps gave a lecture to her history class. The seeds of Marina's Jewish identity were already planted, she recalls, "but her talk was the nourishment. She taught me that I could be a survivor too, no matter if it's one day or 80 years."

Jordan Elgrably, "In Your Faith," *Los Angeles Times*, May 13, 1996, p. E-1. Reprinted by permission.

E X E R C I S E

Name

Section

Date

EXERCISE 5.2: "BODY" LANGUAGE

1. Tattoos have had various meanings through time and space. List some of the meanings given for tattoos in the article "People Illustrated."

2. Why were tattoos considered dangerous in the past?

3. What meanings have tattoos had in the past in your society?

4. What meanings do tattoos have in your society today?

5. Who would have been likely to have a tattoo in your society in the past?

(continued on the next page)

6.   Who would be likely to have a tattoo in your society today?

7.   Has this changed? If so, how?

8.   Do you have a tattoo? If so, what type(s) do you have? What does it mean?

9.   If not, is there a reason that you do not?

10. Do you think your professor has one? Why or why not? Would you ask him/her?

KEY TERMS

Name _____

Section _____

Date _____

Black English Vernacular (BEV):

Body art:

Dialects:

Ebonics:

Ethnic labels:

Graffiti:

Grammar:

Language:

Linguistic invariants:

197

LANGUAGE

Non-verbal communication:

Pidgin:

Slang:

Sociolinguistics:

Sociolinguistic subcultures:

Symbolism (symbolic media):

Tattoos:

6 FAMILY

Sex in the City

Although kinship relations are more important in some cultures over others, it is the most important aspect of social structure for all societies. **Kinship** is based on blood (consanguineal) relations and marriage (affinal) relationships. Most societies recognize some type of **fictive kin**, whereby kinship terms and obligations are applied to non-family members.

A feature of all kinship systems is that they group relatives into certain categories, assign specific names to that relationship (i.e., aunt or cousin) and expect certain behaviors. There are six types of kinship systems based on how the society distinguishes different categories of relatives.

Due to differences in classification of kinship systems, it is not always easy to define the terms family and marriage. The **family** is a social unit; the members of which cooperate economically, manage reproduction and child rearing, and most often live together. **Marriage**—a process by which families are formed—refers to a socially approved union between two or more individuals.

I'm My Own Grandpaw— *Dwight B. Latham and Moe Jaffe*

Many many years ago, when I was 23,
I was married to a widow as pretty as can be.

This widow had a grown-up daughter who had hair of red.
My father fell in love with her and soon the two were wed.

This made my dad my son-in-law and changed my very life,
For my daughter was my mother, for she was my father's wife.

To complicate the matter, even though it brought me joy,
I soon became the father of a bouncing baby boy.

My little baby thus became a brother-in-law to Dad,
And so became my uncle, though it made me very sad.

For if he was my uncle; then that also made him brother
To the widow's grown-up daughter, who of course was my step-mother.

Father's wife then had a son who kept him on the run,
And he became my grandchild for he was my daughter's son.

My wife is now my mother's mother and it makes me blue,
Because although she is my wife, she's my grandmother too!

Oh, if my wife's my grandmother, then I am her grandchild,
And every time I think of it, it nearly drives me wild.

For now I have become the strangest case you ever saw.
As the husband of my grandmother, I am my own grandpaw.

(Chorus)

I'm my own grandpaw,
I'm my own grandpaw.

It sounds funny, I know,
But it really is so
I'm my own grandpaw.

Dwight Latham and Moe Jaffe, 1948, "I'm My Own Grandpaw," EMI Virgin Songs, Inc. EMI Music Publishing. Reprinted by permission of Hal Leonard Corporation.

Brady Bunch Nirvana—
Conrad Kottak

One teaching technique we started using several years ago, taking advantage of students' familiarity with television, is to demonstrate changes in American kinship and marriage patterns by contrasting the TV programs of the 50s with more recent ones. (Students know about the history of sitcom families from syndicated reruns, especially on the cable channel Nickelodeon.) In the 1950s, the usual TV family was a nuclear family consisting of employed dad, homemaker mom, and kids. Examples include *Father Knows Best*, *Ozzie and Harriet*, and *Leave It to Beaver*. These programs, appropriate for the 1950s market, are dramatically out of sync with today's social and economic realities. Only 16 million American women worked outside the home in 1950, compared with three times that number today.

Today, less than 7 percent of American households fit the former ideal: breadwinner father, homemaker mother, and two children.

Most students have watched reruns of the 1960s family series *The Brady Bunch*, whose social organization offers an instructive contrast with 1950s programs. Here, a new, blended family forms when a widow with three daughters marries a widower with three sons. **Blended families** have been increasing in American society because of more frequent divorce and remarriage. When *The Brady Bunch* first aired, divorce was too controversial to give rise to a prime-time TV family. Widow(er)-hood had to be the basis of the blended family, as it was in *The Brady Bunch*.

The Brady husband-father was a successful architect. The Bradys were wealthy enough to employ a housekeeper, Alice. Mirroring American culture when the program was made, the wife's career was part-time and subsidiary. Women lucky enough to find wealthy husbands didn't compete with other women—even professional housekeepers—in the work force.

Each time we begin the kinship lecture using sitcom material, a few people in the class immediately recognize (from reruns) the nuclear families of the 1950s, especially the Beaver Cleaver family. And when we start diagramming the Bradys, students start shouting out their names: "Jan," "Bobby," "Greg," "Cindy," "Marsha," "Peter," "Mike," "Carol," "Alice." As the cast of characters nears completion, my class, filled with TV-enculturated natives, is usually shouting out in unison names made almost as familiar as their parents' through exposure to TV reruns. Students almost seem to find **nirvana** (a feeling of religious ecstasy) through their collective remembrance of the Bradys and in the ritual-like incantation of their names.

Given its massive penetration of the modern home (at least 98 percent of all households), television's effects on our socialization and enculturation can hardly be trivial. Indeed, the common information and knowledge we acquire by watching the same TV programs is indisputably culture in the anthropological sense. Culture is collective, shared, meaningful. It is transmitted by conscious and unconscious learning experiences acquired by humans not through their genes but as a result of growing up in a particular society. Of the hundreds of culture bearers who have passed through a course in Cultural Anthropology, many have been unable to recall the full names of their parents' first cousins. Some have forgotten their grandmother's maiden name. But most have absolutely no trouble identifying names and relationships in a family that exists only in television land.

Conrad Kottak, 2000, "Brady Bunch Nirvana," *Cultural Anthropology*, Chapter 6—"Blood Is Thicker Than Water." New York: McGraw-Hill. Copyright © 2000 The McGraw-Hill Companies. Reprinted with permission of The McGraw-Hill Companies.

FAMILY

Let's Ponder...

How would *The Brady Bunch* show be received in the 1960s if the family was created after a divorce, rather than after the death of two parents?

During the hit show *I Love Lucy*, Ricky and Lucy never shared beds. This was the norm in the 1950s. Also, this was the first time a female was ever seen pregnant on television. How do audiences today explain such behaviors? How are the roles of males and females in this show similar or different by modern standards?

During the 2000 Presidential Campaign, the Gores shared the famous kiss, onstage in front of all Americans. Some members of our society were against this obvious show of affection. Explain how kissing can be viewed negatively in our society.

Does your answer from the previous question remain the same for all people, including teens, unmarried adults, and homosexual couples? Why?

FAMILY

E X E R C I S E

Name

Section

Date

EXERCISE 6.1: SHINING STARS

In 2008, stars and personalities like Lindsay Lohan and Paris Hilton change boyfriends more often than shoes. Do we as a society respect their decisions? Why or why not? How do the decisions of "stars" impact your life?

FAMILY

Marriage and the Family—
Gary Ferraro

In all known societies, people recognize a certain number of relatives who make up the basic social group generally called the family. This is not to imply, however, that all societies view the family in the same way. In fact, humans have developed a wide variety of types of families. To most middle-class North Americans, the family includes a husband and a wife and their children. To an East African herdsman, the family might include several hundred kin related through both blood and marriage. Among the Hopi, the family would be made up of a woman and her husband and their unmarried sons and married daughters, along with the daughters' husbands and children. This chapter examines the variety of family types found throughout the world and the process of marriage that is responsible for the formation of families.

MARRIAGE AND THE FAMILY: SOME DEFINITIONS

Even though we use the terms *family* and *marriage* routinely, their meanings are ambiguous. Because social scientists and laypeople alike use these terms indiscriminately, it will be helpful to define them in more detail. A **family** is a social unit characterized by economic cooperation, the management of reproduction and child rearing, and common residence. It includes both male and female adults who maintain a socially approved sexual relationship. Family members, both adults and children, recognize certain rights and obligations toward one another. The family is distinct from the institution of **marriage**, which we can define as a series of customs formalizing the relationship between male and female adults within the family. Marriage is a socially approved union between a man and a woman that regulates the sexual and economic rights and obligations between them. Marriage usually involves an explicit contract or understanding and is entered into with the assumption that it will be a permanent arrangement.

Although our definition of marriage holds true for most situations found in the world, it is not universally inclusive of all marital arrangements. Because our definition defines marriage as establishing legitimate relationships between men and women, it tends to assume that all marriages are heterosexual. However, some cultures recognize marriages of men to men and women to women as being legitimate. Indeed, in certain industrialized countries (such as Canada and the Netherlands), same-sex relationships are recognized as legal and, consequently, are protected under the law in the same way as heterosexual unions. In

parts of West Africa successful women merchants, who may already be married to a husband, will take a wife to help with the domestic duties while she is at work (Amadiume 1987). Moreover, among the Nandi of Kenya, a woman can marry a woman (female husband) when her father has only daughters and no male heirs. Under such conditions the female husband arranges for a male consort to father children biologically for her bride. Among the Cheyennes of the Great Plains, warriors were permitted to take male transvestites as second wives (Hoebel 1960).

Sexual Union

As with any term, the definition of marriage often must be qualified. **Marriage**, according to our definition, is a socially legitimate sexual union. When a man and a woman are married, it is implied that they are having a sexual relationship or that the society permits them to have one if they desire it. Although this is generally true, we should bear in mind that this social legitimacy is not absolute, for there may be specified periods during which sexual relations with one's spouse may be taboo. To illustrate, in many societies, sexual relations between spouses must be suspended during periods of menstruation and pregnancy. After a child is born, women in many societies are expected to observe a **postpartum sex taboo**, lasting in some cases until the child is weaned, which can be as long as several years. As William Stephens has suggested, "there may be other sex taboos in honor of special occasions: before a hunting trip, before and after a war expedition, when the crops are harvested, or during various times of religious significance" (1963:10). Given this wide range of occasions where sex with one's spouse is illegitimate, it is possible that in some societies, husbands and wives will be prevented from having sexual relations for a significant segment of their married lives.

Permanence

A second qualification to our definition relates to the permanence of the marital union. Often, as part of the marriage vows recited in Western weddings, spouses pledge to live together in matrimony "until death do us part." Even though it is difficult to ascertain a person's precise intentions or expectations when entering a marriage, an abundance of data suggests that the permanence of marriage varies widely, and in no societies do all marriages last until death. For example, recent statistics indicate that more than one of every two marriages in the United States ends in divorce. Impermanent marriages can also be found in smaller-scale societies. Dorothea Leighton and Clyde

FAMILY

Kluckhohn report that they often encountered Navajo men who had "six or seven different wives in succession" (1948:83). In short, when dealing with the permanence of marriage, there is always a discrepancy between ideal expectations and actual behavior.

Common Residence

A qualifying statement must also be added about the notion that family members share a common residence. Although family members usually do live together, there are some obvious definitional problems. If we define "sharing a common residence" as living under the same roof, a long list of exceptions can be cited. In Western society, dependent children sometimes live away from home at boarding schools and colleges. Additionally, in this age of high-speed transportation and communication, it is possible for a husband and wife to live and work in two different cities and see each other only on weekends. On a more global scale, 94 of the 240 African societies listed in George Murdock's *Ethnographic Atlas* (1967) are characterized by wives and their children living in separate houses from the husband. In some non-Western societies, adolescent boys live with their peers apart from their families; and in some cases, such as the Nyakyusa (Wilson 1960), adolescent boys have not only their own houses but their own villages. In each of these examples, family membership and participation are not dependent on living under the same roof.

Thus, as we are beginning to see, the terms *marriage* and *family* are not easy to define. For years, anthropologists have attempted to arrive at definitions of these terms that will cover all known societies. Anthropologists have often debated whether families and the institution of marriage are universals. The Nayar of southern India are an interesting case. According to some (Gough 1959), they did not have marriage in the conventional sense of the term. Although pubescent Nayar girls took a ritual husband in a public ceremony, the husband took no responsibility for the woman after the ceremony, and often he never saw her again. Instead of cohabitating with her "husband" the Nayar bride continued to live with her mother, mother's sister, and mother's brother while being visited over the years by other "husbands." The bride's family retained full responsibility for the woman and whatever children she bore during her lifetime. Thus, it appears that the Nayar do not have marriage according to our definition in that there is no economic cooperation, regulation of sexual activity, co-habitation, or expectation of permanency.

MARRIAGE AND THE FAMILY: FUNCTIONS

Whether or not marriage is a cultural universal found in all societies depends on the level of abstraction in our definitions. Without entering into that debate here, suffice it to say that the formation of families through marriage serves several important functions for the societies in which the families operate. One social benefit that marriage provides is the creation of fairly stable relationships between men and women that regulate sexual mating and reproduction. Because humans are continually sexually receptive, and (in the absence of contraceptives) sexual activity usually leads to reproduction, it is imperative that societies create and maintain unions that will regulate mating, **reproduction**, and child rearing in a socially approved manner.

A second social benefit of marriage is that it provides a mechanism for regulating the sexual **division of labor** that exists to some extent in all societies. For reasons that are both biological and cultural, men in all societies perform some tasks, and women perform others. To maximize the chances of survival, it is important for a society to arrange the exchange of goods and services between men and women. Marriage usually brings about domestic relationships that facilitate the exchange of these goods and services.

Third, marriage creates a set of family relationships that can provide for the material, educational, and emotional **needs of children** for a long period of time. Unlike most other animal species, human children depend on adults for the first decade or more of their lives for their nourishment, shelter, and protection. Moreover, human children require adults to provide the many years of cultural learning needed to develop into fully functioning members of the society. Even though it is possible for children to be reared largely outside a family (as is done on the kibbutzim of Israel), in most societies marriage creates a set of family relationships that provide the material, educational, and emotional support children need for their eventual maturity.

MATE SELECTION: WHO IS OUT OF BOUNDS?

Every society known to anthropology has established for itself rules regulating mating (sexual intercourse). The most common form of prohibition is mating with certain types of kin who are defined by the society as being inappropriate sexual partners. The prohibition on mating with certain categories of relatives is known as the **incest taboo**.

Following the lead of Robin Fox (1967), it is important to distinguish between sexual relations and marriage. Incest taboos are prohibitions against having sexual relations with certain categories of kin. This is not exactly the same thing as rules prohibiting marrying certain kin. Although incest taboos and rules prohibiting marrying certain kin often coincide with each other (that is, those who are forbidden to have sex are also forbidden to marry), it cannot be assumed that they always coincide.

The most universal form of incest taboo involves mating between members of the immediate (nuclear) family—that is, mothers and sons, fathers and daughters, and brothers and sisters—although there are several notable yet limited exceptions. For political, religious, or economic reasons, members of the royal families among the ancient Egyptians, Incas, and Hawaiians were permitted to mate with and marry their siblings, although this practice did not extend to the ordinary members of those societies. The incest taboo invariably extends beyond the scope of the immediate or nuclear family, however. In a number of states in the United States, people are forbidden by law from mating with the children of their parents' siblings (that is, first cousins). In some non-Western societies, the incest taboo may extend to large numbers of people on one side of the family but not on the other. And in still other societies, a man is permitted (even encouraged) to mate with and marry the daughter of his mother's brother (a **cross cousin** and a first cousin) but is strictly prohibited from doing so with the daughter of his mother's sister (also a first cousin but a **parallel cousin**). Thus, although it seems clear that every society has incest taboos, the relatives that make up the incestuous group vary from one society to another. Given that incest taboos are universally found throughout the world, anthropologists have long been interested in explaining their origins and persistence. A number of possible explanations have been set forth.

Natural Aversion Theory

One such theory, which was popular about a hundred years ago, rests on the somewhat unsatisfying concept that there is a natural aversion to sexual intercourse among those who have grown up together. Although any natural (or genetically produced) aversion to having sexual relations within the nuclear family is rejected today, there is some evidence to suggest that such an aversion may be developed. For example, according to Yohina Talmon (1964), sexual attraction between Israelis reared on the

same **kibbutz** is extremely rare, a phenomenon attributed by the kibbutz members themselves to the fact that they had grown up together. Another study (Wolf 1968) of an unusual marital practice in Taiwan, whereby infant girls are given to families with sons to be their future brides, found that these marriages were characterized by higher rates of infidelity and sexual difficulties and fewer children. Thus, it appears that in at least some situations, people who have grown up together and have naturally experienced high levels of familiarity have little sexual interest in each other. Nevertheless, this familiarity theory does not appear to be a particularly convincing explanation for the existence of the incest taboo.

If familiarity does lead to sexual aversion and avoidance, how do we explain why incest does occur with considerable regularity throughout the world? Indeed, in our own society, it has been estimated that 10 to 14 percent of children under 18 years of age have been involved in incestuous relationships (Whelehan 1985). In short, the familiarity theory does not explain why we even need a strongly sanctioned incest taboo if people already have a natural aversion to incest.

Inbreeding Theory

Another theory that attempts to explain the existence of the incest taboo focuses on the potentially deleterious effects of inbreeding on the family. This inbreeding theory, proposed first in the late nineteenth century, holds that mating between close kin, who are likely to carry the same harmful recessive genes, tends to produce a higher incidence of genetic defects (which results in an increased susceptibility to disease and higher mortality rates). This theory was later discredited because it was argued that sharing the same recessive genes could produce adaptive advantages as well as disadvantages. However, recent genetic studies have given greater credence to the older theory that inbreeding does lead to some harmful consequences for human populations. Conversely, outbreeding, which occurs in human populations with strong incest taboos, has a number of positive genetic consequences. According to Bernard Campbell (1979), these include increases in genetic variation, a reduction in lethal recessive traits, improved health, and lower rates of mortality.

Even though it is generally agreed today that inbreeding is genetically harmful to human populations, the question still remains whether prehistoric people understood this fact. After all, the science of Mendelian genetics did not become established until the start of the twentieth century. However, it is not necessary for early people to have recognized the adaptive advantages of avoiding inbreeding through an incest taboo. Rather, the incest taboo could have persisted through time for the simple reason that it was adaptively advantageous. That is, groups that practiced the incest taboo would have more surviving children than societies without the incest taboo. Thus, this greater reproductive success would explain, if not the origins of the incest taboo, at least why it has become a cultural universal.

Family Disruption Theory

Whereas the inbreeding theory focuses on the biological consequences of incest, a third theory centers on its negative social consequences. This theory, which is most closely linked with Bronislaw Malinowski (1927), holds that mating between a mother and son, father and daughter, or brother and sister would create such intense jealousies within the nuclear family that the family would not be able to function as a unit of economic cooperation and socialization. For example, if adolescents were permitted to satisfy their sexual urges within the nuclear family unit, fathers and sons and mothers and daughters would be competing with one another, and, consequently, normal family role relationships would be seriously disrupted. The incest taboo, according to this theory, originated as a mechanism to repress the desire to satisfy one's sexual urges within the family.

In addition to causing disruption among nuclear family members through sexual competition, incest creates the further problem of **role ambiguity**. For example, if a child is born from the union of a mother and her son, the child's father will also be the child's half-brother, the child's mother will also be the child's grandmother, and the child's half sister will also be the child's aunt. These are just some of the bizarre roles created by such an incestuous union. Because different family roles, such as brother and father, carry with them vastly different rights, obligations, and behavioral expectations, the child will have great difficulty deciding how to behave toward his or her immediate family members. Does the child treat the male who biologically fathered him or her as a father or as a brother? How does the child deal with the woman from whose womb he or she sprung—as a mother or a grandmother? Thus, the incest taboo can be viewed as a mechanism that prevents this type of role ambiguity or confusion.

Theory of Expanding Social Alliances

Incest avoidance can also be explained in terms of positive social advantages for societies that practice it. By forcing people to marry out of their immediate family, the incest taboo functions to create a wider network of interfamily alliances, thereby enhancing cooperation, social cohesion, and survival. Each time one of your close relatives mates with a person from another family, it creates a new set of relationships with whom your family is less likely to become hostile. This theory, first set forth by Edward Tylor (1889) and later developed by Claude Lévi-Strauss (1969), holds that it makes little sense to mate with someone from one's own group with whom one already has good relations. Instead, there is more to be gained, both biologically and socially, by expanding one's networks outward. Not only does mating outside one's own group create a more peaceful society by increasing the number of allies, but it also creates a larger gene pool, which has a greater survival advantage than a smaller gene pool.

The extent to which wider social alliances are created by requiring people to mate and marry outside the family is illustrated by a study of Rani Khera, a village in northern India. In a survey of the village population (Lewis 1955), it was found that the 226 married women residing in the village had come from approximately 200 separate villages and that roughly the same number of village daughters married out. Thus, the village of Rani Khera was linked through marriage to hundreds of other northern Indian villages. In fact, this pattern of mating and marrying out side one's own group (created out of a desire to avoid incest) is an important factor integrating Indian society.

MATE SELECTION: WHOM SHOULD YOU MARRY?

As we have seen, every society has the notion of incest that defines a set of kin with whom a person is to avoid marriage and sexual intimacy. In no society is it permissible to mate with one's parents or siblings (that is, within the nuclear family), and in most cases the restricted group of kin is considerably wider. Beyond this notion of incest, people in all societies are faced with rules either restricting one's choice of marriage partners or strongly encouraging the selection of other people as highly desirable mates. These are known as rules of **exogamy** (marrying outside of a certain group) and **endogamy** (marrying within a certain group).

The Anthropological Study of Skid Row

In the social science literature the term *skid row men* refers to indigents who regularly consume inexpensive alcoholic beverages as a way of life, are frequently picked up by the police for public drunkenness, and find themselves repeatedly in "detox" centers. According to most studies (Parsons 1951; Rooney 1961; Spradley 1970), the skid row men have lost all significant involvement with their kinsmen. They are, in short, men without families and men who do not want families.

This general perception that skid row men do not maintain their family ties may be more the result of failing to investigate this aspect of their lives than a true measure of reality. Prompted by such a possibility, Merrill Singer (1985) decided to conduct ethnographic interviews with 28 skid row men who had been admitted to an alcohol detoxification center in Washington, D.C. The interview schedule, composed of 100 open-ended questions, was designed to collect information on family background, drinking history, current lifestyle, and social networks. Singer reasoned that if, in fact, these skid row men do maintain kinship ties, then it might be possible to use these kinship links as part of the strategy for therapeutic intervention.

Interestingly, the data revealed that this sample of skid row men maintained fairly regular contact with relatives. Specifically, 93 percent of the men both stayed in regular contact with, and felt emotionally close to, at least one kinsman; 90 percent received nonmaterial aid from relatives; and 86 percent received material assistance from kinsmen. Despite numerous disappointments caused by the alcoholics' inability to stay out of trouble, ties with certain kin (mostly female) were both persistent and emotionally laden. The skid row men were found to both respect and care for their supportive kin.

Based on these findings from the ethnographic interviews, Singer concluded that these female supportive kinsmen may be an important link in the alcoholic rehabilitation programs for skid row men. Some of the men interviewed stated that some of their kinsmen had not given up on them and would be willing to participate in family therapy. Because there is general agreement in the therapeutic community that successful alcoholic rehabilitation requires the involvement of caring significant others, these findings encourage the use of family therapy for the treatment of skid row alcoholics.

Rules of Exogamy

Because of the universality of the incest taboo, all societies to one degree or another have rules for marrying outside a certain group of kin. These are known as rules of exogamy.

In societies such as the United States, which are not based on the principle of unilineal descent groups, the exogamous group extends only slightly beyond the nuclear family. It is considered either illegal or immoral to marry one's first cousin and, in some cases, one's second cousin, but beyond that one can marry other more distant relatives with only mild disapproval. In societies that are based on unilineal descent groups, however, the exogamous group is usually the **lineage**, which can include many hundreds of people, or even the **clan**, which can include thousands of people who are unmarriageable. Thus, when viewed cross-culturally, rules of exogamy based on kinship do not appear to be based on genealogical proximity.

Rules of Endogamy

In contrast to exogamy, which requires marriage outside one's own group, the rule of endogamy requires a person to select a mate from within one's own group. Hindu castes found in traditional India are strongly endogamous, believing that to marry below one's caste would result in serious ritual pollution. Caste endogamy is also found in a somewhat less rigid form among the Rwanda and Banyankole of eastern Central Africa. In addition to being applied to caste, endogamy can be applied to other social units, such as the village or local community, as was the case among the Incas of Peru, or to racial groups, as has been practiced in the Republic of South Africa for much of the twentieth century.

Even though there are no strongly sanctioned legal rules of endogamy in the United States, there is a certain amount of marrying within one's own group based on class, ethnicity, religion, and race. This general de facto endogamy found in the United States results from the fact that people do not have frequent social contacts with people from different backgrounds. Upper-middle-class children, for example, tend to grow up in the suburbs, take golf and tennis lessons at the country club, and attend schools designed to prepare students for college. By contrast, many lower-class children grow up in urban housing projects, play basketball in public playgrounds, and attend schools with low expectations for college attendance. This general social segregation by class, coupled with parental and peer pressure to "marry your own kind" results in a high level of endogamy in many complex Western societies such as our own.

It should be noted that rules of exogamy and rules of endogamy are not opposites or mutually exclusive. Indeed, they can coexist in the same society provided the endogamous group is larger than the exogamous group. For example, it is quite possible to have an endogamous ethnic group (that is, one must marry within one's ethnic group) while at the same time having exogamous lineages (that is, one must marry outside one's own lineage).

Arranged Marriages

In Western societies, with their strong emphasis on individualism, mate selection is largely a decision made jointly by the prospective bride and groom. Aimed at satisfying the emotional and sexual needs of the individual, the choice of mates in Western society is based on such factors as physical attractiveness, emotional compatibility, and romantic love. Even though absolute freedom of choice is constrained by such factors as social class, ethnicity, religion, and race, individuals in most contemporary Western societies are free to marry whomever they please.

In many societies, however, the interests of the families are so strong that marriages are arranged. Negotiations are handled by family members of the prospective bride and groom, and for all practical purposes, the decision of whom one will marry is made by one's parents or other influential family members. In certain cultures, such as parts of traditional Japan, India, and China, future marriage partners are betrothed while they are still children. In one extreme example—the Tiwi of North Australia—females are betrothed or promised as future wives *before* they are born (Hart and Pilling 1960). Because the Tiwi believe that females are liable to become impregnated by spirits

at any time, the only sensible precaution against unmarried mothers is to betroth female babies before birth or as soon as they are born.

All such cases of **arranged marriage**, wherever they may be found, are based on the cultural assumption that because marriage is a union of two kin groups rather than merely two individuals, it is far too significant an institution to be based on something as frivolous as physical attractiveness or romantic love.

Arranged marriages are often found in societies with elaborate social hierarchies, perhaps the best example of which is Hindu India. Indeed, the maintenance of the caste system in India depends largely on a system of arranged marriages. As William Goode reminds us,

> Maintenance of caste was too important a matter to be left to the young, who might well fall prey to the temptations of love and thus ignore caste requirements. To prevent any serious opposition, youngsters were married early enough to ensure that they could not acquire any resources with which to oppose adult decisions. The joint family, in turn, offered an organization which could absorb a young couple who could not yet make their own living... This pattern of marriage has always been common among the nobility, but in India it developed not only among the wealthy, who could afford early marriages and whose unions might mark an alliance between two families, but also among the poor, who had nothing to share but their debts. (1963:208)

Arranged marriages in India are further reinforced by other traditional Indian values. Fathers, it was traditionally held, sinned by failing to marry off their daughters before puberty. Indeed, both parents in India shared the common belief that they were responsible for any sin the daughter might commit because of a late marriage. For centuries, Hindu civilization, with its heritage of eroticism expressed in the sexual cult of Tantricism, has viewed women as lustful beings who tempt men with their sexual favors. Thus, a girl had to be married at an early age to protect both herself and the men who might become sinners. And, if girls were to become brides before reaching adolescence, they could hardly be trusted to select their own husbands. Prompted by this belief, in certain parts of India girls marry at a very young age. According to a government survey of 5,000 women in Rajastan in northern India, more than half were married before they were 15 years old, and of these, 14 percent married before they were 10 and three percent before they were five. Even though the Indian government passed a law in 1978 setting a minimum age of marriage for females at 18, the law has been largely unenforced.

Anthropologist Serena Nanda (1992) reminds us that arranging marriages in India is serious business and should not be taken frivolously. In addition to making certain that a mate is selected from one's own caste, parents must be careful to arrange marriages for their children that take into consideration such factors as level of education, physical attractiveness, compatibility with future in-laws, and level of maturity. Requiring seriousness, hard work, and patience, arranging marriages may take years to bring about, as one of Nanda's Indian informants explains:

> This is too serious a business. If a mistake is made we have not only ruined the life of our son or daughter, but we have spoiled the reputation of our family as well. And, that will make it much harder for their brothers and sisters to get married. (1992:142)

Even though mate selection in North America generally is a matter of individual choice, many singles are not opposed to seeking help. As we begin the new millennium, there are dozens of web sites devoted to matchmaking, including such alluring sites as "Cupid's Network," "Authoritative Matchmaker," and "Match.com" For those who need assistance in finding a mate along the Information Superhighway, Jodie Gould and Lisa Skriloff have written a handbook, largely for women, entitled *Men Are from Cyberspace*, which offers advice on making the leap from mouse to spouse. Now, according to Alex Kuczynski (1999), even Wall Street has its own matchmaker. Fast-track financial types with little time to look for Mr. or Ms. Right can hire Janis Spindel, a New York City "romantic headhunter." Even though the notion of traditional matchmaking is antiquated, it somehow fits in very nicely with the pressures of the modern business world. Particularly when financial markets have been active (as they have for most of the 1990s), investment bankers, managing directors, corporate lawyers, and other financial high rollers simply don't have time to find a mate. So for $10,000, Spindel offers a dozen dates over the course of a year. Having brokered

294 monogamous relationships and 70 marriages, Spindel says this about her personal service business: "Who wants to look around all the time when you can hire me, your own personal shopper" (Kuczynski 1999:11).

Preferential Cousin Marriage

A somewhat less coercive influence on mate selection than arranged marriages is found in societies that specify a preference for choosing certain categories of relatives as marriage partners. A common form of preferred marriage is **preferential cousin marriage**, which is practiced in one form or another in most of the major regions of the world. Unlike our own kinship system, kinship systems based on lineages distinguish between two different types of first cousins: cross cousins and parallel cousins. This distinction rests on the gender of the parents of the cousin. **Cross cousins** are children of siblings of the opposite sex—that is, one's mother's brothers' children and one's father's sisters' children. **Parallel cousins**, on the other hand, are children of siblings of the same sex (the children of one's mother's sisters and one's father's brothers). In societies that make such a distinction, parallel cousins, who are considered family members, are called "brother" and "sister" and thus are excluded as potential marriage partners. However, because one's cross cousins are not thought of as family members, they are considered by some societies as not just permissible marriage partners but actually preferred ones.

The most common form of preferential cousin marriage is between cross cousins because it functions to strengthen and maintain ties between kin groups established by the marriages that took place in the preceding generation. That is, under such a system of cross cousin marriage, a man originally would marry a woman from an unrelated family, and then their son would marry his mother's brother's daughter (cross cousin) in the next generation. Thus, because a man's wife and his son's wife come from the same family, the ties between the two families tend to be solidified. In this respect, cross cousin marriage functions to maintain ties between groups in much the same way that exogamy does. The major difference is that exogamy encourages the formation of ties with a large number of kinship groups, whereas preferential cross cousin marriage solidifies the relationship between a more limited number of kin groups over a number of generations.

FAMILY

A much less common form of cousin marriage is between parallel cousins, the child of one's mother's sister or father's brother (Murphy and Kasdan 1959). Found among some Arabic-speaking societies of the Middle East and North Africa, it involves the marriage of a man to his father's brother's daughter. Because parallel cousins belong to the same group, such a practice can prevent the fragmentation of family property.

The Levirate and Sororate

Individual choice also tends to be limited by another form of mate selection that requires a person to marry the husband or wife of deceased kin. The **levirate** is the custom whereby a widow is expected to marry the brother (or some close male relative) of her dead husband. Usually, any children fathered by the woman's new husband are considered to belong legally to the dead brother rather than to the actual genitor. Such a custom serves as a form of social security for the widow and her children and preserves the rights of the husband's family to her sexuality and future children. The levirate, practiced in a wide variety of societies found in Oceania, Asia, Africa, and India, is closely associated with placing high value on having male heirs. Hindu men, for example, needed sons to perform certain family ceremonies, and ancient Hebrews placed a high value on sons so that a man's lineage would not die out. In both cases, men were under great pressure to marry their dead brothers' widows.

The **sororate**, which comes into play when a wife dies, is the practice of a widower's marrying the sister (or some close female relative) of his deceased wife. If the deceased spouse has no sibling, the family of the deceased is under a general obligation to supply some equivalent relative as a substitute. For example, in some societies that practice the sororate, a widower may be given as a substitute wife the daughter of his deceased wife's brother.

NUMBER OF SPOUSES

In much the same way that societies have rules regulating whom one may or may not marry, they have rules specifying how many mates a person may or should have. Cultural anthropologists have identified three major types of marriage based on the number of spouses permitted: **monogamy** (the marriage of one man to one woman at a time), **polygyny** (the marriage of a man to two or more women at a time), and **polyandry** (the marriage of a woman to two or more men at a time).

Monogamy

The practice of having only one spouse at a time is so widespread and rigidly adhered to in the United States that most people would have great difficulty imagining any other marital alternative. We are so accustomed to thinking of marriage as an exclusive relationship between husband and wife that for most North Americans, the notion of sharing a spouse is unthinkable. Any person who chooses to take more than one marriage partner at a time is in direct violation of conventional norms, religious standards, and the law and, if caught, will probably be fined or sent to jail.

So ingrained is this concept of monogamy in Western society that we often associate it with the highest standards of civilization, while associating plural marriage with social backwardness and depravity. Interestingly, many societies that practice monogamy circumvent the notion of lifelong partnerships by either permitting extramarital affairs (provided they are conducted discreetly) or practicing **serial monogamy** (taking a number of different spouses one after another rather than at the same time). In fact, serial monogamy is very common in the United States, Canada, and much of western Europe.

Polygyny

Even though monogamy is widely practiced in the United States and generally in the Western world, the overwhelming majority of world cultures do not share our values about the inherent virtue of monogamy. According to Murdock's *World Ethnographic Sample*, approximately seven out of every 10 cultures of the world permit the practice of polygyny. In fact, in most of the major regions of the world, polygyny is the preferred form of marriage. It was practiced widely in traditional India and China and remains a preferred form of marriage throughout Asia, Africa, and the Middle East. There is also evidence to support the idea that polygyny played a significant role in our own Western background by virtue of the numerous references to polygyny in the Old Testament of the Bible.

Many Westerners, steeped in a tradition of monogamy, interpreted the very existence of polygyny as having its basis in the male sex drive. Because they presumed that men had a stronger sex drive than women, polygyny was seen as a mechanism for men to satisfy themselves at the expense of women. This interpretation is flawed on a number of counts. First, there is little hard evidence to suggest that the sex drive is innately stronger for men than for women. Moreover, if men were interested in increasing their sexual options, it is not likely that they would choose multiple wives as a way of solving the problem. Instead, they would resort to multiple extramarital liaisons, which would be far less complicated than taking on the responsibilities of multiple wives.

To suggest that approximately 70 percent of the world's cultures practice polygyny is not tantamount to saying that 70 percent of the world's population practices polygyny. We must bear in mind that many of the cultures that practice polygyny are small-scale societies with small populations. Moreover, even in polygynous societies, the majority of men at any given time still have only one wife. Even in societies where polygyny is most intensively practiced, we would not expect to find more than 35 to 40 percent of the men actually having two or more wives. Polygyny in these societies is the preferred, not the usual, form of marriage. It is something for which men strive but only some attain. Just as the ideal of becoming a millionaire is usually not realized in the United States, so too in polygynous societies, only some men actually practice polygyny.

There are a number of reasons why most men in polygynous societies never acquire more than one wife. First, marriage in many polygynous societies requires the approval (and financial support) of large numbers of kinsmen, and this support is not always easy to obtain. Second, in some polygynous societies it is considered inappropriate for men of low rank to seek additional wives, thereby restricting a certain segment of the males in the society to monogamy. And third, being the head of a polygynous household, which invariably carries with it high prestige, is hard work. The management of two or more wives and their children within a household requires strong administrative skills, particularly if relations between the wives are not congenial. A recent study of polygyny among the present-day Zulu of South Africa (Moller and Welch 1990) indicates that Zulu men tend to opt for monogamy over polygyny for the additional reasons that they are under increasing pressure to accept the socially dominant values of South African Whites, and the dominant White Christian churches have opposed polygyny militantly. In short, most men in polygynous societies, for a variety of reasons, have neither the inclination, family power base, nor social skills needed to achieve the high status of being a polygynist.

Economic Status of Women in Polygynous Societies

The rate of polygyny varies quite widely from one part of the world to another. A critical factor influencing the incidence of polygyny is the extent to which women are seen as economic assets (where they do the majority of labor) or liabilities (where men do the majority of work). To illustrate, in such areas of the world as sub-Saharan Africa where women are assets, it has been estimated (Dorjahn 1959) that the mean rate of polygyny is approximately 35 percent, ranging from a low of 25 percent (!Kung) to a high of 43 percent (Guinea Coast). Conversely, in societies where women are an economic liability (such as among the Inuit, where only about 5 percent of the men practice polygyny), few men can afford the luxury of additional wives (Linton 1936).

Sex Ratio in Polygynous Societies

For polygyny to work, a society must solve the very practical problem of the sex ratio. In most human populations, the number of men and women is roughly equal. The question therefore arises: Where do the excess women who are needed to support a system of polygyny come from? It is theoretically possible that the sex ratio could swing in favor of females if males were killed off in warfare, if women were captured from other societies, or if the society practiced male infanticide. All of these quite radical solutions may account for a small part of the excess of women needed for a polygynous marriage system in some societies.

More commonly, this numerical discrepancy is alleviated quite simply by postponing the age at which men can marry. That is, if females can marry from age 14 on and males are prohibited from marrying until age 26, a surplus of marriageable women always exists in the marriage pool. In some traditional societies, such as the Swazi of southern Africa, young adult men were required by their regimental organizations (that is, age groups) to remain unmarried until the inauguration of the next regiment. Generally, this meant that men were not free to marry until their mid- to late-20s. Because women were able to marry in their teens, the Swazi society had solved the numerical dilemma presented by polygyny by simply requiring men to marry later in life than women.

Advantages of Polygyny

Having two or more wives in a polygynous society is usually seen as a mark of prestige or high status. In highly stratified kingdoms, polygyny is one of the privileges of royalty and aristocrats, as was the case with the late King Sobhuza of Swaziland, who, it was estimated, had well over a hundred wives. In societies that are stratified more on age than on political structure, such as the Azande of the Sudan and the Kikuyu of Kenya, polygyny is a symbol of prestige for older men. Whether aristocrat or commoner, however, having multiple wives means wealth, power, and high status for both the polygynous husband and the wives and children. That is, a man's status increases when he takes additional wives, and a woman's status increases when her husband takes additional wives. For this reason, women in some African societies actually urge their husbands to take more wives. Clearly, these African women do not want to be married to a nobody.

The old anthropological literature (written before the 1970s) gave the impression that women in polygynous societies generally favored polygyny over monogamy. However, such a conclusion was to some extent the result of male bias because the majority of ethnographers for the first half of the twentieth century were men. As Philip Kilbride (1997:284) suggests,

> There is evidence that women, in fact, do traditionally value polygyny. There is also evidence that suggests that men value it even more. There is also strong evidence that modernizing or westernizing women most likely value it not at all.

Sometimes multiple wives are taken because they are viewed by the society as economic and political assets. Each wife not only contributes to the household's goods and services but also produces more children, who are valuable economic and political resources. The Siuai of the Solomon Islands provide an excellent example of how having multiple wives can be an economic advantage for the polygynous husband. Pigs are perhaps the most prized possession of Siuai adults. According to Douglas Oliver, "To shout at a person 'you have no pigs' is to offer him an insult" (1955:348). Women are particularly valuable in the raising of pigs, for the more wives, the more hands to work in the garden, the more pig food, and, consequently, the more pigs. Oliver continues,

> It is by no mere accident that polygynous households average more pigs than monogamous ones. Informants stated explicitly that some men married second and third wives in order to enlarge their gardens and increase

their herds...Opisa of Turunom did not even trouble to move his second wife from her village to his own. She, a woman twenty years his senior, simply remained at her own home and tended two of his pigs. (1955:352–353)

Competition Among Wives

Despite the advantages just discussed, living in a polygynous household has drawbacks. Even though men desire multiple wives, they recognize the potential pitfalls. The major problem is jealousy among the wives, who often compete for the husband's attention, sexual favors, and household resources. In fact, in some African societies, the word for *co-wife* is derived from the root word for *jealousy*. As related here, jealousy and dissension among wives are common among the Gusii of western Kenya:

> Each wife tends to be the husband's darling when she is the latest, and to maintain that position until he marries again...This tendency in itself causes jealousy among the wives. In addition, any inequality in the distribution of gifts or money or in the number of children born and died, or the amount of education received by the children, adds to the jealousy and hatred. A woman who becomes barren or whose children die almost always believes that her co-wife has achieved this through witchcraft or poisoning. She may then attempt retaliation. (LeVine quoted in Stephens 1963:57)

Even though competition among wives in polygynous societies can be a threat to domestic tranquility, there are several ways to minimize the friction. First, some societies practice a form of polygyny called **sororal polygyny**, where a man marries two or more sisters. It is possible that sisters, who have had to resolve issues of jealousy revolving around their parents' attention, are less likely to be jealous of one another when they become wives. Second, wives in many polygynous societies are given their own separate living quarters. As Paul Bohannan and Philip Curtin (1988) remind us, because women may have more difficulty sharing their kitchens than their husbands, jealousy can be minimized by giving each wife her own personal space. Third, dissension is lessened if the rights and obligations among the wives are clearly understood. Fourth, potential conflict among wives can be reduced by establishing a hierarchy among the wives. Because the senior wife often exerts considerable authority over more junior wives, she can run a fairly smooth household by adjudicating the various complaints of the other wives.

Not only can the jealousies among wives be regulated, but some ethnographic reports from polygynous societies reveal considerable harmony and cooperation among the wives. Elenore Smith Bowen (1964:127–128) relates the story of Ava, a Tiv woman who was the senior of five wives:

> The women were fast friends. Indeed it was Ava who had picked out all the others. She saved up forty or fifty shillings every few years, searched out an industrious girl of congenial character, then brought her home and presented her to her husband: "Here is your new wife." Ava's husband always welcomed her additions to his household and he always set to work to pay the rest of the bridewealth, for he knew perfectly well that Ava always picked hard-working, healthy, handsome, steady women who wouldn't run away.

Although North America is adamantly monogamous, the practice of having more than one wife at a time does exist, particularly in the state of Utah. Although the Mormon church outlawed polygyny in 1890, the practice persists on a small scale, and, in fact, has experienced a resurgence over the last 30 years. Officially, polygyny remains a felony in Utah, but because it is considered benign, it is no longer prosecuted. Although accurate statistics on the incidence of polygyny in the United States are not available, it is estimated that as many as 30,000 people practice polygyny. Some Mormons practice polygyny today because of its deep-seated religious significance. Others practice it because it provides considerable social security, particularly for women. But, whatever the motivation, there are growing numbers of middle-class polygynists in parts of the United States. Some of the polygynist homesteads in this subculture are quite elaborate. The *Charlotte Observer* (Williams 1998) ran a picture of one such home: a 35,000 square foot structure with 37 bathrooms and 31 bedrooms, which housed a wealthy Mormon fundamentalist, his 10 wives, and 28 children!

Polyandry

Polyandry involves the marriage of a woman to two or more men at a time. A much rarer form of plural marriage, polyandry is found in less than one percent of the societies of the world, most notably in Tibet, Nepal, and India. Polyandry can be fraternal (where the husbands are brothers) or nonfraternal.

Perhaps the best-known case of polyandry is found among the Toda of southern India, who practice the fraternal variety. When a woman marries a man, she also becomes the wife of all of his brothers, including even those who have not yet been born. Marriage privileges rotate among the brothers. Even though all of the brothers live together with the wife in a single household, there is little competition or sexual jealousy. Whenever a brother is with the wife, he places his cloak and staff at the door as a sign not to disturb him. When the wife becomes pregnant, paternity is not necessarily ascribed to the biological father (genitor) but is determined by a ceremony that establishes a social father (pater), usually the oldest brother. After the birth of two or three children, however, another brother is chosen as the social father for all children born to the woman thereafter.

Toda society is characterized by a shortage of females brought about by the traditional practice of female infanticide, and this shortage of women maybe one of the reasons for the existence of polyandry among the Toda. Because of the influence of both the Indian government and Christian missionaries, however, female infanticide has largely disappeared today, the male-female sex ratio has become essentially balanced, and polyandry among the Toda is, for all practical purposes, a thing of the past.

In addition to explaining the existence of polyandry by the shortage of women, there are certain economic factors to consider. According to William Stephens (1963), senior husbands among the wealthier families in Marquesans society recruited junior husbands as a way of augmenting the manpower of the household. It has also been suggested (Goldstein 1987) that Tibetan serfs practice polyandry as a solution to the problem of land shortage. To prevent the division of small plots of land among their sons, brothers could keep the family land intact by marrying one woman. By marrying one woman, two or more brothers are able to preserve the family resources; that is, if all of the sons split up to form their own monogamous households, the family would rapidly multiply and the family land would rapidly fragment. In such a monogamous situation, the only way to prevent this rapid fragmentation of family land is to practice primogeniture (all land is inherited by the oldest son only). Such a system, though keeping the land intact, does so at the expense of creating many landless male offspring. In contrast, the practice of **fraternal polyandry** does not split up the family land but rather maintains a steady ratio of land to people.

ECONOMIC CONSIDERATIONS OF MARRIAGE

Most societies view marriage as a binding contract between at least the husband and wife and, in many cases, between their respective families. Such a contract includes the transfer of certain rights between the parties involved—rights of sexual access, legal rights to children, and rights of the spouses to each other's economic goods and services. Often the transfer of rights is accompanied by the transfer of some type of economic consideration. These transactions, which may take place either before or after the marriage, can be divided into five categories: **bridewealth, bride service, dowry, woman exchange,** and **reciprocal exchange**.

Bridewealth

Bridewealth is the compensation given upon marriage by the family of the groom to the family of the bride. According to Murdock's *World Ethnographic Sample* (reported in Stephens 1963:211), approximately 46 percent of all societies give substantial bridewealth payment as a normal part of the marriage process. Although bridewealth is practiced in most regions of the world, it is perhaps most widely found in Africa, where it is estimated (Murdock 1967) that 82 percent of the societies require the payment of bridewealth; most of the remaining 18 percent practice either token bridewealth or **bride service** (providing labor, rather than goods, to the bride's family).

Bridewealth is paid in a wide variety of currencies, but in almost all cases, the commodity used for payment is highly valued in the society. For example, reindeer are given as bridewealth by the reindeer-herding Chukchee, horses by the equestrian Cheyenne of the Central Plains, sheep by the sheep-herding Navajo, and cattle by the pastoral Masai, Samburu, and Nuer of eastern Africa. In other societies, marriage payments take the form of blankets (Kwakiutl), pigs (Alor), mats (Fiji), shell money (Kurtachi), spears (Somali), loincloths (Toda), and even the plumes of the bird of paradise (Siane).

Just as the commodities used in bridewealth transactions vary considerably, so does the amount of the transaction. To illustrate, an indigent Nandi of Kenya, under certain circumstances, can obtain a bride with no more than a promise to transfer one animal to the bride's father. A suitor from the Jie tribe of Uganda, on the other hand, normally transfers 50 head of cattle and 100 head of small stock (sheep and goats) to the bride's family before the marriage becomes official. Large amounts of bridewealth, as found among the Jie, are significant for several reasons. First, the economic stakes are so high that the bride and groom are under enormous pressure to make the marriage work. Second, large bridewealth payments tend to make the system of negotiations between the two families more flexible and, consequently, more cordial. When the bridewealth is low, the addition or subtraction of one item becomes highly critical and is likely to create hard feelings between the two families.

Not only do bridewealth payments vary between different cultures, but variations also exist within a single cultural group. In a study of bridewealth payments among the Kipsigis of western Kenya, Monique Mulder (1988) found that intragroup variations depended on several key factors. First, high bridewealth is given for brides who mature early and are plump because such women are thought to have greater reproductive success. Second, lower bridewealth is given for women who have given birth previously. And third, women whose natal homes are far away from their marital homes command higher bridewealth because they spend less time in their own mother's household and therefore are more available for domestic chores in their husband's household.

The meaning of bridewealth has been widely debated by scholars and nonscholars for much of the twentieth century. Early Christian missionaries, viewing the practice of bridewealth as a form of wife purchase, argued that it was denigrating to women and repugnant to the Christian ideal of marriage. Many colonial administrators, taking a more legalistic perspective, saw bridewealth as a symbol of the inferior legal status of women in traditional societies. Both of these negative interpretations of bridewealth led to a number of vigorous yet unsuccessful attempts to stamp out the practice.

Less concerned with moral or legal issues, cultural anthropologists saw the institution of bridewealth as a rational and comprehensible part of traditional systems of marriage. Rejecting the interpretation that bridewealth was equivalent to wife purchase, anthropologists tended to concentrate on how the institution operated within the total cultural context of which it was a part. Given such a perspective, cultural anthropologists identified a number of important **functions** that the institution of bridewealth performed for the well-being of the society. For example, bridewealth was seen as security or insurance for the good treatment of the wife, as a mechanism to stabilize marriage by reducing the possibility of divorce, as a form of compensation to the bride's lineage for the loss of her economic potential and her childbearing capacity, as a symbol of the union between two large groups of kin, as a mechanism to legitimize traditional marriages in much the same way that a marriage license legitimizes Western marriages, as the transference of rights over children from the mother's family to the father's family, and as the acquisition by the husband of uxorial (wifely) rights over the bride.

To avoid the economic implications of "wife purchase," E. E. Evans-Pritchard (1940) suggested that the term *bridewealth* be substituted for the term *bride price*, and Alfred Radcliffe-Brown (1950:47) used the word *prestation*, a term with even fewer economic connotations. Although a much-needed corrective to the earlier interpretations of bridewealth as wife purchase, much of the anthropological literature has overlooked the very real economic significance of bridewealth. It was not until near the end of the colonial period that Robert Gray (1960) reminded social scientists that it was legitimate to view bridewealth as an integral part of the local exchange system and that in many traditional societies, wives are dealt with in much the same way as other commodities. It is now generally held that a comprehensive understanding of the practice of bridewealth is impossible without recognizing its economic as well as its noneconomic functions.

Since the mid-1980s a number of studies in different parts of the world have documented the monetization of bridewealth (that is, the use of money as the medium of exchange). The transition from subsistence-based economies to cash-based economies has had a profound effect in recent times on traditional bridewealth practices and on the institution of marriage itself. As we have pointed out in this section, traditional bridewealth was an exchange of (often valuable) commodities from the groom's lineage to the bride's lineage. Because traditional bridewealth is a matter of solidifying long-term ties between two entire lineages, the actual pair to be married did not benefit directly from the exchange. However, when bridewealth becomes tied to cash payments that individual prospective grooms are able to earn on the open market, the close interdependence of family members (and their sanctioning of the marriage) becomes much less important. Today a growing number of wage earners in societies that practiced traditional bridewealth are becoming independent of their kinship group when it comes time to get married.

This monetization of bridewealth in Oceania is particularly well described in a recent edited volume called *The Business of Marriage* (Marksbury 1993). Contributing authors show how people from Panam, the Fiji Islands, and Papua New Guinea are viewing marriage increasingly as a financial transaction. This transition of bridewealth from being symbolic of alliances between kin groups to more commercial in nature is having a number of important consequences on the entire marital process. According to Richard Marksbury (1993), people are postponing getting married until a later age, marriage payments are being used more for personal fulfillment rather than being redistributed among a wide range of kin, men are incurring serious debts in their attempts to meet their payments, marriages are becoming less stable, and traditional husband-wife roles are changing.

Whatever the medium of exchange may be, bridewealth is still widely practiced today in certain parts of the world. In the 1970s this author conducted a study of changing patterns of bridewealth among the Kikuyu of East Africa and found that the traditional practice of bridewealth had survived amazingly well in the face of significant forces of change. More than two decades later, Bert Adams and Edward Mburugu (1994), studying a sample of 297 Kikuyu interviewees, reported that over 90 percent claimed that bridewealth was still being paid. Interestingly, neither educational level nor long-standing urban residence seemed to reduce the likelihood or amount of bridewealth. These data are consistent with studies of bridewealth in other parts of Africa (Ferraro 1983; Mwamwenda and Monyooe 1997), which indicate similar resilience of bridewealth in rapidly changing societies.

Bride Service

In societies with considerable material wealth, marriage considerations take the form of bridewealth and, as we have seen, are paid in various forms of commodities. But because many small-scale, particularly nomadic, societies cannot accumulate capital goods, men often give their labor to the bride's family instead of material goods in exchange for wives. This practice, known as bride service, is found in approximately 14 percent of the societies listed in Murdock's *World Ethnographic Sample.*

In some cases, bride service is practiced to the exclusion of property transfer; in other cases, it is a temporary condition, and the transfer of some property is expected at a later date. When a man marries under a system of bride service, he often moves in with his bride's family, works or hunts for them, and serves a probationary period of several weeks to several years. This custom is similar to that practiced by Jacob of the Old Testament (Genesis, Chapter 29), who served his mother's brother (Laban) for his two wives, Leah and her sister Rachel. In some cases where bride service is found, other members of the groom's family, in addition to the groom himself, may be expected to give service, and this work may be done not only for the bride's parents but also for her other close relatives, as is the case with the Taita of Kenya (Harris 1972).

Dowry

In contrast to bridewealth, a **dowry** involves a transfer of goods or money in the opposite direction, from the bride's family to the groom or to the groom's family. The dowry is always provided by the bride or the bride's family, but the recipient of the goods varies from one culture to another. In some societies, the dowry was given to the groom, who then had varying rights to dispose of it. In rural Ireland, it was given to the father of the groom in compensation for land, which the groom's father subsequently bequeathed to the bride and groom. The dowry was then used, wholly or in part, by the groom's father to pay the dowry of the groom's sister.

More often than not, the dowry was not given to the husband but was something that the bride brought with her into the marriage. In traditional society in Cyprus the dowry often consisted of a house or other valuable property. If the husband mistreated his wife or if the marriage ended in divorce, the woman was entitled to take the dowry with her. The dowry in this sense, very much like bridewealth, functioned to stabilize the marriage by providing a strong economic incentive not to break up.

The dowry is not very widely practiced throughout the world. Less than three percent of the societies in Murdock's sample actually practice it. It is confined to Eurasia, most notably in medieval and renaissance Europe and in northern India.

In certain European countries, where it is still practiced to some extent today, substantial dowry payments have been used as a means of upward mobility, that is, as a way to marry a daughter into a higher status family. Around the beginning of the twentieth century, a number of daughters of wealthy U.S. industrialists entered into mutually beneficial marriage alliances with European nobles who were falling upon hard economic times. The U.S. heiresses brought a substantial dowry to the marriage in exchange for a title.

Even though bridewealth is the usual form of marriage payment in Africa, there are several instances where the direction of payment is in the opposite direction. One such case is found among the Nilo-Hamitic Barabaig of Tanzania. Although a small number of goods are given to the bride's kin group, her family confers on her a dowry of two to 40 head of large stock, depending on their means. These dowry cattle, which often outnumber the cattle held originally by the groom, are kept in trust as inheritance cattle for the bride's sons and as dowry cattle for the bride's daughters. Because the Barabaig are patrilocal, the wife and her dowry cattle reside at the husband's homestead. Even though the husband has nominal control over the herd, he still must ask his wife's permission to dispose of any of the cattle, for technically the herd belongs to his wife's father. Until the herd is finally redistributed among their own children, it will remain a source of friction between the husband and wife because the very existence of such a dowry gives the wife considerable economic leverage in her marital relations.

Woman Exchange

Another way of legitimizing marriage by means of economic considerations is the practice of **woman exchange**, whereby two men exchange sisters or daughters as wives for themselves, their sons, or their brothers. This practice, which is limited to a small number of societies in Africa and the Pacific, is found in less than three percent of the world's societies. According to Edward Winter (1956), woman exchange was the primary means by which marriages were legitimized among the traditional Bwamba of Uganda. Such a system suffers from a considerable disadvantage: the exchange of one woman for another allows little room for individual variation. Bwamba women differ, as do women elsewhere, in terms of age, beauty, and procreative powers. Bwamba men prefer young, attractive, industrious, and fertile women. The exchange system cannot accommodate variations in these qualities.

In a system using conventional material objects such as bridewealth cattle, a man's preference may be reflected to a certain degree by the quality and quantity of his gifts. We should also bear in mind that the system of woman exchange has different implications for the distribution of women (especially in polygynous societies) than does a system using more conventional objects of exchange. Under the latter system, it is the wealthy man in the society who is able to obtain a large number of wives, whereas under the exchange system, the number of wives a man can obtain is limited to the number of sisters and daughters at his disposal.

Reciprocal Exchange

Reciprocal exchange is found in approximately six percent of the societies listed in Murdock's *Ethnographic Atlas*, most prominently in the Pacific region and among traditional Native Americans. It involves the roughly equal exchange of gifts between the families of both the bride and the groom. Such a custom was practiced by the traditional Vugusu people of western Kenya, who exchanged a large variety of items between a sizable number of people from both families. According to Gunter Wagner, the gifts made and the expenses incurred were basically reciprocal, with only "a slight preponderance on the bride's side" (1949:423). The variety of the reciprocal gift giving and the number of people involved in Vugusu society tend to emphasize the generally valid tenet that marriages in many parts of the world are conceived not simply as a union between a man and a woman but rather as an alliance between two families.

RESIDENCE PATTERNS: WHERE DO WIVES AND HUSBANDS LIVE?

In addition to establishing regulations for mate selection, the number of spouses one can have, and the types of economic considerations that must be attended to, societies set guidelines regarding where couples will live when they marry. When two people marry in North American society, it is customary for the couple to take up residence in a place of their own, apart from the relatives of either spouse. This residence pattern is known as **neolocal residence** (that is, a new place). As natural as this may appear to us, by global standards it is a rare type of residence pattern, practiced in only about five percent of the societies of the world. The remaining societies prescribe that newlyweds will live with or close to relatives of the wife or the husband.

One question facing these societies is, "Which children stay at home when they marry, and which ones leave?" Also, of those who leave, with which relative are they expected to reside? Although these questions can be answered in a number of ways, most residence patterns fall into one of five patterns (percentages based on tabulations from Murdock's *Ethnographic Atlas [1967]*):

Patrilocal residence: The married couple lives with or near the relatives of the husband's father (69 percent of the societies).

Matrilocal residence: The married couple lives with or near the relatives of the wife (13 percent of the societies).

Avunculocal residence: The married couple lives with or near the husband's mother's brother (four percent of the societies).

Ambilocal (bilocal) residence: The married couple has a choice of living with either the relatives of the wife or the relatives of the husband (nine percent of the societies).

Neolocal residence: The married couple forms an independent place of residence away from the relatives of either spouse (five percent of the societies).

To a significant degree, residence patterns have an effect on the types of kinship systems found in any society. For example, there is a reasonably close correlation between patrilocal residence and patrilineal descent (tracing one's important relatives through the father's side) and between matrilocal residence and matrilineal descent (tracing one's important relatives through the mother's side). To be certain, residence patterns do not determine kinship ideology, but social interaction between certain categories of kin can be facilitated if those kin reside (and play out their lives) in close proximity to one another.

It should be kept in mind that these five residence patterns, like most other aspects of culture, are ideal types. Consequently, how people actually behave—that is, where they reside—doesn't always conform precisely to these ideals. Sometimes, normative patterns of residence are altered or interrupted by events such as famines or epidemics that force newlyweds to reside in areas that will maximize their chances for survival or their economic security. To

FAMILY

illustrate, during the Depression years of the 1930s, the normal neolocal pattern of residence in the United States was disrupted when many young married adults moved in with one set of parents to save money. And, because of the high cost of living for young adults during the 1990s, the same pattern may be developing again.

FAMILY STRUCTURE

Cultural anthropologists have identified two fundamentally different types of family structure: the nuclear family and the extended family. The **nuclear family** is based on marital ties, and the **extended family**, a much larger social unit, is based on blood ties among three or more generations of kin.

The Nuclear Family

Consisting of husband and wife and their children, the nuclear family is a two-generation family formed around the conjugal or marital union. Even though the nuclear family to some degree is part of a larger family structure, it remains an autonomous and independent unit. That is, the everyday needs of economic support, childcare, and social interaction are met within the nuclear family itself rather than by a wider set of relatives. In societies based on the nuclear family, it is customary for married couples to live apart from both sets of parents (neolocal residence). The married couple is also not particularly obliged or expected to care for their aging parents in their own home. Generally, parents are not actively involved in mate selection for their children, in no way legitimize the marriages of their children, and have no control over whether their children remain married.

The nuclear family is most likely to be found in societies with the greatest amount of geographic mobility. This certainly is the case in the United States and Canada, which currently have both considerable geographic mobility and the ideal of the nuclear family. During much of our early history, the extended family—tied to the land and working and on the family farm—was the rule rather than the exception. Today, however, the family farm—housing parents, grandparents, aunts, uncles, cousins, and siblings—is a thing of the past. Now, in response to the forces of industrialization, most adults move to wherever they can find suitable employment. Because one's profession largely determines where one will live, adults in the United States and Canada often live considerable distances from their parents or other nonnuclear family members.

In addition to being found in such highly industrialized societies as our own, the nuclear family is found in certain societies located at the other end of the spectrum. In certain foraging societies residing in environments where resources are meager (such as the Inuit of northern Canada and the Shoshone of Utah and Nevada), the nuclear family is the basic food-collecting unit. These nuclear families remain highly independent foraging groups that fend for themselves. Even though they cannot expect help from the outside in an emergency, they have developed a family structure that is well adapted to a highly mobile life. Thus, both U.S. society and some small-scale food-collecting societies have adopted the nuclear family pattern because of their need to maintain a high degree of geographic mobility.

Although the independent nuclear family has been the ideal in the United States for much of the twentieth century, significant changes have occurred in recent years. According to the U.S. Census, less than one in three households consists of the nuclear family (parents and one or more children), a sharp decline from earlier decades. The other two-thirds of the U.S. households are made up of married couples without children, single adults, single parents, unmarried couples, roommates, extended family members, or adult siblings. As Conrad Kottak (1987) has suggested, these changing patterns of family life have been reflected in a number of television sitcoms. For example, during the 1950s the family was depicted by Ozzie and Harriet Nelson and their sons, David and Ricky; and by Ward and June Cleaver and their sons, Wally and the Beaver. Within the last several years, however, an increasing number of TV shows have featured alternative living arrangements such as roommates, single adults, working mothers, and single parents. In fact, some of the most popular TV sitcoms in recent years feature characters who are neither related to nor living with one another (such as *Seinfeld*, *Friends*, and *Ally McBeal*).

There are several explanations for the decline of the nuclear family in the United States as we begin the twenty-first century. First, as more and more women complete higher education and enter the job market, they are more likely to delay marrying and having children. Second, the increasing cost of maintaining a middle-class household that includes the parents, children, a three- or four-bedroom house, a cocker spaniel, and a car or two has caused some couples to opt for remaining childless altogether.

CHAPTER **6**

Hawaiian Children at School and at Home

A basic premise of educational anthropology is that the cultural patterns students bring with them into the classroom must be taken into account if these students are to be successfully integrated into the culture of the school. This is precisely the objective that educational anthropologist Cathie Jordan brought to her work with the Kamehameha Elementary Education Program (KEEP), a privately funded educational research effort designed to develop more effective methods for teaching Hawaiian children in the public schools.

For decades children of Hawaiian ancestry, particularly those from low-income families, have been chronic under-achievers in the public school system. Classroom teachers often describe Hawaiian children as lazy, uncooperative, uninvolved, and disinterested in school. Differences do exist between their dialect, known as Hawaiian Creole English, and the Standard English used by teachers, but the linguistic differences are minimal. Thus, Cathie Jordan and her colleagues at KEEP needed to look beyond linguistic differences to find an explanation for why Hawaiian children were not succeeding in school. Accordingly, KEEP focused on the wider Hawaiian culture—particularly interaction patterns within the family—in order to discover learning skills the children had developed at home that could be used and built upon in the classroom.

When dealing with parents and siblings at home, Hawaiian children behave very differently than when interacting with teachers and classmates. From a very early age, Hawaiian children contribute significantly to the everyday work of the household. Tasks that all children are expected to perform regularly include cleaning, cooking, laundry, yard work, caring for younger siblings, and (for male siblings) earning cash from outside employment. Working together in cooperative sibling groups, brothers and sisters organize their own house holdwork routines with only minimal supervision from parents.

Young children learn to perform their household tasks by observing their older siblings and adults. And, according to Jordan and her colleagues (1992:6), these chores are performed willingly within a "context of strong values of helping, cooperation, and contributing to the family."

The paradox facing KEEP was, "How could children be so cooperative and responsible at home and yet so disengaged and lazy in school?" A comparison of the home and school cultures revealed some major structural differences, When a mother wants her children to do a job around the house, she makes that known and then allows the children to organize how it will get done. In other words, she hands over the responsibility of the job to the children. In contrast, the classroom is almost totally teacher dominated. The teacher makes the assignments, sets the rules, and manages the resources of the classroom. Children are controlled by the classroom rather than being responsible for it. Once these cultural differences between home and school were revealed by anthropological fieldwork, the educational anthropologist was able to suggest some changes for improving student involvement in school. The solution was fairly straightforward: have teachers run their classrooms in much the same way as Hawaiian mothers run their households. Specifically, teachers should minimize verbal instructions, withdraw from direct supervision, and allow students to take responsibility for organizing and assigning specific tasks. When these changes were made, Hawaiian students became more actively involved in their own education, and consequently their achievement levels improved.

Here, then, is an example of how educational anthropologists can apply their findings to improve the learning environment for Hawaiian children. Interestingly, this case of applied anthropology did not follow the traditional solution to problems of minority education, which involves trying to change the child's family culture to make it conform to the culture of the classroom. Rather, Jordan and her colleagues at KEEP solved the problem by modifying the culture of the classroom to conform to the skills, abilities, and behaviors that the Hawaiian students brought with them from their family culture.

FAMILY

Third, the ever-increasing divorce rate in the United States has contributed to the increase in nonnuclear families in recent decades.

The Extended Family

In societies based on extended families, blood ties are more important than ties of marriage. Extended families consist of two or more families that are linked by blood ties. Most commonly, this takes the form of a married couple living with one or more of their married children in a single household or homestead and under the authority of a family head. Such extended families, which are based on parent-child linkages, can be either patrilineal (comprising a man, his sons, and the sons' wives and children) or matrilineal (comprising a woman, her daughters, and her daughters' husbands and children). It is also possible for extended families to be linked through sibling ties rather than parent-child ties, such as extended families consisting of two or more married brothers and their wives and children. According to Murdock's *Ethnographic Atlas* (1967), approximately 46 percent of the 862 societies listed have some type of extended family organization.

When a couple marries in a society with extended families, there is little sense that the newlyweds are establishing a separate and distinct family unit. In the case of a patrilineal extended family, the young couple takes up residence in the homestead of the husband's father, and the husband continues to work for his father, who also runs the household. Moreover, most of the personal property in the household is not owned by the newlyweds but is controlled by the husband's father. In the event that the extended family is large, it may be headed by two or more powerful male elders who run the family in much the same way that a board of directors runs a corporation. Eventually, the father (or other male elders) will die or retire, allowing younger men to assume positions of leadership and power within the extended family. Unlike the nuclear family, which lasts only one generation, the extended family is a continuous unit that can last an indefinite number of generations. As old people die off, they are replaced through the birth of new members.

It is important to point out that in extended family systems, marriage is viewed more as bringing a daughter into the family than acquiring a wife. In other words, a man's obligations of obedience to his father and loyalty to his brothers are far more important than his relationship to his wife. When a woman marries into an extended family, she most often comes under the control of her mother-in-law, who allocates chores and supervises her domestic activities.

In some extended family systems, the conjugal relationship is suppressed to such an extent that contact between husband and wife is kept to a minimum. Among the Rajputs of northern India, for example, spouses are not allowed to talk to each other in the presence of family elders. Public displays of affection between spouses are considered reprehensible; in fact, a husband is not permitted to show open concern for his wife's welfare. Some socities take such severe measures to subordinate the husband-wife relationship because it is feared that a man's feelings for his wife could interfere with his obligations to his own blood relatives.

Why do so many societies in the world have extended families? There is some indication that extended families are more likely to be found in certain types of economies than others. As previously mentioned, economies based on either foraging or wage employment (which require considerable geographic mobility) are more likely to be associated with nuclear than with extended families. In addition, a rough correlation exists between extended family systems and an agricultural way of life. Several logical explanations have been suggested for this correlation. First, extended families provide large numbers of workers, who are necessary for success in both farm production and the marketing of surpluses. Second, in farm economics, where cultivated land is valuable, an extended family system prevents the land from being continually subdivided into smaller and less productive plots. As an alternative explanation, Burton Pasternak, Carol Ember, and Melvin Ember (1976) have suggested that extended family systems develop in response to what they call "incompatible activity requirements." That is, extended families are likely to prevail in societies where there is a lack of man- and woman-power to simultaneously carry out subsistence and domestic tasks.

Modern-day Family Structure

Most Western social thinkers over the past century have been in general agreement concerning the long-term effects of urbanization and modernization on the family. In general, they see a progressive nuclearization of the family in the face of modernization. This position is perhaps most eloquently presented by William Goode, who has stated that industrialization and urbanization have brought about "fewer kinship ties with distant relatives and a greater emphasis on the 'nuclear' family unit of couple and children" (1963:1). Although in many parts of the world we can observe the association between modernization and fewer extended kinship ties, there are a number of exceptions, most notably in certain developing countries. To illustrate, in the Kenya Kinship Study (KKS), no significant differences were found in the extended family interaction between rural Kikuyu and Kikuyu living in Nairobi. This retention of extended family ties in this urban, industrialized setting could be explained by several relevant economic factors. First, the combination of a fiercely competitive job market and few or no employment benefits (such as workers' compensation, retirement, and unemployment insurance) means that the average urban worker has little job security. Second, despite the creation of freehold land tenure in Kenya in recent years, land inheritance still generally takes place within the extended family. Urban workers who sever ties with their rural-based extended kin relinquish their rights to inherit land, which for many remains the only haven from the insecurities of urban employment.

Interestingly, we do not need to focus on developing countries to find the retention of extended kin ties in urban, industrialized areas. For example, Carol Stack (1975) and Jagna Sharff (1981) have shown how urban Blacks in the United States use extended kinship ties as a strategy for coping with poverty. Moreover, at least one immigrant group in the United States—the Vietnamese—has used modern technology to help maintain and strengthen its traditional family values. Jesse Nash (1988) reports that immigrant Vietnamese families routinely rent Chinese-made films (dubbed in Vietnamese) for their VCRs. Whereas most films and TV programming in the United States tend to glorify the individual, Chinese films tend to emphasize the traditional Confucian value of family loyalty.

For at least the first half of the twentieth century, popular opinion (buttressed by the Judeo-Christian tradition) upheld a fairly uniform notion of what form the typical U.S. family should take. The natural family, according to this view, was a nuclear family consisting of two monogamous heterosexual parents (the breadwinning male and the female homemaker) with their children. In the past five decades, however, this so-called typical family has become

harder to find. In fact, there is no longer a "typical family" in the United States. According to census data for 1990, fewer than 27 percent of all families in the United States are made up of married couples with children under 18 years of age. Moreover, even fewer (approximately 20 percent) of all U.S. families fit the typical model with the breadwinning husband and the homemaking wife. As we begin the twenty-first century, nearly three out of every four families are atypical in that they are headed by a female single parent, a male single parent, unmarried partners, or childless or post-child-rearing couples. There are also stepfamilies, extended families, homosexual families, and communal families, all of which are accepted alternative family forms.

From Instructor's Edition for *Cultural Anthropology*, 4th edition, by Gary Ferraro. Copyright © 2001 Wadsworth, a part of Cengage Learning, Inc. Reproduced by permission. www.cengage.com/permissions.

The Rise of the Gay Family: More and More American Children Are Growing up with Same-sex Parents—
Dan Gilgoff

"We were afraid people out here would be skeptical of us," says Sheri Ciancia, sipping a glass of iced tea outside the four-bedroom house she and her partner bought last fall in Tomball, Texas, a half-hour's drive from Houston. "Afraid they wouldn't let their kids play with ours."

"But we've got to take chances," adds Stephanie Caraway, Ciancia's partner of seven years, sitting next to her on their concrete patio as their 8-year-old daughter, Madison, attempts to break her own record for consecutive bounces on a pogo stick. "We're not going to live in fear."

A trio of neighborhood boys pedal their bikes up the driveway, say hello to the moms, and ask Madison if they can use her bike ramp. The boys cruise up and down the ramp's shallow slopes while Madison continues bouncing, the picture of suburban serenity. Despite their misgivings about relocating from Houston to this tidy subdivision, the family has yet to encounter hostility from their neighbors. "We have to give straight people more credit," Caraway says with a wry smile. "I'm working on that."

Tomball—its roads lined with single-room Baptist churches and the occasional sprawling worship complex, known to some locals as "Jesus malls"—may seem an unlikely magnet for gay couples raising kids. A year before Caraway and Ciancia moved here, activists in the neighboring county got a popular children's book that allegedly "tries to minimize or even negate that homosexuality is a problem" temporarily removed from county libraries. So imagine Caraway's and Ciancia's surprise when, shortly after moving in, their daughter met another pair of moms rollerblading down their block: a lesbian couple who had moved into the neighborhood with their kids just a few months earlier.

Growing. Gay families have arrived in suburban America, in small-town America, in Bible Belt America—in all corners of the country. According to the latest census data, there are now more than 160,000 families with two gay parents and roughly a quarter of a million children spread across some 96 percent of U.S. counties. That's not counting the kids being raised by single gay parents, whose numbers are likely much higher—upwards of a million, by most estimates, though such households aren't tracked.

This week, the commonwealth of Massachusetts will recharge the gay-marriage debate by becoming the first state to offer marriage licenses to same-sex couples. The move has raised the ire of conservatives who believe gay marriage tears at the fabric of society—and earned support from progressives who think gay men and lesbians deserve the same rights as heterosexuals. But the controversy is not simply over the bond between two men or two women; it's about the very nature of the American family.

Gay parents say their families are much like those led by their straight counterparts. "I just say I have two moms," says Madison, explaining how she tells friends about her parents (whom she refers to as "Mom" and "Mamma Sheri"). "They're no different from other parents except that they're two girls. It's not like comparing two parents with two trees. It's comparing two parents with two other parents."

Many of today's gay parents, who grew up with few gay-parent role models, say their efforts have helped introduce a culture of family to the gay community. "In the straight community, adoption is a secondary choice," says Rob

Calhoun, 35, who adopted a newborn daughter with his partner 20 months ago. "But in the gay community, it's like, 'Wow, you've achieved the ultimate American dream.'"

The dream has not been without cost, though. Gay parents and their kids in many parts of the country frequently meet with friction from the outside world, in the form of scornful family members, insensitive classmates, and laws that treat same-sex parents differently from straight parents. In general, Americans are split on the subject. A national poll this winter found that 45 percent believe gays should have the right to adopt; 47 percent do not.

Many traditional-marriage advocates argue that marriage is first and foremost about procreation. "It is the reason for marriage," Pennsylvania Sen. Rick Santorum said last summer. "Marriage is not about affirming somebody's love for somebody else. It's about uniting together to be open to children." Other critics call gay and lesbian couples who are raising kids—whether from previous marriages, adoption, or artificial insemination—dangerously self-centered. "It's putting adult desires above the interest of children," says Bill Maier, psychologist in residence at Focus on the Family and coauthor of the forthcoming *Marriage on Trial: The Case Against Same-Sex Marriage and Parenting*. "For the first time in history, we're talking about intentionally creating permanently motherless and fatherless families."

Evidence? Three decades of social science research has supplied some ammunition for both sides of the gay-parent debate. Many researchers say that while children do best with two parents, the stability of the parents' relationship is much more important than their gender. The American Psychological Association, the American Academy of Pediatrics, the National Association of Social Workers, and the American Bar Association have all released statements condoning gay parenting. "Not a single study has found a difference [between children of gay and straight parents] that you can construe as harmful," says Judith Stacey, a professor of sociology, gender, and sexuality at New York University and a gay-rights advocate.

Stacey and other researchers even suggest that gay and lesbian parents who form families through adoption, artificial insemination, or surrogacy may offer some advantages over straight parents. "In the lesbian and gay community,

Gay Nuptials in the Bay State

Planning a wedding is tough under pretty much any circumstances, but for thousands of gay and lesbian couples in Massachusetts hoping to marry this week, the path to the altar has been littered with lawsuits, constitutional amendments, and other legal bric-a-brac.

When the Massachusetts high court sanctioned same-sex marriage last November, it gave the state six months to brings laws into line. Opponents of the ruling used that time to attempt to block the measure, first by crafting a civil-union plan like Vermont's, then, when that failed, initiating an amendment to the state's constitution that would define marriage as solely between a man and woman. This amendment passed the legislature once but must take another pass in the 2005–6 session before going to the voters, in the fall of 2006. Gov. Mitt Romney asked for a stay on the gay-marriage decision until the 2006 vote, but the state's attorney general refused.

Wedding bells. So barring an 11th-hour appeal, Massachusetts will probably be issuing same-sex marriage licenses this week. Marriages performed in Oregon, California, New Mexico, and New York are still clouded by litigation. For his part, President Bush is backing an amendment to the U.S. Constitution that would limit marriage to heterosexual couples, but it's apt to be a tough sell.

Romney, meanwhile, has cited an obscure 1913 miscegenation law to make marriages for out-of-state couples, who would not be legally recognized in their home states, illegal. Defiant clerks in Provincetown, Worcester, and Somerville say they will nevertheless marry all comers, despite the governor's threat of legal action. "I think there're still statutes against witches in the books," says Worcester Mayor Timothy Murray. "Why don't we enforce those?"

—Caroline Hsu

parents are a self-selecting group whose motivation for parenthood is high," says Charlotte Patterson, a psychologist and researcher at the University of Virginia. But studies on the subject have so far examined relatively few children (fewer than 600, by some counts) and virtually no kids of gay dads.

One study coauthored by Stacey and widely cited by both supporters and opponents of gay parenting found that children of lesbians are more likely to consider homosexual relationships themselves (though no more likely to identify as homosexuals as adults) and less likely to exhibit gender-stereotyped behavior. "If we could break down some of society's gender stereotypes, that would be a good thing," says Ellen Perrin, professor of pediatrics at the Floating Hospital for Children at Tufts-New England Medical Center. Focus on the Family's Maier disagrees: "They don't have rigid gender stereotypes? That's gender identity confusion."

While the debate continues, the number of kids with gay parents keeps growing. According to Gary Gates, an Urban Institute demographer, 1 in 3 lesbian couples was raising children in 2000, up from 1 in 5 in 1990, while the number of male couples raising kids jumped from 1 in 20 to 1 in 5 during the same period. The uptick is partly due to changes in the census itself, which in 1990 tabulated most same-sex couples that identified themselves as married on census forms as straight married couples. In the 2000 census, though, those couples were tabulated as gay and lesbian partners. But the leap in such couples with children is large enough to suggest a real spike. And because gay and lesbian couples are sometimes reluctant to identify themselves as such on census forms, actual figures could be much higher.

Moving in. What's perhaps most surprising is that gay- and lesbian-headed families are settling in some of the most culturally conservative parts of the country. According to the *Gay and Lesbian Atlas* published earlier this month by the Urban Institute, Alaska, Arizona, Georgia, Louisiana, and New Mexico are among the 10 states with the largest number of gay families—along with more historically gay-friendly New York, California, and Vermont. States where gay and lesbian couples are most likely to have children (relative to the state's total number of gay couples) are

Mississippi, South Dakota, Alaska, South Carolina, and Louisiana, in that order. "Same-sex couples who live in areas where all couples are more likely to have children" may simply be more likely to have children themselves, according to the atlas. And couples with children—regardless of their sexual orientation—are looking for good schools, safe streets, and outdoor green space. "It's gay couples who don't have kids whose behavior tends to be different: they live in more-distressed areas of cities, with higher crime and more racial diversity," says Gates. "But a large portion of gay people own their homes, live in the suburbs, and are raising two children.

Most of these children are the products of previous heterosexual relationships. Madison, for one, is Caraway's daughter by a former boyfriend. Caraway says the pregnancy forced her to come to terms with her homosexuality; she started dating Ciancia soon after her daughter's birth. "If you stay in a relationship but you're not in love or committed to the person, children sense that," says Caraway, now 31. "What kind of message does that send?"

But as these children enter middle and high school, their peers are more likely to inquire about their parents' sexuality—and not always politely. The Tufts-New England Medical Center's Perrin, who authored the American Academy of Pediatrics' policy on gay parenting, says that children of same-sex parents "get stigmatized because of who their parents are. It's the biggest problem they face by far." Just like many gays and lesbians themselves, children of homosexuals speak of "coming out" as a long and often difficult ordeal. "You are, on a day-to-day basis, choosing if you're out or if you're going to be hiding the whole truth," says Abigail Garner, author of the recently released *Families Like Mine*, about children of homosexuals. "Is she your mom's roommate or your aunt or your mom's friend?"

During middle school and part of high school, A. J. Costa, now a freshman at Texas Lutheran University outside San Antonio, kept his mother's relationship with a live-in partner secret. He grew close to his mom's partner, even preferred the arrangement to his mom's previous marriage, which ended when he was 7, but never invited friends to the house. "I didn't want anyone to make fun of me," says Costa. "Nobody was going to mess with my family."

Costa's fears were reinforced by some classmates who did find out and referred to his moms as "dykes." But in the summer before his junior year in high school, Costa visited Provincetown, Mass., for "Family Week," an annual gathering of gay parents and their children. "I couldn't get over how many families there were, all like mine," he recalls. "I realized that it wasn't about whether I have two gay moms. It was that I have two *moms*. It was getting past the fact that they're gay."

Support. In recent years, support networks for children of gay parents and for parents themselves have expanded dramatically. Children of Lesbians and Gays Everywhere, or COLAGE, has chapters in 28 states. The Family Pride Coalition, whose dozens of local affiliate organizations attract gay parents who want their kids to meet other children of gays and lesbians, has doubled its member and volunteer base in the past five years, to 17,000. Vacation companies like Olivia, founded 30 years ago for lesbian travelers, now offer packages specifically for gays and lesbians with children, and R Family Vacations, underwritten by former talk-show host Rosie O'Donnell, will launch its inaugural cruise this summer. Tanya Voss, a 36-year-old college professor in Austin who, with her partner, has two young boys through artificial insemination, plans to attend the first Family Pride Coalition weekend at Disney World next month. Kids need environments where "they don't have to explain their families," she says, "a safe place where they could just be."

Still, neither COLAGE nor Family Pride Coalition has affiliate groups in Mississippi, South Dakota, or Alaska, the states where gay and lesbian couples are most likely to have kids. ("The way you manage in a more hostile environment," says Gates, "is to go about your business and not draw much attention to yourself.") Many such states also present the highest legal hurdles for those families. Roughly two thirds of children with same-sex parents live in states where second-parent or joint adoptions—which allow the partner of a child's biological or adoptive parent to adopt that child without stripping the first parent of his or her rights, much like stepparent adoption—has been granted only in certain counties or not at all.

Absent such arrangements, a biological or adoptive parent's partner could be powerless to authorize emergency medical treatment or denied custody if the other parent dies. When

Voss and her partner were planning to have their first child, they decided Voss wouldn't carry the baby because her parents—who disapprove of Voss's homosexuality—would have likely claimed custody in the event that their daughter died during childbirth.

Gay-rights advocates argue that it's often children who end up suffering from laws restricting gay parenting—and same-sex marriage. If a parent without a legal relationship with his or her partner's child dies, a 10-year-old child whose nonlegal parent was earning $60,000 at the time of death, for example, would forgo nearly $140,000 in Social Security survivor benefits paid to children of married couples, according to the Urban Institute and the Human Rights Campaign. That's on top of the more than $100,000 in Social Security paid to a widow—but not a gay partner—whose spouse earned $60,000. And without laws recognizing them as legitimate parents, nonlegal parents are unlikely to be required to pay child support if they leave their partner.

Recently, some states have further restricted adoption. Earlier this year, a federal appeals court upheld Florida's ban on homosexuals adopting children, the only one of its kind in the nation. Arkansas now bans gay foster parenting, Mississippi bans same-sex couples from adopting, and Utah bans adoptions by all unmarried couples. "State legislatures that opposed gay marriage are going to push to replicate what Florida has done," says lawyer John Mayoue, author of *Balancing Competing Interests in Family Law*. "We'll see more of this as part of the backlash against gay marriage."

Even so, more gay couples—especially male couples—are adopting than ever before. A study last year found that 60 percent of adoption agencies accept applications from homosexuals, up from just a few a decade ago. The 2000 census showed that 26 percent of gay male couples with children designate a stay-at-home parent, compared with 25 percent of straight parents. "When you have children, whether you're gay or straight, you spend lots of time wondering how good a job you're doing for your kids; you lose sleep over it," says Mark Brown, 49, whose partner stays home with their two young adopted kids. "It doesn't leave much time to worry about how we're being perceived by straight society."

Dan Gilgoff, "The Rise of the Gay Family," *U.S. News and World Report*, May 24, 2004, pp. 40–45. Copyright © 2004 U.S. News and World Report, L.P. Reprinted with permission.

TIL DEATH DO US PART?

The fact is that monogamous species on this planet are rare at best. While 90% of bird species share long-term pair bonds, in mammalian species it has been estimated that 3% are considered monogamous. For primates (which is a category made up of over 200 species, including humans), the rate of monogamy is approximately 12%. This includes borderline cases, such as humans.

Most human cultures world wide practice some ritual or ceremony associated with committed bonding. While in Western societies we take the vow "until death do us part" this is hardly adhered to in all cultures. And more important, what does "taking the vow" mean to most Americans? With a U.S. divorce rate of almost 50% (over 65% in the state of California) and the potential for remarriage, how do humans fit into the concept of monogamy?

Anthropologist Bobbi Low of the University of Michigan states that we as a species practice **serial monogamy**—which means that the first partner might be succeeded by another partner, and even possibly replaced by a third, and so on. Humans are not necessarily true monogamists, forming life-time pair bondings. In fact, based upon ethnographic accounts, anthropologists have discovered that a vast number of cultures, approximately 83%, allow for some type of **polygamy**, meaning more than one sexual partner. Even though this is not necessarily sanctioned in the United States, it does occur.

FAMILY

CHAPTER 6

Mormon Polygyny: Love, Duty, and Salvation—
William Jankowiak

INTRODUCTION

Romantic passion is a complex, multifaceted, emotional phenomenon that is a byproduct of an interplay between biology, self, and society. It is this complexity that separates romantic passion from other more basic emotions (e.g., enjoyment, anger, fear, sadness, disgust, and surprise) that are readily experienced, easily recognized, and thus, understandable around the world (Fisher 2004). Romantic passion draws on several psychological processes that range from erotic stimulation, emotional attachment, and idealization. Like all complex emotions, it is mediated by social learning which shapes its expression in specific ways. In short, it had a cultural face. Before examining that face, I want to explore those elements that contribute to making it, in its most rudimentary form on the level of private experience, a cross-culturally identifiable, emotional state.

In this article, I will examine how the desire for emotional exclusivity in love impacts the way Mormon polygamous women and men relate to one another. Specifically, I want to know if there are ubiquitous, albeit illicit, monogamous emotional entanglement(s) between a co-wife and her husband, or can members in this religious community overcome this impulse and find meaning and emotional fulfillment in their commitment to the larger plural family?

ANGEL PARK: THE SOCIAL COMMUNITY

Angel Park is one of six polygamous communities found in North America and northern Mexico. Each community is separately governed and maintains only nominal, if any, contact with the others. The population of Angel Park is approximately 6,500, with over half of the population under twelve years old. Unlike 19th century Mormonism, where an estimated 10 to 20 percent of the families were polygamous (Foster 1992), in 1996, more than forty-five percent (158 out of 350 Angel Park families) form a polygamous household. Because people strive to practice "Big House" polygamy where everyone lives together, the houses range in size from three bedroom mobile trailers to huge 35,000 square foot mansions that are in various stages of completion or renovation.

Angel Park lacks a well-developed economy which necessitates most residents seek employment outside the community. Most men work in the booming regional construction and inter-state trucking industries, while women and other men work in a variety of jobs that include accountants, architects, janitors, masseuses, caretakers, nurses, mechanics, and until the First Ward's recent rejection of public school education, principals and teachers. Despite the inconvenience of working outside the community, most people do seek and find employment outside of Angel Park. Angel Park is, however, not a wealthy town. Its average income is $14,500, making it one of the lowest median incomes in the western United States (Zoellner 1998, p.A1).

MORMON THEOLOGY, CHRISTIANITY, AND HONORING THY FATHER

There are several non-negotiable tenets at the core of the fundamental Mormon religious theology. One, God is a polygamist who loves all his children but confers on men, in particular, an elevated spiritual essence which insures that men who live "righteously" will obtain a higher spiritual standing in the next life. Two, men occupy leadership positions in their families and on the church council as well as have the potential, in the next life, to become god-heads with dominion over all their descendants. A woman's standing, on the other hand, is determined by her performance in the highly valued complimentary roles of mother and wife. Like Southern Baptists, Mormon fundamentalists interpret the scripture literally, "A woman should submit herself graciously to her husband's leadership" and a husband should "provide for, protect, and lead his family."

The fundamentalists' conviction is that they are God's chosen people, born to live "the fullness of the Gospel" and, thus, to create what the prophet Joseph Smith declared was God's ideal: the Celestial Kingdom organized around the polygamous family on Earth (Baur 1988). In fundamentalism, women achieve salvation through obedience, first to their fathers and then to their husbands, by becoming sister-wives (i.e., co-wives) in a "celestial," or plural, family. The marital contract "seals" a man and woman together "for time and eternity" in the Heavenly Kingdom (Musser 1944). Because this bond extends beyond the grave into an eternal world, it is in a woman's "best interest to advance her husband's interests" (i.e.,

233

she should bear a large number of children [Bohannan 1985:81]), while at the same time strive to uphold her husband's authority, especially in front of his children.

PLACEMENT MARRIAGE: AN EFFORT TO CONTROL ROMANTIC LOVE'S IMPULSE

Mormon cosmology holds that, before birth, everyone lives with God as a spirit (Bennion 1996). Unlike the Church of the Latter Day Saints, however, there is a belief that individuals may meet someone they had been promised to but much more likely was to meet family members rather than a specific spouse. Individuals must, therefore, strive to find their "true love" and, in a sense, remarry their heavenly spouse. Failure to strive in such a way can potentially lead to an awkward situation whereby one's earthly spouse will differ from one's heavenly spouse. To this end, the priesthood's council members as God's representatives are eagerly sought in matters of the heart. One of the council's most important functions is to help community members find their celestial mates.

So strong is this conviction that the community prefers to admonish its youth "not to get involved in 'puppy love' or other kinds of opposite sex stuff." In spite of this value, I found that after 10 p.m. a large number of teenagers had slipped out of their homes and were strolling around in deep conversations with one another. For the more adventurous, there were regular bonfire parties held some distance from the settlement. These parties were known for heavy beer drinking, flirting and heavy kissing, with occasional sexual trysts. These casual meetings and possible developing love encounters are often held in check by the belief in the power of the priesthood elders to know who an individual had been promised to (in the previous life and thus who they will be with in their future life). It is a point emphasized in a ninth grade boy's observation that "it is important to pray to God and ask for a sign [as to whom you are promised to]." He noted that "I recently did this and a feeling came over me and I know I am in love. She is older than I am. She is eighteen years old. But we must wait as I am too young. I will go to the head of the priesthood council and see if he thinks my feeling is an authentic one. If it is, he will be able to tell her to wait for me. If not, then she was not the one for me." In this case, he was told that he was not the one, as she had been promised as a second wife to another man. The ninth grader accepted the decision with regret.

The validity of dreams as a vehicle of truth is so strong that they are often the critical guide one uses in making important decisions. A middle-aged woman, for example, who had recently terminated a short but difficult marriage and was hesitant to become emotionally involved again, changed her mind when she, by chance, met a man who resembled a man that she dreamed about as a young girl. She recalls that, "I dreamt of a man with blue eyes and curly blond hair. Neither of my first two husbands had blue eyes nor curly hair. When I saw him standing with blond hair and blue eyes, I knew he was the man in my dreams and I wanted to immediately marry him. It did not matter what others might think, he was my true love."

In another case a woman who had recently divorced her husband met her future husband by chance when she was assisting an ill workmate. She told me, "I did not want to meet him [her future husband]. He was divorced. A big no-no for a man [but not for a woman] in our community. Because of that, I refused to meet him. By chance when we came together in the man's hospital room, I was intensely aware of being drawn to him. Years ago I had a dream of my ideal man and he fitted that image. He later told me he was sweating and could not look at me."

While some placement marriage deliberations can be a straightforward process in which the individuals readily accept their own or a priesthood council elder's "vision," there are other cases where personal convictions can result in the rejection of an elder's "vision." Twenty years age difference between spouses do not trouble most fundamentalist women. They are troubled, however, when the age difference exceeds twenty years. For example, a twenty-year-old woman was deeply troubled about the possibility of being placed with an old man. She told me, "I thought about this, prayed on it, and realized that nothing was coming from my prayers. So I just picked a young man" (who was the son of the man who her two older sisters had married). "I did not want to be placed with an old man, I know so many girls who cry for years after the wedding, 'cause they were placed with an old man and could have a young man whom they preferred (i.e., had a "love crush" on). I got a young man who is nice and I am happy." Another case found a twenty-two-year-old woman who had run away from the community, then returned and asked that she be placed in a plural family. At first she thought that she was going to be placed with a seventy-year-old man. If this happened, she informed me, she would have rejected the placement. She remembered, "I did not want to be married to that old man. I was set to refuse. However, when it turned out to be Ron [who was twenty years older than she and married to her older sister], I agreed to marry him. In fact, I felt relieved and sank back into the couch in a state of calmness. I knew it would be okay."

From this and other accounts, it should not be assumed that placement marriages result in unhappiness and misery. Some do and others do not. In these marriages individuals, particularly teenage women, follow the matrimonial recommendations of their parents and the priesthood council. Usually not deeply emotionally involved with a spouse, the individual enters marriage expecting, as in many cultures, that in time "love with come." As a twenty-seven-year-old woman who on the eve of her tenth wedding anniversary, admitted, "During the first three years of my marriage I did not even like my husband. But now I can say I truly love him." Hers is not an atypical case. Several couples acknowledged that they fell in love after they were placed. One woman acknowledged that "It was wonderful; without placement we never would have found one another." Other couples remained optimistic, noting that "God would have directed them to each other anyway."

"LOVE CRUSHES": MEN AND WOMEN'S ANXIETIES
In spite of religious doctrine, advanced most adamantly by men, that harmonious or comfort love is superior to romantic love, women regularly use the intensity of their husband's affection as the primary base to assess the quality of their marriage. In this way, Angel Park residents are similar to 19th century Mormon polygamists whose love letters were also filled with romantic yearnings, emotional turmoil, and heart-rending disclosures (Young 1954). This was especially so if the women strove to become her husband's "favorite wife."

The "favorite wife" can easily manipulate her husband, and thereby receive a greater share of his emotional time and financial investment for herself and her children. As one man who had three wives noted, "I do not know why I always give into Alice (his favorite wife). It seems that my other wives do not have the same ability to get me to agree with them." His comment is representative of other men in Angel Park. My research found that while some husbands (usually the more educated) strove to be fair in their dealings with all their wives, only three wealthy families were men able to meet all their material obligations and, thus, prevent wives from competing over the shortage of material resources. For most Angel Park families, there are insufficient material or emotional resources to distribute to everyone's satisfaction. Choices have to be made, some members have to do without. Inevitably the favorite wife and her children's needs are met first. In most families, wives learn to accept or, at least, grudgingly tolerate the family's division of affection.

Although men maintain a stoic, if not cynical, posture toward romantic love, they also have fears of emotional vulnerability. Many men dismissed or downplayed the value of emotional love, stressing that it was, at bottom, an illusion and not the best basis for a marriage. The strength and consistency in which this sentiment was expressed originally convinced me that fundamentalist men seldom felt romantic passion for a spouse. However, more in-depth probing found that two-thirds of the men I interviewed had been romantically rejected as young men in high school. The experience was so distressing that they became determined never to become emotionally involved again. I asked one man if on his wedding day he was in love with any of his three wives. He indicated that he was not, but acknowledged that when in high school he had fallen in love with two women who rejected his overtures. He admitted that "it hurt so much I decided never again to let myself experience that feeling." Twenty years later he found a deep, and at times, passionate love with his second of three wives. Still, his fear is common in Angel Park.

Men's anxiety over the possibility of losing emotional intimacy through abandonment is revealed in the following account. A middle-aged woman recalls the anxiety of her beloved husband and his words on their wedding night: "Have you ever wanted something your whole life and, when you finally have it, you feel that it is going to be taken away from you?" "No," she replied, "I guess I have not lived long enough to desire something that much." Then he told her he was "so afraid of losing me because he loved me so much." That night she promised never to leave him. Twenty years later her husband, bedridden from old age, could no longer control his bowel movements. Whenever she grew weary of the tedious duties involved in bathing, feeding, and cleaning him, she remembered her wedding night promise never to leave him. She asserted that, "I stayed with him because in the end I realized that I loved him. I know right now he is preparing a place for me on the other side and, when I die, he will come and take me back with him, but only if I am worthy."

An example of men's propensity to quietly endure emotional loss is found in the torment of a man whose second wife left him to join another polygamous community. The man did not want to discuss the incident for fear of emotionally retrieving it. However, his son told us that "my father was depressed for months. He lost the woman he loved." Another wife revealed that her husband was devastated when his third wife left the family, remarking that "when Sam's third wife left him for another man who had been secretly courting her, if affected his health. He cried for three straight weeks and simply deteriorated into an invalid. We buried him six months later."

FAMILY CONFLICT AND RELIGIOUS GUILT

Social relations in the Mormon polygamous family, like many other polygamous societies, revolve around personal sentiment as much as duty. There is a twin pull of almost equal force. For women, romantic love's presence or absense, much more than role equity, constitutes the primary measure of quality of their relationship. Its primacy is movingly revealed in the following personal accounts of what happens when a husband's love is lost. A man who had two wives notes that "my wives are not upset over sex, but they are over the amount of time I spend with each wife. They seem to count the time and measure it. It is the source of many of our family disagreements." It also accounts for the heightened guilt and shame men and women often feel striving to live up to the principle of plural marriage. If a husband can avoid pursuing only personal interests and struggle or, in their words, "sacrifice," to uphold the religious principles, the household ambience will be relatively harmonious and content. A polygamist husband knows that if he becomes too attached to any particular woman, it may result in the disruption of family bonds and damage to his reputation within the community for being unable to manage his family. The burden of this management falls heavily on the man. Men know that, if the family has the reputation of being disharmonious, it may be more difficult to attract a future wife. Further, it can result in something ever more important: the loss of the love of his favorite wife.

It is a dilemma for men and women. They embrace the polygamous principle and its call for plurality, while simultaneously seeking to hold onto, or rekindle, the romantic passion once felt toward a particular spouse. The tensions that erupt around this dilemma are the source of drama found in daily life at Angel Park. The reality is that the majority of Angel Park's polygamous families seldom achieve genuine long-lasting harmony. Instead they remain, at best, a cauldron of competing interests that periodically rupture the fragile balance that unites a man, his wives, and children together in their religiously inspired and unified cultural system. For most Mormon polygamous men and women, their anxiety never completely goes away. In this way, polygamy has become for the vast majority of residents of Angel Park the embodiment of their religious convictions anchored in an ethos of self-sacrifice that sustains an effort to achieve a humble spirit. For most, there is not greater sacrifice than that involved with denying a basic human need to merge with another in an exclusive emotional and physical bond. The continuous struggle to achieve and maintain a humble state represents, for most residents of Angel Park, a symbol and heavenly sign of their failing to achieve God's plan for humanity.

ACKNOWLEDGEMENTS

I would like to thank Lauren Arenson, Jim Bell, Helen Gerth, Libby Hinson, Jennifer Miller, and Tom Paladino for their encouragement, feedback, and thoughtful replies to portions of this paper.

ENDNOTE

1. Recent disagreements within the community have resulted in the split of Angel Park into two rival religious communities or Wards (e.g., First and Second Ward). Until 2000, with the exception of some theological differences concerning political succession within the church organization, both Wards were similar in their cultural orientation. This changed with the death of the First Ward's leader or prophet. His son (Warren Jeffs, who has a warrant for his arrest) took control of the community and instituted a series of policies that strengthened his authority and control over its members. The First Ward has completely withdrawn from mainstream society, while the Second Ward continues to interact, albeit in a restrictive fashion, with mainstream society. By 2005, the First Ward leaders

were in hiding and federal courts were preparing to give power to women who lived in the First Ward. If this happens it will constitute a fundamental departure from Angel Park's history of being a male-centered, family-oriented, theologically-governed, religious community. The Second Ward has not violated any local or state laws and continues to be a male-centered governed community.

REFERENCES

Baur, H. 1988. *Utopia in the Desert*. New York: SUNY Press.

Bennion, J. 1998. *Women of Principle: Female Networking in Contemporary Mormon Polygyny*. New York: Oxford University Press.

Bohannan, P. 1985. *All the Happy Families*. New York: McGraw Hill.

Fisher, H. 2004. *Why we love?* New York: Henry Holt Company.

Foster, Lawrence. 1992. *Women, Family, and Utopia*. Syracuse: Syracuse University Press.

Jankowiak, W. 1995. "Introduction." In *Romantic Passion*, William Jankowiak, ed. New York: Columbia University Press, pgs. 1–20.

Musser, Joseph. 1944. *Celestial or Plural Marriage*. Salt Lake City: Truth Publishing Co.

Young, Kimball. 1954. *Isn't One Wife Enough?* New York: Henry Holt and Company.

Zoellner, Tom. 1998. "Polygamy on the Dole." *Salt Lake Tribune*, June 28.

FAMILY

The New "Mixed" Marriage: Working with a Couple When One Partner Is Gay—
Joe Kort

When we think of a "mixed marriage," we typically imagine two individuals of different races or religions. But the mixed-orientation marriage—with one straight spouse and one who's gay or lesbian—is just as real, though far more likely to operate underground. This long-shrouded partnership burst into public view in August 2004, when New Jersey Governor James McGreevey went on national TV to come out as a "gay American," while his wife, Dina, stood stock-still by his side, her mouth arranged in a frozen smile. More recently, best-selling author Terry McMillan (*How Stella Got Her Groove Back*) publicly denounced her husband, Jonathan Plummer, for carrying on clandestine affairs with male lovers. Suddenly, America was buzzing about the "horror" and "tragedy" of straight and gay individuals united by marriage.

Let me be clear at the outset: I'm not against mixed-orientation marriages per se. They can, and do, work well for some couples. What I don't support are mixed marriages that are steeped in secrecy, which is how these relationships too commonly operate.

LIVING A LIE

During my first appointment with Eric, he told me that he'd had some homosexual experiences and wasn't sure whether he was gay, bisexual, or a sex addict. The manager of a major export company, 48-year-old Eric had been married to his wife, Ann, for 25 years, and the couple had a teenage son and daughter. But even before he'd gotten married, Eric admitted, he'd had frequent and elaborate sexual fantasies about men.

When he was 21 years old, a college therapist told him what he badly wanted to hear: that his urges were simply sexual perversions that would pass. The therapist further advised him not to act on these "perversions," but to go forth and lead a healthy heterosexual life. Deeply relieved, Eric decided to marry Ann, whom he'd dated during his senior year of college, and to keep his homoerotism to himself.

At first, Eric felt he pulled it off pretty well. He loved his wife and enjoyed sex with her, though he often used images of men to stay aroused and reach orgasm. For a number of years, he didn't act on his homosexual urges, so he didn't feel bad about them. Occasionally, he's masturbate to porn, but he was careful to throw the magazines out afterward. Overall, Eric's lack of romantic feelings for other men convinced him that his urges were "simply" sexual, not part of full-fledged gay identity. He told himself he was "heterosexual with a bit of kink."

Then, several years into the marriage, the couple bought a home computer, and Eric's delusions quickly began to unravel. Secretly, he began surfing gay-porn sites and entering chat rooms. Before long, he found himself meeting men for anonymous sexual encounters. "But all this time, I loved Ann and believed in monogamy, so I felt horribly guilty for cheating," he told me.

One night, as he surfed the web, he stumbled upon an internet club expressly for married gay men who wanted monogamy with another man without leaving their wives. He immediately joined the group, and soon afterward met Harris, who lived in a nearby city and was also married. They "clicked" online, met soon afterward, and agreed that they'd found the perfect arrangement. They told their wives they'd met at a business conference and discovered that they both enjoyed fly fishing, which gave them the excuse to spend whole weekends alone together, for enthusiastic sex and—for Eric, at least—deepening intimacy.

But their idyll was short-lived, for Harris soon announced that he wanted to have sex with other men. Eric was devastated. He plunged into a depression so black that Ann couldn't help but notice. Finally, sleepless and distraught, he called me.

After listening to his story, I pulled no punches. "You're not living with integrity," I told him.

He exploded. "This from a gay therapist? For a response like that, I could have called Dr. Laura!"

I assured him that I didn't necessarily disapprove of his having an intimate relationship with a man, even though he was married. "The issue is that you're keeping secrets, deceiving your wife, and aren't being congruent with yourself," I said. "If you both had an open relationship, with informed consent on her side, that would be different."

"You have no idea what my life is like!" Eric shouted. "You've never had a wife and kids you loved, and because of it, faced giving up someone you're mad about." He started crying. 'Maybe you're not the right therapist for me," he said between sobs. "I need someone to support me and help me make this work."

"Make what work?" I inquired.

"Having a relationship with both my wife *and* my boyfriend. I don't want to lose either of them."

I gently told Eric that if he wanted someone to approve his living a lie with his wife and himself, he was correct—I wasn't the right therapist for him. "Until you get honest with yourself and your wife," I said, "I can't support your belief that having sex with someone outside of marriage is okay." Even more important, I told him, "Until you act from a place of integrity, I don't think you'll feel any happier or more whole than you are right now."

If Eric wasn't prepared to tell his wife, I said, there was another viable option—to stay married and make a commitment to never again act on his homosexual urges. I made very clear that my perspective on this was different from practitioners of Reparative Therapy (RT), who tell gay people that sexual reorientation is possible and, indeed, highly advisable. I believe that's nonsense. However, I do believe that people who self-identify as homosexual, but don't wish to come out as gay, can choose to create a heterosexual lifestyle.

But Eric wasn't open to this option, either. At the end of the session he left quickly, mumbling over his shoulder that he'd call if he wanted to reschedule. I figured there was a good chance I'd never hear from him again. But a month later, he called, sounding desperate. His depression and anxiety had worsened. "I gotta tell her," he said.

COMING OUT

When a gay person comes out to his or her straight spouse, the couple is likely to embark on a roller-coaster ride of emotional stages that often encompass humiliation, revenge, renewed hope, rage, and, finally, resolution. While each couple is unique, these stages can serve as a rough road map for therapists trying to help mixed-orientation couples make sense of their feelings, communicate honestly, and, ultimately, make informed, healthy decisions about their future.

When Eric told Ann that he was homosexual, she was stunned and horrified. "Did you marry me just to have kids?" she railed. "Were you just using me all along?" When he then admitted that he'd been having an affair with Harris, her hurt and horror turned to cold fury. Blaming him for ruining her life, she ordered him out of the house and threatened to tell their two teenage children and their families of origin. She also planned to see a divorce lawyer to get full custody of the kids. "You do realize," she hissed, "that no judge would let a homosexual even have visitation rights!"

Beneath Ann's rage was a deep sense of humiliation. "What kind of a person was she to choose a homosexual husband?" she wondered. Eric, in turn, felt humiliated by Ann's accusatory response, which only reinforced a lifetime of shame about his essential "wrongness." I explained to Eric that Ann was trying to shame him because of the humiliation she felt, but that he needed to take her threats of reprisal seriously. At my suggestion, he asked her to join him for a therapy session, and she reluctantly agreed.

Before they came in, Ann sent me a long e-mail detailing everything she knew about Eric's dysfunctional childhood, neurotic personality traits, inadequate fathering, problematic work and sleep habits, and more. This wasn't unusual. Typically, when spouses learn that their partner is gay; their first response is to focus on their partner's failings.

As the joint session got underway, Ann was quick to let me know that she didn't trust me. "Why would a gay therapist be interested in helping us decide whether to stay together?" she demanded. She wasn't sure she wanted to stay with Eric, she said, but she wanted to keep the possibility open. Her concerns made sense to me, and I explained my perspective on mixed-orientation marriages. "If you both want it to work, then so do I," I assured her.

For most of that first session, I listened to, and validated, Ann's flood of thoughts and feelings. Both Ann and Eric wept, insisting that they wanted to stay together but weren't sure it was possible.

I then appealed to Ann's sense of integrity. If she wanted to remain married, it needed be a conscious choice free of shame and darkness. But Ann was unwilling to look at her contribution to the issues in the marriage. Spouses in all marriages—gay or straight—choose partners, in part, to meet certain unconscious needs. I tried to explain to Ann that straight individuals rarely marry gay people accidentally. Either they have sexual issues themselves or they need emotional distance from their partners. Ann didn't want to hear any of this. Instead, she projected all of their problems as a couple onto Eric. I spent our next several meetings trying to facilitate clear, open communication between them. What did each of them want? Ann made it clear that she couldn't tolerate Eric's having a relationship with both her and Harris. "You'll have to choose," she told him. But soon afterward, Harris made the choice for Eric by breaking off with him. Eric was crushed, although his boyfriend's decision also clarified for Eric what he wanted—or at least what he thought he wanted. Now that he'd lost Harris, he couldn't face the possibility of losing Ann, too. He apologized for hurting her, and told her he wanted to stay married. "I love you, and I promise to stay faithful," he said.

THE HONEYMOON

This new pledge of fidelity initiated the next stage of the coming-out process for Eric and Arm as a couple: a kind of honeymoon period of renewed hope and mutual appreciation. Because Eric truly loved Ann, and because he'd empathized with her pain, she began to feel she'd been reunited with the man she married. Eric, for his part, was profoundly grateful that Ann was willing to take him back. "She's a saint!" he told me, his voice edged with awe.

Shortly after they reunited, Ann stopped coming to see me. She also refused to see another therapist or attend a support group for straight partners married to gay partners. But Eric continued on in therapy. Before long, he acknowledged that he'd begun to feel restless and dissatisfied. He loved Ann and his kids; there was no question about that. But with no homosexual outlet, his life felt flat and empty.

Eric's growing dissatisfaction initiated the next stage of the couple's process, when they become aware of the limits of the possible. While still hurt, Ann was genuinely happy

to have Eric back. But, the absence of a man's emotional and sexual companionship weighed increasingly heavily on him. Increasingly depressed, he found himself surfing internet porn sites once again, and drifting into chat rooms. Before long, he was telephoning men and meeting them for sex—and, he hoped, for love.

Late one night, Ann caught Eric making arrangements online to hook up with a new man. After an explosive fight, they returned to my office together. "I love you," he told her in that session, "but I have to be who I am. I want to stay married to you and have affairs with men." I still remember my sense of foreboding when Ann, looking strained and pale, agreed to his terms. This type of arrangement can sometimes work out, but only when the straight spouse is willing to take a long, close look at herself. So far, I hadn't seen any willingness on Ann's part to do that. I strongly recommended she get some individual therapy, but she assured me, "I can handle this on my own."

Eric continued to meet men, but now told Ann the truth about his plans. Between dates, he'd often sit in their driveway for hours talking on his cell phone with guys he'd met online. From Eric's vantage point, Ann seemed to be adjusting pretty well to their "new marriage." Then one night Eric returned home from a date to discover that Ann had told their son and daughter that their father was gay. He was stunned and furious. "How dare you tell them without my permission," he raged, "and without letting me be part of the process!"

"What was I supposed to do?' Ann countered bitterly. "You're out all hours meeting guys, and I'm left here worrying sick you'll be killed!"

Back into therapy they came.

Ann stubbornly held to her position that she'd told the kids only because she was worried out of her mind, not because she was furious at Eric. Firmly, I told them that I believed that neither one of them was behaving either with respect to themselves or their relationship. As far as I could tell, I said, Ann wanted a full-time, monogamous husband—sexually and emotionally. Eric wanted a boyfriend as well as a wife who was reasonably happy with the arrangement. Their aims were incompatible.

For the next few sessions, I worked on encouraging both of them to examine and identify their authentic relationship needs. Within a few weeks, Eric decided to come out as a gay man—in his words, to live "as the person I've been all along." Ann, for her part, realized that it was impossible to make the marriage work. They decided to divorce.

GETTING REAL

When I work with people in mixed-orientation marriages like Eric and Ann's, my goal is neither to help them to stay married nor to get divorced. Instead, it's to help partners come back into integrity with themselves and each other. It's truly up to the couple, not to me, to discover what's right for them.

That said, I tend to start from a place of hope for the relationship. Unless one partner definitely wants out of the marriage, I start by asking a couple how their marriage can continue. I work with each partner on what he or she really wants.

I realize that many therapists disapprove of a gay husband and straight wife staying together under any circumstances. Sign of an intimacy disorder. Some might urge the couple to consider divorce to allow both parties to move on with their lives. Other clinicians might advise the gay husband to remain the sexually faithful partner he promised to be on his wedding day. I once held this belief myself—that anything less than monogamy betrayed the relationship. Now I'm open to the various arrangements that couples adopt.

The principal reason I've changed my mind is that I've now sat with many couples who've struggled long and hard over a divorce or separation when, in the end, that wasn't at all what they wanted. So I've come to accept that there are a number of instances in which responsible nonmonogamy between partners is a viable option. One such instance is when the couple is older, has invested emotionally, financially, and psychologically in each other, and want to be together in their later years. Another is when the couple has become best friends, and the marriage is sacred to them. A third is when the man is emotionally heterosexual and physically homosexual.

The idea here isn't to change the orientation of the gay spouse. That's impossible. Rather, it's to accept the couple they are and honor what they want.

In doing this kind of work, taking a thorough history on both partners is essential. While Ann refused to participate, I was able to do some effective family-of-origin work with Eric. He grew up in a family that demanded obedience, and therefore Eric learned early on to get his needs met underground. I helped him see that his depression stemmed, in part, from his inability to openly make decisions for himself and allow himself to experience the consequences of those decisions. Gradually, I helped him feel safe enough to do this.

Ann still hasn't gotten help. She remains angry at Eric for "ruining her life." This outcome isn't the norm: many gay and straight spouses who divorce ultimately become friends. While Eric wants friendship, particularly for his children's sake, Ann has made it clear she's not interested. Meanwhile, Eric has done his best to talk with his teenage kids about who he is, why he's made the decisions he has, and how much he loves them. At this point, they're more aligned with their mother.

In the meantime, Eric has met a man with whom he wants to spend the rest of his life. He continues to regularly visit his children, but doesn't talk about his gay life or bring his partner around, at their request. I hope that, eventually, the children will develop a separate relationship with Eric and accept his life as a gay man with a new partner, just as they would if their parents had divorced and Eric had married another woman.

It's often hard for me to sit with mixed-orientation couples, since I get in touch with my anger at living in a society that shames gays and lesbians into role-playing heterosexuality. If gays were treated with respect and empathy to begin with, much personal suffering and chaos could be spared. As comedian Jason Stuart says, "I wish you straight people would let us gay people get married. If you did, we'd stop marrying you!"

CASE COMMENTARY—
MICHELE WEINER-DAVIS

Couples decide their marriages are doomed for a litany of reasons. Some say that, though they love their spouses, they're no longer *in love*. Others find the spark has gone out of their sexual relationships. Still others feel that the endless arguments about children, in-laws, and money are so divisive that the marriage has been drained of mutual respect and caring. To me, a psychotic optimist about the possibility of personal and relationship change, these are nothing more than garden-variety problems that, with a heavy dose of problem-solving, can easily be resolved.

But because sex is such a fundamentally important part of marriage, what happens when one spouse finds him- or herself yearning to be with a same-sex partner, despite many years of marriage? No amount of "I-messages," active listening, or willingness to compromise alters sexual orientation.

This is the problem Joe Kort faces on a regular basis, and I have great respect for his interest in helping these couples find their way. Nonetheless, there were times in reading about Eric and Ann that I found myself wondering, "How might I have handled this case differently?" As I reflected on this, several major issues emerged.

One of the most important lessons I've learned in my work with 11th-hour couples is that, regardless of my personal opinions, unless I join equally with *both* spouses, change becomes unlikely and resistance almost inevitable. I've become convinced that the art of doing good marital work lies in our ability to have both spouses leave our offices feeling that we're on his or her side. After all, we often ask people to stretch outside their comfort zones. But, unless they see us as genuine allies, why should they?

With that in mind, I wondered whether Kort really connected with Ann. Let's face it, she was inappropriate and irritating. Her anger and blaming would easily push the buttons of even the most accepting of therapists. But I put myself in her shoes for a moment and tried to imagine what it would be like to discover in an instant that the man I married and thought I knew more intimately than anyone in the world wasn't who I thought he was. Talk about having the rug pulled out from under you!

So, while I'd draw a line in the sand about Ann's anger and threats, I'd try to help both Ann and Eric see how her cruel behavior was really a symptom of the shock, grief, and fear she was undoubtedly feeling. Normalizing in this way might have softened the blow of her actions for Eric, while, at the same time, painting a more humane picture of Ann. This might have allowed them to join in their shared pain, rather than become opponents.

Also, I suspect that marital work may have been doomed from the start because of a theoretical belief held by Kort—that mixed marriages can only work if straight spouses are willing to examine the underlying dysfunctional reasons they marry gays. I know many, many people who simply don't have "gaydar"; they don't pick up on their spouses' homosexual tendencies. And I don't think this means they have an unconscious need for emotional/sexual distance in their relationships.

If owning up to her own reasons for marrying a gay man was the sort of personal growth Kort was expecting of Ann, I can completely understand why she resisted it, along with his other suggestions for individual therapy and support groups. From my perspective, since both Ann and Eric were interested in saving their marriage if at all possible, what they needed was help in defining the parameters of their newly emerging relationship, which was headed toward uncharted territory. I couldn't help but wonder whether Ann's meltdown resulted, not from her inability to cope with her anger about having to develop a mixed marriage, but from poor communication regarding their mutual expectations around his dating behavior.

Kort's work shines a light on one other issue that's become increasingly clear to me over the years—a marriage is about more than the person to whom you're wedded. I recently worked with a man who loved his wife, but was not in love with her, and was wildly passionate about the woman with whom he'd been having an affair. He admitted he didn't understand why he felt so confused and stuck, because he knew he'd rather be with his affair partner. I explained that, in life, our choices are never simply about one issue versus another: every choice in life is about package deals. I asked him to weigh the attributes not of the women in his life, but of the packages they encompassed. When he did so, his marital package won hands down, despite the sizzle of his affair.

How does this relate to Kort's work with Ann and Eric? Marriage isn't always about achieving personal satisfaction. While I'd certainly encourage Eric to honor and explore his need for same-sex relationships, I'd work overtime to help preserve the family unit, and not simply for the reasons Kort proposes—a shared history, friendship, companionship in old age, etc.—all personally driven goals. What about the kids? Conspicuously missing from Kort's list of acceptable reasons to stay in the marriage is a relationship with your children.

Am I suggesting Eric stay for the sake of the kids? That would be okay with me, but that's not what I'm proposing here. Nevertheless, I can't help but wonder how Eric feels now, months or even years later, having sated his homosexual yearnings and become a "regular visitor" of his not-yet-accepting children? Is that the package he wanted?

AUTHOR'S RESPONSE

Weiner-Davis' commentary is comparing apples to oranges: she juxtaposes her heterosexual male client's affair with a woman to the affair of a gay husband with another man. But for the gay spouse, cheating isn't just an indication of a relationship issue; it's his attempt to resolve a personal identity crisis about his fundamental sexual and romantic orientation. Eric had to decide not just whether he could make some changes in his marriage, but whether his marital partner was the wrong gender.

My work with couples assumes that each partner has an equal investment in creating and maintaining the type of closeness or distance—including emotional and sexual—that exists between them. Straight spouses often look back at themselves and admit they unconsciously needed a partner who couldn't be fully available to them. In mixed marriages, these spouses happen to be gay. Nevertheless, Ann was unwilling to examine anything other than Eric's "bad" behaviors. Try as I did to join with her, she was unwilling to accept any insights about herself from support groups or individual therapy with myself or another therapist. Had she been willing to do so, she could have come to understand her own personal and relational dynamics.

With all couples, my work is about *shared* responsibility. When one partner in a relationship has an addiction, they're an addicted couple. When the woman is pregnant, they're pregnant. When one has an affair, they both share the burden of how it evolved and how to resolve it.

I would never advise anyone, gay or straight, to stay in a marriage only for the sake of the kids. This burdens the children and would have denied Eric's fundamental identity as a gay man, keeping him invisible.

Weiner-Davis supports my concern about a therapist's countertransference with these couples when she writes, "I put myself in [Ann's] shoes…and tried to imagine what it would be like to discover in an instant that the man I married and thought I knew more intimately than anyone in the world wasn't who I thought he was." As therapists, our job is to put on our clients' shoes and take off our own. Doing this is no easy task, but it's mandatory if we're to do good work. Weiner-Davis winds up by doing what too many do to gay spouses: giving them all the blame for their situation, rather than having empathy for both partners within the context of the culture as a whole.

JOE KORT, M.S.W., is an openly gay psychotherapist in Royal Oak, Michigan. His forthcoming book, *10 Smart Things Gay Men Can Do To Find Real Love*, includes a chapter on heterosexually married gay men. For more information, go to www.gayaffirmativepsychotherapy.com. Contact joekort@joekort.com.

MICHELE WEINER-DAVIS, M.S.W., is a marriage and family therapist in Woodstock, Illinois, and author of *The Sex-Starved Marriage*; *The Divorce Remedy*; and the bestsellers *Divorce Busting*; *Change Your Life and Everyone In It*; and *Getting Through to the Man You Love*. Contact dbusting@aol.com.

From Joe Kort, 2005, "The New 'Mixed' Marriage," *Psychotherapy Networker*, September/October, pp. 83–89. Reprinted by permission.

KEY TERMS

Name

Section

Date

Ambilocal (bilocal) residence:

Arranged marriages:

Avunculocal residence:

Bride service:

Bridewealth:

Cross cousins:

Dowry:

Endogamy:

Exogamy:

247

FAMILY

Extended family:

Family:

Fraternal plyandry:

Incest taboo:

Kin:

Levirate:

Marriage:

Matrilocal residence:

Mixed marriage:

Monogamy:

Mormon Fundamentalists:

Natural aversion theory:

KEY TERMS

 Name _____

 Section _____

 Date _____

Neolocal residence:

Nuclear family:

Parallel cousins:

Patrilocal residence:

Polyandry:

Polygamy:

Polygyny:

Preferential cousin marriage:

Reciprocal exchange:

FAMILY

Serial monogamy:

Sororate:

Woman exchange:

7 KINSHIP

Kinship Bonds and Family Classification

In the United States, it is not uncommon for married couples to establish a place of residence separate from parents or relatives. This differs from about 95% of all cultures' traditional residence patterns, which are for the couple to settle with or close to the household of parents or close relatives of either the bride or the groom. Contrary to the norm of setting up an independent residence, **Romas** (also known as Gypsies) living in the United States often take residence with the groom's family (*familia*) after marriage. An investigation of the Gypsy culture allows us to understand wedding arrangements that differ from the norm, yet exist in the United States.

No one knows the exact number of Romas living in the United States, since members of this culture often move around, using different names and aliases, and are secretive about their whereabouts. Paul Maas, author of *King of the Gypsies*, states that there are perhaps a million or more Romas in the United States—nobody knows exactly how many, not even the government. He continues on to state that they no longer live in horse-drawn caravans on dusty roads; they live in cities, drive cars, have telephones and credit cards. Yet they do not go to school, neither read nor write, don't pay taxes, and keep themselves going by means of time-honored ruses and arrangements. Romas themselves, Maas states, recognize the contrast they make with typical American culture, and they are proud of it.

Roma culture stresses the importance of group rather than individual activity. This is true with their marriage rituals, which stress not just the commitment of the bride to the groom, but rather the lifetime alliance built between two extended families. Parents play a major role in the mate selection process, and the arrangements for the **bride price** (*daro*) are entirely up to them.

The wedding ceremony for Romas is private in that it involves neither religious nor civil officiates, and they generally occur in rented halls. The festivities are often elaborate affairs, yet unlike most weddings, no formal invitations are ever issued. It is understood that all Romas in the community are welcome.

Arranged marriages normally include a *daro*, a payment by the groom's family to the bride's family. The actual figure varies from less than $1,000 to $10,000 or more. The higher the status of the young woman's *familia*, and the greater her attractiveness, the higher will be the asking price. Although a *daro* of several thousand dollars is quite common, part of the money is spent on wedding festivities and gifts for the couple. Additionally, part of the money may be returned to the groom's father as a gesture of good will.

KINSHIP

The *daro* has traditionally served as a protection for the young wife. Thus, if she should be mistreated by her husband or his *familia*, she can return home—and the money may not be returned. This is important, since the wife is generally quite young, between the ages of twelve to sixteen. While this is under the legal age for marriage in the United States, it does not present a problem for the Romas. As a culture, the Romas do not seem overly concerned about marriage and divorce records, birth certificates, and other statistics vital to the United States government.

After the wedding ceremony, it is customary for the wife to live with her husband's *familia*. She is now referred to as a *bori* and comes under the direct supervision of her mother-in-law. It is also expected that the bride be older than the groom, so that she can fulfill all duties, including generating an income for her husband until he is fully mature. The following quote by Gropper in the text entitled *Gypsies in the City* demonstrates this point:

> The groom now has a wife who caters to his needs and whom he orders about, so his mother and sisters may devote less time to him. The bride, on the other hand, is now a *bori*, to be ordered around by all. She is expected to be the first one to awake in the morning and the last one to go to bed.

> She should do much of the housework as well as work as a fortune-teller, giving her earnings to her husband and mother-in-law. She should eat sparingly and only after everyone else has finished. She must ask neither for clothing nor for an opportunity to go out. She should be grateful if she gets either. (Gropper 1975:162)

Kinship and Descent—
Robert Lavenda and Emily Schultz

People in all societies live in worlds of social ties. They consider themselves to be connected to other people in a variety of different ways, and also consider that there are some people to whom they are not connected at all. Some anthropologists refer to these socially recognized connections as **relatedness**. There are many forms of relatedness that may be recognized in a given society,

based on such categories as friendship, marriage, adoption, procreation, descent from a common ancestor, common labor, co-residence, sharing food, and sharing some kind of substance (blood, spirit, or nationality, for example). One of the most important forms of relatedness that has interested anthropologists since the birth of the field in the late nineteenth century has been **kinship**: the various systems of social organization that societies have constructed on principles derived from the universal human experiences of mating, birth, and nurturance. Members of Western societies influenced by the sciences of biology and genetics frequently believe that kinship relationships are (or should be) a direct reflection of the biology and genetics of human reproduction. Nevertheless, they are aware that, even in their own societies, kinship is not the same thing as biology.

KINSHIP VS. BIOLOGY

Europeans and North Americans know that in their societies mating is not the same as marriage, although a valid marriage encourages mating between the partners. Similarly, all births do not constitute valid links of descent; in some societies, children whose parents have not been married according to accepted legal or religious specifications do not fit the cultural logic of descent, and many societies offer no positions that they can properly fill. Finally, not all acts of nurturance are recognized as adoption. Consider, for example, the status of foster parents in the United States, whose custody of the children they care for is officially temporary and can terminate if someone else clears the hurdles necessary to adopt those children legally.

Thus, mating, birth, and nurturance are ambiguous human experiences, and culturally constructed systems of kinship try to remove some of that ambiguity by paying selective attention to some aspects of these phenomena while downplaying or ignoring others. For example, one society may emphasize the female's role in childbearing and base its kinship system on this, paying little formal attention to the male's role in conception. Another society may trace connections through men, emphasizing the paternal role in conception and reducing the maternal role to that of passive incubator for the male seed. A third society may encourage its members to adopt not only children to rear but adult siblings for themselves, thus blurring the link between biological reproduction and family creation. Even though they contradict one another, all three understandings can be justified with reference to the panhuman experiences of mating, birth, and nurturance.

Every kinship system, therefore, emphasizes certain aspects of human reproductive experience and culturally constructs its own theory of human nature, defining how people develop from infants into mature social beings. Put another way, kinship is an *idiom*: a selective interpretation of the common human experiences of mating, birth, and nurturance. The result is a set of coherent principles that allow people to assign one another membership in particular groups. These principles normally cover several significant issues: how to carry out the reproduction of group members (marriage or adoption), where group members should live after marriage (residence rules), how to establish links between generations (descent or adoption), and how to pass on social positions (succession) or material goods (inheritance). Collectively, kinship principles define social groups, locate people within those groups, and position the people and groups in relation to one another both in space and over time. While this set of principles may be coherent, it is also open to modification, negotiation and even legal challenge, as is shown by the ambiguities and questions raised by the consequences of **new reproductive technologies**—technologically mediated reproductive practices such as in vitro fertilization, surrogate parenthood, and sperm banks.

DESCENT

Discussions in anthropology tend to specialize in different aspects of kinship. Culturally defined connections based on mating are usually called *marriage* and are often referred to as *affinal* relationships (the term is based on *affinity*, which means "personal attraction"). In this chapter, we will consider culturally defined relationships based on birth and nurturance, which anthropologists traditionally call **descent**. People related to one another by descent are what English speakers often refer to as "blood" relations and are socially relevant connections based on either parent-child relationships or sibling relationships. Anthropologists use the term **consanguineal kin** to refer to all those people who are linked to one another by birth as blood relation (the word comes from the Latin *sanguineus*, meaning "of blood"). In addition, however, a consanguineal kinship group, may include individuals whose membership in

the group was established not by birth but by means of culturally specific rituals of incorporation that resemble what Euro-Americans call **adoption**. Incorporation via adoption often is seen to function in a way that parallels consanguinity, because it makes adopted persons and those who adopt them of the "same flesh." The transformation that incorporates adoptees frequently is explained in terms of *nurturance*: feeding, clothing, sheltering, and otherwise attending to the physical and emotional well-being of an individual for an extended period.

Ethnographers have shown repeatedly that kinship bonds established by adoption can be just as strong as bonds established through birth. An interesting recent example comes from research among groups of gay and lesbian North Americans who established enduring "families by choice" that include individuals who are not sexual partners and who are unrelated by birth or marriage. Given that these chosen family ties are rooted in ongoing material and emotional support over extended periods of time, one might reasonably suggest that the people involved have based their relationships on nurturance and have "adopted" one another.

Because they are based on parent-child links that connect the generations, relations of descent have a time depth. In establishing patterns of descent, the cultures of the world rely on one of two basic strategies: either people are connected to one another through *both* their mothers and fathers, or they are connected by links traced *either* through the mother *or* the father, but not both.

BILATERAL DESCENT

When people believe themselves to be just as related to their father's side of the family as to their mother's side, the term that is used is **bilateral descent** (this is sometimes also referred to as **cognatic descent**). Anthropologists have identified two different kinds of kinship groups based on bilateral descent. One is the *bilateral descent group*, an unusual form that consists of a set of people who claim to be related to one another through descent from a common ancestor, some through their mother's side and some through their father's; the other is the *bilateral kindred*, a much more common form that consists of all the relatives, related through males or females, of one person or group of siblings.

KINSHIP

Figure 7.1 Hawaiian kinship terminology

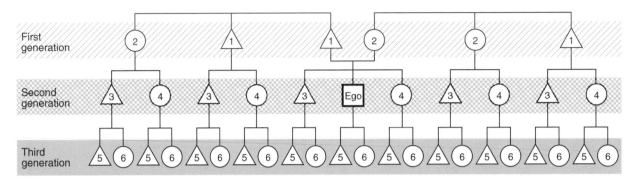

The **bilateral kindred** is the kinship group that most Europeans and North Americans know. A bilateral kindred forms around particular individuals and includes all the people linked to that individual through kin of both sexes—people usually called *relatives* in English. These people form a group only because of their connection to the central person, known in the terminology of kinship as *Ego*. In North American society, bilateral kindreds assemble at events associated with Ego: when he or she is baptized, confirmed, bar or bat mitzvahed, married, or buried. Each person within Ego's bilateral kindred has his or her own separate kindred. For example, Ego's father's sister's daughter has a kindred that includes people related to her through her father and her father's siblings—people to whom Ego is not related. This is simultaneously the major strength and major weakness of bilateral kindreds. That is, they have overlapping memberships, and they do not endure beyond the lifetime of an individual Ego. But they are widely extended, and they can form broad networks of people who are somehow related to one another. (Figure 7.2, Eskimo [Inuit] kinship terminology, also illustrates a bilateral kindred.)

Kinship systems create social relationships by defining sets of interlocking statuses and roles. Thus, a man is to behave in the same way to all his "uncles" and in another way to his "father," and they are to behave to him as "nephew" and "son." (Perhaps he owes labor to anyone he calls "uncle" and is owed protection and support in return.) In anthropology, these are referred to as the *rights and obligations of kinship*. In a bilateral kindred, the "broad networks of people who are somehow related to one another" means that no matter where a person may be, if he or she finds kin there, the person and the kin have a basis for social interaction. This basis for interaction is different from the possible social interactions that the person might have with strangers (in this case, non-kin).

Figure 7.2 Eskimo (Inuit) kinship terminology

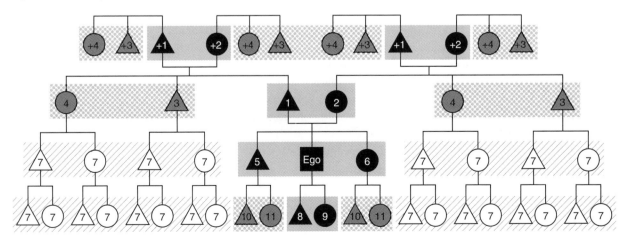

Figure 7.3 Iroquois kinship terminology

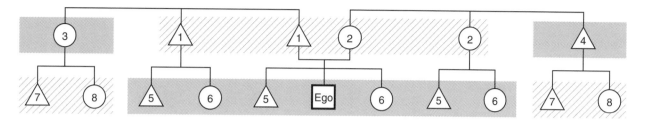

Organization in bilateral kindreds is advantageous when members of social groups need flexible ways of establishing ties to kin who do not live in one place. They are also useful when valued resources, such as farmland, are limited and every generation must be distributed across available plots in an efficient and flexible manner. Bilateral kindreds become problematic, however, in at least four kinds of social circumstances: when clear-cut membership in a particular social group must be determined, when social action requires the formation of groups that are larger than individual families, when conflicting claims to land and labor must be resolved, and when people are concerned with perpetuating a specific social order over time. In societies that face these dilemmas, unilineal descent groups usually are formed.

UNILINEAL DESCENT

The second major descent strategy, **unilineal descent**, is based on the principle that the most significant kin relationships must be traced through *either* the mother *or* the father but not both. Unilineal descent groups are found in more societies today than are any other kind. Those unilineal groups that are based on links traced through a person's father (or male kin) are called **patrilineal** (or **agnatic**); those traced through a mother (or female kin) are called **matrilineal** (or **uterine**). (Note that lineages are institutions—people do not choose whether they'd like to be patrilineal or matrilineal; these are the standardized long-established social forms through which they learn about individuals and groups to whom they are related and how to interact with them.)

Unilineal descent groups are found all over world. They are all based on the principle that significant-relationships are created via links through one parent rather than the other. Membership in a unilineal descent group is based on the membership of the appropriate parent in the group.

In a patrilineal system, an individual belongs to a group formed by links through males, the lineage of his or her father. In a matrilineal system, an individual belongs to a group formed by links through females, the lineage of his or her mother. "Patrilineal" and "matrilineal" do not mean that only men belong to one and only women to the other; rather, the terms refer to the principle by which membership is conferred. In a patrilineal society, women and men belong to a **patrilineage** formed by father-child links; similarly, in a matrilineal society, men and women belong to a **matrilineage** formed by mother-child connections. In other words, membership in the group is, in principle, unambiguous: an individual belongs to only one lineage. This is in contrast to a bilateral kindred, in which an individual belongs to overlapping groups. (Figure 7.4, Crow kinship terminology also illustrates a matrilineage; 7.5, Omaha kinship terminology also illustrates a patrilineage.)

Talk of patrilineal or matrilineal descent focuses attention on the kind of social group created by this pattern of descent: the lineage. A **lineage** is composed of all those people who believe they can specify the parent-child links that connect them to one another through a common ancestor. Typically, lineages vary in size from twenty or thirty members to several hundred or more.

Many anthropologists have argued that the most important feature of lineages is that they are corporate in organization. That is, a lineage has a single legal identity such that, to outsiders, all members of the lineage are equal in law to all others. In the case of a blood feud, for example, the death of any opposing lineage member avenges the death of the lineage member who began the feud; the death of the actual murderer is not required. Lineages are also corporate in that they control property, such as land or herds, as a unit.

KINSHIP

Figure 7.4 Crow kinship terminology

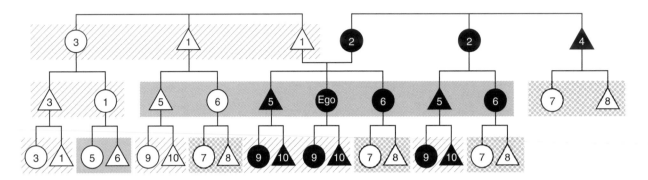

Finally, lineages are the main political associations in the societies that have them. Individuals have no political or legal status in such societies except through lineage membership. They have relatives who are outside the lineage, but their own political and legal status derives from the lineage to which they belong.

Because membership in a lineage is determined through a direct line from father or mother to child, lineages can endure over time and in a sense have an independent existence. As long as people can remember their common ancestor, the group of people descended from that common ancestor can endure. Most lineage-based societies have a time depth that covers about five generations: grandparents, parents, Ego, children, and grandchildren.

When members of a descent group believe that they are in some way connected but cannot specify the precise genealogical links, they compose what anthropologists call a **clan**. Usually, a clan is made up of lineages that the larger

society's members believe to be related to one another through links that go back to mythical times. Sometimes the common ancestor is said to be an animal that lived at the beginning of time. The important point to remember in distinguishing lineages and clans is that lineage members can specify the precise genealogical links back to their common ancestor ("Your mother was Eileen, her mother was Miriam, her sister was Rachel, her daughter was Ruth, and I am Ruth's son"), whereas clan members ordinarily cannot ("Our foremother was Turtle who came out of the sea when this land was settled. Turtle's children were many and for many generations raised sweet peas on our land. So it was that Violet, mother of Miriam and Rachel, was born of the line of the Turtle..."). The clan is thus larger than any lineage and also more diffuse in terms of both membership and the hold it has over individuals.

Because people are born into them, lineages endure over time in societies in which no other form of organization lasts, and therefore, the system of lineages becomes the

Figure 7.5 Omaha kinship terminology

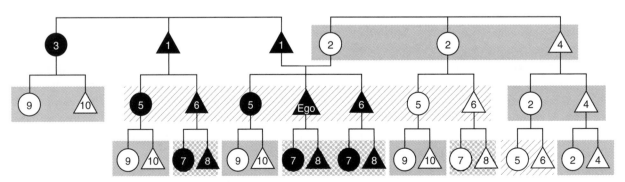

256

foundation of social life in the society. Although lineages might be the foundation of social life, however, this does not mean that they are immovable and inflexible. People can use lineage and clan membership to pursue their interests. Because lineage depth frequently extends to about five generations, the exact circumstances of lineage origins can be hazy and open to negotiation. Perhaps "Miriam" and "Rachel" from the preceding example have another sister whom everyone "forgot about" until someone appears who claims lineage membership as a descendant of the forgotten sister. If there are good reasons for including this descendant in the lineage, this claim might well be accepted.

By far the most common form of lineage organization is the patrilineage, which consists of all the people (male and female) who believe themselves to be related to one another because they are related to a common male ancestor by links through men. The prototypical kernel of a patrilineage is the father-son pair. Female members of patrilineages normally leave the lineage to marry, but in most patrilineal societies, women do not give up their membership in their own lineages. In a number of societies, women play an active role in the affairs of their own patrilineages for many years—usually until their interest in their own children directs their attention toward the children's lineage (which is, of course, the lineage of their father, the woman's husband).

By contrast, in a matrilineal society, descent is traced through women rather than through men. Superficially, a matrilineage is a mirror image of a patrilineage, but certain features make it distinct. First, the prototypical kernel of a matrilineage is the sister-brother pair—a matrilineage may be thought of as a group of brothers and sisters connected through links made by women. Brothers marry out and often live with the families of their wives, but they maintain an active interest in the affairs of their own lineage. Second, the most important man in a boy's life is not his father (who is not in his lineage) but his mother's brother, from whom he will receive his lineage inheritance. Third, the amount of power women exercise in matrilineages is still being hotly debated in anthropology. A matrilineage is not the same as a *matriarchy* (a society in which women rule); brothers often retain what appears to be a controlling interest in the lineage. Some anthropologists claim that the male members of a matrilineage are supposed to run the lineage, even though there is more autonomy for

women in matrilineal societies than in patrilineal ones; they suggest that the day-to-day exercise of power tends to be carried out by the brothers or sometimes the husbands. A number of studies, however, have questioned the validity of these generalizations. Trying to say something about matrilineal societies in general is difficult, since they vary a great deal. The ethnographic evidence suggests that matrilineages must be examined on a case-by-case basis.

KINSHIP TERMINOLOGIES

People everywhere use special terms to address and refer to people they recognize as kin; anthropolgists call these **kinship technologies**. Consider the North American kinship term *aunt*. This term seems to refer to a woman who occupies a unique biological position, but in fact, it refers to a woman who may be related to a person in one of four ways: as father's sister, mother's sister, father's brother's wife, or mother's brother's wife. From the perspective of North American kinship, all those women have something in common, and they are all placed into the same kinship category and called by the same kin term. Prototypically, one's aunts are women one generation older than oneself and are sisters or sisters-in-law of one's parents. However, North Americans may also refer to their mother's best friend as "aunt." By doing so, they recognize the strength of this system of classification by extending it to include **fictive kin**.

Despite the variety of kinship systems in the world, anthropologists have identified six major patterns of kinship terminology based on how people categorize their cousins. The six patterns reflect common solutions to structural problems faced by societies organized in terms of kinship. They provide clues concerning how the vast and undifferentiated world of potential kin may be organized. Kinship terminologies suggest both the external boundaries and the internal divisions of the kinship groups, and they outline the structure of rights and obligations assigned to different members of the society.

The major criteria that are used for building kinship terminologies are listed here, from the most common to the least common:

- **Generation**. Kin terms distinguish relatives according to the generation to which the relatives belong. In English, the term *cousin* conventionally refers to someone of the same generation as Ego.

KINSHIP

- **Gender**. The gender of the individual is used to differentiate kin. In Spanish, *primo* refers to a male cousin, and *prima* to a female cousin. In English, cousins are not distinguished on the basis of gender, but *uncle* and *aunt* are distinguished on the basis of both generation and gender.

- **Affinity**. A distinction is made on the basis of connection through marriage, or affinity. This criterion is used in Spanish when *suegra* (Ego's spouse's mother) is distinguished from *madre* (Ego's mother). In matrilineal societies, Ego's mother's sister and father's sister are distinguished from each other on the basis of affinity. The mother's sister is a direct, lineal relative, and the father's sister is an affine; they are called by different terms.

- **Collaterality**. A distinction is made between kin who are believed to be in a direct line and those who are "off to one side," linked to Ego through a lineal relative. In English, the distinction of collaterality can be seen in the distinction between mother and aunt or between father and uncle.

- **Bifurcation**. Bifurcation distinguishes the mother's side of the family from the father's side. The Swedish kin terms *morbror* and *farbror* are bifurcating terms, one referring to the mother's brother and the other to the father's brother.

- **Relative age**. Relatives of the same category may be distinguished on the basis of relative age—that is, whether they are older or younger than Ego. Among the Ju/'hoansi of southern Africa, for example, speakers must separate "older brother" (*!ko*) from "younger brother" (*tsin*).

- **Sex of linking relative**. This criterion is related to collaterality. The sex of linking relative distinguishes cross relatives (usually cousins) from parallel relatives (also usually cousins). Parallel relatives are linked through two brothers or two sisters. **Parallel cousins**, for example, are Ego's father's brother's children or Ego's mother's sister's children. **Cross relatives** are linked through a brother-sister pair. **Cross cousins** are Ego's mother's brother's children or Ego's father's

sister's children. The sex of either Ego or the cousins does not matter; the important factor is the sex of the linking relatives.

The six major patterns of kinship terminology that anthropologists have identified in the world are based on how cousins are classified. These patterns were named after the societies that represent the prototypes. The first two patterns discussed here are found in association with bilateral descent systems.

Bilateral Patterns

The **Hawaiian** pattern is based on the application of the first two criteria: generation and gender. The kin group is divided horizontally by generation, and within each generation are only two kinship terms, one for males and one for females (Figure 7.1). In this system, Ego maintains a maximum degree of flexibility in choosing the descent group with which to affiliate. Ego is also forced to look for a spouse in another kin group because Ego may not marry anyone in the same terminological category as a genetic parent, sibling, or offspring.

The **Eskimo** (Inuit) pattern reflects the symmetry of bilateral kindreds. A lineal core—the **nuclear family**—is distinguished from collateral relatives, who are not identified with the father's or the mother's side. Once past the immediate collateral line (aunts and uncles, great-aunts and great-uncles, nephews and nieces), generation is ignored. The remaining relatives are all "cousins," sometimes distinguished by *number* (second or third) or by *removal* (generations away from Ego[1]) (Figure 7.2). This is the only terminological system that sets the nuclear family apart from all other kin. If the Hawaiian system is like a cake made up of horizontal layers of kin, this system is like an onion, with layers of kin surrounding a core.

Unilineal Patterns

The **Iroquois** pattern is sometimes known in the literature as bifurcate merging, because it merges Ego's mother's and father's parallel siblings with Ego's parents. The sex of the linking relatives is important in this system: The parents' parallel siblings are grouped together with the parents, whereas cross siblings are set apart. This is repeated on

---

[1] Ego's "first cousin once removed" can be one generation older or younger than Ego. For example, your cousin Suzanne's daughter is your first cousin once removed, but so is your father's cousin Arnold. Arnold's son, Eric, is your second cousin.

CHAPTER 7

Figure 7.6 Sudanese kinship terminology

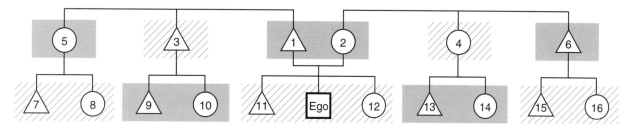

the level of cousins. In a bilateral system, these distinctions would mirror the lines of lineage membership. If Ego is a male, he will use one term to refer to all women of his matrilineage who are one generation older than he is. Their children are all referred to by another set of terms, one for males and one for females. Similarly, in his father's matrilineage, all men in the father's generation are referred to by one term. Their children are called by the same set of terms used for the cousins on the mother's side.

The **Crow** pattern is a matrilineal system named after the Crow people of North America, but it is found in many other matrilineal societies. This system distinguishes the two matrilineages that are important to Ego: Ego's own and that of Ego's father (Figure 7.4). As in the Iroquois system, the gender of the linking relative is important, and both parents and their same-sex siblings are grouped together. Their children—Ego's parallel cousins—are in the same category as Ego's siblings. The terms or cross cousins follow lineage membership, which is more important than generation. In Ego's own matrilineage, all the children of males are referred to by the same term regardless of their generation; their fathers are in Ego's matrilineage, but *they* are not. On the side of the Ego's father's matrilineage, all male members are distinguished by one term, and all female members by another, regardless of generational relationship to Ego.

The system known as **Omaha**, found among some patrilineal peoples, is the mirror image of the Crow system. All the members of Ego's mother's patrilineage are distinguished only by gender, and all the children of women in Ego's patrilineage are referred to by the same term, one for males and one for females (Figure 7.5). Lineage membership again is more important than generation, a principle that often is hard for people living in bilateral kindreds to grasp.

Finally, in the **Sudanese** pattern, each related person is referred to by a separate term (Figure 7.6). While this was originally seen as a relatively rare terminological pattern found in patrilineal societies, especially in northern Africa, it is also a very common pattern in south Asia and southwest Asia, where it is found among speakers of Turkish, Arabic, Urdu, and Hindi, as well as other northern Indian languages. (Table 7.1 lists the basic patterns of kinship terminology.)

Table 7.1 Patterns of Kinship Terminology

Bilateral Descent	Unilineal Descent
Hawaiian	Iroquois
Eskimo	Crow
	Omaha
	Sudanese

Robert Lavenda and Emily Schultz, 2007, "Kinship and Descent," *Core Concepts in Cultural Anthropology*, 3rd ed., pp. 153–173, 177–179. McGraw-Hill. Copyright © 2007 The McGraw-Hill Companies. Reprinted with permission of The McGraw-Hill Companies.

259

KINSHIP

EXERCISE

Name

Section

Date

EXERCISE 7.1: FAMILY TREE

Interview a classmate about his/her family. Diagram three generations using unilineal descent on either their mother's or their father's side of the family. Shade in members of the depicted line of descent. You may wish to utilize the diagram on the following page for assistance with this project.

Describe which of the six kinship systems of classification explained in the previous article best represents their family, and explain why.

KINSHIP

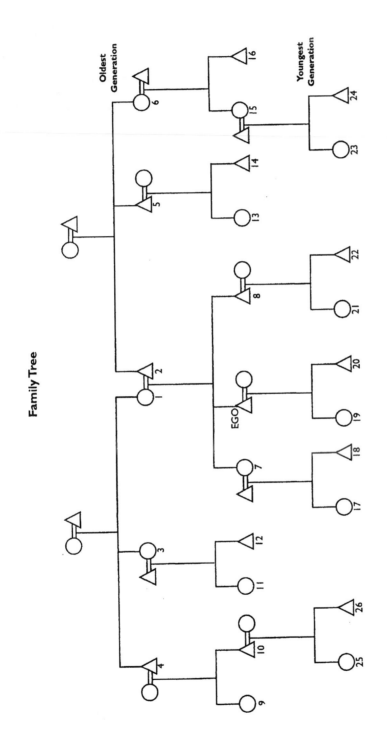

EXERCISE

Name

Section

Date

EXERCISE 7.2: WE ARE FAMILY

Create a kinship diagram of your family (or of the family of a friend) going back a minimum of four generations. This diagram may represent either unilineal or bilateral descent, which ever you prefer. Clearly mark the **ego**. Include all **affinal** and **consanguineal** relationships. For the sake of this assignment, please be sure to distinguish kin by generation.

After creating the diagram, please answer the following questions in a manner which best suits your family. Be sure to make cross-cultural comparisons, as expected from trained cultural anthropologists.

1. Are you tracing in your diagram unilineal (patrilineal or matrilineal) or bilateral descent? Is this a true representation of your family's practices?

2. Which of the six kinship systems most closely resembles your family, and why?

3. Would you define relationships as exogamous or endogamous? Please determine what factors you are using to define "the particular group." Have beliefs changed through the generations?

4. What role is played by fictive kin members?

5. Are the roles of males and females (gender differentiation) clearly defined in your family? Have expectations changed over the generations?

Fathering: Paradoxes, Contradictions, and Dilemmas—
Scott Coltrane

The beginning of the 21st century offers a paradox for American fathers: Media images, political rhetoric, and psychological studies affirm the importance of fathers to children at the same time that men are becoming less likely to live with their offspring. Although the average married father spends more time interacting with his children than in past decades, marriage rates have fallen, and half of all marriages are predicted to end in divorce. Additionally, the proportion of births to unmarried mothers has increased dramatically for all race and ethnic groups, and single-mother households have become commonplace. These contradictory tendencies—more father-child interaction in two-parent families but fewer two-parent families in the population—have encouraged new research on fathers and spawned debates about how essential fathers are to families and normal child development (Blankenhorn, 1995; Silverstein & Auerbach, 1999).

Scholars attribute the current paradox in fathering to various economic and social trends. Whereas most men in the 20th century were sole breadwinners, contemporary fathers' wages can rarely support a middle-class standard of living for an entire family. The weakening of the good-provider model, coupled with trends in fertility, marriage, divorce, and custody, has resulted in the average man spending fewer years living with children (Eggebeen, 2002). Simultaneously, however, men rank marriage and children among their most precious goals, single-father households have increased, and fathers in two-parent households are spending more time with co-resident children than at any time since data on fathers were collected (Pleck & Masciadrelli, 2003). Although married fathers report that they value their families over their jobs, they spend significantly more time in paid work and less time in family work than married mothers, with most men continuing to serve as helpers to their wives, especially for housework and child maintenance activities (Coltrane, 2000). Personal, political, religious, and popular discourses about fathers reveal similar ambivalence about men's family involvements, with ideals ranging from stern patriarchs to nurturing daddies, and public portrayals frequently at odds with the actual behavior of average American fathers (LaRossa, 1997). We can understand these contradic- tions by recognizing that fatherhood has gained symbolic importance just as men's family participation has become more voluntary, tenuous, and conflicted (Griswold, 1993; Kimmel, 1996).

In this [article], I summarize how fathering practices have varied across cultures and through history; highlight how different social, economic, and political contexts have produced different types of father involvement; review how social scientists have measured father involvement; and examine findings about causes and consequences of father involvement. I end with a short analysis of debates over family policy and offer tentative predictions about the future of fathering in America.

CROSS-CULTURAL VARIATION

Fatherhood defines a biological and social relationship between a male parent and his offspring. *To father* means to impregnate a woman and beget a child, thus describing a kinship connection that facilitates the intergenerational transfer of wealth and authority (at least in patrilineal descent systems such as ours). Fatherhood also reflects ideals about the rights, duties, and activities of men in families and in society and generalizes to other social and symbolic relationships, as when Christians refer to "God the Father," Catholics call priests "Father," and Americans label George Washington "the Father" of the country. Fatherhood thus reflects a normative set of social practices and expectations that are institutionalized within religion, politics, law, and culture. Social theories have employed the concept of *social fatherhood* to explain how the institution of fatherhood links a particular child to a particular man (whether father or uncle) in order to secure a place for that child in the social structure (Coltrane & Collins, 2001).

Fathering (in contrast to *fatherhood*) refers more directly to what men do with and for children. Although folk beliefs suggest that fathering entails behaviors fixed by reproductive biology, humans must learn how to parent. In every culture and historical period, men's parenting has been shaped by social and economic forces. Although women have been the primary caretakers of young children in all cultures, fathers' participation in child rearing has varied from virtually no direct involvement to active participation in all aspects of children's routine care. Except for breastfeeding and the earliest care of infants, there are no cross-cultural universals in the tasks that mothers and fathers perform (Johnson, 1988). In some societies, the social worlds of fathers and mothers were so separate that they rarely had contact and seldom performed the same tasks; in other societies, men participated in tasks like infant care and women participated in tasks like hunting (Coltrane, 1988; Sanday, 1981).

Drawing on worldwide cross-cultural comparisons, scholars have identified two general patterns of fathers' family involvement, one intimate and the other aloof. In the intimate pattern, men eat and sleep with their wives and children, talk with them during evening meals, attend births, and participate actively in infant care. In the aloof pattern, men often eat and sleep apart from women, spend their leisure time in the company of other men, stay away during births, and seldom help with child care (Whiting & Whiting, 1975). Societies with involved fathers are more likely than societies with aloof fathers to be peaceful, to afford women a role in community decision making, to have intimate husband–wife relationships, to feature more gender equality in the society, and to include nurturing deities of both sexes in their religions. Aloof-father societies are more likely to have religious systems with stern male gods, social institutions that exclude women from community decision making, marriage systems in which husbands demand deference from wives, and public rituals that focus on men's competitive displays of masculinity (Coltrane, 1988, 1996; Sanday, 1981).

Research on fathering among indigenous peoples such as the African Aka suggests why involved fathering and gender egalitarianism are associated (Hewlett, 1991). Anthropologists such as Hewlett have drawn on Chodorow's (1974) work to suggest that when fathers are active in infant care, boys develop an intimate knowledge of masculinity, which makes them less likely to devalue the feminine, whereas when fathers are rarely around, boys lack a clear sense of masculinity and construct their identities in opposition to things feminine by devaluing and criticizing women (Hewlett, 2000). In reviews of data on father involvement over the past 120,000 years, Hewlett concluded that fathers contribute to their children in many ways, with the relative importance of different contributions varying dramatically; that different ecologies and modes of production have a substantial impact on the contributions of fathers to their children; and that fathers' roles today are relatively unique in human history (Hewlett, 1991, 2000).

HISTORICAL VARIATION

Historical studies have focused on practices in Europe and North America, chronicling and emphasizing men's public lives: work, political exploits, literary accomplishments, scientific discoveries, and heroic battles. This emphasis shows how various economic, political, and legal practices have structured privileges and obligations within and beyond families. For example, the historical concept of family in the West is derived from the Latin *famulus*, meaning servant, and the Roman *familia*, meaning the man's domestic property. Linking institutional arrangements with linguistic forms tells us something important about men's relationships to families. Recent historical studies have focused more directly on men's ideal and actual behaviors in families, thereby documenting complexity and diversity in past fathering practices (e.g., Griswold, 1993; Kimmel, 1996; LaRossa, 1997; Mintz, 1998; Pleck & Pleck, 1997).

Before these studies, many scholars erroneously assumed that changes in fatherhood were linear and progressive (Coltrane & Parke, 1998). For example, early family history emphasized that peasant families were extended and governed by stern patriarchs, whereas market societies produced nuclear families, companionate marriages, and involved fathers. In fact, historical patterns of fathering have responded to a complex array of social and economic forces, varying considerably across regions, time periods, and ethnic or cultural groups. Although it is useful to identify how men's work and production have shaped their public and private statuses, actual family relations have been diverse, and fatherhood ideals have followed different trajectories in different regions of the same country (Griswold, 1993; Mintz, 1998; Pleck & Pleck, 1997).

The economy of the 17th and 18th centuries in Europe and America was based on agriculture and productive family households. For families that owned farms or small artisan shops, their place of work was also their home. Slaves, indentured servants, and others were expected to work on family estates in return for food, a place to live, and sometimes other rewards. In this pattern of household or family-based production, men, women, and children worked together. Regional variations could be large, and fathers and mothers often did different types of work, but many tasks required for subsistence and family survival were interchangeable, and both mothers and fathers took responsibility for child care and training (Coltrane & Galt, 2000).

Because most men's work as farmers, artisans, and tradesmen occurred in the family household, fathers were a visible presence in their children's lives. Child rearing was a more collective enterprise than it is today, with family behaviors and attitudes ruled primarily by duty and obligation. Men introduced sons to farming or craft work within the household economy, oversaw the work of others, and were responsible for maintaining harmonious household relations. The preindustrial home was a system of control as well as a center of production, and both functions reinforced the father's authority (Griswold, 1993). Though mothers provided most direct care for infants and young children, men tended to be active in the training and tutoring of children. Because they were moral teachers and family heads, fathers were thought to have greater responsibility for and influence on children than mothers and were also generally held responsible for how the children acted outside the home (Pleck & Pleck, 1997).

Because the sentimental individualism of the modern era had not yet blossomed, emotional involvement with children in the Western world during the 17th and early 18th centuries was more limited than today. Prevailing images of children also were different from modern ideas about their innocence and purity. Religious teachings stressed the corrupt nature and evil dispositions of children, and fathers were admonished to demand strict obedience and use swift physical punishment to cleanse children of their sinful ways. Puritan fathers justified their extensive involvement in children's lives because women were seen as unfit to be disciplinarians, moral guides, or intellectual teachers. Griswold (1997) pointed out, however, that stern unaffectionate fathering, though not confined to Puritans, was not representative of all of the population. In fact, most American fathers attempted to shape and guide their children's characters, not break them or beat the devil out of them. As more privileged 18th-century fathers gained enough affluence to have some leisure time, many were affectionate with their children and delighted in playing with them (Griswold, 1997).

As market economies replaced home-based production in the 19th and 20th centuries, the middle-class father's position as household head and master and moral instructor of his children was slowly transformed. Men increasingly sought employment outside the home, and their direct contact with family members declined. As the wage labor economy developed, men's occupational achievement outside the household took on stronger moral overtones. Men came to be seen as fulfilling their family and civic duty, not by teaching and interacting with their children as before, but by supporting the family financially. The middle-class home, previously the site of production, consumption, and virtually everything else in life, became a nurturing, child-centered haven set apart from the impersonal world of work, politics, and other public pursuits. The separate-spheres ideal became a defining feature of the late 19th and early 20th centuries (Bernard, 1981; Coltrane & Galt, 2000; Kimmel, 1996).

The ideal that paid work was only for men and that only women were suited to care for family members remained an unattainable myth rather than an everyday reality for most families. Many working-class fathers were not able to earn the family wage assumed by the separate-spheres ideal, and a majority of African American, Latino, Asian American, and other immigrant men could not fulfill the good-provider role that the cultural ideal implied. Women in these families either had to work for wages, participate in production at home, or find other ways to make ends meet. Although the emerging romantic ideal held that women should be sensitive and pure keepers of the home on a full-time basis, the reality was that women in less advantaged households had no choice but to simultaneously be workers and mothers. In fact, many working-class and ethnic minority women had to leave their homes and children to take care of other people's children and houses (Dill, 1988). Even during the heyday of separate spheres in the early 20th century, minority women, young single women, widows, and married women whose husbands could not support them worked for wages.

As noted above, attempts to understand the history of fatherhood have often painted a simple before-and-after picture: *Before* the Industrial Revolution, families were rural and extended, and patriarchal fathers were stern moralists; *after* the Industrial Revolution, families were urban and nuclear, and wage-earning fathers became companionate husbands, distant breadwinners, and occasional playmates to their children. This before-and-after picture captures something important about general shifts in work and family life, but its simple assumption of unidirectional linear change and its binary conceptualization contrasting men's patriarchal roles in the past with egalitarian roles in the present is misleading (Coontz, 1992). Stage models of family history have ignored the substantial regional and race/ethnic differences that encouraged different family patterns (Pleck & Pleck, 1997). For example, as most of the United States was undergoing industrialization, large pockets remained relatively untouched by it. The experience of white planters in the antebellum South was both like and unlike that of men in the commercial and industrial North (Griswold, 1993). Another major drawback of early historical studies is the tendency to over-generalize for the entire society on the basis of the experience of the white middle class. Even during the heyday of separate spheres at the turn of the 20th century, minority and immigrant men were unlikely to be able to support a family. Race and class differences also intersect with regional differences: Not only did southern fathering practices differ from northern ones, but slave fathers and freedmen in the South had much different experiences than either group of white men (Griswold, 1993; McDaniel, 1994).

THE EMERGENCE OF MODERN FATHERING

Throughout the 20th century, calls for greater paternal involvement coexisted with the physical presence, but relative emotional and functional absence, of fathers (LaRossa, 1997). Nevertheless, some fathers have always reported high levels of involvement with their children. By the 1930s, even though mothers bore most of the responsibility for care of homes and families, three out of four American fathers said they regularly read magazine articles about child care, and nearly as many men as women were members of the PTA (Kimmel, 1996). Increases in women's labor force participation during the 1940s briefly challenged the ideal of separate family and work roles, but in the postwar era, high rates of marriage and low rates of employment reinforced the ideology of separate spheres for men and women. The ideal father at mid-century was seen as a good provider who "set a good table, provided a decent home, paid the mortgage, bought the shoes, and

kept his children warmly clothed" (Bernard, 1981, pp. 3–4). As they had during the earlier Victorian era, middle-class women were expected to be consumed and fulfilled by wifely and motherly duties. With Ozzie and Harriet-style families as the 1950s model, women married earlier and had more children than any group of American women before them. Rapid expansion of the U.S. economy fueled a phenomenal growth of suburbs, and the consumer culture from that era idolized domestic life on radio and television. Isolated in suburban houses, many mothers now had almost sole responsibility for raising children, aided by occasional reference to expert guides from pediatricians and child psychologists (Hays, 1996).

Fathers of the 1950s were also told to get involved with child care—but not *too* involved (Kimmel, 1996). The separate spheres of white middle-class men and women were thus maintained, though experts deemed them permeable enough for men to participate regularly as a helper to the mother (Coltrane & Galt, 2000; Hays, 1996).

During the mid-20th century, separate-spheres ideology and the popularity of Freud's ideas about mother-infant bonding led to widespread acceptance of concepts like *maternal deprivation*, and few researchers asked who besides mothers took care of children, although some researchers began to focus on father absence during the baby boom era (roughly 1946–64). Empirical studies and social theories valued the symbolic significance of fathers' breadwinning, discipline, and masculine role modeling, even though few studies controlled for social class or measured what fathers actually did with children. Studies including fathers found that they were more likely than mothers to engage in rough and tumble play and to give more attention to sons than daughters (Parke, 1996; Pleck, 1997). In general, research showed that child care was an ongoing and taken-for-granted task for mothers but a novel and fun distraction for fathers (Thompson & Walker, 1989).

Compared to the wholesome but distant good-provider fathers pictured on television programs like *Ozzie and Harriet* and *Father Knows Best* in the 1950s, a new father ideal gained prominence in the 1980s (Griswold, 1993). According to Furstenberg (1988), "[T]elevision, magazines, and movies herald the coming of the modern father—the nurturant, caring, and emotionally attuned parent....Today's father is at least as adept at changing diapers as changing tires" (p. 193). No longer limited to being protectors and providers, fathers were pictured on television and in magazines as intimately involved in family life. Fatherhood proponents focused on the potential of the new ideals and practices (Biller, 1976), but researchers in the 1980s reported that many fathers resisted assuming responsibility for daily housework or child care (Thompson & Walker, 1989).

Some researchers claimed that popular images far exceeded men's actual behaviors (LaRossa, 1988), and others suggested that men, on the whole, were less committed to families than they had been in the past (Ehrenreich, 1984). In the 1990s, researchers also began to examine how the modern ideal of the new father carried hidden messages about class and race, with some suggesting that the image of the sensitive and involved father was a new class/ethnic icon because it set middle-class fathers apart from working-class and ethnic minority fathers, who presented a more masculine image (Messner, 1993). Others suggested that the sensitive or androgynous parenting styles of new fathers might lead to gender identity confusion in sons (Blankenhorn, 1995).

MEASURING FATHER INVOLVEMENT

Before the 1980s, the rare researchers who included fathers focused on simple distinctions between father-present and father-absent families, finding that children from families with co-resident fathers generally fared better, on average, than those without co-resident fathers. Although the structural aspects of fatherhood (marriage, paternity, co-residence) sometimes correlate with various child and family outcomes, most researchers now agree that what fathers do with and for children is more important than co-residence or legal relationship to the mother and recommend that dichotomous measures (e.g., father presence/absence) be replaced by more nuanced ones.

The most influential refinement in fathering measurement was offered by Lamb, Pleck, Charnov, and Levine (1987), who suggested three components: (a) interaction, the father's direct contact with his child through caregiving and shared activities; (b) availability (or accessibility), a related concept concerning the father's potential availability for interaction, by virtue of being accessible to the child (whether or not direct interaction is occurring); and

(c) responsibility, the role the father takes in ascertaining that the child is taken care of and in arranging for resources to be available for the child. Within each of these categories, two further distinctions should be made. First, it is critical to distinguish the amount from the quality of involvement: Both are important to child development and parental well-being (Parke, 1996). Second, absolute as well as relative (in relation to partner) indices of involvement are independent and may affect children and adults in different ways (Pleck, 1997).

A recent tabulation of father involvement assessment in 15 large social science family data sets showed that all but one measured father "presence/absence," with most also measuring some aspects of fathers' "availability," "teaching," "monitoring," or "affection." About half measured the fathers' "communication" or "emotional support," only a few measured "thought processes" (e.g., worrying, dreaming) or "planning" (e.g., birthdays, vacations, friend visits), and none measured "sharing interests" (e.g., providing for instruction, reading together) or "child maintenance" (e.g., cleaning or cooking for the child) (Federal Interagency Forum, 1998, pp. 144, 400; Palkovitz, 1997, pp. 209–210). Structural availability is thus the most common fathering indicator, with various routine parent-child interactions and support activities sometimes assessed, and with fathers' planning and responsibility rarely measured. In addition, many studies collect fathering data from just one reporter, even though self-reports of fathers' involvement tend to be higher than mothers' reports of fathers' involvement, especially for nonresident fathers (Coley & Morris, 2002; Smock & Manning, 1997).

LEVELS AND PREDICTORS OF FATHERS' INVOLVEMENT

Research on fathering in two-parent households shows a noticeable and statistically significant increase in men's parenting involvement, both in absolute terms and in relation to mothers. Simultaneously, however, average levels of fathers' interaction with, availability to, and responsibility for children lag well behind those of mothers. (Maxsiglio, Amato, Day, & Lamb, 2000; Parke, 1996; Pleck & Masciadrelli, 2003). Measurement strategies vary, with time-use diaries generally producing the most accurate estimates of fathers' interaction and availability. On average, in the 1960s to early-1980s, fathers interacted with their children about a third as much as mothers and were available about half as much as mothers (Lamb et al., 1987). During the mid 1980s to early 1990s, the average co-resident father interacted about two fifths as much as mothers and was available to his children almost two thirds as much (Pleck, 1997). In the late 1990s, he was available to his children about three fourths as much as mothers, interacting on weekdays about two thirds as often, but over four fifths as much on weekends (Pleck & Masciadrelli, 2003; Yueng, Sandberg, Davis-Kean, & Hofferth, 2001). In an estimated 20% of two-parent families, men are now about as involved as mothers interacting with and being available to their children. At the same time, in most families, fathers share much less of the responsibility for the planning, scheduling, emotional management, housework, and other maintenance activities associated with raising children (Deutsch, 1999; Hochschild, 1989).

Researchers have begun to isolate the effects of income, race/ethnicity, education, family structure, marriage, employment, work schedules, and other factors on father involvement, though results are often incomplete or contradictory. For example, the relation between socioeconomic status and father involvement is complex. Income is often found to be positively correlated with father involvement among various ethnic groups (Fagan, 1998; Parke, 1996). Relative income contributions by wives are also associated with higher proportionate levels of father involvement in housework and child care (Coltrane, 2000; Yeung et al., 2001), though some studies still find that financially dependent husbands do less domestic work than others (Brines, 1994). Wealthier men do little routine family work, but the amount their wives do varies dramatically, with higher-earning wives more likely to purchase domestic services (e.g., child care, house cleaning, laundry) (Cohen, 1998; Oropesa, 1993).

Although most contemporary studies of fathering have been based on white, middle-class, two-parent families, we are beginning to get a more complete picture about similarities and differences across family types. When financial stability is hard to achieve, fathers only minimally involved with their children may nevertheless see themselves as "good fathers" because they work hard to provide financially. Because of inequities in the labor market, men of color are disproportionately likely to face difficulties being adequate providers (Bowman & Sanders,

1998; Hamer & Marchioro, 2002). Comparisons between white, African American, and Latino fathers suggest similar levels of involvement with infants and similar styles of engagement with young children (e.g., proportionately more play and less caretaking than mothers; Coltrane, Parke, & Adams, 2001; Toth & Xu, 1999). Contrary to cultural stereotypes, some research also shows that Latino fathers are more likely than their European American counterparts to spend time in shared activities with children, to perform housework and personal care, and to engage in monitoring and supervising children's activities (Coltrane et al., 2001; Toth & Xu, 1999; Yeung et al., 2001). Results for African-American fathers in two-parent households are mixed, with most reporting levels of father-child interaction comparable to other race/ethnic groups, and several studies finding that black men do more housework than white men, net of other predictors (Ahmeduzzaman & Roopnarine, 1992; Broman, 1991; Hossam & Roopnarine, 1993; John & Shelton, 1997), and that nonresident black fathers contribute more to children than nonresident white fathers (Wilson, Tolson, Hinton, & Kiernan, 1990). Studies of African-American and Latino fathers reveal a wide range of behaviors across families, depending on employment, income, education, gender and religious ideology, family structure, marital status, age of children, immigration status, neighborhood context, cultural traditions, and presence of extended or fictive kin, and a similar pattern of association between social contextual variables and levels and styles of paternal participation (Auerbach, Silverstein, & Zizi, 1997; Cabrera, Tamis-LeMonda, Bradley, Hofferth, & Lamb, 2000; Hossain & Roopnarine, 1993; Hunter & Davis, 1994; Padgett, 1997; Pleck & Steuve, 2001; Silverstein, 2002).

Fathers tend to spend more time with young children than they do with older children and adolescents, probably because younger children require more attention and care, even though many men feel more comfortable interacting with older children. Most research finds that a father's availability (as determined by work hours) is a strong predictor of his involvement in child care. When mothers of preschool children are employed, a father's time availability predicts whether he will serve as a primary caregiver (Brayfield, 1995; Casper & O'Connell, 1998). Fathers and mothers with non-overlapping work shifts are the most likely to share child care (Presser, 1995). When mothers of school-aged children are employed more hours, their husbands tend to do a greater portion of the child care and housework, and fathers tend to be more involved to the extent that they view their wives' career prospects more positively (Pleck, 1997). For instance, Brewster (2000) found that fathers in the late 1980s and 1990s were likely to use nonworking discretionary hours for child care, whereas in the late 1970s and early 1980s they tended to use those hours for other activities.

As demonstrated in comprehensive reviews (Pleck, 1997; Pleck & Masciadrelli, 2003), father involvement is multiply determined, with no single factor responsible for the different types of involvement. In addition, studies often report contradictory effects of factors like income, education, age, family size, and birth timing. One of the most consistent findings is that men are more involved with sons than with daughters (Harris, Furstenberg, & Marmer, 1998; Harris & Morgan, 1991, Marsiglio, 1991; McBride, Schoppe, & Rane, 2002), especially with older children (Pleck, 1997). However, some recent studies have found no differences in father involvement by sex of child (Fagan, 1998; Hofferth, 2003), leading Pleck and Masciadrelli (2003) to suggest that fathers' preference for sons may be weakening. Some researchers also find that if fathers get involved during pregnancy or early infancy they tend to sustain that involvement later in children's lives (Coltrane, 1996; Parke, 1996).

Lamb, Pleck, and colleagues suggested that for fathers to become actively involved, they required four facilitating factors: (a) motivation, (b) skills and self-confidence, (c) social approval, and (d) institutional support (Lamb et al., 1987; see also Pleck, 1997). Many studies find that fathers are more involved and show more warmth if they believe in gender equality (Cabrera et al., 2000; Hofferth, 1998), though others find no significant association (Marsiglio, 1991; Pleck, 1997). Others find that fathers get more involved when they have a strong fatherhood identity or actively embrace the father role (Beitel & Parke, 1998; Hawkins, Christiansen, Sargent, & Hill, 1993; Pasley, Ihinger-Tallman, & Buehler, 1993; Rane & McBride, 2000; Snarey, 1993). In general, fathers feel more competent as parents when they are more involved with their children, though it is difficult to say whether this competence is a precursor or a result of active fathering (Beitel & Parke, 1998; McHale & Huston, 1984). Evidence suggesting that competence leads to involvement comes from interven-

tions designed to develop fathers' parenting skills (e.g., Cowan & Cowan, 2000; McBride, 1990). In terms of social support, fathers tend to be more involved when the children's mothers facilitate it, when the mothers had positive relationships with their own fathers when they were children (Allen & Hawkins, 1999; Cowan & Cowan, 2000; McBride & Mills, 1993; Parke, 1996), and when kin and other community members support father involvement (Pleck, 1997). Finally, institutional supports can include factors such as fewer work hours and more flexible work schedules (Pleck, 1993).

Another approach to identifying predictors of father involvement is based on a process model of parenting (Belsky, 1984; McBride et al., 2002). This framework suggests that fathering is shaped by three categories of influence: (a) characteristics of the father (e.g., personality, attitudes toward child rearing), (b) characteristics of the child (e.g., temperament, age, gender), and (c) contextual sources of stress and support (e.g., marital relationships, social support networks, occupational experiences). Many of these facilitating influences overlap with factors in the Lamb and Pleck model, but this approach also includes consideration of things like child temperament and parental stress. Emergent findings suggest that child temperament or other characteristics may have a larger influence on father-child involvement than mother-child involvement, probably because fathering is seen as more discretionary than mothering (Cabrera et al., 2000; McBride et al., 2002).

The nature of the marital relationship is also associated with paternal involvement, though causality is sometimes difficult to assess. Some find that greater marital satisfaction leads to greater father involvement (Parke, 1996), and others suggest that higher levels of men's relative contributions to child care lead to women's greater marital satisfaction (Brennan, Barnett, & Gareis, 2001; Ozer, Barnett, Brennan, & Sperling, 1998). In addition, satisfaction with men's levels of family involvement appears to be strongly related to mothers' and fathers' gender ideals and expectations. We cannot simply assume that more father involvement is better for all families. As the emerging gatekeeping literature (e.g., Allen & Hawkins, 1999; Beitel & Parke, 1998) attests, too much involvement by fathers can be interpreted as interference rather than helpfulness. In general, if family members want a father to be more involved, his participation has positive effects on family functioning. If family members feel that fathers should not change diapers or do laundry, then such practices can cause stress (Coltrane, 1996).

THE POTENTIAL INFLUENCE OF FATHERS

As scholars pay more attention to fathers, they are beginning to understand what influence their involvement might have on child development. Most researchers find that father-child relationships are influential for children's future life chances (Federal Interagency Forum, 1998; Parke, 1996; Pleck & Masciadrelli, 2003). The focus of this research tends to be on the positive aspects of fathers' involvement, though it should be noted that because men are more likely than women to abuse children or to use inappropriate parenting techniques, increased male involvement can lead to increased risk and negative outcomes for children, particularly if the father figure does not have a long-term relationship with the mother (Finkelhor, Hotaling, Lewis, & Smith, 1990; Margolin, 1992; National Research Council, 1993; Radhakrishna, Bou-Saada, Hunter, Catellier, & Kotch, 2001).

Many researchers continue to focus on fathers' economic contributions to children and report that fathers' resources improve children's life chances. Longitudinal research shows that children from one-parent households (usually mother headed) are at greater risk for negative adult outcomes (e.g., lower educational and occupational achievement, earlier childbirth, school dropout, health problems, behavioral difficulties) than those from two-parent families (Marsiglio et al., 2000; McLanahan & Sandefur, 1994). Although comparisons between children of divorced parents and those from first-marriage families show more problems in the former group, differences between the two are generally small across various outcome measures and do not necessarily isolate the influence of divorce or of father involvement (Crockett, Eggebeen, & Hawkins, 1993; Furstenberg & Harris, 1993; Seltzer, 1994). For children with nonresident fathers, the amount of fathers' earnings (especially the amount that is actually transferred to children) is a significant predictor of children's well-being, including school grades and behavior problems (Amato & Gilbreth, 1999; McLanahan, Seltzer, Hanson, & Thomson, 1994; Marsiglio et al., 2000). Because the great majority of children from single-parent homes turn out to be happy, healthy, and productive adults, debates continue about how such large-group comparisons should

be made and how we should interpret their results in terms of fathers' economic or social contributions (Amato, 2000; Coltrane & Adams, 2003).

Earlier reviews suggested that the level of father involvement has a smaller direct effect on infant attachment than the quality or style of father interaction, though time spent parenting is also related to competence (Lamb et al., 1987; Marsiglio et al., 2000). Preschool children with fathers who perform 40% or more of the within-family child care show more cognitive competence, more internal locus of control, more empathy, and less gender stereotyping than preschool children with less involved fathers (Lamb et al., 1987; Pleck, 1997). Adolescents with involved fathers are more likely to have positive developmental outcomes such as self-control, self-esteem, life skills, and social competence, provided that the father is not authoritarian or overly controlling (Mosley & Thomson, 1995; Pleck & Masciadrelli, 2003). Studies examining differences between the presence of biological fathers versus other father figures suggest that it is the quality of the father-child relationship rather than biological relationship that enhances the cognitive and emotional development of children (Dubowitz et al., 2001; Hofferth & Anderson, 2003; Silverstein & Auerbach, 1999). Reports of greater father involvement when children were growing up have also been associated with positive aspects of adult children's educational attainment, relationship quality, and career success (Amato & Booth, 1997; Harris et al., 1998; Nock, 1998; Snarey, 1993). Because of methodological inadequacies in previous studies such as not controlling for maternal involvement, most scholars recommend more carefully controlled studies using random samples and multi-rater longitudinal designs, as well as advocating caution in interpreting associations between fathering and positive child outcomes (Amato & Rivera, 1999; Parke, 1996; Pleck & Masciadrelli, 2003). It will take some time to isolate the specific influence of fathers as against the influence of mothers and other social-contextual factors such as income, education, schools, neighborhoods, communities, kin networks, and cultural ideals.

We do know that when fathers share child care and housework with their wives, employed mothers escape total responsibility for family work, evaluate the division of labor as more fair, are less depressed, and enjoy higher levels of marital satisfaction (Brennan et al., 2001; Coltrane 2000;

Deutsch, 1999). When men care for young children on a regular basis, they emphasize verbal interaction, notice and use more subtle cues, and treat sons and daughters similarly, rather than focusing on play, giving orders, and sex-typing children (Coltrane, 1996, 1998; Parke, 1996). These styles of father involvement have been found to encourage less gender stereotyping among young adults and to encourage independence in daughters and emotional sensitivity in sons. Most researchers agree that these are worthy goals that could contribute to reducing sexism, promoting gender equity, and curbing violence against women (but see Blankenhorn, 1995).

DEMOGRAPHIC CONTEXTS FOR FATHER INVOLVEMENT

As Furstenberg (1988) first noted, conflicting images of fathers are common in popular culture, with nurturing, involved "good dads" contrasted with "bad dads" who do not marry the mother of their children or who move out and fail to pay child support. Recent research suggests that both types of fathers are on the rise and that the demographic contexts for fatherhood have changed significantly over the past few decades. In many industrialized countries, at the same time that some fathers are taking a more active role in their children's lives, growing numbers of men rarely see their children and do not support them financially. In the United States, for example, single parent households are increasing, with only about half of U.S. children eligible for child support from nonresident parents via court order, and only about half of those receive the full amount (Scoon-Rogers, 1999). Both trends in fatherhood—toward more direct involvement and toward less contact and financial support—are responses to the same underlying social developments, including women's rising labor force participation and the increasingly optional nature of marriage.

Marriage rates have fallen in the past few decades, with people waiting longer to get married and increasingly living together without marrying. Women are having fewer children than they did just a few decades ago, waiting longer to have them, and not necessarily marrying before they give birth (Eggebeen, 2002; Seltzer, 2000). One of three births in the United States is to an unmarried woman, a rate that is three times higher than it was in the 1960s, with rates for African-American women highest, followed by Latinas, and then non-Hispanic whites (National Cen-

ter for Health Statistics, 2000). It is often assumed that non-marital births produce fatherless children, but recent studies show that most of the increase in non-marital childbearing from the 1980s to the 1990s is accounted for by the increase in the number of cohabiting women getting pregnant and carrying the baby to term without getting married. Historically, if an unmarried woman became pregnant, she would marry to legitimate the birth. Today, only a minority of women do so.

In addition, an increasingly large number of American fathers live apart from their children because of separation or divorce. Because most divorcing men do not seek (or are not awarded) child custody following divorce, the number of divorced men who are uninvolved fathers has risen (Eggebeen, 2002; Furstenberg & Cherlin, 1991), although recent research shows that the actual involvement of fathers with children after divorce varies enormously, sometimes without regard to official post-divorce court orders (Braver, 1998; Hetherington & Stanley-Hagan, 1999; McLanahan & Sandefur, 1994; Seltzer, 1998). The number of men with joint physical (residential) custody has grown, though joint legal (decision-making) custody is still a more common post-divorce parenting arrangement (Maccoby & Mnookin, 1992; Seltzer, 1998). And although single-father households have increased in recent years, single-mother households continue to outpace them five to one. Demographers suggest that because of all these trends, younger cohorts will be less likely to experience sustained involved fathering than the generations that immediately preceded them (Eggebeen, 2002).

Marriage and the traditional assumption of fatherhood have become more fragile, in part because an increasing number of men face financial difficulties. Although men continue to earn about 30% higher wages than women, their real wages (adjusted for inflation) have declined since the early 1970s, whereas women's have increased (Bernstein & Mishel, 1997). As the U.S. economy has shifted from heavy reliance on domestic manufacturing to global interdependence within an information and service economy, working-class men's prospects of earning a family wage have declined. At the same time, women's labor force participation has risen steadily, with future growth in the economy predicted in the areas where women are traditionally concentrated (e.g., service, information, health care, part-time work). The historical significance of this shift cannot be overestimated. For most of the 19th and 20th centuries, American women's life chances were determined by their marriage decisions. Unable to own property, vote, or be legally independent in most states, daughters were dependent on fathers and wives were dependent on their husbands for economic survival. Such dependencies shaped family relations and produced fatherhood ideals and practices predicated on male family headship. As women and mothers have gained independence by entering the labor force in record numbers, it is not surprising that older ideals about marriage to a man legitimating childbearing have been challenged.

GENDER AND THE POLITICS OF FATHERHOOD

In the 1990s, popular books and articles revived a research and policy focus that had been popular in the 1960s: father absence. For example, Popenoe (1996) suggested that drug and alcohol abuse, juvenile delinquency, teenage pregnancy, violent crime, and child poverty were the result of fatherlessness and that American society was in decline because it had abandoned traditional marriage and child-rearing patterns. Such claims about father absence often rely on evolutionary psychology and sociobiology and define fathers as categorically different from mothers (Blankenhorn, 1995; Popenoe, 1996). Even some proponents of nurturing fathers warn men against trying to act too much like mothers (Pruett, 1993). Following this reasoning, some argue for gender-differentiated parenting measurement strategies: "[T]he roles of father and mother are different and complementary rather than interchangeable and thus the standards for evaluating the role performance of fathers and mothers should be different" (Day & Mackey, 1989, p. 402). Some label the use of measures developed on mothers to study fathers and the practice of comparing fathers' and mothers' parenting as the *deficit model* (Doherty, 1991) or the *role inadequacy perspective* (Hawkins & Dollahite, 1997).

Because parenting is a learned behavior for both men and women, most social scientists focus on the societal conditions that create gender differences in parenting or find proximate social causes of paternal investment that outweigh assumed biological causes (e.g., Hofferth & Anderson, 2003). Nevertheless, questioning taken-for-granted cultural ideals about families can cause controversy. When Silverstein and Auerbach (1999) challenged assertions about essential differences between fathers and mothers in an *American Psychologist* article entitled "Deconstructing the Essential Father," they received widespread public and academic criticism. Their scholarly article (based on a review of research findings) was ridiculed as "silliness" and "junk science" by Wade Horn (1999; formerly of the National Fatherhood Initiative and now Assistant Secretary in the U.S. Department of Health and Human Services), and the U.S. House of Representatives debated whether to pass a resolution condemning the article (Silverstein, 2002). Clearly, debates about fathers, marriage, and family values carry symbolic meanings that transcend scientific findings. The contentious political and scholarly debates about fathers that emerged in the 1990s appear to be framed by an older political dichotomy: Conservatives tend to focus on biological parenting differences and stress the importance of male headship and breadwinning, respect for authority, and moral leadership (Blankenhorn, 1995; Popenoe 1996), whereas liberals tend to focus on similarities between mothers and fathers and stress the importance of employment, social services, and possibilities for more equal marital relations (Coontz, 1992; Silverstein & Auerbach, 1999; Stacey, 1996).

A full analysis of contemporary family values debates is beyond the scope of this [article], but elsewhere I analyze marriage and fatherhood movements using data and theories about political opportunities, resource mobilization, and the moral framing of social issues (Coltrane, 2001; Coltrane & Adams, 2003; see also Gavanas, 2002). In general, cultural tensions in the larger society are mirrored in policy proposals and academic debates about the appropriate roles of fathers and the importance of marriage. One cannot adjudicate among various scholarly approaches to fathering without acknowledging gendered interests and understanding the political economy of expert knowledge production. Recent policies and programs promoting marriage and fatherhood using faith-based organizations are designed to advance a particular vision of fatherhood. Whether they will benefit the majority of American mothers and children is a question that cannot be resolved without more sophisticated research with controls for mothers' parenting and various other economic and social-contextual issues (Marsiglio et al., 2000; Marsiglio & Pleck, in press).

PROSPECTS FOR THE FUTURE

The forces that are driving changes in fathers' involvement in families are likely to continue. In two-parent households (both married and cohabiting), men share more family work if their female partners are employed more hours, earn more money, and have more education. All three of these trends in women's attainment are likely to continue for the foreseeable future. Similarly, fathers share more family work when they are employed fewer hours and their wives earn a greater portion of the family income. Labor market and economic trends for these variables are also expected to continue for several decades. Couples also share more when they believe that family work should be shared and that men and women should have equal rights. According to national opinion polls, although the country has become slightly more conservative about marriage and divorce than it was in the 1970s and 1980s, the belief in gender equality continues to gain acceptance among both men and women. In addition, American women are waiting longer, on average, to marry and give birth, and they are having fewer children—additional factors sometimes associated with more sharing of housework and child care. Thus, I predict that increasing economic parity and more equal gender relations will allow women to buy out of some domestic obligations and/or recruit their partners to do more. Middle- and upper-class wives and mothers will rely on working-class and immigrant women to provide domestic services (nannies, housekeepers, child care workers, fast food employees, etc.), thereby reducing their own hours of family labor but simultaneously perpetuating race, class, and gender hierarchies in the labor market and in the society. Some fathers in dual-earner households will increase their contributions to family work, whereas others will perform a greater proportion of housework and child care by virtue of their wives' doing less. Other men will remain marginal to family life because they do not stay connected to the mothers of their children, do not hold jobs allowing them to support their children, or do not seek custody or make regular child support payments. These two ideal types—of involved and marginalized fathers—are likely to continue to coexist the popular culture and in actual practice.

The context in which American couples negotiate fathering has definitely changed. The future is likely to bring more demands on fathers to be active parents if they want to stay involved with the mothers of their children. For fathers to assume more responsibility for active parenting, it may be necessary to change cultural assumptions that men are entitled to domestic services and that women are inherently predisposed to provide them. Further changes in fathering are likely to be driven by women's increasing independence and earning power. Ironically, women's enhanced economic position also makes them able to form families and raise children without the father's being present. In the future, men will be even less able to rely on their superior earning power and the institution of fatherhood to maintain their connection to families and children. Increasingly, they will need to adopt different fathering styles to meet specific family circumstances and to commit to doing things men have not been accustomed to doing. Some men will be able to maintain their economic and emotional commitments to their children, whereas others will not. Some men will participate in all aspects of child rearing, whereas others will hardly see their children. Unless living wages and adequate social supports are developed for all fathers (as well as for mothers and children), we can expect that the paradoxes, contradictions, and dilemmas associated with fathering described in this [article] will continue for the foreseeable future.

Author's Note: This [article] incorporates some material from a November 21, 2002, National Council on Family Relations (NCFR) Annual Conference Special Session Prospects for Increasing Father Involvement in Child "Future Rearing and Household Activities," reprinted as "The Paradox of Fatherhood: Predicting the Future of Men's Family Involvement" in *Vision 2003* (Minneapolis, MN: NCFR/Allen Press). I thank Marilyn Coleman, Lawrence Ganong, Joseph Pleck, Carl Auerbach, and two anonymous reviewers for valuable feedback on an earlier draft of this chapter.

REFERENCES

Abmeduzzaman, M., & Roopnarine, J. L. (1992). Sociodemographic factors, functioning style, social support and fathers' involvement with preschoolers in African-American intact families. *Journal of Marriage and the Family, 54,* 699–707.

Allen, S. M., & Hawkins, A. J. (1999). Maternal gatekeeping. *Journal of Marriage and the Family, 61,* 199–212.

Amato, P. (2000). Diversity within single-parent families. In D. H. Demo, K. R. Allen, & M. A. Fine (Eds.), *Handbook of family diversity* (pp. 149–172). New York: Oxford University Press.

Amato, P., & Booth, A. (1997). *A generation at risk: Growing up in an era of family upheaval.* Cambridge, MA: Harvard University Press.

Amato, P., & Gilbreth, J. (1999). Nonresident fathers and children's well-being: A meta-analysis. *Journal of Marriage and the Family, 61,* 557–573.

Amato, P., & Rivera, F. (1999). Paternal involvement and children's behavior problems. *Journal of Marriage and the Family, 61,* 375–384.

Auerbach, C., Silverstein, L., & Zizi, M. (1997). The evolving structure of fatherhood. *Journal of African-American Men, 2,* 59–85.

Beitel, A. H., & Parke, R. D. (1998). Paternal involvement in infancy: The role of maternal and paternal attitudes. *Journal of Family Psychology, 12,* 268–288.

Belsky, J. (1984). The determinants of parenting. *Child Development, 55,* 83–96.

Bernard, J. (1981). The good provider role: Its rise and fall. *American Psychologist, 36,* 1–12.

Bernstein, J., & Mishel, L. (1997). Has wage inequality stopped growing? *Monthly Labor Review, 120,* 3–17.

Biller, H. B. (1976). The father and personality development. In M. E. Lamb (Ed.), *The role of the father in child development.* New York: John Wiley.

Blankenhorn, D. (1995). *Fatherless America.* New York: Basic Books.

Bowman, P. J., & Sanders, R. (1998). Unmarried African-American fathers. *Journal of Comparative Family Studies, 29,* 39–56.

Braver, S. L. (1998). *Divorced dads.* New York: Jeremy Tarcher/Putnam.

Brayfield, A. (1995). Juggling jobs and kids. *Journal of Marriage and the Family, 57,* 321–332.

Brennan, R. T., Barnett, R. C., & Gareis, K. C. (2001). When she earns more than he does: A longitudinal study of dual-earner couples. *Journal of Marriage and the Family, 63,* 168–182.

Brewster, K. L. (2000, March). *Contextualizing change in fathers' participation in child care.* Paper presented at "Work and Family" Conference, San Francisco.

Brines, J. (1994). Economic dependency, gender, and the division of labor at home. *American Journal of Sociology, 100,* 652–688.

Broman, L. L. (1991). Gender, work, family roles, and psychological well-being of blacks. *Journal of Marriage and the Family, 53,* 509–520.

Cabrera, N., Tamis-LeMonda, C., Bradley, R., Hofferth, S., & Lamb, M. (2000). Fatherhood in the 21st century. *Child Development, 71,* 127–136.

Casper, L. M., & O'Connell, M. (1998). Work, income, the economy, and married fathers as child-care providers. *Demography, 35,* 243–250.

Chodorow, N. (1974). Family structure and feminine personality. In M. Z. Rosaldo & L. Lamphere (Eds.), *Woman, culture and society* (pp. 43–66). Palo Alto, CA: Stanford University Press.

Cohen, P. N. (1998). Replacing housework in the service economy: Gender, class, and race-ethnicity in service spending. *Gender and Society, 12,* 219–231.

Coley, R. L., & Morris, J. E. (2002). Comparing father and mother reports of father involvement among low-income minority families. *Journal of Marriage and the Family, 64,* 982–997.

Coltrane, S. (1988). Father-child relationships and the status of women. *American Journal of Sociology, 93,* 1060–1095.

Coltrane, S. (1996). *Family man.* New York: Oxford University Press.

Coltrane, S. (1998). *Gender and families.* Newbury Park, CA: Pine Forge/Alta Mira.

Coltrane, S. (2000). Research on household labor. *Journal of Marriage and the Family, 62,* 1209–1233.

Coltrane, S. (2001). Marketing the marriage "solution." *Sociological Perspectives, 44,* 387–422.

Coltrane, S., & Adams, M. (2003). The social construction of the divorce "problem": Morality, child victims, and the politics of gender. *Family Relations, 52,* 21–30.

Coltrane, S., & Collins, R. (2001). *Sociology of marriage and the family* (5th ed.). Belmont, CA: Wadsworth/Thomson Learning.

Coltrane, S., & Galt, J. (2000). The history of men's caring. In M. H. Meyer (Ed.), *Care work: Gender, labor, and welfare states* (pp. 15–36). New York: Routledge.

Coltrane, S., & Parke, R. D. (1998). *Reinventing fatherhood: Toward an historical understanding of continuity and change in men's family lives* (WP 98–12A). Philadelphia: National Center on Fathers and Families.

Coltrane, S., Parke, R. D., & Adams, M. (2001, April). *Shared parenting in Mexican-American and European-American families.* Paper presented at the biennial meeting of the Society for Research in Child Development, Minneapolis, MN.

Coontz, S. (1992). *The way we never were.* New York: Basic Books.

Cowan, C. P., & Cowan, P. A. (2000). *When partners become parents.* Mahwah, NJ: Lawrence Erlbaum.

Crockett, L. J., Eggebeen, D. J., & Hawkins, A. J. (1993). Fathers' presence and young children's behavioral and cognitive adjustment. *Journal of Family Issues, 14,* 355–377.

Day, R. D., & Mackey, W. C. (1989). An alternate standard for evaluating American fathers. *Journal of Family Issues, 10,* 401–408.

Deutsch, F. (1999). *Halving it all.* Cambridge, MA: Harvard University Press.

Dill, B. T. (1988). Our mother's grief: Racial ethnic women and the maintenance of families. *Journal of Family History, 13,* 415–431.

Doherty, W. J. (1991). Beyond reactivity and the deficit model of manhood. *Journal of Marital and Family Therapy, 17,* 29–32.

Dubowitz, H., Black, M. M., Cox, C. E., Kerr, M. A., Litrownik, A. I., Radhakrishna, A., English, D. J., Schneider, M. W., & Runyan, D. K. (2001). Father involvement and children's functioning at age 6 years: A multisite study. *Child Maltreatment, 6,* 300–309.

Eggebeen, D. (2002). The changing course of fatherhood. *Journal of Family Issues, 23,* 486–506.

Ehrenreich, B. (1984). *The hearts of men.* Garden City, NY: Anchor Press/Doubleday.

Fagan, J. A. (1998). Correlates of low-income African American and Puerto Rican fathers' involvement with their children. *Journal of Black Psychology, 3,* 351–367.

Federal Interagency Forum on Child and Family Statistics. (1998). Report of the Working Group on Conceptualizing Male Parenting (Marsiglio, Day, Evans, Lamb, Braver, & Peters). In *Nurturing fatherhood* (pp. 101–174). Washington, DC: Government Printing Office.

Finkelhor, D., Hotaling, G., Lewis, I., & Smith, C. (1990). Sexual abuse in a national survey of adult men and women. *Child Abuse and Neglect, 14,* 19–28.

Furstenberg, F. F. (1988). Good dads—bad dads. In A. Cherlin (Ed.), *The changing American family and public policy* (pp. 193–218). Washington, DC: Urban Institute Press.

Furstenberg, F. F., & Cherlin, A. (1991). *Divided families.* Cambridge, MA: Harvard University Press.

Furstenberg, F. F., & Harris, K. (1993). When and why fathers matter. In R. Lerman & T. Ooms (Eds.), *Young unwed fathers* (pp. 150–176). Philadelphia: Temple University Press.

Gavanas, A. (2002). The fatherhood responsibility movement. In B. Hobson (Ed.), *Making men into fathers* (pp. 213–242). New York: Cambridge University Press.

Griswold, R. L. (1993). *Fatherhood in America: A history.* New York: Basic Books.

Griswold, R. L. (1997). Generative fathering: A historical perspective. In A. J. Hawkins & D. Dollahite (Eds.), *Generative fathering* (pp. 71–86). Thousand Oaks, CA: Sage.

Hamer, J., & Marchioro, K. (2002). Becoming custodial dads: Exploring parenting among low-income and working-class African American fathers. *Journal of Marriage and the Family, 64,* 116–129.

Harris, K. H., Furstenberg, F. F., & Marmer, J. K. (1998). Paternal involvement with adolescents in intact families. *Demography, 35,* 201–216.

Harris, K. H., & Morgan, S. P. (1991). Fathers, sons, and daughters: Differential paternal involvement in parenting. *Journal of Marriage and the Family, 53,* 531–544.

Hawkins, A. J., Christiansen, S. L., Sargent, K. P., & Hill, E. J. (1993). Rethinking fathers' involvement in child care. *Journal of Family Issues, 14,* 531–549.

Hawkins, A. J., & Dollahite, D. C. (1997). Beyond the role-inadequacy perspective of fathering. In A. J. Hawkins & D. C. Dollahite (Eds.), *Generative fathering: Beyond deficit perspectives* (pp. 3–16). Thousand Oaks, CA: Sage.

Hays, S. (1996). *The cultural contradictions of motherhood.* New Haven, CT: Yale University Press.

Hetherington, E. M., & Stanley-Hagan, M. M. (1999). Stepfamilies. In M. E. Lamb (Ed.), *Parenting and child development in "nontraditional" families* (pp. 137–159). Mahwah, NJ: Lawrence Erlbaum.

Hewlett, B. S. (1991). *The nature and context of Aka pygmy paternal infant care.* Ann Arbor: University of Michigan Press.

Hewlett, B. S. (2000). Culture, history, and sex: Anthropological contributions to conceptualizing father involvement. *Marriage and Family Review, 29,* 59–73.

Hochschild, A. R. (1989). *The second shift.* New York: Viking.

Hofferth, S. L. (1998). *Healthy environments, healthy children: Children in families.* Ann Arbor: Institute for Social Research, University of Michigan.

Hofferth, S. L. (2003). Race/ethnic differences in father involvement in two-parent families: Culture, context, or economy? *Journal of Family Issues, 24,* 185–216.

Hofferth, S. L., & Anderson, K. G. (2003). Are all dads equal? Biology versus marriage as a basis for paternal investment. *Journal of Marriage and the Family, 65,* 213–232.

Horn, W. (1999). Lunacy 101: Questioning the need for fathers. Retrieved April 29, 2003, from the Smart Marriages Web site: http://listarchives.his.com/smartmarriages/smartmarriages.9907/msg000111.html.

Hossain, Z., & Roopnarine, J. L. (1993). Division of household labor and child care in dual-earner African-American families with infants. *Sex Roles, 29,* 571–581.

Hunter, A. G., & Davis, J. E. (1994). Hidden voices of black men: The meaning, structure, and complexity of manhood. *Journal of Black Studies, 25,* 20–40.

John, D., & Shelton, B. A. (1997). The production of gender among black and white women and men: The case of household labor. *Sex Roles, 36,* 171–193.

Johnson, M. (1988). *Strong mothers, weak wives.* Berkeley: University of California Press.

Kimmel, M. (1996). *Manhood in America: A cultural history.* New York: Free Press.

Lamb, M. E., Pleck, J., Charnov, B., & Levine, J. (1987). A biosocial perspective on parental behavior and involvement. In J. B. Lancaster, J. Altman, & A. Rossi (Eds), *Parenting across the lifespan* (pp. 11–42). New York: Academic Press.

LaRossa, R (1988) Fatherhood and social change. *Family Relations, 37,* 451–457.

LaRossa, R. (1997). *The modernization of fatherhood: A social and political history.* Chicago: University of Chicago Press.

Maccoby, E., & Mnookin, R. (1992). *Dividing the child.* Cambridge, MA: Harvard University Press.

Margolin, L. (1992) Child abuse by mother's boyfriends. *Child Abuse and Neglect, 16,* 541–551.

Marsiglio, W. (1991). Paternal engagement activities with minor children. *Journal of Marriage and the Family, 53,* 973–986.

Marsiglio, W., Amato, P., Day, R. D., & Lamb, M. E. (2000). Scholarship on fatherhood in the 1990s and beyond. *Journal of Marriage and the Family, 62,* 1173–1191.

Marsiglio, W., & Pleck, J. H. (in press). Fatherhood and masculinities. In R. W. Council, J. Hearn, & M. Kimmel (Eds.), *The handbook of studies on men and masculinities.* Thousand Oaks, CA: Sage.

McBride, B. A. (1990). The effects of a parent education/play group program on father involvement on child rearing. *Family Relations, 39,* 250–256.

McBride, B. A., & Mills, G. (1993). A comparison of mother and father involvement with their preschool age children. *Early Childhood Research Quarterly, 8,* 457–477.

McBride, B. A., Schoppe, S., & Rane, T. (2002). Child characteristics, parenting stress, and parental involvement: Fathers versus mothers. *Journal of Marriage and the Family, 64,* 998–1011.

McDaniel, A. (1994). Historical racial differences in living arrangements of children. *Journal of Family History, 19,* 57–77.

McHale, S. M., & Huston, T. L. (1984). Men and women as parents: Sex role orientations, employment, and parental roles with infants. *Child Development, 55,* 1349–1361.

McLanahan, S., & Sandefur, G. (1994). *Growing up with a single parent: What hurts, what helps.* Cambridge, MA: Harvard University Press.

McLanahan, S., Seltzer, J., Hanson, T., & Thomson, E. (1994). Child support enforcement and child well-being. In I. Garfinkel, S. S. McLanahan, & P. K. Robins (Eds.). *Child support and child well-being* (pp. 285–316). Washington, DC: Urban Institute.

Messner, M. (1993). "Changing men" and feminist politics in the U.S. *Theory and Society, 22,* 723–737.

Mintz, S. (1998). From patriarchy to androgyny and other myths. In A. Booth & A. C. Crouter (Eds.), *Men in families* (pp. 3–30). Mahweh, NJ: Lawrence Erlbaum.

Mosley, J., & Thomson, E. (1994). Fathering behavior and child outcomes. In W. Marsiglio (Ed.), *Fatherhood* (pp. 148–165). Thousand Oaks, CA: Sage.

National Center for Health Statistics. (2000, January). Nonmarital birth rates, 1940–1999. Retrieved on April 29, 2003, from the Centers for Disease Control and Prevention Web site: www.cdc.gov/nchs/data/nvsr/nvsr48.

National Research Council. (1993). *Understanding child abuse and neglect*. Washington, DC: National Academy Press.

Nock, S. (1998). *Marriage in men's lives*. New York: Oxford University Press.

Oropesz, R. S. (1993). Using the service economy to relieve the double burden: Female labor force participation and service purchases. *Journal of Family Issues, 14*, 438–473.

Ozer, E. M., Barnett, R. C., Brennan, R. T., & Sperling, J. (1998). Does childcare involvement increase or decrease distress among dual-earner couples? *Women's Health: Research on Gender, Behavior, and Policy, 4*, 285–311.

Padgett, D. L. (1997). The contribution of support networks to household labor in African American families. *Journal of Family Issues, 18*, 227–250.

Palkovitz, R. (1997). Reconstructing "involvement." In A. Hawkins & D. Dollahite (Eds.), *Generative fathering* (pp. 200–216). Thousand Oaks, CA: Sage.

Parke, R. D. (1996). *Fatherhood*. Cambridge, MA: Harvard University Press.

Pasley, K., Ihinger-Tallman, M., & Buehler, C. (1993). Developing a middle-range theory of father involvement postdivorce. *Journal of Family Issues, 14*, 550–576.

Pleck, E. H., & Pleck, J. H. (1997). Fatherhood ideals in the United States: Historical dimensions. In M. E. Lamb (Ed.), *The role of the father in child development* (3rd ed., pp. 33–48). New York: John Wiley.

Pleck, J. H. (1993). Are "family-supportive" employer policies relevant to men? In J. C. Hood (Ed.), *Men, work, and family* (pp. 217–237). Newbury Park, CA: Sage.

Pleck, J. H. (1997). Paternal involvement: Levels, sources, and consequences. In M. E. Lamb (Ed.), *The role of the father in child development* (3rd ed., pp. 66–103). New York: John Wiley.

Pleck, J. H., & Masciadrelli, B. P. (2003). Paternal involvement: Levels, sources, and consequences. In M. E. Lamb (Ed.), *The role of the father in child development* (4th ed.). New York: John Wiley.

Pleck, J. H., & Steuve, J. L. (2001). Time and paternal involvement. In K. Daly (Ed.), *Minding the time in family experience* (pp. 205–226). Oxford, UK: Elsevier.

Popenoe, D. (1996). *Life without father: Compelling new evidence that fatherhood and marriage are indispensable for the good of children and society*. New York: Free Press.

Presser, H. B. (1995). Job, family, and gender. *Demography, 32*, 577–598.

Pruett, K. D. (1993). The paternal presence. *Families in Society, 74*, 46–50.

Radhakrishna, A., Bou-Saada, I. E., Hunter, W. M., Catellier, D. J., & Kotch, J. B. (2001). Are father surrogates a risk factor for child maltreatment? *Child Maltreatment, 6*, 281–289.

Rane, T. R., & McBride, B. A. (2000). Identity theory as a guide to understanding father's involvement with their children. *Journal of Family Issues, 21*, 347–366.

Sanday, P. R. (1981). *Female power and male dominance*. New York: Cambridge University Press.

Scoon-Rogers, L. (1999). Child support for custodial mothers and fathers. *Current Population Reports*, P60–196. Washington, DC: U.S. Bureau of the Census.

Seltzer, J. A. (1994). Consequences of marital dissolution for children. *Annual Review of Sociology, 20*, 235–266.

Seltzer, J. A. (1998). Father by law: Effects of joint legal custody on nonresident fathers' involvement with children. *Demography, 35*, 135–146.

Seltzer, J. A. (2000). Families formed outside of marriage. *Journal of Marriage and the Family, 62*, 1247–1268.

Silverstein, L. B. (2002). Fathers and families. In J. McHale & W. Grolnick (Eds.), *Retrospect and prospect in the psychological study of fathers* (pp. 35–64). Mahwah, NJ: Lawrence Erlbaum.

Silverstein, L. B., & Auerbach, C. F. (1999). Deconstructing the essential father. *American Psychologist, 54*, 397–407.

Smock, P., & Manning, W. (1997). Nonresident parents' characteristics and child support. *Journal of Marriage and the Family, 59*, 798–808.

Snarey, J. (1993). *How fathers care for the next generation.* Cambridge, MA: Harvard University Press.

Stacey, J. (1996). *In the name of the family.* Boston: Beacon.

Thompson, L., & Walker, A. J. (1989). Gender in families: Women and men in marriage, work, and parenthood. *Journal of Marriage and the Family, 51*, 845–871.

Toth, J. F., & Xu, X. (1999). Ethnic and cultural diversity in fathers' involvement: A racial/ethnic comparison of African American, Hispanic, and white fathers. *Youth and Society, 31*, 76–99.

Whiting, J., & Whiting, B. (1975). Aloofness and intimacy of husbands and wives. *Ethos, 3*, 183–207.

Wilson, M. N., Tolson, T. F. J., Hinton, I. D., & Kiernan, M. (1990). Flexibility and sharing of childcare duties in black families. *Sex Roles, 22*, 409–425.

Yueng, W. J., Sandberg, J. F., Davis-Kean, P. E., & Hofferth, S. L. (2001). Children's time with fathers in intact families. *Journal of Marriage and Family, 63*, 136–154.

Marilyn Coleman and Lawrence Ganong, eds., 2004, *Handbook of Contemporary Families: Considering the Past, Contemplating the Future*, pp. 224–243. Thousand Oaks, CA: Sage Publications. Reprinted by permission via the Copyright Clearance Center.

The Child-man—
Kay Hymowitz

Today's single young men hang out in a hormonal limbo between adolescence and adulthood

It's 1965, and you're a 26-year-old white guy. You have a factory job, or maybe you work for an insurance broker. Either way, you're married, probably have been for a few years now; you met your wife in high school, where she was in your sister's class. You've already got one kid, with another on the way. For now, you're renting an apartment in your parents' two-family house, but you're saving up for a three-bedroom ranch house in the next town. Yup, you're an adult!

Now meet the 21st-century you, also 26. You've finished college and work in a cubicle in a large Chicago financial-services firm. You live in an apartment with a few single guy friends. In your spare time, you play basketball with your buddies, download the latest indie songs from iTunes, have some fun with the Xbox 360, take a leisurely shower, massage some product into your hair and face—and then it's off to bars and parties, where you meet, and often bed, girls of widely varied hues and sizes. Wife? Kids? House? Are you kidding?

Not so long ago, the average mid-twentysomething had achieved most of adulthood's milestones—high school degree, financial independence, marriage and children. These days, he lingers—happily—in a new hybrid state of semi-hormonal adolescence and responsible self-reliance. Decades in unfolding, this limbo may not seem like news to many, but in fact it is to the early 21st century what adolescence was to the early 20th: a momentous sociological development of profound economic and cultural import.

It's time to state what is now obvious to legions of frustrated young women: The limbo doesn't bring out the best in young men.

With women, you could argue that adulthood is in fact emergent. Single women in their 20s and early 30s are joining an international New Girl Order, hyper-achieving in both school and an increasingly female-friendly workplace, while packing leisure hours with shopping, traveling and dining with friends. Single young males, or SYMs, by contrast, often seem to hang out in a playground of drinking, hooking up, playing Halo 3 and, in many cases, underachieving. With them, adulthood looks as though it's receding.

Freud famously asked: "What do women want?" Notice that he didn't ask what men wanted—perhaps he thought he'd figured that one out. But that's a question that ad people, media execs and cultural entrepreneurs have pondered a lot in recent years. They're particularly interested in single young men, for two reasons: There are a lot more of them than before, and they tend to have some extra change.

Consider: In 1970, 69 percent of 25-year-old and 85 percent of 30-year-old white men were married; in 2000, only 33 percent and 58 percent were, respectively. And the percentage of young guys tying the knot is declining as you read this. Census Bureau data show that the median age of marriage among men rose from 26.8 in 2000 to 27.5 in 2006—a dramatic demographic shift for such a short time period.

That adds up to tens of millions more young men blissfully free of mortgages, wives and child-care bills. Historically, marketers have found this group an "elusive audience"— the phrase is permanently affixed to "men between 18 and 34" in adspeak—largely immune to the pleasures of magazines and television, as well as to shopping expeditions for the products advertised there.

A signal cultural moment came in April 1997, when *Maxim*, a popular British "lad magazine," hit American shores. *Maxim* plastered covers and features with pouty-lipped, tousled-haired pinups in lacy underwear and, in case that didn't do the trick, block-lettered promises of *sex! lust! naughty!* And it worked.

What really set *Maxim* apart from other men's mags was its voice. It was the sound of guys hanging around the *Animal House* living room. *Maxim* asked the SYM what he wanted and learned that he didn't want to grow up. And now the *Maxim* child-man voice has gone mainstream. You're that 26-year-old who wants sophomoric fun and macho action? Now the culture has a groaning table of entertainment with your name on it.

That sound you hear is women not laughing. Oh, some women get a kick out of child-men and their frat/fart jokes. But for many, the child-man is either an irritating mystery or a source of heartbreak. In contemporary female writing and conversation, the words "immature" and "men" seem united in perpetuity.

Naturally, women wonder: How did this perverse creature come to be? The most prevalent theory comes from feminist-influenced academics and cultural critics, who view dude media as symptoms of backlash, a masculinity crisis. Men feel threatened by female empowerment, these thinkers argue, and in their anxiety, they cling to outdated roles.

Insofar as the new guy media reflect a backlash against feminism, they're part of the much larger story of men's long, uneasy relationship with bourgeois order. In *A Man's Place*, historian John Tosh locates male resistance to bourgeois domesticity in the early 19th century, when middle-class expectations for men began to shift away from the patriarchal aloofness of the bad old days.

Under the newer bourgeois regime, the home was to be a haven in a heartless world, in which affection and intimacy were guiding virtues. But in Mr. Tosh's telling, it didn't take long before men vented frustrations with bourgeois domestication: They went looking for excitement and male camaraderie in empire building, in adventure novels and in going to "the club."

By the early 20th century, the emerging mass market in the U.S. offered new outlets for the virile urges that sat awkwardly in the bourgeois parlor; hence titles like *Field & Stream* and *Man's Adventure*, as well as steamier fare like *Escapade* and *Caper*. When television sets came on the market in the late 1940s, it was the airing of heavyweight fights and football games that led Dad to make the big purchase; to this day, sports events—the battlefield made civilized—glue him to the Barcalounger when he should be folding the laundry.

But this history suggests an uncomfortable fact about the new SYM: He's immature because he can be. We can argue endlessly about whether "masculinity" is natural or constructed—whether men are innately promiscuous, restless and slobby or socialized to be that way—but there's no denying the lesson of today's media marketplace: Give young men a choice between serious drama on the one hand, and Victoria's Secret models, battling cyborgs, exploding toilets and the NFL on the other, and it's the models, cyborgs, toilets and football by a mile.

For whatever reason, adolescence appears to be the young man's default state, proving what anthropologists have discovered in cultures everywhere: It is marriage and children that turn boys into men. Now that the SYM can put off family into the hazily distant future, he can—and will—try to stay a child-man. Not only is no one asking that today's twenty- or thirtysomething become a responsible husband and father—that is, grow up—but a freewheeling marketplace gives him everything he needs to settle down in pig's heaven indefinitely.

Now, you could argue that the motley crew of *Maxim*, Comedy Central and Halo 3 aren't much to worry about, that extended adolescence is what the word implies: a temporary stage. Most guys have lots of other things going on and will eventually settle down. Men know the difference between entertainment and real life. At any rate, like gravity, growing up happens; nature has rules.

That's certainly a hope driving the sharpest of recent child-man entertainments, Judd Apatow's hit movie *Knocked Up*. What sets *Knocked Up* apart from, say, *Old School*, is that it invites the audience to enjoy the SYM's immaturity even while insisting on its feebleness. The potheaded 23-year-old Ben Stone accidentally impregnates Alison, a gorgeous stranger he was lucky enough to score at a bar. He is clueless about what to do when she decides to have the baby, not because he's a "badass"—actually, he has a big heart—but because he dwells among social retards. In the end, though, Ben understands that he needs to grow up. He gets a job and an apartment and learns to love Alison and the baby. This is a comedy, after all.

The important question that Mr. Apatow's comedy deals with only obliquely is what extended living as a child-man does to a guy—and to the women he collides with along the way.

For the problem with child-men is that they're not very promising husbands and fathers. They suffer from a proverbial "fear of commitment," another way of saying that they can't stand to think of themselves as permanently attached to one woman. Sure, they have girlfriends; many are even willing to move in with them. But cohabiting can be just another Peter Pan delaying tactic. Women tend to see cohabiting as a potential path to marriage; men view it as another place to hang out or, as Barbara Dafoe Whitehead observes in *Why There Are No Good Men Left*, a way to "get the benefits of a wife without shouldering the reciprocal obligations of a husband."

And here's what may be the deepest existential problem with the child-man—a tendency to avoid not just marriage but any deep attachments. This is British writer Nick Hornby's central insight in his novel *About a Boy*. The book's anti-hero, Will, is an SYM whose life is as empty of passion as of responsibility. He has no self apart from pop-culture effluvia, a fact that the author symbolizes by having the jobless 36-year-old live off the residuals of a popular Christmas song written by his late father. Mr. Hornby shows how the media-saturated limbo of contemporary guyhood makes it easy to fill your days without actually doing anything.

Will's unemployment is part of a more general passionlessness. To pick up women, for instance, he pretends to have a son and joins a single-parent organization; the plight of the single mothers means nothing to him. For Will, women are simply fleshy devices that dispense sex, and sex is just another form of entertainment, a "fantastic carnal alternative to drink, drugs and a great night out, but nothing much more than that."

The superficiality, indolence and passionlessness evoked in Mr. Hornby's novels haven't triggered any kind of cultural transformation. The SYM doesn't read much, remember, and he certainly doesn't read anything prescribing personal transformation. The child-man may be into self-mockery; self-reflection is something else entirely.

That's too bad. Young men especially need a culture that can help them define worthy aspirations.

Adults don't emerge. They're made.

Hymowitz, Kay. "The Child-Man." Adapted from article appearing in the Manhattan Institute's City Journal. Reprinted by permission of the author.

Say It in a Soap

Could a foreign visitor to the United States learn anything about American family life from watching our soap operas? Consider the following plot line:

> Holden is having an affair with Lilly while his wife Angel is undergoing psychiatric treatment because she had been sexually molested by her father, who was shot and killed by Kalib, Holden's brother. In the meantime, Darryl is having an affair with Francine while he and his wife, Carol, are arranging to have a child through a surrogate mother. Francine's sister Sabrina has run off with Antonio, an apparent drug dealer who has shot Bob, the sister's father.

How does this depict the average American family? A visitor might conclude from the popularity of soap operas that Americans like to watch stories of illicit love, incest, infidelity, greed, and marital and family conflict. While the behaviors of these soap opera characters may not really represent daily lives of American family members, they must represent enough of reality to allow viewers to identify and sympathize with the characters throughout their every trial and tribulation.

It is important to know that Americans are not alone in their fascination with soap opera plots. Most societies have fictional dramas and tales about family life that reveal the concerns of members of that culture. Brazilians, for example, like Americans, are fanatical soap opera watchers, but the characters, situations, and plots are different from what is shown to American audiences. The focus of Brazilian soap operas tends to be on the **family of orientation**—father, mother, self, and siblings—rather than on the **family of procreation**—husband, wife, and children—as depicted on American television. The theme of class mobility dominates Brazilian soaps, as do plots about women from poor, rural families marrying wealthy men from the city. Love is depicted as dangerous and often unrequited, as when a woman is hopelessly in love with a man destined to marry someone else.

In Brazilian soap operas, characters almost always interact with family and friends; American soap operas display interactions more frequently between strangers. In addition, the setting for Brazilian soaps is usually the home, representing a place of private life. For American soaps, the setting is often the workplace, a bar, or some other location associated with public life.

KINSHIP

E X E R C I S E

Name

Section

Date

EXERCISE 7.3: SLIPPERY SOAP

Soap operas, like other tales and traditional dramas, reveal character motivations, choices, and actions that impact others. Such stories are an interesting way for the cultural anthropologist to learn about the dynamics of family life. Plot out your own story line for a new soap opera scheduled to air in the United States. What character traits must first be assigned in order to grasp the attention of your audience? Describe the setting for the first episode and how you wish to introduce the main characters.

How could visitors from Brazil learn about family life from your main plot? Is it an accurate portrayal of the typical American family?

KINSHIP

KEY TERMS

Adoption:

Bilateral descent:

Bilateral kindred:

Bride price:

Clan:

Cognatic descent:

Consanguineal kin:

Descent:

Family of orientation:

KINSHIP

Family of procreation:

Fictive kin:

Generation:

Lineage:

Man-child:

Matrilineage:

New reproductive technologies:

Patrilineage:

Romas:

KEY TERMS

Name _____

Section _____

Date _____

Six kinship classification:

       * Inuit (Eskimo)

       * Hawaiian

       * Iroquois

       * Crow

       * Omaha

       * Sudanese

Unilineal descent groups:

KINSHIP

8 ECONOMIC ANTHROPOLOGY

The Price Is Right

Four basic types of economy are found in non-industrial societies: food collectors (also known as hunters and gatherers), pastoralists, horticulturalists, and agriculturalists. Humans relied on **foraging** (hunting and gathering) to make their living until food production emerged around 10,000 years ago. The life ways of the hunters and gatherers have changed drastically with the introduction of more modern tools, the increase in population, and the spread of Westernized belief systems.

Pastoralism is an economy oriented toward herds of domesticated animals. Most often these cultures only eat the meat on special occasions (if at all). Generally, the herd animals offer blood and milk to members of these cultures. But making a living from animals alone is difficult. Therefore, pastoralists often take on another economic system in order to ensure their survival.

Horticulture and agriculture are two forms of food production based on cultivation or the domestication of crops. **Horticulture** always has a fallow period, but **agriculturalists** farm the same piece of land for long periods. This is because agriculture incorporates systems of irrigation, tilling of soil, laborers and domesticated animals.

Industrialized societies are distinct due to our sedentary nature, our large populations, and our ability to utilize chemicals in the manufacturing of food. Spam is a perfect example of an industrialized delicacy!

With a more sedentary lifestyle and the introduction of a labor force comes **social stratification**. In the United States, we have a class system which separates people by their level of income and personal possessions. By definition, any person can move up (or down) the social class ladder. Yet factors such as sex, age, religion, sexual preference, and ethnicity make such potential growth highly unlikely.

ECONOMIC ANTHROPOLOGY

CHAPTER 8

Making a Living—
Conrad Kottak

OVERVIEW

Four basic economic types are found in nonindustrial societies: foraging, horticulture, agriculture, and pastoralism. Food production eventually supplanted foraging in most world areas. Among foragers the band is a basic social unit. Ties of kinship and marriage link its members. Men usually hunt and fish. Women usually gather.

Horticulture and agriculture are two forms of farming, representing different ends of a continuum based on land and labor use. Horticulture always has a fallow period, but agriculturalists farm the same land year after year. Agriculturalists also use labor intensively, in irrigation and terracing, and by maintaining domesticated animals. The mixed nature of pastoralism, based on herding, is evident. Nomadic pastoralists trade with farmers. Among **transhumant pastoralists**, part of the population farms, while another part takes the herds to pasture.

Economic anthropologists study systems of production, distribution (exchange), and consumption. **Economics** has been defined as the science that studies the allocation of scarce means to alternative ends. Western economists assume that the idea of scarcity is universal—which it isn't—and that in making choices, people strive to maximize personal profit. However, people may and do maximize values other than individual profit.

There are three forms of **exchange**. **Market exchange** is based on impersonal purchase and sale, motivated by profit. With **redistribution**, goods are collected at a central place, with some eventually given back to the people. **Reciprocity** governs exchanges between social equals. Reciprocity, redistribution, and the market principle may coexist in the same society. The primary exchange mode in a society is the one that allocates the **means of production**.

ADAPTIVE STRATEGIES

The anthropologist Yehudi Cohen (1974b) used the term **adaptive strategy** to describe a group's system of economic production. Cohen argued that the most important reason for similarities between two (or more) unrelated societies is their possession of a similar adaptive strategy. For example, there are clear similarities among societies that

have a foraging (hunting and gathering) strategy. Cohen developed a typology of societies based on correlations between their economies and their social features. His typology includes these five adaptive strategies: foraging, horticulture, agriculture, pastoralism, and industrialism. The present chapter focuses on the first four adaptive strategies.

FORAGING

Until 10,000 years ago, people everywhere were foragers, also known as hunter-gatherers. However, environmental differences did create contrasts among the world's foragers. Some, such as the people who lived in Europe during the ice ages, were big-game hunters. Today, hunters in the Arctic still focus on large animals and herd animals; they have much less vegetation and variety in their diets than do tropical foragers. In general, as one moves from colder to warmer areas, there is an increase in the number of species. The tropics contain tremendous biodiversity, a great variety of plant and animal species, many of which have been used by human foragers. Tropical foragers typically hunt and gather a wide range of plant and animal life. The same may be true in temperate areas, such as the North Pacific Coast of North America, where Native American foragers could draw on a variety of land and sea resources, including salmon, other fish species, berries, mountain goats, seals, and sea mammals. Nevertheless, despite differences due to environmental variation, all foraging economies have shared one essential feature: People rely on nature to make their living.

Animal domestication (initially of sheep and goats) and plant cultivation (of wheat and barley) began 10,000 to 12,000 years ago in the Middle East, a period of time known as the **Neolithic period**. Cultivation based on different crops, such as maize, manioc (cassava), and potatoes, arose independently some 3,000 to 4,000 years later in the Americas. In both hemispheres the new economy spread rapidly. Most foragers eventually turned to food production. Today, almost all foragers have at least some dependence on food production or on food producers (Kent 1992).

The foraging way of life survived in certain environments (see Figure 8.1), including a few islands and forests, along with deserts and very cold areas—places where food production was not practicable with simple technology (see Lee and Daly 1999). In many areas, foragers had been exposed to the "idea" of food production but never adopted it because their own economies provided a perfectly adequate and nutritious diet—with a lot less work. In some areas, people reverted to foraging after trying food production and abandoning it. In most areas where hunter-gatherers did survive, foraging should be described as "recent" rather than "contemporary." All modern foragers live in nation-states, depend to some extent on government assistance, and have contacts with food-producing neighbors, as well as missionaries and other outsiders. We should not view contemporary foragers as isolated or pristine survivors of the Stone Age. Modern foragers are influenced by regional forces (e.g., trade and war), national and international policies, and political and economic events in the world system.

Although foraging is disappearing as a way of life, the outlines of Africa's two broad belts of recent foraging remain evident. One is the Kalahari Desert of southern Africa. This is the home of the *San* (!Kung Bushmen), who include the *Ju/'hoansi* (see Kent 1996; Lee 1993). The other main African foraging area is the equatorial forest of central and eastern Africa, home of the Mbuti, Efe, and other "pygmies" (Bailey et al. 1989; Turnbull 1965).

People still do subsistence foraging in certain remote forests in Madagascar; in Southeast Asia, including Malaysia and the Philippines; and on certain islands off the Indian coast (Lee and Daly 1999). Some of the best-known recent foragers are the indigenous people of Australia. Those Native Australians lived on their island continent for more than 40,000 years without developing food production.

The Western Hemisphere also had recent foragers. The Eskimos, or Inuit, of Alaska and Canada are well-known hunters. These (and other) northern foragers now use modern technology, including rifles and snowmobiles, in their subsistence activities (Pelto 1973). The native populations of California, Oregon, Washington, British Columbia, and Alaska were all foragers, as were those of

Figure 8.1 Worldwide Distribution of Recent Hunter-Gatherers. SOURCE: Adapted from a map by Ray Sim, in Göran Burenhult, ed., Encyclopedia of Humankind: People of the Stone Age *(McMahons Point, NSW, Australia: Weldon Owen Pty LTD, 1933), p. 193.*

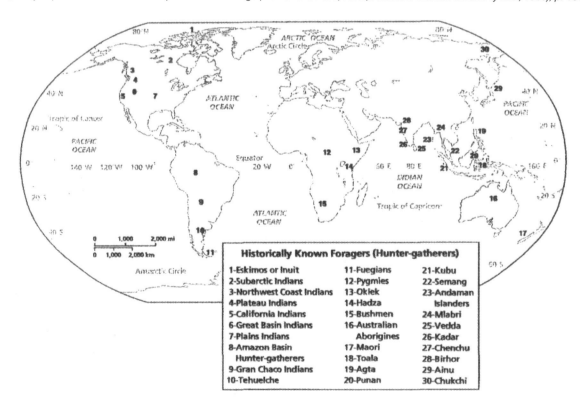

inland subarctic Canada and the Great Lakes. For many Native Americans, fishing, hunting, and gathering remain important subsistence (and sometimes commercial) activities.

Coastal foragers also lived near the southern tip of South America, in Patagonia. On the grassy plains of Argentina, southern Brazil, Uruguay, and Paraguay, there were other hunter-gatherers. The contemporary Aché of Paraguay are usually called "hunter-gatherers" even though they get just a third of their livelihood from foraging. The Ache also grow crops, have domesticated animals, and live in or near mission posts, where they receive food from missionaries (Hawkes et al. 1982; Hill et al. 1987).

Throughout the world, foraging survived mainly in environments that posed major obstacles to food production. (Some foragers took refuge in such areas after the rise of food production, the state, colonialism, or the modern world system.) The difficulties of cultivating at the North Pole are obvious. In southern Africa, the Dobe Ju/'hoansi San area studied by Richard Lee is surrounded by a waterless belt 70 to 200 kilometers in breadth. The Dobe area is hard to reach even today, and there is no archaeological evidence of occupation of this area by food producers before the 20th century (Solway and Lee 1990). However, environmental limits to other adaptive strategies aren't the only reason foragers survived. Their niches have one thing in common: their marginality. Their environments haven't been of immediate interest to groups with other adaptive strategies.

The hunter-gatherer way of life did persist in a few areas that could be cultivated, even after contact with cultivators. Those tenacious foragers, such as indigenous foragers in what is now California, did not turn to food production because they were not supporting themselves adequately by hunting and gathering. As the modern world system spreads, the number of foragers continues to decline.

CORRELATES OF FORAGING

Typologies, such as Cohen's adaptive strategies, are useful because they suggest **correlations**—that is, association or covariation between two or more variables. (Correlated variables are factors that are linked and interrelated, such as food intake and body weight, such that when one increases or decreases, the other tends to change, too.) Ethnographic studies in hundreds of societies have revealed many correlations between the economy and social life. Associated (correlated) with each adaptive strategy is a bundle of particular cultural features. Correlations, however, are rarely perfect. Some foragers lack cultural features usually associated with foraging, and some of those features are found in groups with other adaptive strategies.

What, then, are the usual correlates of foraging? People who subsist by hunting, gathering, and fishing often live in band-organized societies. Their basic social unit, the **band**, is a small group of fewer than a hundred people, all related by kinship or marriage. Band size varies between cultures and often from one season to the next in a given culture. In some foraging societies, band size stays about the same year-round. In others, the band splits up for part of the year. Families leave to gather resources that are better exploited by just a few people. Later, they regroup for cooperative work and ceremonies.

Several examples of seasonal splits and reunions are known from ethnography and archaeology. In southern Africa, some San aggregate around waterholes in the dry season and split up in the wet season, whereas other bands disperse in the dry season (Barnard 1979; Kent 1992). This reflects environmental variation. San who lack permanent water must disperse and forage widely for moisture-filled plants. In ancient Oaxaca, Mexico, before the advent of plant cultivation there around 4,000 years ago, foragers assembled in large bands in summer. They collectively harvested tree pods and cactus fruits. Then, in fall, they split into much smaller family groups to hunt deer and gather grasses and plants that were effectively foraged by small teams.

One typical characteristic of the foraging life is mobility. In many San groups, as among the Mbuti of Congo, people shift band membership several times in a lifetime. One may be born, for example, in a band where one's mother has kin. Later, one's family may move to a band where the father has relatives. Because bands are exogamous (people marry outside their own band), one's parents come from two different bands, and one's grandparents may come from four. People may join any band to which they have kinship or marriage links. A couple may live in, or shift between, the husband's band and the wife's band.

One also may affiliate with a band through **fictive kinship**—personal relationships modeled on kinship, such as that between godparents and godchildren. San, for example, have a limited number of personal names. People with the same name have a special relationship; they treat each other like siblings. San expect the same hospitality in bands where they have **namesakes** as they do in a band in which a real sibling lives. Namesakes share a strong identity. They call everyone in a namesake's band by the kin terms the namesake uses. Those people reply as if they were addressing a real relative. Kinship, marriage, and fictive kinship permit San to join several bands, and nomadic (regularly on-the-move) foragers do change bands often. Band membership therefore can change tremendously from year to year.

(continued on page 301)

E X E R C I S E

Name _____

Section _____

Date _____

EXERCISE 8.1: GARBOLOGY

Garbage can tell anthropologists a lot about the people who threw it away. These material remains often give clues about the consumers, such as use patterns, buying patterns, food/diet patterns, social status, economic status, religious beliefs, gender, age, ethnicity, etc. The more you know about the culture throwing the trash away the better your interpretation of the garbage will be; however, it is important to note that unless you are observing who is actually using these items and discarding them, your interpretations are only hypotheses or guesses about these people and their cultural patterns.

With this in mind, this assignment is a "practice" garbology exercise where you will be able to collect data (the trash), analyze it and draw hypotheses about the site/people/culture represented by it.

Process
1. Break up into groups of 5–6 people each. Each group will take a bag of "midden" (i.e., garbage) from the sample brought to class (either by the students or by the teacher, each group should have a bag of trash that does not belong to them to make the analysis more interesting). This will be the team's data.

2. Take the bag back to your designated area and examine the contents. Record the description of the contents onto a piece of paper. Be sure to include details such as shape, color, texture, size, smell, designs, pictures, words, etc. Sketching the items might also be useful if you have the time.

3. Create categories for the items according to their attributes or types to help organize them. Then make a list of the groupings and name each grouping with a heading such as "food," "beauty," "healthcare," "technology," "paper," "metal," "plastic," etc. Try to create discrete groups so that each item only fits into one category. You can make different lists with different categories to help you gain the most information from your artifacts.

(continued on the next page)

ECONOMIC ANTHROPOLOGY

4. Use this list to make inferences and/or hypotheses about the behavior and/or culture at the site where this data was produced. For example, try to answer the following questions:

Can you tell the ages of this group? (i.e., older, younger, children, adults)

Can you tell ethnicity from the items?

Can you tell sex and gender from the items?

Can you tell what type of group it was? (i.e., roommates, families, single, married, etc.)

Can you tell anything else about the people using these items, such as economic status, social status, religious affiliation, language spoken, dietary patterns, use patterns?

Use only the information that you see in the material remains of your site. Remember to reference each inference with examples of artifacts from your site (to support your hypothesis or conclusion).

Making a Living—
Conrad Kottak (continued)

UNDERSTANDING OURSELVES

How do we use **fictive kinship**? Although most of us are born in families, most of the people in our lives are non-relatives. This is a major contrast with a kin-based society, such as that of the San. There is a human tendency to be social, to seek friends, to make alliances, and to convert nonrelatives to whom we are especially close into something more—something like kin. Do you have godparents? Often godparents are close friends of one's parents. Or they may be actual relatives to whom one's parents felt especially close, and so they sought to strengthen the relationship. Adoptive parents and siblings are fictive kin who become legal kin. Fraternities and sororities have fictive kin including "brothers," "sisters," and house "mothers." Priests are addressed as "father"; nuns, as "sister." What other fictive kin can you think of? In our society, how is fictive kinship like and unlike the San namesake system?

All human societies have some kind of division of labor based on gender. Among foragers, men typically hunt and fish while women gather and collect, but the specific nature of the work varies among cultures. Sometimes women's work contributes most to the diet. Sometimes male hunting and fishing predominate. Among foragers in tropical and semitropical areas, gathering tends to contribute more to the diet than hunting and fishing do—even though the labor costs of gathering tend to be much higher than those of hunting and fishing.

All foragers make social distinctions based on age. Often old people receive great respect as guardians of myths, legends, stories, and traditions. Younger people value the elders' special knowledge of ritual and practical matters. Most foraging societies are **egalitarian**. This means that contrasts in prestige are minor and are based on age and gender.

When considering issues of "human nature," we should remember that the egalitarian band was a basic form of human social life for most of our history. Food production has existed less than one percent of the time *Homo* has spent on earth. However, it has produced huge social differences. We now consider the main economic features of food-producing strategies.

CULTIVATION

In Cohen's typology, the three adaptive strategies based on food production in nonindustrial societies are horticulture, agriculture, and pastoralism. In non-Western cultures, as is also true in modern nations, people carry out a variety of economic activities. Each adaptive strategy refers to the main economic activity. **Pastoralists** (herders), for example, consume milk, butter, blood, and meat from their animals as mainstays of their diet. However, they also add grain to the diet by doing some cultivating or by trading with neighbors. Food producers also may hunt or gather to supplement a diet based on domesticated species.

Horticulture

Horticulture and agriculture are two types of cultivation found in nonindustrial societies. Both differ from the farming systems of industrial nations like the United States and Canada, which use large land areas, machinery, and petro-chemicals. According to Cohen, **horticulture** is cultivation that makes intensive use of *none* of the factors of production: land, labor, capital, and machinery. Horticulturalists use simple tools such as hoes and digging sticks to grow their crops. Their fields are not permanently cultivated and lie *fallow* for varying lengths of time.

Horticulture often involves **slash-and-burn techniques**. Here, horticulturalists clear land by cutting down (slashing) and burning forest or bush or by setting fire to the grass covering the plot. The vegetation is broken down, pests are killed, and the ashes remain to fertilize the soil. Crops are then sown, tended, and harvested. Use of the plot is not continuous. Often it is cultivated for only a year. This depends, however, on soil fertility and weeds, which compete with cultivated plants for nutrients.

When horticulturalists abandon a plot because of soil exhaustion or a thick weed cover, they clear another piece of land, and the original plot reverts to forest. After several years of fallowing (the duration varies in different societies), the cultivator returns to farm the original plot again. Horticulture is also called **shifting cultivation**. Such shifts from plot to plot do not mean that whole villages must move when plots are abandoned. Horticulture can support large permanent villages. Among the Kuikuru of the South American tropical forest, for example, one village of 150 people remained in the same place for 90 years (Carneiro 1956). Kuikuru houses are large and well made. Because the work involved in building them is great, the Kuikuru would rather walk farther to their fields than construct a new village. They shift their plots rather than their settlements. On the other hand, horticulturalists in the montaña (Andean foothills) of Peru live in small villages of about 30 people (Carneiro 1961/1968). Their houses are small and simple. After a few years in one place, these people build new villages near virgin land. Because their houses are so simple, they prefer rebuilding to walking even a half mile to their fields.

Agriculture

Agriculture is cultivation that requires more labor than horticulture does, because it uses land intensively and continuously. The greater labor demands associated with agriculture reflect its common use of domesticated animals, irrigation, or terracing.

Domesticated Animals Many agriculturalists use animals as **means of production**—for transport, as cultivating machines, and for their manure. Asian farmers typically incorporate cattle and/or water buffalo into agricultural economies based on rice production. Rice farmers may use cattle to trample pretilled flooded fields, thus mixing soil and water, prior to transplanting. Many agriculturalists attach animals to plows and harrows for field preparation before planting or transplanting. Also, agriculturalists typically collect manure from their animals, using it to fertilize their plots, thus increasing yields. Animals are attached to carts for transport, as well as to implements of cultivation.

Irrigation While horticulturalists must await the rainy season, agriculturalists can schedule their planting in advance, because they control water. Like other irrigation experts in the Philippines, the Ifugao irrigate their fields with canals from rivers, streams, springs, and ponds. Irrigation makes it possible to cultivate a plot year after year. Irrigation enriches the soil because the irrigated field is a unique ecosystem with several species of plants and animals, many of them minute organisms, whose wastes fertilize the land.

An irrigated field is a capital investment that usually increases in value. It takes time for a field to start yielding; it reaches full productivity only after several years of cultivation. The Ifugao, like other irrigators, have farmed the same fields for generations. In some agricultural areas, including the Middle East, however, salts carried in the irrigation water can make fields unusable after 50 or 60 years.

Terracing Terracing is another agricultural technique the Ifugao have mastered. Their homeland has small valleys separated by steep hillsides. Because the population is dense, people need to farm the hills. However, if they simply planted on the steep hillsides, fertile soil and crops would be washed away during the rainy season. To prevent this, the Ifugao cut into the hillside and build stage after stage of terraced fields rising above the valley floor. Springs located above the terraces supply their irrigation water. The labor necessary to build and maintain a system of terraces is great. Terrace walls crumble each year and must be partially rebuilt. The canals that bring water down through the terraces also demand attention.

Costs and Benefits of Agriculture Agriculture requires human labor to build and maintain irrigation systems, terraces, and other works. People must feed, water, and care for their animals. Given sufficient labor input and management, agricultural land can yield one or two crops annually for years or even generations. An agricultural field does not necessarily produce a higher single-year yield than does a horticultural plot. The first crop grown by horliculturalists on long-idle land may be larger than that from an agricultural plot of the same size. Furthermore, because agriculturalists work harder than horticulturalists do, agriculture's yield relative to labor is also lower. Agriculture's main advantage is that the long-term yield per area is far greater and more dependable. Because a single field sustains its owners year after year, there is no need to maintain a reserve of uncultivated land as horticulturalists do. This is why agricultural societies tend to be more densely populated than are horticultural ones.

The Cultivation Continuum

Because nonindustrial economies can have features of both horticulture and agriculture, it is useful to discuss cultivators as being arranged along a **cultivation continuum**. Horticultural systems stand at one end—the "low-labor, shifting-plot" end. Agriculturalists are at the other—the "labor intensive, permanent-plot" end.

We speak of a continuum because there are today intermediate economies, combining horticultural and agricultural features—more intensive than annually shifting horticulture but less intensive than agriculture. These recall the intermediate economies revealed by archaeological sequences leading from horticulture to agriculture in the Middle East, Mexico, and other areas of early food production. Unlike nonintensive horticulturalists, who farm a plot just once before fallowing it, the South American Kuikuru grow two or three crops of *manioc*, or cassava—an edible tuber—before abandoning their plots. Cultivation is even more intense in certain densely populated areas of Papua New Guinea, where plots are planted for two or three years, allowed to rest for three to five, and then recultivated. After several of these cycles, the plots are abandoned for a longer fallow period. Such a pattern is called *sectorial fallowing* (Wolf 1966). Besides Papua New Guinea, such systems occur in places as distant as West Africa and highland Mexico. Sectorial fallowing is associated with denser populations than is simple horticulture. The simpler system is the norm in tropical forests, where weed invasion and delicate soils prevent more intensive cultivation.

The key difference between horticulture and agriculture is that horticulture always uses a fallow period where agriculture does not. The earliest cultivators in the Middle East and in Mexico were rainfall-dependent horticulturalists. Until recently, horticulture was the main form of cultivation in several areas, including parts of Africa, Southeast Asia, the Pacific islands, Mexico, Central America, and the South American tropical forest.

Intensification: People and the Environment

The range of environments available for food production has widened as people have increased their control over nature. For example, in arid areas of California, where Native Americans once foraged, modern irrigation technology now sustains rich agricultural estates. Agriculturalists live in many areas that are too arid for nonirrigators or too hilly for nonterracers. Many ancient civilizations in arid lands arose on an agricultural base. Increasing labor intensity and permanent land use have major demographic, social, political, and environmental consequences.

Thus, because of their permanent fields, intensive cultivators are sedentary. People live in larger and more permanent communities located closer to other settlements.

Growth in population size and density increases contact between individuals and groups. There is more need to regulate interpersonal relations, including conflicts of interest. Economies that support more people usually require more coordination in the use of land, labor, and other resources.

Intensive agriculture has significant environmental effects. Irrigation ditches and paddies (fields with irrigated rice) become repositories for organic wastes, chemicals (such as salts), and disease microorganisms. Intensive agriculture typically spreads at the expense of trees and forests, which are cut down to be replaced by fields. Accompanying such **deforestation** is loss of environmental diversity. Agricultural economies grow increasingly specialized—focusing on one or a few caloric staples, such as rice, and on the animals that are raised and tended to aid the agricultural economy. Because tropical horticulturalists typically cultivate dozens of plant species simultaneously, a horticultural plot tends to mirror the botanical diversity that is found in a tropical forest. Agricultural plots, by contrast, reduce ecological diversity by cutting down trees and concentrating on just a few staple foods. Such crop specialization is true of agriculturalists both in the tropics (e.g., Indonesian paddy farmers) and outside the tropics (e.g., Middle Eastern irrigated farmers).

At least in the tropics, the diets of both foragers and horticulturalists are typically more diverse, although under less secure human control, than the diets of agriculturalists. Agriculturists attempt to reduce risk in production by favoring stability in the form of a reliable annual harvest and long-term production. Tropical foragers and horticulturalists, by contrast, attempt to reduce risk by relying on multiple species and benefiting from ecological diversity. The agricultural strategy is to put all one's eggs in one big and very dependable basket.

Of course, even with agriculture, there is a possibility that the single staple crop may fail, and famine may result. The strategy of tropical foragers and horticulturalists is to have several smaller baskets, a few of which may fail without endangering subsistence. The agricultural strategy makes sense when there are lots of children to raise and adults to be fed. Foraging and horticulture, of course, are associated with smaller, sparser, and more mobile populations.

ECONOMIC ANTHROPOLOGY

Agricultural economies also pose a series of regulatory problems—which central governments often have arisen to solve. How is water to be managed—along with disputes about access to and distribution of water? With more people living closer together on more valuable land, agriculturalists are more likely to come into conflict than foragers and horticulturalists are. Agriculture paved the way for the origin of the state, and most agriculturalists live in **states**: complex sociopolitical systems that administer a territory and populace with substantial contrasts in occupation, wealth, prestige, and power. In such societies, cultivators play their role as one part of a differentiated, functionally specialized, and tightly integrated sociopolitical system.

PASTORALISM

Pastoralists live in North Africa, the Middle East, Europe, Asia, and sub-Saharan Africa. These herders are people whose activities focus on such domesticated animals as cattle, sheep, goats, camels, and yak. East African pastoralists, like many others, live in symbiosis with their herds. (**Symbiosis** is an obligatory interaction between groups—here humans and animals—that is beneficial to each.) Herders attempt to protect their animals and to ensure their reproduction in return for food and other products, such as leather. Herds provide dairy products, meat, and blood. Animals are killed at ceremonies, which occur throughout the year, and so beef is available regularly.

People use livestock in a variety of ways. Natives of North America's Great Plains, for example, didn't eat, but only rode, their horses. (Europeans reintroduced horses to the Western Hemisphere; the native American horse had become extinct thousands of years earlier.) For Plains Indians, horses served as "tools of the trade," means of production used to hunt buffalo, a main target of their economies. So the Plains Indians were not true pastoralists but *hunters* who used horses—as many agriculturalists use animals—as means of production.

Unlike the use of animals merely as productive machines, pastoralists typically make direct use of their herds for food. They consume their meat, blood, and milk, from which they make yogurt, butter, and cheese. Although some pastoralists rely on their herds more completely than others do, it is impossible to base subsistence solely on animals. Most pastoralists therefore supplement their diet by hunting, gathering, fishing, cultivating, or trading.

To get crops, pastoralists either trade with cultivators or do some cultivating or gathering themselves.

Unlike foraging and cultivation, which existed throughout the world before the Industrial Revolution, pastoralism was almost totally confined to the Old World. Before European conquest, the only pastoralists in the Americas lived in the Andean region of South America. They used their llamas and alpacas for food and wool and in agriculture and transport. Much more recently, Navajo of the southwestern United States developed a pastoral economy based on sheep, which were brought to North America by Europeans. The populous Navajo are now the major pastoral population in the Western Hemisphere.

Two patterns of movement occur with pastoralism: nomadism and transhumance. Both are based on the fact that herds must move to use pasture available in particular places in different seasons. In **pastoral nomadism**, the entire group—women, men, and children—moves with the animals throughout the year. The Middle East and North Africa provide numerous examples of pastoral nomads. In Iran, for example, the Basseri and the Qashqai ethnic groups traditionally followed a nomadic route more than 300 miles (480 kilometers) long. Starting each year near the coast, they took their animals to grazing land 17,000 feet (5,400 meters) above sea level.

With **transhumance**, part of the group moves with the herds, but most people stay in the home village. There are examples from Europe and Africa. In Europe's Alps, it is just the shepherds and goat herds—not the whole village—who accompany the flocks to highland meadows in summer. Among the Turkana of Uganda, men and boys accompany the herds to distant pastures, while much of the village stays put and does some horticultural farming. Villages tend to be located in the best-watered areas, which have the longest pasture season. This permits the village population to stay together during a large chunk of the year.

During their annual trek, pastoral nomads trade for crops and other products with more sedentary people. Transhumants don't have to trade for crops. Because only part of the population accompanies the herds, transhumants can maintain year-round villages and grow their own crops. Table 8.1 (on the following page) summarizes the main features of Cohen's adaptive strategies.

MODES OF PRODUCTION

An **economy** is a system of production, distribution, and consumption of resources; **economics** is the study of such systems. Economists tend to focus on modern nations and capitalist systems, while anthropologists have broadened understanding of economic principles by gathering data on nonindustrial economies. **Economic anthropology** studies economics in a comparative perspective (See Gudeman 1999; Plattner 1989; Wilk 1996).

A **mode of production** is a way of organizing production—"a set of social relations through which labor is deployed to wrest energy from nature by means of tools, skills, organization, and knowledge" (Wolf 1982, p. 75). In the capitalist mode of production, money buys labor power, and there is a social gap between the people (bosses and workers) involved in the production process. By contrast, in nonindustrial societies, labor is not usually bought but is given as a social obligation. In such a *kin-based* mode of production, mutual aid in production is one among many expressions of a larger web of social relations.

Societies representing each of the adaptive strategies just discussed (e.g., foraging) tend to have a similar mode of production. Differences in the mode of production within a given strategy may reflect the differences in environments, target resources, or cultural traditions. Thus, a foraging mode of production may be based on individual hunters or teams, depending on whether the game is a solitary or a herd animal. Gathering is usually more individualistic than hunting, although collecting teams may assemble when abundant resources ripen and must be harvested quickly. Fishing may be done alone (as in ice or spear fishing) or in crews (as with open sea fishing and hunting of sea mammals).

Production in Nonindustrial Societies

Although some kind of division of economic labor related to age and gender is a cultural universal, the specific tasks assigned to each sex and to people of different ages vary. Many horticultural societies assign a major productive role to women, but some make men's work primary. Similarly, among pastoralists, men generally tend large animals, but in some cultures women do the milking. Jobs accomplished through teamwork in some cultivating societies are done by smaller groups or individuals working over a longer period of time than others.

The Betsileo of Madagascar have two stages of teamwork in rice cultivation: transplanting and harvesting. Team size varies with the size of the field. Both transplanting and harvesting feature a traditional division of labor by age and gender that is well known to all Betsileo and is repeated across the generations. The first job in transplanting is the trampling of a previously tilled flooded field by young men driving cattle, in order to mix earth and water. They bring cattle to trample the fields just before transplanting.

The young men yell at and beat the cattle, striving to drive them into a frenzy so that they will trample the fields properly. Trampling breaks up clumps of earth and mixes irrigation water with soil to form a smooth mud into which women transplant seedlings. Once the tramplers leave the field, older men arrive. With their spades, they break up the clumps that the cattle missed. Meanwhile, the owner and other adults uproot rice seedlings and bring them to the field.

At harvest time, four or five months later, young men cut the rice off the stalks. Young women carry it to the clearing above the field. Older women arrange and stack it. The

Table 8.1 Vehudi Cohen's Adaptive Strategies (Economic Typology) Summarized

Adaptive Strategy	Also Known as	Key Features/Varieties
Foraging	Hunting-gathering	Mobility, use of nature's resources
Horticulture	Slash-and-burn, shifting cultivation, swiddening, dry farming	Fallow period
Agriculture	Intensive farming	Continuous use of land, intensive use of labor
Pastoralism	Herding	Nomadism and transhumance
Industrialism	Industrial production	Factory production, capitalism, socialist production

oldest men and women then stand on the stack, stomping and compacting it. Three days later, young men thresh the rice, beating the stalks against a rock to remove the grain. Older men then attack the stalks with sticks to make sure all the grains have fallen off.

Most of the other tasks in Betsileo rice cultivation are done by individual owners and their immediate families. All household members help weed the rice field. It's a man's job to till the fields with a spade or a plow. Individual men repair the irrigation and drainage systems and the earth walls that separate one plot from the next. Among other agriculturalists, however, repairing the irrigation system is a task involving teamwork and communal labor.

Means of Production

In nonindustrial societies, there is a more intimate relationship between the worker and the means of production than there is in industrial nations. **Means, or factors of production** include land (territory), labor, and technology.

Land Among foragers, ties between people and land are less permanent than they are among food producers. Although many bands have territories, the boundaries are not usually marked, and there is no way they can be enforced. The hunter's stake in an animal that is being stalked or has been hit with a poisoned arrow is more important than where the animal finally dies. A person acquires the rights to use a band's territory by being born in the band or by joining it through a tie of kinship, marriage, or fictive kinship. In Botswana in southern Africa, Ju/'hoansi San women, whose work provides over half the food, habitually use specific tracts of berry-bearing trees. However, when a woman changes bands, she immediately acquires a new gathering area.

Among food producers, rights to the means of production also come through kinship and marriage. Descent groups (groups whose members claim common ancestry) are common among nonindustrial food producers, and those who descend from the founder share the group's territory and resources. If the adaptive strategy is horticulture, the estate includes garden and fallow land for shifting cultivation. As members of a descent group, pastoralists have access to animals to start their own herds, to grazing land, to garden land, and to other means of production.

Labor, Tools, and Specialization Like land, labor is a means of production. In nonindustrial societies, access to both land and labor comes through social links such as kinship, marriage, and descent. Mutual aid in production is merely one aspect of ongoing social relations that are expressed on many other occasions.

Nonindustrial societies contrast with industrial nations in regard to another means of production: technology. In bands and tribes, manufacturing is often linked to age and gender. Women may weave and men may make pottery or vice versa. Most people of a particular age and gender share the technical knowledge associated with that age and gender. If married women customarily make baskets, all or most married women know how to make baskets. Neither technology nor technical knowledge is as specialized as it is in states.

However, some tribal societies do promote specialization. Among the Yanomami of Venezuela and Brazil, for instance, certain villages manufacture clay pots and others make hammocks. They don't specialize, as one might suppose, because certain raw materials happen to be available near particular villages. Clay suitable for pots is widely available. Everyone knows how to make pots, but not everybody does so. Craft specialization reflects the social and political environment rather than the natural environment. Such specialization promotes trade, which is the first step in creating an alliance with enemy villages (Chagnon 1997). Specialization contributes to keeping the peace, although it has not prevented intervillage warfare.

Alienation in Industrial Economies

There are some significant contrasts between industrial and nonindustrial economies. When factory workers produce for sale and for their employer's profit, rather than for their own use, they may be alienated from the items they make. Such alienation means they don't feel strong pride in or personal identification with their products. They see their product as belonging to someone else, not to the man or woman whose labor actually produced it. In nonindustrial societies, by contrast, people usually see their work through from start to finish and have a sense of accomplishment in the product. The fruits of their labor are their own, rather than someone else's.

In nonindustrial societies, the economic relation between coworkers is just one aspect of a more general social relation. They aren't just coworkers but kin, in-laws, or celebrants in the same ritual. In industrial nations, people don't usually work with relatives and neighbors. If coworkers are friends, the personal relationship usually develops out of their common employment rather than being based on a previous association.

Thus, industrial workers have impersonal relations with their products, coworkers, and employers. People sell their labor for cash, and the economic domain stands apart from ordinary social life. In nonindustrial societies, however, the relations of production, distribution, and consumption are *social relations with economic aspects*. Economy is not a separate entity but is *embedded* in the society.

ECONOMIZING AND MAXIMIZATION

Economic anthropologists have been concerned with two main questions:

1. How are production, distribution, and consumption organized in different societies? This question focuses on *systems* of human behavior and their organization.

2. What motivates people in different cultures to produce, distribute or exchange, and consume? Here the focus is not on systems of behavior but on the motives of the *individuals* who participate in those systems.

Anthropologists view both economic systems and motivations in a cross-cultural perspective. Motivation is a concern of psychologists, but it also has been, implicitly or explicitly, a concern of economists and anthropologists. Economists tend to assume that producers and distributors make decisions rationally using the *profit motive*, as do consumers when they shop around for the best value.

Although anthropologists know that the profit motive is not universal, the assumption that individuals try to maximize profits is basic to the capitalist world economy and to much of Western economic theory. In fact, the subject matter of economics is often defined as **economizing**, or the rational allocation of scarce means (or resources) to alternative ends (or uses). What does that mean? Classical economic theory assumes that our wants are infinite and that our means are limited. Since means are limited, people must make choices about how to use their scarce resources: their time, labor, money, and capital. Economists assume that when confronted with choices and decisions, people tend to make the one that maximizes profit. This is assumed to be the most rational (reasonable) choice.

The idea that individuals choose to maximize profits was a basic assumption of the classical economists of the 19th century and one that is held by many contemporary economists. However, certain economists now recognize that individuals in Western cultures, as in others, may be motivated by many other goals. Depending on the society and the situation, people may try to maximize profit, wealth, prestige, pleasure, comfort, or social harmony. Individuals may want to realize their personal or family ambitions or those of another group to which they belong.

Understanding Ourselves

What motivates us? Do we have the same motives our parents had? People must choose among alternatives, and economists think such choices are guided mainly by the desire for economic gain. Do you agree? Such an assumption isn't evident among the Betsileo. Is it true of individual Americans? Think about the choices your parents have made. Did they make decisions that maximized their incomes, their lifestyles, their individual happiness, family benefits, or what? What about you? What factors were involved when you chose to apply to and attend a college? Did you want to stay close to home, to attend college with friends, or to maintain a romantic attachment (all social reasons)? Did you seek the lowest tuition and college costs—or get a generous scholarship (economic decisions)? Did you choose prestige, or perhaps the likelihood that one day you would earn more money because of the reputation of your alma mater (maximizing prestige and future wealth)? The profit motive may predominate in contemporary North America, but different individuals, like different cultures, may choose to pursue other goals.

Alternative Ends

To what uses do people in various societies put their scarce resources? Throughout the world, people devote some of their time and energy to building up a *subsistence fund* (Wolf 1966). In other words, they have to work to eat, to replace the calories they use in their daily activity. People also must invest in a *replacement fund*. They must maintain their technology and other items essential to production. If a hoe or plow breaks, they must repair or replace it. They also must obtain and replace items that are essential not to production but to everyday life, such as clothing and shelter.

People also have to invest in a *social fund*. They have to help their friends, relatives, in-laws, and neighbors. It is useful to distinguish between a social fund and a *ceremonial fund*. The latter term refers to expenditures on ceremonies or rituals. To prepare a festival honoring one's ancestors, for example, requires time and the outlay of wealth.

Citizens of nonindustrial states also must allocate scarce resources to a *rent fund*. We think of rent as payment for the use of property. However, rent fund has a wider meaning. It refers to resources that people must render to an individual or agency that is superior politically or economically. Tenant farmers and sharecroppers, for example, either pay rent or give some of their produce to their landlords, as peasants did under feudalism.

Peasants are small-scale agriculturalists who live in nonindustrial states and have rent fund obligations (Kearney 1996). They produce to feed themselves, to sell their produce, and to pay rent. All peasants have two things in common:

1. They live in state-organized societies.

2. They produce food without the elaborate technology—fertilizers, tractors, airplanes to spray crops, and so on—of modern farming or agribusiness.

In addition to paying rent to landlords, peasants must satisfy government obligations, paying taxes in the form of money, produce, or labor. The rent fund is not simply an *additional* obligation for peasants. Often it becomes their foremost and unavoidable duty. Sometimes, to meet the obligation to pay rent, their own diets suffer. The demands of paying rent may divert resources from subsistence, replacement, social, and ceremonial funds.

Motivations vary from society to society, and people often lack freedom of choice in allocating their resources. Because of obligations to pay rent, peasants may allocate their scarce means toward ends that are not their own

but those of government officials. Thus, even in societies where there is a profit motive, people are often prevented from rationally maximizing self-interest by factors beyond their control.

DISTRIBUTION AND EXCHANGE

The economist Karl Polanyi (1968) stimulated the comparative study of exchange, and several anthropologists followed his lead. To study exchange cross-culturally, Polanyi defined three principles orienting exchanges: the market principle, redistribution, and reciprocity. These principles can all be present in the same society, but in that case they govern different kinds of transactions. In any society, one of them usually dominates. The principle of exchange that dominates in a given society is the one that allocates the means of production.

The Market Principle

In today's world capitalist economy, the **market principle** dominates. It governs the distribution of the means of production: land, labor, natural resources, technology, and capital. "Market exchange refers to the organizational process of purchase and sale at money price" (Dalton 1967). With market exchange, items are bought and sold, using money, with an eye to maximizing profit, and value is determined by the *law of supply and demand* (things cost more the scarcer they are and the more people want them).

Bargaining is characteristic of market principle exchanges. The buyer and seller strive to maximize—to get their "money's worth." In bargaining, buyers and sellers don't need to meet personally. But their offers and counteroffers do need to be open for negotiation over a fairly short time period.

Redistribution

Redistribution operates when goods, services, or their equivalent move from the local level to a center. The center may be a capital, a regional collection point, or a storehouse near a chief's residence. Products often move through a hierarchy of officials for storage at the center. Along the way, officials and their dependents may consume some of them, but the exchange principle here is *re*distribution. The flow of goods eventually reverses direction—out from the center, down through the hierarchy, and back to the common people.

CHAPTER **8**

One example of a redistributive system comes from the Cherokee, the original owners of the Tennessee Valley. Productive farmers who subsisted on maize, beans, and squash, supplemented by hunting and fishing, the Cherokee had chiefs. Each of their main villages had a central plaza, where meetings of the chief's council took place, and where redistributive feasts were held.

According to Cherokee custom, each family farm had an area where the family, if they wished, could set aside a portion of their annual harvest for the chief. This supply of corn was used to feed the needy, as well as travelers and warriors journeying through friendly territory. This store of food was available to all who needed it, with the understanding that it "belonged" to the chief and was dispersed through his generosity. The chief also hosted the redistributive feasts held in the main settlements (Harris 1978).

Reciprocity

Reciprocity is exchange between social equals, who are normally related by kinship, marriage, or another close personal tie. Because it occurs between social equals, it is dominant in the more egalitarian societies—among foragers, cultivators, and pastoralists. There are three degrees of reciprocity: **generalized, balanced, and negative** (Sahlins 1968, 1972; Service 1966). These may be imagined as areas of a continuum defined by these questions:

1. How closely related are the parties to the exchange?

2. How quickly and unselfishly are gifts reciprocated?

Generalized reciprocity, the purest form of reciprocity, is characteristic of exchanges between closely related people. In *balanced reciprocity*, social distance increases, as does the need to reciprocate. In *negative reciprocity*, social distance is greatest and reciprocation is most calculated.

With **generalized reciprocity**, someone gives to another person and expects nothing concrete or immediate in return. Such exchanges (including parental gift giving in contemporary North America) are not primarily economic transactions but expressions of personal relationships. Most parents don't keep accounts of every penny they spend on their children. They merely hope that the children will respect their culture's customs involving love, honor, loyalty, and other obligations to parents.

Among foragers, generalized reciprocity tends to govern exchanges. People routinely share with other band members (Bird-David 1992; Kent 1992). A study of the Ju/'hoansi San found that 40 percent of the population contributed little to the food supply (Lee 1968/1974). Children, teenagers, and people over 60 depended on other people for their food. Despite the high proportion of dependents, the average worker hunted or gathered less than half as much (12 to 19 hours a week) as the average American works. Nonetheless, there was always food because different people worked on different days.

So strong is the ethic of reciprocal sharing that most foragers lack an expression for "thank you." To offer thanks would be impolite because it would imply that a particular act of sharing, which is the keystone of egalitarian society, was unusual. Among the Semai, foragers of central Malaysia (Dentan 1979), to express gratitude would suggest surprise at the hunter's generosity or success (Harris 1974).

Balanced reciprocity applies to exchanges between people who are more distantly related than are members of the same band or household. In a horticultural society, for example, a man presents a gift to someone in another village. The recipient may be a cousin, a trading partner, or a brother's fictive kinsman. The giver expects something in return. This may not come immediately, but the social relationship will be strained if there is no reciprocation.

Exchanges in nonindustrial societies also may illustrate **negative reciprocity**, mainly in dealing with people outside or on the fringes of their social systems. To people who live in a world of close personal relations, exchanges with outsiders are full of ambiguity and distrust. Exchange is one way of establishing friendly relations with outsiders, but especially when trade begins, the relationship is still tentative. Often, the initial exchange is close to being purely economic; people want to get something back immediately. Just as in market economies, but without using money, they try to get the best possible immediate return for their investment.

Generalized and balanced reciprocity are based on trust and a social tie. But negative reciprocity involves the attempt to get something for as little as possible, even if it means being cagey or deceitful or cheating. Among the most extreme and "negative" examples of negative reciprocity was 19th-century horse thievery by North American Plains Indians. Men would sneak into camps and villages of neighboring tribes to steal horses. A similar pattern of cattle raiding continues today in East Africa, among tribes like the Kuria (Fleisher 2000). In these cases, the party that starts the raiding can expect reciprocity—a raid on their own village—or worse. The Kuria hunt down cattle thieves and kill them. It's still reciprocity, governed by "Do unto others as they have done unto you."

Coexistence of Exchange Principles

In today's North America, the market principle governs most exchanges, from the sale of the means of production to the sale of consumer goods. We also have redistribution. Some of our tax money goes to support the government, but some of it also comes back to us in the form of social services, education, health care, and road building. We also have reciprocal exchanges. Generalized reciprocity characterizes the relationship between parents and children. However, even here the dominant market mentality surfaces in comments about the high cost of raising children and in the stereotypical statement of the disappointed parent: "We gave you everything money could buy."

Exchanges of gifts, cards, and invitations exemplify reciprocity, usually balanced. Everyone has heard remarks like: "They invited us to their daughter's wedding, so when ours gets married, we'll have to invite them" and, "They've been here for dinner three times and haven't invited us yet. I don't think we should ask them back until they do." Such precise balancing of reciprocity would be out of place in a foraging band, where resources are communal (common to all) and daily sharing based on generalized reciprocity is an essential ingredient of social life and survival.

POTLATCHING

One of the most thoroughly studied cultural practices known to ethnography is the **potlatch**, a festive event within a regional exchange system among tribes of the North Pacific Coast of North America, including the Salish and Kwakiutl of Washington and British Columbia and the Tsimshian of Alaska. Some tribes still practice the potlatch, sometimes as a memorial to the dead (Kan 1986, 1989). At each such event, assisted by members of their communities, potlatch sponsors traditionally gave away food, blankets, pieces of copper, or other items. In return for this, they

got prestige. To give a potlatch enhanced one's reputation. Prestige increased with the lavishness of the potlatch, the value of the goods given away in it.

The potlatching tribes were foragers, but atypical ones. They were sedentary and had chiefs. And unlike the environments of most other recent foragers, theirs was not marginal. They had access to a wide variety of land and sea resources. Among their most important foods were salmon, herring, candlefish, berries, mountain goats, seals, and porpoises (Piddocke 1969).

If classical economic theory is correct that the profit motive is universal, with the goal of maximizing material benefits, then how does one explain the potlatch, in which wealth is given away? Many scholars once cited the potlatch as a classic case of economically wasteful behavior. In this view, potlatching was based on an economically irrational drive for prestige. This interpretation stressed the lavishness and supposed wastefulness, especially of the Kwakiutl displays, to support the contention that in some societies people strive to maximize prestige at the expense of their material well-being. This interpretation has been challenged.

Ecological anthropology, also known as *cultural ecology*, is a theoretical school in anthropology that attempts to interpret cultural practices, such as the potlatch, in terms of their long-term role in helping humans adapt to their environments. A different interpretation of the potlatch has been offered by the ecological anthropologists Wayne Suttles (1960) and Andrew Vayda (1961/1968). These scholars see potlatching not in terms of its apparent wastefulness, but in terms of its long-term role as a cultural adaptive mechanism. This view not only helps us understand potlatching, it also has comparative value because it helps us understand similar patterns of lavish feasting in many other parts of the world. Here is the ecological interpretation: customs like the potlatch are cultural adaptations to alternating periods of local abundance and shortage.

How does this work? The overall natural environment of the North Pacific Coast is favorable, but its sources fluctuate from year to year and place to place salmon and herring aren't equally abundant every year in a given locality. One village can have a good year while another is experiencing a bad one. Later their fortunes reverse. In this context, the potlatch cycle of the Kwakiutl and Salish had adaptive value, and the potlatch was not a competitive display that brought no material benefit.

A village enjoying an especially good year had a surplus of subsistence items, which it could trade for more durable wealth items, like blankets, canoes, or pieces of copper. Wealth, in turn, by being distributed, could be converted into prestige. Members of several villages were invited to any potlatch and got to take home the resources that were given away. In this way, potlatching linked villages together in a regional economy—an exchange system that distributed food and wealth from wealthy to needy communities. In return, the potlatch sponsors and their villages got prestige. The decision to potlatch was determined by the health of the local economy. If there had been subsistence surpluses, and thus a buildup of wealth over several good years, a village could afford a potlatch to convert its food and wealth into prestige.

The long-term adaptive value of intercommunity feasting becomes clear when we consider what happened when a formerly prosperous village had a run of bad luck. Its people started accepting invitations to potlatches in villages that were doing better. The tables were turned as the temporarily rich became temporarily poor and vice versa. The newly needy accepted food and wealth items. They were willing to receive rather than bestow gifts and thus to relinquish some of their stored-up prestige. They hoped their luck would eventually improve so that resources could be recouped and prestige regained.

The potlatch linked local groups along the North Pacific Coast into a regional alliance and exchange network. Potlatching and intervillage exchange had adaptive functions, regardless of the motivations of the individual participants. The anthropologists who stressed rivalry for prestige were not wrong. They were merely emphasizing motivations at the expense of an analysis of economic and ecological systems.

The use of feasts to enhance individual and community reputations and to redistribute wealth is not peculiar to populations of the North Pacific Coast. Competitive feasting is widely characteristic of nonindustrial food producers. But among most foragers, who live, remember, in marginal areas, resources are too meager to support feasting on such a level. In such societies, sharing rather than competition prevails.

Like many other cultural practices that have attracted considerable anthropological attention, the potlatch does not, and did not, exist apart from larger world events. For example, within the spreading world capitalist economy of the 19th century, the potlatching tribes, particularly the Kwakiutl, began to trade with Europeans (fur for blankets, for example). Their wealth increased as a result. Simultaneously, a huge proportion of the Kwakiutl population died from previously unknown diseases brought by the Europeans. As a result, the increased wealth from trade flowed into a drastically reduced population. With many of the traditional sponsors dead (such as chiefs and their families), the Kwakiutl extended the right to give a potlatch to the entire population. This stimulated very intense competition for prestige. Given trade, increased wealth, and a decreased population, the Kwakiutl also started converting wealth into prestige by destroying wealth items such as blankets, pieces of copper, and houses (Vayda 1961/1968). Blankets and houses could be burned, and coppers could be buried at sea. With dramatically increased wealth and a drastically reduced population, Kwakiutl potlatching changed its nature. It became much more destructive than it had been previously and than potlatching continued to be among tribes that were less affected by trade and disease.

In any case, note that potlatching also served to prevent the development of socioeconomic stratification, a system of social classes. Wealth relinquished or destroyed was converted into a nonmaterial item: prestige. Under capitalism, we reinvest our profits (rather than burning our cash), with the hope of making an additional profit. However, the potlatching tribes were content to relinquish their surpluses rather than use them to widen the social distance between themselves and their fellow tribe members.

CONCLUSION

Economies comprise systems of production, distribution, and consumption. In other words, all economies, wherever they may be found, involve organized and systematic ways of producing goods, distributing them to the members of the society, and then using those goods to satisfy basic human and societal needs. Anthropologists have traditionally

ECONOMIC ANTHROPOLOGY

studied consumption patterns as part of their analyses of economies. Recently, the business world has discovered that anthropologists' insights can be helpful, particularly in the area of market research.

In recent years, anthropologists have become increasingly important players in the market research industry. Market research aimed at learning how and why people use certain products or fail to do so. Manufacturers need this information so they can modify their products in ways that will make them more attractive to consumers. During the 1980s, anthropologist Steve Barnett served as senior vice president of Planmetrics Cultural Analysis Group, a market research firm in New York that studied consumer behavior through direct observations (See Baba 1986). Many market researchers gather data by interviewing people randomly in shopping malls, but Barnett and his associates used a number of innovative techniques designed to learn what people *actually* do rather than what they say they do. To illustrate, in order to learn more about dishwashing practices in the United States, Barnett put video cameras in people's kitchens for a period of three weeks. The information gathered by this direct observational research enabled Procter and Gamble to alter its television commercials to bring them more into line with actual dishwashing behavior. In addition to videotaping actual behavior, Barnett's anthropological approach to market research helped him develop another technique, which he calls the "unfocus group." This technique involves asking a target group of consumers to solve a problem related to the product. The purpose is to discover unconscious cultural codes and assumptions about the product.

One such exercise, conducted on behalf of a utility company, involved asking the unfocus group to build a nuclear power plant out of building blocks and other household items. Interestingly, all of the participants in this exercise enclosed their nuclear plant models in cake covers, suggesting that they believed enclosed plants were safer than those that are not enclosed. The unfocus group is a very subtle and unobtrusive way of getting at people's attitudes about various consumer products. This type of market research, which draws on traditional anthropological techniques and concerns with behavior patterns, attitudes, and cultural assumptions, provides us with an excellent example of how cultural anthropology is being applied to careers in the private sector.

Conrad Kottak, 2004, "Making a Living," *Cultural Anthropology*, 10th ed., pp. 189–214. New York: McGraw-Hill. Copyright © The McGraw-Hill Companies. Reproduced with permission of The McGraw-Hill Companies.

EXERCISE

EXERCISE 8.2: SUBSISTENCE TECHNOLOGY

Objective
To illustrate the relationship between subsistence technology and several other aspects of culture. A secondary objective is to give students practice in speaking in front of the entire class.

Rationale
By having to reason out the relationship between a subsistence technology and other aspects of culture, students will see for themselves that many aspects of culture are a logical adaptation to both the environment and subsistence technology.

Procedures
1. Put students into groups of four.

2. Give each group one of the handouts—either hunter/gatherer, horticulturalist, agriculturalist, or industrialist.

3. Instruct them to answer the questions on the handout.

4. After they finish answering all the questions, meet as an entire class.

5. Have students from each subsistence group present their answers and explain why they chose the answers they did. Make sure the students in each group take turns answering the questions for the entire class.

6. Construct a chart on the board which shows the comparable cultural elements for each subsistence group.

ECONOMIC ANTHROPOLOGY

HUNTERS AND GATHERERS
Hunt wild animals, collect wild plants.

Technology—simple tools, no machinery, no knowledge of how to grow food.

Environment—sparse. Seasonal movement of animals, seasonal plant growth.

Questions
Choose from the answers following each point. Answer in comparison to the other types of subsistence economies:

- population size/density (high, med, low)*
- family size (large, med, small)
- mobility (yes, some, no)
- shelter (temporary or permanent)
- land ownership (yes, no)
- warfare (yes, no)
- sexual mores (strict, moderate, lenient)**
- social stratification (yes, some, no)
- degree of specialization (high, med, low)***
- number of non-subsistence related activities (high, some, low)

*   Consider how many people the land can feed/support.

**   What are the society's attitudes toward pre-marital and extra-marital sex? Consider how strictly the society (not individuals) will punish the individual who transgresses.

***   Do different people do different jobs?

EXERCISE

HORTICULTURALISTS

Extensive farming.

Technology—hand tools, knowledge of how to grow food, but no irrigation, fertilizer or draft animals. Can't replenish soil. Slash-and-burn agriculture.

Questions

Choose from the answers following each point. Answer in comparison to the other types of subsistence economies.

- population size/density (high, med, low)*
- family size (large, med, small)
- mobility (yes, some, no)
- shelter (temporary or permanent)
- land ownership (yes, no)
- warfare (yes, no)
- sexual mores (strict, moderate, lenient)**
- social stratification (yes, some, no)
- degree of specialization (high, med, low)***
- number of non-subsistence related activities (high, some, low)

  *   Consider how many people the land can feed/support.
  ** What are the society's attitudes toward pre-marital and extra-marital sex? Consider how strictly the society (not individuals) will punish the individual who transgresses.
  *** Do different people do different jobs?

ECONOMIC ANTHROPOLOGY

AGRICULTURALISTS
Intensive farming.

Technology—use of plow, domestication of draft animals, irrigation, fertilizer.

Note: Not modern U.S. farming. More like third world countries or the U.S. in the 1800s. (cf., "Little House on the Prairie").

Questions
Choose from the answers following each point. Answer in comparison to the other types of subsistence economies.

- population size/density (high, med, low)*
- family size (large, med, small)
- mobility (yes, some, no)
- shelter (temporary or permanent)
- land ownership (yes, no)
- warfare (yes, no)
- sexual mores (strict, moderate, lenient)**
- social stratification (yes, some, no)
- degree of specialization (high, med, low)***
- number of non-subsistence related activities (high, some, low)

    * Consider how many people the land can feed/support.
   ** What are the society's attitudes toward pre-marital and extra-marital sex? Consider how strictly the society (not individuals) will punish the individual who transgresses.
*** Do different people do different jobs?

E X E R C I S E

INDUSTRIALISTS

Industrialization.

Technology—heavy machinery, chemicals, food processing, factories.

Example—the United States today.

Questions

Choose from the answers following each point. Answer in comparison to the other types of subsistence economies.

- population size/density (high, med, low)*
- family size (large, med, small)
- mobility (yes, some, no)
- shelter (temporary or permanent)
- land ownership (yes, no)
- warfare (yes, no)
- sexual mores (strict, moderate, lenient)**
- social stratification (yes, some, no)
- degree of specialization (high, med, low)***
- number of non-subsistence related activities (high, some, low)

     *   Consider how many people the land can feed/support.
   **   What are the society's attitudes toward pre-marital and extra-marital sex? Consider how strictly the society (not individuals) will punish the individual who transgresses.
 ***   Do different people do different jobs?

Exercise: "Subsistence Technology," by Geri-Ann Galanti, California State University, Los Angeles. Reprinted by permission.

ECONOMIC ANTHROPOLOGY

Inside the Life of the Migrants Next Door—
Nathan Thornburgh

On a crisp Saturday night in early winter, an armada of Hyundais and Saturns arrived at the colonnaded Bridge-hampton Community House in the center of the Hamptons, a thin necklace of ultra-wealthy hamlets at the tip of New York's Long Island.

The Hamptons are best known as a summer playground for Manhattan millionaires. But this night, the people who service the lavish Hamptons lifestyle were throwing their own party. They caravanned from a nearby church, little girls in frilly dresses and pomaded boys in squeaky shoes, shepherded by their parents—the roofers who tack gray slate to colonial homes, the maids who scrub toilets and dusk Swarovski stemware, and the gardeners who feed the Hamptons' endless appetite for formal English gardens and straight hedgerows.

The hundred or so guests had gathered for a *quinceañera*—a souped-up Latino version of a sweet 16 party, thrown for a girl's 15th birthday. But this was a coming-of-age celebration not just for the birthday girl but also for the Mexican community that has grown up in the Hamptons. Nearly all the attendees come from a town called Tuxpan in the green hills of the central-Mexican state of Michoacán, which has seen several generations of young workers move to this far, affluent corner of the U.S. They came with nothing, and many have managed to build a solid facsimile of middle-class American life. Still, most of them are—in the hard parlance of the immigration debate—illegal aliens, part of an emerging presence that was once seen as a blessing but has turned into one of the Hamptons' biggest controversies.

The same souring dynamic echoes in cities and towns from Tuscaloosa, Ala., to Tacoma, Wash., as migrants push into new communities with increasing numbers and confidence. Their ascension has caused a thousand brushfires of resentment throughout the country. A TIME poll found that 63% of respondents consider illegal immigration a very serious or extremely serious problem in the U.S.

Washington, having heard the call, is creaking into action. President George W. Bush has made it a New Year's resolution to pass a guest-worker program, coupled with robust policing of the border. Under his proposal, undocumented workers already in the U.S. would register here, work for as many as six more years and then return to their native country to reapply if they want to continue living in the U.S. Immigrant advocates oppose the idea, saying that a full amnesty giving permanent legal status is the only practical way to deal with the estimated 11 million illegal aliens in the U.S. without sending the economy, not to mention its poorest workers, into shock. But neither the President nor the amnesty crowd has a bill already rolling through Congress. That distinction belongs to House conservatives, who passed a hard-line border-security measure, stripped of any nod to guestworker status, in December. The Senate will likely consider it this month.

In the meantime, an estimated 700,000 undocumented immigrants from around the world continue to enter the U.S. each year according to the Pew Hispanic Center. TIME followed the fortunes of those from Tuxpan—both in the U.S. and in Mexico—and found that American misgivings about illegal immigration are mirrored by the illegals. Again and again, the immigrants asked themselves the question: Is coming to the U.S. worth it? The wages are undeniably good, as much as $15 an hour for manual labor in the Hamptons, 10 times the rate for the same work in Tuxpan. But even among the relatively well-off guests at the *quinceañera*, there has been a heavy price to pay for the opportunity: estranged marriages, wayward children, hostile neighbors here in the U.S. and a beloved home town in Mexico whose long-term prospects seem to dim with each worker lost to the north.

THE TRAILBLAZER
The story of Tuxpan's transformation from a provincial town of 30,000 into a major conduit of cheap labor for the Hamptons begins with a single wanderer. Mario Coria, 55, grew up so poor in Tuxpan that at age 11 he left for Mexico City to work in construction, a skinny kid carrying 80-pound bags of cement and mortar on ramshackle scaffolding, sending nearly all his earnings back to Tuxpan. In January 1977, when he was 26, Coria had a chance encounter that would change his life—and that of Tuxpan—forever. He ran into a vacationing restaurateur from Bridgehampton who was asking directions to the Palace of Fine Arts in downtown Mexico City. Coria showed him the way, the men struck up a halting conversation in Spanish,

and within two years, Coria had accepted the American's invitation to work as a gardener in the Hamptons. A tourist visa to the U.S. came included with his plane ticket, both easily arranged by a Mexico City travel agency.

The Hamptons, like much of the U.S., had a very different relationship to illegal immigrants 30 years ago. Back then, Coria was one of only a handful of Spanish-speaking immigrants who lived in the area. His blend of industry, attention to detail and, eventually, confidence in his vision as a landscaper made him a hit with the wealthy Hamptonites. One family liked him so much that they had their personal attorney help him apply for legal residency. But even after he was legal, he still found it tricky being gardener to the rich and famous. He is fond of recalling how he walked out on the actress Lauren Bacall after, he says, she yelled at him for cutting a clutch of lilies too short. Overall, however, his perseverance has been richly rewarded. Coria started out making just $3.25 an hour, but today he is a U.S. citizen and owns a house in the Hamptons town of Wainscott. He bought it for $125,000 in 1996, but similar homes are selling for more than half a million dollars today.

A trip to Ororicua, the shantytown in the mountains outside Tuxpan where his grandmother was born, highlights just how far Coria has come. His grandmother's people still live in sloping clapboard shacks with dirt floors. Coria's home in Tuxpan is a porticoed five-bedroom residence in the center of town, and he drives a late-model Nissan Pathfinder. In the front of his vast garden are orchids and lilies he brought from the Hamptons. In the back are groves of guava, orange and avocado. But Coria's pursuit of success has taken a heavy toll. Being just about the only Mexican gardener in the Hamptons when he first arrived meant less competition, but it also made him more homesick. He returned to Tuxpan in the winters, but "every March when I went back to America, there would be two weeks when I just didn't want to get out of bed," he says.

In 2005, the depression came and didn't leave. The more financially secure he was, Coria says, the more overwhelmed he became by memories of his bitter past: the beatings he suffered as a boy working construction in Mexico City; the disapproval of his mother, who never seemed satisfied with the money he sent back every week. Coria fled the Hamptons abruptly last year in the middle of the busy summer season to recuperate in Tuxpan. Once a week, he makes the six-hour round-trip drive to see a therapist in Mexico City. He's planning on returning to the Hamptons in March to begin buying seeds and drawing up plans for his clients' summer 2006 gardens. But even if he goes back, he says, he doesn't think he can spend more than two additional seasons in the Hamptons. "Walking the streets of Tuxpan, I know who I am," he says. "Over there, even after all these years, I am just a stranger."

THE NEWCOMERS

The darker complexities of building a life abroad are lost on most Tuxpeños, who see Coria's mansion in Mexico and his new truck as tangible evidence of his success. Early on, friends and relatives asked how they could make their way to the Hamptons. In 1985, he brought over his half brother Fernando. Fernando invited two friends, who started bringing their relatives. A handful became dozens. Dozens become hundreds. There are no reliable estimates, but workers in the Hamptons say there are as many as 500 Tuxpeños living full-time in the area, and scores more show up during the work-filled summer months. Many of the new arrivals cross by foot near Douglas, Ariz., and then get rides to big cities where they catch vans, buses or even airplanes to New York. (Southwest Airlines is a popular choice for its fares, as low as $99 one-way.) The lucky ones with tourist visas can fly directly from Mexico City to New York City's J.F.K. Airport. But whether they travel by land or by air, relatively few get caught or even delayed. Their safety comes in numbers: hundreds of thousands of migrants will always win a game of Red Rover with a little more than 11,000 border-patrol agents.

Of course, people are not just coming from Tuxpan. Workers have been flooding into the Hamptons from other parts of Mexico, from Colombia, Costa Rica, Guatemala and Honduras. And the Hamptons, like so many suburban areas facing the same deluge, are feeling the strain.

The community's complaints against the newcomers are varied and vigorous. Neighbors rail against single-family homes that are carved into hostels housing a dozen or more men at a time. Uninsured drivers, some of whom display the daredevil driving style of rural Latin America, anger local motorists. Day laborers looking for work clog parking lots, and they are more than just an inconvenience. Flooding the market with cheap labor, they're driving down wages for everyone. Even some of the more established undocumented workers are critical of the newcomers. "A hard worker used to be able to make $15 an hour here," says Gabriel, 33, a Tuxpan native who owns a small gardening business and who, like many of the people interviewed for this story, asked not to be identified by surname. "But there are too many workers here now. They're working for $10 an hour."

A crowd of Ecuadorian day laborers gathered at the East Hampton train station in the fall were asking $12 an hour. The employers who stopped by ranged from heating repairmen to housemoms. Homeowners and renters make up almost half of those who hire day laborers, according to a recently published UCLA study. The day laborers, who exist on the bottom of the undocumented-worker food chain, say they feel slightly shut out by those immigrants who already have a foothold in the Hamptons. "Their attitude is, we were here first," says a worker named Oscar. "But we deserve the same chance they had."

The old-timers, for their part, complain about the newcomers' work ethic. "The people who come these days just see the nice cars or the money on the streets of Tuxpan," says Coria. "They don't know how much hard work it takes to make it in the Hamptons. So many of them come, get disillusioned very quickly and return to Mexico empty handed."

Octavio, 19, a shy mechanic from a poor settlement outside Tuxpan, knows how hard it can be, and he is trying to hold on. In March he paid $2,200 to a door-to-door smuggling service that picked him up in Tuxpan and dropped him off in the Hamptons. But it was no luxury ride. The trip took eight days, including three days and nights of nonstop driving from Douglas, Ariz., where he walked across the border, to the Hamptons. The Chevy Astro van that took him through the U.S. was crammed with 13 people—11 other Tuxpeño passengers and two alternating drivers. "I wasn't ever scared," Octavio says about the journey. "Just very tired." After he arrived, it took only a few weeks for his English-speaking uncle to find him a job in an auto-repair shop and a room to rent. Octavio now lives in a single-family home that got the illegal immigrant make over: slap a lock on every bedroom and try to squeeze in as many families and workers as possible. He pays $500 a month to share his home with eight other workers he doesn't know and barely trusts.

But Octavio knows he's one of the lucky ones. His spot at the garage spares him the insecurity of hustling for temporary jobs as a day worker. The UCLA study reported that even when laborers find work, 49% say they have been cheated out of at least some of their pay in the past two months. Octavio recently got a raise to $10 an hour and supplements his income by doing freelance car repairs after hours, but after paying his rent and sending more than $1,000 a month to his mother (who plans to build a bathroom with running water), he doesn't have much money left. His only furniture is a mattress and a milk crate. Cardboard does the job of window shades. Octavio speaks just a few words of English and says he lives in fear of his Anglo neighbors, who seem to be constantly scolding him on the street. He thinks they might be mistaking him for one of his housemates, who disrupted the quiet neighborhood with repeated attempts to do body repair work on old cars in the driveway.

UNEASY NEIGHBORS

The Hamptons have long cultivated a climate of easygoing tolerance, and for years town leaders dealt with illegal immigration by simply looking the other way. But that too is changing, as the numbers grow larger and the complaints grow louder. Last November, in a crackdown that has been lauded by anti-immigration groups around the country, police began taking down information about the vehicles that came to the East Hampton railroad station to pick up day laborers. They traced the plates and sent letters to the IRS and Federal Immigration and Customs Enforcement agency, saying that the cars' owners might be hiring illegal contractors and should be investigated. "Sure, it's unlikely that the feds would take action," says East Hampton village police chief Gerard Larsen Jr., "but put it this way: Would you want a letter from your local police department to the IRS saying that you're probably paying people off the books?"

Larsen sees the crackdown as a way of targeting the problem without going after the workers directly—an acceptable solution for the sensitive political ecosystem of the Hamptons. Suffolk County Executive Steve Levy, who mainly oversees the more working-class communities west of the Hamptons, takes a more direct approach. Levy, a Democrat, has initiated sting operations on local contractors and helped towns bust lawbreaking landlords.

His police also forcibly removed day laborers from a Farmingville 7-Eleven parking lot. Levy says the voters in his county appreciate his strong arm. "There's a tremendous disconnect between the public and these do-nothing politicians," he says. "You're seeing the beginnings of a citizens' uprising."

The tensions are most evident in the complex relationship between the Hispanic immigrants and the German, Italian and Irish families that for a century formed the area's working-class backbone. Those locals were the ones who did the gardening, cleaning and cooking in the Hamptons before Latinos started showing up and working longer for less. And it's the working-class residents, not the wealthy summer-estate owners, who end up not only competing for work with but also living next door to the newcomers. "We have up to 60 single men being stuffed into homes of up to 900 sq. ft. That's not an exaggeration. Single-family neighborhoods have been turned upside down," says Levy. "It's very politically incorrect to say, but that's not what those homeowners signed up for in suburbia." Despite their grievances, however, many of those same working-class families have become addicted to the cheap labor. As a landscaper, Jeremy Samuelson has seen starting hourly wages for gardeners fall from $14 to $12 in the past decade, but he admits that he and his neighbors view cheap labor as a perk of living in the Hamptons. "People are making less, maybe, but now lots of people have house cleaners come once a week," he says. "And if you want your roof redone, you can just go to the corner, round up 20 guys, and they'll have it done in an afternoon for less than $3,000."

RESTLESS EXILES

As crossing the border has become more difficult and expensive, workers are staying longer and bringing their children to live with them in the U.S. Julio, 18, and Carlos, 15, moved to the Hamptons from Tuxpan almost a decade ago with their parents Julio Sr. and Yadira. The boys grew up on PlayStations, sledding in the winter and pool parties in the summer. They speak accentless English and for most of their childhood were average happy-go-lucky small-town kids. But because the brothers were born in Mexico, they have no legal American papers, no Social Security numbers. And that means they are not able to apply for federal college loans or even prove that they meet the residency requirements of the local community college. Their parents have seen enough to know that without a college degree the boys would get no further

than their parents had. So just before Julio was about to enter the 10th grade, the decision was made for the boys to go back to Tuxpan with their mother to finish high school there, which would make them eligible to attend a Mexican university. Their father would keep working in New York alone.

Finding their place in Tuxpan has been hard for the brothers. In America they were too Mexican. In Mexico they are too American. Julio, for example, started out wearing the baggy clothes he bought at Banana Republic and the Gap before he left the Hamptons, but he quickly found out that what passes for universal teenage fashion in the U.S. is viewed as the indelible mark of a hoodlum in Tuxpan. Even his friends greet him with "What's up, gringo?" So Julio and Carlos spend a lot of time hanging out with other kids who, like them, are Americans in exile. There's Flor, 15, a cousin who also grew up in the Hamptons and speaks a rapid teenage patois. There's her boyfriend Luis, also 15, a basketball-crazy redhead who grew up outside L.A. "People get mad at us when we speak English together," says Julio. "They think we trying to act all big. But it's just how we are."

As part of their return plan, Julio and Carlos' parents have built their dream house just outside Tuxpan. It is a grand two-story affair with granite counters in the kitchen and views of the mountains from the boys' bedrooms. But cash is tight. In the U.S., Yadira had moved up from cleaning houses to working as a manicurist for an upscale spa in Bridgehampton. With tips from her wealthy clients, she made up to $200 a day. But returning to Tuxpan, she quickly found out that sustainable income is hard to come by in small-town Mexico. Yadira tried running a small convenience store—selling sodas, lollipops, toilet paper—from the ground floor of her house. Those abarrotes can be found, it seems, in every other house in Tuxpan, and nobody appears to sell much of anything. After nine months, Yadira shut hers down. She now operates a clothing store. It is doing better than the convenience store, although on a typical afternoon, a few teenage girls stop in after school but don't have any money to buy anything. An elderly woman comes by to call a relative in Mexico City from one of the row of telephones in back. Yadira collects 20 cents for the call. To supplement her income, Yadira does manicures and facials when she can. She has also started to think about returning to New York, not solely for the money but because, like her sons, she has in many ways simply outgrown the town where cockfighting is the major pastime. "I thought it would be different coming back," she says with a sigh. "It can be so boring in this town."

AN ENDLESS CYCLE

A quick glance at the economy of a small Mexican town like Tuxpan makes it clear why undocumented workers continue to head north. Tuxpan's heyday was in the 1950s and '60s, when it gained fame throughout Mexico for its gladiolus. But overproduction slowly poisoned the soil, leaving Tuxpan in a slow decline. In the past decade, flowers have made a comeback, but the salary for working in the greenhouses or out in the field still averages only $10 a day. At the same time, the cost of living is comparatively high in Tuxpan. As in much of small-town Mexico, the large influx of cash from the U.S. has thrown the economy out of balance. According to Pew Hispanic Center estimates, almost half the 10.6 million adult Mexican immigrants living in the U.S. sent at least some money back to their relatives last year, for a 2005 total of $20 billion.

In Tuxpan, as in many other towns in Mexico, the money is rarely used for bettering the community. Instead, there seen to be two impulses competing for those hard-earned dollars: a deep love of one's own family and a desire to show up everyone else's. Everyone buys Mom a house. Everyone buys a truck. Many buy subwoofers and chrome packages for their trucks. When the returning workers descend on Tuxpan for the holidays in December, the local Yamaha motorcycle dealer has a field day. Rents in Tuxpan now average around $250 a month; completed houses can cost well over $100,000. Nike shoes cost up to $200 a pair. Seafood restaurants in town charge $10 a plate. "In America, we could go to restaurants whenever we wanted to," says the teenager Carlos. "Here, we can't afford it any more." And the cycle of migration is self-propelling. Bartender Alfonso Mayo Lopez, 43, lost his job in the fall when the last bar in Tuxpan closed because all its customers had gone up north. Lopez now sees fewer and fewer reasons not to leave his daughter and wife and join his brother in the Hamptons. "The more difficult it gets here," he says, "the more I think about going there."

Roberto Suro, director of the Pew Hispanic Center in Washington, says the great irony of Mexican migration is that it often feeds the same problems that sent people north in the first place. "Many towns have lost the best of

their labor force. There's money coming in [from the U.S.] but no job creation back home," he says. "It just shows that migration does not solve migration."

The governments of the U.S. and Mexico are trying to encourage people to put the remittances to better use. In 2004 the U.S. Agency for International Development began a five-year, $10 million program to help Mexican microlenders boost small businesses. And the Mexican government is proud of its 3x1 initiative, a project that aims to unite the federal, state and local governments in Mexico with immigrants in the U.S. to fund programs for improving life in Mexico. But Tuxpan's Mayor Gilberto Coria Gudiño (no relation to Mario) says he doesn't know of any 3x1 projects in the region. When asked if he has a plan for ensuring that the next generation of Tuxpeños won't be lost to the U.S., he says his administration has paid $20,000 for a gigantic Mexican flag to be placed on the highest peak above Tuxpan. "This will send a message to all those who are working up north that they should be proud to be Mexican, not ashamed," he says. "It will tell them that Tuxpan welcomes them home with open arms!"

There are some signs of change, but they're planted in rocky soil. Like Mario Coria, a Tuxpeño named Pancho found wealthy patrons who valued his hard work in the Hamptons. He worked as a gardener at one family's East Hampton estate for more than a decade while his wife Ruth worked as their housekeeper. When the matriarch of the family died, she left Pancho, his wife and three daughters a fair sum of money. Pancho won't say exactly how much, but it was enough to seed his American Dream for Tuxpan: state-of-the-art greenhouses for growing roses, orchids and gladiolus to be sold around Mexico. He hoped to supplement his inheritance with low-interest loans that the state of Michoacán earmarked for returning emigrants. He says the loans would allow him to employ up to 40 people. "When this greenhouse gets going," says Pancho, "I hope to be able to save many people from having to go to the Hamptons, myself included." Right now, however, the several plots of land he bought in the hills outside Tuxpan lie fallow. Applying for the loans proved more complicated than Pancho anticipated, and he has no backup plan. He ended up spending much of a recent visit to Tuxpan driving his beat-up Dodge Caravan around town, drinking with old friends, trying to figure out how to raise more money.

ECONOMIC ANTHROPOLOGY

THE PRICE OF PROGRESS

Despite the flood of American money streaming into towns like Tuxpan, there is a palpable lack of vitality on the streets. In the summer working season, Tuxpan feels as if there's some great war on: all the fighting-age men have gone to battle the hedgerows up north. Only women, children and the elderly remain. That emptiness is felt acutely by Lucila, 75, mother of 13, eight of whom live in the U.S. She proudly gives a tour of her renovated house on one of the town's main streets. The back of the building is neat and thoroughly modern, with tile floors in the living room, modern appliances in the kitchen. Still standing in the front part are the three tiny adobe-walled rooms that used to be the entire house. Lucila and her husband slept in one room. The five girls slept in another. The eight boys slept in the third. Out back, just past where the refrigerator now stands, was a large pen that held up to 70 pigs. Besides tending the pigs, Lucila's husband grew corn and beans and did odd jobs as a tailor. Lucila taught knitting classes at her house to help the family scrape by.

Nowadays Lucila doesn't have to worry about money—her children paid for the renovations in cash, a 50th wedding anniversary present in 1995 for her and her late husband—but she is lonely. Four of her daughters live in the U.S. permanently; three are citizens by marriage. Five sons work in the Hamptons; the other three are scattered across Mexico. Visits outside of Christmas are rare. Lucila occasionally talks on the phone with her children, but she spends most of her time walking through the enclosed town market and waiting for visits from the local priest. She keeps a bowl of salsa on the table at all times, just in case he stops by unexpectedly. "The padre loves spicy things," she says. But most days, not even the padre shows up. "There are times when I really miss my children," she says.

The northern migration has taken its toll on nuclear family life in towns like Tuxpan. Countless men have girlfriends in the north, while their wives and children remain in the south. And the women left behind in Mexico are faced with the same temptations. Workers in the U.S. regard this threat with black humor. The idea that there's a guy who's back home in Mexico drinking your beer, sleeping with your wife and spending your hard-earned money looms large in their mythology. He has even been given a name: Sancho. Taking a break from sodding a lawn in the Hampton town of Springs, a worker named Neftali jokes that he has to wire some money to Mexico that weekend because, he says with a grin, "Sancho needs new shoes."

The relentless separations put particular stress on children. When schoolteacher Claudia Gonzalez's husband returned after a two-year stint as a farmworker in Texas, her young daughter chased her father out of the house, yelling, "You don't live here. Go back to Texas!" Says Gonzalez: "No amount of money from up north can bring those years back."

TIGHTENING BORDERS

Before the U.S. began cracking down on illegal immigration in the early 1990s, a push only accelerated by 9/11, many Tuxpeños flew back and forth easily on 10-year tourist visas. But as those visas expire, they're not being renewed under policies that seek to control more closely who gets into the U.S. The heightened border security has not, however, stopped undocumented Mexicans from getting in. The Pew Hispanic Center found that even though immigration is down since its peak in 2000, about 485,000 undocumented Mexicans were still crossing each year from 2000 to '04. In fact, the tougher restrictions have been a boon for the smugglers who sneak human traffic across the border. When Mario Coria's half-brother Fernando went to the U.S. in 1985, the trip from Tuxpan cost $200. Now the same trip costs more than $2,000.

For Pancho, the rising profitability of human smuggling is proving too tempting. He used to work as an *enganchador*, ore wrangler, in Tuxpan, earning $200 for each would-be migrant he steered toward his friends who worked as coyotes, smuggling people across the Arizona border. Now, with the business plan for his greenhouses in disarray, he says he plans to move to Phoenix, Ariz., and work as a facilitator for the coyotes, watching over the newcomers and arranging bus or plane tickets for them to their final destination. Pancho estimates he could clear close to $1,000 a week. Working as a facilitator isn't as dangerous as sneaking through the desert with a group of immigrants as the coyotes do, but under the tough new laws aimed at traffickers, Pancho could face felony time of up to 20 years if he's caught. It's a stunning risk for a family man to take, but Pancho just shrugs. "I think it will be fine," he says. "And besides, where am I going to get that kind of money in Tuxpan?"

For those who are crossing, the traveling has become more arduous. The first time Gabriel, one of the guests at the Bridgehampton *quinceañera*, crossed the border in 1990, he left Tijuana at 6 p.m. and reached his sister in Los Angeles by 8 a.m. the next day. But after the border crackdowns of the mid-1990s, he has had to seek out new routes. In 1999 he flew from Mexico City to Montreal and went to a random downtown McDonald's, where he thought he could bump into Hispanics. If he found some Mexicans there, he reasoned, one of them would know how to sneak across the nearby U.S. border. Before long, he got a ride to a secluded place in the woods just north of the border, but an off-duty U.S. customs agent getting lunch at a Burger King drive-through spotted Gabriel as he walked out of the trees. He was fingerprinted, handed a summons to appear before a judge and released. The judge later issued Gabriel a voluntary departure order, giving him two months to arrange his affairs and move back to Mexico. For an already overburdened immigration system, voluntary departure keeps the U.S. from having to pay for jailing or deporting low-risk illegal immigrants like Gabriel. He did fly back to Tuxpan at his own expense but stayed only a couple months before illegally crossing once again, this time through Arizona, to rejoin his family up north.

For anti-immigration advocates, the episode is typical of the leniency on both the northern and southern borders that is killing the system. Their outrage was directed at Mexico's National Human Rights Commission last week for its plan—scrapped a few days later—to distribute maps showing safe routes into the U.S. For Gabriel, however, the prospect of creeping and crawling through the woods just to reach his wife and two children in New York is humiliating. "I've got 15 years here," he says. "And crossing like that makes you feel like trash, like you're worth nothing."

Rather than run the risk and expense of going home in the winter, many Tuxpeños, particularly the families, simply choose to stay year round, putting even more pressure on the educational, health and social-service agencies in the Hamptons. The East Hampton school system now has a population that is 25% Hispanic, including legal and illegal kids. At East Hampton High School, new students who don't speak a word of English drop in so frequently that the school has developed a two-week crash course in basic phrases and American culture. There are signs of backlash from local taxpayers. A $90 million construction bond meant to alleviate overcrowding in East Hampton schools was rejected by voters last June, and some locals attribute the defeat to anger at the perceived costs of educating the kids of immigrant workers.

BACK AT THE *QUINCEAÑERA* in Bridgehampton, the festivities continued, yet the price and the promises of immigration were never far out of mind. Julio Sr. was there, but his wife and sons were 2,000 miles away in Tuxpan. Pancho was still in Mexico, so his wife Ruth waltzed with their daughter Samantha, 3. Gabriel sat with his arm around his wife Jani and talked about how their daughter Lena, 8, born in the Hamptons, could petition to obtain permanent legal residency for her parents in 2015, when she turns 18. "But by then," he said, as if suddenly remembering, "I really hope we're living in Tuxpan."

Nathan Thornburgh, "Inside the Life of the Migrants Next Door." *Time*, February 6, 2006, p. 34. Copyright © 2006, Time, Inc. Reprinted by permission.

ECONOMIC ANTHROPOLOGY

KEY TERMS

Name _____

Section _____

Date _____

Adaptive strategy:

Agriculturalists:

Allocation of resources:

Balanced reciprocity:

Cultivation continuum:

Division of labor:

Economic anthropologist:

Economic anthropology:

Economy:

ECONOMIC ANTHROPOLOGY

Exchange:

Fallow:

Fictive kinship:

Foragers:

Generalized reciprocity:

Horticulturalists:

Industrialists:

Market exchange/principle:

Means of production:

Migration:

Modes of production:

Namesakes:

Negative reciprocity:

KEY TERMS

Name _____

Section _____

Date _____

Nomadic:

Pastoralists:

Pastoral nomadism:

Peasants:

Potlatch:

Production:

Reciprocity:

Redistribution:

Sedentary:

Shifting cultivation:

ECONOMIC ANTHROPOLOGY

Slash and burn techniques:

Symbiosis:

Transhumance:

Transhumant pastoralists:

9 POLITICAL ORGANIZATION

Class versus Caste: Another Lesson in Inequality

Cultural Anthropology: A Problem-Based Approach—
Richard H. Robbins

THE RATIONALE FOR SOCIAL INEQUALITY

The maldistribution of wealth, status, and privilege is a significant problem in the modern world. To Americans it is visible in the starving faces that stare out from our television screens in documentaries and on the evening news, interspersed with advertisements for luxuries such as automobiles, cosmetics, and household conveniences. Some people can purchase the finest amenities, while others lack the basic necessities of life, such as food, shelter, and health care. There are few, if any, modern nations in which one portion of the population does not in some way enjoy privileges that other portions do not share. In most of these cases, inequality follows from the assumption that certain people are somehow better than others. Individuals are judged by traits—gender, age, physical appearance, occupation, wealth, group membership, and so on—that seem to make them more or less worthy compared to others.

Some people believe that the hierarchical ordering of people and groups is unavoidable. In their view, scarce resources, occupational specialization, and the power of an elite group to control the behavior of others necessarily result in some form of social stratification. Others maintain that **stratification** is not only avoidable, but is counter to human nature. According to anthropologist Thomas Belmonte:

> Since the emergence of stratification, man's history (his changing ways of relating to nature and other men) has stood opposed to his humanity. The emergence of power-wielding elites...laid the basis for a new kind of anti-collective society whose vastly accelerated growth was founded, not on the reconciliation of antagonisms between men, but on their origination and amplification in slavery, caste, and class. (Belmonte 1989:137)

Those who support Belmonte's view note that in societies such as those of the Inuit, there are no "poor," "rich," "inferior," or "superior" people. This is not to say that these societies are totally **egalitarian**; even in small-scale societies, valued statuses are not available to some members. Rather, the question is why modern societies are characterized by such extremes of poverty and wealth.

POLITICAL ORGANIZATION

HOW DO SOCIETIES RANK PEOPLE IN SOCIAL HIERARCHIES?

Social hierarchies in different societies vary along several dimensions: the criteria used to differentiate people into one level of society or another, the number of levels that exist, the kinds of privileges and rights that attach to people at different levels, and the strength of the social boundaries that separate the different levels. In American society, for example, people are stratified by income and personal possessions into social classes (e.g., lower-class, middle-class, and upper-class). They are classified by cultural or family background into ethnic groups (e.g., Italian, Jewish, Hispanic, or white Anglo-Saxon Protestant), or by physical appearance or skin color into racial categories (e.g., black or white). They are also classified by gender and age, as well as by standards such as education. People in the United States may move from class to class, and they may choose to emphasize or deemphasize their ethnic group membership, but generally their racial category and gender are fixed.

In India, the population is stratified into hundreds of different **castes**. In a caste system, individuals are assigned at birth to the ranked social and occupational groups of their parents. A person's place in the social order is fixed; there is no mobility from one caste to another. Castes are separated from one another by strict rules that forbid intermarriage and other forms of interaction, such as eating together, speaking to each other, or working together.

In any stratified society, people's access to jobs, wealth, and privilege is determined largely by their position in the hierarchy. Castes in India are based on traditional roles, for example. The *Brahmins*, priests whose lives were devoted to worship and teaching, occupied the top of the caste hierarchy. Directly under them were the *Kshattriya* castes, whose members comprised the soldiers, politicians, and administrators. Next were the *Vaisya* castes, made up of farmers and merchants. At the bottom of the hierarchy were the *Sudra* castes, which were devoted to the service of other castes. The *Sudra* castes included "untouchable" or "unclean" persons whose occupations were believed to be polluting to others. Untouchables included washermen, tanners, shoemakers, and sweepers, people whose occupations required them to come into contact with animal or human wastes. The Indian government has outlawed discrimination against untouchables based on caste membership, but it persists nevertheless.

THE FEMINIZATION OF POVERTY

In the United States, sex and age are significantly related to whether or not a person lives in poverty. In *Women and Children Last*, Ruth Sidel draws an analogy between the doomed ship *Titanic* and American society at the end of the 1980s. Both, she says, were gleaming symbols of wealth that placed women and children at a disadvantage. When the *Titanic* went down, women and children were indeed saved first, but only those who were traveling in first-class or second-class accommodations. Women and children in third-class and steerage were not saved. While only eight percent of the women and three percent of the children in first- and second-class drowned the night the *Titanic* sunk, 45 percent of the women and 70 percent of the children in steerage died. As with the *Titanic*, Sidel says, certain women and children in the United States are not the first to be saved; instead, they are the first to fall into poverty.

There have been dramatic changes in the role of women in the United States over the past half century. One measure is their steadily increasing participation in the work force. In 1960, only 32 percent of married women worked outside the home; in 1989, 58 percent were wage earners. Yet women in American society make up a disproportionate share of the poor. Americans are witnessing what sociologists call the **feminization of poverty**. According to the U.S. Bureau of the Census, in 1990 more than 15 percent of all Americans had incomes at or below the amount established by the federal government as the official **poverty** level, and this level is set well below what is required for basic subsistence. In 1990, the poverty level was $12,195 for a family of four, the pretax annual income for a person working full time for $6.10 an hour. Two out of every three poor adults were women, including more than a quarter of all women over 65 who were not living in families. The 16 percent of all American families that were headed by females represented 53 percent of the families officially classified as living below the poverty level.

Children pay an even greater price than women do. In 1990, one out of every four preschoolers and one out of every five children under the age of 12 were living in poverty. Nearly 40 percent of the American poor are children under 12 years of age, and more than half of these are living in families headed by females. In other words, women and children make up the majority of America's poor. If in addition to being a child and a female, a person is African-American, Hispanic-American, or

Native-American, the chances of being among America's poor are even greater. For African-American children, the poverty rate was almost 50 percent in 1990, and for African-American and Hispanic-American children in female headed households it was higher than 70 percent. The greatest stigma in American society is to be a child, a female, and either African-American, Hispanic-American, or Native-American.

There are various explanations for the unequal distribution of resources in the United States and in other countries. Americans, who are highly **individualistic**, tend to believe that if people live in poverty it's probably their own fault, a rationale often referred to as "blaming the victim." In the case of children, most say poverty is their parents' fault. But since the surest predictor of a person's income is the income of his or her parents, it should be obvious that more than individual work effort and motivation are responsible for social stratification. There must be reasons why societies construct social hierarchies.

WHY DO SOCIETIES CONSTRUCT SOCIAL HIERARCHIES?

The construction of a social hierarchy is not a necessary feature of all human societies. Groups such as the Inuit, for example, are not totally egalitarian; however, people go out of their way not to appear better than others. Moreover, there seems to be no universal inclination to rank people by one criterion or another; in some societies skin color makes a difference, and in others it doesn't. In some societies men are accorded far greater status than women; in others there is little if any difference in gender rank. Even the use of age as a criterion of rank varies from society to society. The only general rule that seems to hold is that as societies become more complex and populous, their propensity for social stratification increases.

There are various explanations for the existence of social hierarchies. Some claim social stratification emerged with the origin of private property; others claims it was created to satisfy the organizational needs of war. We will explore two explanations here: the **integrative theory of social stratification**, based on the assumption that social hierarchy is necessary for the smooth functioning of modern society; and the **exploitative theory of social stratification**, which presumes that hierarchy exists because one group of individuals seeks to take advantage of another group for economic purposes.

Proponents of the integrative theory of social stratification assume that as societies grow and there are more people to feed, house, and clothe, more labor-efficient or technologically sophisticated means are required to produce enough food and other necessities and to erect the necessary infrastructure. Unlike the smaller societies of hunters and gatherers and horticulturists, larger-scale societies require individuals to specialize in certain tasks or occupations. This results in a **division of labor** that requires greater coordination of tasks, more efficient management, and more complex leadership systems, all of which inevitably lead to some form of social stratification. In addition, as societies become more complex, they need to organize systems of defense against other groups when they attack them, and the development of a military organization requires the centralization of power, which again leads to the emergence of an elite group. As resources become scarce, an internal policing system may also be required to keep order and prevent crime. In any case, the integrative theory of social stratification is based on the assumption that society's need for greater integration, along with the need to assert greater controls on individual behavior, necessitates some form of centralized authority that offers its citizens security, protection, means of settling disputes, defense against other groups, and sustenance. All these are offered in exchange for the people's acceptance of and loyalty to state authorities and officials.

In the integrative theory, society is likened to a living organism whose parts must be regulated by a controlling device if they are to function efficiently for the survival of the whole. The nineteenth-century social philosopher Herbert Spencer suggested that complex societies, like complex living organisms, exhibit greater differentiation as they evolve. With greater differentiation there follows a greater degree of interrelation among parts, which in turn requires greater control by government, management, and the military. Without control, society, like a living organism, would cease to exist.

In American society, proponents of the integrative theory of hierarchy might point to the military to illustrate the necessity for stratification. Without generals or commissioned officers, they would say, privates, corporals, and sergeants could not function efficiently to do their jobs, and the military would therefore disintegrate. They might point to industry as another illustration of the need for hierarchy; if there were no executives to direct those who do the work, industry would collapse. The reason the Ju/'hoansi require no hierarchy, integrationists might say, is because each person or family is self-sufficient, and there is no need for the coordination or control of activities. As societies become more complex and the division of labor increases, greater control is necessary. The fact that those who assume the responsibility of control are given greater rewards is simply a way of assuring the survival of the society as a whole.

The Indian caste system, for example, is sometimes said to perform an integrative function by providing benefits to both higher-caste landowners and lower-caste workers. Landowners get workers to cultivate their land, and the lower castes are assured economic security.

Other scholars agree that in complex societies it is necessary for integration to occur, but they disagree that social hierarchy is required for integration. Proponents of the exploitative theory of social stratification claim that stratification arises when one group seeks to exploit the resources or labor of others. The exploitation might take the form of military conquest, as it did during the Spanish conquest of South America, when thousands of indigenous people were forced to labor on farms or in mines to increase the wealth of Spanish conquerors, or it might take other forms of manipulation and control. Members of India's lower castes, for example, have tried to change their status, only to bring a violent reaction from the higher castes.

KARL MARX AND THE ORIGIN OF CLASS

The most influential and controversial of the exploitative theories of social stratification is that of Karl Marx and Friedrich Engels. As witnesses to the teeming squalor of British cities during the industrial revolution, Marx and Engels concluded that landlords and factory owners (*capitalists*, in their terms) were able to use their control of resources to exploit the unlanded laborers in the newly emerging factories and mines of England. To understand how landlords and factory owners were able to exploit the masses, it is necessary to grasp the meaning of some key concepts in Marxist theory. The most important of these concepts is *social class*.

Social classes are an outgrowth of capitalism, not a necessary feature of modern society. According to Marx, classes arise when a group—a ruling class, landlords, bosses, and

so on—gains control of the **means of production**. The means of production consist of the materials, such as land, machines, or tools, that people need to produce things. A group that controls the means of production can maintain or increase its wealth by taking advantage of the **surplus value of labor**.

The idea of the surplus value of labor works something like this: take a product or commodity such as bricks. Say that the labor value of bricks on the open market is $300 per 1,000 bricks; that is, people are willing to pay $300 above the cost of materials for each 1,000 bricks they purchase. If the same people both make the bricks and sell 1,000 of them for $300 plus the cost of materials, they are getting a 100 percent return on their labor. But what if the person who owns or controls the means of production for bricks hires some people to make the bricks and only pays them $30 for every 1,000 bricks they make? The value of the labor to produce the bricks is still $300 per 1,000, but the laborers are getting only one-tenth ($30) of what their labor is worth, while the person who controls means of production is getting the surplus value of labor, or the other nine-tenths of the labor value of the bricks ($270). In other words, the capitalist, the person who controls the means of production (the brickworks, in this case), is expropriating $270 worth of labor from the worker who produced the bricks.

Why would a worker labor under such conditions? The reason is **political or social repression**, which occurs because the ruling class, the group that controls the means of production, also makes the rules of the society. Members of this class elect or choose representatives who pass laws that serve their interests. Such laws may require people to work for the ruling class, prohibit workers from organizing into labor unions, require them to accept whatever wages they are offered, and forbid them from protesting these laws or the working conditions they produce. Because the ruling class can enforce these rules with the threat of joblessness, jail, or even death, most people allow themselves to be exploited. Moreover, the workers readily accept their situation if the ruling class also controls the distribution of information so it can create for its own benefit an **ideology of class**.

The ideology of class is a belief that the division of society into classes is both natural and right. According to Marx and Engels, if the ruling class controls the institutions that are responsible for determining how people view the world (institutions such as the churches, schools, and newspapers) it can promote the view that their dominance of society is in the best interests of all. The church, for example, can encourage the lower class to accept its fate because it is "God's will," or it can teach poor people that their poverty is not the fault of the ruling class but reflects their own "fall from grace." The ruling class may allow only children of its own class to go to school and at the same time make education a criterion for membership in the ruling class. Or, through its control of educational institutions and mass communications media, it may convince people who don't have an education that they are unworthy of being members of the ruling class, while it makes education so expensive that only the rich can afford it. The ruling class may use the media to tell people that the whole society would perish without it, or it could promote an ideology based on the belief that if you are poor, it's your own fault. As a result of an ideology of class, members of the lower class come to believe that their position in society is as it should be and that there is nothing they can (or should) do about it.

The ideology of class thus produces a society in which a few people control the means of production through the expropriation of the surplus value of labor, maintaining their position of control through repression and the manipulation of ideology through religion, education, and the media. The only way the lower class can rectify this situation, according to Marx and Engels, is through **violent revolution**. Violent revolution is necessary because the ruling class controls the means of repression (e.g., police, militia, and military), and it won't relinquish its privileges and positions of control unless it is violently overthrown. Thus, repression and poverty brought about by the existence of social classes ultimately push the lower class (the workers), in desperation, to revolt to regain control of the means of production in order to regain the surplus value of their labor.

Two points about Marx and Engel's views are particularly relevant today; first, the position that class structure is very resistant to change seems to be corroborated by income distribution figures in the United States over the past decade. The information is summarized in the table below.

The table shows how total income in the United States has been distributed among the total population from 1980 to 1993. For example, in 1980, the 20 percent of the population with the highest income accounted for 44.1 percent of the total income received, while the 20 percent of the population with the lowest income accounted for 4.2 percent of the total. In 1993, the highest 20 percent took in 48.9 percent of the total income earned, while the lowest 20 percent took in 3.6 percent. In other words, the rich have been getting richer and the poor have been getting poorer. This phenomenon is not new to the 1980s and '90s; it is a trend that goes back at least to the 1950s.

A second major theoretical contribution to Marx and Engels lies in their ideas about the ideology of class: the notion that people in class societies come to believe that social stratification is "natural."

Income Distribution in the United States from 1980 to 1993

Percentage of Money Received by Each Quintile and the Top 5%

Year	Lowest Fifth	Second Fifth	Third Fifth	Fourth Fifth	Fifth Fifth	Top 5%
1993	3.6	9.0	15.1	23.5	48.9	21.0
1992	3.8	9.4	15.8	24.2	46.9	18.6
1991	3.8	9.6	15.9	24.2	46.5	18.1
1990	3.9	9.6	15.9	24.0	46.6	18.6
1989	3.8	9.5	15.8	24.0	46.8	18.9
1988	3.8	9.6	16.0	24.3	46.3	18.3
1987	3.8	9.6	16.1	24.3	46.2	18.2
1986	3.8	9.7	16.2	24.3	46.1	18.0
1985	3.9	9.8	16.2	24.4	45.6	17.6
1984	4.0	9.9	16.3	24.6	45.2	17.1
1983	4.0	9.9	16.4	24.6	45.1	17.1
1982	4.0	10.0	16.5	24.5	45.0	17.0
1981	4.1	10.1	16.7	24.8	44.4	16.5
1980	4.2	10.2	16.8	24.8	44.1	16.5

Source: U.S. Bureau of the Census. CD-ROM, "Income and Poverty: 1993."

From *Cultural Anthropology*, 2nd edition, by Richard Robbins. Copyright © 1997, Wadsworth, a part of Cengage Learning, Inc. Reproduced by permission. www.cengage.com/permissions.

Poverty in the United States: 2001

Poverty data offer an important way to evaluate the nation's economic well-being. Because poor people in the United States are too diverse to be characterized along any one dimension, this report illustrates how poverty rates vary by selected characteristics—age, race and origin, nativity, family composition, work experience, and geography. The data reveal how many people were poor and how the poverty population has changed.

Whether one is in poverty or not provides but one perspective on economic well-being.

The estimates in this report are based on interviewing a sample of the population. Respondents provide answers to the best of their ability, but as with all surveys, the estimates may differ from the actual values.

HIGHLIGHTS

- The poverty rate in 2001 was 11.7 percent, up from 11.3 percent in 2000.

- In 2001, people below the poverty thresholds numbered 32.9 million, a figure 1.3 million higher than the 31.6 million poor in 2000.

- At 16.3 percent, the poverty rate for children remained higher that that of other age groups, but did not change between 2000 and 2001.

- For people 18 to 64 years old, the poverty rate rose to 10.1 percent in 2001, up from 9.6 percent in 2000.

- In 2001, there were 6.8 million poor families (9.2 percent), up from 6.4 million (8.7 percent) in 2000.

- For non-Hispanic Whites, the poverty rate rose between 2000 and 2001 (from 7.4 percent to 7.8 percent), as did the number who were poor (from 14.4 million to 15.3 million). Poverty rates for Blacks, Hispanics, and Asians and Pacific Islanders did not change between 2000 and 2001. However, the number of poor Hispanics rose to 8.0 million in 2001, up from 7.7 million in 2000.

- The poverty rate in the South increased from 12.8 percent in 2000 to 13.5 percent in 2001. The poverty rates in the Northeast, Midwest, and Western United States did not change.

- The poverty rate for people living in the suburbs rose from 7.8 percent in 2000 to 8.2 percent in 2001; the poverty rate did not change in central cities or in non-metropolitan areas.

- How poverty is measured affects one's perception of who is poor. Six experimental measures showed lower poverty rates for children, Blacks, and people in female-householder families than under the official measure, while poverty rates for those 65 and over varied greatly according to how medical expenses were taken into account.

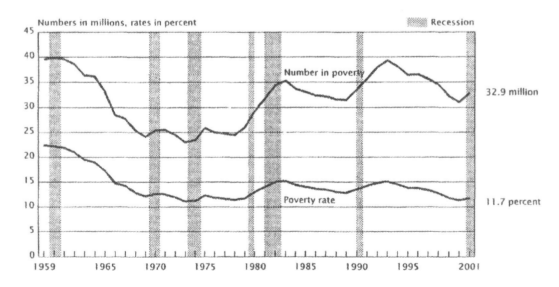

Note: The data points represent the midpoints of the respective years. The latest recession began in March 2001.
Source: U.S. Census Bureau. Current Population Survey. 1960–2002 Annual Demographic Supplements.

CHAPTER 9

Figure 9.1 Poverty in the United States 2001

People and Families in Poverty by Selected Characteristics: 2000 and 2001

(Numbers in thousands)

Characteristic	2001 below poverty				2000 below poverty[1]				Difference (2001 minus 2000)[2]			
	Number	90-percent C.I. (±)	Percent	90-percent C.I. (±)	Number	90-percent C.I. (±)	Percent	90-percent C.I. (±)	Number	90-percent C.I. (±)	Percent	90-percent C.I. (±)
PEOPLE												
Total	32,907	644	11.7	0.2	31,581	633	11.3	0.2	*1,325	669	*0.4	0.2
Family Status												
In families	23,215	551	9.9	0.2	22,347	542	9.6	0.2	*868	623	*0.3	0.3
Householder	6,813	172	9.2	0.2	6,400	165	8.7	0.2	*413	192	*0.5	0.3
Related children under 18	11,175	323	15.8	0.5	11,005	321	15.6	0.5	170	367	0.1	0.5
Related children under 6	4,188	207	18.2	1.0	4,066	204	17.8	0.9	121	235	0.4	1.1
In unrelated subfamilies	466	82	39.8	7.6	581	45	41.2	3.7	*-116	78	-1.4	7.2
Reference person	172	50	36.4	11.4	223	27	39.0	5.6	*-50	48	-2.7	10.8
Children under 18	292	57	44.6	9.8	348	62	43.7	8.8	-57	68	0.9	10.6
Unrelated individual	9,226	207	19.9	0.5	8,653	199	19.0	0.5	*573	213	*0.9	0.5
Male	3,833	122	17.3	0.6	3,426	115	15.7	0.6	*407	124	*1.6	0.6
Female	5,393	149	22.3	0.7	5,227	146	22.0	0.7	*165	155	0.3	0.7
Race[3] and Hispanic Origin												
White	22,739	546	9.9	0.2	21,645	534	9.5	0.2	*1,094	616	*0.4	0.3
Non-Hispanic	15,271	454	7.8	0.2	14,366	441	7.4	0.2	*905	511	*0.4	0.3
Black	8,136	300	22.7	0.8	7,982	297	22.5	0.8	154	313	0.1	0.9
Asian and Pacific Islander	1,275	129	10.2	1.0	1,258	129	9.9	1.0	17	135	0.3	1.1
Hispanic[4]	7,997	300	21.4	0.8	7,747	295	21.5	0.8	*250	249	-0.1	0.7
Age												
Under 18 years	11,733	329	16.3	0.5	11,587	328	16.2	0.5	146	344	0.1	0.5
18 to 64 years	17,760	483	10.1	0.3	16,671	469	9.6	0.3	*1,089	500	*0.5	0.3
65 years and over	3,414	129	10.1	0.4	3,323	127	9.9	0.4	91	134	0.2	0.4
Nativity												
Native	27,698	597	11.1	0.2	26,680	587	10.8	0.2	*1,018	621	*0.3	0.3
Foreign born	5,209	308	16.1	1.0	4,901	299	15.4	0.9	307	319	0.6	1.0
Naturalized citizen	1,186	148	9.9	1.2	1,060	140	9.0	1.2	126	151	0.9	1.3
Not a citizen	4,023	271	19.7	1.3	3,841	265	19.2	1.3	181	281	0.5	1.4
Region												
Northeast	5,687	266	10.7	0.5	5,474	261	10.3	0.5	212	277	0.4	0.5
Midwest	5,966	278	9.4	0.4	5,916	274	9.3	0.4	50	290	-	0.5
South	13,515	458	13.5	0.5	12,705	444	12.8	0.5	*810	473	*0.7	0.5
West	7,739	364	12.1	0.6	7,485	358	11.8	0.6	254	379	0.2	0.6
Residence												
Inside metropolitan areas	25,446	575	11.1	0.3	24,603	566	10.8	0.3	*843	598	*0.3	0.3
Inside central cities	13,394	427	16.5	0.5	13,257	425	16.3	0.5	137	447	0.2	0.6
Outside central cities	12,052	406	8.2	0.3	11,346	394	7.8	0.3	*706	420	*0.4	0.3
Outside metropolitan areas	7,460	394	14.2	0.8	6,978	382	13.4	0.7	*482	407	0.8	0.8
FAMILIES												
Total	6,813	172	9.2	0.2	6,400	165	8.7	0.2	*413	192	*0.5	0.3
White	4,579	135	7.4	0.2	4,333	131	7.1	0.2	*246	158	*0.4	0.3
Non-Hispanic	3,051	108	5.7	0.2	2,896	105	5.4	0.2	*155	125	*0.3	0.2
Black	1,829	81	20.7	1.0	1,686	78	19.3	0.9	*144	91	*1.4	1.1
Asian and Pacific Islander	234	28	7.8	1.0	233	28	7.8	1.0	-	32	-	1.1
Hispanic[4]	1,649	77	19.4	0.9	1,540	74	19.2	1.0	*109	72	0.2	0.9
Type of Family												
Married-couple	2,760	102	4.9	0.2	2,637	99	4.7	0.2	*124	115	*0.2	0.2
White	2,242	91	4.5	0.2	2,181	89	4.4	0.2	61	107	0.1	0.2
Non-Hispanic	1,477	73	3.3	0.2	1,435	72	3.2	0.2	42	85	0.1	0.2
Black	328	33	7.8	0.8	266	30	6.3	0.7	*62	36	*1.4	0.9
Asian and Pacific Islander	156	23	6.6	1.0	142	22	5.9	0.9	13	26	0.7	1.1
Hispanic[4]	799	53	13.8	0.9	772	52	14.2	1.0	26	50	-0.4	0.9
Female householder, no husband present	3,470	116	26.4	1.0	3,278	112	25.4	0.9	*191	130	1.0	1.1
White	1,939	84	22.4	1.1	1,820	81	21.2	1.0	*118	98	1.2	1.2
Non-Hispanic	1,305	68	19.0	1.1	1,226	66	17.8	1.0	*80	79	1.2	1.2
Black	1,351	69	35.2	2.0	1,300	68	34.3	2.0	51	78	0.9	2.3
Asian and Pacific Islander	61	14	14.6	3.6	81	16	22.2	5.0	*-20	18	*-7.6	5.1
Hispanic[4]	711	50	37.0	2.9	664	48	36.4	3.0	*47	46	0.6	2.8
Male householder, no wife present	583	45	13.1	1.1	485	41	11.3	1.0	*98	49	*1.8	1.2
White	398	37	11.7	1.1	332	34	10.1	1.1	*66	42	*1.6	1.3
Non-Hispanic	270	30	10.3	1.2	236	28	9.2	1.2	34	35	1.1	1.4
Black	150	23	19.4	3.1	120	20	16.3	3.0	*31	24	3.1	3.5
Asian and Pacific Islander	17	8	9.1	4.2	10	6	5.4	3.1	7	8	3.7	4.2
Hispanic[4]	139	22	17.0	2.9	104	19	13.6	2.6	*35	19	*3.5	2.6

-Represents zero.   *Statistically significant at the 90-percent confidence level.
For explanation of confidence intervals (C.I.), see "Standard errors and their use" at *www.census.gov/hhes/poverty/poverty01/pov01src.pdf.*

[1]Consistent with 2001 data through implementation of Census 2000-based population controls and a 28,000 household sample expansion.
[2]As a result of rounding, some differences may appear to be slightly higher or lower than the differences of the reported rates.
[3]Data for American Indians and Alaska Natives are not shown separately in this table because of the small sample of that population.
[4]Hispanics may be of any race.

Source: U.S. Census Bureau, Current Population Survey, 2001 and 2002 Annual Demographic Supplements.

POLITICAL ORGANIZATION

Politics and Leadership—
Barbara D. Miller

When cultural anthropologists consider the concept of politics, they tend to take a broader view than a political scientist because their cross-cultural data indicate that many kinds of behavior and thought are political in addition to formal party politics, voting, and government. Cultural anthropologists offer important examples of political systems that might not look like political systems at all to people who have grown up in large states. This section explores basic political concepts from an anthropological perspective and raises the question of whether political systems are universal to all cultures.

POLITICS AND CULTURE

British anthropologists, especially Bronislaw Malinowski and A.R. Radcliffe-Brown, long dominated theory-making in political anthropology. Their approach, referred to as **functionalism**, emphasized how institutions such as political organization and law promote social cohesion. Later, the students of these two teachers developed divergent theories. For example, in the late 1960s, some scholars began to look at aspects of political organization that pull societies apart. The new focus on disputes and conflict prompted anthropologists to gather information on dispute "cases" and to analyze the actors involved in a particular conflict, "processual analysis."

The processual approach to micropolitics has been countered by a swing toward a more macro view (Vincent 1996), which examines politics, no matter how local, within a global context (Asad 1973). This global perspective has prompted many studies of colonialism and neocolonialism in political anthropology and historical anthropology. Ann Stoler's book, *Capitalism and Confrontation in Sumatra's Plantation Belt, 1870–1979* (1985), on the history and cultural impact of Dutch colonialism in Indonesia, is a classic study in this genre. In the 1980s, the experiences of "subaltern" peoples (those subordinated by colonialism) and "subaltern movements" in former colonized regions attracted research attention, particularly from native anthropologists of decolonizing countries. The history of political anthropology in the twentieth century illustrates the theoretical tensions between the actor-as-agent approach (processual approach) and the structurist perspective that sees actors as constrained in their choices by larger forces.

Politics: The Use of Power, Authority, and Influence

What, first, do we mean by the word *politics*? The term **politics** refers to public power, as opposed to the more private, micropolitics of family and domestic groups. **Power** is the ability to bring about results, often through the possession or use of forceful means. Closely related to power are authority and influence. **Authority** implies "the right to take certain forms of action" (M. Smith 1966:3). It is usually based on a person's achieved or ascribed status, moral reputation, or other basis for respect. Authority differs from power in that power "is the capacity to take autonomous action in the face of resistance... It is the capacity to pursue one's will effectively, if necessary, by imposing it on others." Power is backed up by the potential use of force.

Influence is yet another way of achieving a desired end, through exerting social or moral pressure, not force, on someone or some group. Compared to authority, influence may be reinforced by social position and status, but it may also be exerted from a low-status and marginal position. All three terms are relational. A person's power, authority, or influence exists in relation to others. Power implies the greatest likelihood of a coercive and hierarchical relationship, and authority and influence offer the most scope for consensual, cooperative decision making. Power, authority, and influence are all related to politics, with power being the strongest basis for action and decision making.

Politics: Cultural Universal?

Is politics a human universal? Some anthropologists would say "No." They point to instances of cultures with scarcely any institutions that can be called political, with no durable ranking systems and very little aggression. Foraging lifestyles, as a model for early human evolution, suggest that nonhierarchical social systems characterized human life for 90 percent of its existence. Only with the emergence of private property, surpluses, and other changes did ranking systems, government, formal law, and organized group aggression emerge. Also, studies show how dominance-seeking and aggression are learned behaviors, emphasized in some cultures and among some segments of the population such as the military, and de-emphasized among others such as religious leaders, healers, and child care providers. Being a good politician or a five-star general is a matter of socialization.

Other anthropologists argue that, despite a wide range of variation, politics is a human universal. Every society is organized to some degree by kinship relationships, and many anthropologists would not draw a clear boundary between how kinship organizes power and how political organization organizes power.

This chapter takes the approach that there is a continuum of political structures, starting with the minimal forms that are found among foraging groups.

POLITICAL ORGANIZATION AND LEADERSHIP

Political organization refers to groups that exist for purposes of public decision making and leadership, maintaining social cohesion and order, protecting group rights, and ensuring safety from external threats. Power relationships situated in private, within the household for example, may be considered "political" and may be related to wider political realities, but they are not forms of political organization. Political organizations have several features:

- *Recruitment principles*: criteria for determining admission to the unit.

- *Perpetuity*: assumption that the group will continue to exist indefinitely.

- *Identity markers*: particular characteristics that distinguish it from others, such as costume, membership card, or title.

- *Internal organization*: an orderly arrangement of members in relation to each other.

- *Procedures*: prescribed rules and practices for behavior of group members.

- *Autonomy*: ability to regulate its own affairs. (Tiffany 1979:71–72)

Cultural anthropologists cluster the many forms of political organization that occur cross-culturally into four major types. The four types of political organization correspond, generally, to the major economic forms. Recall that the categories of economies represent a continuum, suggesting that there is overlap between different types rather than clear boundaries; this overlap exists between types of political organization as well.

Bands

Anthropologists use the term *band* to refer to the political organization of foraging groups. Since foraging has been the predominant mode of production for almost all of human history, the band has been the most longstanding form of political organization. A **band** comprises a small

Figure 9.2 Economies and Political Organization

	Foraging	Horticulture	Pastoralism	Agriculture	Industrialism (Capitalist)
POLITICAL ORGANIZATION	Band	Tribe	Chiefdom	Confederacy · State	State
LEADERSHIP	Band leader	Headman/Headwoman · Big-man · Big-woman	Chief	Paramount chief	King/Queen/President · Prime Minister/ Emperor
SOCIAL CHANGE	More surpluses of resources and wealth ————→ Increased population density and residential centralization ————→ More social inequality/ranking ————→ Less reliance on kinship relations as the basis of political structures ————→ Increased internal and external social conflict ————→ Increased power and responsibility of leaders ————→ Increased burdens on the population to support political organization ————→				

POLITICAL ORGANIZATION

group of households, between twenty and a few hundred people at most, who are related through kinship. These units come together at certain times of the year, depending on their foraging patterns and ritual schedule.

Band membership is flexible: If a person has a serious disagreement with another person or a spouse, one option is to leave that band and join another. Leadership is informal in most cases, with no one person being named as a permanent leader for the whole group at all times. Depending on the events at hand, such as organizing the group to relocate or to send people out to hunt, a particular person may come to the fore as a leader for that time. That person's advice and knowledge about the task may be especially respected.

There is no social stratification between leaders and followers. A band leader is the "first among equals." Leadership is informal and is based on the quality of the individual's advice and personality. If a person gives bad advice, people will not continue to listen. Band leaders have limited authority or influence, but no power. They cannot enforce their opinions. Social leveling mechanisms prevent anyone from accumulating much authority or influence, since strong values of self-effacement prevail over self-aggrandizement. Political activity in bands involves mainly decision making about migration, food distribution, and interpersonal conflict resolution. External conflict between groups is rare since territories of different bands are widely separated and the population density is low.

The band level of organization barely qualifies as a form of political organization since groups are flexible, leadership ephemeral, and there are no signs or emblems of political affiliation. In fact, some anthropologists argue that "real" politics did not exist in undisturbed band societies such as the Ju/wasi of southern Africa, the Inuit of northern Canada and Alaska, and the Andaman Islanders of India.

Tribes

A tribe is a more complex form of political organization than the band. Typically associated with horticulture and pastoralism, tribal organization developed only about 10,000 to 12,000 years ago with the advent of these modes of production. A **tribe** is a political group that comprises several bands or lineage groups, each with similar language and lifestyle and occupying a distinct territory.

These groups may be connected through a **clan** structure in which most people claim descent from a common ancestor, although they may be unable to trace the exact relationship. Kinship, as in the band, is the primary basis of membership. Tribal groupings contain from a hundred to several thousand people. Tribes are found in the Middle East, South Asia, Southeast Asia, the Pacific, Africa, and among Native Americans.

In terms of group leadership, a tribal **headman** or **headwoman** (most are male) is a more formal leader than a band leader. Key qualifications for this position are being hardworking and generous, and possessing good personal skills. A headman is a political leader on a part-time basis only. Like all other group members, he is primarily involved in production. Yet this role is more demanding than being a band leader. Depending on the mode of production, a headman will be in charge of determining the times for moving herds, planting and harvesting, and setting the time for seasonal feasts and celebrations. Internal and external conflict resolution is also his responsibility. A headman relies mainly on authority and persuasion rather than power. These strategies are effective because tribal members are all kin and have a certain loyalty to each other. Furthermore, exerting force on kinspersons is generally avoided.

Among horticulturalists of the Amazonian rain-forest, tribal organization is the dominant political pattern. Each local tribal unit, which is itself a lineage, has a headman (or perhaps two or three). Each tribal group is autonomous, but recently many have united temporarily into larger groups, in reaction to threats to their environment and lifestyle from outside forces.

Pastoralist tribal formations are often linked into a confederacy, with local units or segments maintaining substantial autonomy. The local segments meet together rarely, usually at an annual festival. But in case of an external threat, the confederacy gathers together. Once the threat is removed, local units resume their autonomy. The equality and autonomy of units along with their ability to unite and then disunite, is referred to as a **segmentary model** of political organization. This form of tribal organization is found among pastoralists from Morocco to Mongolia (Eickelman 1981). For example, the Qashqa'i, pastoralists of Iran, have three levels of political organization—subtribe, tribe, and confederacy:

CHAPTER **9**

Leaders at all levels of the Qashqa'i political hierarchy dealt with wider authorities and external forces on behalf of the tribespeople and communicated information to higher and lower levels in the system....From the perspective of the Qashqa'i people, tribal and confederacy memberships brought benefits...They gained relatively secure and protected access to pastures...and leaders assisted them in times of economic need. Relations with external powers were mediated for them...and they profited from the military power and political authority of their leaders. (Beck 1986:201)

Leadership combines both ascribed and achieved features. Subtribe headmen's positions were mainly based on achievement. Both *khans* (tribe leaders) and *ilkhanis* (confederacy leaders) were members of noble lineages and achieved their position through patrilineal descent, with the eldest son favored. The role of the *ilkhani* merges into that of chiefs (described in the next section).

The increased power of the state in most places has reduced the role of leaders such as Borzu Qermezi, headman of one segment of the Qashqa'i tribe (Beck 1991). Decreases in the role of headman occurred rapidly:

Borzu and the people of the Qermezi group faced many difficulties in 1970 and 1971... Expected winter rains did not fall, and the pastures and crops on which the people depended did not grow. The drought caused their debts to urban merchants and moneylenders to mount. Iran's government was increasing its control over the Qashqa'i, and the Qermezi group could not escape the expanding jurisdiction of central authorities. The government's application of new policies concerning pastures, migratory schedules, animals, prices of pastoral products, and tribal leadership was jeopardizing the people's ability to conduct viable nomadic pastoralism. Non-Qashqa'i agriculturalists and livestock investors were encroaching on land upon which the group depended...Borzu's role as tribal headman shifted in response to political and economic changes in Iran as a whole. He gradually lost some of the political support upon which he had relied... They withdrew from him because of outside pressures that not only affected economic conditions but also made part of his role as headman obsolete (1–2).

Big-Man Leadership

The **big-man system** or **big-woman system** is a form of political organization in which key individuals devote much of their efforts to developing a political following through a system of redistribution based on personal ties and grand feasts. Anthropological research in Melanesia, a large region in the South Pacific, established the big-man type of politics, and most references to it are from this region (Sahlins 1963, Strathern 1971). Nevertheless, personalistic, favor-based political groupings are found elsewhere.

Compared to a tribal headman, a big-man or big-woman has an expanded following that includes people in several villages. A big-man tends to have greater wealth than his followers, although people continue to expect him to be generous. The core supporters of a big-man tend to be kin, with extended networks including non-kin. A big-man has heavy responsibilities in regulating both internal affairs—cultivation—and external affairs—intergroup feasts, exchanges of goods, and war. In some instances, a big-man is assisted in carrying out his responsibilities by a group of other respected men. These councils include people from the big-man's different constituencies.

Big-man political organization is common in Papua New Guinea. In several tribes in the Mount Hagen area of the New Guinea highlands, an aspiring big-man develops a leadership position through making **moka** (Strathern 1971). Making moka involves exchanging gifts and favors with individuals and sponsoring large feasts where further gift-giving occurs. A social factor in big-manship in the Mount Hagen area is having at least one wife. An aspiring big-man urges his wives to work harder than ordinary women in order to grow more food to feed more pigs. (Pigs are an important measure of a man's status and worth.) The role of the wife is so important that a man whose parents died when he was young is at an extreme disadvantage. He has impaired chances of getting a wife or wives since he lacks financial support from his parents for the necessary bridewealth.

Using his own wife's (or wives') production as an exchange base, the aspiring big-man begins to extend his moka relationships, first with kin and then beyond. By giving goods to people, he gains prestige over them. The recipient, later will make a return gift of somewhat greater value: "One of the most striking features of the moka is the basic rule that to make moka one must give more than one has received. It is strictly the increment that entitles a man to say he has made moka" (Strathern 1971:216). The exchanges continue to go back and forth, over the years. The more one gives, and the more people in one's exchange network, the greater prestige the big-man develops. Degrees of big-manship exist throughout the Pacific region. In the Mt. Hagen region, there are "minor big-men" and "major big-men."

Strictly speaking, big-manship is an achieved position. However, analysis of the family patterns of big-manship in the Mt. Hagen area shows that most big-men are the sons of big-men. This is especially true of major big-men, of whom over three-quarters were sons of former big-men. It is unclear whether this pattern is the result of the greater wealth and prestige of big-man families to begin with, socialization into big-manship through paternal example, or a combination of these aspects. This is what the Hageners have to say about sons of big-men and their political chances:

> The sons of a big-man may emulate him. We watch them as they grow up, and see if they are going to be big-men or not. Promising boys are those who speak well, learn quickly to make exchanges and to ask for things, and whose eyes are like a pig's, taking in everything around them...it may turn out to be any one or none of a big-man's sons who will themselves become big-men. We decide by the skill they show in moka and speaking (208–209).

Table 9.1 Family Background of Big-Men in Mt. Hagen, Papua New Guinea

	Father was a big man	Father was not a big man	Totals
Major big-men	27	9	36
Minor big-men	31	30	61
Total	58	39	97

Big-Woman Leadership

With few exceptions, the early anthropological literature about Melanesian tribal politics portrays men as dominating public exchange networks and the public political arenas. Women as wives are mentioned as being important in providing the material basis for men's political careers. Maria Lepowsky's (1990, 1993) study of Vanatinai, a Pacific island which is gender-egalitarian, reveals the existence of big-women as well as big-men. In this culture, both men and women can gain power and prestige by sponsoring feasts at which valuables are distributed, especially mortuary feasts (feasts for the dead):

> On Vanatinai, any individual, male or female, may choose to exert the extra effort to go beyond the minimum contributions to the mortuary feasts expected of every adult. He or she accumulates ceremonial valuables and other goods both in order to give them away in acts of public generosity and to honor obligations to exchange partners from the local area as well as distant islands. These people are the giagia...

> A woman may have considerably more prestige and influence than her husband due to her reputation for acquiring and redistributing valuables. There are more men than women who are extremely active in ceremonial exchange, but there are also some women who are far more active in exchange and feasting than the majority of men.... Vanatinai women may lead expeditions by sailing canoes to distant islands to visit their exchange partners, who are both male and female....Women as well as men host mortuary feasts, mobilizing kin, affines, and exchange partners to plant extra large yam gardens to feed guests sumptuously. (41–42)

As in other parts of Melanesia, exchanging and feasting are not the only paths to power and leadership roles. On Vanatinai, big-women also include powerful sorcerers, famous healers, and successful gardeners. Sometimes these people are also giagia, big-women who accumulate wealth and redistribute valuables, and sometimes they are not.

Contact with European colonial culture gave men a political edge that they had not had before on Vanatinai. The Europeans traded with men for goods and approached the women only for sexual relations. Formal government councils were established. Thus far, councilors from Vanatinai have all been male. Many officials from outside the area have a more patriarchal tradition and wish to deal with men only. In addition, some Vanatinai men have received some training in the English language, the language of government, and thus have another advantage. In other cases, European domination led to more political equality between men and women with the imposition of "pacification," which ended local warfare and thereby eliminated traditional paths to power for men.

CHIEFDOMS

A **chiefdom** is a political grouping of permanently allied tribes and villages under one recognized leader. Compared to most tribes, chiefdoms have larger populations, often numbering in the thousands, and are more centralized and socially complex. Heritable systems of social ranking and economic stratification are found in chiefdoms (Earle 1991) with social divisions existing between the chiefly lineage or lineages and non-chiefly groups. Chiefs and their descendants are considered to be superior to commoners, and intermarriage between the two strata is forbidden. Chiefs are expected to be generous, but they may have a more luxurious lifestyle than the rest of the people; they are not simply a "first among equals." The chiefship is an "office" that must be filled at all times. When a chief dies or retires, he or she must be replaced. In contrast, the death of a band leader or big-man or big-woman does not require that someone else be chosen as a replacement. A chief has more responsibilities than a band or tribal leader. He or she regulates production and redistribution, solves internal conflicts, and plans and leads raids and warring expeditions. Criteria for coming a chief are more clearly defined. Besides ascribed criteria (birth in a chiefly lineage, or being first son or daughter of the chief), achievement is still important. Achievement is measured in terms of personal leadership skills, charisma, and accumulated wealth. Chiefdoms have existed in many places, including the Ashanti of West Africa and the Cahokia chiefdom in the area of present-day St. Louis, Missouri.

Anthropologists and archaeologists are interested in how and why chiefdom systems evolved as an intermediary unit between tribes and states, and what the political implications of this evolution are (Earle 1991). Several political strategies support the expansion of power in chiefdoms: controlling more internal and external wealth and distributing feasting and gift exchanges that create debt ties; improving local production systems; applying force internally; forging stronger and wider external ties; and controlling ideological legitimacy. Research on many chiefdoms historically and in contemporary times shows that depending on local conditions, different strategies were employed. Internal control of irrigation systems was the most important factor in the emergence of chiefdoms in prehistoric southeastern Spain, while control of external trade was more important in the prehistoric Aegean region (Gilman 1991).

Gender and Leadership

Much evidence about leadership patterns in chiefdoms comes from historical examples. Prominent chiefs—men and women—are documented in colonial archives and missionary records. Many historic examples of women chiefs and women rulers come from West Africa, including the Queen Mother of the Ashanti of Ghana and of the Edo of Nigeria (Awe 1977). Oral histories and archival records show that Yoruba women had the institution of the *iyalode*, chief of the women. The iyalode was the women's political spokesperson in the "council of kingmakers," the highest level of government. She was a chief in her own right, with chiefly insignia including the necklace of special beads, wide-brimmed straw hat, shawl, personal servants, special drummers, and bell ringers. She had her own council of subordinate chiefs. The position of iyalode was completely based on achievement. The most important qualifications were her proven ability as a leader, economic resources to maintain her new status as chief, and popularity. Tasks included dispute settlement in her court and meeting with women to formulate women's stands on such policy issues as the declaration of war and the opening of new markets. Although she represented all women in the group and had widespread support among women, she was outnumbered at the council of king-makers because she was the only female and the only representative of all women.

The Iroquois of central New York provide a case of women's political importance in other than chiefly roles (J. K. Brown 1975). Men were chiefs, but women and men councilors were the appointing body. Most adult males were away for extended periods, waging long-distance war as far away as Delaware and Virginia. Women controlled production and distribution of the staple crop, maize. If the women did not want warriors to leave for a particular campaign, they would refuse to provide them with maize, thereby vetoing the plan. Some have said that the Iroquois are an example of a **matriarchy**, or a society in which women are dominant in terms of economics, politics, and ideology. But most anthropologists would agree that the Iroquois are better characterized as an egalitarian society, since women did not control the society to the exclusion of men nor did they oppress men as a group. Men and women participated equally on the councils.

Why do women play greater political roles in some chiefdoms than others? The most successful answers point to women's economic roles as the primary basis for political power, as among the Iroquois and many African horticultural societies. In contrast, the dominant economic role of men in Native American groups of the prairies, following the introduction of the horse by the Spanish and the increased importance of buffalo hunting by men, supported male-dominated political leadership in such groups as the Cheyenne.

A marked change in leadership patterns in chiefdoms in the past few hundred years is the decline of women's political status due to European and North American colonial and missionary influences (Etienne and Leacock 1980). For example, British colonialists redefined the institution of iyalode in Nigeria. Now "she is no longer a member of any of the important councils of government. Even the market, and therefore the market women, have been removed from her jurisdiction, and have been placed under the control of the new local government councils in each town" (146). Ethnohistorical research on chiefdoms in Hawaii provides another view of formerly powerful women chiefs (Linnekan 1990). Following Captain Cook's arrival in 1778, a Western-model monarchy was established. By the time the United States annexed the islands in 1898, indigenous Hawaiian leaders had been displaced by westerners.

Confederacies

An expanded version of the chiefdom occurs when several chiefdoms are joined in a confederacy, headed by a chief of chiefs, "big chief," or paramount chief. Many prominent confederacies have existed, for example, in Hawaii in the late 1700s, and in North America, the Iroquois league of five nations that stretched across New York state, the Cherokee of Tennessee, and the Algonquins who dominated the Chesapeake region in present-day Virginia and Maryland. In the Algonquin confederacy, each village had a chief, and the regional council was composed of local chiefs and headed by the paramount chief. Powhatan, father of Pocahontas, was paramount chief of the Algonquins when the British arrived in the early 1600s. Confederacies were supported financially by contributions of grain from each local unit. Kept in a central storage area where the paramount chief lives, the grain was used to feed warriors during external warfare that both maintained and expanded the confederacy's borders. A council building existed in the central location, where local chiefs came together to meet with the paramount chief to deliberate on questions of internal and external policy.

STATES

A **state** is a centralized political unit encompassing many communities and possessing coercive power. Earliest evidence of the state form of political organization comes from Mesopotamia, China, India, and Egypt, perhaps as early as 4000 BCE. States emerged in these several locations with the development of intensive agriculture, increased surpluses, and increased population density. The state is now the form of political organization in which all people live. Band organizations, tribes, and chiefdoms still exist, but they are incorporated, to a greater or lesser degree, within state structures.

Origins of the State

Many theories exist for why the state evolved (Trigger 1996). Demographic theory says that population density drove the need for central mechanisms for social control. Economic theory argues that the state emerged in response to the increased surpluses of food production in the neolithic era, which produced sufficient wealth to support a permanent ruling class. Political theory says that the state arose as a necessary structure to manage increases as competition for land and access to food surpluses. Marxist theory says that the state emerged to maintain ruling-class dominance.

Rather than emphasizing a single causal factor, most scholars now include multiple causes in their theories. Another development is that scholars have moved from the "why" question to the "how" question (Trigger 1996). New areas of inquiry include the state's increased bases for central power, such as finances and information management.

Powers of the State

The state and its leaders have much more power and responsibility than leaders of other categories of political organization. The increased powers of the state include:

- *States define citizenship and its rights and responsibilities.* In complex nations, since early times, not all residents were granted equal rights as citizens.

- *States monopolize the use of force and the maintenance of law and order.* Internally, the state controls the population through laws, courts, and the police. Externally, the state uses force to defend the nation's borders and offensively to extend territory.

- *States maintain standing armies and police* (as opposed to part-time forces).

- *States keep track of their citizens in terms of number, age, gender, location, and wealth through census systems that are regularly updated.* A census allows the state to maintain formal taxation systems, military recruitment, and policy planning such as population settlement, immigration quotas, and social benefits such as old-age pensions.

- *States have the power to extract resources from citizens through taxation.* All political organizations are supported by contributions of the members, but variations occur in the rate of contributions expected, the form in which they are paid, and the return that members get in terms of services. In bands, people voluntarily give time or labor for "public projects" such as a group hunt or a planned move. Public finance in states is based on formal taxation that takes many forms. **In-kind taxation** is a system of mandatory, non-cash contributions to the state. For example, the Inca state used the *corvee*, a labor tax, to finance public works such as roads and monuments and to provide agricultural labor on state lands. Another form of in-kind taxation in early states required that farmers pay a percentage of their crop yield. Cash taxes, such as the income tax that takes a percentage of wage, emerged only in the past few hundred years.

- *States manipulate information.* Control of information to protect the state and its leaders can be done directly through censorship and restricting access to certain information by the public and promotion of favorable images through propaganda, and indirectly through pressure on journalists and television networks to present information in certain ways.

POLITICAL ORGANIZATION

E X E R C I S E

EXERCISE 9.1: GENDER AND ECONOMICS

Economic anthropologists have recognized two trends in the American business world. The first is known as the **glass ceiling**. This refers to the fact that women often can only reach a certain level in management, and cannot progress any farther, regardless of skills and training. While this is slowly changing, women are still earning about $.80 to each male's dollar earning potential.

The second trend is known as the **glass elevator**. This concept refers to the fact that males are often depicted as taking a quick ride straight to the top of the business world. Again, regardless of skill, males seem to be on the fast track to success more frequently than their female counterparts.

Part 1

Since the 1980s, women have begun to move into high-rank positions in smaller companies, while men continue to fill the boardrooms in larger corporations. While this statement may be a generalization, what are your thoughts on the subject? Support your response with the facts supplied in class readings and discussions.

How does the media portray males and females in the business world? How realistic are these media portrayals and how do they shape our views of the differing social classes in the United States?

Part 2

Search the Internet for five large companies in the United States owned and managed by males. List them below. Then do the same exercise for companies owned and managed by females. Is it harder to find examples of women-operated businesses than for males?

(continued on the next page)

347

POLITICAL ORGANIZATION

According to your Internet search, are business strategies different for the males versus the females in terms of their leadership styles?

Should sex determine one's professional rank? What role does culture play in your investigation of business executives?

Part 3

If both parents work, who is generally expected to care for the home and the children? Why is this so?

Recent studies suggest that females perceive themselves as needing to deal with more pressures than males due to the numerous roles they play daily—including worker, mother, wife, caregiver, chauffeur, friend, etc. Do you agree with this analysis? Why or why not?

White Privilege and Male Privilege: A Personal Account of Coming to See Correspondences through Work in Women's Studies—
Peggy McIntosh

Through work to bring materials and perspectives from Women's Studies into the rest of the curriculum, have often noticed men's unwillingness to grant that they are overprivileged in the curriculum, even though they may grant that women are disadvantaged. Denials that amount to taboos surround the subject of advantages that men gain from women's disadvantages. These denials protect male privilege from being fully recognized, acknowledged, lessened, or ended.

Thinking through unacknowledged male privilege as a phenomenon with a life of its own, I realized that since hierarchies in our society are interlocking, there was most likely a phenomenon of white privilege that was similarly denied and protected, but alive and real in its effects. As a white person, I realized I had been taught about racism as something that puts others at a disadvantage, but had been taught not to see one of its corollary aspects, white privilege, which puts me at an advantage.

I think whites are carefully taught not to recognize white privilege, as males are taught not to recognize male privilege. So I have begun in an untutored way to ask what it is like to have white privilege. This paper is a partial record of my personal observations and not a scholarly analysis. It is based on my daily experiences within my particular circumstances.

I have come to see white privilege as an invisible package of unearned assets that I can count on cashing in each day, but about which I was "meant" to remain oblivious. White privilege is like an invisible weightless knapsack of special provisions, assurances, tools, maps, guides, codebooks, passports, visas, clothes, compass, emergency gear, and blank checks.

Since I have had trouble facing white privilege, and describing its results in my life, I saw parallels here with men's reluctance to acknowledge male privilege. Only rarely will a man go beyond acknowledging that women are disadvantaged to acknowledging that men have unearned advantage, or that unearned privilege has not been good for men's development as human beings, or for society's development, or that privilege systems might ever be challenged and *changed*.

I will review here several types or layers of denial that I see at work protecting, and preventing awareness about, entrenched male privilege. Then I will draw parallels, from my own experience, with the denials that veil the facts of white privilege. Finally, I will list forty-six ordinary and daily ways in which I experience having white privilege, by contrast with my African American colleagues in the same building. This list is not intended to be generalizable. Others can make their own lists from within their own life circumstances.

Writing this paper has been difficult, despite warm receptions for the talks on which it is based.[1] For describing white privilege makes one newly accountable. As we in Women's Studies work reveal male privilege and ask men to give up some of their power, so one who writes about having white privilege must ask, "Having described it, what will I do to lessen or end it?"

The denial of men's overprivileged state takes many forms in discussions of curriculum change work. Some claim that men must be central in the curriculum because they have done most of what is important or distinctive in life or in civilization. Some recognize sexism in the curriculum but deny that it makes male students seem unduly important in life. Others agree that certain *individual* thinkers are male oriented but deny that there is any *systemic* tendency in disciplinary frameworks or epistemology to overempower men as a group. Those men who do grant that male privilege takes institutionalized and embedded forms are still likely to deny that male hegemony has opened doors for them personally. Virtually all men deny that male over-reward alone can explain men's centrality in all the inner sanctums of our most powerful institutions. Moreover, those few who will acknowledge that male privilege systems have overempowered them usually end up doubting that we could dismantle these privilege systems. They may say they will work to improve women's status, in the society or in the university, but they can't or won't support the idea of lessening men's. In curricular terms, this is the point at which they say that they regret they cannot use any of the interesting new scholarship on women because the syllabus is full. When the talk turns to giving men less cultural room, even the most thoughtful and fair-minded of the men I know will tend to reflect, or fall back on, conservative assumptions about the inevitability of present gender relations and distributions of power, calling on precedent or sociobiology and psychobiology to demonstrate that male domination is natural and follows inevitably from evolutionary pressures. Others resort to arguments from "experience" or religion or social responsibility or wishing and dreaming.

After I realized, through faculty development work in Women's Studies, the extent to which men work from a base of unacknowledged privilege, I understood that much of their oppressiveness was unconscious. Then I remembered the frequent charges from women of color that white women whom they encounter are oppressive. I began to understand why we are justly seen as oppressive, even when we don't see ourselves that way. At the very least, obliviousness of one's privileged state can make a person or group irritating to be with. I began to count the ways in which I enjoy unearned skin privilege and have been conditioned into oblivion about its existence, unable to see that it put me "ahead" in any way, or put my people ahead, overrewarding us and yet also paradoxically damaging us, or that it could or should be changed.

My schooling gave me no training in seeing myself as an oppressor, as an unfairly advantaged person, or as a participant in a damaged culture. I was taught to see myself as an individual whose moral state depended on her individual moral will. At school, we were not taught about slavery in any depth; we were not taught to see slaveholders as damaged people. Slaves were seen as the only group at risk of being dehumanized. My schooling followed the pattern which Elizabeth Minnich has pointed out: whites are taught to think of their lives as morally neutral, normative, and average, and also ideal, so that when we work to benefit others, this is seen as work that will allow "them" to be more like "us." I think many of us know how obnoxious this attitude can be in men.

After frustration with men who would not recognize male privilege, I decided to try to work on myself at least by identifying some of the daily effects of white privilege in my life. It is crude work, at this stage, but I will give here a list of special circumstances and conditions I experience that I did not earn but that I have been made to feel are mine by birth, by citizenship, and by virtue of being a conscientious law-abiding "normal" person of goodwill. I have chosen those conditions that I think in my case *attach somewhat more to skin-color privilege* than to class, religion, ethnic status, or geographical location, though these other privileging factors are intricately intertwined. As far as I can see, my Afro-American co-workers, friends, and acquaintances with whom I come into daily or frequent contact in this particular time, place, and line of work cannot count on most of these conditions.

1. I can, if I wish, arrange to be in the company of people of my race most of the time.

2. I can avoid spending time with people whom I was trained to mistrust and who have learned to mistrust my kind or more.

3. If I should need to move, I can be pretty sure of renting or purchasing housing in an area which I can afford and in which I would want to live.

4. I can be reasonably sure that my neighbors in such a location will be neutral or pleasant to me.

5. I can go shopping alone most of the time, fairly well assured that I will not be followed or harassed by store detectives.

6. I can turn on the television or open to the front page of the paper and see people of my race widely and positively represented.

7. When I am told about our national heritage or about "civilization," I am shown that people of my color made it what it is.

8. I can be sure that my children will be given curricular materials that testify to the existence of their race.

9. If I want to, I can be pretty sure of finding a publisher for this piece on white privilege.

10. I can be fairly sure of having my voice heard in a group in which l am the only member of my race.

11. I can be casual about whether or not to listen to another woman's voice in a group in which she is the only member of her race.

12. I can go into a book shop and count on finding the writing of my race represented, into a supermarket and find the staple foods that fit with my cultural traditions, into a hairdresser's shop and find someone who can deal with my hair.

13. Whether I use checks, credit cards, or cash, I can count on my skin color not to work against the appearance that I am financially reliable.

14. I could arrange to protect our young children most of the time from people who might not like them.

15. I did not have to educate our children to be aware of systemic racism for their own daily physical protection.

16. I can be pretty sure that my children's teachers and employers will tolerate them if they fit school and workplace norms; my chief worries about them do not concern others' attitudes toward their race.

17. I can talk with my mouth full and not have people put this down to my color.

18. I can swear, or dress in secondhand clothes, or not answer letters, without having people attribute these choices to the bad morals, the poverty, or the illiteracy of my race.

19. I can speak in public to a powerful male group without putting my race on trial.

20. I can do well in a challenging situation without being called a credit to my race.

21. I am never asked to speak for all the people of my racial group.

22. I can remain oblivious to the language and customs of persons of color who constitute the world's majority without feeling in my culture any penalty for such oblivion.

23. I can criticize our government and talk about how much I fear its policies and behavior without being seen as a cultural outsider.

24. I can be reasonably sure that if I ask to talk to "the person in charge," I will be facing a person of my race.

25. If a traffic cop pulls me over or if the IRS audits my tax return, I can be sure I haven't been singled out because of my race.

26. I can easily buy posters, postcards, picture books, greeting cards, dolls, toys, and children's magazines featuring people of my race.

27. I can go home from most meetings of organizations I belong to feeling somewhat tied in, rather than isolated, out of place, outnumbered, unheard, held at a distance, or feared.

28. I can be pretty sure that an argument with a colleague of another race is more likely to jeopardize her chances for advancement than to jeopardize mine.

29. I can be fairly sure that if I argue for the promotion of a person of another race, or a program centering on race, this is not likely to cost me heavily within my present setting, even if my colleagues disagree with me.

30. If I declare there is a racial issue at hand, or there isn't a racial issue at hand, my race will lend me more credibility for either position than a person of color will have.

31. I can choose to ignore developments in minority writing and minority activist programs, or disparage them, or learn from them, but in any case, I can find ways to be more or less protected from negative consequences of any of these choices.

32. My culture gives me little fear about ignoring the perspectives and powers of people of other races.

33. I am not made acutely aware that my shape, bearing, or body odor will be taken as a reflection on my race.

34. I can worry about racism without being seen as self-interested or self-seeking.

35. I can take a job with an affirmative action employer without having my co-workers on the job suspect that I got it because of my race.

36. If my day, week, or year is going badly, I need not ask of each negative episode or situation whether it has racial overtones.

37. I can be pretty sure of finding people who would be willing to talk with me and advise me about my next steps, professionally.

38. I can think over many options, social, political, imaginative, or professional, without asking whether a person of my race would be accepted or allowed to do what I want to do.

39. I can be late to a meeting without having the lateness reflect on my race.

40. I can choose public accommodation without fearing that people of my race cannot get in or will be mistreated in the places I have chosen.

41. I can be sure that if I need legal or medical help, my race will not work against me.

42. I can arrange my activities so that I will never have to experience feelings of rejection owing to my race.

43. If I have low credibility as a leader, I can be sure that my race is not the problem.

44. I can easily find academic courses and institutions that give attention only to people of my race.

45. I can expect figurative language and imagery in all of the arts to testify to experiences of my race.

46. I can choose blemish cover or bandages in "flesh" color and have them more or less match my skin.

I repeatedly forgot each of the realizations on this list until I wrote it down. For me, white privilege has turned out to be an elusive and fugitive subject. The pressure to avoid it is great, for in facing it I must give up the myth of meritocracy. If these things are true, this is not such a free country; one's life is not what one makes it; many doors open for certain people through no virtues of their own. These perceptions mean also that my moral condition is not what I had been led to believe. The appearance of being a good citizen rather than a troublemaker comes in large part from having all sorts of doors open automatically because of my color.

A further paralysis of nerve comes from literary silence protecting privilege. My clearest memories of finding such analysis are in Lillian Smith's unparalleled *Killers of the Dream* and Margaret Andersen's review of Karen and Mamie Fields' *Lemon Swamp*. Smith, for example, wrote about walking toward black children on the street and knowing they would step into the gutter; Andersen contrasted the pleasure that she, as a white child, took on summer driving trips to the south with Karen Fields' memories of driving in a closed car stocked with all necessities lest, in stopping, her black family should suffer "insult, or worse." Adrienne Rich also recognizes and writes about daily experiences of privilege, but in my observation, white women's writing in this area is far more often on systemic racism than on our daily lives as light-skinned women.[2]

In unpacking this invisible knapsack of white privilege, I have listed conditions of daily experience that I once took for granted, as neutral, normal, and universally available to everybody, just as I once thought of a male-focused curriculum as the neutral or accurate account that can speak for all. Nor did I think of any of these perquisites as bad for the holder. I now think that we need a more finely differentiated taxonomy of privilege, for some of these varieties are only what one would want for everyone in a just society, and others give license to be ignorant, oblivious, arrogant, and destructive. Before proposing some more finely tuned categorization, I will make some observations about the general effects of these conditions on my life and expectations.

In this potpourri of examples, some privileges make me feel at home in the world. Others allow me to escape penalties or dangers that others suffer. Through some, I escape fear, anxiety, insult, injury, or a sense of not being welcome, not being real. Some keep me from having to hide, to be in disguise, to feel sick or crazy, to negotiate each transaction from the position of being an outsider or, within my group, a person who is suspected of having too close links with a dominant culture. Most keep me from having to be angry.

I see a pattern running through the matrix of white privilege, a pattern of assumptions that were passed on to me as a white person. There was one main piece of cultural turf; it was my own turf, and I was among those who could control the turf. I could measure up to the cultural standards and take advantage of the many options I saw around me to make what the culture would call a success of my life. *My skin color was an asset for any move I was educated to want to make*. I could think of myself as "belonging" in major ways and of making social systems work for me. I could freely disparage, fear, neglect, or be oblivious to anything outside of the dominant cultural forms. Being of the main culture, I could also criticize it fairly freely. My life was reflected back to me frequently enough so that I felt, with regard to my race, if not to my sex, like one of the real people.

Whether through the curriculum or in the newspaper, the television, the economic system, or the general look of people in the streets, I received daily signals and indications that my people counted and that others *either didn't exist or must be trying, not very successfully, to be like people of my race*. I was given cultural permission not to hear voices of people of other races or a tepid cultural tolerance for hearing or acting on such voices. I was also raised not to suffer seriously from anything that darker-skinned people might say about my group, "protected," though perhaps I should more accurately say *prohibited*, through the habits of my economic class and social group, from living in racially mixed groups or being reflective about interactions between people of differing races.

In proportion as my racial group was being made confident, comfortable, and oblivious, other groups were likely being made unconfident, uncomfortable, and alienated. Whiteness protected me from many kinds of hostility, distress, and violence, which I was being subtly trained to visit in turn upon people of color.

For this reason, the word "privilege" now seems to me misleading. Its connotations are too positive to fit the conditions and behaviors which "privilege systems" produce. We usually think of privilege as being a favored state, whether earned, or conferred by birth or luck. School graduates are reminded they are privileged and urged to use their (enviable) assets well. The word "privilege" carries the connotation of being something everyone must want. Yet some of the conditions I have described here work to systemically overempower certain groups. Such privilege simply *confers dominance*, gives permission to control, because of one's race or sex. The kind of privilege that gives license to some people to be, at best, thoughtless and, at worst, murderous should not continue to be referred to as a desirable attribute. Such "privilege" may be widely desired without being in any way beneficial to the whole society.

Moreover, though "privilege" may confer power, it does not confer moral strength. Those who do not depend on conferred dominance have traits and qualities that may never develop in those who do. Just as Women's Studies courses indicate that women survive their political circumstances to lead lives that hold the human race together, so "underprivileged" people of color who are the world's majority have survived their oppression and lived survivors' lives from which the white global minority can and must learn. In some groups, those dominated have actually become strong through *not* having all of these unearned advantages, and this gives them a great deal to teach the others. Members of so-called privileged groups can seem foolish, ridiculous, infantile, or dangerous by contrast.

I want, then, to distinguish between earned strength and unearned power conferred systemically. Power from unearned privilege can look like strength when it is, in fact, permission to escape or to dominate. But not all of the privileges on my list are inevitably damaging. Some, like the expectation that neighbors will be decent to you, or that your race will not count against you in court, should be the norm in a just society and should be considered as the entitlement of everyone. Others, like the privilege not to listen to less powerful people, distort the humanity of the holders as well as the ignored groups. Still others, like finding one's staple foods everywhere, may be a function of being a member of a numerical majority in the population. Others have to do with not having to labor under pervasive negative stereotyping and mythology.

We might at least start by distinguishing between positive advantages that we can work to spread, to the point where they are not advantages at all but simply part of the normal civic and social fabric, and negative types of advantage that unless rejected will always reinforce our present hierarchies. For example, the positive "privilege" of belonging, the feeling that one belongs within the human circle, as Native Americans say, fosters development and should not be seen as privilege for a few. It is, let us say, an entitlement that none of us should have to earn; ideally it is an *unearned entitlement*. At present, since only a few have it, it is an *unearned advantage* for them. The negative "privilege" that gave me cultural permission not to take darker-skinned. Others seriously can be seen as arbitrarily conferred dominance and should not be desirable for anyone. This paper results from a process of coming to see that some of the power that I originally saw as attendant on being a human being in the United States consisted in *unearned advantage* and *conferred dominance*, as well as other kinds of special circumstance not universally taken for granted.

In writing this paper I have also realized that white identity and status (as well as class identity and status) give me considerable power to choose whether to broach this subject and its trouble. I can pretty well decide whether to disappear and avoid and not listen and escape the dislike I may engender in other people through this essay, or interrupt, answer, interpret, preach, correct, criticize, and control to some extent what goes on in reaction to it. Being white, I am given considerable power to escape many kinds of danger or penalty as well as to choose which risks I want to take.

There is an analogy here, once again, with Women's Studies. Our male colleagues do not have a great deal to lose in supporting Women's Studies, but they do not have a great deal to lose if they oppose it either. They simply have the power to decide whether to commit themselves to more

equitable distributions of power. They will probably feel few penalties whatever choice they make; they do not seem, in any obvious short-term sense, the ones at risk, though they and we are all at risk because of the behaviors that have been rewarded in them.

Through Women's Studies work I have met very few men who are truly distressed about systemic, unearned male advantage and conferred dominance. And so one question for me and others like me is whether we will be like them, or whether we will get truly distressed, even outraged, about unearned race advantage and conferred dominance and if so, what we will do to lessen them. In any case, we need to do more work in identifying how they actually affect our daily lives. We need more down-to-earth writing by people about these taboo subjects. We need more understanding of the ways in which white "privilege" damages white people, for these are not the same ways in which it damages the victimized. Skewed white psyches are an inseparable part of the picture, though I do not want to confuse the kinds of damage done to the holders of special assets and to those who suffer the deficits. Many, perhaps most, of our white students in the United States think that racism doesn't affect them because they are not people of color; they do not see "whiteness" as a racial identity. Many men likewise think that Women's Studies does not bear on their own existences because they are not female; they do not see themselves as having gendered identities. Insisting on the universal "effects" of "privilege" systems, then, becomes one of our chief tasks, and being more explicit about the *particular* effects in particular contexts is another. Men need to join us in this work.

In addition, since race and sex are not the only advantaging systems at work, we need to similarly examine the daily experience of having age advantage, or ethnic advantage, or physical ability, or advantage related to nationality, religion, or sexual orientation. Professor Marnie Evans suggested to me that in many ways the list I made also applies directly to heterosexual privilege. This is a still more taboo subject than race privilege: the daily ways in which heterosexual privilege makes some persons comfortable or powerful, providing supports, assets, approvals, and rewards to those who live or expect to live in heterosexual pairs. Unpacking that content is still more difficult, owing to the deeper imbeddedness of heterosexual advantage and dominance and stricter taboos surrounding these.

But to start such an analysis I would put this observation from my own experience: the fact that I live under the same roof with a man triggers all kinds of societal assumptions about my worth, politics, life, and values and triggers a host of unearned advantages and powers. After recasting many elements from the original list I would add further observations like these:

1. My children do not have to answer questions about why I live with my partner (my husband).

2. I have no difficulty finding neighborhoods where people approve of our household.

3. Our children are given texts and classes that implicitly support our kind of family unit and do not turn them against my choice of domestic partnership.

4. I can travel alone or with my husband without expecting embarrassment or hostility in those who deal with us.

5. Most people I meet will see my marital arrangements as an asset to my life or as a favorable comment on my likability, my competence, or my mental health.

6. I can talk about the social events of a weekend without fearing most listeners' reactions.

7. I will feel welcomed and "normal" in the usual walks of public life, institutional and social.

8. In many contexts, I am seen as "all right" in daily work on women because I do not live chiefly with women.

Difficulties and dangers surrounding the task of finding parallels are many. Since racism, sexism, and heterosexism are not the same, the advantages associated with them should not be seen as the same. In addition, it is hard to isolate aspects of unearned advantage that derive chiefly from social class, economic class, race, religion, region, sex, or ethnic identity. The oppressions are both distinct and interlocking, as the Combahee River Collective statement of 1977 continues to remind us eloquently.[3]

One factor seems clear about all of the interlocking oppressions. They take both active forms that we can see and embedded forms that members of the dominant group are taught not to see. In my class and place, I did not see myself as racist because I was taught to recognize racism only in individual acts of meanness by members of my group, never in invisible systems conferring racial dominance on my group from birth. Likewise, we are taught to think that sexism or heterosexism is carried on only through intentional, individual acts of discrimination, meanness, or cruelty, rather than in invisible systems conferring unsought dominance on certain groups. Disapproving of the systems won't be enough to change them. I was taught to think that racism could end if white individuals changed their attitudes; many men think sexism can be ended by individual changes in daily behavior toward women. But a man's sex provides advantage for him whether or not he approves of the way in which dominance has been conferred on his group. A "white" skin in the United States opens many doors for whites whether or not we approve of the way dominance has been conferred on us. Individual acts can palliate, but cannot end, these problems. To redesign social systems, we need first to acknowledge their colossal unseen dimensions. The silences and denials surrounding privilege are the key political tool here. They keep the thinking about equality or equity incomplete, protecting unearned advantage and conferred dominance by making these taboo subjects. Most talk by whites about equal opportunity seems to me now to be about equal opportunity to try to get into a position of dominance while denying that *systems* of dominance exist.

Obliviousness about white advantage, like obliviousness about male advantage, is kept strongly enculturated in the United States so as to maintain the myth of meritocracy, the myth that democratic choice is equally available to all. Keeping most people unaware that freedom of confident action is there for just a small number of people props up those in power and serves to keep power in the hands of the same groups that have most of it already. Though systemic change takes many decades, there are pressing questions for me and I imagine for some others like me if we raise our daily consciousness on the prerequisites of being light-skinned. What will we do with such knowledge? As we know from watching men, it is an open question whether we will choose to use unearned advantage to weaken invisible privilege systems and whether we will use any of our arbitrarily awarded power to try to reconstruct power systems on a broader base.

NOTES

1. This paper was presented at the Virginia Women's Studies Association conference in Richmond in April, 1986, and the American Education Research Association conference in Boston in October, 1986, and discussed with two groups of participants in the Dodge seminars for Secondary School Teachers in New York and Boston in the spring of 1987.

2. Andersen, Margaret, "Race and the Social Science Curriculum: A Teaching and Learning Discussion." *Radical Teacher*, November, 1984, pp. 17–20. Smith, Lillian, *Killers of the Dream*, New York: W. W. Norton, 1949.

3. "A Black Feminist Statement," The Combahee River Collective, pp. 13–22 in G. Hull, P. Scott, B. Smith, Eds., *All Women Are White, All the Blacks Are Men, But Some of Us Are Brave: Black Women's Studies*, Old Westbury, NY: The Feminist Press, 1982.

E X E R C I S E

Name

Section

Date

EXERCISE 9.2: PRIVILEGES

Write five privileges you have due to your race, ethnicity, religion, age, sex, gender, and/or sexuality

1.

2.

3.

4.

5.

Write five disadvantages you have due to your race, ethnicity, religion, age, sex, gender, and/or sexuality

1.

2.

3.

4.

5.

Write two paragraphs answering the following questions:

What do you think these privileges and disadvantages mean to your life experiences and opportunities? What does it mean to your "group" (i.e., race, ethnicity, religion, age, sex, gender, sexuality)? What does it mean to Americans?

POLITICAL ORGANIZATION

ANTHROPOLOGISTS AND THE LAW:
Culture and Culpability: A Study of Contrasts—
Allison Renteln

In a pluralistic society it is common to encounter "**culture conflict**." When new citizens arrive, they bring with them legal standards which may differ significantly from those of their new homeland. The question which inevitably arises is whether or not the new citizens should be held criminally liable for conduct which violates American law. Is it justifiable to punish a person in the United States for engaging in activities which were customary in his or her country of origin? This kind of situation in which multiple legal systems are to be found is called legal pluralism. It is the conflict among the various systems that has given rise to a theory of criminal responsibility known as the **cultural defense**.

This article concentrates on some of the conceptual problems associated with the cultural defense. In particular I will take the view that: (1) the ideology of cultural pluralism does not require the adoption of the cultural defense, (2) mechanisms already exist within the American legal system which can take culture into account, and (3) the consequences of utilizing the cultural defense would be highly undesirable. The cultural defense will be discussed in the context of the United States and of other countries by examining selected cases. Some analysis of the problems in general will be made, paying attention to the distinction between immigrants and indigenous peoples. Although there are many types of crimes for which the cultural defense might be used, such as polygamy in nations that permit only monogamy, the analysis below will focus primarily on cases involving homicide. While cultural sensitivity is arguably an admirable posture, pluralism (actually relativism) does not require the rejection of one's own legal standards. Ultimately, it appears that the cultural defense is a dangerous and unnecessary doctrine.

UNITED STATES CASES—IMMIGRANTS

Two factors appear to be primarily responsible for the recent (1980s) resurgence of interest in the cultural defense. The first is the unusually large influx of (mainly Southeast) Asians into the United States, especially Southern California. The second is the highly publicized case of *People v. Kimura*.[1] This case illustrates not only the context in which the cultural defense has been considered as a pos-

sible device for denying responsibility for criminal action but also the way in which American commentators have misinterpreted cultural differences.

Fumiko Kimura discovered that her husband had deceived her by keeping a mistress and had thus shamed the family. On January 29,1985, she attempted to commit *oyako-shinju*, the Japanese custom of parent-child suicide. She took her two children, a daughter, Yuri, six months old, and her son, Kazutaka, four years old, on a bus ride from their Los Angeles home to the beach in Santa Monica. Then, carrying Yuri and leading Kazutaka by the hand, she walked into the ocean. This was a culturally accepted course of action in the Japanese tradition, not to leave the children behind to bear the shame alone. Although onlookers on the shore managed to rescue Kimura, her two children died.

The district attorney charged Kimura with first-degree murder in their deaths. Four thousand members of the Los Angeles Japanese-American community signed a petition stating that her act would not be treated as murder in Japan and urging officials to apply modern Japanese law. This would mean charging her with involuntary manslaughter at most. The district attorney refused the request, however, and left a first degree murder charge in place which could have brought the death penalty. The district attorney rejected the use of Japanese law but indicated that Kimura's background could, in fact, be taken into account in determining her mental state at the time of the incident. The crime itself could not be mitigated by legal or cultural standards from another country.

The issue was whether or not a person from another culture should be judged according to standards other than those in force in the United States. Kimura's attorney evidently considered but chose not to use the cultural defense. Interestingly, he relied instead on testimony from six psychiatrists to show that Kimura was "ill" and "mentally deranged," and therefore lacked the intent necessary for first degree murder because the element of malice was absent. A plea bargain ultimately reduced the charge to voluntary manslaughter, and Kimura received five years probation, intensive psychiatric treatment and one year in the county jail (with credit for time already served). It is hard to say whether it was culture or (attributed) insanity which helped change her fate.

Several observations are in order. First, Kimura's act is not legally acceptable in Japan. It is simply more culturally acceptable. Even in Japan, ritual parent-child suicide is still a crime. The culture conflict here is not based on an act which is entirely legitimate in country A but illegal in country B. Rather, the conflict is over the proportionality, *i.e.*, what is the appropriate punishment which corresponds to the crime. Second, even though the defense attorney did not explicitly invoke the cultural defense, the fact that there was a plea bargain suggests that culture was taken into account to some extent. Third, the legal system, as exemplified in this case, treats the logic of another culture as analogous to insanity. Kimura was ordered to undergo intensive psychiatric counseling. In spite of the absence of a formal cultural defense, Kimura's cultural background was influential in determining the disposition of her case. She was treated with compassion though as if mentally disturbed. Finally, Kimura raises another issue worthy of consideration. For what period of time would a "new" citizen be permitted to avail herself of the cultural defense? Would it be necessary to establish a "presumption" of assimilation after a specified period of time elapsed? Kimura herself had lived in the United States for nine years but had not become fully "Americanized" because she had remained extremely isolated.

UNITED STATES CASES—REFUGEES

Refugees arriving in the United States from other countries have had their share of legal problems. In some instances they commit acts that are not considered crimes in their native lands but which violate American law.

In the last several years almost thirty thousand Hmong, a people from Laos, have settled in the area of Fresno, California. Some of their traditions involve activities which are illegal here, such as polygamy and the use of opium. The Hmong also have a habit of butchering pigs in their backyards in violation of local ordinances. It seems that, among other things, the pigs' squealing disturbs the neighbors.

A more serious matter concerns a practice called *zij poj niam* which, loosely translated, means marriage by capture. *People v. Moua*[2] centered on the interpretation of the traditional courtship ritual among the Hmong. According to custom, there is an exchange of gifts between the man and the woman who are to be married. It is expected that

the man will exercise his right to abduct his chosen bride and then consummate the marriage at his family's home. Custom requires that the woman display resistance by weeping and moaning and declaring that she is not ready. Otherwise, she will not appear virtuous enough. The man is supposed to show force or else he will not appear strong enough. After the event, the woman is viewed as "unmarriagable" by other Hmong men.

In this case Kong Moua followed custom but his "wife," Xeng Xiong, an "Americanized" nineteen-year-old, rejected tradition and called the police. Consequently, Moua was charged with kidnapping and rape but these charges were dropped when he agreed to plead guilty to a misdemeanor charge of false inprisonment. After hearing testimony about traditional Laotian marriage rituals and after reviewing a doctoral dissertation on the subject, the judge reduced the sentence for Moua from 180 days to 90 days.[3] Some have claimed that the judge implicitly recognized the cultural defense.[4]

Even though the cultural defense was not officially used, it appears that culture played a role in this case. The rule in American law is that if a reasonable, good faith belief in the woman's consent was evident, the act would not constitute rape. This means that although the conduct may not be excused because it is motivated by cultural tradition, it is possible that the motivation may be relevant in establishing the defendant's state of mind.[5] Culture served not to absolve Moua of responsibility altogether but to mitigate the sentence, as in *Kimura*.

We can see the undeniable influence of enculturation and the power of moral injunction in another case, also called *People v. Moua*.[6] In this case, a Hmong man by the name of Tou Moua killed his wife when he learned that she planned to take a job working for another man. Evidently, this is an act tantamount to adultery in Hmong culture. Moua's defense attorney explained that in his culture a wife's adultery is punishable by death and that it was "culturally demanded that he [Moua] execute justice, even if it meant his own personal pain and personal loss to do so."[7] Moua's attorney argued for a mitigation of the sentence because of the cultural circumstances involved. The sentencing judge denied the request, however, and sentenced the defendant to eight years in prison.

BELIEF/ACTION DISTINCTION

While the American ideology of cultural tolerance has instructed citizens to respect different ways of life, there is a longstanding commitment in the American legal system to a belief/action distinction. As early as 1879 in *Reynolds v. US*,[8] the Supreme Court refused to overturn a conviction for bigamy where this was mandated by the defendant's religious beliefs. The court held that to allow such an excuse of illegal conduct would be:

> ...to make the professed doctrines of religious belief superior to the law of the land, and in effect to permit every citizen to become a law unto himself. Government could exist only in name under such circumstances.[9]

Not only have Mormons been denied the right to have polygamous marriages, but Jehovah's Witnesses have been compelled by the law to have blood transfusions.[10] In the case of *In re Application of Jamaica Hospital*[11] the court ordered a competent adult woman who was eighteen weeks pregnant and suffering from internal bleeding to accept blood transfusions for the sake of her fetus. Because she was a Jehovah's Witness, a religious group which believes that the Scriptures forbid "drinking blood" and that receiving a blood transfusion is the equivalent of "drinking blood," she refused on religious grounds. But the court held: "The state has a highly significant interest in protecting the life of a mid-term fetus, which outweighs the patient's right to refuse a blood transfusion on religious grounds."[12]

The law will reject or require actions based on beliefs if they lead to harming others. In the case just mentioned the court was willing to intervene when the one at risk was a previable fetus. In another case a court ordered a woman to undergo childbirth by Cesarean section when she refused on religious grounds.[13] The physician had predicted that a vaginal delivery would have a 99% risk of the infant dying and a 50% chance for the mother. After the court order was issued, she fled and gave birth to a healthy child a few days later, uneventfully without intervention.[14]

Snake-handling for religious purposes has also been denied by the courts.[15] In *Swann v. Pack*,[16] for example, the Supreme Court of Tennessee held that the handling of dangerous and poisonous snakes in a crowded church (with virtually no safeguards and with children roaming around unattended and with handlers in trances) meant that the Pastor had, in fact, committed a public nuisance.

The Court remanded the case so that the trial court could enter an injunction perpetually enjoining and restraining all parties from handling snakes. Although the Court recognized that the decision would impose stringent limitations on a religious practice,[17] it concluded that "paramount considerations of public policy" precluded less stringent solutions.

The courts have been unwilling to allow drug use for religious rites. The freedom to believe is virtually absolute whereas the freedom to act is not. This distinction is central to the analysis of the cultural defense. Cultural pluralism encourages us to recognize the existence of other value-systems but does not force us to relinquish our own standards for judging action. Even where an action is arguably an integral part of the belief system, the legal system has consistently acted to sustain its own legitimacy.

IGNORANCE OF THE LAW IS NO EXCUSE

Some of the opponents of the cultural defense base their argument on the traditional maxim—ignorance of the law—the mistaken belief that one's conduct is lawful—is no excuse for criminal behavior. They maintain that the court should not create an exception to this rule because of cultural differences. The notion that the cultural defense depends on ignorance suggests that there is a lack of understanding as to the basic premise of the defense. The cultural defense does not presuppose ignorance of the law. Even if the defendants are aware of American legal standards, their cultural conditioning is so powerful that they cannot discard their own standards in favor of American ones. Enculturation shapes their perceptions to such an extent that they cannot readily embrace those of another culture.

In the cases already discussed, it was apparent that the lawyers were not arguing on the basis of ignorance. The prosecutors and judges were not asked to excuse the defendants because they did not comprehend that their actions were considered criminal in the eyes of Americans. The point of the cultural defense is to recognize that the power of enculturation makes it exceedingly difficult for someone from another culture to make his conduct conform to standards of the dominant American culture. The underlying notion is that a person's criminal behavior should be judged according to the legal standards of his or her culture.

POLITICAL ORGANIZATION

GOVERNMENTAL RESPONSIBILITY

Since the government arranged to bring refugees to the United States, one could advance the argument that the government is responsible for ensuring that new citizens become familiar with particularly important American laws. When it becomes known that certain communities, e.g., the Hmong, engage in activities which are not compatible with American legal standards, then there is all the more reason to expect the government to establish some form of educational programs. Even though the cultural defense does not depend on ignorance, in some instances ignorance may be a factor. Moreover, even where refugees are cognizant of American crimes, they may not be as fully aware of the punishments which they face for violation. When the American government brings a large refugee population within its borders, it bears some measure of responsibility for providing information about American customs and laws.

In some cases the duty to inform may turn out to be problematic. There may not be any words or concepts in the language of the new group which can capture the idea of the American crime. And besides technical difficulties the government has to contend with the negative symbolic dimensions, specifically of having Americans trying to indoctrinate newly arrived citizens. Despite these problems, however, the government can obviate the need for the cultural defense to some extent by ensuring knowledge of both crimes and punishments.

UNITED STATES CASES—NATIVE AMERICANS

Since immigrants and refugees make a conscious decision to move to a new country, one might argue that they should adhere to the legal standards of the new country. But even if one decides that these groups ought to be bound by American law, this does not necessarily mean that indigenous peoples who controlled the territory first should have to surrender to the colonial or dominant legal regime.

That there are major conceptual differences in traditional Native and modern American legal ideals is known.[19] In fact, Native Americans have experienced an unusual legal status, i.e., semi-sovereign status. Federal law has allowed Native American societies some limited rights of self-government but has retained control insofar as violent crimes are concerned (18 U.S.C. 1153). For the most part, state courts have jurisdiction unless a Native American commits a proscribed act on Native American land in which case the federal courts have jurisdiction.

There are numerous cases in which the conduct of Native Americans has been judicially evaluated, and in some of them courts have been willing to take culture into account. For example, the case of United States v. Whaley[20] in 1888 makes this clear. The defendants were all Native Americans charged with the murder of Juan Baptista, also a Native American. Baptista was a doctor but not a very good doctor. In fact, he was so unsuccessful that the members of the tribe were convinced that he had been systematically poisoning his patients. All of his patients, approximately twenty, had died.

Finally, Hunter Jim, who was extremely popular within the tribe, fell ill and had to be treated by the doctor. The members of the tribe decided to hold a council at which time they informed the doctor that if Hunter Jim died, they would kill him. Hunter Jim died, and so the four defendants were appointed by the council to carry out its determination. They shot the doctor the following morning.

The court decided that the law did apply to Native Americans (which was somewhat in question) but felt that the defendants had not committed murder because malice was absent, an essential element for the crime of murder. Though the offense if committed by a "white man" would certainly have been murder, the court said that in view of the "Indian nature," customs, superstition, and ignorance, they had not committed murder. The prosecutor did not press for a murder charge but for manslaughter. The judge decided that justice should be tempered with mercy and imposed a sentence of five years of imprisonment for each, as well as a one dollar fine.

A 1985 Oregon case raises a slightly different set of issues because the murder did not involve only Native Americans. In State v. Butler[21] three members of the Siletz tribe were accused of murdering a man who was caught desecrating Native American burial grounds. It was alleged that when they found him digging up Native American artifacts to sell in local antique shops, they smashed his fingers and cut his throat as punishment. The presumption seems to be that this was the culturally determined proportionality, but this is not made clear in what has been written about the case.

Defense counsel stated that he would not use the cultural defense because he did not think it would be fruitful. Instead, he intended to show that they did not commit the act charged. But some of the Native Americans in the area felt that the acts committed against the grave-robber could be regarded as justifiable acts of war or self-defense. In the end it appeared that all three defendants were acquitted based on insufficient evidence, rather than cultural considerations. Although the judge did not want the case to center on the culture conflict, he did allow a member of the Siletz tribe to explain their religious convictions concerning burial traditions.[22]

A PRINCIPLE

The central question is what principle should govern culture conflict. There are two choices: (1) Might makes right—meaning that the dominant legal system controls or (2) Who arrived first—meaning that the indigenous peoples ought, at the very least, to be permitted to retain control over their own matters. Since it is admittedly quite unrealistic to expect colonial regimes or their descendants to relinquish control because the second principle is determined to be correct, it is possible that the cultural defense ought to function for indigenous groups. Perhaps there should be some guarantee that culture will be considered to mitigate sentences. Since immigrants have come voluntarily to the United States, they should be educated about American law and expected to abide by it. Indigenous peoples, however, made no such choice and should, in theory, have the right to handle legal matters within their own system. When it is necessary for them to enter American courts, culture should probably be taken into account in mitigating sentences.

THE CULTURAL DEFENSE IN OTHER COUNTRIES

Killings based on a belief in the supernatural are found across the globe and have been documented in such places as Colombia, Fiji, Papua New Guinea, South Africa, as well as in various countries in Africa.[23] But where defenses are tried in such cases, they generally fail. For example, a number of cases involving sorcery killings have arisen in Papua New Guinea and defenses of all kinds are rejected because the courts take an extremely inflexible view of such killings.[24] In Africa there are also many cases in which the courts rigidly apply common law doctrines in witchcraft, juju, and other supernatural cases despite widespread belief in these practices. One legal scholar attests to the depth of commitment to the beliefs, even among the educated and Westernized. Aremu found in one of his criminal law classes in Nigeria that more than 90% of the students (aged 20 and older) believed strongly in witchcraft. Nevertheless, the (formerly colonial) courts in their administration of criminal justice refuse to recognize the supernatural to the dismay of some African legal scholars:

> This attitude, apart from being patently unjust to the accused who had killed under the influence of such forces, also failed to take into consideration prevailing views on criminal law and culture conflicts...[25]

It seems that these scholars favor a **cultural defense** because it represents the only realistic possibility for invoking traditional norms. One wonders whether they would support the reinstitution of traditional courts.

The device which the courts have employed to avoid any consideration of culture is the so-called reasonable man standard. Because they rely on an "objective" version of it, they simply define the state of mind of the person (who killed to defend himself against witchcraft) as unreasonable. For instance, in the Nigerian case of *Gadam v. R.*[26] (1954) the Court held that "though prevalent, such a belief is unreasonable, being fraught as it is with such terrible results." In this case the defendant's wife had a miscarriage and became mortally ill. The man attributed this unhappy turn of events to two women. He struck one of them on the head with a hoe-handle in the belief that by so doing he would destroy the spell cast over his wife. The woman whom he hit died, and he was soon convicted of murder, which was affirmed on appeal. Because the belief was considered to be "unreasonable" by the court in its consequentialist reasoning, he was held responsible.

Although the courts will not entertain a cultural defense, they recognize how pervasive supernatural beliefs are. Oddly enough, this undermines attempts to use the insanity defense as can be seen in the Kenyan case of *Philip Muswi v. R.*[27] (1956). The defendant had been having trouble with his first wife after he took a second one. He believed that his first wife was practicing witchcraft against him. In fact, she was trying to alienate their children from him. When she took away their young son from his home, he became so furious that he killed her.

At the trial he testified that he did not know what he was doing and that it was not even until the next day that he remembered having killed his wife. The insanity defense was not persuasive because a belief in witchcraft does not prove insanity where it is so common:

> Even if the defendant believed he was justified in killing his wife because she was practicing witchcraft, there is again no evidence that such belief arose from any mental defect; it is a belief sometimes held by entirely sane Africans. The question whether the appellant's act was or was not contrary to tribal law is irrelevant.[28]

The defendant in such a court finds himself in a dilemma: there is no cultural defense because a belief in the supernatural is not reasonable: but it is not unreasonable enough to warrant the insanity defense.

In some places courts have been willing to mitigate sentences on the basis of culture in witchcraft cases. For instance, in March 1985 in Oakland, California, an Ethiopian man, Hagos Gebreamlak, was accused of attempting to kill a woman whom he claimed had placed a spell over him.[29] There were suggestions that the shooting had followed a lovers' quarrel. At the trial the public defender relied on the defense that beliefs concerning the bouda, voodoo and spells could arise from the man's background. Over strenuous objections from the prosecution, the judge allowed the defense to call an anthropologist as a witness to testify on Ethiopian customs. A psychologist also testified that the man was depressed and under considerable stress. The jury found the defendant not guilty of attempted murder but convicted him of a lesser charge, assault with a deadly weapon. It may be that the jury was more sympathetic to him because he did not actually kill the woman at whom he fired.

The degree to which cultural beliefs are accepted varies considerably. One way to anticipate whether or not culture will be considered is to ascertain what kind of reasonable-man standard is used. Where the standard is an "objective" one, cultural beliefs are treated as irrelevant. But where it is "subjective," culture is taken into account. In the Enga Jury case in Papua New Guinea, two village surgeons were charged with manslaughter after they operated on an ailing man with bamboo knives who then died. At first they were acquitted because no local Enga jury would have thought they had acted with reckless disregard for human life. But on appeal the court relied on an "objective" standard:

> It is sufficient, in my opinion, to state that the reasonable man is for the purposes of this case to be presumed to be one whose state of knowledge and prudence is such that appreciates the difference in training and skill between the qualified doctor and "the village surgeon" without any medical qualification.[30]

In the case of *R. v. Noboi-Bosai* (1971–1972)[31] a "subjective" reasonable-man standard was used. Here the accused were charged with improperly or indecently interfering with a corpse. They cooked and ate parts of the body from another village. The judge explicitly applied a standard which was based on the "reasonable primitive Gabusi villager of Daldalibi and Yulabi in early 1971." He concluded that eating the body of the deceased villager was "neither improper nor indecent behavior on their part, being normal and reasonable behavior on their part." For the most part the "objective" standard convicts whereas the "subjective" one will acquit or at least mitigate the sentence.

WESTERNERS IN ASIAN COURTS

Two Australians were convicted of drug trafficking in Malaysia. They received the death penalty and were executed. Since the death penalty was approved in 1975 and made mandatory in 1983, 36 men and women have been hanged in Malaysia for the offense of drug trafficking. Although some foreigners were hanged, all were Asians. More than 70 others have been sentenced to death, some of whom are foreigners, including some Westerners.

Capital punishment remains the norm in Asia. Both Thailand and Singapore also provide for the death penalty for drug offenses. These countries are trying to cope with the severe drug problems they experience because they are geographically near the "Golden Triangle," famous for the growth of heroin. One estimate of the number of narcotics addicts in Malaysia was 500,000 of the total 15 million population. Should one expect Malaysian courts to use Australian or Western guidelines in sentencing?

ANALYSIS

Most of the debate about the cultural defense takes place in the language of pluralism.[33] The language tends to obscure the real issues underlying culture conflict, issues which are most appropriately addressed in the framework of relativism. Pluralism simply means that a given society is composed of various groups with different mores. The concept of relativism, on the other hand, focuses less on the structural relationships and more on the psychological disposition of individuals within the group. Relativism holds that each person perceives reality in accordance with inculcated standards that have been uncritically accepted and may be unconscious. It is not simply the existence of different groups which gives rise to culture conflict. Rather, it is the power of enculturation which leads each group to perceive reality according to internal standards.

Many of those who see relativism as the issue fail to understand what acceptance of the theory does and does not require. In particular, many anthropologists, philosophers, and social scientists erroneously believe that relativism logically entails tolerance. They cast the theory of relativism as a value or prescriptive theory, which it is not. Unfortunately, this has caused great difficulty for the theory as a whole and for those who mistakenly believe that, by accepting the theory of relativism, they are automatically committed to endorsing the cultural defense.

Relativism is actually a descriptive theory and not connected to any particular value:

> ...the two parts of the doctrine are not logically or necessarily interdependent. The first part says that people are brought up to see the value in things that their local experience has suggested. The second part says that we should respect all cultures. But there is no true "therefore" between these two parts. It cannot be proved from the proposition that all values are relative, that we ought to respect all systems of values. We might just as well hate them all.[34]

In essence, relativism asks us to acknowledge that there are different ways of looking at the world; but taking a relativist approach certainly does not require us to surrender our own standards. Because enculturation leads to ethnocentrism, if anything, relativism reinforces our commitment to our own standards. So, the argument advanced by some that pluralism (relativism) compels us to adopt the cultural defense is seen to be a misguided one. Cultural sensitivity does not involve abandoning one's own laws.

Secondly, the cultural defense is not needed because culture is already taken into account at the various stages of charging and sentencing. Prosecutors, for example, often will not press charges against Laotian defendants because members of the community are reluctant to testify against one another and prefer to settle disputes by traditional mechanisms. In a number of cases such as *Whaley*, *Kimura*, and *Moua* (Kong), the sentences were mitigated, most likely because of culture.

One advocate of the cultural defense argues that a formal cultural defense is preferable to the informal use of culture.[35] The allegation is that where discretion exists in the United States legal system, it works most often to the disadvantage of minorities. But the cases show this proposition to be false. Moreover, if there is a problem of having prejudiced judges within the system, that should be remedied. It does not necessarily justify having a cultural defense. Furthermore, if judges are unwilling to consider culture, it remains unclear how a formal cultural defense would force them to take culture into account. Judges need not, for instance, accept the insanity defense.

For immigrants there is no real justification for having a cultural defense. But where individualized justice merits it, judges can use culture to mitigate sentences. In the case of individuals upon whom a system of legal norms has been imposed, the cultural defense may not be feasible. This is because adherence to an "objective" reasonable-man standard prevents the consideration of culture. For these societies two solutions are possible: (1) restore traditional courts which follow customary law (unless the traditional system is no longer desired), or (2) modify the Western judicial structure so that it incorporates traditional norms. For example, perhaps self defense ought to be allowed in witchcraft killings if the vast majority of citizens want it. Although some may be uncomfortable with the idea of sanctioning defenses for such crimes as witchcraft killings, using the law to force social change is equally troublesome.[36]

Finally, it is necessary to recognize the negative consequences that would follow the adoption of the cultural defense. Anarchy would reign if each person could claim a different cultural immunity from prosecution. One extreme reaction to the attempted use of the cultural defense in the *Moua* (Tou) case was a claim that acceptance of it would lead to a rash of wife killings. While this may seem far-fetched, it is possible that in the absence of any deterrent whatsoever, immigrants might be less circumspect when continuing their customary ways in the United States. Moreover, those who prefer not to follow the traditional way of life would fall prey to the cultural defense. If the perpetrator is not held responsible, women who seek their rights will have no recourse. Women's rights and children's rights will never be protected if their traditions follow them wherever they go.

Even if we assume for the sake of argument that the cultural defense is desirable because it reflects **cultural sensitivity**, we must acknowledge the overwhelming negative connotations it has. The cultural defense is often compared to the insanity defense. This seems to suggest that different cultural logics are viewed as being delusional.

The use of the cultural defense also presents dangers of distortion. If Americans mistakenly believe that Japanese women kill their children whenever their husbands take mistresses, this could trigger intensified racial prejudice. In fact, the inexcusable treatment of Japanese-Americans in the 1940s stemmed from racial stereotypes. Not only is there a possibility that the culture itself will be distorted, but the facts in a particular case may be molded to accommodate the cultural defense. Some argue that the trial of Hagos Gebreamlak illustrates this occurrence. It is possible that his beliefs in the bouda were not genuine, suggested by his failure to apply traditional remedies such as using garlic and wearing amulets to break the spell. The district attorney in that case maintained that the public defender had invented the bouda defense merely to absolve Gebreamlak of responsibility.[37] In the long term the cultural defense would probably have serious and detrimental effects, even upon the individuals it was designed to protect.

CONCLUSION

Some contend that the cultural defense is necessary if we are a truly pluralistic society. This is erroneous. American law recognizes an important distinction between belief and action: the former is absolute, while the latter is not. A culturally sensitive outlook does not require that we relinquish our standards. Others argue that we must reject the cultural defense because we must force new citizens to become assimilated as soon as possible. This is an example of cultural arrogance because retaining our criminal laws does not mean that we should impose *all* of the beliefs in the dominant value-system upon new citizens! While it is true that punishment educates and socializes, there are certainly less repressive ways to achieve the same result.

We can be culturally sensitive and retain our standards. There is no need for a cultural defense because mechanisms already exist which can take culture into account. The negative consequences of the defense such as undercutting the legitimacy of government, undermining women's and children's rights, and treating the logic of other cultures as insane all represent good reasons for rejecting the cultural defense.

NOTES

[1] *People v. Kimura*, No. A-091133 (Los Angeles City. Super. Ct., filed April 24, 1985).

[2] *People v. Moua* (Kong), No. 315972-0 (Fresno Cnty. Super. Ct., Feb. 7, 1985); Alan Dershowitz, 'Marriage by Capture' Runs into the Law of Rape, *Wall Street Journal*, June 14, 1985, at 5, col. 1.

[3] Julia B. Sams, The Availability of the "Cultural Defense" as an Excuse for Criminal Behavior, 16 *Georgia Journal of International and Comparative Law*, 335, 336–337 (1986).

[4] Mark R. Thompson, Immigrants Bring Cultural Defense into U.S. Courts, *Wall Street Journal*, June 6, 1985, p. 28; Mark R. Thompson, Cultural Defense, 14(1) Student Lawyer 24, 213 (1985).

[5] John C. Lyman, Cultural Defense: Viable Doctrine or Wishful Thinking, 9 *Criminal Law Review* 87, 94 (1986).

[6] *People v. Moua* (Tou, F-9083403 (Fresno Municipal Court (1985); 328-106-0 Fresno County 1985).

[7] Anon., Cultural Defense Fails to Mitigate Wife-Slayer's Sentence, *Los Angeles Daily Journal*, Nov. 29, 1985, col. 1, p. 15.

[8] *Reynolds v. United States*, 98 U.S. 145 (1879).

[9] *Id.* 167.

[10] Ford, Refusal of Blood Transfusions by Jehovah's Witnesses, 10 *Catholic Lawyer* 232(1964); Cantor, A Patient's Decision to Decline Life-Saving Medical Treatment: Bodily Integrity Versus the Preservation of Law, 26 *Rutgers Law Review* 228 (1973).

[11] In re Application of Jamaica Hospital, 128 Misc. 2d 1006, 491 N.Y.S. 2d 898 (N.Y. Sup. Ct. 1985).

[12] *Id.*, at 1008; at 899.

[13] *Jefferson v. Griffin Spalding County Hospital Authority*, 247 S.E. 2d 457 (1981).

[14] Lawrence Nelson, Brian Buggy, and Carol Weil, Forced Medical Treatment of Pregnant Women: 'Compeling Each to Live as Seems Good to the Rest.' 86 *Hastings Law Journal* 703. 707 (1986); George J. Annas, Forced Cesareans: The Most Unkindest Cut of All, 23 (3) *Hastings Center Report* 16 (1982).

[15] *Lawson v. Commonwealth*, 164 S.W2d 972 (Ky 1942).

[16] *Swann v. Pack*, 527 S.W.2d 114 (1975).

[17] *Id.*, at 114.

[18] *US v. Kuch*, 288 S.W.2d 972 (Ky 1942), *US. v. Leary*, 383 F.2d 851 (1967).

[19] Sandra R. Weber, Native-Americans Before the Bench: The Nature of Contrast and Conflict in Native-American Law Ways and Western Legal Systems. 19 *Social Science Journal* 47(1982); Laurence French (ed.) *Indians and Criminal Justice*. Totowa, New Jersey: Allanheld, Osmun (1982).

[20] *United States v. Whaley*, 37 F. 145 (1888).

[21] *State v. Butler*, No. 44496 (Lincoln Cty. Cir. Ct. filed Mar. 11, 1981).

[22] Tia Nichols, Belief in the Way: Native Americans in the Western Legal System, 1987, unpublished paper.

[23] Bernard M. Narokobi, Adaptation of Western Law in Papua New Guinea, 5 *Melanesian Law Journal* 52 (1977); Kharisu S. Chukkol, Supernatural Beliefs and Criminal Law in Nigeria, 25 *Journal of the Indian Law Institute* 444 (1983); L.O. Aremu,

Criminal Responsibility for Homicide in Nigeria and Supernatural Beliefs, 29 *International and Comparative Law Quarterly* 112 (1980); David S. Clark, Witchcraft and Legal Pluralism: The Case of Celimo Miquirucama, 15 *Tulsa Law Journal* 679 (1980). For more general references on the cultural defense in other countries, see Sebastian Poulter, *English Law and Ethnic Minority Customs*. London: Butterworths, 1986, Sebastian Poulter, Hyde v. Hyde—A Reappraisal. *International and Comparative Law Quarterly* 475 (1976); Sebastian Poulter, Foreign Customs and the English Criminal Law 24 *International and Comparative Law Quarterly* 136 (1975). Alec Samuels, Legal Recognition and Protection of Minority Customs in a Plural Society in England, 10 *Anglo-American Law Review* 241 (1981); Justin Lewis, The Outlook for a Devil in the Colonies. 1958 *Criminal Law Review* 661 (1958); A. Gledhill, The Reception of English Law in India, In William B. Hamilton (ed), *The Transfer of Institutions* (pp. 165–191). Durham, N.C.: Duke University Press, 1964: David Weisbrot, Note: Law Reform Commission Working Paper No. 6—Criminal Responsibility: Taking Customs, Perceptions and Beliefs into Account. 5 *Melanesian Law Journal* 164(1977); T.O. Elias Customary Law: The Limits of Its Validity in Colonial Law, 13 *African Studies* 97 (1954).

[24] Narokobi, *Id.*, at 60.

[25] Aremu *supra* note 23, at 113.

[26] *Gadam v. R.*, 14 WA.C.A. 442 (1954).

[27] *Philip Muswi s/o Musele v. R.*, 23, E.A.C.A. 622 (1956).

[28] *Id.*, at 625.

[29] Anon., Profile, *Los Angeles Daily Journal*, Oct. 25, 1985, pp. 1,17.

[30] Narokobi, *supra* note 23, at 60.

[31] *R. v. Noboi-Bosai* (1971-1 972), P. & N.G.L.R., 271; see Narokobi, *supra* note 23 at 58; see also, Howard, What Colour is the "Reasonable Man"? 1961 *Criminal Law Review* 41.

[32] Nick B. Williams, Malaysia Standing Firm on Drug Laws, *Los Angeles Times*, July 5, 1986; anon., 2 Australians Hanged by Malaysia for Drug Crimes, *Los Angeles Times*, July 6, 1986, p. 4.

[33] Milton E. Gordon, Models of Pluralism: The New American Dilemma. 454 *Annals, American Academy of Political and Social Science* 178 (1981); Charles M. Lamb, Legal Foundations of Civil Rights and Pluralism in America, 454 *Annals, American Academy of Political and Social Science* 13 (1981).

[34] Robert Redfield, *The Primitive World and Its Transformations*. Ithaca, New York: Cornell University Press, 1962 at 146–147; see also Alison Dundes Renteln, Relativism and the Search for Human Rights, 90 *American Anthropologist* (1988).

[35] Anon., The Cultural Defense in the Criminal Law, 99 *Harvard Law Review* 1293 (1986).

[36] Studies indicate that it can be disastrous to employ law as a vehicle for social change when the values in the society support the retention of traditional legal norms. See, for example, Gregory Massell, Revolutionary Change in Soviet Central Asia. In D. Black and M. Mileski (eds.), *The Social Organization of Law* (pp. 226–261). New York: Seminar Press, 1973; Haleh Afshar, The Legal, Social, and Political Position of Women in Iran, 13 *International Journal of the Sociology of Law* 47(1985); F.J.M. Feldbrugge, The Role of Soviet Law in the Integration of Non-Slavic Peoples, 3 *Review of Socialist Law* 3 (1977).

[37] Lauren Arenson, *Hagos Gebreamlak v. California*, 1987, unpublished paper.

From Allison Renteln, 1988, "Culture and Culpability: A Study of Contrasts," *Beverly Hills Bar Association Journal*, Vol. 22, No. 1. Reprinted by permission.

E X E R C I S E

Name

Section

Date

EXERCISE 9.3: THE CULTURAL DEFENSE

Objective
To understand the kinds of legal issues that result from the cultural diversity found in the United States.

Rationale
To discuss real legal issues that have arisen as a result of cultural differences, and to understand the complexity of the effect of cultural diversity on our legal system.

Instructions
1. Form groups of four or five.

2. Give each group a brief written description (following page) of an actual case where a crime was committed in the U.S. by an immigrant, and in which cultural factors were a mitigating influence.

3. Decide the defendant's guilt or innocence, and the punishment.

4. Present the case, decisions, and reasoning behind the decision.

5. Afterwards, review the court's decisions as they compare with the groups' decisions.

(Continued on the next page)

POLITICAL ORGANIZATION

THE CULTURAL DEFENSE

Instructions: Read the following case as described in the newspaper. If you were the judge/jury, how would you decide the case? If you determined that the defendant was guilty, how would you punish him/her? Would you treat him/her the same as a native born American who committed the crime? Be ready to defend your reasoning to the class.

Cases

1. A Japanese woman in Los Angeles acted out the old Japanese custom of parent-child suicide, *oyako-shinju*, in response to the shame of hearing that her husband had a mistress. She walked into the ocean in Santa Monica, carrying her 6-month-old daughter and holding the hand of her four-year-old son. The children drowned, but the mother was rescued and subsequently charged with first degree murder.

   Outcome: 4,000 members of the Japanese-American community signed a petition saying that though such acts are no longer legally acceptable in Japan, the Japanese courts would charge her with no more than involuntary manslaughter. But the D.A. refused to reduce the charge. Her attorney used the testimony of six psychiatrists to show she was mentally deranged at the time. The attorney was thus treating a foreign cultural perspective as delusional. The case was plea-bargained down to voluntary manslaughter, and the woman received a sentence of one year in county jail, less time already served, five years probation, and mandatory psychiatric treatment.

2. A Hmong refugee from Laos killed his wife because she was going to take a job working for another man. His attorney argued that in Hmong culture, the wife's intended action was tantamount to adultery, which in that culture, had to be punished by death.

   Outcome: He was convicted of murder, and sentenced to 8 years.

3. Laotian man in Fresno engaged in the ritualistic act of abducting his Laotian fiancée and bringing her to his family's home so he could consummate their relationship—thus ensuring she would not be available for any other man. The fiancée was rather Americanized, and resisted. The man was charged with kidnapping and rape.

   Outcome: He was allowed to plea-bargain the charge to a misdemeanor of false imprisonment, and the judge handed down a comparatively mild sentence of 90 days.

4. A Korean born merchant in Los Angeles was raided by game wardens and charged with selling wild animal parts, including sliced elk, deer antlers, animal horns, bear gallbladders, skins and paws. In Korea, people have relied on folk remedies made from rare animal parts for thousands of years. He claims he didn't know it was illegal.

   Outcome (not decided): If convicted, he could face up to 3 years in state prison and a $5,000 fine.

5. A Chinese man in New York killed his wife by hitting her in the head with a hammer eight times after she admitted to him that she was having an affair. His lawyer argued that the overwhelming sense of shame and humiliation brought on by his wife's adultery put him in a frame of mind where he was no longer in control of his actions. In China, adultery is an "enormous stain" which also reflects on the aggrieved husband's ancestors and descendants.

   Outcome: In a nonjury trial, he was found guilty of second-degree manslaughter, after reducing a charge of second-degree murder. Legally, the lesser manslaughter charge means that he did not intentionally kill his wife.

Exercise: "Cultural Relativism and the Law," by Geri-Ann Galanti, California State University, Los Angeles. Reprinted by permission.

POLITICAL ORGANIZATION

KEY TERMS

Name

Section

Date

Authority:

Big-man/Big-woman leadership system:

Capitalists:

Caste:

Class:

Cultural conflict:

Cultural defense:

Cultural relativism:

Division of labor:

POLITICAL ORGANIZATION

Egalitarian:

Exploitative theory of social stratification:

Functionalism:

Glass ceiling:

Glass elevator:

Hierarchy:

Idealogy of class:

Influence:

Integrative theory of social stratification:

Leadership:

Matriarchy:

Moka:

KEY TERMS

Political organization:

> ** Band:*

> ** Tribe:*

> ** Chiefdom:*

> ** State:*

Politics:

Power:

Poverty:

Privilege:

Rank:

Segmentary model:

Social stratification:

POLITICAL ORGANIZATION

Status:

Surplus value of labor:

Taxation:

Wealth:

10 RELIGION

Religions of the United States

The number of religions practiced in the United States is great, and the diversity in beliefs is just as astounding. Yet, again, religion is a product of culture.

Anthropologists have long observed that societies around the globe have recognizable sets of beliefs and behaviors that are classified as religious. **Religion** can be defined as a set of beliefs and patterned behaviors concerned with the supernatural and/or forces beyond human control. As you can see by this definition, religion is a matter of both belief and action. It is not always a tangible object that can clearly be recognized as being religious.

Religion is often interpreted through symbolic meaning. Since we today cannot be present with Buddha at the Bodhi Tree or with Moses while receiving the Ten Commandments, we symbolically participate in such religious events through our actions, ritualized objects, and sacred narratives.

We express our participation in religious events through plays, acts of confession, religious dances, etc. We thus demonstrate our connectedness to previous generations and to each other through shared symbolic activities. Ritualized objects such as a Jewish star, a copy of the Quar'an, or a mask demonstrate such symbolism, and are important to religious practice. And lastly, sacred narratives, referred to as **myths**, are stories that transmit culturally meaningful messages—from one generation to the next—about the natural and supernatural worlds and a person's place within the universe.

A specific type of myth, known as the **creation myth**, explains how we came to be. While the myth of creation may differ according to each culture, all explain the importance of a society in terms of its worldview. In addition, a religion may offer the prospect of an afterlife, it may provide a means of conflict resolution, and it may intensify group solidarity and instill psychological comfort to the individual practitioner.

RELIGION

Religion is a cultural universal: it exists in virtually all human societies. It consists of beliefs and behaviors concerned with supernatural beings, powers, and forces. Like ethnicity, language, kinship practices, economics and politics, religion may be associated with social divisions within and between societies and nations. Religious behavior and beliefs may unite or divide. Participation in common practices may affirm and promote social solidarity. On the other hand, religious differences may be associated with ethnocentrism and bitter enmity between practitioners.

When studying religion cross-culturally, anthropologists pay attention to the social roles of religion as well as to the content and nature of religious acts, events, practitioners, and organization. We also investigate verbal and nonverbal manifestations of religious beliefs through prayer, myths, and religious artifacts.

Religious beliefs are ideas that people may hold fast to or find important. **Beliefs** differ from facts, since facts are scientifically proven to have validity and reliability.

LET'S PONDER...

Let's Ponder...

WRITING AN ETHNOGRAPHY (OF A RELIGIOUS SITE)

Visit a place of worship, like a church, temple, mosque or sacred site. During your visit, collect data and form a big idea (thesis). Record your objective findings (etic) and subjective impressions (emic). You will want to spend at least one hour at your chosen site.

Part One—The Walkaround:

Spend some time walking around the religious site, actively observing. What do you see, hear, smell, feel? What is your general impression of the place? Are you drawn to a certain area, object or person? Why?

Choose a location where you can sit and observe the behavior of the practitioners. Describe, in detail, the area in which you are seated and the behaviors you are witnessing.

Part Two—Objective Analysis:

Be descriptive when answering each of the following questions. Also, be sure to remain objective in your responses.

Place—Describe why you chose this location. What do you see?

People—Describe the actions of those around you. Do you feel included in their practices? How are they dressed? How are they interacting with one another, objects and the space?

(continued on the next page)

RELIGION

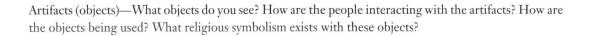

Artifacts (objects)—What objects do you see? How are the people interacting with the artifacts? How are the objects being used? What religious symbolism exists with these objects?

Part Three—Impressions Count!

What are your impressions concerning the religious site and its practitioners? How do you feel? Are you comfortable at this location? Why or why not?

Part Four—Constructing a Brief Ethnography:

Just as with any ethnography (a written document based upon the collection of accurate notes taken while conducting field research) the anthropologist cannot only focus on description. Interpretation is also essential. Also, you must narrow your scope when sharing your facts with the reader. Be sure to include an introduction, body, and conclusion in your essay.

Based upon data you have collected, produce an essay (minimum of 150 words) that focuses on specific aspects of the religious site and the practitioners you observed.

"Let's Ponder" exercises reprinted by permission of Professor Brock Klein, Pasadena City College.

Religion—
Marvin Harris and Orna Johnson

Now we are entering the inner sanctum of superstructure: the domain of religion, myth, magic, ritual, and all the other aspects of cultures that are intended to mediate between ordinary beings and forces, on the one hand, and extraordinary beings and forces, on the other. First some basic definitions will be needed. Then we will try to classify the basic types of religious organizations and rituals. Finally, we will range over the vast variety of religious behaviors, from puberty rites to messianic cults, from prayer to cannibal feasts, and from abominable pigs to sacred cows.

Can aspects of religion be explained in terms of structure and infrastructure? To a considerable degree. Yet religion can frequently become a powerful force in its own right. Although infrastructural and structural conditions provide means for understanding the origin of many specific beliefs and rituals, religion frequently plays a crucial role in strengthening the impulses leading toward major transformations in social life.

ANIMISM

The earliest anthropological attempt to define religion was that of E. B. Tylor (1871). In his book *Primitive Culture*, he demonstrated that members of every society believe that inside the ordinary, visible, tangible body of a human or other life form, there is a normally invisible, normally intangible being: the soul. He named this belief **animism**.

Animism is the belief that humans share the world with a population of extraordinary, mostly invisible beings.

Animism is spiritual belief originated from the experience of dreaming in which a phantom version appears. Sleep, fainting, madness, and death all lead to the notion of a world of spirits who enter and leave human bodies at will. Once imagined, this world of spirits can explain anything: The power of this impersonal power increases in the human mind to the point where humans find themselves captive in an imaginary world and become the vassal of the spiritual forces that they created.

Why is animism universal? Tylor reasoned that if a belief recurred again and again in virtually all times and places, it could not be a product of mere fantasy. Rather, it must have grounding in evidence and in experiences that were equally recurrent and universal. What were these experiences? Tylor pointed to dreams, trances, visions, shadows, reflections, and death. During dreams, our body stays in bed, yet another part of us gets up, talks to people, and travels to distant lands. Trances and drug-induced visions also bring vivid evidence of another self, distinct and separate from one's body. Shadows and mirror images reflected in still water point to the same conclusion, even in the full light of normal wakefulness.

The concept of an inner being—a **soul**—makes sense of all this. It is the soul that wanders off when we sleep, that lies in the shadows, and that peers back at us from the surface of the pond. Most of all, the soul explains the mystery of death: A lifeless body is a body permanently deprived of its soul.

Tylor has been criticized by twentieth-century anthropologists for his suggestion that animism arose merely as a result of the attempt to understand puzzling human and natural phenomena. Today, we know that religion is much more than an attempt to explain puzzling phenomena. Like other aspects of superstructure, religion serves a multitude of economic, political, and psychological functions.

Another important criticism of Tylor's stress on the puzzle-solving function of religion concerns the role of hallucinations in shaping religious beliefs. During drug-induced trances and other forms of hallucinatory experience, people "see" and "hear" extraordinary things that seem even more real than ordinary people and animals. One can argue, therefore, that animistic theories are not intellectual attempts to explain trances and dreams but direct expressions of extraordinary psychological experiences. Nonetheless, it cannot be denied that religion and the doctrine of souls also provides people with answers to fundamental questions about the meaning of life and death and the causes of events (Pandian 1992:88).

Although certain animistic beliefs are universal, each culture has its own distinctive animistic beings and its own specific elaboration of the soul concept. Even the number of a person's souls varies cross-culturally:

- The ancient Egyptians had two and so do many West African cultures: one from the mother's ancestors and one from the father's.

- The J'varo of Ecuador (Harner 1984) have three souls. The first soul—the *mekas*—gives life to the body. The second soul—the *arutam*—has to be captured through a drug-induced visionary experience at a sacred waterfall. It confers bravery in battle to the possessor. The third soul—the *musiak*—forms inside the head of a dying warrior and attempts to avenge his death. It is to gain control over the musiak soul that the J'varo cut off the fallen warrior's head, "shrink" it, and bring it back to their village, where it is the focus of rituals designed to transfer its powers to its captor.

- The Dahomey say that women have three souls and that men have four. Both sexes have an ancestor soul, a personal soul, and a *mawn* soul. The ancestor soul gives protection during life, the personal soul is accountable for what people do with their lives, and the mawn soul is a bit of the creator god, Mawn, who supplies divine guidance. The exclusively male fourth soul guides men to positions of leadership in their households and lineages.

- The Fang of Gabon have seven: a brain soul, a heart soul, a name soul, a life force soul, a body soul, a shadow soul, and a ghost soul (Riviere 1987).

ANIMATISM AND MANA

Robert Marett (1914) complained that Tylor's definition of religion as animism was too narrow. When people attribute lifelike properties to rocks, pots, storms, and volcanoes, they do not necessarily believe that souls cause the lifelike behavior of these objects. Hence, Marett introduced the term **animatism** to designate a supernatural force that does not derive its effect from souls.

Animatism is the belief in diffuse impersonal power that people can control under certain conditions.

Marett uses the Melanesian word **mana** to refer to a concentrated form of animatistic force.

Mana is the possession of a concentrated animatistic force that gives certain objects, animals, and people extraordinary powers independent of the power derived from souls and gods.

An adze that makes intricate carvings, a fishhook that catches large fish, a club that kills many enemies, and a horseshoe that brings good luck all have large amounts of mana. People, too, may be spoken of as having more or less mana. A woodcarver whose work is especially intricate and beautiful possesses mana, whereas a warrior captured by the enemy has obviously lost his mana.

In its broadest range of meaning, mana simply indicates belief in a powerful force. In Western cultures, the concepts of luck and charisma closely resemble the idea of mana. A horseshoe posesses a concentrated power that brings good luck. Vitamin pills are consumed by many millions of people in the expectation that they will exert a powerful effect on health and well-being. Soaps and detergents are said to clean because of "cleaning power," gasolines provide engines with "starting power" or "go-power," salespeople are prized for their "selling power," and politicians are said to have charisma or "vote-getting power." Many people fervently believe that they are "lucky" or "unlucky," which can be interpreted as a belief that they control varying quantities of mana.

NATURAL AND SUPERNATURAL

Marett's idea that religion involves a belief in mana is problematic because the distinction between natural and supernatural is culturally defined. If a belief in a powerful supernatural force constitutes religion, then what prevents a belief in the natural force of gravity, electricity, or other concepts of physics from being regarded as religious beliefs? Saying that mana is a supernatural force outside the realm of the observable world, whereas electricity is a natural force because it can be scientifically tested, does not solve this problem.

Most cultures do not distinguish between natural and supernatural realms.

In a society where people believe ghosts are always present, it is not necessarily either natural or supernatural to provide dead ancestors with food and drink. The culture may simply lack emic categories for natural and supernatural. Similarly, when a shaman blows smoke over a patient and triumphantly removes a sliver of bone allegedly inserted by the patient's enemy, the question of whether the performance is natural or supernatural may have no emic meaning.

Writing of the Gururumba of the highlands of western New Guinea, Philip Newman noted that they "have a series of beliefs postulating the existence of entities and forces we would call supernatural." Yet the contrast between natural and supernatural is not emically relevant to the Gururumba themselves:

> It should be mentioned that our use of the notion "supernatural" does not correspond to any Gururumba concept: they do not divide the world into natural and supernatural parts. Certain entities, forces, and processes must be controlled partially through *lusu*, a term denoting rituals relating to growth, curing, or the stimulation of strength, while others need only rarely be controlled in this way. However, *lusu* does not contrast with any term denoting a realm of control where the nature of controls differ from *lusu*. Consequently *lusu* is simply part of all control techniques and what it controls is simply part of all things requiring human control. (1965:83)

MAGIC AND RELIGION

In his famous book *The Golden Bough* (1911–1915), Sir James Frazer attempted to define religion. For Frazer, the question of whether a belief was religious or not centered on the extent to which the participants felt they could make an entity or force do their bidding. If the participants felt insecure and humble and were inclined to supplicate and request favors and dispensations, their beliefs and actions were essentially religious. If they thought they were in control of the entities and forces governing events, felt no uncertainty about the outcome, and experienced no need for humble supplication, their beliefs and practices were examples of **magic**, rather than of religion.

Religion refers to beliefs and actions that are based on the assumption that the world is under the control of supernatural forces that humans must please.

Magic refers to a practice intended to manipulate supernatural forces to achieve a specific result. Magic is less spiritual and less ethical than religion.

Frazer regarded prayer as the essence of religious ritual and magic as a more primitive form that preceded religion. But prayers are not always rendered in a mood of supplication, and magic is still prominent in a wide range of modern-day pursuits. Thus, the line between prayers and magical spells is actually hard to draw.

Not all cultures approach their gods as supplicants. In many cultures, people try to intimidate, bribe, and lie to their gods. The Tsimshian of the Canadian Pacific Coast stamp their feet and shake their fists at the heavens and call their gods "slaves" as a term of reproach. The Manus of the Bismarck Archipelago keep the skulls of their ancestors in a corner of the house and try their best to please "Sir Ghost." However, if someone gets sick, the Manus may angrily threaten to throw Sir Ghost out of the house. This is what they tell Sir Ghost: "This man dies and you rest in no house. You will but wander about the edges of the island [used for excretory functions]" (Fortune 1965:216).

Religion and magic are both symbolic systems that help people cope with the ambiguities and anxieties of everyday life. Religion, however, emphasizes explanation and is practiced regularly, whereas magic is a means of manipulation that targets specific, immediate problems. When people face danger or uncertainty, they turn to magic. According to Malinowski (1935), magic provides psychological safety, allowing people to perform tasks without being distracted by fears.

One can find an analogous use of magic in the little rituals and routines that baseball players engage in as they come up to bat, such as touching their caps, spitting in the dirt, and rubbing their hands. Other rituals include eating the same food at the same time of day, taking the same route to the ballpark, wearing the same clothes, and carrying certain good luck charms in order to keep a winning streak going (Gmelch 1971). None of this has any real connection with getting a hit, but constant repetition reduces anxiety and can improve a player's performance.

RELIGION

THE ORGANIZATION OF RELIGIOUS BELIEFS AND PRACTICES

Anthropologist Anthony Wallace (1966) distinguished four principal varieties of religious *cults*—that is, forms of organization of religious doctrines and activities—that have broad evolutionary implications. The passage of time has not brought forth a better classification. Wallace's four principal forms are (1) individualistic cults, (2) shamanistic cults, (3) communal cults, and (4) ecclesiastical cults (see Table 10.1).

Individualistic Cults

Individualistic cults do not make distinctions between specialists and laypeople. One might call this "do-it-yourself" religion.

In **individualistic cults**, all people are their own specialists.

As is common among native North and South Americans, individuals acquire a personal guardian spirit or supernatural protector—typically by means of a visionary experience induced by fasting, self-inflicted torture, or hallucinogenic drugs.

The Inuit. The individualism of much of Inuit belief and ritual parallels the individualism of the Inuit mode of production. Hunters alone or in small groups constantly match their wits against the cunning and strength of animal prey and confront the dangers of travel over the ice and the threats of storms and month-long nights. The Inuit hunter is equipped with an ingenious array of technological devices that make life possible in the Arctic, but the outcome of the daily struggle remains in doubt. From the Inuit's point of view, it is imperative to be well equipped to handle both the danger of the harsh physical elements and the danger of offending or not properly warding off unseen spirits and forces.

Table 10.1 Principal Types of Cults

Cult Type	Role Specialization	Political Complexity	Examples
Individualistic	No role specialization. Most basic form of religious life. Each person enters into relationship with animistic being when in need of control or protection.	Egalitarian band and village societies	Inuit hunters, Crow warrior vision quest
Shamanistic	Part-time specialization. Shamans work in direct communication with supernatural as diviners, curers, spirit mediums, and magicians. They serve people in need in exchange for gifts, fees, prestige, or power.	Egalitarian band and village societies	!Kung, J'varo, and Tapirapé
Communal	Groups of nonspecialists perform rites for community, deemed vital to well-being of individuals and society.	Lineage-based societies	Rites of solidarity; rites of passage among Ndembu
Ecclesiastical	Full-time professional clergy who work as intermediaries between society and supernatural in hierarchical organization under control of centralized church.	State societies	Aztec, Incas (also Egyptians, Christianity, Judaism, Buddhism, and Islam)

Source: Based on Wallace 1966.

Vigilant individual effort is needed to deal with wandering human and animal souls, place spirits, Sedna (the Keeper of the Sea Animals), the Sun, the Moon, and the Spirit of the Air. Part of each hunter's equipment is his hunting song, a combination of chant, prayer, and magic formula that he inherits from his father or father's brothers or purchases from some famous hunter or shaman. In return for protection and hunting success given by his spirit helpers, the hunter has to observe certain taboos, refrain from hunting or eating certain species, or avoid trespassing in a particular locale. Moreover, a hunter should never sleep out on the ice edge. Note that some of these superstitions may alleviate psychological stress or have a practical value for hunting or some other aspect of Inuit life. Not sleeping out on the ice, for example, is a safety precaution.

The Crow. For many native North Americans, a hallucinatory vision is the central experience of life. Young men need this hallucinatory experience to be successful in love, warfare, horsestealing, trading, and all other important endeavors. In keeping with their code of personal bravery and endurance, they seek these visions primarily through self-inflicted torture.

Among the Crow, a youth who craves the visionary experience of his elders goes alone into the mountains, strips off his clothes, and abstains from food and drink. If this is not sufficient, he chops off part of the fourth finger of his left hand. Coached from childhood to expect that a vision would come, most Crow vision-seekers are successful. A buffalo, snake, chicken hawk, thunderbird, dwarf, or mysterious stranger appears; miraculous events unfold; and then these strange beings "adopt" the vision-seeker and disappear.

Scratches-Face, who was one of Robert Lowie's informants, prayed to the morning star: "Old woman's grandson, I give you this (finger joint). Give me something good in exchange....A good horse...a good-natured woman...a tent of my own to live in" (Lowie 1948 [1924]:6). Lowie reported that after cutting off his finger, Scratches-Face saw six men riding horses. One of them said, "You have been poor, so I'll give you what you want." Suddenly the trees around them turned into enemy warriors, who began to shoot at the six horsemen. The horsemen rode away but returned unscathed. The spokesman then said

to Scratches-Face, "If you want to fight all the people on the earth, do as I do, and you will be able to fight for three days or four days and yet not be shot." The enemy attacked again, but Scratches-Face's benefactor knocked them down with a spear. According to Lowie (1948 [1924]:6), "In consequence of his blessing Scratches-Face struck and killed an enemy without ever getting wounded. He also obtained horses and married a good-tempered and industrious woman."

Although each Crow's vision had some unique elements, they were usually similar in the following regards:

*   Some revelation of future success in warfare, horse-raiding, or other acts of bravery was involved.

*   The visions usually occurred at the end of the fourth day—four being a sacred number.

*   Practically every vision was accompanied by the acquisition of a sacred song.

*   The friendly spirits in the vision adopted the youth.

*   Trees or rocks often turned into enemies who vainly shot at the invulnerable spirit being.

Lowie concluded:

> He sees and hears not merely what any faster, say in British Columbia or South Africa would see and hear under like conditions of physiological exhaustion and under the urge of generally human desires, but what the social tradition of the Crow tribe imperatively suggests. (1948 [1924]:14)

Shamanistic Cults

To become a **shaman**, an individual must undergo a difficult apprenticeship to acquire the ability of entering into trance states. In trance, the shaman's powers increase. He or she can then heal the sick.

Shamans are women and men who are socially recognized as having special abilities for entering into contact with spirit beings and for controlling supernatural forces.

There are broad similarities in the techniques used by shamans to cure their patients. The shaman goes into a trance by smoking tobacco, taking drugs, beating on a drum, dancing monotonously, or simply by closing his or her eyes and concentrating. The trance begins with rigidity of the body, sweating, and heavy breathing. While in the trance, the shaman may act as a medium, transmitting messages from the ancestors. With the help of friendly spirits, shamans predict future events, locate lost objects, identify the cause of illness, battle with spirits on behalf of the patient, prescribe cures, and give advice on how clients can protect themselves against the evil intentions of enemies.

There is a close relationship between shamanistic cults and individualistic vision quests. Shamans are usually personalities who are psychologically predisposed toward hallucinatory experiences. In cultures that use hallucinogenic substances freely in order to penetrate the mysteries of the other world, many people may claim shamanistic status. Among the J'varo, one out of every four men is a shaman because the use of hallucinogenic vines makes it possible for almost everyone to achieve the trance states essential for the practice of shamanism (Harner 1972:154). Elsewhere, becoming a shaman may be restricted to people who are prone to having auditory and visual hallucinations.

An important part of shamanistic performance in many regions of the world consists of simple tricks of ventriloquism, sleight of hand, and illusion. Siberian shamans, for example, signaled the arrival of the possessing spirit by secretly shaking the walls of a darkened tent. Throughout South America, the standard shamanistic curing ceremony involves the sleight-of-hand removal of slivers of bone, pebbles, bugs, and other foreign objects from the patient's body.

The practice of these tricks should not be regarded as evidence that the shaman has a cynical or disbelieving attitude toward the rest of the performance. Michael Harner (1980), a modern proponent of shamanic rituals, insists there is nothing fraudulent about the sucking cure. It is not the object itself that is in the patient's body and causing the trouble; rather, it is the object's spiritual counterpart.

Shamans put the material object in their mouth during the sucking cure because this helps withdraw its spiritual counterpart.

Although trance is part of the shamanistic repertory in hundreds of cultures, it is not universal. Many cultures have part-time specialists who do not make use of trance but who diagnose and cure disease, find lost objects, foretell the future, and confer immunity in war and success in love. Such persons may be referred to variously as magicians, seers, sorcerers, witch doctors, medicine men or medicine women, and curers. The full shamanistic complex embodies all these roles (Atkinson 1992; but see Winkelman 1990).

The !Kung. The !Kung use a method of healing based on the principle of **n/um**, which is the healing energy that originates from the gods. *N/um* is accessed during an all-night dance. As dancing intensifies, the n/um of the healers is activated in the healers through the *kia* (trance)— an enhanced state of consciousness that is both painful and feared. Healing is a routine cultural event among the !Kung, open to everyone. But to become a healer, a person must undergo intense training. By the time they reach adulthood, about half the men and 10 percent of the women have become healers.

The *kia*, or activated *n/um*, is said to boil fiercely within the healer (Katz 1982). Those who learn to heal are called the "masters" or "owners" of *n/um*. Healers are able to access the realm where the gods and spirits of dead ancestors live. These are the spirits that try to carry off the sick into their own realm by bringing misfortune and death. In the *kia*, healers express the wishes of the living by entering into a struggle with the spirits to rescue the souls of the sick.

Healers who are in *kia* lay their hands on a person to pull out the sickness. They shriek and howl, expressing the pain and difficulty of healing work. Then they shake their hands toward the outside of the dance circle to cast away the sickness they have taken from the person being treated. Such healing may go on for several hours. Healers plead and argue with the gods to save the people from illness, demanding that the spirits of their dead ancestors spare the sick person. They plead and yell at the spirits to leave the sick person alone, saying that he or she is not ready to go and wants to remain with loved ones. If the healer's *n/um* is strong, the spirits will retreat and the sick person will live.

The Tapirapé. Among the Tapirapé, a village people of central Brazil (Wagley 1977), shamans derive their powers from dreams in which they encounter spirits who become their helpers. Dreams are caused by the soul leaving the body and going on a journey. Frequent dreaming is a sign of shamanistic talent. Mature shamans, with the help of the spirit familiars, can turn into birds or launch themselves through the air in gourd "canoes," visit with ghosts and demons, or travel to distant villages forward and backward through time.

Tapirapé shamans are frequently called on to cure illness. This they do with sleight of hand and the help of their spirit familiars while in a semitrance condition induced by gulping huge quantities of tobacco, which makes them vomit. It is interesting to note in conjunction with the discussion of the widespread use of tobacco in Native American rituals that tobacco contains hallucinogenic alkaloids and may induce visions when consumed in large quantities.

Charles Wagley (1943:73–74) provided the following description of a Tapirapé shaman:

> A shaman comes to his patient, and squats near the patient's hammock; his first act is always to light his pipe. When the patient has a fever or has fallen unconscious from the sight of a ghost, the principal method of treatment is by massage. The shaman blows smoke over the entire body of the patient; then he blows smoke over his own hands, spits into them, and massages the patient slowly and firmly, always toward the extremities of the body. He shows that he is removing a foreign substance by quick movement of his hands as he reaches the end of an arm or leg.

> The more frequent method of curing, however, is by the extraction of a malignant object by sucking. The shaman squats alongside the hammock of his patient and begins to "eat smoke"—swallow large gulps of tobacco smoke from his pipe. He forces the smoke with great intakes of breath deep down into his stomach. Soon he becomes intoxicated and nauseated; he vomits violently and smoke spews from his stomach. He groans and clears his throat in the manner of a person gagging with nausea but unable to vomit. By sucking back what he vomits, he accumulates saliva in his mouth.

> In the midst of this process he stops several times to suck on the body of his patient and finally, with one awful heave, he spews all the accumulated material on the ground. He then searches in this mess for the intrusive object that has been causing the illness.

Wagley reports that

> Never once did I see a shaman show the intrusive object to observers. At one treatment a Tapirapé [shaman] usually repeats this process of "eating smoke," sucking, and vomiting several times. Sometimes, when a man of prestige is ill, two or even three shamans will cure side by side in this manner and the noise of violent vomiting resounds throughout the village. (1943:73–74)

Communal Cults

No society is completely without communally organized religious beliefs and practices. Even the Inuit have group rites. Under the cross-examinations of shamans, frightened and sick individuals publicly confess violations of taboos that have made them ill and that have endangered the rest of the community.

Communal cults use rituals to strengthen group continuity by communicating socially constructed meaning signifying the continuity of the group.

Communal rites fall into two major categories: (1) rites of solidarity and (2) rites of passage. In **rites of solidarity**, participation in dramatic public rituals enhances the sense of group identity, coordinates the actions of the individual members of the group, and prepares the group for immediate or future cooperative action. **Rites of passage** celebrate the social movement of individuals into and out of groups or into or out of statuses of critical importance to the individual and to the community. Reproduction, the achievement of manhood and womanhood, marriage, and death are the principal worldwide occasions for rites of passage.

The performance of **rituals** is an integral part of religion.

Rituals are formal, stylized, and repetitive acts that are performed in special, sacred places at set times.

Most rituals are performed in special places under specific conditions removed from the ordinary world. Rituals convey information that is repeated time after time and convey messages and sentiments and translate them into action. As such, rituals are social acts. They are powerful forces that bring participants to accept a common social and moral order that transcends their status as individuals. By reinforcing group norms, they bring about homogeneity. A uniformity of beliefs helps bind people together and reinforces group identity.

Communal Rites of Solidarity. Rites of solidarity are common among clans and other descent groups.

Rites of solidarity are directed toward the welfare of the community, rather than the individual. They reaffirm the power of the group, which transcends individuals.

Such groups usually have names and emblems that identify group members and set one group off from another. Animal names and emblems predominate, but insects, plants, and natural phenomena such as rain and clouds also occur. These group-identifying objects are known as **totems**.

Totems are objects, such as animals and plants, that serve as the emblems or symbols of a kinship group or a person.

Members of each totemic group believe they were descendents of their totem. They view their totem with awe and refrain from harming or eating their totem. Each group sees their totem as their companion and protector. Though it is generally agreed that totemism is not a religion, totemism contains religious elements—the cult of ancestors, ideas of the soul, beliefs in spirits—in varying degrees. The specific forms of totemic belief, however, vary greatly, and no single totemic complex can be said to exist.

The Arunta of Australia provide one of the classic cases of totemic ritual. Here, an individual identifies with the totem of the sacred place near which one's mother passed shortly before becoming pregnant. These places contain the stone objects known as **churinga**, which are the visible manifestations of each person's spirit. The churinga are believed to have been left behind by the totemic ancestors as they traveled about the countryside at the beginning of the world. The ancestors later turned into animals, objects, and other entities. The sacred places of each totem are visited annually.

These totemic rituals have many meanings and functions. The participants are earnestly concerned with protecting their totems and ensuring their reproduction. But the exclusive membership of the ritual group also indicates that they are acting out the mythological dogma of their common ancestry.

The totem ceremonies reaffirm and intensify the sense of common identity of the members of a regional community.

The handling of the churinga confirms the fact that the totemic group has "stones" or, in a more familiar metaphor, "roots" in a particular land.

In contemporary U.S. society, rites of solidarity are mostly secular events, such as the Fourth of July parades and football games. Groups meet for traditional barbecues or watch college and professional games. These events become unifying cultural traditions that symbolize key features of American life. On Super Bowl Sunday, for example, millions of Americans from diverse cultural backgrounds come together to watch televised football. Although the symbolism of football—teamwotk and reward for consistency—are important, it is the common experience of participating in a national event that reinforces group solidarity.

Communal Rites of Passage. The most common occasions for rites of passage are birth, puberty, marriage, and death.

Rites of passage are ceremonies that mark changes in a person's social position that are of general public concern.

The individual who is born, who reaches adulthood, who takes a spouse, or who dies is not the only one implicated in these events. Many other people must adjust to these momentous changes. Being born not only defines a new life but also brings into existence or modifies the position of parent, grandparent, sibling, heir, age-mate, and many other domestic and political relationships. Rites of passage are important public rituals that recognize a wider set of altered social relationships. Contemporary passage rites include confirmations, baptisms, bar and bat mitzvahs, and fraternity hazings (see Box 10.1).

Rites of passage conform to a remarkably similar pattern among widely dispersed cultures (Eliade 1958; Schlegel and Barry 1979).

The three phases of rites of passage are separation, transition, and incorporation.

First, the principal performers are separated from the routines associated with their earlier life and prepare to move from one place or status to another. Second, decisive physical and symbolic steps are taken to extinguish the old status. Often, depersonalization accompanies separation; a person may leave his or her group and experience a symbolic death. Army boot camp is a good example of this process. Inductees are stripped of their former identity; they are issued numbers, dressed in identical uniforms, and given short haircuts. All ties are severed during their confinement. Often, these steps include the notion of killing the old personality. To promote "death and transfiguration," old clothing and ornaments are exchanged for new, and the body is painted or mutilated.

The second phase, known as the **liminal phase**, is a period of ambiguity during a person's transition between one status and another.

The **liminal phase** is a temporary ritual state, during which the individual is cut off from normal social contacts to demarcate a contrast from regular social life.

According to Victor Turner (1967), liminality involves the suspension of social norms; a person's past and future positions in society are ignored and he or she is subjected to experiences that are different or even reversed from what they are in the ordinary world.

Sometimes passage rites are collective. Collective liminality, called **communitas**, creates a community spirit and feeling of togetherness.

Box 10.1 No Rites Hurt, Too

Westerners are likely to be shocked and dismayed by examples of painful puberty rituals, but the system that has been substituted for such rituals may not have any clear advantage as far as eliminating pain and suffering. The passage from child to adult in advanced industrial societies is not marked by any rituals at all. No one is quite sure when adulthood begins. As a result, the young girl or boy must pass through a prolonged period of stress, known as **adolescence**, which is marked by high rates of accidents, suicides, and antisocial behavior. Which system is more cruel?

The Jewish bar mitzvah and bat mitzvah, held at age 13 for boys and girls, respectively, creates boy–men and girl–women for whom adult status lies many years ahead. Similarly, the Christian rite of confirmation, also performed in the teen years, is only vaguely associated with the passage to adulthood.

Communitas is an intense community spirit, a feeling of social solidarity, equality, and togetherness that is achieved through liminality.

People who experience communitas form a community of equals that is symbolically marked by reversals of ordinary behavior, such as fasting and seclusion. Permanent liminal groups, such as cults and sects, are found in complex societies. They are set apart from other religious groups and from society as a whole. Members become submerged in the collective group and abide by such liminal features as sexual abstinence, poverty, and silence.

Ecclesiastical Cults

Ecclesiastical cults or groups have a professional clergy or priesthood organized into a bureaucracy. This bureaucracy is usually associated with and under the control of a central temple. At secondary or provincial temple centers, the clergy may exercise a considerable amount of independence.

Ecclesiastical religion is found in highly centralized political systems.

RELIGION

The ecclesiastic specialists differ from both the Tapirapé shamans and the Ndembu circumcisers and guardians (see Profile 10.1). They are formally designated persons who are elected or appointed to devote themselves to conducting rituals at regular intervals. These rituals usually include a wide variety of techniques for reinforcing support for the supremacy of the ruling class.

Throughout history, the ecclesiastical specialists have generally lived much better than the population at large.

In many cases, it has been common for them to be part of the ruling class; material support for these full-time specialists is usually closely related to the power of taxation. It is therefore no surprise that in class societies, religion reflects the ideology of the dominant class. Among the Inca, the state and the priesthood were both supported by the rent and tribute extracted from the peasants (see Profile 10.2). Under feudalism, feudal lords received rights to land from the king, who was granted the right to rule by God. The priests of that time supported feudalism by endorsing the God-given rights of the nobility. The peasants had to work the land in exchange for the right to cultivate for themselves, while the priesthood preached humility and acceptance of one's station in life. In modern ecclesiastical religions such as Christianity, Judaism, and Buddhism, a full time professional clergy is supported through dues, donations, and gifts.

It must be stressed, however, that the congregation does not altogether abandon individualistic shamanistic and communal beliefs and rituals. These practices are all continued, sometimes secretly, in neighborhoods, villages, and households, side by side with the higher rituals, despite efforts by state-sanctioned religions to stamp out what it often calls superstitious, pagan, or heathen beliefs and performances.

Although it is considered controversial, Michael Harner's (1977) explanation of the Aztec state's unique ecclesiastical cannibalism is a viable theory. Harner starts from the fact that as a result of millennia of intensification and population growth, the Central Mexican highlands had lost their best domesticable animal species. Unlike the Inca, who obtained animal foods from llama, alpaca, and guinea pigs—or the Old World states that had sheep, goats, pigs, and cattle—the Aztec had only semidomesticated ducks and turkeys and hairless dogs. Wild fauna, such as deer and migrating waterfowl, were not abundant enough to provide the Aztecs with more than one or two grams of animal protein per capita per day (compared with over 60 grams in the United States). The depleted condition of the natural fauna is shown by the prominence in the Aztec diet of bugs worms, and "scum cakes," which were made out of algae skimmed off the surface of Lake Texcoco (see M. Harris 1979b; Sahlins 1978).

According to Harner, the severe depletion of animal resources made it uniquely difficult for the Aztec state to prohibit the consumption of human flesh. Human flesh, rather than animal flesh, was redistributed as a means of rewarding loyalty to the throne and bravery in combat.

According to Tim White (1997), there is no doubt that cannibalism was a common practice. At archeological digs all over the globe, researchers have found evidence of cannibalism. Human bones were broken open for their marrow and smaller fragments were boiled to extract fatty residues. White concludes that it used to be thought that the Spanish made up (as propaganda, to justify their own cruelty) the stories of the Aztecs eating their prisoners. But now excavations in Mexico City are finding evidence, such as carefully splintered bones, that the Aztecs really were cannibals (see Box 10.2).

BOX 10.2 The Evidence for Aztec Cannibalism

Bernadino de Sahagun, who started collecting data on the Aztecs in the 1540s, is generally considered to be the most honest and reliable historian and ethnographer of Aztec culture. In his *General History of the Things of New Spain*, he repeatedly describes the fate of the Aztec's sacrificial victims as follows:

"After they had slain them and torn out their hearts, they took them away gently, rolling them down the steps.... They carried the bodies to the houses...where they divided them up in order to eat them" (Sahagun 1951:24).

PROFILE 10.1: NDEMBU COMMUNAL RITES OF CIRCUMCISION

Communitas can be seen in the male initiation ceremonies of the Ndembu of northern Zambia. Here, as in many African and Middle Eastern cultures, the transition from boyhood to manhood involves the rite of circumcision. Young boys are taken from their separate villages and placed in a special bush "school." They are circumcised by their own kinsmen or neighbors, and after their wounds heal, they are returned to normal life. Among the Ndembu, the process of publicly transforming boys to men takes four months and is known as *mukanda*.

Victor Turner (1967) have a detailed account of a *mukanda* that he was permitted to witness in 1953. It began with the storage of food and beer. Then a clearing was made in the bush and a camp established. This camp included a hearth, at which the mothers of the boys undergoing circumcision cooked for them. On the day preceding the circumcision, the circumcisers danced and sang songs in which they expressed antagonism to the boys' mothers and made reference to the "killing" that was about to take place. The boys and their families assembled at the campsite, fires were lit, and a night of dancing and sexual license was begun.

According to Turner, "Suddenly the circumcisers entered in procession, carrying their apparatus…. All the rest of the gathering followed them as they danced crouching, holding up different items of apparatus, and chanting hoarsely. In the firelight and moonlight the dance got wilder and wilder" (1967:205). Meanwhile, "those who were about to die" sat in a line attended by their mothers and fathers. During the night, they were repeatedly awakened and carried about by their male relatives. The next morning, they were given a "Last Supper" (a last breakfast) by their mothers, "each mother feeding her son by hand as though he were an infant." The boys tried not to look terrified, as after breakfast, the circumcisers, their brows and foreheads daubed with red clay, danced about brandishing their knives.

The actual circumcision took place in another clearing some distance away from the cooking camp. The boys remained in seclusion at this site, which was known as the "place of dying." They slept in a brush lodge, watched over and ordered about by a group of male "guardians." After their "last breakfast," the boys were marched down the trail toward the "place of dying." The guardians came rushing out, seized them, and tore off their clothes. The mothers were chased back to the cooking camp, where they began to wail as at the announcement of a death. The boys were held by the guardians while the circumcisers "stretch out the prepuce, make a slight nick on top and another underneath as guides, then cut through the dorsal section with a single movement and follow this by slitting the ventral section, then removing sufficient amount of the prepuce to leave the glans well exposed" (Turner 1967:216).

PROFILE 10.2: THE RELIGION OF THE AZTECS

The Aztecs of Mexico had an ecclesiastical religion whose priests were held responsible for the maintenance and renewal of the entire universe. By performing annual rituals, priests could obtain the blessing of the Aztec gods, ensure the well-being of the Aztec people, and guard the world against collapse into chaos and darkness. According to Aztec theology, the world had already passed through four ages, each of which ended in cataclysmic destruction. The fifth age was in progress, ruled over by the sun god and doomed to destruction sooner or later by earthquakes.

The principal function of the 5,000 priests living in the Aztec capital was to ensure that the gods governing the world were sufficiently pleased so that the end of the world would come later, rather than sooner. The best way to please the gods was to give them gifts, the most precious being fresh human hearts—especially the hearts of war captives, because they were won only at great expense and risk.

Aztec ceremonial centers were dominated by large pyramidal platforms topped by temples. These structures were vast stages on which the drama of human sacrifice was enacted at least once a day throughout the year. First the victim would ascend to the top of the pyramid, where four priests would seize the victim and place him or her over the sacrificial stone. A fifth priest cut the victim's chest open with an obsidian knife and wrenched out the beating heart. The heart was smeared over the statue of the god and later burned. During a four-day dedication ceremony of the main Aztec temple in Tenochtitlán, some 20,000 prisoners of war were sacrificed in this manner.

It is estimated that nearly 15,000 people were sent to death annually to placate the blood-thirsty gods. Most of these victims were prisoners of war, although local youths, maidens, and children were also sacrificed from time to time (Coe 1977; Berdan 1982; Vaillant 1966 [1941]). After being killed, the bodies of most of those who were sacrificed were dismembered and probably cooked and eaten (Harner 1977; see also Box 10.2 for evidence of Aztec cannibalism).

Prior to the emergence of states, many societies, especially chiefdoms, practiced human sacrifice and ritually consumed all or parts of the bodies of prisoners of war. (M. Harris 1985, 1989). Lacking the political-military means to tax and conscript large populations, chiefdoms had little interest in preserving the lives of their defeated enemies. With the advent of the state, however, cannibalism and human sacrifice tended to disappear.... Conquering territories were incorporated into the state, and the labor power of defeated populations was tapped through taxation, conscription, and tribute. Thus, preserving the lives of defeated peoples became an essential part of the process of state expansion.

The Aztecs, however, were an exception to this general trend. Instead of making human sacrifice and cannibalism taboo, the Aztec state made them the main focus of ecclesiastical beliefs and rituals. As the Aztecs became more powerful, they sacrificed increasing numbers of prisoners of war and became more rather than less cannibalistic (see also E. Wolf 1998).

RELIGION AND POLITICAL ECONOMY: HIGH GODS

Full-time specialists, monumental temples, dramatic processions, and elaborate rites performed for spectator congregations are incompatible with the infrastructure and political economy of hunters and gatherers. Similarly, the complex astronomical and mathematical basis of ecclesiastical beliefs and rituals is never found among band and village peoples.

The level of political economy also influences the way in which gods are thought to relate to each other and to human beings. For example, the idea of a single high god who created the universe is found among cultures at all levels of economic and political development. These high gods, however, play different kinds of roles in running the universe after they have brought it into existence. Among hunter-gatherers and other nonstate peoples, the high gods

CHAPTER **10**

tend to become inactive after their creation task is done (Sullivan 1987). To obtain assistance, one must turn to a host of lesser gods, demons, and ancestor souls (see Hayden 1987). In stratified societies, the high god bosses the lesser gods and tends to be a more active figure, to whom priests and commoners address their prayers (Swanson 1960), although ordinary people may still revere the lesser gods more actively.

Societies whose rulers rely on religious indoctrination to secure and legitimize their position of power have a different reward system than secular societies. In such societies, conformity is reinforced through the promise of spiritual rewards, especially promises of rewards in the afterlife or martyrdom in exchange for deprivation in this world or sacrifice in battle.

A plausible explanation for this difference is that nonstate cultures have no need for the idea of a central or supreme authority. Just as centralized control over people and strategic resources is absent in life, so in religious belief the inhabitants of the spirit world lack decisive control over each other. They form a more or less egalitarian group.

The belief that superordination and subordination characterize relationships among the gods helps obtain the cooperation and submission of the commoner classes in stratified societies.

One way to achieve conformity in complex stratified societies is to convince commoners that the gods demand obedience to the state. Myths and rituals express the commoners' dependence on the rulers' well-being. To challenge the ruler would be like challenging the very order of the universe. The priesthood dazzles, mystifies, and intimidates the commoners through the performance of highly intricate rituals and the construction of grandiose temples in order to discourage the commoners from opposing their rulers. Disobedience and nonconformity result not only in retribution administered through the state's police military apparatus but also in punishments in the present or future life, administered by the high gods themselves. In nonstate societies (for reasons discussed in Chapter 18), law and order are rooted in common interest. Consequently, there is little need for high gods to administer punishments to those who have been "bad" and rewards to those who have been "good."

REVITALIZATION MOVEMENTS

The relationship of religion to structure and infrastructure can also be seen in the process known as **revitalization**.

Revitalization movements occur during times of change, in which religious leaders emerge to bring forth positive change.

Anthony Wallace (1970) defines **revitalization movements** as "deliberate and organized attempts by some members of a society to construct a more satisfying culture through rapid acceptance of a pattern of multiple innovations." Most revitalization movements follow a fairly uniform process:

- A society is in the state of equilibrium.

- A society is pushed out of equilibrium by various forces, such as climatic or biotic change, epidemic disease, war and conquest, and so forth.

- The society becomes disillusioned and disorganized.

- Social deterioration sets the stage for a revitalization movement to appear in an effort to bring about a more satisfying society.

- An individual or group constructs a new, idealistic image of culture that forms the basis for social action.

Under the severe stresses associated with colonial conquest and intense class or minority exploitation, religions tend to become movements concerned with achieving drastic improvements in the immediate conditions of life or in the prospects for an afterlife. These movements are sometimes referred to as **nativistic**, **revivalistic**, **millennarian**, and **messianic**. The concept of revitalization is intended to embrace all the specific cognitive and ritual variants implied by these terms (Wallace 1966).

Revitalization occurs during times of cultural stress brought about by rapid change, foreign domination, and perceived deprivation.

RELIGION

Revitalization is a process of political and religious interaction among a depressed caste, class, ethnicity, or other subordinate social group and a superordinate group. Some revitalization movements emphasize passive attitudes, the adoption of old rather than new cultural practices, or salvation through rewards after death; others advocate more or less open resistance or aggressive political or military action (see Profile 16.3). These differences largely reflect the extent to which the subordinate groups are prepared to cope with the challenge to their power and authority. Re vitalizations that take place under conditions of massive suffering and exploitation sooner or later result in political and even military confrontations, even though both sides may overtly desire to avoid conflict (Worsley 1968).

Native American Revitalizations

Widespread revitalizations were provoked by the European invasion of the New World, the conquest and expulsion of the Native American peoples, and the destruction of their natural resources. The native peoples of the American West had been mostly confined to reservations by the 1870s; their economic base was ruined with the destruction of buffalo herds and occupation of their lands. The coercive authority imposed on them brought an atmosphere of total defeat and discouragement, which provided the conditions for numerous revitalization movements.

The most famous of the nineteenth-century revitalization movements was the **Ghost Dance** that began among the Piute Indians and then spread across the Plains. The main phase of the Ghost Dance began in 1889 under the inspiration of a prophet named Wovoka. Wovoka and his followers envisioned a day when all their ancestors would return to life. Songs and dances revealed to Wovoka would make this happen. The Ghost Dance prophecy was in the tradition of myths about the dead returning to life and the beginning of a life of plenty.

The **Ghost Dance**, Native Americans believed, would place dancers in contact with the spirit world and hasten the time when people would be reunited with their dead ancestors. This meant that they would outnumber the Whites and hence be more powerful.

Ostensibly, Wovoka's teachings lacked political content, and as the Ghost Dance spread eastward across the Rockies, its political implications remained ambiguous.

The Sioux interpreted the vision differently and initiated a version of the Ghost Dance that included the return of all the bison and the extermination of the Whites under a huge landslide. The Sioux led pure lives and believed that violence was no longer necessary because the world would change by itself. They put on Ghost Dance shirts, believing they would make them invulnerable to bullets. Nevertheless, the Ghost Dance frightened settlers, who feared that the movement would spark a political uprising. After the Sioux leader Sitting Bull was arrested and killed, the U.S. Army ended the Ghost Dance movement by massacring 200 members of the Lakota Sioux—mainly women and children—at Wounded Knee, South Dakota, on December 29, 1890 (Mooney 1965).

After all chance of military resistance was crushed, the Native American revitalization movement became more introverted and passive. Visions in which all the Whites were wiped out ceased to be experienced, confirming once again the responsiveness of religion to political reality.

The development and spread of beliefs and rituals centering on peyote, mescal, and other hallucinogenic drugs is characteristic of many current Native American revitalizations. Peyote ritual, as practiced in the Native American Church, involves a night of praying, singing, peyote eating, and ecstatic contemplation followed by a communal breakfast. Peyote, which is a small cactus that grows in northern Texas, produces vivid hallucinations. The peyote eaters are not interested in bringing back the buffalo or making themselves invulnerable to bullets; they seek self-knowledge, personal moral strength, and physical health (Stewart 1987).

RELIGION AND SOCIETY

Emile Durkheim believed the essence of religion is a moral system that enables individuals to function as coordinated units. Religion originates in the experience by which people feel a moral force exterior to themselves—a state of consciousness affected by social conditions of which the individual remains unaware. Religion is a unified system of beliefs and practices relative to sacred things that unite those who adhere to them into a moral community (Durkheim 1995 [1912]:76–77).

PROFILE 10.3: MELANESIAN CARGO CULTS

In New Guinea and Melanesia, revitalization is associated with the concept of cargo. The typical vision of the leaders of Melanesian revitalization movements is that of a ship bringing back the ancestors and a cargo of European goods. Over the years, airplanes and spaceships have become the favorite means of delivering the cargo.

Inspired by the adundance of goods U.S. military forces displayed during the Pacific Island campaigns of World War II, Melanesians developed the belief that they too would become wealthy. Some revitalizations stressed the return of the Americans. In 1944, a local leader named Tsek urged his people to destroy all trade goods and throw away their clothes in preparation for the return of the mysteriously departed Americans. Some of the U.S.-oriented revitalizations had placed specific U.S. soldiers in the role of cargo deliverers. On the island of Tana in the New Hebrides, the John Frumm cult cherished an old GI jacket as the relic of one John Frumm, whose identity is not otherwise known. The followers of John Frumm built landing strips, bamboo control towers, and grass-thatched cargo sheds. In some cases, beacons were kept ablaze at night and radio operators stood ready with tin-can microphones and earphones to guide the cargo planes to a safe landing. The natives were waiting for a total upgrading of their lives. They believed the phantom ships and planes would mark the beginning of a whole new era.

The Melanesians had several revitalization scenarios. Some believed that the cargo planes and ships had been successfully loaded by their ancestors at U.S. ports and were on their way but that the local authorities had refused to permit the cargo to be landed. In another version, the cargo planes had been tricked into landing at the wrong airport. In a metaphorical sense, these sentiments applied to the actual conditions under colonialism. The peoples of the South Seas were indeed often tricked out of their lands and resources.

The confusion of the Melanesian revitalization prophets stemmed from naiveté about the workings of cultural systems. The prophets did not understand how modern industrial wage labor societies were organized, nor could they comprehend how law and order were maintained among state-level peoples. Their leaders dismissed the standard European explanation of hard work equaling wealth as a calculated deception. Anyone could see that the European "big men," unlike their native prototypes, scarcely worked at all. The natives insisted that the material wealth of the industrial age was really created in some distant place, not by humans but by supernatural means. To the Melanesians, the material abundance of the industrial nations and the poverty of others constituted an irrational flaw, a massive contradiction in the structure of the world.

The belief system of the cargo cults vividly demonstrates why we can't assume that all people distinguish between natural and supernatural categories. Cargo leaders who had been taken to see modern Australian stores and factories, in the hope that they would give up their beliefs, returned home more convinced than ever that they were following the best prescription for obtaining cargo. With their own eyes, they had observed the fantastic abundance the authorities refused to let them have (Lawrence 1964).

Westerners were impressed by the natives' inability to understand European economic lifestyles. The implication was that the natives were too backward or superstitious to grasp the principles of civilization. However, it was not that these natives could not grasp the principles in question; rather, it was that they found them unacceptable. When their leaders learned more about how Europeans produced wealth, they were less prepared to accept their explanation of why their people were unable to share in it. Without the cheapness of native labor and the expropriation of native lands, the colonial powers would never have gotten so rich. In one sense, the natives were entitled to the products of the industrialized nations, even though they couldn't pay for them. The cargo cult was their way of saying this.

RELIGION

Durkheim saw the fundamental psychological aspect of religion as the elimination of the self and the denial of individuality for the purpose of the social group, which is greater than the self.

Religion is a symbolic representation of society.

When people come together in social assemblies, a social effervescence is created, out of which religious ideas are confirmed and given greater emotional meaning.

Religion emerges through the distinction between **sacred** and **profane**. Human actions take on special meaning through the realm of the *sacred*—that which pertains to the transcendental and extraordinary. Sacred objects may look like *profane* ones; the distinction between sacred and profane does not reside in the intrinsic properties of the object but in its symbolic representation and meaning.

The sacred is the realm of human experience that evokes an attitude of awe and reverence.

The profane is the realm of the secular. It is the world of everyday domestic duties that are essentially utilitarian.

For example, sacramental wine symbolizing the blood of Christ may not differ from ordinary table wine, yet it is defined as holy and treated in a reverential manner. Religious beliefs and social behaviors are guided by what a culture deems sacred. Sacred propositions are taken to be unquestionably true because their sacred meanings elicit a sense of certainty in the validity of the propositions that is beyond question. A sanctified message is certified, so there is no need to prove it.

Sanctity is the quality of unquestionable truthfulness credited by the faithful to unverifiable propositions.

Sanctity ensures that participants will fulfill their commitments and greatly increases the likelihood of conformity. Religion reinforces group norms by defining what is proper and improper behavior. If individuals do the proper things in life, they will earn approval of the gods. Otherwise,

they will suffer supernatural retribution. Religion has been used to affect action and mobilize people to support certain views or policies. Similarly, religion has been used to persuade people that groups who hold different views are threatening and dangerous. This is why throughout history, political leaders have used religion to instill fear and hatred for political purposes. This is evident in the case of Holy Wars such as the Crusades, aimed at recapturing Jerusalem from Islam, and jihad, a duty imposed on Muslims to spread Islam by waging war.

Witchcraft accusations are another means of instilling social control through fear….[A]ntisocial or otherwise deviant behavior can result in an individual being labeled as a witch. Since witches are feared, they are often ostracized or killed. During the sixteenth and seventeenth centuries in Germany, the witch craze was directly aimed at demobilizing protests by the poor and deflecting their demands for redistribution of wealth (Harris 1974:239).

Roy Rappaport (1975, 1979) has shown that sacred propositions also provide a means of expression for ecological adaptation by maintaining the predominance of certain conventions against the challenge of alternatives. The conventions through which societies are regulated are sanctified, but they themselves are not sacred. "To sanctify statements is to certify them" (1973:69). If people are more likely to accept sanctified messages as unquestionable, then their response will be more predictable. Sanctity, as we will see, takes behavior out of the hands of individual decision makers and increases the likelihood of compliance.

Incest Taboo

If religious sanctions evoke a sense of the sacred, it follows that an appeal to the sacred nature of a rule governing interpersonal relations will resolve the uncertainties about what people should do or how they should behave. For example, the prohibition on incest is widely regarded as a sacred obligation. One plausible explanation is that people are strongly tempted to commit incest but that the short-run satisfactions would have long-term negative consequences for them and for the community….By surrounding incest prohibitions with the aura of sacredness, the long-term individual and collective interest comes to prevail, and the ambiguities and doubts that the individual feels about renouncing the prohibited relationship are resolved more decisively than would otherwise be possible.

This does not mean that incest does not occur or that all psychological doubts are removed but that such doubts are brought under effective social control.

Taboos against Eating Pork

Anthropologists have debated the issue of whether strongly held religious beliefs are ecologically adaptive. Do various religiously sanctioned taboos on the consumption of certain foods, for example, have negative nutritional consequences? Do such taboos sometimes actually contribute to a more efficient use of a society's infrastructural potential? In answering these questions, both the costs and benefits of not eating a particular food and the availability of more efficient alternatives must be considered.

A tension between short-run and long-run costs and benefits may also explain the origin of certain food taboos that are regarded as sacred obligations. Consider, for example, the ancient Israelite prohibition on the consumption of pork. Pigs require shade and moisture to regulate their body temperature. Moreover, unlike the domesticated ruminants, such as cattle, sheep, and goats, pigs don't give milk. They also can't pull carts or plows, nor can they subsist on grass. With the progressive deforestation and desertification of the Middle East caused by the spread and intensification of agriculture and stock raising and by population growth, habitat zones suitable for pig rearing became scarce. Hence, an animal that was at one time reared and consumed as a relatively in expensive source of fat and protein could no longer be reared and consumed by large numbers of people without reducing the efficiency of the main system of food production (M. Harris 1985). The temptation to continue the practice of pig raising persisted, however—hence, the invocation of sacred commandments in the ancient Hebrew religion.

Note that the explanation of the ancient origins of this taboo does not account for its perpetuation into the present. Once in existence, the taboo against pork (and other foods) acquired the function of demarcating or bounding Jewish ethnic minorities from other groups and of increasing their sense of identity and solidarity. Outside the Middle East, the taboo no longer served an ecological function, but it continued to be useful on the level of structural relationships.

The Sacred Cow

The case of the sacred cattle of India conforms to the general theory that the flesh of certain animals is made taboo when it becomes very expensive as a result of ecological changes. Like pigs in the Middle East, cattle were sacrificed and eaten quite freely in India during the Neolithic period. With the rise of the state and of dense rural and urban populations, however, cattle could no longer be raised in sufficient numbers to be used both as a source of meat and as the principal source of traction power for pulling plows. But as the taboo on cattle use developed, it took a form quite different from the Israelite taboo on the pig.

Whereas the pig was valued almost exclusively for its flesh, cattle were also valued for their milk and especially for their traction power. When pigs became too costly to be raised for meat, the whole animal became taboo and an abomination. But as cattle in India became too costly to be raised for meat, their value as a source of traction power increased. (The land had to be plowed more intensively as population grew.) Therefore, they had to be protected and so the Hindu religion came to emphasize everyone's sacred duty to refrain from killing cattle or eating beef. The Hindu doctrine of *ahimsa* puts the full power of religion in support of the command not to kill cattle or eat beef, even in times of extreme food scarcity. Interestingly, the Brahmans…who at one time were the caste responsible for ritually slaughtering cattle, later became the caste most concerned with their protection and most opposed to the development of a beef-slaughtering industry in India (M. Harris 1977, 1979a, 1985; cf. Simoons 1979).

What about sacred cattle today? Are the religious ban on the slaughter of cows (female cattle) and oxen (castrated male cattle) and the taboo against the consumption of beef functionally useful features of modern Hinduism? Everyone agrees that the human population of India needs more calories and proteins, yet the Hindu religion still bans the slaughter of cattle and taboos the eating of beef. These taboos are often held responsible for allowing large numbers of aged, decrepit, barren, and useless cattle. Such animals are depicted as roaming aimlessly across the Indian countryside, clogging the roads, stopping the trains, stealing food from the marketplace, and blocking city streets. A closer look at some of the details of the ecology and economy of the Indian subcontinent, however, suggests that the taboo in question does not decrease the capacity of the present Indian system of food production to support human life.

The basis of traditional Indian agriculture is the ox-drawn plow. Each peasant farmer needs at least two oxen to plow the fields at the proper time of the year. Despite the impression of surplus cattle, there is in fact a shortage of oxen, because one-third of the peasant households own less than the minimum pair. It is true that many cows are too old, decrepit, and sick and the Hindu farmer is depicted as ritually obsessed with preserving the life of each sacred beast, rather than killing dry, barren, and weak cattle, no matter how useless it may become. But from the point of view of the poor farmer, these creatures may be quite useful. The farmer would prefer to have more vigorous cows but is prevented from achieving this goal not by the taboos against slaughter but by the short age of land and pasture (Chakravarti 1985a, 1985b; George 1990).

Even barren and weak cattle are by no means a total loss. Their dung makes an essential contribution to the energy system as fertilizer and as cooking fuel. Millions of tons of artificial fertilizer, at prices beyond the reach of the small farmer, would be required to make up for the loss of dung if substantial numbers of cattle were sent to slaughter. Because cattle dung is also a major source of cooking fuel, the slaughter of substantial numbers of animals would require the purchase of expensive dung substitutes, such as wood, coal, or kerosene. Cattle dung is relatively cheap because the cattle do not eat foods that can be eaten by people. Instead, they eat the stubble left in the fields and the marginal patches of grass on steep hillsides, roadside ditches, railroad embankments, and other nonarable lands. This constant scavenging gives the impression that cows are roaming around aimlessly, devouring everything in sight. But most cattle have an owner, and in the cities, after poking about in the market refuse and nibbling on neighbors' lawns, each animal returns to its stall at the end of the day.

In a study of the bioenergetic balances involved in the cattle complex of villages in West Bengal, Stuart Odend'hal (1972) found that "basically, the cattle convert items of little direct human value into products of immediate human utility." Their gross energetic efficiency in supplying useful products was several times greater than that characteristic of agroindustrial beef production. He concluded that "judging the productive value of Indian cattle based on Western standards is inappropriate."

Another crucial question is whether the taboo on slaughter accounts for the ratio of cows to oxen. Despite the ban on slaughter, Hindu farmers cull their herds and adjust sex ratios according to regional needs. The cattle are killed by various indirect means of neglect…culling unwanted female calves results in having over 200 oxen for every 100 cows in the Gangetic plain in northern India, where oxen are needed for traction, despite the fact that the region is one of the most religiously orthodox in India (Vaidyanathan et al. 1982).

There are additional reasons for concluding that the Hindu taboo has a positive effect on the carrying capacity of the ecosystem. Cows seldom go to waste because animals that die a natural death are consumed by the untouchables, who are not obligated by the beef-eating taboos, and their skin is preserved as leather. Moreover, the function of the ban on slaughter is critical during famines. When hunger strikes the Indian countryside, the taboo on slaughter helps the peasants resist the temptation to eat their cattle.

If the temptation to eat their cattle were to win out over their religious scruples, the Indian peasants would be unable to plant new crops when the rains begin again. Thus, the intense resistance among Hindu saints to the slaughter and consumption of beef takes on a new meaning in the context of the Indian infrastructure. In the words of Mohandas Gandhi: "Why the cow was selected for apotheosis is obvious to me. The cow was in India the best companion. She was the giver of plenty. Not only did she give milk but she also made agriculture possible" (1954:3).

Marvin Harris; Orna Johnson, *Cultural Anthropology* (book alone), 7th edition. Copyright © 2007, pages 271–280, 282–291. Reprinted by permission of Pearson Education, Inc., Upper Saddle River, NJ.

E X E R C I S E

Name

Section

Date

EXERCISE 10.1: RELIGION AND POLITICS

Describe your thoughts concerning religion and politics. Write an article of 150 words or less as though you are to submit this to the opinion section of your school newspaper. Demonstrate your opinions and ground them in the beliefs of your religion. Presenting these papers before the class will demonstrate the diversity of religions practiced in the United States as well as help you understand beliefs and myths which may differ from your own.

RELIGION

400

The Permanent Record—
Jim Bell, Ph.D.

It was cloudy and heavily overcast as I recall. The school and church structures loomed menacingly against the darkened sky, like those black and white images in the Rod Sterling opening of the *Twilight Zone* television program. Like the television show, the playground was devoid of the usual cacophony associated with children at play. This morning was still, even surreal, wrapped in a murky haze of shadows and an oppressive mist. Looking back over forty-seven years, or so, I remember the whole scene as ghostly in a way. I remember a chilly breeze floating down from the San Gabriel Mountains. We were in the midst of those horrific Winter storms that terrorized us from the Pacific northwest, hitting southern California one right after the other, sometimes with just a half hour reprieve between them. During the 1950s and early 1960s, these tempests always frightened the children. (It seemed to rain for two weeks straight without any let up in those days.) Loud booms and bangs, the ear-splitting crackling of thunder which seemed to roll across the sky forever, and quick flashes of lightening piercing the darkness in steel-gray configuration like the road maps in our classroom Atlas. This punctuated the school day. A sobering demand for us children during those periods was to continue our normal routine, to maintain ordinary activities as much as possible—and we did receive some sense of security from the regularity in the behavior of both adults and children.

Sister Mary Gladys was at her post as the crossing guard. She was one of the most pleasant people in the world, when she wanted to be. Sister "Happy Bottom," as we called her behind her back, was tall and thin. She was the principal and the school's detective of sorts, ferreting out "truth" and virtue from the most hardened of the school's criminals. At least we thought so. Whenever two children were in conflict over anything, she would come to settle the issue in the same manner. Her Ben Franklin glasses added an air of authority to her physical presence, particularly when confronting small children, who had to stretch their necks to look up at this tall wisp of saintliness. During her interrogation sessions, those penetrating blue eyes perpetually found their way over the rims of her glasses and she would stare into the eyes of her "little people" and pierce their very souls with this examination, which was guaranteed to find the "truth." As she saw it, "her children" would never willingly provide accuracy in their individual accounts until she had sorted out the facts for herself. It would not take much of the famous "Happy Bottom" stare before the offending culprit(s) would confess and wait for his or her punishment. Sister Mary Gladys was always fair. Usually both children would receive yard clean up duty, with one child, however, receiving more yard to clean up than the other. "There is," she would say, "nothing like the utterance of an untruth to keep our school yard clean." She would recite this, her favorite axiom, to each and every class at least twice a week.

Father O'Hagen, an Irishman who spoke with the thickest of brogues, would come in each morning to lead us in prayer and to prepare us for First Communion. He was a fine, roly-poly, sort of a gentleman. His bulbous nose was slightly red with tiny veins going through it, like the switching-tracks down at the rail yards. On this particular day, Father O'Hagan changed the routine and, instead of First Communion practice, he told us about the thing which altered the worldview of every second-grader in the class. He informed us of: **THE PERMANENT RECORD!**

This thing, this profane object from the depths of Hell, would follow each of us throughout life. No matter where we went, people would know all about each one of us and our individual deeds. Our grades from school, our work habits, our illnesses, our faults... all would be in this record for anyone and everyone to see.

A new storm began to rage outside. Thunder crackled, lightning streaked across an ebony sky. I envisioned a trail of paper similar to the lightning, hiding everywhere behind me, carried on the winds of an eternal storm, and striking just when I least expected it. No matter where I went in life, it would be there. Everyone would know what kind of Catholic I was, what kind of child I had been, and what sort of a parent I would become. It was terrifying. It occurred to me that I had to be good from then until forever. "How come they didn't tell us about this permanent record before now," I wondered to myself. "Why did they let some of us start accumulating bad materials on our record before telling us of its existence? Who was the diabolical person that thought this up?" A flash of light and a loud KABOOM from the Heavens rattled the windows, stopped my heart and my thoughts. "Did the yard clean up duties imposed by Sister Mary Gladys go into this record? Does calling her 'Happy Bottom' get into the record as well? Who was in charge of this record? Was this another of those things of which God kept score?"

Another nearby strike and the floor seemed to roll and shake. I was sure that God was listening to my thoughts, just as the nuns had told us He does. "Would a visit to the confessional erase a portion of this permanent record each time you went? If not, how did one clear this record before it was too late? Could one ever do that?" I had a lot to comprehend about this permanent record business and there was the storm outside; and I was only seven years old. I was very concerned about the morning's light and sound show, and about the permanent record. This had not been a regular morning routine at all. Something was going on, I was sure.

My grandfather was the first person I would see every day after school. He was an elevator operator in one of the tall buildings in downtown Los Angeles. He was a smart man. I knew that because he knew everything about everything. "He knows more about white people than any other Negro alive," my uncle Tommy would say. Papa, as we called him, was from a family who had known their share of lynchings and burnings, killings, and the night riding klansmen who frightened him as a child back in the Midwest. If anyone could tell me about this permanent record thing, he would be the one.

Papa usually came in from work around the time I came home from school. He was a comfortable soul to be around. He had stories and jokes that made him laugh harder than anyone else. If he had a joke, we all had to wait long minutes for the punch line because he was so tickled himself that he could not get it out without first twisting himself up with laughter. Carrol Lewis Robinson was his given name and his history within the Catholic Church could be characterized as a perpetual war with the clergy, the dogma out of Rome, and the "nerve of God to place so much hurt" on him. Still, he was wrapped up in "his Church." He would "put the Church on the straight and narrow someday," he often said.

Papa listened as I told him about the permanent record as I had learned about it from Father O'Hagan that morning as the storm waned outside. He made no comment

immediately, but seemed first to gather his thoughts. He could evidently see that I was very concerned about this matter and so he decided that we would have to engage in a family meeting.

Family meetings were a serious thing when I was growing up. Every person in the family had to come and speak, listen, debate, and/or vote on issues which often meant the very survival of individuals in the family. I was more puzzled then ever. My father was a waiter on the Santa Fe Railroad at that time and was on a run from Los Angeles to Chicago. He would not be at the meeting. He was the one person who could have enlightened me as to why a family meeting was needed here.

At supper that night, my mother and grandmother, brothers, Mr. Curry (our boarder), young Mr. Frazier (a bachelor neighbor who paid to eat the evening meal with us), and old Mrs. Johnstone (who lived in the back house) were all listening to Papa relay the story of the permanent record. I watched their faces for any signs of distress, any meaningful facial expressions. There were none. Most everyone was pretty quiet. Nana (my grandmother) talked about asking Sister Mary Elizabeth but, in his usual wisdom, Papa believed that might be a mistake. "Dizzy Lizzy," as he liked to call her, was "not a member of the true human family." Papa always thought she was too ugly to be a real person. To him, she was some sort of a gargoyle slipped into the parish by the Cardinal to keep the "colored folk in line." Papa had a lot of these kind of impressions. Most of them were dismissed by us kids as Papa being—well, being Papa.

The next day was Wednesday and the family meeting would not be held until Saturday. I had to stay on the alert so that nothing went on my permanent record before the family had a chance to meet. No one told me this. I just figured it out for myself. I would not even take a chance playing with the other kids, for fear that something could be recorded on my record. Sister Mary Joseph had playground duty that week so I could get away with not playing. She was very old. Papa said that "she was three days older than God." Anyway, she sat in a kind of a lifeguard chair up high so she could see more of the school yard but, often, she sort of dozed off and missed much of the children's real mischief; at least we thought she did. I watched to see if she was keeping a record under her sleeve.

Saturday finally came. The women shopped in the morning and began cooking as soon as they returned from the supermarket. Our family meetings were always a big festival of sorts. Supper, which was eaten around three or four in the afternoon, was followed later in the evening by beer and snacks, loud debates, and quiet whispers. Sometimes a family meeting caused someone to cry, or a person to beg forgiveness from other individuals. Sometimes the meetings centered on how one was being discriminated against on the job, at a particular store or movie theater, or when and where a member should purchase a home. These were all issues of major concern to the family in those days, well before passage of the Civil Rights Act. It was important for the family to maintain close watch on each others' lives. Family meetings were just about the most important event we had.

Now this family meeting was being called for me, to discuss my problem concerning the permanent record. I felt a little fear and apprehension but was very proud that my Papa had called a family meeting on my behalf. That had never happened to me before. Now I could see that I was really part of the family, not just a child who "should be seen and not heard."

Heavy rain and a strong wind punctuated the day and evening. Supper had been the usual family meeting feast. Everyone had eaten "hardily" and a polyrhythmic chorus of a few muffled belches and resonant complaints of being "full to the top" accentuated the termination of the meal. Laughter and good-natured ribbing were the normal order of the day. Nothing appeared out of the ordinary. Still, the family had gathered to resolve my problem and that made it all a memorable occasion. Big fat Aunt Helen had come straight from her job as a domestic for a television executive. Uncle Jess had closed his barber shop early to attend this meeting. Several of the others had canceled important Saturday night plans just to deliberate on my behalf.

Papa was in fine spirits as he sat at the head of the dining-room table. Mother and grandmother had put in the extra leaves so that the table would accommodate a total of fourteen people. Chairs were brought in from the living room and den so that the ten or so guests not seated at the table could be a part of this conclave. Great Uncle Robert sat at the other end of the table. He was the oldest living member of the family. He had been in the Spanish American War and repeatedly told how he and the rest of the "Buffalo Soldiers" attacked "Kettle Hill" at San Juan, Cuba, and waited for Teddy and his Rough Riders to come along and take the glory. If Sister Mary Jo was three days older than God, my great Uncle Robert was at least two days older than Sister Mary Jo.

All the members were seated, the opening prayer was administered by Papa (who claimed a direct line to God because he and the Lord had been at war off and on during his entire life) and minor business was dispensed with. Aunt Claudine and Uncle Moss had repaid the last installment on their loan from the family account. My mother's cousin Ellen was unable to get the promotion at the Helm's Bakery where she and Uncle Harry were employed part-time. My Uncle Gregory was appointed to see a man named Del Vecchio about union rules and cousin Ellen's right to have the promotion. Aunt Johnnie wanted to borrow six hundred dollars from the family account to get some new machines for her beauty parlor business that she had started with one of her girl friends from beauty college. Great Uncle Robert wanted to discuss his funeral arrangements.

Every family meeting had a moment when Great Uncle Robert wanted to make clear his "laying out" plans. We all knew which suit of clothes he wanted, how his hands were to be folded, which song was to be sung, and how his army medal was to be placed on his chest. Everyone knew, but he would repeat it every time there was a family meeting. Mr. Frazier always reminded him that he was "too cantankerous to die like a proper gentleman." Papa also kidded him about how God "didn't take old soldiers who rode mules and ate horses." I guess that was some kind of a joke in the old cavalry. Great Uncle Robert was proud of his years as a "horse soldier" and he polished his antique silver spurs every day and hung them on his bedpost. Soon this banter would give way to the more serious reason for the meeting: The Permanent Record.

THE MOMENT HAD ARRIVED

The beer and soda were placed on the table by my grandmother. Snacks had already been arranged on platters (cold cuts, cheeses, crackers, sweet pickles, several pieces of sliced breads, a bowl of fruit balls, and the finest raw vegetables money could buy). This was a real important deliberation for the family, I could tell. No expense had been spared. We even had three kinds of ice-cream and two kinds of cake. This was a serious meeting, I just knew it.

Papa called the members to order with the tinkling of a spoon on his beer stein. The room fell into a hush. A stillness captured the air. I sat perfectly quiet. Papa allowed for the famous pause. He had learned that as a sergeant in the army. A flash of light outside the window followed by a crash of thunder broke the silence in the room. It was so dramatic. All eyes were on Papa as he began to recount the purpose for this gathering. The older people looked at me as Papa told them about my encounter with Father O'Hagan and the tale of the permanent record. When Papa had finished, he asked me to express my thoughts on the matter. I wanted to be real grown up at that moment and say something brilliant, but all I could muster was a soft "I don't know." My grandmother hugged me. Papa clinked his stein once again with his spoon and said, "Teeny leave the boy speak for himself. Stop mauling him."

I eventually expressed myself on the matter and the floor was open for discussion. Uncle Bill wanted to seek out "this priest" and give him "a swift kick in the…" Great Uncle Robert begged his young nephew to not even think of such action. "We should pray for the man like good Catholics," the old wise great uncle asserted, "and then give him a swift kick in the…" The image of Father O'Hagan's plump body being kicked in the rear was at first frightening. When all the adults laughed, I realized it was all said in jest…maybe. Perhaps this was something that needed further thought.

Aunt Peal (not a relative, but a friend of my grandmother's since they were children) suggested that Papa and Dit (my father) should make an appointment to meet with Father O'Hagan and have my permanent record cleared of any prior offenses, since I was not made aware of its existence and be allowed to start over again. Everyone thought that was a good idea. "What if the kindly servant of God doesn't wish to cooperate in such a plan?" Mr. Frazier chimed in. "Then," Uncle Bill said, "we can start the…kickin'." Everyone laughed again.

The discussion moved to exactly when the meeting with Father O'Hagan should take place and what precisely should be said. This continued for quite a while amidst beer and snacks, and the occasional lightning and thunder from the new storm. I felt better about the permanent record already. My family was not going to let this miscarriage of justice pass. They were not going to leave me alone with this messy record. They would come to my defense. They loved me very much. The women decided on their own that they would approach a few of the nuns and tell them something about how this permanent record issue was a fearful thing to several of the children and that it should be dealt with prior to any real harm coming from it. I was so pleased that the storms meant nothing to me anymore. Everyone smiled at me as I began to devour my bowl of ice-cream and cake. It was a wonderful family meeting. "The best we ever had," I thought. I knew I would never forget it, ever.

CONCLUSION

Several days after our family meeting, at school one morning, Father O'Hagan came to our classroom and interupted our arithmetic lesson. He wanted to discuss the "finer points of the permanent record," and we were to "listen very carefully to what I'll be sayin' about that now." That was the best morning of the whole school year. It seems that he "had checked into the finer points of the thing and there was no doubt that often the permanent record doesn't contain everything one does after all." Some of these records, according to him, had been known to actually be changed during one's lifetime so that a person can be forgiven certain social faults and minor school infractions occurring while one was under the age of twenty-one, or so. The good Father made it perfectly clear that we were not to worry about the permanent record until well after we had become adults. He further assured us that the "good sisters," and many others in the Church, would assist us in our quest toward proper High School training and entrance into fine colleges and universities when that time came.

Father O'Hagan had made it seem like we had all misunderstood him the first time he spoke of the permanent record, but I knew in my heart that my family, my Papa, had straightened him out on this issue. I believed that they must have checked very carefully into this permanent record thing and found out these little distinctions existed. My chest was stuck out a mile all that day. At recess and lunch break, I wanted so much to tell the other children what my family had done for me, for them, for all of us, but mama had told me not to say a word if Father O'Hagan came back to talk about the permanent record.

I was happy all day. My family had listened to me, they had come to my defense, and they had let me know that I was an important member of the group. It was one of the greatest days of my life.

When I was a little older, and a bit more mature, I learned from my grandmother that Papa had never spoken to Father O'Hagan about the permanent record. No one in my family had ever said anything to any of the clergy about it. Sister Margaret Mary, our teacher at the time, had noticed our faces and knew that we did not quite understand the meaning behind a "permanent record." Several of us moped around the playground for a few days after his first conversation with us and old Sister "Mary Jo" had caught the subtle change in our playground behavior over those few days, and informed Sister Margaret Mary that some of her children were troubled about something. Sister Mary Jo saw a lot while snoozing in her lifeguard chair. Anyway, Sister Maggie Mae (Margaret Mary) figured it out and spoke to Father O'Hagan about his first talk concerning the permanent record, the impression it seemed to have made on some of us, and she asked him to come and "lift the curse" he had placed on the class. And he did. We all felt much better about that record business once he cleared the air.

Still, my family did have a meeting to discuss my problem, they did allow me a moment in the center of the group, and they did prop me up, emotionally. My psyche was not damaged by the expression of their concern for my well-being; and my pride in who I was and where I belonged was enhanced by their small effort to teach me that lesson and to let me know that I was loved no matter what the permanent record might say about me.

The nuns were good also. They, whom we thought were there only to teach, to scream and punish, and to help save our souls, were very good for our mind and our humanity. They cared about us in ways we never saw, we never knew. They channeled kindness and concern into the classroom, onto the playground, and into our hearts without so much as a whisper.

In the final analysis, there is a generational permanent record of sorts. Older relatives and their friends, nuns and priests, working in long-ago neighborhoods linked by ethnicity and religion, did their share of bringing me along in the interconnected cultures of family and Church. The authentic permanent record of my childhood is that the best part of those days and the best part of those people remain a part of me.

Jim Bell, "The Permanent Record." Reprinted by permission of the Estate of James R. Bell, III.

RELIGION

E X E R C I S E

Name

Section

Date

EXERCISE 10.2: RITES OF PASSAGE

Compare a cultural practice with the transition to adulthood in your family. How is it similar or different? Is the practice you are describing associated with your ethnic group, religious identity, or family? What is the purpose of this event? What transition is being celebrated? Is this an important event in maintaining your cultural identity?

RELIGION

Neighboring Faiths: How Will Americans Cope with Increasing Religious Diversity?— *Diana L. Eck*

I first came to Harvard as a student of the culture and religions of India. I was fascinated by India's many religious traditions—the interrelations, tensions, and movements of Hindu, Buddhist, Jain, Muslim, and Sikh traditions over many centuries in a complex culture. But never did I imagine as I began teaching here in the late 1970s that the very interests that drew me to India would lead me in the 1990s to the study of the United States. So how is it that a scholar of comparative religion and Indian studies has spent the past five years studying America—furtively at first, fearful to be treading on the territory of some of Harvard's most distinguished scholars, then unapologetically, flagrantly, even zealously?

That intellectual passage from India to America began here at Harvard. The circumstances that drove me to study America raise important issues—for Harvard, for the United States, and perhaps for the world. They are issues all of us will encounter in a world shaped by a new geopolitical and a new "georeligious" reality.

For me, this journey began in the academic year 1989–90. Suddenly the contextual ground under my own feet as a scholar and teacher began to shift. In the past, I had always had several students from India in my classes on India, but in that year, their numbers increased. Only now, they were not from India, but were Indian Americans, born and raised in San Antonio, Baltimore, or Cleveland. They were, as I discovered, the children of the first generation of immigrants who had settled in America after the passage of the 1965 immigration act. That historic event finally removed the legal legacy of racism that had been built into immigration legislation from the first Chinese exclusion act in 1882 to the Johnson Reed Act in 1924, which effectively barred Asian immigrants for four decades. The 1965 policy opened the door again for immigration from Asia and from other parts of the world.

As a scholar of India, I had taken note of the effects of the new immigration on that country, the so-called "brain drain," as thousands of Indian professionals, doctors, and scientists left India for the United States. I have to admit, however, that I had never stopped to think what this would mean for the United States until the children of this first generation of Indian immigrants reached college age and enrolled in my classes at Harvard that year. There were Muslims from Providence, Hindus from Baltimore, Sikhs from Chicago, Jains from New Jersey. They represented the emergence in America of a new cultural and religious reality.

Some came from very secular families and knew little of their Indian heritage. Others had grown up in the new Hindu or Muslim culture of temples and Islamic centers their parents had begun to establish here in the United States. Some had been to Muslim youth leadership camps, organized by the Islamic Society of North America. Some had been to a Hindu summer camp at Rajarajeswari Pitha in the Poconos, or to a family Vedanta camp at Arsha Vidya Gurukulam in Saylorsburg, Pennsylvania. Some were involved as founding members of the Jain Youth of North America. Straddling two worlds, critically appropriating two cultures, they lived in perpetual inner dialogue between the distinctive cultures of their parents and grandparents and the forceful multiple currents of American culture. In their own struggles with identity lay the very issues that were beginning to torment the soul of the United States.

The new questions that arose were not only those that under-lay the foreign cultures requirement of the Core Curriculum—how we might understand some "other" civilization so different from our own. Other questions pushed themselves to the fore: What does it mean to speak of "our own" culture? Who do "we" mean when we say "we?" How are "difference" and "otherness" defined, and by whom? The word "multicultural" signaled the fact that every dimension of American culture had become more complex. Racial issues became multisided, with Hispanic and Latino, Korean and Filipino, Chinese and Indian perspectives. Religious diversity shattered the paradigm of an America the sociologist Will Herberg had confidently described as a "three religion country"—Protestant, Catholic, and Jewish. By the 1990s, there were Hindus and Sikhs, Buddhists and Jains. There were more Muslims than Episcopalians, more Muslims than Presbyterians, perhaps soon more Muslims than Jews.

RELIGION

The sons and daughters of the first generation from South Asia rose at Harvard to become some five percent of the Harvard undergraduate population. In the spring of 1993, when that first class graduated, I slipped into the balcony at Memorial Church for the Baccalaureate service and sat with the families of Mukesh Prasad and Maitri Chowdhury, the first marshals of the Harvard and Radcliffe graduating classes that year—both Hindus. Maitri recited a hymn from the Rig-Veda in ancient Sanskrit. It was a new Harvard. It had happened in four years.

The Puritans founded Harvard College to provide an educated Christian ministry for the churches. Before Judah Monis, a Sephardic Jew, was hired to teach Hebrew in 1722, he publicly converted to Christianity. But both Judah Monis and Cotton Mather would be astounded at Harvard in the 1990s—its Chinese and Korean Christian fellowships, its diverse and vibrant Jewish community, its rapidly growing Islamic Society. In December 1994, the newly founded Harvard Buddhist Community observed the Buddha's Enlightenment Day for the first time ever at Harvard. There in the Divinity School's Braun Room, beneath the august portraits of a long lineage of divinity deans, some 50 Harvard students from a dozen Buddhist lineages sat on rows of square zabutons, listening to Pali, Tibetan, and Vietnamese chanting and rising, one by one, to make offerings of incense.

What has happened at Harvard has happened at major universities throughout the country. In the 1990s, universities have become the microcosms and laboratories of a new multicultural and multireligious America. It is not uncommon to have Hindu and Jew, Muslim and Christian in a single rooming group. These changes in university demographics have come not from abroad, but from the rapidly changing cultural and religious landscape of the United States. Harvard's issues, America's issues, have become, increasingly, a fresh recasting of many of India's issues, the world's issues: race, culture, religion, difference, diversity, and whether it is possible to move from diversity to pluralism.

I knew in 1990 that my own teaching context had radically changed and the scope of my academic work would have to change, too. Increasingly, it became clear to me that the very shape of traditional fields of study was inadequate to this new world. In my field, those of us who study Buddhism, Islam, or Hinduism all earn our academic stripes, so to speak, by intensive study in Japan, Egypt, or India, doing language studies, textual editions and translations, fieldwork. And those who study religion in America focus largely on the Protestant mainstream, or perhaps on Catholics, or American Judaism—but not on American Buddhism, not on the Muslims of America, not on the Sikhs of America. And those historians who focus their work on what has become known as ethnic studies are curiously silent about the religious traditions of America's ethnic minorities—the old Islamic traditions of the African slaves, the old Chinese temples in Montana and Idaho, or the early Sikh communities in California's Imperial Valley.

In 1991, the pluralism project at Harvard set out to study multireligious America, beginning right here in Boston. Our research seminar visited the mosque in Quincy built in the shadow of the great cranes of the shipyards by Lebanese immigrants who came early in the century, and we found that there were some 20 other mosques and Islamic centers that are part of the Islamic Council of New England—in Dorchester, Wayland, Cambridge. We went to the spectacular new Sri Lakshmi temple in Ashland, a temple designed by Hindu ritual architects with tall towers decorated with the images of the gods and consecrated with the waters of the Ganges mingled with the waters of the Mississippi, the Colorado, and the Merrimack rivers. We visited half a dozen other Hindu communities in Boston, and two Sikh gurdwaras in Millis and Milford, and a Jain temple in Norwood, housed in a former Swedish Lutheran church. We found a dozen Buddhist meditation centers, with their respective Tibetan, Burmese, Korean and Japanese lineages of instruction. And we visited the temples of the Cambodian Buddhists in Lowell and Lynn, the Vietnamese in Roslindale and Revere, the Chinese in Quincy and Lexington. Eventually, we published *World Religions in Boston*, a documentary guide to a city whose Asian population had doubled in 10 years, now a multi-religious city.

It was clear that what was true of Boston might well be true of many other American cities. So the Pluralism Project sent a research team of students, multiethnic and multreligious, to study "hometown" America, fanning out across the United States every summer for three years. We were guided by three kinds of questions. First, who is here now in the 1990s? How many Hindu temples are there in Chicago? How many mosques in Oklahoma City? How many Buddhist temples in Houston? Second, how are these traditions changing as they take root in American soil? And third, how is America changing as Americans of many religions begin to appropriate this new multireligious reality and come to terms once again with our foundational commitment to religious freedom and, consequently, religious pluralism?

We found many remarkable developments. For example, Buddhist communities widely separated in Asia are now neighbors in Los Angeles, Seattle, and Chicago—Vietnamese, Cambodian, Thai, Chinese, Japanese, Korean, and Tibetan Buddhists. Here in America, these Buddhist communities are just beginning to know one another and to meet the distinctive communities of "new Buddhists"—Americans of all races who have come to Buddhism through its meditation practices and its ethics. The Buddhist Sangha Council of Southern California, the Buddhist Council of the Midwest, the Texas Buddhist Association are evidence of the beginning of a new "ecumenical" Buddhism. There are American Buddhist newspapers and magazines, feminist Zen sitting groups, exemplary Buddhist AIDS hospice projects. Today Buddhism is an American religion.

We visited communities that represent the entire spectrum of Islam in America: African American communities, Muslim immigrants from Syria and Lebanon whose forebears came in the early 1900s, and new immigrant Muslims from Africa and South Asia. All of them are in the process of working out what it is to be both Muslim and American. They gather in huge annual conventions in Dayton or in Kansas City to discuss the Muslim family in America or the American public schools. The Islamic Medical Association tackles ethical issues in medical practice, while the Washington-based American Muslim Council facilitates Islamic participation in the American political process.

We found that most of the new religious institutions are invisible. The first generation of American mosques could be found in places like a former watch factory in Queens, a U-Haul dealership in Pawtucket, Rhode Island, a gymna-

sium in Oklahoma City, and a former mattress showroom in Northridge, California. There were Hindu temples in a huge warehouse in Queens, a former YMCA in New Jersey, or a former Methodist church in Minneapolis. Most of the Vietnamese Buddhist temples of Denver, Houston, and Orange County were in ranch-style homes. Because of the invisibility of these first-generation religious institutions, many Americans, understandably, have remained quite unaware of these new communities.

The past decades, however, have also seen the beginnings of a striking new visible landscape. There are new mosques and Islamic centers in Manhattan and Phoenix, rising from the corn fields outside Toledo and from the suburbs of Chicago and Houston. There are multimillion-dollar Hindu temples, like the Sri Venkateswara temple in Pittsburgh, the Bharatiya Temple in the northern suburbs of Detroit, the spectacular Sri Meenakshi Temple south of Houston, the Ganesha temple in Nashville, and dozens of others. The Buddhists have made a striking architectural imprint, with, for example, the huge Hsi Lai temple in Hacienda Heights, California, and the Jade Temple in Houston. In the western Chicago suburb of Bartlett, the Jains have built a large new temple. To the north in Palatine is a striking new hexagonal gurdwara of the Sikhs.

There are some neighborhoods where all this is visible in short compass. For example, driving out New Hampshire Avenue, one of the great spokes of Washington, D.C., into Silver Spring, Maryland, just beyond the Beltway there is a stretch of road a few miles long where one passes the new Cambodian Buddhist temple with its graceful, sloping tiled roof, the Ukrainian Orthodox Church, the Muslim Community Center with its new copper-domed mosque. Farther along is the new Gujarati Hindu temple called Mangal Mandir. The many churches along the way also reveal the new dimensions of America's Christian landscape: Hispanic Pentecostal, Vietnamese Catholic, and Korean evangelical congregations sharing facilities with more traditional English-speaking "mainline" churches.

The diversity of New Hampshire Avenue, however, is not simply a curiosity for a Sunday drive. What it represents has profound implications for every aspect of American public life. What is happening to America as all of us begin to renegotiate the "we" of "We, the people"? That "we" in the United States is increasingly complex, not only culturally and racially, but also religiously. What will this religious diversity mean for American electoral politics, for the continuing interpretation of "church-state" issues by the Supreme Court, for American public education and the controversies of school boards, for hospitals and health-care programs with an increasingly diverse patient population, and for colleges and universities with an increasingly multireligious student body? While many Americans are only dimly aware of the changing religious landscape, the issues this new diversity has raised are already on the agenda of virtually every public institution, including Harvard.

New Hampshire Avenue dramatizes the new diversity, but building a pluralist society from that diversity is no easy matter in a world in which the "politics of identity" is busy minting our identities in smaller and smaller coins, and in a world in which religious markers of identity are often presumed to be the most divisive of all differences. American public debate is charged with the power of these issues. Some say such a multicultural and multireligious society is impossible. Their voices have been raised at each and every stage of American immigration—too many Catholics, too many Jews, too many Chinese and Japanese. Those voices are present today, and some of the most extreme have called for the repeal of the 1965 immigration act. Others have insisted there is simply too much *pluribus* and not enough *unum*. And still others would insist that this is a secular society, so why make a point of looking at religious differences at all?

But to ascertain how we—all of us—are doing in this new struggle for America's soul, we have to look not only at race, not only at ethnicity, but at religion. The history of prejudice and stereotype demonstrates that religious insignia and institutions often become key markers of "difference." The persistent attacks on synagogues and Jewish graveyards provide ample testimony to the tactics of hatred. So does the long and continuing history of racist attacks on black churches. Religious insignia, religious markers of identity, and religious institutions come to stand in a public way for the very heart of the community and often become the most visible targets for bigotry and violence.

And so it is as America's new immigrants become increasingly visible as religious minorities. In New Jersey, the dot or *bindi* on the forehead, worn by many Hindu women, stood for the strangeness of the whole Indian immigrant community in the eyes of a racist group calling themselves the "Dotbusters." Those who beat Navroze Mody to death in 1987, shouting "Hindu, Hindu, Hindu," did not know or care whether he was a Hindu, but conflated race, religion, and culture in one cry of hatred.

The Pluralism Project has documented the ways in which today's minority religious communities have experienced the violence of attacks on their visible religious institutions. In February 1983, for example, vandals broke into the newly constructed Hindu-Jain Temple in Pittsburgh and smashed all the white marble images of the Hindu deities. The sacred scripture of the Sikhs, housed on a side altar, was torn to pieces. "Leave!" was written across the main altar. In 1993, the temple of a tiny Cambodian Buddhist community in Portland, Maine, was vandalized with an axe, its doorjambs hacked, its doors broken, the contents of the Buddha hall strewn in the front yard, and the words "Dirty Asian Chink, Go Home!" written on the walls. In September 1994, a nearly completed mosque in Yuba City, California, was burned to the ground, leaving its dome and minaret in the ashes of a fire that the sheriff deemed to be arson. There are dozens of these incidents every year, some of them now documented by such groups as the Council on American-Islamic Relations, but most of them noted only in the pages of local newspapers.

The documentary register of acts of violence is easier to assemble than the register of new initiatives of cooperation and understanding, for violence is still deemed more "news-worthy" than cooperation. Yet assembling the evidence of new patterns of interreligious encounter, cooperation, and relationship is also important in discerning how the "we" is being reconfigured in multireligious America. For example, on April 2, 1993, a groundbreaking in Sharon, Massachusetts, brought Jews, Christians, and Muslims together from the Greater Boston area. There on a hillside overlooking the fields of a former horse farm, rabbis and priests, imams and Muslim leaders each turned a shovel of earth for the new Islamic Center of New England. Two weeks later, across the country in Fremont, California, Saint Paul's United Methodist Church and the Islamic Society of the East Bay broke ground together for a new church and a new mosque, to be built side by side on the same property. They named their common access road "Peace Terrace," and they are now next-door neighbors. "We want to set an example for the world," said one of the Muslim leaders.

All across America, there are new interreligious councils—in cities like Tulsa, Oklahoma, and Lincoln, Nebraska. The Interreligious Council of Southern California supported the appointment of a Buddhist chaplain in the California State Senate and backed the Sikhs in their petition to the Los Angeles Police Department to be allowed to wear the turban while serving as policemen. The Interfaith Conference of Metropolitan Washington, D.C., brought people of all religious communities together in March 1994 in the wake of the Hebron massacre. Because of new relationships of trust, the head of the Washington board of rabbis offered prayers right there on New Hampshire Avenue at the Muslim Community Center.

The public symbolic acknowledgment of America's diversity is also becoming more visible. In April 1990, for example, the city council of Savannah, Georgia, issued a proclamation in which Islam was recognized as having been "a vital part of the development of the United States of America and the city of Savannah." On June 25, 1991, for the first time in history, a Muslim imam, Siraj Wahaj of Brooklyn, opened a session of the U.S. House of Representatives with prayer. On February 20, 1996, at the end of the month of Ramadan, Hillary Clinton welcomed Muslims to the White House for the first Eid celebration ever to take place there. She said, "This celebration is an American event. We are a nation of immigrants who have long drawn on our diverse religious traditions and faiths for the strength and courage that make America great."

A few years ago, my Harvard colleague Samuel Huntington, a distinguished political scientist, wrote of the deep religious currents that so profoundly shape the great civilizations of the world.* In the new post-Cold War era, he predicted that "civilizational identity" will have a major role in the coming political realignment. He contended that the Confucian, Islamic, and Hindu worlds will be forces to reckon with in the geopolitical arena and he foresees a "clash of civilizations." But

where exactly are these worlds and civilizations, we might ask, with Hindus in Leicester, Durban, Toronto, and Houston? With huge mosques in Paris, London, Chicago, and Toledo? One of the decisive facts of the 1980s and 1990s has been the tremendous migration of peoples from one nation to another, both as immigrants and as refugees. Every part of the globe is experiencing the demographic changes of these migrations. Today, the Islamic world is no longer somewhere else, in some other part of the world; instead Chicago, with its 50 mosques and nearly half a million Muslims, is part of the Islamic world. America today is part of the Islamic, the Hindu, the Confucian world. It is precisely the interpenetration of ancient civilizations and cultures that is the hallmark of the late twentieth century. *This* is our new georeligious reality. The map of the world in which we now live cannot be color-coded as to its Christian, Muslim or Hindu identity, but each part of the world is marbled with the colors and textures of the whole.

The plurality of religious traditions and cultures challenges people in every part of the world today, including the United States, which is now the most religiously diverse country on earth. Diversity we have—here in America and here at Harvard. It is not an ideology invented by the multicultural enthusiasts of the left. It is the new reality of our society. Diversity we have. But what is pluralism? First, **pluralism** is not diversity alone, but the energetic engagement with that diversity. Diversity can and has meant the creation of religious ghettoes with little traffic between or among them. In this new world of religious diversity pluralism is not a given, but an achievement. In the world into which we now move, diversity without engagement, without a fabric of relationship, will be increasingly difficult and increasingly dangerous.

Second, pluralism will require not just tolerance, but the active seeking of understanding. Tolerance is a necessary public virtue, but it does not require Christians and Muslims, Hindus, Jews, and ardent secularists to know anything about one another. Tolerance is simply too thin a foundation for a world of religious differences. It does nothing to remove our ignorance of one another, and leaves in place the stereotype, the half-truth, the fear that underlie old patterns of division and violence. In the world into which we now move, our ignorance of one another will be increasingly costly.

---

*Samuel P. Huntington, "The Clash of Civilizations?" Foreign Affairs, volume 72, number 3 (summer, 1993).

And finally, pluralism is not simply relativism. The new paradigm of pluralism does not require us to leave our identities and our commitments behind, for pluralism is the encounter of commitments. It means holding our deepest differences, even our religious differences, not in isolation, but in relationship to one another. The language of pluralism is that of dialogue and encounter, give and take, criticism and self-criticism. In the world into which we now move, it is a language we will have to learn.

Whether in India or America, whether on New Hampshire Avenue or at Harvard University, the challenge for all of us today is how to shape societies, nations, neighborhoods, and universities that now replicate and potentially may reconfigure the differences that have long divided humankind.

Diana L. Eck, "Neighboring Faiths: How Will Americans Cope With Increasing Religious Diversity?" *Harvard Magazine*, September/October 1996, pp. 38–44. Reprinted by permission of the author.

Superstitions

Baseball is as American as apple pie…but are superstitions woven into the very fabric of American society? A **superstition** refers to a belief that is maintained despite all evidence that it is unfounded and irrational. A superstition is not based on fact, but rather consists of a particular practice or thought that one may hope will increase their likelihood of a pre-determined outcome.

In our culture, there are many superstitions that are practices: if you walk under a ladder or break a mirror it will lead to bad luck; the number 13 is said to represent bad luck and crossing the path of a black cat can lead to negative ramifications.

Superstitions seem to be a cross-cultural phenomenon. From where do you think superstitions originated?

Baseball Magic—
George Gmelch

On each pitching day for the first three months of a winning season, Dennis Grossini, a pitcher on a Detroit Tiger farm team, arose from bed at exactly 10:00 a.m. At 1:00 p.m. he went to the nearest restaurant for two glasses of iced tea and a tuna fish sandwich. When he got to the ballpark at 3:00 p.m., he put on the sweatshirt and jock he wore during his last winning game; one hour before the game he chewed a wad of Beech-Nut chewing tobacco. After each pitch during the game he touched the letters on his uniform and straightened his cap after each ball. Before the start of each inning he replaced the pitcher's rosin bag next to the spot where it was the inning before. And after every inning in which he gave up a run, he washed his hands.

When I asked which part of his ritual was most important, he said, "You can't really tell what's most important so it all becomes important. I'd be afraid to change anything. As long as I'm winning, I do everything the same."

Trobriand Islanders, according to anthropologist Bronislaw Malinowski, felt the same way about their fishing magic. Trobrianders fished in two different settings: in the *inner lagoon* where fish were plentiful and there was little danger, and on the *open sea* where fishing was dangerous and yields varied widely. Malinowski found that magic was not used in lagoon fishing, where men could rely solely on their knowledge and skill. But when fishing on the open sea, Trobrianders used a great deal of magical ritual to ensure safety and increase their catch.

Baseball, America's national pastime, is an arena in which players behave remarkably like Malinowski's Trobriand fishermen. To professional ballplayers, baseball is more than just a game, it is an occupation. Since their livelihoods depend on how well they perform, many use magic in an attempt to control the chance that is built into baseball. There are three essential activities of the game—pitching, hitting, and fielding. In the first two, chance can play a surprisingly important role. The pitcher is the player least able to control the outcome of his efforts. He may feel great and have good stuff warming up in the bullpen and then get in the game and get clobbered. He may make a bad pitch and see the batter miss it for a strike or see it hit hard but right into the hands of a fielder for an out.

Conversely, his best pitch may be blooped for a base hit. He may limit the opposing team to just a few hits yet lose the game, and he may give up many hits and win. And the good and bad luck don't always average out over the course of a season. For instance, this past season Jeriome Robertson gave up 1.4 more runs per game than his teammate Tim Redding but had a better won-lost record. Robertson went 15-9, while Redding was only 10-14. Both pitched for the same team—the Houston Astros—which meant they had the same fielders behind them. Regardless of how well a pitcher performs, the outcome of the game also depends upon the proficiency of his teammates, the ineptitude of the opposition, and luck.

Hitting, which many observers call the single most difficult task in the world of sports, is also full of uncertainty. Unless it's a home run, no matter how hard the batter hits the ball, fate determines whether it will go into a waiting glove or find a gap between the fielders. The uncertainty is compounded by the low success rate of hitting: the average hitter gets only one hit in every four trips to the plate, while the very best hitters average only one hit in every three trips. Fielding, which we will return to later, is the one part of baseball where chance does not play much of a role.

How does the risk and uncertainty in pitching and hitting affect players? How do they try to control the outcomes of their performance? These are questions that I first became interested in many years ago both as a ballplayer and as an anthropology student. I had devoted much of my youth to baseball, and played professionally as a first baseman in the Detroit Tiger organization in the 1960s. It was shortly after the end of one baseball season that I took an anthropology course called "Magic, Religion, and Witchcraft." As I listened to my professor describe the magical rituals of the Trobriand Islanders, it occurred to me that what these so-called "primitive" people did wasn't all that different from what my teammates and I did for luck and confidence at the ballpark.

ROUTINES AND RITUALS
The most common way players attempt to reduce chance and their feelings of uncertainty is to develop a daily routine—a course of action which is regularly followed. Talking about the routines of ballplayers, Pittsburgh Pirates coach Rich Donnelly said:

They're like trained animals. They come out here [ballpark] and everything has to be the same, they don't like anything that knocks them off their routine. Just look at the dugout and you'll see every guy sitting in the same spot every night. It's amazing, everybody in the same spot. And don't you dare take someone's seat. If a guy comes up from the minors and sits here, they'll say, 'Hey, Jim sits here, find another seat.' You watch the pitcher warm up and he'll do the same thing every time…You got a routine and you adhere to it and you don't want anybody knocking you off it.

Routines are comforting, they bring order into a world in which players have little control. And sometimes practical elements in routines produce tangible benefits, such as helping the player concentrate. But some of what players do goes beyond mere routine. These actions become what anthropologists define as ritual—prescribed behaviors in which there is no empirical connection between the means (e.g., tapping home plate three times) and the desired end (e.g., getting a base hit). Because there is no real connection between the two, rituals are not rational. Sometimes they are quite irrational. Similar to rituals are the nonrational beliefs that form the basis of taboos and fetishes, which players also use to bring luck to their side. But first let's take a close look at rituals.

Baseball rituals are infinitely varied. Most are personal, performed by individuals rather than by a team or group. Most are done in an unemotional manner, in much the same way players apply pine tar to their bats to improve the grip or dab eye black on their upper cheeks to reduce the sun's glare. A ballplayer may ritualize any activity that he considers important or somehow linked to good performance. Recall the variety of things that Dennis Grossini does, from specific times for waking and eating to foods and dress. White Sox Jason Bere listens to the same song on his Walkman before he pitches. Atlanta Brave Denny Neagle goes to a movie on days he is scheduled to start. Baltimore Oriole Glenn Davis used to chew the same gum every day during hitting streaks, saving it under his cap. Astros Infielder Julio Gotay always played with a cheese sandwich in his back pocket (he had a big appetite, so there might also have been a measure of practicality here). Red Sox Wade Boggs ate chicken before every game during his career, and that was just one of many elements in his pre- and postgame routine, which also included leaving his house for the ballpark at precisely the same time each day (1:47 for a 7:05 game).

Many hitters go through a series of preparatory rituals before stepping into the batter's box. These include tugging on their caps, touching their uniform letters or medallions, crossing themselves, and swinging, tapping, or bouncing the bat on the plate a prescribed number of times. Consider Cubs shortstop Nomar Garciaparra. After each pitch he steps out of the batters box, kicks the dirt with each toe, adjusts his right batting glove, adjusts his left batting glove, and touches his helmet before getting back into the box. Mike Hargrove, former Cleveland Indian first baseman, had so many time-consuming elements in his batting ritual that he was nicknamed "the human rain delay." Both players believe their batting rituals helped them regain their concentration after each pitch. But others wondered if the two had become prisoners of their superstitions. Another ritual associated with hitting is tagging a base when leaving and returning to the dugout between innings. Some players don't "feel right" unless they tag a specific base on each trip between dugout and field. One of my teammates added some complexity to his ritual by tagging third base on his way to the dugout only after the third, sixth, and ninth innings.

Players who have too many or particularly bizarre rituals risk being labeled as flakes, and not just by teammates but by fans and the media as well. For example, Mets pitcher Turk Wendell's eccentric rituals, which include wearing a necklace of teeth from animals he has killed, made him a cover story subject in the *New York Times Sunday Magazine*.

Baseball fans observe a lot of this ritual behavior, such as pitchers smoothing the dirt on the mound before each new batter, never realizing its importance to the player. The one ritual many fans do recognize, largely because it's a favorite of TV cameramen, is the "rally cap"—players in the dugout folding their caps and wearing them bill up in hopes of sparking a rally.

Most rituals grow out of exceptionally good performances. When a player does well, he seldom attributes his success to skill alone; he knows that his skills don't change much from day to day. So, then, what was different about today which can explain his three hits? He may attribute his success, in part, to an object, a food he ate, not having shaved, a new shirt he bought that day, or just about any behavior out of the ordinary. By repeating those behaviors, the player seeks to gain control over his performance, to bring more good luck. Outfielder John White explained how one of his rituals started:

> I was jogging out to centerfield after the national anthem when I picked up a scrap of paper. I got some good hits that night and I guess I decided that the paper had something to do with it. The next night I picked up a gum wrapper and had another good night at the plate... I've been picking up paper every night since.

When outfielder Ron Wright played for the Calgary Cannons he shaved his arms once a week. It all began two years before when after an injury he shaved his arm so it could be taped, and then hit three homers. Now he not only has one of the smoothest swings in the minor leagues, but two of the smoothest forearms. Wade Boggs' routine of eating chicken before every game began when he was a rookie in 1982 and noticed a correlation between multiple-hit games and poultry plates (his wife has 40 chicken recipes). One of Montreal Expo farmhand Mike Saccocio's rituals also concerned food: "I got three hits one night after eating at Long John Silver's. After that when we'd pull into town, my first question would be, "Do you have a Long John Silver's?" Unlike Boggs, Saccocio abandoned his ritual and looked for a new one when he stopped hitting well.

When in a slump, most players make a deliberate effort to change their routines and rituals in an attempt to shake off their bad luck. One player tried taking different routes to the ballpark, another tried sitting in a different place in the dugout, another shaved his head, and several reported changing what they ate before the game. Years ago, some of my teammates rubbed their hands along the handles of the bats protruding from the bat bin in hopes of picking up some power or luck from the bats of others. I had one manager who would rattle the bat bin when the team was not hitting well, as if the bats were in a stupor and could be aroused by a good shaking.

TABOO

Taboos (the word comes from a Polynesian term meaning prohibition) are the opposite of rituals. These are things you shouldn't do. Breaking a taboo, players believe, leads to undesirable consequences or bad luck. Most players observe at least a few taboos, such as never stepping on the white foul lines. A few, like Nomar Garciaparra, leap over the entire basepath. One teammate of mine would never watch a movie on a game day, despite the fact that we played nearly every day from April to September. Another teammate refused to read anything before a game because he believed it weakened his batting eye.

Many taboos take place off the field, out of public view. On the day a pitcher is scheduled to start, he is likely to avoid activities he believes will sap his strength and detract from his effectiveness. Some pitchers avoid eating certain foods, others will not shave on the day of a game, refusing to shave again as long as they are winning. Early in one season Oakland's Dave Stewart had six consecutive victories and a beard by the time he lost.

Taboos usually grow out of exceptionally poor performances, which players, in search of a reason, attribute to a particular behavior. During my first season of pro ball I ate pancakes before a game in which I struck out three times. A few weeks later I had another terrible game, again after eating pancakes. The result was a pancake taboo: I never again ate pancakes during the season. Pitcher Jason Bere has a taboo that makes more sense in dietary terms: after eating a meatball sandwich and not pitching well, he swore off them for the rest of the season.

While most taboos are idiosyncratic, there are a few that all ballplayers hold and that do not develop out of individual experience or misfortune. These form part of the culture of baseball, and are sometimes learned as early as Little League. Mentioning a no-hitter while one is in progress is a well-known example.

FETISHES

Fetishes are charms, material objects believed to embody supernatural power that can aid or protect the owner. Good-luck charms are standard equipment for some ballplayers. These include a wide assortment of objects from coins, chains, and crucifixes to a favorite baseball hat. The fetishized object may be a new possession or something a player found that coincided with the start of a streak and which he holds responsible for his good fortune. While playing in the Pacific Coast League, Alan Foster forgot his baseball shoes on a road trip and borrowed a pair from a teammate. That night he pitched a no-hitter, which he attributed to the shoes. Afterwards he bought them from his teammate and they became a fetish. Expo farmhand Mark LaRosa's rock has a different origin and use:

I found it on the field in Elmira after I had gotten bombed. It's unusual, perfectly round, and it caught my attention. I keep it to remind me of how important it is to concentrate. When I am going well I look at the rock and remember to keep my focus. The rock reminds me of what can happen when I lose my concentration.

For one season Marge Schott, former owner of the Cincinnati Reds, insisted that her field manager rub her St. Bernard "Schotzie" for good luck before each game. When the Reds were on the road, Schott would sometimes send a bag of the dog's hair to the field manager's hotel room. Religious medallions, which many Latino players wear around their necks and sometimes touch before going to the plate or mound, are also fetishes, though tied to their Roman Catholicism. (Also relating to their religion, some players some make the sign of the cross or bless themselves before every at bat (a few like Pudge Rodriguez do so before every pitch), and a few point to the heavens after hitting a home run.

Some players regard certain uniform numbers as lucky. When Ricky Henderson came to the Blue Jays in 1993, he paid teammate Turner Ward $25,000 for the right to wear number 24. Don Sutton got off cheaper. When he joined the Dodgers he convinced teammate Bruce Boche to give up number 20 in exchange for a new set of golf clubs. Oddly enough, there is no consensus about the effect of wearing number 13. Some players shun it, while a few request it. When Jason Giambi arrived with the Oakland A's his favorite number 7 was already taken, so he settled for 16 (the two numbers add up to 7). When he signed with the Yankees, number 7 (Mickey Mantle's old number) was retired and 16 was taken, so he settled for 25 (again, the numbers add up to 7).

RELIGION

Number preferences emerge in different ways. A young player may request the number of a former star, sometimes hoping that it will bring him the same success. Or he may request a number he associates with good luck. Colorado Rockies' Larry Walker's fixation with the number 3 has become well known to baseball fans. Besides wearing 33, he takes three practice swings before stepping into the box, he showers from the third nozzle, sets his alarm for three minutes past the hour and he was wed on November 3 at 3:33 p.m.[1] Fans in ballparks all across America rise from their seats for the seventh-inning stretch before the home club comes to bat because the number 7 is lucky, although the specific origin of this tradition has been lost.[2]

Clothing, both the choice and the order in which it is put on, combine elements of both ritual and fetish. Some players put on the part of their uniform in a particular order. Expos farmhand Jim Austin always puts on his left sleeve, left pants leg, and left shoe before the right. Most players, however, single out one or two lucky articles or quirks of dress for ritual elaboration. After hitting two home runs in a game, for example, ex-Giant infielder Jim Davenport discovered that he had missed a buttonhole while dressing for the game. For the remainder of his career he left the same button undone. Phillies' Len Dykstra would discard his batting gloves if he failed to get a hit in a single at-bat. In a hitless game, he might go through four pair of gloves. For outfielder Brian Hunter the focus is shoes: "I have a pair of high tops and a pair of low tops. Whichever shoes don't get a hit that game, I switch to the other pair." At the time of our interview, he was struggling at the plate and switching shoes almost every day. For Birmingham Baron pitcher Bo Kennedy the arrangement of the different pairs of baseball shoes in his locker is critical:

> I tell the clubbies [clubhouse boys] when you hang stuff in my locker don't touch my shoes. If you bump them move them back. I want the Ponys in front, the turfs to the right, and I want them nice and neat with each pair touching each other…Everyone on the team knows not to mess with my shoes when I pitch.

During hitting or winning streaks players may wear the same clothes day after day. Once I changed sweatshirts midway through the game for seven consecutive nights to keep a hitting streak going. Clothing rituals, however, can become impractical. Catcher Matt Allen was wearing a long sleeve turtle neck shirt on a cool evening in the New York-Penn League when he had a three-hit game. "I kept wearing the shirt and had a good week," he explained. "Then the weather got hot as hell, 85 degrees and muggy, but I would not take that shirt off. I wore it for another ten days—catching—and people thought I was crazy." Former Phillies, Expos, Twins, and Angels manager Gene Mauch never washed his underwear or uniform after a win. Perhaps taking a ritual to the extreme, Leo Durocher, managing the Brooklyn Dodgers to a pennant in 1941, spent three and a half weeks in the same gray slacks, blue coat, and knitted blue tie. Losing can produce the opposite effect, such as the Oakland A's players who went out and bought new street clothes in an attempt to break a 14-game losing streak.

Baseball's superstitions, like most everything else, change over time. Many of the rituals and beliefs of early baseball are no longer observed. In the 1920s–30s sportswriters reported that a player who tripped en route to the field would often retrace his steps and carefully walk over the stumbling block for "insurance." A century ago players spent time on and off the field intently looking for items that would bring them luck. To find a hairpin on the street, for example, assured a batter of hitting safely in that day's game. A few managers were known to strategically place a hairpin on the ground where a slumping player would be sure to find it. Today few women wear hairpins—a good reason the belief has died out. In the same era, Philadelphia Athletics manager Connie Mack hoped to ward off bad luck by employing a hunchback as a mascot. Hall of Famer Ty Cobb took on a young black boy as a good luck charm, even taking him on the road during the 1908 season. It was a not uncommon then for players to rub the head of a black child for good luck.

To catch sight of a white horse or a wagon-load of barrels were also good omens. In 1904 the manager of the New York Giants, John McGraw, hired a driver with a team of white horses to drive past the Polo Grounds around the time his players were arriving at the ballpark. He knew that if his players saw white horses, they would have more confidence and that could only help them during the game. Belief in the power of white horses survived in a few backwaters until the 1960s. A gray-haired manager of a team I played for in Drummondville, Quebec, would drive around the countryside before important games and during the playoffs looking for a white horse. When he was successful, he would announce it to everyone in the clubhouse.

One belief that appears to have died out recently is a taboo about crossed bats. Some of my Latino teammates in the 1960s took it seriously. I can still recall one Dominican player becoming agitated when another player tossed a bat from the batting cage and it landed on top of his bat. He believed that the top bat might steal hits from the lower one. In his view, bats contained a finite number of hits. It was once commonly believed that when the hits in a bat were used up no amount of good hitting would produce any more. Hall of Famer Honus Wagner believed each bat contained only 100 hits. Regardless of the quality of the bat, he would discard it after its 100th hit. This belief would have little relevance today, in the era of light bats with thin handles—so thin that the typical modern bat is lucky to survive a dozen hits without being broken. Other superstitions about bats do survive, however. Position players on the Class A Asheville Tourists would not let pitchers touch or swing their bats, not even to warm up. Poor-hitting players, as most pitchers are, were said to pollute or weaken the bats.

UNCERTAINTY AND MAGIC

The best evidence that players turn to rituals, taboos, and fetishes to control chance and uncertainty is found in their uneven application. They are associated mainly with pitching and hitting—the activities with the highest degree of chance—and not fielding. I met only one player who had any ritual in connection with fielding, and he was an error-prone shortstop. Unlike hitting and pitching, a fielder has almost complete control over the outcome of his performance. Once a ball has been hit in his direction, no one can intervene and ruin his chances of catching it for an out (except in the unlikely event of two fielders colliding). Compared with the pitcher or the hitter, the fielder has little to worry about. He knows that in better than 9.7 times out of 10 he will execute his task flawlessly. With odds like that there is little need for ritual.

Clearly, the rituals of American ballplayers are not unlike those of the Trobriand Islanders studied by Malinowski many years ago.[3] In professional baseball, fielding is the equivalent of the inner lagoon while hitting and pitching are like the open sea.

While Malinowski helps us understand how ballplayers respond to chance and uncertainty, behavioral psychologist B. F. Skinner sheds light on why personal rituals get established in the first place.[4] With a few grains of seed Skinner could get pigeons to do anything he wanted. He merely waited for the desired behavior (e.g., pecking) and then rewarded it with some food. Skinner then decided to see what would happen if pigeons were rewarded with food pellets regularly, every fifteen seconds, regardless of what they did. He found that the birds associate the arrival of the food with a particular action, such as tucking their head under a wing or walking in clockwise circles. About ten seconds after the arrival of the last pellet, a bird would begin doing whatever it associated with getting the food and keep doing it until the next pellet arrived. In short, the pigeons behaved as if their actions made the food appear. They learned to associate particular behaviors with the reward of being given seed.

Ballplayers also associate a reward—successful performance—with prior behavior. If a player touches his crucifix and then gets a hit, he may decide the gesture was responsible for his good fortune and touch his crucifix the next time he comes to the plate. Unlike pigeons, however, most ballplayers are quicker to change their rituals once they no longer seem to work. Skinner found that once a pigeon associated one of its actions with the arrival of food or water, only sporadic rewards were necessary to keep the ritual going. One pigeon, believing that hopping from side to side brought pellets into its feeding cup, hopped ten thousand times without a pellet before finally giving up. But, then, didn't Wade Boggs eat chicken before every game, through slumps and good times, for seventeen years?

Obviously the rituals and superstitions of baseball do not make a pitch travel faster or a batted ball find the gaps between the fielders, nor do the Trobriand rituals calm the seas or bring fish. What both do, however, is give their practitioners a sense of control, and with that added confidence. And we all know how important that is. If you really believe eating chicken or hopping over the foul lines will make you a better hitter, it probably will.

RELIGION

BIBLIOGRAPHY

Gmelch, G. Inside Pitch: Life in Professional Baseball (Smithsonian Institution Press, 2001).

Malinowski, B. Magic, Science and Religion and Other Essays (Glencoe, III., 1948).

Skinner, B.F. Behavior of Organisms: An Experimental Analysis (D. Appleton-Century Co., 1938).

Skinner, B.F. Science and Human Behavior (New York: Macmillan, 1953).

Torrez, Danielle Gagnon. High Inside: Memoirs of a Baseball Wife. New York: G.P. Putnam's Sons, 1983.

NOTES

1. *Sports Illustrated* ..... , 48

2. Allen, The Superstitions of Baseball Players," 104.

3. Malinowski, B. *Magic, Science and Religion and Other Essays*

4. Skinner, B.F. *Behavior of Organisms: An Experimental Analysis*

From George Gmelch, 1992, "Baseball Magic," (Revised version of "Superstition and Ritual in American Baseball"), *Elysian Fields Quarterly*, Vol. 11, No. 3, pp. 25–36. McGraw-Hill/Dushkin. © September, 2000. Reprinted by permission.

KEY TERMS

Name _____

Section _____

Date _____

Ancestral spirits:

Animism:

Beliefs:

Cargo cults:

Communal cults:

Creation myth:

Diviners:

Ecclesiastical cults:

Fetishes:

Functions of religion:

RELIGION

Ghosts:

Individualistic cults:

Magic:

Myth:

Permanent record:

Priests:

Profane:

Religion:

Religious rites:

Revitalization movements:

Rituals:

Sacred:

Shamans:

KEY TERMS

Name _____

Section _____

Date _____

Spirits:

Supernatural:

Superstition:

Taboo:

Totemic animal spirits:

Witchcraft:

RELIGION

11 APPLIED AND MEDICAL ANTHROPOLOGY

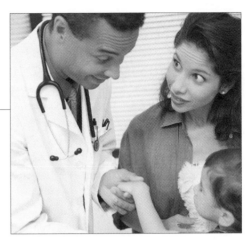

Put Your Knowledge to Work

Cultural anthropologists investigate human behaviors and cultural traditions. Researchers can be found working in both the academic world as well as in a variety of applied contexts, including business, law, medicine, military, and government positions within and outside the United States. **Applied anthropology** uses anthropological methodology, knowledge, and theories to solve contemporary human problems.

APPLIED AND MEDICAL ANTHROPOLOGY

A Brief History of Applied Anthropology—
Alexander M. Ervin

Authors such as Harris (1968) and Voget (1975) provide rich histories of academic anthropology, but the neglect of similar accounts of anthropology's application is quite striking. This oversight contributes to a hazy impression of where applied anthropoiogy really fits within the discipline. Some may see it as an appendix to academia or even as an enterprise born out of a shortage of university jobs. In contrast, I claim, as do some others (see van Willigen 1993), that application has been more at the forefront both in the earliest visions and through subsequent activities. Nonetheless, it is true that applied anthropology has waxed and waned in its 150 years of existence.

NINETEENTH-CENTURY BEGINNINGS

Anthropology emerged by the middle of the 1800s through the efforts of amateurs, including British abolitionists who were concerned about the status of peoples native to the British colonies. They established the Ethnological Society of London in 1843 and then a factionalized offshoot, the Anthropological Society of London, in 1863. According to Reining, members of both groups advocated the application of anthropological knowledge to policy with the hope that it "…would aid in the emancipation of the human mind from preconceived notions" (Reining 1962: 595). However, this early rush toward applicable knowledge became mired down because of inflammatory controversies surrounding issues of race and poverty—crudely formed social Darwinism justifying social inequality dominated the Anthropological Society, and moderate liberalism motivated the Ethnological Society.

One response to the division was to firmly establish anthropology as a respectable academic science by withdrawing it from the more divisive issues of the day. This was accomplished in part through a re-amalgamation of the two societies into a forerunner of the Royal Anthropological Society of Great Britain and Ireland, shepherded by the famous biologist Sir Thomas Huxley. Legitimacy was further strengthened with the appointment of E. B. Tylor as an anthropologist at Oxford in 1883. But even Tylor saw anthropology as a reformer's science. One of his goals was to educate colonial officials about native customs. However, British anthropology turned to less practical topics until the mid-1920s. Yet Reining (1962)

reminds us that anthropology's original vision was practical, intended to explore vital issues of human welfare such as poverty and conflict.

One of American anthropology's earliest forebears was Henry Schoolcraft. Schoolcraft was commissioned by Congress to report on the circumstances and prospects of Indian tribes in the United States. The results, contained in a six-volume report (Schoolcraft 1852–1857), gave background and direction to Indian policy (van Willigen 1993:19). That expectation continued with Congress' 1879 establishment of the Bureau of American Ethnology attached to the Smithsonian Institution. The first director, Major John Wesley Powell, felt that inductive knowledge of tribal peoples was needed to ease their transition to the next stages of civilization and to rectify some problems that "civilized" people had created during contacts. But Congress expected usable information more quickly than it was received, even as researchers wanted longer periods to accumulate the information of their choice. Conflict over timing and content still plagues anthropologists and policy makers. After Powell removed himself from the controversy, the Bureau strayed from its original mandate to serve the more antiquarian curiosity of its staff (Hinsley 1979). However, one researcher, James Mooney (1896), can be cited for his remarkably advanced research on the Ghost Dance Religion. As a form of advocacy, he sympathetically portrayed the Ghost Dance, widespread among Western tribes, as a genuinely religious expression of coping with the severe dislocations produced by the U.S.–Indian wars and confinement to reservations.

In the nineteenth century, anthropology eventually became successful in gaining a foothold of respectability. Yet its professional numbers were minuscule, and the scope of its task enormous. The most important contributor to that venture was Franz Boas, who held the first North American appointment in anthropology at Clark University, later moving to Columbia. Boas did not consider himself an applied anthropologist, being primarily concerned with salvaging information about tribal cultures before they disappeared, but he did prepare the way for effective demonstrations of the uses of anthropology for policy. For instance, with scientific rigor and research, he attacked notions of **racial determinism**, claiming a more important role for culture and context. As a physical anthropologist, he submitted results from two massive studies to the U.S. Commissioner of Education. These works were a form of scientific advocacy, demonstrating that even physical growth and development of immigrants were strongly influenced by new social environments. Within a few generations immigrant physical characteristics approximated those of British North Americans. He provided factual arguments against the current policies to restrict immigration to British and Northwestern Europeans (Stocking 1979).

APPLIED ANTHROPOLOGY BETWEEN THE WORLD WARS

By the mid-1920s, as the Boasian concern with documenting cultural history waned, anthropology turned to the study of contemporary societies. Part of this was due to the stimulus of British anthropologists Bronislaw Malinowski and Alfred Reginald Radcliffe-Brown. Both delivered their visions of anthropological enquiry during sojourns at American universities until the 1940s. Their versions of structural functionalism regarded present-day societies as organic entities that were maintained by interconnected institutions. To use an anatomical analogy, the main task for the anthropologist was to map the institutional "organs" of society and then to analyze their "bodily" functions in the style similar to that of physiology. British anthropologists directed their research at tribal societies within the British Empire and the Dominions of New Zealand, South Africa, and Australia.

At the same time, the changes and disruptions on North American Indian reservations increasingly attracted the attention of American anthropologists. One breakthrough was Margaret Mead's (1932) study of the deteriorating conditions among the "Antlers" a pseudonym for a Plains tribe. A new strategy, the **acculturation approach**, gradually developed for the investigation of change among American Indians. It was an inductive perspective that incorporated some assumptions of the structural functionalist approach but also focused on changes in indigenous societies following sustained contact with European and American societies. In bare outline, the study begins by reconstructing a "baseline culture" and then describes significant events and strategies initiated by intruders (e.g., settlement, wars, trade). It details particular effects of cultural contact on areas such as language, socialization, subsistence, religion, values, authority, and land uses of the indigenous societies. Acculturation studies described reservation sociocultural systems as by-products of these dynamics, outlining dimensions of both persistence and change. The study of

acculturation was prominent in anthropology through the late 1960s and guided much of the work done by North Americans (see Bee 1974; Redfield et al. 1936; Social Science Research Council 1954; Spicer 1961).

Both acculturation and functionalist approaches were associated with applied work that started in the 1930s and continued through the 1960s. In Britain, Malinowski encouraged the funding and training of anthropologists in applied research. In an article titled "Practical Anthropology," Malinowski (1929) laid out much of the agenda for that kind of work. He suggested that anthropologists provide information on land tenure, jurisprudence, health, demographics, and ongoing change. In far-flung and populous colonies with few British administrators available to govern them directly, it was thought best to leave intact as many indigenous customs that were broadly compatible with British policy as possible, allowing limited self-rule in tribal contexts. Any changes should be made as compatible with local customs as was feasible. Ethnographic information was valuable for such purposes. If, for instance, a new cash crop was introduced, cultivation should not seriously violate indigenous systems of land distribution because of the amount of internal conflict it might generate. Out of this era and extending well into the 1950s, a significant amount of data was generated, sometimes coming out of regional centers such as the Rhodes-Livingstone Institute (see Wilson 1940) in Central Africa. Evans-Pritchard's classic (1940) and influential study of the Nuer was done as background information for the Anglo-Egyptian administration of the Sudan. Some other highlights included Raymond Firth's (1936) analysis of over population in Tikopia, Schapera's (1947) investigations of the effects of labor migration in Bechuanaland, and various studies by Lucy Mair (1957) in Africa.

In the United States, anthropologists advised the Bureau of Indian Affairs (BIA) during the New Deal. Activated by the vision of John Collier, the new commissioner, the BIA undertook new policies for improvement. These were mandated by the Wheeler-Howard Act or Indian Reorganization Act of 1934. American Indian reservations had been devastated by disease, cultural disintegration, and demoralization. Indians had lost much land when the Allotment Act divided many reservations into 160-acre plots to be individually owned. The 1934 Act provided the means to recover land by drawing from the public domain and consolidating holdings under the control of elected tribal councils. The Act also made provisions for new forms of tribal government and promoted reforms in education and economic development. To get the information needed, Collier turned to the Bureau of American Ethnology, which started an Applied Anthropology Unit to study tribal social organization and to provide information about the needs for land acquisition. Some of the well-known anthropologists who served with that unit included Edward H. Spicer, Julian Steward, Morris Opler, Clyde Kluckhohn, Oscar Lewis, Gordon MacGregor, Laura Thompson, and Dorothea Leighton. Again, it was difficult to quickly provide the knowledge needed, and conflicts emerged between bureaucrats and anthropologists. Yet even after the unit disbanded, Collier continued to contract some policy research from anthropologists at the University of Chicago (McNickle 1979).

One project reveals the dilemmas for anthropologists working with New Deal Indian policy. It involved problems of overgrazing and soil erosion on the Navaho reservation (Kimball 1979). A joint program for tackling the problem engaged the BIA and the Soil Conservation Service, which sought to restrict livestock ownership by Navaho. The bureaucrats' approach was heavy-handed, paternalistic, and bitterly resisted by the Navaho. Anthropologists John Provinse and Sol Kimball were brought in to ease conflict and foster cooperation between the bureaucrats and Indians. Among their useful findings was a corporate grouping of linked families that they called the "land-use community." They recommended that officials cooperate with those units rather than impose arbitrary restrictions upon individual stockholders. The anthropologists developed a working arrangement with one such group, but the plan was abruptly scuttled by bureaucrats who resented threats to their prerogative for centralized planning. Unfortunately, many contemporary applied anthropologists can recount similar frustrations today.

According to Julian Steward (1969), a disillusioned participant, Collier's New Deal policies were based on a misplaced paternalism and a romantic image of American Indians. Steward maintains that much of the relatively uniform policy was unrealistic and unfair because there was diversity of opinion among Indians with, for example, factions on reservations representing "traditionalist" versus "progressive" interests. Sometimes the provisions of government were incompatible with the desires of particular groups, as Clemmer (1969, 1974) documents

in his portrayal of the imposition of a united reservation system upon the Hopi, who saw their separate communities as sovereign.

It is tempting to harshly criticize this era of applied anthropology, most especially with regard to Britain, and perceive anthropology as a handmaiden of imperialism (Gjessing 1968; Willis 1974). However, the actions might be better evaluated according to the standards and values of the times. In the case of Britain, the concept of indirect rule, maintaining the essence of tribal customs and institutions whenever possible, was morally defensible to most anthropologists faced with colonial realities. For instance, Firth (1981) denies that Malinowski was the archlackey of colonialism as some have portrayed him. He was capable of severely criticizing colonial practices that damaged tribal peoples. It should also be remembered that he did help educate Jomo Kenyatta, the first president of Kenya, who was most certainly an anti-imperialist. Still, as Asad (1973) suggests, it is important to objectively review anthropology's role in the colonial encounter, especially in the context of unbalanced power relationships.

Anthropologists who participated in New Deal BIA policies wished to mitigate its more heavy-handed approaches. Also, to maintain a sense of perspective, consider some of the alternative assimilationist policies that preceded and followed the New Deal. The Dawes Act led to the selling of previously Indian-owned lands, and the Termination Acts of the 1950s led to the elimination of several complete reservations. New Deal Indian policy definitely shored up land rights for many and provided consistent, albeit sometimes flawed, tribal government.

Also as part of the New Deal, anthropological studies were done by the Bureau of Agricultural Economics, an agency of the U.S. Department of Agriculture. The Bureau was set up to examine the problems of rural poverty and the relationship of farming to community viability. A set of ethnographies with a common research design (see Olen and Loomis 1941; Kollmorgen 1942; Macleish and Young 1942; Moe and Taylor 1942; Bell 1942; Wynne 1943) examined dairy, wheat, corn, and cotton farmers in the Midwest, New England, the Southwest, and the South. They all took into account factors of ethnicity (e.g., Amish and Mexican Americans), scale and mechanization of farm operations, class, values, local conflicts, and community cohesion. Also among the Bureau's reports was Walter

Goldschmidt's (1947) study, which showed the huge discrepancies in the implementation of federal irrigation policy in California. Small producers, the intended beneficiaries of irrigation, produced more per acre, yet large corporate farms gained much more from public irrigation while proportionately producing less. Another study, by Horace Miner (1949), demonstrated how certain federal farm policies (e.g., payments for not growing surplus crops) were counterproductive to local value systems. Unfortunately, the Bureau of Agricultural Economics was eventually terminated for political reasons.

One other advanced branch of applied anthropology, that of business and industrial anthropology, originated during the 1930s. W. Lloyd Warner, newly appointed to the Harvard School of Human Relations, was interested in extending the ethnographic approach to complex societies. An opportunity arose with a study overseen by psychologist Elton Mayo, of industrial productivity and worker morale at the massive Hawthorne Electric Company plant in Chicago. Separate work groups were ethnographically observed and their members interviewed as if they were participants in small-scale societies. This research demonstrated that there were many more motivators of workers' behavior than just wages. Workers could no longer be seen as analogous to functioning parts of a machine. Worker morale and productivity needed to be perceived as more organic, based on shared values and interactions within small groups. Furthermore, with regard to the more contemporary anthropological study of business, industry, and organizations, the importance of effective informal organization was clearly recognized in any successes. Warner and some colleagues went on to do anthropological research on complex American communities through the Yankee City series (Warner 1941–1947). Associates such as Burleigh Gardner (1945), F. L. W. Richardson (1955), and William Whyte (1948) used anthropological principles in various industrial and commercial ventures. For more information on this era, see Baba (1986), Richardson (1979), and Schwartzman (1993).

WORLD WAR II AND ITS AFTERMATH

In 1941, an exceptionally significant event in the development of applied anthropology occurred, the founding of the Society for Applied Anthropology (SfAA). This was the first professional association devoted to the application of anthropology. Various anthropologists and sympathetic colleagues in a few other cognate disciplines, such as rural sociology and social psychology, gathered at Harvard and Washington for two spring meetings to form a professional association with the primary objective of "...scientific investigation of the principles controlling the relations of human beings to one another. . . and the wide application of these principles to practical problems." At the second meeting, papers on colonial or Indian administration, social welfare, mental health, national morale, diet, and industry were delivered. The participants included Margaret Mead, Gregory Bateson, William F. Whyte, George P. Murdock, Ruth Underhill, Ruth Benedict, and fifty others. The following year an influential journal, *Applied Anthropology* (later *Human Organization*), began publication. In 1949, the Society produced its code of ethics, an essential guide for applied anthropologists. Current and future practitioners of applied anthropology owe a tremendous debt to the founders of the SfAA. Without its influence, applied anthropology would not be as coherent and effective as it is today.

American anthropologists made significant contributions to the war effort. Margaret Mead (1979) tells how anthropologists and other social scientists met with high-level administration officials in 1940 to discuss ways to maintain national morale should the United States declare war. After Pearl Harbor, Mead was placed in charge of the Committee on Food Habits attached to the National Research Council. Her group (including Lloyd Warner and Ruth Benedict) advised on programs for emergency feeding and rationing and measured public opinion about aid to allies. Mead also studied the social impact of having over a million U.S. servicemen stationed in Britain, focusing on the clash of values between American soldiers and British civilians and military, and making recommendations for the improvement of relations (Mead 1944).

Another group, prominently involving British anthropologist Gregory Bateson, established areal institutes at universities across the country, focusing on regions such as the Far East, Oceania, the Middle East, Latin America, Africa, and the Soviet Union. The idea was to teach foreign-service officers, the military, and others the region's history, language, culture, society, and politics relevant to national defense and U.S. participation in global affairs. Most immediate were preparations for military intelligence and language study, especially for the Pacific theater.

APPLIED AND MEDICAL ANTHROPOLOGY

Bateson, in 1943, was employed by the Office of Strategic Services along with Rhoda Métraux, Geoffrey Gorer, Clyde Kluckhohn, and Ruth Benedict. Here, "enemy" societies were studied at a distance through interviews, written materials, and films. Important work was done on the Japanese by Ruth Benedict and her associates. Their insight made it possible to understand the culturally based behavior of the Japanese during the U.S. liberation of Pacific islands. It also helped prepare for the postwar occupation of Japan and influenced the decision not to depose Emperor Hirohito (see Benedict 1946; Mead 1979; Mead and Métraux 1953; Yans-McLaughlin 1980).

Through the Smithsonian Institution and the Social Science Research Council, anthropologists established databases relevant to small-scale societies that the Allies were encountering in their war efforts. Some anthropologists used their anthropological knowledge while serving in the military. For instance, Demitri Shimkin, as an officer in the U.S. Army Intelligence Corps, advised and helped maintain a liaison with Russians in Siberia, especially in transferring military supplies there. Appropriately, Northern Eurasia and its peoples were among Shimkin's many academic specialties.

Exceptionally painful for social scientists and many people in the United States was the wartime relocation of 110,000 Japanese Americans from California to the American Southwest. Also present in Canada, this discrimination did not extend to citizens descended from other "enemy" nationalities. It was generated by misguided motives of some overly influential generals and commercial interests on the West Coast. To administer this regrettable policy, the War Relocation Authority (WRA) was established. According to Spicer (1979), the agency did not have a concentration-camp mentality but, instead, tried to make the best of a very bad policy and intended to relocate and integrate Japanese Americans back into society as soon as possible. Relocation camps were viewed only as temporary way stations, to be dismantled quickly when feasible. Yet some (Willis 1974) harshly criticize anthropological participation in this program as collusion with imperialism. One of the camps was established under the joint authority of the WRA and the BIA on an Indian reservation at Poston on the Colorado River. John Collier arranged to have an applied social science unit established there under the direction of psychiatrist/anthropologist Alexander Leighton and anthropologists Edward H. Spicer and

Elizabeth Colson. Just as the unit was being established, major conflicts occurred among the residents and also between the residents and the bureaucrats. Leighton and colleagues were put to the test in resolving these issues. Later Leighton (1945), in his *Governing of Men*, wrote of the insights gained under a theoretical framework explicating social stress.

The use of applied social scientists, including thirteen other anthropologists, such as Margaret Lantis and Weston Labarre, increased with the establishment of the Bureau of Sociological Research and the Community Analysis Section, which were carefully integrated into the total program. Both units reported to John Provinse, an anthropologist operating at the highest levels of the WRA. The units formulated and monitored policies and acted as cross-cultural interpreters (for more information, see Spicer 1952, 1979; Leighton 1945).

One immediate aftermath of World War II was the use of anthropological expertise in the administration of the Trust Territory of Micronesia, including the islands of Truk, Yap, Palau, Ponape, and the Marshalls. The work had begun during the war, when anthropologists George P. Murdock and Felix Keesing provided background and intelligence materials to the U.S. Navy for the eventual liberation of the islands from the Japanese. Right after the war, an extensive program of anthropological background research began. In 1951 the Navy turned the Trust Territory over to the U.S. Department of the Interior. In both administrations, several dozen anthropologists served as researchers and district anthropologists, providing in-depth studies of problems associated with relocation, devastated economies, communication, housing, and other topics. They supervised particular tasks, such as arranging for wages and royalties from development to go to clans instead of individuals. Some prominent anthropologists who served in these applied roles included Ward Goodenough, Homer Barnett, David Schneider, Philip Drucker, Douglas Oliver, and Thomas Gladwin (for more details, see Barnett 1956; Fischer 1979).

ACADEMIC APPLIED ANTHROPOLOGY AND CONSULTING FOR DEVELOPMENT, 1950–1970

After the war, anthropologists returned to universities. Because of the tremendous expansion in higher education that continued through the 1960s, anthropologists had many opportunities for career advancement, and research grants for scholarly studies were readily accessible. There was also growing disillusionment about associating with policy makers and the possible corrupted use of scientific information. Two things contributed to this 1950s pessimism: the dropping of atomic bombs on Japan and Senator Joseph McCarthy's attacks on left-leaning intellectuals, scholars, and artists (Yans-McLaughlin 1980).

Academic anthropology flourished. More domains of study, such as economic, political, medical, and urban anthropology, enculturation, and education, were either initiated or became more sophisticated. Important new methodological contributions, such as network and componential analyses, were developed, and the collection of sophisticated ethnographic information greatly expanded.

Applied anthropology did not disappear during this era. Working out of university settings, an effective minority of anthropologists did applied anthropology largely on a part-time, consulting, and public-service basis. Work continued with Native North Americans. Anthropologists served as expert witnesses on behalf of tribes making land claims before the U.S. Indian Land Claims Commission (see Lithe 1955) and spoke in defense of religious freedoms as associated with the Native American Church or Peyote Cult (see Stewart 1983).

It was on behalf of American Indians that *Action Anthropology* was devised by Sol Tax. In 1948 Tax had begun a field school for six University of Chicago graduate students at the Fox or Mesquawkie Indian reservation in Iowa. He saw the Fox informants as *co-investigators* and the investigators as *students* of the Fox. The approach was to engage the Fox themselves in the fieldwork, to establish with them the directions in which their society was going, what their principal needs were, and then attach value and priority to them. Together, they were to engage in action after determining desired courses of action. The beliefs and opinions of the Fox always had precedence over any suggestions by outside investigators. Projects included a craft industry centered around the designs of a talented artist and a program for Fox students to attend college (see Tax 1958; Gearing 1960; Peattie 1960; Piddington 1960).

Another historically significant project, with a different approach, was the Vicos Project, directed by Allan Holmberg. Holmberg (1958) refers to his method as the "research and development" approach to change. Definitely a form of interventionist strategy, it is based on the assumptions that progress can be made toward the realization of human dignity and that people can use scientific knowledge to further social goals. Here, power and knowledge gained from research were used by social scientists to improve the lives of a dominated and impoverished people. Power was to be gradually shared until the scientists could completely devolve it to community members. In the case of Vicos, community-based research was used to identify desired changes; the results of the changes were monitored for further refinement or use elsewhere.

This experiment is not likely to be repeated today. Through funds from the Cornell University Board of Governors, Holmberg purchased a lease on a 40,000-acre Peruvian hacienda that included almost 2,000 Quechua serfs whose ancestors had been bonded to the land for about 400 years. Previously, serfs had to provide weekly labor to the patron. The medieval-like serfdom had left Vicos residents with the lowest economic, health, and political status in Peru. The Vicos experiment, 1952–1957, was supported by Peruvian anthropologists and the Peruvian Indianist Institute. In the end, the people of Vicos were allowed to buy out their own lease, thus achieving autonomy from the hacienda system. Along the way, much was accomplished. Scientists and villagers collaborated to establish a local authority system and gained collective ownership of the manor land. Profits were used for the public good. Schooling increased significantly; economic production by individual families went up four or five times, and a new clinic improved health. The Vicos Project remains a unique and fascinating project in applied anthropology. Yet it raises questions about ethics and styles of intervention still discussed in classrooms. Was it too paternalistic? Was it proper for anthropologists to conduct experiments of any kind?

Development, both for impoverished American communities and through U.S.-sponsored international aid programs, was a major focus for some university-based anthropologists. Cornell University's anthropology program, under the direction of Alexander Leighton, Morris Opler, John Adair, and Allan Holmberg, along with Edward H. Spicer and colleagues at the University of Arizona, were leaders in these areas. One especially important contribution was Spicer's (1952) edited collection, *Human Problems in Technological Change*, which systematically explored the unintended consequences of community modernization and technological intervention in India, Australia, Micronesia, Alaska, and the American Southwest. A related approach was taken by George Foster at Berkeley (1962, 1969), who outlined the significant dimensions of social and cultural change; cultural, psychological, and social barriers to planned change; and possible stimulants for positive change. Foster consulted with United Nations and U.S. aid agencies for several decades, especially on the interplay between Western medical systems and indigenous health beliefs and practices (see Foster and Anderson 1978). Other landmarks were Margaret Mead's *Cultural Patterns and Technological Change* (1955) and *New Lives for Old* (1956), Charles J. Erasmus' (1961) critique of U.S. aid programs, and Edward Hall's (1959) advice on the subtleties of cross-cultural encounters.

Of all of the anthropological overviews of development, the most influential may have been Ward Goodenough's (1963) *Cooperation in Change*, which charts the fundamental factors of culture, society, values, beliefs, identity, and the principal dimensions of change that may face development agents. Its anthropological expertise is blended with a psychological and cognitive approach focusing on factors such as identity that helps agents of change anticipate obstacles as well as recognize opportunities for initiating change. Goodenough underscores the necessity to understand wants and needs as perceived by the local people. Using Anthony F. C. Wallace's (1956) concept of revitalization movements, he suggests that development works best, if at all, when its agents conform to strongly felt local needs that are ideologically or even religiously driven by the desire for improvement.

APPLIED ANTHROPOLOGY IN CANADA

Canadian applied anthropology developed much later because, until the 1960s, there were few anthropologists in a vast country. It was sustained only by the ethnographic and archaeological activities of the National Museum in Ottawa, two widely separated small departments of anthropology (Toronto and British Columbia), and a handful of social anthropologists scattered within sociology departments.

The first notable applied work in Canada was done by Harry Hawthorn of the University of British Columbia. In 1947, he arranged a conference of British Columbian Indian chiefs to discuss issues of Indian welfare and how

anthropologists could contribute. This effort continued during the 1950s through government-commissioned studies of the conditions of British Columbian Indians, the feasability of extending federal Social Security benefits to Indians (Hawthorn et al. 1958), and a special study of the social conditions of the conflict between a culturally distinct religious sect, the Doukabhours, and mainstream rural residents of interior British Columbia (Hawthorn 1955).

Another 1950s hallmark of Canadian applied anthropology was the establishment of the longitudinal Stirling County Study of community mental health in southern Nova Scotia. This interdisciplinary applied research program was developed by Alexander and Dorothea Leighton (Leighton 1959). Although American, the Leightons maintained very close collaborative links with Canadian researchers. Some significant leaders in Canadian anthropology, including Marc-Adélard Tremblay (see Hughes et al. 1960), got their starts through this project. Tremblay (1990) went on to found the modern Quebec version of social anthropology and participated in many other applied projects.

One of these projects was done jointly with Harry Hawthorn in the 1960s. In 1961, the Canadian Indian Act was revised to discontinue earlier repressions such as outlawing the Potlatch and Sun Dance. Indians were granted citizenship and more opportunities to participate in the larger society. Following this legislation, Hawthorn and Tremblay (Hawthorn et al. 1967), along with fifty other researchers, conducted a countrywide survey examining social, political, economic, and cultural conditions with recommendations to the federal government. During the same period, a series of applied anthropological studies was done in Canada's Arctic and Subarctic territories to advise the government on aspects of development (see, for instance, Vallee 1962; van Stone 1963).

Most significant, though, was the remarkable growth of anthropology in Canada during the 1960s. Where there had been only two departments at the beginning of the decade, there were twenty-six as well as thirteen augmented departments of sociology and anthropology by the end of the 1960s, with corresponding increases in the number of anthropologists and their work. Through the 1970s, 1980s, and 1990s, the domains of application rapidly expanded in areas such as indigenous self-determination and land uses (see Freeman 1976; Salisbury 1986; Dyck and Waldram 1993; Hedican 1995); multiculturalism, immigration, and refugee settlement (Buchignani 1982; Gilad 1990); agriculture (Ervin 1985; Hedly 1976), mining (Rouse 1993) and fishing (Anderson 1978; Davis 1989); medical anthropology (O'Neil et al. 1993); and other topics. In the 1990s, applied anthropology in Canada was proportionately on a rough par with the United States. Its relative strengths today are the developmentof anthropological advocacay and participatory-action research. Its weaknesses are gaps in the development of specific application-oriented training programs and a relative lack of interest in fostering the practicing domain (see Ervin 1997a for more details).

THE EMERGENCE OF THE "NEW APPLIED ANTHROPOLOGY" OF POLICY AND PRACTICE: 1970 TO THE PRESENT

Michael Angrosino (1976) refers to the "New Applied Anthropology," an anthropology that focuses on policy and practice. This multifaceted approach emerged during the early 1970s, became crystallized in the 1980s, and is currently receiving even more attention.

Its foundations were laid in the 1960s, which saw a rising public consciousness of social issues. This was an era of anti-imperialistic struggles, manifested in the emergence of nationalism, the establishment of new African states, the Cold War, and the outbreak of nationalistic wars such as Vietnam. Domestically, it was expressed through movements focusing on civil rights, feminism, gay rights, environmentalism, and Native self-determination, as well as a growing awareness of the negative consequences of development, consumerism, enforced dependencies, and ravages of the environment. The 1960s were years of significant social criticism as well as confidence in the possibilities for humane and effective public policy.

This resulted in an unparalleled period of growth and activity for the social sciences. In both Canada and the United States, increases in university enrollments were phenomenal. Anthropology, one of the smallest of disciplines, benefited from a great hiring boom in universities. Many students entered graduate school, and many new MA and PhD programs were established. Anthropologists did an enormous amount of productive research in this era. Growing numbers of students and faculty brought strongly felt pressures for relevance and attention to social responsibilities.

It was becoming clear that anthropologists could no longer study or conceptualize isolated communities with undisturbed traditional cultures and social structures. Nor could social scientists comfortably expect to attach themselves to the status quo. Some called for social science models that explained or critiqued social inequalities, social conflict, revolution, illness, and urban migration, and emphasized commitment and advocacy for the oppressed (see Berreman 1968; Gjessing 1968; Gough 1968; Hymes 1974). The actual results of this foment fell short of the original hopes and, sometimes, radical visions, although there was doubtless some shifting of consciousness toward the aspirations of the oppressed and colonialized.

During that time, many anthropologists got drawn into applied activities on a part-time basis, sometimes being called upon for advice by government or international aid agencies. This situation arose largely because of the cultural and linguistic knowledge that anthropologists had about specific groups affected by policy proposals that included the building of dams, extensions of health care or education, attempts to introduce market crops, proposals for relocation, campaigns to get local people to participate in literacy and disease-control campaigns, and many other projects. More significantly, anthropologists frequently became involved in working for groups affected by proposed development. This was so especially in North America, as such groups became more organized in attempts at resistance or self-determination. The involvement might be motivated by humanitarian concerns or by a recognition that they owed their burgeoning academic careers to the cooperation of the peoples they studied. Many anthropologists adopted a style of application combining expertise with advocacy and learned to take more subordinate or background roles as the indigenous leaders of such movements found their own voices in policy arenas. Among anthropologists, the importance of self-determination and consultation was more firmly established.

Urban problems surrounding poverty and racism became a research and applied topic for anthropologists (see Valentine 1968). In addition, many members of minorities were now becoming social scientists and working with formal organizations devoted to helping impoverished minority peoples. In a few large departments, such as those at Cornell, Chicago, UCLA, Arizona, Columbia, McGill, Illinois, Pennsylvania, Berkeley, and North Carolina, some distinguished faculty continued to provide role models of application.

Then another factor entered into the picture. Large numbers of people were graduating with PhDs and MAs in anthropology, but the available academic positions had been filled as of the early 1970s. Often by choice as well as necessity, many graduates sought other jobs, and this crisis of hiring led to a surge of creativity among anthropologists in opening new niches of practice. Many entered government; others began working for international development agencies, private companies, and nonprofit human service agencies; still others went into business for themselves as consultants. Some were hired by universities but in settings in which their knowledge was used for practical tasks or training. Schools of medicine, architecture, social work, nursing, and public health provided some new jobs. Some anthropologists saw the practical value of second graduate degrees, often a master's in public health or urban planning. Many of these pioneers upgraded their skills on the job, developing competence in their domains of practice but also in quantitative methodologies and interdisciplinary fields such as program evaluation and social impact assessment.

At the same time, the social and policy sciences or professions were undergoing a convergence that would make anthropological approaches less marginal. Here was the arena for the discussions of organizational and corporate cultures that were common in the early to mid-1980s (see Peters and Waterman 1982). It was recognized that an organization's effectiveness depended on the nature of its collective values, which were not necessarily products of rational, technocratic, or standard ways of organizing businesses or institutions. Although anthropologists may justly criticize these excursions into "corporate culture" as superficial poaching into anthropological domains, nonetheless, they may have helped to bring about a wider understanding of the value of anthropological-like investigations.

Also crucial to a new applied anthropology of policy and practice was the establishment of specialized training programs for work in nonacademic and nontraditional anthropology. Anthropology programs tended to beget other academic anthropologists. The pioneers in practicing niches reported that they had to learn many things through an enormous amount of on-the-job training. They also had to shed many academic habits. As a result, some people started to consider other forms of explicitly practical training. One of the first of these was established in the late 1960s—a program in applied anthropology at the University of Kentucky. Then, in an attempt to more directly prepare anthropologists for service for society, the first training program for nonacademic practitioners was established at the University of South Florida in Tampa in 1974. Conceived and implemented by Gilbert Kushner and his colleagues, most prominently Alvin Wolfe, Robert Wulff, and Erve Chambers, that program at first emphasized the specialty tracks of urban and medical anthropology as well as cultural resource management or public archaeology. Students learned the core literature of issues and theory for each of their practical tracks, as well as applied methods from anthropology and interdisciplinary contexts. Students also took courses from relevant cognate areas such as urban planning or public health. Capping the training was an internship program in which the students worked on a problem defined and completed in collaboration with an institution or agency. The product was both an agency report and an MA thesis. Later the South Florida department instituted a PhD program in applied anthropology along the same lines. By now about thirty departments in the United States have similar programs, for the most part at the MA level (for more information on training programs, see Kushner 1994; Kushner and Wolfe 1993; Trotter 1988; Wolfe et al. 1981).

During the 1980s, textbooks by Chambers (1985) and van Willigen (1986) effectively charted the new field of policy and practice for the first time. The Society for Applied Anthropology supplemented *Human Organization* by sponsoring a second journal, *Practicing Anthropology* (also innovated at the University of South Florida), which was devoted to the experiences of applied anthropologists outside of academic settings. In the early 1980s, the American Anthropological Association developed a new unit, the National Association for the Practice of Anthropology, for similar purposes.

OTHER NATIONAL TRADITIONS OF ANTHROPOLOGICAL PRACTICE

In this North American-focused text, it is difficult to do justice to applied anthropology in other countries. Yet practitioners should consider becoming more aware of it. Through globalization, joint collaboration with anthropologist counterparts in other countries is becoming frequent, especially in projects involving development and business anthropology. It also should be remembered that anthropology is a cosmopolitan discipline, and perspectives beyond North America most certainly add to the collective growth of the subject and its practice. For instance, policy issues and innovations relevant to indigenous peoples in Australia and New Zealand can inform those regarding American and Canadian Native peoples and vice versa. Also, many countries have health, social welfare, and justice policies that could positively influence American anthropologists seeking improvement for poor and marginalized peoples in the United States. It is not just a matter of helpful North Americans bringing their solutions to the rest of the world. It can and should be the other way around too.

To date, little has been written about non-North American applied anthropology, but a major breakthrough came in 1993 with the establishment of the Commission on Policy and Practice, a branch of the International Union of Anthropological and Ethnological Sciences (IUAES). Coming out of its first conference was a collection, *The Global Practice of Anthropology* (Baba and Hill 1997), which outlines a dozen national traditions. Also, *Practicing Anthropology* has published issues and articles devoted to practice in Israel (Halper and Nudelman 1993), China (Guan and Young 2002), Australia (Toussaint 2001), Mexico (Santos 2001), and Latin America (Guerrón-Montero 2002). To orient readers, I will make a few points about some of these traditions.

Australian anthropologists have been called upon, often in the context of court cases, to clarify Aboriginal rights, primarily in Western Australia and often in the face of development proposals (Mardiros 1997; McIntosh 1999, 2000). Given its regional sphere of influence in Southeast Asia and Oceania, Australian anthropologists have assisted in development projects, most notably in the health field (Manderson 2001), as well as being involved in issues of social welfare on the home front (Smith 2001). A small number of very active applied anthropologists are rapidly expanding the range of anthropological practice in Australia.

Anthropology in China (Guan and Young 2002) is experiencing a profound renascence. China has over 60 million members of culturally distinct Nationalities: some quite advanced, such as the Manchus and Tibetans, but many that could be considered at kin, tribal, and subsistence

levels. Since the major opening up to the West and massive liberalization of economic structures, there have been phenomenal rates of sociocultural change in China, probably unsurpassed anywhere at any time in history. Most of that change has been centered in the southern and central coastal regions. With some controversy on the international stage (e.g., the Tibet issue), the Chinese Government in its various Five Year Plans has been trying to monitor and mitigate the rates of development for the Nationalities so that they too can benefit from the changes in Chinese economy and society. Anthropologists at the Institute of Nationality Studies of the Chinese Academy of Social Sciences are conducting a massive, longitudinal, applied study of these impacts—including factors such as local markets, development, agricultural transitions, education, and many other things (Hao 2002). Its research design and collection of an enormous amount of data have a real potential to provide advanced theoretical foundations for the study of sociocultural change, development, and applied anthropology beyond China.

Applied anthropology in Mexico and Central America has some commonality. In Mexico for a long time, an acculturation/assimilation model dominated government policy. That approach frequently tried to co-opt Mexican anthropologists into assisting in getting Indigenous peoples and peasants to comply with nationally articulated, top-down, capitalist-oriented development schemes. With the rise of a predominately Marxist anthropology in the 1960s and 1970s, this led to a major crisis, with many actively promoting the self-determination rights of Mexican Indian peoples (Nahmad 1997). This thrust continued with, for instance, significant anthropological support for the Zapatista, or Mayan, self-determination movement in the 1990s. Similarly, in Costa Rica and the rest of Central America there were pressures for directed change involving anthropologists working with peasants and indigenous peoples, such as with village and regional relocations to make room for controversial hydroelectric and irrigation projects. This led to a similar Marxian struggle for the rights of the oppressed by anthropologists and other social scientists. While still maintaining pro-indigenous and peasant advocacy stances, applied anthropologists in Honduras, Costa Rica, and El Salvador have worked in projects to preserve and promote minority traditions and, along with various international aid agencies, to improve health and economic conditions of peoples in the villages

APPLIED AND MEDICAL ANTHROPOLOGY

(De Wille 1997). In Mexico, anthropologists have continued to work in development at a community level but are working even more with a rapidly evolving nongovernment sector, in part generated through the Catholic Church as an offshoot of its Liberation Theology. The focus is now toward helping small communities adjust to the penetrations and dislocations generated by globalization. Mexican applied anthropologists have also turned to issues such as health, violence, violence and gender, education, and urban anthropology (Nahmad 1998). A sophisticated applied anthropology related to business and technology is emerging, with, for instance, analyses of the expansion of the automobile industry as related to the North American Free Trade Agreement (Bueno Castellanos 2001) and a major restructuring of the Mexican national telephone company and other high-tech transformations (Santos and Marquez 2001).

British anthropology has had a long tradition of off-shore application, but one that has been associated with colonialism, a legacy that has had to be downplayed in recent years. While continuing to be involved in international development, a domestic, policy-oriented applied anthropology has emerged to deal with continuous dislocations upon the poor, homeless, youth, elderly, chronically ill, and disabled as related to government downsizing (Shore and Wright 1996, 1997), most especially efforts at deinstitutionalization. Britain probably has the second highest critical mass of applied anthropologists, and they have formed an organization known as Anthropology in Action, with a journal of the same name.

Other traditions—France (Baré 1997), Russia (Yamskov and Dubova 1997; Yamskov 1999), Israel (Kalifon 1997), India (Mahapatra 1997), Nigeria (Dike 1997)—are discussed in the Baba and Hill (1997) collection. Active traditions such as those in Scandinavia and the Netherlands have yet to be described in an accessible literature.

Overall there is a need to create a wider dialogue among applied anthropologists globally. Theory and substance need to be attached to wider formulations of policy and its analysis. This should be quite obvious because of the pressures of globalization, On the one hand, the policies of states, transnational corporations, and international trade agreements can intrude and create enormous dislocations upon peoples that might be conceived as nations within states (see Clay 1994). This requires more policy discussion and advocacy protecting the differential rights of these nations, yet does not preclude them from some of the benefits of global connections. On the other hand, policy directions need to be formulated that draw us all closer together to deal with emerging challenges of global warming and emerging pandemics.

SUMMARY

For students of applied anthropology, this history is important for several reasons. For one, some of the approaches of earlier applied anthropologists are still strikingly insightful (see Goodenough 1963, for example). Although additional positive lessons can be learned from these examples, aspiring applied anthropologists need to be alerted to the pitfalls and occasional excesses of the past, especially those associated with paternalism and colonialism. Those warnings are appropriate in a subject that requires scrupulous attention to matters of social responsibility. A history of application is also significant, because the reader gains insight about the shifts in topical interests and the steady opening of new domains for practice—ranging from colonialized tribal societies to complex organizations in modern societies.

L E T ' S   P O N D E R . . .

Let's Ponder...

You have obtained the tools necessary to become a successful anthropologist...now it is time to put your knowledge to the test. How would you respond to the situations described in the following articles?

APPLIED AND MEDICAL ANTHROPOLOGY

ANTHROPOLOGISTS IN MEDICINE:
Cultural Approaches in Medical Anthropology—
Peter J. Brown

Cultural approaches form the core of medical anthropological research and theory. Most people who identify themselves as medical anthropologists are trained in cultural anthropology and most medical anthropological studies utilize some form of ethnographic methodology. There is probably more theoretical diversity in culturally oriented medical anthropology than in the biocultural orientation. Cultural approaches consider the systems of ideas, beliefs, and values of a particular social group. In regard to health and illness, culture provides ways of explaining and combating sickness. Medicine is a cultural system of knowledge and practice.

Culture is the most important concept in anthropology, and most anthropological studies of health, healing, and medicine utilize some type of cultural approach. Ironically, despite the centrality of culture, there is little agreement among cultural anthropologists concerning the exact definition of culture. Philosophers of science say that this means that culture is an orienting concept in anthropology. **Culture** refers to the learned patterns of thought and behavior characteristic of a social group—but that covers a lot of territory. Anthropologists are interested in culture in a myriad of domains—religion, kinship, economy, art, law, child-rearing practices, markets, and conceptions of the self, just to name a few. Some anthropologists emphasize materialistic aspects of culture like the productive economy; others emphasize social relations and the way that political power is organized in a group; still others are interested in the interpretation of symbols and meaning in a cultural context.

All cultural anthropologists agree, however, that the best way to collect information about culture is through ethnographic fieldwork—living in another society, observing, interviewing, and learning from the local people. Some of the most important cultural anthropological work is ethnographic description of peoples' lives and their cultural beliefs and behaviors. These ethnographic descriptions, typically published in book form, are called **ethnographies**. Most ethnographies have some description of the local culture's beliefs and practices regarding medicine. This is largely because medicine is not a separate category from religion in many cultures that anthropologists have traditionally studied.

It is impossible to do a pure or complete description of another culture or to do an ethnography that is theory-free. For one thing, despite the goal of **holism**, it is impossible for a single anthropologist to describe and understand everything in another society. Additionally, the anthropologist's preexisting theoretical orientation determines what that anthropologist finds interesting and pays attention to during field research. Today, nearly all cultural anthropological studies are still ethnographic, but they focus on a particular question in a particular cultural context, and they use an explicit theoretical orientation that informs the analysis of that question. To understand cultural anthropology and culturally oriented medical anthropology, therefore, it is very useful to have some idea of the variety of theoretical orientations that are being used by researchers.

All anthropologists enjoy **cross-cultural comparisons**. They like to know about a wide variety of customs and practices, some of which seem exotic and extremely different from our own way of doing things. Cross-cultural comparisons tell us about both similarities and differences in customs and ways of thinking. But whether there are more similarities or differences between societies depends on one's point of view. All humans face the problems of getting adequate food and shelter; all humans face a similar life cycle of childhood dependence, growth, reproduction, sickness, and death; all humans live in social groups marked by family ties, conformity, and conflict. The variation in the ways humans solve these problems—not only in behaviors but in ways of thinking—is enormous.

There are very few things that anthropologists regard as **cultural universals**; the cultural prohibition about incest always comes to mind, even though the definition of incest varies from society to society. Another cultural universal is the fact that all societies have systems of belief and ritual that we can call religion. Similarly, most medical anthropologists would argue that all societies have a cultural system for explaining and struggling against the inevitability of sickness and death. The cultural beliefs and practices that are learned and shared by a group of people can be called a **medical system**. Most societies have specific people who know about sickness and disease, people who are able to diagnose and treat. These people may be shaman, *curanderos*, "medicine men," folk healers, or physicians. People come to these practitioners in times of difficulty; they are treated with respect and sometimes fear. Curers have special knowledge that gives them power.

APPLIED AND MEDICAL ANTHROPOLOGY

In general, curers are perceived to have courage that gives them strength in the struggle against sickness and death. All people in all cultures have to cope with sickness in themselves and their loved ones. Cultural systems of belief help people cope with those difficult, inevitable times. Our culture provides explanations for how and why we get sick. Our medical systems, as part of culture, tell us what to do when confronted with illness.

Culturally constructed medical systems are generally called **ethnomedicine** by anthropologists. People used to think of ethnomedicine as limited to exotic, non-Western systems for healing that medical anthropologists have traditionally described and studied. But over the last two decades, people have come to recognize that Western allopathic or scientific medical practices (the regular medicine at regular doctors' offices and hospitals) are also products of a particular culture. Anthropologists use the label "biomedicine" to refer to this medical system, but what they mean is that scientific Western medicine is actually just another type of ethnomedicine. In other words, biomedicine is based on a set of cultural assumptions about the nature of reality and the nature of health. Most biomedical treatments (especially surgeries) and therapies, in fact, have not been subjected to adequate scientific testing to prove their utility. Most Americans do not know, for example, that the practice of biomedicine in the United States is quite different from medical practice in France, Germany, or England. Lynn Payer (1988) has described U.S. biomedicine as aggressive and based on a metaphor of the body as a machine. It is for this cultural reason that U.S. treatments use heavier dosages of drugs and more frequent and more invasive surgeries. In all likelihood, actual healing in biomedicine depends on dynamic somatic [physical] and psychological processes based on beliefs. In other words, belief in the power of the doctor and the medicine creates a placebo effect that is remarkably powerful. The body heals itself most of the time, but we give medicine the credit for the cure.

Most anthropologists are cultural anthropologists, and, similarly, most medical anthropologists have a cultural orientation. But there is so much variation in this part of medical anthropology that I have divided this section into five areas based on theoretical themes. As you will see from the selections, however, there is a good deal of overlap among these themes, and they all emphasize the social and cultural aspects of medical systems.

BELIEF AND ETHNOMEDICAL SYSTEMS

These selections revolve around the question of ethnomedical systems and the power of belief. In general, ethnomedical systems provide three elements: a theory of the etiology (causation) of illness, mechanisms for the diagnosis of those causes; and, finally, the prescription of appropriate therapy based on that diagnosis. The practice of medicine depends on the art of diagnosis and the craft of therapy. The theory of the causation of health and illness represents the cultural knowledge based upon which a medical system is built. A theory of health and illness and the medical practices based on it are generally logically coherent: The theory provides the categories and symptomatology of diagnosis, and the therapy is based on the diagnosis. In actual practice, however, things are not that simple. People often use multiple medicine systems (called "medical pluralism") simultaneously. A classic on the topic of ethnomedicine is selection 12 [in the original text, not in this one] by George Foster, in which he describes the variation in ethnomedical systems across cultures. A more recent case study based in Mexico, by Kaja Finkler, compares a medical system based on sacred healing with bio-medicine. Both selections are good examples of cross-cultural comparison. The actual phenomenon of healing, however, may be a different story—one linking mind, belief, and body. There are two selections on this theme: Claude Levi-Strauss analyzes three elements of belief necessary for sorcery as well as curing, and Robert Hahn, an epidemiologist-anthropologist, reviews scientific evidence of the "nocebo" phenomenon—how beliefs can make people sick—which is the analogue to placebo in curing.

THE SOCIAL CONSTRUCTION OF ILLNESS AND THE SOCIAL PRODUCTION OF HEALTH

The second thematic area within cultural anthropological approaches concerns the social construction of illness and the social production of health. A standard conceptual distinction in medical anthropology is the difference between **disease** and **illness**. Although this distinction has been criticized and refined recently (Hahn 1995), the basic difference is between objectively defined disease based on clinical signs and the patient's perception of not being well and having an illness. Many anthropologists and social philosophers think that *all* of reality is socially constructed; that is, based on a culturally learned set of assumptions about how and why the world works. There is little doubt that illness categories are culturally agreed upon and that these categories change over time and through cultural circumstances. One example of an illness that has not always been considered legitimate is chronic fatigue syndrome (Ware 1992). Another example involves the social factors surrounding leprosy (Hansen's disease) as it is experienced in the United States and other cultures. (Social stigma, classically associated with leprosy but extended to many other social and medical conditions, is an important theme in medical anthropology.)

Another important theme in medical social science is the examination of the illness behavior of people as they seek treatment. This approach involves medical decision making: When do people seek help when they are sick, and whom do they go to first? To what extent are gender and poverty influential in people's decisions to seek medical care? Is it possible to identify cognitive rules that help us understand the social organization of health-seeking behavior? This approach involves researching the sick role and the individual's strategies for getting help. A quantitative approach can be applied to study treatment decision making (Weller and Romney 1988); a good example of this is James Young's *Medical Choice in a Mexican Village* (1981). Anthropologists have made an important contribution to this literature by emphasizing the household production of health (Kendall 1990). Ethnography adds an "experience-near" dimension of people's lives to medical social science, as seen in Lauren Clark's study of poor Latina women in the United States.

HEALERS IN CROSS-CULTURAL PERSPECTIVE

The next kind of cultural approach to medical anthropology involves the ethnographic description of the world of healers themselves. Many anthropologists have studied healers in other societies very closely; some anthropologists, in fact, have become shaman. **Shamanism** has gained popularity with the New Age movement, but anthropologists like Michael Brown remind us of the importance of understanding healers within their wider social and cultural context. We see the anthropologist as a participant-observer, for example, when Melvin Konner goes into a trance in the curing ritual of the !Kung San people of Botswana or to demonstrate the shaman's tricks (magical sleight of hand) in a ritual of Filipino "psychic surgery."

CULTURE, ILLNESS, AND MENTAL HEALTH

Issues of mental health and illness entail cultural questions about the definition of normal. How do we presume that we are normal? How do we decide when someone is crazy? Why are there different rates of mental illness in different societies? Is it possible to find cross-culturally valid categories of mental illness? All of these are thorny questions in cross-cultural psychiatry. A classic case study of the epidemiology of a particular folk illness—*susto*, or soul loss illness—in a Latin American context indicates that anthropological analysis of the etic cause of this illness revolves around the concept of social stress.

CRITICAL MEDICAL ANTHROPOLOGY

Critical medical anthropology (CMA) refers to the application of critical theories in looking at medical systems, particularly biomedicine. Although we have already seen similar critical theories applied to political-ecological studies of disease, a classic by Nancy Scheper-Hughes and Margaret Lock questions the underlying cultural assumptions about the nature of mind-body dualism, for example, that permeate biomedicine. This epistemologically different approach to the study of the body applies a critical perspective to biomedicine and the study of emotions, as well as to the politics and social processes linked with health questions.

In all five of these approaches there is an emphasis on social and cultural variables affecting health, illness behavior, medicinal practices, and medical beliefs. I hope that these cultural approaches, particularly because of their cross-cultural comparisons, challenge most students' beliefs about medical systems in the United States and other countries. The selections should also challenge ethnocentric assumptions that the U.S. biomedical system is the correct or the best system. Culture is all around us, like the water in a goldfish bowl. If we were the goldfish in the bowl, it would be hard, if not impossible, for us to be aware of the water. But by taking a step back, often through cross-cultural comparison, we can come to see the wider context and to recognize our own cultural blinders.

In summary, there are two basic approaches within medical anthropology. The biocultural and cultural approaches complement each other, but they do not necessarily share the same epistemological assumptions or research methodologies. Nevertheless, medical anthropologists might

APPLIED AND MEDICAL ANTHROPOLOGY

use one orientation to discuss one type of problem, like emerging infectious diseases, and a completely different orientation to discuss another phenomenon, like faith healing. One exciting aspect of medical anthropology is that it provides us with multiple ways of examining questions of health and illness. There may be central concepts in medical anthropology, but there is no central dogma.

Peter J. Brown, 1998, "Cultural Approaches to Medical Anthropology," *Understanding and Applying Medical Anthropology*, pp. 6–9. Mayfield Publishing Co. Copyright © 1998 The McGraw-Hill Companies. Reproduced with permission of The McGraw-Hill Companies.

Health-care Differences—
Dan Zuberi

Money is important, health is more important. If you are millionaire, but you are poor in health, you are not good. Your health is more important.

—George Chan, fifty-year-old Chinese immigrant and houseman at the Globe Hotel Vancouver

Canada and the United States have developed very different health-care systems over the past fifty years. The Canadian universal system of health insurance mitigates the financial stress around health care, whereas the current U.S. system keeps financial considerations linked to health care, with deleterious consequences for the working poor and their families. Accessing health care and treatment creates much greater financial stress for the working poor and their families in Seattle than in Vancouver. The problems with the current health insurance system in the United States go well beyond people simply lacking insurance. The financial stresses surrounding health care in Seattle also translate into lower levels of preventive care and higher levels of health hardship among hotel workers. Because of the many interacting factors that contribute to health outcomes, we should be cautious about attributing poorer health outcomes among Seattle workers to differences in health policy; however, it is no doubt an important factor.

CROSS-NATIONAL COMPARATIVE RESEARCH ON HEALTH AND HEALTH CARE

Previous U.S. and Canadian research on the topics of health and health care has focused on several issues, including comparative health quality and outcomes; policy lessons for the United States based on Canadian policy; and health-care development, care, and outcomes within each country.

Public health and medical researchers have completed a number of studies comparing health outcomes, such as avoidable mortality, life expectancy, infant mortality, and mortality from specific diseases, in Canada and the United States. The lack of health insurance coverage, even temporarily, has developed into a major crisis for many Americans. Canada's universal health insurance system, in contrast, covers all residents at lower per-capita cost. Many national-level statistics show better health outcomes for Canadians in general compared to Americans, with lower infant mortality and higher life expectancy (see Table 11.1).

Table 11.1 U.S. and Canadian comparative health-care statistics

	United States	Canada
Individuals without health insurance[a]	41 million (14.6%)	None (0%)
Individuals without health insurance for some period in 2001–2002[a]	75 million (26.7%)	None (0%)
Infant mortality, 1995 (per 1,000 births)[b]	8	6
Health expenditure per person, 1998 (US$)	4,270	2,250

[a]From McLellan (2003).

[b]Before one year old. From Marmor and Sullivan (2000).

Much of the cross-national comparative literature discusses the current problems with the health system in the United States, with a focus on the increasing number of Americans lacking health insurance and the skyrocketing costs of the system. These works discuss how Canada's single-payer (government-funded) universal system of health insurance covers all residents and controls health-care costs. Many "health policy lessons from Canada" books and articles have been published in the United States over the past twenty years. These works encourage U.S. policy makers to learn from the successes of the Canadian health system.

There have also been a large number of non-comparative studies on many aspects of each nation's health-care system. These studies cover a diverse range of issues, including the development of the current system, potential directions for reform, investment in new health technology; spiraling prescription medicine costs, and private provision of health services.

Health Insurance and Care in the United States

The current U.S. health insurance system is a complex mix of public and private insurance and services. The defeat of the Clinton administration's proposed universal health insurance legislation in the early 1990s has been followed by a wave of incremental health policy reforms. These reforms include the regulation of private insurance providers through Consolidated Omnibus Budget Reconciliation Act (COBRA) legislation in an attempt to increase the portability of private insurance for those between jobs. Many states have also implemented their own health insurance legislation, such as Children's Health Insurance Programs (CHIP), aimed at providing health insurance for currently uninsured children. These reforms have failed to stem the increase in the percentage of Americans lacking health insurance. The current mixed system in the United States is among the most expensive per capita in the world, and the U.S. government spent more per capita on health care in 1998 (excluding the huge private expenditures) than the Canadian government spent to provide the entire universal system of insurance and provision.

At sixty-five years of age, all Americans become eligible to apply for Medicare, relatively high-quality, publicly funded health insurance. Even though they have Medicare, many elderly purchase extended health insurance privately to ensure that they are covered in case they require long-term care. Public-assistance recipients in the United States can apply to receive more restricted public health insurance from the Medicaid program, which also provides some coverage for basic dental and vision needs. Some U.S. states now have child health insurance programs, which provide health insurance for children under eighteen who lack insurance.

Most Americans get their health insurance through workplace benefit packages. Often they must pay a subsidized monthly premium for these services. Some Americans also purchase private health insurance independently from insurers. The premiums for coverage range dramatically in cost; they are based on an individual's previous medical history and can be extremely expensive for those with preexisting medical conditions. Those without health insurance risk having to pay for extremely expensive health-care services, especially for emergency or chronic care. According to Katherine Newman in *No Shame in My Game*, "Kids in working poor families go without health insurance at a much higher rate than any other group of American children. In 1994, 27 percent of the kids from working-poor families had neither public nor private medical insurance."

The problems with the current U.S. health system go well beyond the large percentage of American's who lack insurance. Spiraling health-care costs threaten the financial well-being of even insured families. According to Elizabeth Warren and Amelia Warren Tyagi in *The Two Income Trap*, "Over the past twenty years, the number of families declaring bankruptcy in the wake of a serious illness has multiplied more than twenty-fold, or *2,000 percent*."

Growing evidence points to the severe costs in terms of the overall health of Americans under the current health-care system. Ichiro Kawachi and Bruce P. Kennedy in *The Wealth of Nations* find that "The poor are also denied access to screening and preventative services that could make the difference in terms of the early detection and treatment of cancer and a host of other serious conditions." The health system in the United States is in crisis. A nonpartisan committee of the National Academy of Sciences recommended that the U.S. government create universal health-care coverage by 2010, because noncoverage is killing 18,000 people per year in the United States and resulting in tremendous economic costs.

The Health-Care System in Canada

Canada's universal system of health insurance evolved after World War II. The universal single-payer Canadian health system developed incrementally through waves of reform—and not without initial opposition from the medical profession, providers, private insurers, business organizations, and even trade unions. Although the federal government proposed a cost-sharing universal program for health insurance in 1945, it was the creation of a "universal, comprehensive system of tax-financed hospitalization insurance" in the province of Saskatchewan by Premier Tommy Douglas, elected by the farmer-dominated Co-operative Commonwealth Federation (CCF) party, that inspired other provinces to begin to implement their own cost-sharing tax-financed systems. By 1961, the nine provinces had similar hospital insurance programs. The current Medicare program was established after the Royal Commission on Health in 1964 led to the Federal Medicare Program in 1966, which all provinces and territories in Canada had joined by 1972.

The current Canadian Medicare system is not a national socialized health system. The health services are provided by nonprofit providers, and each province runs a publicly financed health insurance plan. The current system continues to operate as a mixed public-private system, but with physician and hospital services largely covered by the public system. The public sector covers nearly 100 percent of physician services and most hospital care expenses. The system works to minimize administrative overhead through a single-payer (the government) system, price controls on physician fees, and the bulk purchasing of prescription medications. The savings are substantial: whereas one percent of health-care funding goes to overhead in Canada, 15 to 30 percent goes to overhead in U.S. private insurance companies. Lower overhead and the provision of services through not-for-profit organizations have created a health-care system that provides comparable care for all Canadians and is far less expensive per capita than the U.S. system.

The Current State of the Health-Care System in Canada
The Canadian health-care system is not without problems, many of them the result of a declining federal financial commitment to health-care expenditures. Recently the Canadian health-care system came under the scrutiny of a Federal Commission on Health Care, headed by ex-Saskatchewan Premier Roy Romanow. The Romanow Report makes it clear that the Canadian system is under fiscal strain. The provinces, for example, have picked up a growing percentage of medical expenditures in the past ten years, and the system as a whole is suffering from the federal cutbacks made in the 1990s, the failure to expand home care, and problematic patterns of access in remote rural areas. There is the also growing problem of waiting lists, especially for noncritical services.

Last summer, Statistics Canada produced its first national look at access to health services, ranging from specialists to non-emergency surgery. StatsCan estimated that 4.3 million Canadians had difficulty accessing so-called "first contact" services such as family doctors, and 1.4 million Canadians had difficulty getting specialized care over a 12-month period. Most cited waiting times as the specific problem, ranging from 55 percent of those who had difficulties getting non-emergency surgery to 72 percent of those trying to get a diagnostic test. Almost 60 percent of those affected by delay in seeing a specialist talked about wrenching stress; more than 30 percent said their health deteriorated.

Because the health-care system in Canada is public, the complaints and debate around it are also very public. The federal government currently appears set to legislate some of the proposed reforms outlined in the Romanow Report and infuse a significant surplus of cash into shoring up the system. Despite its weaknesses, the Canadian health-care system clearly provides a level of care for average Canadians, and most especially for the poor, that is more dependable than is available to their counterparts in the United States, who lack health-care coverage.

The differences between living under a universal system of health coverage in Canada and a mixed non-universal private-public system in the United States go beyond standard measurable indicators of health and health-care access. Adam Gopnik, debating Malcolm Gladwell—both Canadians living in the United States—in a *Washington Monthly* article on universal health insurance coverage, sums it up as follows: "The crucial point is, I think, the difference in social tone between a society in which universal access to medical care is taken for granted and one in which it is something that weighs constantly on all of us, even though some of us are lucky to have good insurance, and becomes an omnipresent preoccupation to the lower middle classes and to the working poor. It's enormous." Gopnik relates his sister-in-law's experience having a premature baby to illustrate the impact of the difference between the health-care systems in the United States and Canada:

My wife's sister had a very, very premature baby born in Edmonton six years ago, the kind who normally lives in about 20 percent of cases—and they had eight months of intensive care. I mean really intensive care. And the baby ended up living. It was a pound and a half at birth, the smallest baby that survived in western Canada in that year. The one thing they never thought about, the one thing they never considered, the one thing they never had to pay a moment's attention to was: How much will this cost? When does our insurance run out? It simply was not in the agonizing equation of worry and concern that they had to face. That seems to me, in itself, the most powerful argument you can make for socialized medicine, to put it in the bluntest possible terms.

A universal system of health-care changes the experience of health care by eliminating worries about the cost of care; health crises alone generally create enough worry.

A comparative analysis of data collected on hotel workers in Seattle and Vancouver confirms the essential point of Gopnik's argument: the Canadian health system greatly limits financial stress around health insurance, care, and treatment compared to the United States.

HEALTH CARE IN WASHINGTON VERSUS BRITISH COLUMBIA

Because the hotel workers in this study live under the policies not only of their country but also their state/province, the differences between health care systems in Washington state and British Columbia are also important. Generally, national-level differences between U.S. and Canadian health policies and outcomes are replicated when we compare Washington state and British Columbia.

Every resident of British Columbia is covered 100 percent by the government insurance for medically needed care in physicians' offices and hospitals. Along with health insurance, the province also provides some prescription drug coverage, although the program was recently changed to become more means-tested. The old Pharmacare system paid for medications for low-income people and seniors, as well as prescription expenses over $800 for most other British Columbia residents. For their health insurance, British Columbia residents pay a small monthly premium for their health benefits under the Medical Services Plan (MSP) program.

The new provincial government in British Columbia recently cut income taxes across the board, which has reduced revenues available for health care, and the past two years have seen many unpopular decisions to close

hospitals and long-term senior-care nursing sites, particularly in more rural communities. Because 39 percent of British Columbia's budget went to health care in 2000, the largest expense for the provincial government, it is no surprise that the recent tax cuts have led to hospital closures in British Columbia and other cost-saving measures. At the same time, British Columbia residents are expected to pay for more health-related expenses out of pocket or with extended health benefits.

In recent years, pressure has mounted for Canadians to cover an increasing number of health-related expenses out of pocket (or through workplace extended benefit plans), ranging from physiotherapy to prescription drugs. British Columbians spent an average of $891 per person on private health care in 2000, the fourth highest level of private health expenditures among the provinces and up from $685 in 1997. Overall, BC is also in the middle (compared to other Canadian provinces) in terms of the share of total health expenditures (71.5%) paid for by the public system.

While the provincial government of British Columbia may have scaled back funding for health care, the Canadian federal government's latest commitment to increasing funding in targeted areas, such as homecare, will probably shore up the current system for some time.

In Washington state, 910,000 people (15.8 percent) lacked health insurance coverage in 1999 (see Table 11.2)—slightly higher than the U.S. national average. The state experienced one of the fastest rates of growth in the number of non-insured residents during the late 1990s in the United States. Why is the number of people without health insurance in Washington state increasing? Mirroring the national trend in the United States identified by Ichiro Kawachi and Bruce P. Kennedy, a decreasing percentage of employers in Washington state are providing health benefits to employees.

According to the WA [state] based Economic Opportunity Institute, seven of 10 of the uninsured are members of working families. The proportion of private employers with 100 or more employees providing health benefits dropped from 97 percent in 1980 to 76 percent in 1997. Increasingly, employers are replacing permanent staff with temporary workers in order to avoid responsibility for providing health benefits and other benefits.

Table 11.2 Washington state and British Columbia comparative health-care statistics

	Washington State	British Columbia
Individuals without health insurance, 1999[a]	910,000 (15.8%)	None (0%)
Infant mortality, 1998 (per 1,000 births)[b]	5.7	4.03
Average family expenditure on private health care, 1998 (CA$)[c]	2,267	1,499

[a] From U.S. Census Bureau, *Health Insurance Coverage by State: 1997–1999*, in Vogel (2001, 17).

[b] From British Columbia Vital Statistics Agency, *The State of Washington's Children*, in Vogel (2001, 17).

[c] Includes medical services and supplies, drugs, and medical insurance. Canadian dollars based on 1.3 Purchasing Power Party (PPP). From Vogel (2001, 15).

Despite the increase in the number and percentage of people lacking health insurance, it appears that the government of Washington state does not plan to address the issue due to a revenue crunch: "Facing a revenue shortfall this year Washington's legislators have proposed a budget that would cut health funding. The number of people receiving state subsidies for basic health insurance would be reduced from 133,000 to 100,000 over the next two years. Federal funds that were supposed to go to hospitals that treat the uninsured would be diverted to other purposes." Thus, the current trend of increasing levels of noninsured Washington state residents is not likely to change in the short term.

COMPARATIVE ANALYSIS OF HEALTH INSURANCE, HEALTH CARE, AND OUTCOMES

I analyzed the data on health and health care for hotel workers for three interconnected domains: access to health insurance, access to preventative health care, and health outcomes. These measures are based on commonly used measures in public health research and the health economics literature.

Health insurance coverage is intricately linked to household financial security and psychological well-being as, for example, when a family has a medical crisis requiring extremely expensive catastrophic care. Some of the measures

used to compare access to health insurance are percentage lacking insurance, monthly financial outlays for medical care, financial stress related to health care, and percentage reporting lack of dental and vision benefits.

Health insurance coverage also increases access to the second domain, preventative health care (e.g., regular physical exams). Those without health insurance coverage generally avoid going to the doctor, except when there is a health emergency. Some measures used to compare preventative health care are frequency of visits to a doctor, time since the last visit to a doctor, distance to providers, and sleep deprivation.

The quality of preventative care is generally enhanced by consistency of care, which is improved by having a personal physician or regular doctor. A regular doctor can examine an individual's medical history for patterns to detect, prevent, or provide early treatment for health problems. Other potentially problematic long-term health behaviors, such as smoking, high stress, and sleep deprivation, can be counseled against and possibly addressed by preventative health care. Preventative health care for children can set the stage for lifelong healthy behaviors.

Because high-quality preventative care is associated with better health outcomes, access to this care is an important contributor to individual quality of life. Some measures of health outcomes are life expectancy, self-assessed health status, and reports of health problems.

The following analysis uses comparable data in these three domains, collected through the interviews, to evaluate the impact of health policy differences between Canada and the United States on workers in the hotel industry and their families.

Health Insurance Findings

In my study, I found hotel workers in Vancouver were better off in terms of the percentage with health insurance and regular access to care and they experienced much less financial stress concerning health emergencies. Whereas all the workers interviewed in Vancouver had medical insurance coverage, a significant percentage of Seattle employees lacked health insurance coverage. This was a problem among employees at both the Globe Hotel Seattle and the Hotel Deluxe Seattle, where approximately one in four (25 percent) hotel workers interviewed lacked health insurance coverage.

In both Seattle and Vancouver, workers received benefit packages with health, dental, and vision benefits from the hotel after a certain probationary period, as long as the employee had worked a certain minimum number of hours over a set period of time. In Seattle, the probationary period was for receiving basic health insurance coverage, whereas in Vancouver the probationary period was for extended health benefits, which go beyond the government-provided basic health insurance. Because of the high rate of turnover in the hotel industry, the probationary period for basic health insurance coverage in Seattle results in a significant proportion of employees lacking health insurance coverage. In contrast, in Vancouver employees cannot lose the government-provided universal health insurance and only low-seniority workers can temporarily lose their employee extended health benefits, if their hours are reduced below a certain level or if they are laid off during the slow winter season. Some of these employees simply go without the extended health benefits temporarily; others temporarily purchase extended health coverage for their families for approximately $35–50 per month to cover prescription, dental, and vision expenses.

Despite the surface similarities between the U.S. and Canadian branches of the two multinational hotel chains in my study in terms of health benefit policy, the experiences of the hourly employees appear to differ systematically cross-nationally with regards to health insurance, health-care access, and particularly the financial stress surrounding accessing health care. For example, hotel workers in Seattle report paying higher regular expenses for medical care and insurance than employees in Vancouver, including spending more per month, on average, for medical care and medical insurance.

Whereas only one hotel worker in Vancouver reported having regular medical expenses, 69 percent of Seattle employees reported spending money every month on health expenses, including insurance costs deducted from paychecks, co-pays, and treatment expenses. These reported expenses varied dramatically. Although most were around $50 per month, one hotel employee's household expenditure on medical care and medical insurance averaged $350 per month and another reported spending an average of $750 per month. In contrast, in Vancouver hotel employees were covered by government-provided universal health coverage and also received extended health benefits as part of their employee benefit packages with no premiums deducted from their paychecks.

Conditions such as having to work a minimum number of hours and being subject to probation periods left some Seattle workers without health insurance coverage. The lack of a universal health-care system in the United States has created substantial gaps in health insurance coverage, and these gaps impact nonsalaried hourly employees particularly. The most vulnerable, such as those receiving public assistance, often qualify for government Medicaid programs, and recently arrived refugees receive special health benefits. Alma Meteko, an eighteen-year-old refugee from Ethiopia who works full time as a room attendant at the Globe Hotel Seattle while attending high school full time, is covered by a government health program. According to Kevin Johnson, a twenty-eight-year-old maintenance engineer at the Globe Hotel Seattle, as a former member of the U.S. military he is eligible for Medicare coverage for his family through the Veterans Administration (VA) programs if he does not have access to subsidized health insurance through his job: "if [we] had no other health insurance, I think you could go to the VA." James Allan, a forty-five-year-old African-American banquet houseman at the Hotel Deluxe Seattle, is fortunate to get Social Security Disability for schizophrenia, which provides him with $600 a month (as an income supplement) as well as medical care and coverage through a government program. His co-worker, thirty-four-year-old Amy Luminov, who works as an on-call banquet server in the same department, had a much more difficult time accessing necessary mental health care, therapy, and medication for her bipolar disorder until she became an experimental patient for University of Washington Hospital psychiatry students.

Several of the hotel workers in Seattle who I interviewed were either waiting to get health insurance coverage or do not work enough hours to qualify. Even within families, a husband may be covered by his employer, but his wife and/or children are not. In some cases, a Washington state program temporarily provides health insurance for children, leaving the parents uninsured. Whereas in Canada hotel employees enjoy the protection of the government-provided universal health system as a critical safety net, in the United States workers are one bad work day away from being uninsured medically and extremely vulnerable financially in the event of a major health catastrophe.

Most of the employees who lacked health insurance in Seattle discussed it as a stressful situation, as did Sujita Hassam….Instability of coverage can also cause stress. Hue Chung is a thirty-seven-year-old recent immigrant from Guangdong, China, who works as a room attendant at the Globe Hotel Seattle. She said that she would like to see her job unionized because of "Health care. [We] pay for the kids, the bills, a lot of burden, it's a lot of money." Although Hue Chung and her husband were covered by her hotel benefits, her children were still in a waiting period. "For some reason, the insurance only cover adults, then [I] have to wait for a year to have the kids. Appreciate. Cannot join for one year. [I] think [my] income is not that much already, in fact, even with that, it is going to take out more, and [I] think it will become a problem eventually." At the time of the study, her children were covered temporarily by a Washington state government health program because, "the school, the school actually ask them to apply."

A few workers commented that health insurance coverage prevented them from switching jobs or retiring early. Jane Donaldson, a fifty-nine-year-old Hotel Deluxe Seattle Housekeeping supervisor stated, "I probably still working [five years from now], because now, we really need the insurance. I was going to retire at sixty-two, because my husband is a lot younger than I am, can continue to work, but now he can't work, I don't know, I can never retire at sixty-two."

Even the younger employees who did not have health insurance or who were waiting for coverage reported feeling some stress. Mark Frulo, a twenty-one-year-old banquet houseman at the Hotel Deluxe Seattle and his nineteen-year-old live-in girlfriend Rita Hall, a manager at a major retail store, moved to Seattle from the U.S. territory of Guam to attend Seattle Community College and experience life in the continental United States. Even though both of his parents work at a hospital, Mark Frulo and Rita Hall lack health insurance coverage. He complained that doctor's visits in Seattle without health insurance are "pretty expensive. You pay a sitting fee, and then later on you get billed….The sitting fee is like $40, and then when they bill you, [it's] like [another] $60."

Many on-call banquet servers do not work enough hours to qualify for continuous health benefits and cycle through periods of being on and off coverage. Carrie Fitzpatrick, an on-call banquet server at the Globe Hotel Seattle, described the stress of not having health insurance during probationary periods: "It is kind of stressful, because when you don't have insurance, if something happens…." At the

same time, she said that health insurance coverage can be inadequate: "But then also sometimes when you do have insurance, you feel at ease because you think they'll take care of you and then something happens, and it turns out, they're like, oh, we don't cover that."

Samantha Beck is a thirty-three-year-old Ethiopian immigrant who only recently began working in the food service as a barista (or coffee server) at the Hotel Deluxe Seattle. One day she spilled a pot of boiling water on her arm while cooking at home, but did not go to the doctor or emergency room because she did not have health insurance. Samantha Beck felt she could not afford it, especially since she was already past due on paying for a previous hospital visit. She showed me her serious scar on her arm and reflected that she should have gone to the doctor because now it would probably be permanent: "Yeah, I burn it with hot water and I was a mess, I didn't have money to go to the doctor…. It's about a second-degree burn. It was like all blistered and it was really bad…I didn't have the money. I owed Uptown Hospital still, I couldn't go there." The cycling through periods of being on and off health coverage appears to encourage employees without coverage simply to avoid going to the doctor, if at all possible, and hope that they do not require any medical care.

Problems with the health-care system in the United States go well beyond the number of people lacking health insurance. As Elizabeth Warren and Amelia Warren Tyagi report, "Many families have discovered that the exclusions, co-payments, and caps on health insurance mean that they are on the hook for far more than they anticipated, while others have learned that much needed services such as physical therapy or mental health treatment are scarcely covered at all."

The insufficient coverage provided by some health insurance plans—particularly by 80/20 plans—also causes financial stress for several of the Seattle hotel workers I interviewed. Kevin Johnson, a maintenance engineer at the Globe Hotel Seattle, discussed his previous experience with an 80/20 health care plan, explicitly emphasizing the financial dimension of health and health care.

> Like unfortunately when I worked for Major Soda Company in Indiana, when we had our daughter, the only health care they offered…[was] the 80/20 [plan]. You pay, they pay 80 [percent], you pay 20 [percent].

Well that's the kind of plan we were on in Indiana. And it cost us thousands of dollars to have our child…. Because like when you get an epidural, it's like $1,000. We had to pay $500 of that. Actually it was so we ended up paying thousands of dollars to have our daughter, which if we would have had managed care or whatever it's called, it would have been you know, $15 for every doctor's visit and then like once you went in to have the baby, it would have been like $15.

An 80/20 health insurance plan may sound acceptable to a healthy individual and family, but when a health crisis strikes it can turn out to be inadequate coverage to prevent major financial hardship. Alfred Jones, a long-time maintenance engineer at the Hotel Deluxe Seattle, was diagnosed with terminal prostate cancer that had recently spread to his bones. He was forced to switch to an 80/20 plan:

So they wouldn't offer it [to stay in the General HMO plan] to me. You know, tried, I asked them to make an exception, especially because having the cancer and all that, and plus the fact that I had been on General HMO for all that time [over twenty years]. And they said, we can't do it….

Before…if I had a monthly treatment for my cancer infusion that I get every month, it was twenty bucks. And that went up from ten because the co-pay used to be $10 and then it went to $20. Now, I have to pay, 20 percent of like $3,500….I know that essentially I am going to end up either not paying the bills or I'm going to just pay all my savings away to where I don't have any anymore, which is essentially what they want you to do when you are ill with a terminal disease anyway. They want to bleed you till you don't have any assets so they can stick you in the nursing home and put you on Medicare, at that point.

Trying to arrange your will and stuff too is real hard, because you are trying to give your kids something. And they are waiting to recoup any losses that they make or have. So they can even go back after the fact, and try to recoup it from your kids.

Recent changes also forced Alfred Jones to keep working full-time despite having terminal cancer because the Hotel Deluxe Seattle reduced the amount of pay an employee could receive during extended sick leave from $2,000 to $1,200 per month, a level that is too low for Alfred Jones to make ends meet.

Dental and vision benefits do not differ between Seattle and Vancouver in the same way as medical insurance and prescription coverage. The province of British Columbia does not currently provide dental and vision benefits for residents, except for public-assistance recipients. Until two years ago, British Columbia health insurance covered annual eye examinations, but now residents who are not covered by a work-based or a private dental and vision plan must pay for insurance or pay directly for these services themselves. The Vancouver workers expressed their disappointment at not having the same protection when it comes to vision and oral health care that they do for health care more generally. Americans face the same problem for all health services.

Dental expenses came up frequently during the interviews as one of the main health-related hardships in both countries. In Vancouver, many of the lower-seniority room attendants had lost their extended health, dental, and vision benefits when their hours were cut or when they were laid off in the winter slow season. Whereas all the workers I interviewed at the Hotel Deluxe Vancouver reported having dental benefits at the time of the interview, four out of the twenty-one hotel workers interviewed at the Globe Hotel Vancouver reported they did not have dental benefits because they did not work enough hours to qualify for coverage. These benefits cover the cost of dental visits every six months and 80 percent of other dental expenditures. Tse Leung, a fifty-four-year-old Chinese-immigrant room attendant at the Globe Hotel Vancouver was not able to access dental care because it was too expensive. Kerry Wong, also a Chinese-immigrant room attendant at the Globe Hotel Vancouver, said that dental care was so expensive in Canada that she waited and visited the dentist during her visits to Shanghai.

The subject of vision coverage came up less frequently, although some respondents had also lost access to vision benefits during the slow season. One employee, Hassam Mansour, a maintenance engineer at the Globe Hotel Vancouver, reported that even with the vision benefits provided by the hotel, his wife could not afford to get herself a new pair of glasses. He remarked, "Yeah, my wife actually wanted to get eyeglasses, but we could not afford it, so she didn't get it. She had to use her old ones instead." Until recently, many of the hotel employees could still visit the eye doctor regularly even without extended health benefits from work. Also, perhaps because regular vision check-ups seem less important and are required less frequently than dental cleanings, hotel workers interviewed did not report losing vision benefits as being much of a problem.

In Seattle, 29 percent of the employees interviewed at the Globe Hotel Seattle and 26.7 percent at the Hotel Deluxe Seattle reported not having dental and vision benefits, a slightly higher percentage than for those lacking health insurance. Sheila Chang, a forty-seven-year-old immigrant from Guangdong, China, works as a room attendant at the Globe Hotel Seattle. She said that she spent an average of $220 per month—over $2,000 per year—on dental expenses to fix her "bad teeth." Kevin Johnson, a maintenance engineer at the Globe Hotel Seattle, reported serious problems with the inadequacy of the dental coverage: "Well, even if it is [covered by the employee dental plan], it's like 50 percent of a root canal, which is $1,000. So that's still $500, $500 I don't have." Kevin Johnson's comments were echoed by Sheila Chang, the Globe Hotel Seattle public space supervisor, who emigrated from China and ended up spending thousands of dollars for dental work, despite having dental coverage through the employee benefit plan. Although dental benefits cover preventative work in Seattle, they also leave employees vulnerable to paying a substantial percentage of potentially very expensive dental bills due to the structure of benefits.

Health-Crisis and Financial-Stress Findings

Financial stress as it relates to health care and health crises was virtually nonexistent among Vancouver hotel employees I interviewed. A car accident, sudden illness, or a sports injury can in a single moment create a major crisis for an individual and his or her family, but the physical consequences are not compounded by financial trauma in Canada. Although Vancouver hotel workers had their share of injuries and illness, their positive experience with the Canadian health system and freedom from health-care expenses relieved them of the burdens—psychological and financial—that Americans in the same jobs must constantly bear in mind. For example, Mark Heung, a Vietnamese-immigrant houseman at the Globe Hotel Vancouver described a typical Canadian story about a trip to the emergency room:

Oh, we had a family fondue, you know the Chinese set-up and it was a big family gathering and the dining table wasn't big enough. So what we did, was we cleared the living room floor and we ate on the floor…. And after we were eating, drinking and things, like my oldest daughter,

she was monkeying around. And she somehow fell and she rolled into the center of the dining set-up…. And the soup that was in the center of it, were hot, not boiling hot, but hot, okay and it was enough to scald her on the side of the thigh. So that was a major, major crisis…. Boy, was it stressful…that was one event that we had to go to the hospital under extreme stress.

When I asked him if he had to pay a large medical bill for the visit, Mark replied, "No, it was all covered." His story was typical among Vancouver workers— most reported not having to pay anything for emergency health care.

Tara Wang, a forty-year-old immigrant from Guangdong, China, who works as a room attendant at the Globe Hotel Vancouver, has three boys: twelve-year-old Wa-Jun, eight-year-old Gerry, and four-year-old Alan. One day, she had to take Gerry to the emergency room. When it rains, it pours—after being treated, Gerry broke his leg the next day skating. Tara Wang said, "Two days [in a row] go the same doctor." Despite the misfortune, Tara Wang explained that they did not have to pay anything for the medical care. Health-care emergencies in Vancouver are covered under universal coverage and, thus, do not cause serious financial stress for hotel workers.

Insurance coverage and medical costs were the most frequently mentioned hardships by Seattle employees in terms of accessing health care. A medical crisis can set off a chain of events that can completely undermine a family's financial security as a consequence of uncovered medical costs (deductibles and co-payments) and lost wages. Joey Harrison, a long-time maintenance engineer at the Hotel Deluxe Seattle, owns his home, but piled up significant credit card debt due to lost wages and expenses related to his mother-in-law's cancer, wife's kidney cancer, and the births of and medical expenses for his children.

JOEY: Well, medical you know. Maybe like the mom has medical problems. My wife needs to take a lot of time off work and we are a two-income family and we need that extra income and that's when the credit cards start saving us. So maybe we start charging $1,000 a month on credit cards so she can get to the hospital with her mom. So you know that's kind of a sad deal…. Yeah, yeah, it's saving you, its keeping you to do things, and then all of a sudden like bang, your minimum payment is more than you can afford.

ME: It sounds like you have a lot of debt…and it's because, so your wife's mom got sick?

JOEY: Yeah, and then she passed away. After she passed away, my wife was diagnosed with cancer. . . . Yeah, she has to go through the whole works, for the rest of her life…. Yeah, she gets a CAT scan every three, I mean, six months….

ME: You said at one point, you almost had to declare bankruptcy but you had to cash out your pension?

JOEY: Yeah, that was hard times.

ME: This is when you had one child?

JOEY: Yeah, I had to look at ways we could save money. Should we cancel our AOL, our cable, our cell phones, our storage, you know, should we use less heat. How are we going to save money here and there?

ME: And meanwhile maximizing the amount of hours you worked?

JOEY: Yeah, taking a credit card that's got really high interest rate, 25 percent some of them and looking for one that will handle like six months, one that's like three percent, and that will handle for 6 months. You know, playing the credit card game, transferring everything over to new different credit cards so they can have less minimum payment, so you can make the minimum payment. And trying to do Home Equity Loans. Have you ever been denied on getting a credit card? Well, you get a credit card and you get denied for it. And then you get credit cards that come that will take you no matter what.

ME: Yeah, it's almost surprising.

JOEY: And then you get denied, someone wants to help you with your minimum payments, like those companies.

ME: Yeah, the consumer credit companies.

JOEY: And they look at you and they shake their heads and say you got to be nuts, I'm not doing that for you. Your minimum payments are $2,500 per month and you make, without food and utilities or anything like that, and you make $2,600 per month. How are you going to make that happen, you know. I say, I just make it happen and they don't understand that. They don't understand that I'm not just going to be sitting on the side of the road, I'll just go do gutters, I'll change, I'll go do something to make it happen. Like this interview, I'm making it happen. This will probably be a costume for my son for Halloween.

Joey Harrison's story is both unique and illustrative; a large proportion of the workers interviewed in Seattle described major financial stress resulting from medical crises.

On the other hand, some Seattle hotel employees, particularly younger ones, reported not having any problems in terms of health or health-care, dental, and vision benefits. In Seattle and Vancouver, health and health care were often more of a concern for older workers and those with children. Unless forced to deal with a health crisis, younger hotel workers did not often think about the health system.

Preventive-Care Findings

The higher costs of accessing health-care services in Seattle provide disincentives to seeking preventative treatment, such as regular doctor visits. A greater percentage of employees interviewed in Seattle (20.5 percent) than in Vancouver (7.9 percent) said they had delayed or not received care they thought they needed for themselves or a family member because of difficulties getting medical care. Because they had little or no concern about the financial aspects of accessing health services, hotel workers in Vancouver reported going to the doctor more frequently for regular check-ups and preventative care than similar employees in Seattle. Fewer workers in Vancouver than in Seattle also reported hardships in terms of accessing preventative care.

A higher percentage of workers in Vancouver than in Seattle reported having a regular doctor. Most hotel employees I interviewed in Vancouver had a family doctor that they visited in a non-hospital-based office located less than fifteen minutes driving distance from their home.

Overall more employees in Vancouver than in Seattle said they saw one doctor regularly for care (85 percent compared to 67 percent). The differences are magnified for the children of hotel workers: 100 percent of children in Vancouver had a regular doctor compared to only 56.6 percent of children in Seattle.

Cross-national differences also emerged as to where hotel employees accessed medical services (see Table 11.3). Seattle workers reported relying on a wider range of health-service providers than did Vancouver employees, who almost exclusively saw the doctor in a doctor's office or private clinic, arguably the best option because of the preventive benefits of consistent care.

Table 11.3 Health-care providers of hotel employees

	Seattle	Vancouver
Doctor's office	11 (28%)	31 (82%)
Private clinic	8 (21%)	3 (8%)
Community health center	3 (8%)	4 (11%)
Hospital-based doctor's office	4 (10%)	None (0%)
HMO	7 (18%)	None (0%)
Hospital emergency room	1 (3%)	None (0%)
Don't know	5 (13%)	None (0%)

Hotel workers in Seattle reported visiting the doctor less regularly. They had not visited the doctor as recently, on average, as employees in Vancouver. A higher percentage reported visiting the doctor in the past year: 92.1 percent in Vancouver compared to 79.5 percent in Seattle. Hotel workers in Vancouver also reported more visits to the doctor on average in the past year. There was also a small group of hotel employees in each city who had not visited the doctor in the two years before their interview, in Vancouver 5.3 percent and in Seattle 12.8 percent—more than twice the percentage.

As another dimension of preventative care, hotel employees interviewed in Vancouver reported sleeping longer per night on average and a lower percentage of respondents suffered regular sleep deprivation than in Seattle. A proxy measure of how well employees take care of themselves, a sleep deficit can also lead to deleterious health effects as well as to increased incidences of fatigue, depression, and

rage. Many more Seattle hotel workers reported sleeping fewer than six hours per night—25.6 percent compared to 10.5 percent in Vancouver. Although a combination of personal life stress and preferences may be contributing to this figure, sleeping fewer than six hours per night may contribute to poorer overall physical and mental health in the long term among the respondents in Seattle compared to Vancouver.

HEALTH-OUTCOME FINDINGS

Based on my interviews, hotel workers in Vancouver appear to have somewhat better health outcomes than those in Seattle, but, given the complex interaction of factors that shape health outcomes, it is extremely difficult to draw definitive conclusions about causality from the data collected. It does make sense that differences in the health-care systems make a difference in health outcomes of populations. At a national level, life expectancy is higher and infant and young-child (one- to five-year-olds) mortality rates are lower in Canada than in the United States; this is suggestive. Hotel workers in Vancouver reported having somewhat better perceptions of their own health, physical as well as mental and emotional, relative to others of the same age than did their counterparts in Seattle. They also appear to have slightly better health outcomes based on their answers to questions about health problems and auxiliary measures of health.

Although the results of the Global Hotel study cannot prove that a universal health insurance system results in better health outcomes than the present U.S. health-care system, it does provide evidence of some of the pathways by which these policy differences could translate into outcome differences. For example, early detection is critical to the successful treatment of cancer and other life-threatening diseases. If Americans are delaying going to the doctor because of a fear of the financial consequences of medical care, then more will die prematurely—and unnecessarily—than would under a system that guarantees universal health insurance coverage.

Canada's universal health insurance system decouples health insurance from employment and reduces the financial stress that surrounds health-care insurance and treatment for working-poor families compared to the current mixed public and private system in the United States.

The two health-care systems differ in similar ways on the national level and on the state/province level. The U.S. mixed public and private system leaves many—especially the working poor—without health insurance coverage; despite the provision of health insurance benefits by the hotels, a significant percentage of hotel workers in Seattle lack health insurance. In the realm of dental or vision insurance, however, few differences exist between hotel workers in the two cities.

The universal system of health coverage in Canada strongly mitigates the financial stress surrounding health care, even in health emergencies, for hotel workers in Vancouver. The differences in health policy also appear to foster conditions in which employees in Vancouver and their families are more likely to access preventive health care and have lower levels of health-related hardships than in Seattle.

The current health-care system in the United States leaves a growing number of Americans vulnerable to stressful periods without health insurance and many more susceptible to financial collapse due to inadequate health coverage in the event of a health emergency. The Global Hotel study findings suggest some of the many ways that the United States could benefit from its own version of a universal health insurance system.

From Dan Zuberi, *Differences That Matter: Social Policy and the Working Poor in the United States and Canada*. Copyright © 2006 by Cornell University. Used by permission of the publisher, Cornell University Press.

Chantways: A Song for Healing—
Lori Arviso Alvord, M.D.

> *Music is a healing force*
> *all living spirits sing.*
>
> —Joanna Shenandoah,
> Oneida composer

In many places in the world when a person is ill, a song is sung to heal. For this to be effective, that person must let the song sink into her body, and allow it to penetrate to even the cellular level of her being. In a sense she must breathe it in.

A song, in physical terms, is an action made of breath and sound. It is made by the vibrations of air across a section of membranes in the throat, which are then shaped by the placement of the tongue and mouth. That is a literal description of singing, but of course there is more, much more. A song is also made from the mind, from memory, from imagination, from community, and from the heart. Like all things, a song may be seen in scientific terms or in spiritual terms. Yet neither one alone is sufficient; they need each other to truly represent the reality of the song. Singing comes from that misty place where human physiology, feeling, and spirit collide. It can even be, for some people, a holy act, a religious act, an act with great power.

The notion of singing a person to wellness and health may sound strange. You may think it irresponsible of me, a trained physician, even to mention it. But I am not talking about a New Age or alternative treatment. I am speaking of the medicine ways of my tribe, the Navajo, where a singer is called in when someone is sick. As part of the cure, they perform a "sing" or ceremony, called a **chantway**. The Beauty Way, the Night Chant, the Mountain Way: different kinds of songs cure different kinds of illnesses. A Shooting Way ceremony might be used to cure an illness thought to have been caused by a snake, lightning, or arrows; a Lifeway may cure an illness caused by an accident; an Enemyway heals an illness believed to be caused by the ghosts of a non-Navajo. There even are songs for mental instability.

Not long ago I learned that Navajos are not the only people on earth to recognize the power of the human voice. In places in Africa the people sing to broken bones in order to mend them. Yet the power of a song lies not in a tested, quantifiable, and clinical world and it will not be written about in *The New England Journal of Medicine*. It will not be discussed at meetings of the American Medical Association. Many physicians, good ones, cringe at the very mention of it.

Yet one afternoon, at the hospital where I worked as a surgeon in Gallup, New Mexico, singing was going on at the bedside of Charlie Nez. As I stood in a doorway, watching the medicine man leave, I was surprised to see the elderly man, who had stirred little in the preceding days, sit up straighter, and look attentive. I glanced at his chart: his heart rate was steady, and his blood pressure had stabilized. There was a new red flush of circulation in his cheeks.

Charlie Nez was being treated with chemotherapy, radiation, and surgery for an advanced cancer. I know this because I was one of the doctors participating in his treatment. I had performed surgery on his colon to remove a tumor.

But this treatment was not the entirety of the medicine he received. As I stood in the doorway listening to the song of the medicine man who stood beside him, his voice rising and falling in a familiar range of tones, I saw a minor miracle. In Charlie's eyes, for the very first time since I'd met him, was hope.

Any physician—from an exclusive research program at Massachusetts General, from a team of surgeons in Paris, or with Doctors Without Borders in Afghanistan—will tell you that unless a dying patient has hope and emotional strength, the will to live, a doctor can do little to save him. Watching that hope come back into Charlie Nez's eyes, I realized something else: it would take both medicines to help heal this patient. The only surprising thing about this realization of the two sides of medicine was that it had taken me so long to comprehend this duality, this twoness.

My name is Dr. Lori Arviso Alvord. I am a general surgeon. I am also an enrolled member of my tribe, the *Diné*, or Navajo. I am the first woman in my tribe ever to learn and practice the discipline of surgery, and it has put me in a rare position of being able to see clearly and distinctly two different styles of medicine—and relate to them both.

In my house in Gallup, New Mexico, the dichotomy is striking. My beeper lies on the table, my cellular phone is recharging in its cradle, and a stack of medical journals stands next to a hand-hewn wood-and-leather cradleboard propped against one wall, a menagerie of bear fetishes inhabits the mantelpiece, and through the window I can see the rolling desert peppered with piñon trees beneath the slate-colored sky. I am continually reminded of a simple truth about my life: I live between two worlds. In one of them I am a dispenser of a very technologically advanced Western style of medicine. In the other, people are healed by songs, herbs, sand paintings, and ceremonies held by firelight in the deep of winter.

My father was a full-blooded Navajo, the son of my *shínálí* or grandmother, Grace, and my mother is a *bilagáana*, which in Navajo means a "white person," whose ancestors came from Europe. If you were Navajo, I would introduce myself to you by telling you my clans. My father's mother's clan is *Tsi'naajinii*, the black-streaked wood clan; his father's clan is *Ashiihi Dineé*, the salt clan. This would tell you not only where I come from but whether I am your "sister," because frequently in the Navajo world there are people around who may be one's relatives. When I introduce myself to you in the white world, I tell you I am a doctor, educated at Stanford University, specializing in general surgery.

In my two worlds I am two different people, defined in different ways—in one by my clan and people, in the other by my education and worldly accomplishments. In one by blood, in the other by paper.

Much of the time and in many circumstances, I am reminded of the metaphor of weaving. My life itself feels like a rug I am weaving, where the warp is one culture and the weft another. I pull the strings of my life across itself and make it make sense, like a beautiful rug with the *yei*, or ancient gods, woven into the wool.

The fact that my life is split between cultures was one of my earliest realizations. There is a word for this in Navajo— *'alni*, or a person who is half. The Chinese, who some anthropologists believe are the long-ago Asian ancestors of my tribe, have another way of describing it. They call it *yuckso'*, which is also a thin filament between bamboo layers and is considered "neither here nor there."

Even as I type these words, I am going against a basic understanding of my tribe. The *Diné* strongly discourage talking about or drawing attention to themselves. We are taught from the earliest age to be humble, not to brag or speak of our accomplishments. To talk about myself in a book is to go against this part of myself. Breaking the rule brings me discomfort, but I believe that this story is important—to Navajo girls, who may want to know what possibilities are out there for them; to people who wish to think about healing in a broader sense; to doctors who find their professions somehow lacking, and to sick people who may want to look at their illness in a different way. In a time when there is great confusion about how best to treat the human body, to care for it as it ages or becomes sick, my story may shed light on how two cultures can gain knowledge from each other—knowledge about health and wellness, about the bodies and spirits we are given at our birth, and about ways to care for them.

My mother, a white woman on the reservation, grew to be loved and accepted by our Navajo friends and neighbors. But from her we saw what it meant always to be slightly outside a culture, somewhere on its margin, in a place where we could not completely belong. We learned what it was like to feel peripheral. This was doubly ironic, because we felt peripheral to a culture that was itself peripheral to the larger culture that had engulfed it. We lived on the margin of a margin, which is dangerously close to nowhere at all.

My parents held no college degrees, but they encouraged my sisters and me to get an education. In high school I allowed myself to believe that I might someday hold a college degree. I resisted any larger dreams, for fear they could not come true. In my high school class of fifty-eight students, only six went on to college.

Years later, after medical school, I returned to work for my own tribe, although I could have had a much more lucrative practice elsewhere. I knew that Navajo people mistrusted Western medicine, and that Navajo customs and beliefs, even Navajo ways of interacting with others, often stood in direct opposition to the way I was trained at Stanford to deliver medical care. I wanted to make a difference in the lives of my people, not only by providing surgery to heal them but also by making it easier for them to understand, relate to, and accept Western medicine. By speaking some Navajo with them, by showing respect for their ways, and by being one of them, I could help them. I watched my patients. I listened to them. Slowly I began to develop better ways to heal them, ways that respected their culture and beliefs. I desired to incorporate these traditional beliefs and customs into my practice.

Amazingly enough, as I was gradually allowing my Navajo upbringing to affect my Western medical practice, I found that I myself was changing. I had been trained by a group of physicians who placed much more emphasis on their technical abilities and clinical skills than on their abilities to be caring and sensitive. I had unconsciously adopted

many of these attitudes, but while working with the *Diné* I worked to improve my bedside manner, learning little ways to make my patients feel trusting and comfortable with treatments that were completely alien to them.

Navajo patients simply didn't respond well to the brusque and distanced style of Western doctors. To them it is not acceptable to walk into a room, quickly open someone's shirt and listen to their heart with a stethoscope, or stick something in their mouth or ear. Nor is it acceptable to ask probing and personal questions. As I adapted my practice to my culture, my patients relaxed in situations that could otherwise have been highly stressful to them. As they became more comfortable and at ease, something even more remarkable—astonishing, even—happened. When patients were trusting and accepting before surgery, their operations seemed to be more successful. If they were anxious, distrustful, did not understand, or had resisted treatment, they seemed to have more operative or postoperative complications. Could this be happening? The more I watched, the more I saw it was indeed true. Incorporating Navajo philosophies of balance and symmetry, respect and connectedness into my practice, benefited my patients and allowed everything in my two worlds to make sense.

Navajos believe in *hózhó* or *hózhóni*—"Walking in Beauty"—a worldview in which everything in life is connected and influences everything else. A stone thrown into a pond can influence the life of a deer in the forest, a human voice and a spoken word can influence events around the world, and all things possess spirit and power. So Navajos make every effort to live in harmony and balance with everyone and everything else. Their belief system sees sickness as a result of things falling out of balance, of losing one's way on the path of beauty. In this belief system, religion and medicine are one and the same.

At a certain point I felt quite sure that my relationships with my Navajo patients were directly influencing the outcome of their surgical operations. Moreover, even what happened while a patient was asleep in the operating room seemed to have a direct impact on the outcome of the surgery. If the case did not go smoothly, if members of the operating team were arguing with one another, if there was any discord, the patient would be directly and negatively affected. Harmony seemed to be key in the OR—and just as in Navajo philosophy, one tiny thing amiss could influence everything else that happened. In response to this realization, I took more time to talk to my patients, to establish a bond of trust with them before surgery. I worked to keep the tenor within the OR calm and serene—I worked hard not to allow adverse or negative conditions to arise. I was importing Navajo philosophy into the OR.

Knowing and treating my patients was a very profound privilege, I realized, and as a surgeon I had license to travel to a country no other person can visit—to the inside of another person's body, a sacred and holy place. To perform surgery is to move in a place where spirits are. It is a place one should not enter, if they cannot enter with *hózhó*.

As I have modified my Western techniques with elements of Navajo culture and philosophy, I have seen the wisdom and truth of Navajo medicine too, and how Navajo patients can benefit from it. In this way I am pulling the strands of my life even closer together. The results have been dazzling—*hózhóni*. It has been beautiful.

It is my own private medical experiment, although it has not been proven by the "scientific method"—my hope is eventually to help design studies that demonstrate the truth of what my eyes have seen. But I believe it and have seen at firsthand its effectiveness. As I continue to bring *Diné* ways into the OR, I want to teach other students of surgery these things and instill respect for this incredible honor. They do more than fix broken parts of the human body—they bear the responsibility for life itself. In our era of managed care, because of financial constraints and the technological development of better and better equipment, medicine has drifted away from certain basic practices that improve medical outcomes. Emphasis is placed on training doctors to be efficient, cut costs, and be timely, making bedside manner an afterthought. But patients who feel taken care of and understood fare better. We doctors, like medicine men, are in the business of healing, and we must not lose sight of it.

My insights run counter to Western medical practitioners' training. With the pressures of an increasingly overburdened health care system, the tight scheduling, and budget cuts in hospitals, I do not expect it will be easy for them to receive this message. Medicine is moving in quite a different direction altogether. The Navajo view would mean a 180-degree shift for many doctors. But by implementing certain Navajo ways, I believe doctors can achieve better results in their practices.

Living between two worlds and never quite belonging to either, I have learned from both. Navajo healers use song to carry words of the Beauty Way; the songs provide a blueprint for how to live a healthy, harmonious, and balanced life. I would like to create such a pathway between cultures, so that people can walk across and see the wonders on the other side. The scalpel is my tool, as are all the newer technologies of laparoscopy, but my "Silver Bear," my Navajo beliefs and culture—from my *Tsi'naajinii* and *Ashiihi Dineé* clans and Navajo heritage—are what guide me.

Modern physicians, who have so much technology at their disposal, must somehow find their way back to healing, their primary task. We must treat our patients the same way we would treat our own relatives. We must find what has been lost as we have become so enraptured with scientific advancements: working with communities, and creating bonds of trust and harmony. We must learn how to sing.

EXERCISE

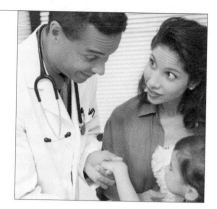

Name _____

Section _____

Date _____

EXERCISE 11.1: FOLK HEALER

Learning Goals: The successful student will apply class concepts to a scholarly journal, synthesize the two, and conclude with the production of a creative persuasion paper.

Description of Assignment: You are to assume the role of a folk healer. Choose a minimum of one scholarly journal article in order to learn more about the medical role of a shaman, curandero/a, diviner, etc. Be sure that your chosen article includes information pertaining to the history of this medical practice, how a person is chosen to become a healer and in what culture your medical system is practiced.

Writing Assignment: While talking with acquaintances, you discover that their friend is quite ill. As a healer of folk medicine, you possess specific healing skills. Write a letter to their friend introducing them to your alternative medical system. Introduce your skills and discuss how this medical system is beneficial in terms of healing. Be sure to include a brief history of this healing technique as well as information pertaining to how you obtained your medicinal knowledge and training. Be sure to offer a persuasive argument, since most people outside of your culture have never heard anything about your healing system.

Specific Requirements for this Assignment:
- 2–4 pages in length (not including title page and works cited page)
- double-spaced
- 12 font
- must have a title page
- must have a works cited page
- must utilize a "scholarly journal" (see librarian for help)
- must attach copy of "scholarly journal" article
- APA or MLA format
- no book reviews
- connect the material to class lectures, videos and readings

APPLIED AND MEDICAL ANTHROPOLOGY

Politics, Economics, and Health: Survival Strategies at the U.S.-Mexican Border— Jennifer Miller-Thayer

The U.S.-Mexican border provides unique challenges and opportunities for healthcare. The lower cost of health care procedures and medications in Mexico make it an attractive health care alternative for low-income populations in the United States. At the same time, the easier access to technology makes certain health care procedures in the United States attractive alternatives for persons with middle and high incomes in Mexico. Thus, segments of both populations practice a transnational medical pluralism, as they attempt to optimize their health by making the best use of the health care resources available in both countries. Economically, this practice has benefits for the populations who access healthcare at an affordable rate, as well as the health care markets of the countries providing the care. However, while this practice is economically beneficial and possibly healthier for both populations, some interests, such as the American Medical Association and the U.S. pharmaceutical companies, do not view this practice as positive or healthy. Stereotypes, misperceptions, and misinformation create further problems associated with this practice. This paper, drawing on my dissertation research conducted between July–August 2002 and April 2004–May 2005,[1] presents some of the complexities and dynamics of the medical pluralism occurring on both sides of the U.S.-Mexican border.

MEDICAL PLURALISM

Medical pluralism is generally defined as the presence of two or more medical systems in one culture. This is often applied to situations where biomedical models are combined with "alternative" models of health and healing providing multiple medical choices for patients. In these cases medical pluralism would be recognized as occurring at the institutional level with individual actors making their medical choices from the options provided to them by their cultural institutions. However, in my work at the U.S.-Mexican border, I observed a different type of medical pluralism—one created by individuals as they crossed the border to use more than one medical system.

This pluralism is also different from "traditional" definitions in that both medical systems accessed by these patients are considered biomedical models, also sometimes referred to as "Western medicine." (There are alternative models on both sides as well, but this paper is only focusing on the biomedical models that were accessed.)

The assumed uniformity in biomedical models masks the variation in the application, practice, ideologies and access to these models in different settings. In the transnational context I observed at the border, the health and healing beliefs are Western biomedical models, but how they are put into practice and accessed are different due to different political economic situations related to aspects of health, healing and care access. For example, in the United States the models of access are based on institutional structures of capitalism where access is based on the patient's ability to pay for services. In Mexico, they are based on socialist structures of nationalized medicine where access to healthcare is a guaranteed right in the constitution, and where the government helps to regulate the cost of care and medications.

Each system offers different benefits to health consumers based on their economic resources. For example, easier access to technology is available in the United States for those who can afford it. Thus, Mexican citizens with higher financial resources cross the border to access better technology, or in some cases to access the same technology available in Mexico more quickly. For instance, heart surgery is available at the same quality, with the same technology in Mexico as it is in the United States. However, it is limited in the quantity of availability, so that a person who qualifies for access to it in Mexico has to go through a 6–9 month process (which also includes a lot of travel) to get the surgery, while someone with more economic capital can cross the border into the United States and access the same surgery in a matter of weeks. So, the quality is the same, but the time to access it is dramatically different. Because in this case, the technology for this procedure is more prolific in the United States than it is in Mexico. Another example of this involves a community called "snowbirds."

WHAT IS A SNOWBIRD?

A **snowbird** is commonly defined as a person from the Northern United States or Canada, 55 years or older, who spends the winter months in the warmer Southwestern United States. Generally, they live in the Southwest for 5–6 months of the year, arriving sometime in October or November and leaving in late March or early April. Most snowbirds own either a trailer or mobile home and stay in the same community or mobile home park year after year. Some have been coming to the same place for 25 years or more and many move to the Southwest permanently as they get older.

APPLIED AND MEDICAL ANTHROPOLOGY

In addition to the snowbirds described above, my research sample included people who came to Mexico for a one day or weekend turn-around trip. Some of the "day/weekend trippers" took tour buses that originated in California or Arizona, while others carpooled with family members and/or friends from as far away as Oregon and Washington. They were also sometimes younger than the 55 years that is often the marker of the "snowbirds" age.

The most common health problems requiring medication for the snowbirds were high blood pressure, arthritis, and high cholesterol. Additionally, they commonly needed dental care and eyeglasses. The insurance coverage for this group varied, but most received Medicare. Some also carried supplemental insurance to their Medicare coverage in order to have some coverage of medications and dental and eye care.

Medicare and Medi-cal did not cover prescriptions at all during my research period, and do not cover it well now, so people run out of medication coverage within 6–9 months and then have to pay the full price for their medications for 3–6 months of the year. In order to continue with their life saving medication regimens, they cross the border and access the pharmacies in Mexico where their medication is available at a much lower cost. They also access eye and dental care for the same reasons. The chart below provides an example of the cost differences between the United States, Canada and Mexico for common medications used by snowbirds at the time of my research.

Medication	US	Canada	Mexico
Vioxx 100 25mg	$357	$149	$48
Premerin 100 .625mg	$32	$19	$8
Lopressor 100 50mg	$17	$14	$8

(2004 field notes from internet site—http://www.RV.NET).

Economically this is a win-win situation for the snowbirds and the medical providers in Mexico. The snowbirds access their necessary medical procedures and medications while the medical industry in Mexico thrives. One small Mexican border town, dubbed "the Mecca of medicine" by local U.S. newspapers, has approximately fifty dental offices, twenty-six pharmacies, twenty optician offices and fourteen doctors offices (Coates, Healy and Morrison 2002) in a six block radius from the border crossing.

The medical markets in the United States also reflect these cross-border usage patterns. For example, a local border area hospital with a "state of the art" birthing facility offers patients from Mexico a discount if they pay for their birthing services ahead of time (most pay in cash) rather than being billed after the birth takes place. Additionally, some doctors, who are licensed to practice in both countries, will recommend that their Mexican patients have their surgery in the United States and then recover in Mexico where costs of recovery are much cheaper.

However, not everyone benefits from this medical pluralism at the border. The U.S. pharmaceutical companies lose money when elderly patients buy their medication south of the border (the elderly are by far the largest consumers of medicine as a group). As a result, the American Medical Association (AMA), U.S. pharmaceutical companies and U.S. media produce "risk" campaigns to "inform" consumers about the risks of buying their medications and accessing services in Mexico. They warn consumers that buying their medication or seeking their healthcare in Mexico is risky and dangerous because they do not have the same regulations that are in place in the United States (Mena 2002:B1). The manufacturing of the drugs along with their purity and quality is questioned. They tell consumers that the medications may be expired, or may not be what they say they are, or may be devoid of any "real" medication at all (placebo/sugar pills). However, if the elderly buy name brand medications, which are patented and must contain the formula in the patent, then they are buying medications that are either manufactured by the U.S. pharmaceutical companies themselves (i.e., Merck, GlaxoSmithKline, Pfizer, Bayer, etc.) or by a licensed manufacturer following the patented formula. Only when they buy generic medications is there any possible question of quality. Furthermore, the people of Mexico are using these medications as well, so is their health compromised when they buy their medications? Additionally, when we examine "risk" in this context the important question to ask is, "What puts a patient more at risk—buying medication that may, according to rumors and speculation, be poor quality, or not being able to buy any medication at all?" (Which is where most of these elderly people are after 6–9 months of the year.) In my research I rarely came across anyone who was unhappy with buying medications in Mexico. And the danger I saw came from people not being very aware consumers of their medications.

For example, Jane[2], a 69-year-old snowbird migrant who lives in the Southwest during the winter and Kansas the rest of the year, explains:

> There could be [problems], you have to have medical knowledge—[like about] side effects of medications. Most of the pharmacists in the U.S. will tell you the side effects when they give you the medication, and they will do that in Mexico if you ask. But if you don't ask, then they probably won't tell you. If the patients are not paying attention to the dosages and side effects, it can be dangerous. Like if you are supposed to take 5 mg of medication, but the pills you get in Mexico are 10 mg instead, you have to cut it in half when you take it or you will take too much. So you have to pay attention because that would not happen in the U.S. They wouldn't do that (Miller-Thayer, J 2004: fieldnotes).

So what may be dangerous is not understanding how the second medical system works, based on the assumption that biomedical models are the same everywhere. This danger is somewhat mitigated by the socialization and networking that occurs between these transnational populations. The previous experience of friends, neighbors, family and healthcare professionals who know the second system is used to educate "newcomers" in the process of accessing their care in the second system. This happens on both sides of the border.

Another type of misinformation comes from U.S. newspaper accounts that tell of Americans arrested in Mexico for purchasing their medications there. This "scares" some potential U.S. consumers from buying their medications in Mexico for fear of being arrested and thrown into a Mexican jail. What is left out of the articles is that those who were arrested were attempting to buy controlled substances in Mexico without a Mexican doctor's prescription, and most of these people were buying substances that are illegal in the United States to sell on the black market. The types of drugs they were purchasing include classes of drugs that are considered narcotic, such as sleeping pills, certain anti-depressants, etc. Additionally, if the purchaser had a prescription from a Mexican doctor then he/she could legally buy them in Mexico in certain quantities. They would, of course, then need a U.S. doctor's prescription to bring up to a 90-day supply into the United States. They were not your typical snowbird or day/weekend tripper consumer. The types of medications that most U.S. consumers are buying in Mexico do not require a Mexican doctor's prescription and are thus, legal to purchase over the counter (they still require a U.S. doctor's prescription to bring up to a 90-day supply back into the United States). During my fieldwork, I did not come across anyone (or stories of anyone) who had been arrested for purchasing their medications in Mexico.

CONCLUSION

From these examples we can see that the transnational medical pluralism occurring at the US-Mexican border is made up of a complex web of connections — it is not just a simple matter of individuals making economic choices for their optimal health, but rather it also involves the larger social institutions that are connected to health ideologies, practices, production and consumption.

REFERENCES CITED

Coates, Healy and Morrison
2002 "Tracking the Snowbirds: Seasonal Migration from Canada to the U.S.A. and Mexico." *American Review of Canadian Studies*. Association for Canadian Studies in the United States. Autumn v32:3 p. 433-452. Electronic Collection: A98124116.

Mena, Jennifer
2002 "U.S. Insurers Tapping a Market for Cross-Border Health Coverage." *Los Angeles Times*. Pgs. B1, B7. July 29.

Miller-Thayer, Jennifer
2004 Dissertation fieldwork, field notes.

RV.Net website
2004 Open Roads Forum–Snowbirds–Drugs in Mexico. Collected on March 5, 2004. Postings from Jan. 29, 2004–Mar. 1, 2004. http://www.RV.NET

Endnotes:
[1] My research was generously funded by grants from UCMEXUS, EGARC, and UCR Humanities.

[2] All names used are pseudonyms.

Jennifer Miller-Thayer, Migration for Health: A Snowbird's Journey.

ANTHROPOLOGISTS IN MEDICINE:
African AIDS Tragedy: Patent Rights versus Human Rights—
Stu Borman

Pharmaceutical researchers have recently developed drugs that have helped extend the life spans of many AIDS patients. These drugs include the human immunodeficiency virus (HIV) protease inhibitors. Unfortunately, many people in African countries and other developing nations cannot afford to use such medicines.

According to both the Joint United Nations Program on HIV/AIDS (UNAIDS) and the World Health Organization (WHO), 70% of people newly infected with HIV in 1998 live in southern Africa. About 83% of all AIDS deaths have occurred there since the epidemic began, although only 10% of the world's population lives there. About 11.5 million southern African AIDS patients had died by the end of last year—almost 2 million in 1998 alone.

With the advent of protease-inhibitor drugs and the concept of combination therapy, many AIDS patients in the U.S. and Europe are now able to live reasonably productive lives. But in many developing countries, "one year's HIV treatment, if it were purchased, would consume 30 years income," says L. Jonathan Quick, WHO director of essential drugs and other medicines.

Some governments and organizations are trying to help. Glaxo Wellcome and other drug companies have reduced prices of AIDS drugs in some African localities. Bristol-Myers-Squibb announced in May a grant of $100 million over five years for AIDS research, prevention, and treatment in Africa—although not for drug discounts. And last week Vice President Al Gore proposed spending $100 million for AIDS prevention and care in Africa.

Nevertheless, "access to essential drugs is a basic human right often denied to people in poor countries," writes Bernard Pecoul and colleagues at Médecins Sans Frontieres, Paris [*J.Am. Med Assoc.*, *281, 361 (1999)*]. They suggest that developing countries "should be able to obtain **compulsory licenses** whereby national authorities allow local manufacturers to circumvent [drug companies'] patent rights, with certain conditions and in return for the payment of royalties to the inventor."

The pharmaceutical industry is frightened by compulsory licensing "because they believe that if it takes hold in South Africa and elsewhere, other countries will do it—and they won't just do it with AIDS drugs, they'll do it with other essential medicines," said *Wall Street Journal* reporter Michael Waldholz in a recent National Public Radio interview on the issue. This would "show the world what these drugs really cost to produce, and there would be tremendous pressure by activists here as well as governments abroad to significantly reduce the amount of money they're paying for these drugs."

African countries are themselves reluctant to establish compulsory licenses because they fear U.S. trade sanctions if they do—a threat Gore has been criticized for backing.

"There are probably a lot of people who think it's not good to mess with companies' patent rights, who find that kind of troubling and disturbing," says James Love, director of the Consumer Project on Technology, Washington, D.C; "On the other hand, so many people are infected in these countries, and millions of them are going to die. This is such a horrific tragedy that the average person can't comprehend it. I think there's going to be a harsh judgment in history when people look back and see that it was an instrument of U.S. government policy that actually made it harder to get access to drugs."

It would set a very bad precedent "if nations were allowed to arbitrarily abrogate patents," says spokesperson Jeff Trewhitt of Pharmaceutical Research & Manufacturers of America. "Patent protection is the lifeblood of this industry. Our companies have increased research spending in just the past 15 years from $4 billion a year in 1985 to $24 billion this year," and research as a percentage of sales has more than doubled in that period, from 10% to 21%. "This has made it that much more difficult to get an adequate return on investment, and patent protection ensures our ability to sustain innovation." Trewhitt also notes that in many developing countries "there are not enough doctors who know how to administer and monitor AIDS medicines properly in patients, and without that AIDS drugs can do more harm than good."

Certainly, African nations are partly responsible for the severity of the AIDS problem there, in that for many years they did not acknowledge the issue forthrightly and did not devote sufficient resources to fight the disease. Nevertheless, the gravity of the African AIDS issue suggests that much more could and should be done.

Western countries just spent billions of dollars lobbing smart bombs at Serbia in an effort to protect a million or so ethnic Albanian Kosovars—a worthy and well-intentioned but not wholly successful effort. Perhaps the world should now devote comparable resources to lobbing some smart drugs at AIDS patients in developing nations—who are literally dying to share in some of the wondrous advances pharmaceutical research has brought about.

For more information and the most recent statistics on this topic, please visit the following websites:

A PowerPoint file:
 http://data.unaids.org/Topics/Epidemiology/Slides02/12-05/Epi-core2005_Dec05_en.ppt

An HTML page that includes the above link is located at:
 http://www.unaids.org/en/HIV_data/Epidemiology/epi_slides.asp

UNAIDS (Joint United Nations Programme on HIV/AIDS at: *http://www.unaids.org/en/* and WHO (World Health Organization) at *http://www.who.int/*

ANTHROPOLOGISTS IN MEDICINE:
AIDS as Human Suffering—
Paul Farmer and Arthur Kleinman

Our environment is constantly changing, and the necessity of adapting to environmental change is a fundamental challenge for every species. Often, when people think of the "environment," they envision trees, mountains, water, and animals. Few people think of invisible life forms, like bacteria and viruses, as part of our environment—but they are. Disease organisms themselves are constantly changing, and the kinds of diseases that afflict a social group are largely determined by their ecology and culture.

In the last two decades, humans have been faced by the challenge of a new virus (HIV) causing a lethal disease—acquired immune deficiency syndrome (AIDS)—that has spread throughout the world. In the United States we tend to think of AIDS as a disease that affects "risk groups" like gay men and intravenous drug users. But on a global basis, an estimated three-quarters of AIDS sufferers contracted the HIV virus through heterosexual intercourse. In the United States, much of the public discussion about AIDS reflects moral judgments about people's lifestyles and places the blame for the disease on the sufferers. For people with AIDS, such cultural attitudes and stigmatization significantly compound their suffering.

Social reactions to AIDS vary among cultures. The cross-cultural comparison of Robert and Anita, both dying from AIDS but in very different settings, has much to tell us about the cultures themselves. In this selection, two prominent medical anthropologists make the case that on a human plane the way that we think about AIDS and its victims compounds the suffering and tragedy of this epidemic.

In the history of this epidemic, anthropologists have played a role in describing and understanding the behavioral practices related to the transmission of the HIV virus. The biomedical challenge of AIDS is great, but the challenge of coping with the human dimensions of AIDS is enormous, requiring both compassion and cross-cultural understanding.

That the dominant discourse on AIDS at the close of the twentieth century is in the rational-technical language of disease control was certainly to be expected and even necessary. We anticipate hearing a great deal about the molecular biology of the virus, the clinical epidemiology of the disease's course, and the pharmacological engineering of effective treatments. Other of contemporary society's key idioms for describing life's troubles also express our reaction to AIDS: the political-economic talk of public-policy experts, the social-welfare jargon of the politicians and bureaucrats, and the latest psychological terminology of mental-health professionals. Beneath the action-oriented verbs and reassuringly new nouns of these experts' distancing terminology, the more earthy, emotional rumblings of the frightened, the accusatory, the hate-filled, and the confused members of the public are reminders that our response to AIDS emerges from deep and dividing forces in our experience and our culture.

AIDS AND HUMAN MEANINGS

Listen to the words of persons with AIDS and others affected by our society's reaction to the new syndrome:

- "I'm 42 years old. I have AIDS. I have no job. I do get $300 a month from social security and the state. I will soon receive $64 a month in food stamps. I am severely depressed. I cannot live on $300 a month. After $120 a month for rent and $120 a month for therapy, I am left with $60 for food and vitamins and other doctors and maybe acupuncture treatments and my share of utilities and oil and wood for heat. I'm sure I've forgotten several expenses like a movie once in a while and a newspaper and a book."[1]

- "I don't know what my life expectancy is going to be, but I certainly know the quality has improved. I know that not accepting the shame or the guilt or the stigma that people would throw on me has certainly extended my life expectancy. I know that being very up-front with my friends, and my family and coworkers, reduced a tremendous amount of stress, and I would encourage people to be very open with friends, and if they can't handle it, then that's their problem and they're going to have to cope with it."

- "Here we are at an international AIDS conference. Yesterday a woman came up to me and said, 'May I have two minutes of your time?' She said, 'I'm asking doctors how they feel about treating AIDS patients.' And I said, 'Well, actually I'm not a doctor. I'm an AIDS patient,' and as she was shaking hands, her hand whipped away, she took two steps backward, and the look of horror on her face was absolutely diabolical."

- "My wife and I have lived here [in the United States] for fifteen years, and we speak English well, and I do O.K. driving. But the hardest time I've had in all my life, harder than Haiti, was when people would refuse to get in my cab when they discovered I was from Haiti [and therefore in their minds, a potential carrier of HIV]. It got so we would pretend to be from somewhere else, which is the worst thing you can do, I think."

All illnesses are metaphors. They absorb and radiate the personalities and social conditions of those who experience symptoms and treatments. Only a few illnesses, however, carry such cultural salience that they become icons of the times. Like tuberculosis in *fin de siècle* Europe, like cancer in the first half of the American century, and like leprosy from Leviticus to the present, AIDS speaks of the menace and losses of the times. It marks the sick person, encasing the afflicted in an exoskeleton of peculiarly powerful meanings: the terror of a lingering and untimely death, the panic of contagion, the guilt of "self-earned" illness.

AIDS has offered a new idiom for old gripes. We have used it to blame others: gay men, drug addicts, inner-city ethnics, Haitians, Africans. And we in the United States have, in turn, been accused of spreading and even creating the virus that causes AIDS. The steady progression of persons with AIDS toward the grave, so often via the poor house, has assaulted the comforting idea that risk can be managed. The world turns out to be less controllable and more dangerous, life more fragile than our insurance and welfare models pretend. We have relegated the threat of having to endure irremediable pain and early death—indeed, the very image of suffering as the paramount reality of daily existence—to past periods in history and to other, poorer societies. Optimism has its place in the scale of American virtues; stoicism and resignation in the face of unremitting hardship—unnecessary character traits in a land of plenty—do not. Suffering had almost vanished from public and private images of our society.

Throughout history and across cultures, life-threatening disorders have provoked questions of control (What do we do?) and bafflement (Why me?). When bubonic plague depopulated fourteenth-century Europe by perhaps as many as half to three-fourths of the population, the black death was construed as a religious problem and a challenge to the moral authority as much or even more than as a public-health problem. In the late twentieth century, it is not surprising that great advances in scientific knowledge and technological intervention have created our chief responses to questions of control and bafflement. Yet bafflement is not driven away by the advance of scientific knowledge, for it points to another aspect of the experience of persons with AIDS that has not received the attention it warrants. It points to a concern that in other periods and in other cultures is at the very center of the societal reaction to dread disease, a concern that resonates with that which is most at stake in the human experience of AIDS even if it receives little attention in academic journals— namely, suffering.

A mortal disease forces questions of dread, of death, and of ultimate meaning to arise. **Suffering** is a culturally and personally distinctive form of affliction of the human spirit. If pain is distress of the body, suffering is distress of the person and of his or her family and friends. The affliction and death of persons with AIDS create master symbols of suffering; the ethical and emotional responses to AIDS are collective representations of how societies deal with suffering. The stories of sickness of people with AIDS are texts of suffering that we can scan for evidence of how cultures and communities and individuals elaborate the unique textures of personal experience out of the impersonal cellular invasion of viral RNA. Furthermore, these illness narratives point toward issues in the AIDS epidemic every bit as salient as control of the spread of infection and treatment of its biological effects.

Viewed from the perspective of suffering, AIDS must rank with smallpox, plague, and leprosy in its capacity to menace and hurt, to burden and spoil human experience, and to elicit questions about the nature of life and its significance. Suffering extends from those afflicted with AIDS to their families and intimates, to the practitioners and institutions who care for them, and to their neighborhoods and the rest of society, who feel threatened by perceived sources of the epidemic and who are thus affected profoundly yet differently by its consequences. If we minimize the significance of AIDS as human tragedy, we dehumanize people with AIDS as well as those engaged in the public-health and clinical response to the epidemic. Ultimately, we dehumanize us all.

ROBERT AND THE DIAGNOSTIC DILEMMA

It was in a large teaching hospital in Boston that we first met Robert, a forty-four-year-old man with AIDS.[2] Robert was not from Boston, but from Chicago, where he had already weathered several of the infections known to strike people with compromised immune function. His most recent battle had been with an organism similar to that which causes tuberculosis but is usually harmless to those with intact immune systems. The infection and the many drugs used to treat it had left him debilitated and depressed, and he had come east to visit his sister and regain his strength. On his way home, he was prevented

from boarding his plane "for medical reasons." Beset with fever, cough, and severe shortness of breath, Robert went that night to the teaching hospital's emergency ward. Aware of his condition and its prognosis, Robert hoped that the staff there would help him to "get into shape" for the flight back to Chicago.

The physicians in the emergency ward saw their task as straightforward: to identify the cause of Robert's symptoms and, if possible, to treat it. In contemporary medical practice, identifying the cause of respiratory distress in a patient with AIDS entails following what is often called an **algorithm**. An algorithm, in the culture of biomedicine, is a series of sequential choices, often represented diagrammatically, which helps physicians to make diagnoses and select treatments. In Robert's case, step one, a chest X-ray, suggested the opportunistic lung parasite *Pneumocystis* as a cause for his respiratory distress; step two, examination of his sputum, confirmed it. He was then transferred to a ward in order to begin treatment of his lung infection. Robert was given the drug of choice, but did not improve. His fever, in fact, rose and he seemed more ill than ever.

After a few days of decline, Robert was found to have trismus: his jaw was locked shut. Because he had previously had oral candidiasis ("thrush"), his trismus and neck pain were thought to suggest the spread of the fungal infection back down the throat and pharynx and into the esophagus—a far more serious process than thrush, which is usually controlled by antifungal agents. Because Robert was unable to open his mouth, the algorithm for documenting esophagitis could not be followed. And so a "GI consult"—Robert had already had several—was called. It was hoped that the gastroenterologists, specialists at passing tubes into both ends of the gastrointestinal tract, would be better able to evaluate the nature of Robert's trismus. Robert had jumped ahead to the point in the algorithm that called for "invasive studies." The trouble is that on the night of his admission he had already declined a similar procedure.

Robert's jaw remained shut. Although he was already emaciated from two years of battle, he refused a feeding tube. Patient refusal is never part of an algorithm, and so the team turned to a new kind of logic: Is Robert mentally competent to make such a decision? Is he suffering from AIDS dementia? He was, in the words of one of those treating him, "not with the program." Another member of the team suggested that Robert had "reached the end of the algorithm" but the others disagreed. More diagnostic studies were suggested: in addition to esophagoscopy with biopsy and culture, a CT scan of the neck and head, repeated blood cultures, even a neurological consult. When these studies were mentioned to the patient, his silent stare seemed to fill with anger and despair. Doctors glanced uncomfortably at each other over their pale blue masks. Their suspicions were soon confirmed. In a shaky but decipherable hand, Robert wrote a note: "I just want to be kept clean."

Robert got a good deal more than he asked for, including the feeding tube, the endoscopy, and the CT scan of the neck. He died within hours of the last of these procedures. His physicians felt that they could not have withheld care without having some idea of what was going on.

In the discourse of contemporary biomedicine, Robert's doctors had been confronted with "a diagnostic dilemma." They had not cast the scenario described above as a moral dilemma but had discussed it in rounds as "a compliance problem." This way of talking about the case brings into relief a number of issues in the contemporary United States—not just in the culture of biomedicine but in the larger culture as well. In anthropology, one of the preferred means of examining culturally salient issues is through **ethnology**: in this case, we shall compare Robert's death in Boston to death from AIDS in a radically different place.

ANITA AND A DECENT DEATH

The setting is now a small Haitian village. Consisting of fewer than a thousand persons, Do Kay is composed substantially of peasant farmers who were displaced some thirty years ago by Haiti's largest dam. By all the standard measures, Kay is now very poor; its older inhabitants often blame their poverty on the massive buttress dam a few miles away and note bitterly that it has brought them neither electricity nor water.

When the first author of this paper began working in Kay, in May of 1983, the word *SIDA*, meaning AIDS, was just beginning to make its way into the rural Haitian lexicon. Interest in the illness was almost universal less than three years later. It was about then that Anita's intractable cough was attributed to tuberculosis.

Questions about her illness often evoked long responses. She resisted our attempts to focus discussions. "Let me tell you the story from the beginning," she once said; "otherwise you will understand nothing at all."

As a little girl, Anita recalls, she was frightened by the arguments her parents would have in the dry seasons. When her mother began coughing, the family sold their livestock in order to buy "a consultation" with a distinguished doctor in the capital. Tuberculosis, he told them, and the family felt there was little they could do other than take irregular trips to Port-au-Prince and make equally irregular attempts to placate the gods who might protect the woman. Anita dropped out of school to help take care of her mother, who died shortly after the girl's thirteenth birthday.

It was very nearly the *coup de grâce* for her father, who became depressed and abusive. Anita, the oldest of five children, bore the brunt of his spleen. "One day, I'd just had it with his yelling. I took what money I could find, about $2, and left for the city. I didn't know where to go." Anita had the good fortune to find a family in need of a maid. The two women in the household had jobs in a U.S.-owned assembly plant; the husband of one ran a snack concession out of the house. Anita received a meal a day, a bit of dry floor to sleep on, and $10 per month for what sounded like incessant labor. She was not unhappy with the arrangement, which lasted until both women were fired for participating in "political meetings."

Anita wandered about for two days until she happened upon a kinswoman selling gum and candies near a downtown theater. She was, Anita related, "a sort of aunt." Anita could come and stay with her, the aunt said, as long as she could help pay the rent. And so Anita moved into Cité Simone, the sprawling slum on the northern fringes of the capital.

It was through the offices of her aunt that she met Vincent, one of the few men in the neighborhood with anything resembling a job: "He unloaded the whites' luggage at the airport." Vincent made a living from tourists' tips. In 1982, the year before Haiti became associated, in the North American press, with AIDS, the city of Port-au-Prince counted tourism as its chief industry. In the setting of an unemployment rate of greater than 60 percent, Vincent could command considerable respect. He turned his attention to Anita. "What could I do, really? He had a good job. My aunt thought I should go with him." Anita was not yet fifteen when she entered her first and only sexual union. Her lover set her up in a shack in the same neighborhood. Anita cooked and washed and waited for him.

When Vincent fell ill, Anita again became a nurse. It began insidiously, she recalls: night sweats, loss of appetite, swollen lymph nodes. Then came months of unpredictable and debilitating diarrhea. "We tried everything — doctors, charlatans, herbal remedies, injections, prayers." After a year of decline, she took Vincent to his hometown in the south of Haiti. There it was revealed that Vincent's illness was the result of malign magic: "It was one of the men at the airport who did this to him. The man wanted Vincent's job. He sent an AIDS death to him."

The voodoo priest who heard their story and deciphered the signs was straightforward. He told Anita and Vincent's family that the sick man's chances were slim, even with the appropriate interventions. There were, however, steps to be taken. He outlined them, and the family followed them, but still Vincent succumbed. "When he died, I felt spent. I couldn't get out of bed. I thought that his family would try to help me to get better, but they didn't. I knew I needed to go home."

She made it as far as Croix-des-Bouquets, a large market town at least two hours from Kay. There she collapsed, feverish and coughing, and was taken in by a woman who lived near the market. She stayed for a month, unable to walk, until her father came to take her back home. Five years had elapsed since she'd last seen him. Anita's father was by then a friendly but broken-down man with a leaking roof over his one-room, dirt-floor hut. It was no place for a sick woman, the villagers said, and Anita's godmother, honoring twenty-year-old vows, made room in her overcrowded but dry house.

Anita was diagnosed as having tuberculosis, and she responded to antituberculosis therapy. But six months after the initiation of treatment, she declined rapidly. Convinced that she was indeed taking her medications, we were concerned about AIDS, especially on hearing of the death of her lover. Anita's father was poised to sell his last bit of land in order to "buy more nourishing food for the child." It was imperative that the underlying cause of Anita's poor response to treatment be found. A laboratory test confirmed our suspicions.

Anita's father and godmother alone were apprised of the test results. When asked what she knew about AIDS, the godmother responded, "AIDS is an infectious disease that has no cure. You can get it from the blood of an infected person." For this reason, she said, she had nothing to fear in caring for Anita. Further, she was adamant that Anita not be told of her diagnosis—"That will only make her suffer more"—and skeptical about the value of the AIDS clinic in Port-au-Prince. "Why should we take her there?" asked Anita's godmother wearily. "She will not recover from this disease. She will have to endure the heat and humiliation of the clinic. She will not find a cool place to lie down. What she might find is a pill or an injection to make her feel more comfortable for a short time. I can do better than that."

And that is what Anita's godmother proceeded to do. She attempted to sit Anita up every day and encouraged her to drink a broth promised to "make her better." The godmother kept her as clean as possible, consecrating the family's two sheets to her goddaughter. She gave Anita her pillow and stuffed a sack with rags for herself. The only thing she requested from us at the clinic was "a beautiful soft wool blanket that will not irritate the child's skin."

In one of several thoughtful interviews accorded us, Anita's godmother insisted that "for some people, a decent death is as important as a decent life.... The child has had a hard life; her life has always been difficult. It's important that she be washed of bitterness and regret before she dies." Anita was herself very philosophic in her last months. She seemed to know of her diagnosis. Although she never mentioned the word *SIDA*, she did speak of the resignation appropriate to "diseases from which you cannot escape." She stated, too, that she was "dying from the sickness that took Vincent," although she denied that she had been the victim of witchcraft—"I simply caught it from him."

Anita did not ask to be taken to a hospital, nor did her slow decline occasion any request for further diagnostic tests. What she most wanted was a radio—"for the news and the music"—and a lambswool blanket. She especially enjoyed the opportunity to "recount my life," and we were able to listen to her narrative until hours before her death.

APPLIED AND MEDICAL ANTHROPOLOGY

AIDS IN CULTURAL CONTEXT

The way in which a person, a family, or a community responds to AIDS may reveal a great deal about core cultural values. Robert's story underlines our reliance on technological answers to moral and medical questions. "Americans love machines more than life itself," asserts author Philip Slater in a compelling analysis of middle-class North American culture. "Any challenge to the technological-over-social priority threatens to expose the fact that Americans have lost their manhood and their capacity to control their environment." One of the less noticed but perhaps one of the farthest-reaching consequences of the AIDS epidemic has been the weakening of North America's traditional confidence in the ability of its experts to solve every kind of problem. In the words of one person with the disorder, "The terror of AIDS lies in the collapse of our faith in technology."[4]

This core cultural value is nowhere more evident than in contemporary tertiary medicine, which remains the locus of care for the vast majority of AIDS patients. Despite the uniformity of treatment outcome, despite the lack of proven efficacy of many diagnostic and therapeutic procedures, despite their high costs, it has been difficult for practitioners to limit their recourse to these interventions. "When you're at Disney World," remarked one of Robert's physicians ironically, "you take all the rides."

Robert's illness raises issues that turn about questions of autonomy and accountability. The concept of autonomous individuals who are solely responsible for their fate, including their illness, is a powerful cultural premise in North American society. On the positive side, this concept supports concern for individual rights and respect for individual differences and achievement. A more ominous aspect of this core cultural orientation is that it often justifies blaming the victims. Illness is said to be the outcome of the free choice of high-risk behavior.

This has been especially true in the AIDS epidemic, which has reified an invidious distinction between "innocent victims"—infants and hemophiliacs—and, by implication, "the guilty"—persons with AIDS who are homosexuals or intravenous drug users. Robert's lonely and medicalized death is what so many North Americans fear: "He was terrified. He knew what AIDS meant. He knew what happens. Your friends desert you, your lover kicks you out into the street. You get fired, you get evicted from your apartment. You're a leper. You die alone."[5] The conflation of correlation and responsibility has the effect of making sufferers feel guilt and shame. The validity of their experience is contested. Suffering, once delegitimated, is complicated and even distorted; our response to the sufferer, blocked.

In contrast, in Haiti and in many African and Asian societies, where individual rights are often underemphasized and also frequently unprotected, and where the idea of personal accountability is less powerful than is the idea of the primacy of social relationships, blaming the victim is also a less frequent response to AIDS. Noticeably absent is the revulsion with which AIDS patients have been faced in the United States, in both clinical settings and in their communities. This striking difference cannot be ascribed to Haitian ignorance of modes of transmission. On the contrary, the Haitians we have interviewed have ideas of etiology and epidemiology that reflect the incursion of the "North American ideology" of AIDS—that the disease is caused by a virus and is somehow related to homosexuality and contaminated blood. These are subsumed, however, in properly Haitian beliefs about illness causation. Long before the advent of AIDS to Do Kay, we might have asked the following question: some fatal diseases are known to be caused by "microbes" but may also be "sent" by someone; is *SIDA* such a disease?

Differences in the responses of caregivers to Robert and Anita—such as whether to inform them of their diagnosis or undertake terminal care as a family or a community responsibility—also reflect the ego-centered orientation in North American cities and the more sociocentric orientation in the Haitian village. An ironic twist is that it is in the impersonal therapeutic setting of North American healthcare institutions that concern for the patient's personhood is articulated. It is, however, a cool bioethical attention to abstract individual rights rather than a validation of humane responses to concrete existential needs. Perhaps this cultural logic—of medicine as technology, of individual autonomy as the most inviolable of rights, and so of individuals as responsible for most of the ills that befall them—helps us to understand how Robert's lonely death, so rich in all the technology applied to his last hours, could be so poor in all those supportive human virtues that resonate from the poverty-stricken village where Anita died among friends.

A core clinical task would seem to be helping patients to die a decent death. For all the millions of words spilled on the denial of death in our society and the various psychotechniques advertised to aid us to overcome this societal silence, AIDS testifies vividly that our secular public culture is simply unable to come to terms with mortality.

A final question might be asked in examining the stories of Robert and Anita: just how representative are they of the millions already exposed to HIV? As a middle-class, white gay male, Robert is thought by many to be a "typical victim of AIDS." But he is becoming increasingly less typical in the United States, where the epidemic is claiming more and more blacks and Hispanics, and Robert would not be sociologically representative of the typical AIDS patient in much of the rest of the world. In many Third World settings, sex differences in the epidemiology of HIV infection are unremarkable: in Haiti, for example, there is almost parity between the sexes. Most importantly, most people with AIDS are not middle-class and insured. All this points to the fact that the virus that causes AIDS might exact its greatest toll in the Third World.

AIDS IN GLOBAL CONTEXT

Although the pandemic appears to be most serious in North America and Europe, per capita rates reveal that fully seventeen of the twenty countries most affected by AIDS are in Africa or the Caribbean. Further, although there is heartening evidence that the epidemic is being more effectively addressed in the North American gay community, there is no indication that the spread of HIV has been curbed in the communities in which women like Anita struggle. Although early reports of high HIV seroprevalence were clearly based on faulty research, even recent and revised estimates remain grim: "In urban areas in some sub-Saharan countries, up to 25% of young adults are already HIV carriers, with rates among those reporting to clinics for sexually transmitted diseases passing 30%, and among female prostitutes up to 90%."[6] In other words, the countries most affected are precisely those that can least afford it.

These figures also remind us that AIDS has felled many like Anita—the poor, women of color, victims of many sorts of oppression and misfortune. Although heterosexual contact seems to be the means of spreading in many instances, not all who contract the disease are "promiscuous," a label that has often offended people in Africa, Haiti, and elsewhere. *Promiscuous* fails utterly to capture the dilemmas of millions like Anita. In an essay entitled "The Myth of African Promiscuity," one Kenyan scholar refers to the "new poor': the massive pool of young women living in the most deprived conditions in shanty towns and slums across Africa, who are available for the promise of a meal, new clothes, or a few pounds."[7]

Equally problematic, and of course related, is the term *prostitute*. It is often used indiscriminately to refer to a broad spectrum of sexual activity. In North America, the label has been misused in investigations of HIV seroprevalence: "the category *prostitute* is taken as an undifferentiated 'risk group' rather than as an occupational category whose members should, for epidemiological purposes, be divided into IV drug users and nonusers—with significantly different rates of HIV infection—as other groups are."[8] A more historical view reminds us that prostitutes have often been victims of scapegoating and that there has long been more energy for investigation of the alleged moral shortcomings of sex workers than for the economic underpinnings of their work.

The implications of this sort of comparative exercise, which remains a cornerstone of social anthropology, are manifold. The differences speak directly to those who would apply imported models of prevention to rural Haiti or Africa or any other Third World setting. A substantial public-health literature, reflecting the fundamentally interventionist perspective of that discipline, is inarguably necessary in the midst of an epidemic without cure or promising treatment. The same must be true for the burgeoning biomedical literature on AIDS. But with what consequences have these disciplines ignored the issue of AIDS as suffering? Whether reduced to parasite-host interactions or to questions of shifting incidence and prevalence among risk groups, AIDS has meant suffering on a large scale, and this suffering is not captured in these expert discourses on the epidemic.

The meaning of suffering in this context is distinctive not only on account of different beliefs about illness and treatment responses but because of the brute reality of grinding poverty, high child and maternal mortality, routinized demoralization and oppression, and suffering as a central part of existence. The response to AIDS in such settings must deal with this wider context of human misery and its social sources. Surely it is unethical—in the broadest sense, if not in the narrow technical biomedical limits to the term—for international health experts to turn their backs on the suffering of people with AIDS in the Third World and to concentrate solely on the prevention of new cases.

DEALING WITH AIDS AS SUFFERING

To what practical suggestions does a view of AIDS as human suffering lead?

Suffering Compounded by Inappropriate Use of Resources

The majority of all medical-care costs for AIDS patients is generated by acute inpatient care. In many ways, however, infection with HIV is more like a chronic disease. Based on cases of transfusion-associated HIV transmission in the United States, the mean time between exposure to the virus and the development of AIDS is over eight years. This period may well be lengthened by drugs already available. And as the medical profession becomes more skilled at managing the AIDS condition, the average time of survival of patients with the full-blown syndrome will also be extended. For many with AIDS, outpatient treatment will be both more cost-effective and more humane. For the terminally ill, home or hospice care may be preferred to acute-care settings, especially for people who "just want to be kept clean." Helping patients to die a decent death was once an accepted aspect of the work of health professionals. It must be recognized and appropriately supported as a core clinical task in the care of persons with AIDS.

Not a small component of humane care for people with AIDS is soliciting their stories of sickness, listening to their narratives of the illness, so as to help them give meaning to their suffering. Restoring this seemingly forgotten healing skill will require a transformation in the work and training of practitioners and a reorganization of time and objectives in health-care delivery systems.

The practitioner should initiate informed negotiation with alternative lay perspectives on care and provide what amounts to brief medical psychotherapy for the threats and losses that make chronic illness so difficult to bear. But such a transformation in the provision of care will require a significant shift in the allocation of resources, including a commitment to funding psychosocial services as well as appropriate providers—visiting nurses, home health aides, physical and occupational therapists, general practitioners, and other members of teams specializing in long-term, outpatient care.

Suffering Magnified by Discrimination

In a recent study of the U.S. response to AIDS, the spread of HIV was compared to that of polio, another virus that struck young people, triggered public panic, and received regular attention in the popular media. "Although these parallels are strong," notes the author, "one difference is crucial: there was little early sympathy for victims of AIDS because those initially at risk—homosexual men, Haitian immigrants, and drug addicts—were not in the mainstream of society. In contrast, sympathy for polio patients was extensive."[9] "This lack of sympathy is part of a spectrum that extends to hostility and even violence, and that has led to discrimination in housing, employment, insurance, and the granting of visas."[10] The victims of such discrimination have been not only people with AIDS or other manifestations of HIV infection but those thought to be in "risk groups."

In some cases, these prejudices are only slightly muted in clinical settings. In our own experience in U.S. hospitals, there is markedly more sympathy for those referred to as "the innocent victims"—patients with transfusion-associated AIDS and HIV-infected babies. At other times, irrational infection-control precautions do little more than heighten patients' feelings of rejection. Blame and recrimination are reactions to the diseases in rural Haiti as well—but there the finger is not often pointed at those with the disease.

Although the President's Commission on AIDS called for major coordinated efforts to address discrimination, what has been done has been desultory, unsystematic, and limited in reach. While legislation is crucial, so too is the development of public-education programs that address discrimination and suffering.

Suffering Augmented by Fear

Underlying at least some of the discrimination, spite, and other inappropriate responses to AIDS is fear. We refer not to the behavior-modifying fear of "the worried well" but to the more visceral fear that has played so prominent a role in the epidemic. It is fear that prompts someone to refuse to get into a taxi driven by a Haitian man; it is fear that leads a reporter to wrench her hand from that of a person with AIDS; it is fear that underpins some calls for widespread HIV antibody testing; and fear that has led some health professionals to react to patients in degrading fashion. The fact that so much of this fear is "irrational" has thus far had little bearing on its persistence.

Dissemination of even a few key facts—by people with AIDS, leaders of local communities, elected officials and other policy-makers, teachers, and health professionals—should help to assuage fear. HIV is transmitted through parenteral, mucous-membrane, or open-wound contact with contaminated blood or body fluids and not through casual contact. Although the risk of transmission of HIV to health-care professionals is not zero, it is extremely low, even after percutaneous exposure (studies show that, of more than 1,300 exposed health-care workers, only four seroconverted[11]).

Suffering Amplified by Social Death

In several memoirs published in North America, persons with AIDS have complained of the immediate social death their diagnosis has engendered. "For some of my friends and family, I was dead as soon as they heard I had AIDS," a community activist informed us. "That was over two years ago." Even asymptomatic but seropositive individuals, whose life expectancy is often better than that of persons with most cancers and many common cardiovascular disorders, have experienced this reaction. Many North Americans with AIDS have made it clear that they do not wish to be referred to as victims: "As a person with AIDS," writes Navarre, "I can attest to the sense of diminishment at seeing and hearing myself referred to as an AIDS victim, an AIDS sufferer, an AIDS case—as anything but what I am, a person with AIDS. I am a person with a condition. I am not that condition." [12]

It is nonetheless necessary to plan humane care for persons with a chronic and deadly disease—"without needlessly assaulting my denial," as a young man recently put it. The very notion of hospice care will need rethinking if its intended clients are a group of young and previously vigorous persons. Similarly, our cross-cultural research has shown us that preferred means of coping with a fatal disease are shaped by biography and culture. There are no set "stages" that someone with AIDS will go through, and there can be no standard professional response.

Suffering Generated by Inequities

AIDS is caused, we know, by a retrovirus. But we need not look to Haiti to see that inequities have sculpted the AIDS epidemic. The disease, it has been aptly noted, "moves along the fault lines of our society."[13] Of all infants born with AIDS in the United States, approximately 80 percent are black or Hispanic.[14] Most of these are the children of IV drug users, and attempts to stem the virus may force us to confront substance abuse in the context of our own society. For as Robert Gallo and Luc Montagnier assert, "efforts to control AIDS must be aimed in part at eradicating the conditions that give rise to drug addiction."[15]

There are inequities in the way we care for AIDS patients. In the hospital where Robert died, AZT—the sole agent with proven efficacy in treating HIV infection—is not on formulary. Patients needing the drug who are not in a research protocol have to send some one to the drugstore to buy it—if they happen to have the $10,000 per year AZT can cost or an insurance policy that covers these costs. Such factors may prove important in explaining the striking ethnic differences in average time of survival following diagnosis of AIDS. In one report it was noted that, "while the average lifespan of a white person after diagnosis is two years, the average minority person survives only 19 weeks."[16]

From rural Haiti, it is not the local disparities but rather the international inequities that are glaring. In poor countries, drugs like AZT are simply not available. As noted above, the AIDS pandemic is most severe in the countries that can least afford a disaster of these dimensions. A view of AIDS as human suffering forces us to lift our eyes from local settings to the true dimensions of this worldwide tragedy.

Compassionate involvement with persons who have AIDS may require listening carefully to their stories, whether narratives of suffering or simply attempts to recount their lives. Otherwise, as Anita pointed out, we may understand nothing at all.

NOTES

We thank Carla Fujimoto, Haun Saussy, and Barbara de Zalduondo for their thoughtful comments on this essay.

[1] The first three of the four quotations cited here are the voices of persons with AIDS who attended the Third International Conference on AIDS, held in Washington, D.C. in June 1987. Their comments are published passim in 4 (1) (Winter/Spring 1988) of *New England Journal of Public Policy*. All subsequent unreferenced quotations are from tape-recorded interviews accorded the first author.

[2] All informants' names are pseudonyms, as are "Do Kay" and "Ba Kay." Other geographical designations are as cited.

[3] Philip Slater, *The Pursuit of Loneliness: American Culture at the Breaking Point* (Boston: Beacon Press, 1970), 49, 51.

[4] Emmanuel Dreuilhe, *Mortal Embrace: Living with AIDS* (New York: Hill and Wang, 1988), 20.

[5] George Whitmore, *Someone Was Here: Profiles in the AIDS Epidemic* (New York: New American Library, 1988), 26.

[6] RenEe Sabatier, *Blaming Others: Prejudice, Race, and Worldwide AIDS* (Philadelphia: New Society Publishers, 1988), 15.

[7] Professor Aina, ibid., 80.

[8] Jan Zita Grover, 'AIDS: Keywords," in *AIDS: Cultural Analysis/ Cultural Activism* (Cambridge: MIT Press, 1988), 25–26.

[9] Sandra Panem, *The AIDS Bureaucracy* (Cambridge: Harvard University Press, 1988), 15.

[10] See Sabatier for an overview of AIDS-related discrimination. As regards Haiti and Haitians, see Paul Farmer, "AIDS and Accusation: Haiti, Haitians, and the Geography of Blame," in *Cultural Aspects of AIDS: Anthropology and the Global Pandemic* (New York: Praeger, in press). The degree of antipathy is suggested by a recent *New York Times*–CBS News poll of 1,606 persons: "Only 36 percent of those interviewed said they had a lot or some sympathy for 'people who get AIDS from homosexual activity,' and 26 percent said they had a lot or some sympathy for 'people who get AIDS from sharing needles while using illegal drugs' " (*New York Times*, 14 October 1988, A12).

[11] Infectious Diseases Society of America, 276.

[12] Max Navarre, "Fighting the Victim Label," in A*IDS: Cultural Analysis/Cultural Activism* (Cambridge: MIT Press, 1988), 143.

[13] Mary Catherine Bateson and Richard Goldsby, *Thinking AIDS: The Social Response to the Biological Threat* (Read ing, Mass.: Addison-Wesley, 1988), 2.

[14] Samuel Friedman, Jo Sotheran, Abu Abdul-Quadar, Beny Primm, Don Des Jarlais, Paula Kleinman, Conrad Mauge, Douglas Goldsmith, Wafaa El-Sadr, and Robert Maslansky, "The AIDS Epidemic Among Blacks and Hispanics," *The Milbank Quarterly* 65, suppl. 2 (1987): 455–99.

[15] Robert Gallo and Luc Montagnier, "AIDS in 1988," *Scientific American* 259 (4) (October 1988):48.

[16] Sabatier, 19.

From Paul Farmer and Arthur Kleinman, "AIDS as Human Suffering," *Daedalus*, Spring 1989, Vol. 118, No. 2. Reprinted by permission.

KEY TERMS

Name _____

Section _____

Date _____

AIDS:

Applied anthropology:

Chantway:

Critical medical anthropology (CMA):

Cross-cultural comparisons:

Disease:

Epidemic:

Ethnomedicine:

Health insurance (U.S. and Canada):

Holism:

APPLIED AND MEDICAL ANTHROPOLOGY

Illness:

Medical anthropology:

Medical pluralism:

Medical system:

Shamanism and medicine:

Snowbird:

Suffering (in relation to AIDS):

Susto:

WHO:

12 GLOBALIZATION AND CULTURE CHANGE

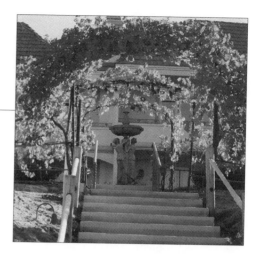

How Sushi Went Global—
Theodore C. Bestor

Cultures are always changing. If we take the broad anthropological view of cultural change in human prehistory and history, it is clear that the world is getting "smaller and smaller." In addition to the remarkable technological advances in electronic media and jet travel, the world is "smaller" because there is less cultural diversity in the world, as evidenced, in part, by the rapid decline in the number of remaining human languages. Particularly in the past decade, societies all around the world have become more closely linked within a single world capitalist system. This type of cultural and economic change has both good and bad aspects, although many people would argue that, in general, the good aspects are enjoyed by the relatively rich and the negative aspects tend to burden the relatively poor. Local societies experience and interpret global changes in different ways: People are influenced not only by their own traditions and customs but also by the attractive, exotic, and luxurious aspects of "modern" cultural traditions.

This selection provides a good illustration of two different processes of culture change that are often discussed under the term globalization. One process links tuna fishermen in Maine with the fresh sushi market in Tokyo (while being influenced by new businesses of tuna-fattening lots off the coast of Spain and Morocco). The second change involves the spread of sushi into societies such as the United States where the raw sliced fish rolls have become a popular, cosmopolitan, and elite food item. When we first started teaching anthropology, students were revolted when they heard of the Japanese cuisine consisting of raw fish, seaweed, and rice. Cultures are always changing.

Globalization is a pattern of economic and cultural change involving the mutual influence of previously separate and distinct societies. This is not a new phenomenon, because the entire period of colonialization was one of unequal transnational economic and cultural exchange. In the postcolonial world, the processes of globalization are made possible by the advent of world capitalism. Multinational corporations are now world powers operating in a world market. On the local level, the flow of investment, profit, and consumer goods across borders can provide access to cash for the producers of some luxury goods. In the long run, however, the evidence indicates that peripheral peoples become less well-off because of globalization, while wealth becomes more and more concentrated in the hands of a small elite.

In this selection we see that fishermen (following an ancient hunting-gathering tradition) do not eat what they catch but rather sell their fish on a world market. Japanese merchants travel halfway around the world to buy the fresh seafood, and the huge tuna is flown to Tokyo to be sold the next day. Indeed, it had become a small world, a global village.

GLOBALIZATION AND CULTURE CHANGE

A 40-minute drive from Bath, Maine, down a winding two-lane highway, the last mile on a dirt road, a ramshackle wooden fish pier stands beside an empty parking lot. At 6:00 p.m. nothing much is happening. Three bluefin tuna sit in a huge tub of ice on the loading dock.

Between 6:45 and 7:00, the parking lot fills up with cars and trucks with license plates from New Jersey, New York, Massachusetts, New Hampshire, and Maine. Twenty tuna buyers clamber out, half of them Japanese. The three bluefin, ranging from 270 to 610 pounds, are winched out of the tub, and buyers crowd around them, extracting tiny core samples to examine their color, fingering the flesh to assess the fat content, sizing up the curve of the body.

After about 20 minutes of eyeing the goods, many of the buyers return to their trucks to call Japan by cellphone and get the morning prices from Tokyo's Tsukiji market—the fishing industry's answer to Wall Street—where the daily tuna auctions have just concluded. The buyers look over the tuna one last time and give written bids to the dock manager, who passes the top bid for each fish to the crew that landed it.

The auction bids are secret. Each bid is examined anxiously by a cluster of young men, some with a father or uncle looking on to give advice, others with a young woman and a couple of toddlers trying to see Daddy's fish. Fragments of concerned conversation float above the parking lot: "That's all?" "Couldn't we do better if we shipped it ourselves?" "Yeah, but my pickup needs a new transmission now!" After a few minutes, deals are closed and the fish are quickly loaded onto the backs of trucks in crates of crushed ice, known in the trade as "tuna coffins." As rapidly as they arrived, the flotilla of buyers sails out of the parking lot—three bound for New York's John F. Kennedy Airport, where their tuna will be airfreighted to Tokyo for sale the day after next.

Bluefin tuna may seem at first an unlikely case study in globalization. But as the world rearranges itself—around silicon chips, Starbucks coffee, or sashimi-grade tuna—new channels for global flows of capital and commodities link far-flung individuals and communities in unexpected new relationships. The tuna trade is a prime example of the globalization of a regional industry, with intense international competition and thorny environmental regulations; centuries-old practices combined with high technology; realignments of labor and capital in response to international regulation; shifting markets; and the diffusion of culinary culture as tastes for sushi, and bluefin tuna, spread worldwide.

GROWING APPETITES

Tuna doesn't require much promotion among Japanese consumers. It is consistently Japan's most popular seafood, and demand is high throughout the year. When the Federation of Japan Tuna Fisheries Cooperative (known as *Nikkatsuren*) runs ad campaigns for tuna, they tend to be low-key and whimsical, rather like the "Got Milk?" advertising in the United States. Recently the federation launched "Tuna Day" (*Maguro no hi*), providing retailers with posters and recipe cards for recipes more complicated than "slice and serve chilled." Tuna Day's mascot is Goro-kun, a colorful cartoon tuna swimming the Australian crawl.

Despite the playful contemporary tone of the mascot, the date selected for Tuna Day carries much heavier freight. October 10, it turns out, commemorates the date that tuna first appeared in Japanese literature, in the eighth-century collection of imperial court poetry known as the *Man'yoshu*—one of the towering classics of Japanese literature. The neat twist is that October 10 today is a national holiday, Sports Day. Goro-kun, the sporty tuna, scores a promotional hat trick, suggesting intimate connections among national culture, healthy food for active lives, and the family holiday meal.

Outside of Japan, tuna, especially raw tuna, hasn't always had it so good. Sushi isn't an easy concept to sell to the uninitiated. And besides, North Americans tend to think of cultural influence as flowing from West to East: James Dean, baseball, Coca-Cola, McDonald's, and Disneyland have all gone over big in Tokyo. Yet Japanese cultural motifs and material—from Kurosawa's *The Seven Samurai* to Yoda's Zen and Darth Vader's armor, from Issey Miyake's fashions to Nintendo, PlayStation, and Pokémon—have increasingly saturated North American and indeed the entire world's consumption and popular culture. Against all odds, so too has sushi.

PROFILE 12.1: STATELESS FISH

As the bluefin business grows ever more lucrative, the risk of overfishing has become ever more real. The question of who profits from the world's demand for sushi makes for battles among fishers, regulators, and conservationists.

Bluefin tuna have been clocked at 50 miles per hour, and tagged fish have crossed the Atlantic in about two months. Since bluefin swim across multiple national jurisdictions, international regulations must impose political order on stateless fish.

Charged with writing those regulations is the International Commission for the Conservation of Atlantic Tunas (IC-CAT), which assigns quotas for bluefin tuna and related species in the North Atlantic and the Mediterranean and directs catch reporting, trade monitoring, and populations assessments. Based in Madrid since its founding in 1969, ICCAT now has 28 members, including Atlantic and Mediterranean fishing countries and three global fishing powers: South Korea, China, and Japan.

In recent years, conservation groups have criticized ICCAT for not regulating more aggressively to prevent or reverse an apparent bluefin population decline in the Western Atlantic. Some activists have campaigned to have bluefin tuna protected under the Convention on International Trade in Endangered Species, or CITES. At least in part to keep that from happening, Japan and ICCAT have implemented new systems to track and regulate trade; "undocumented fish" from nations that fail to comply with ICCAT regulations are now banned from Japanese markets.

Regulations, though, are complicated by how far and fast these fish can travel: No one can say for certain whether there is one bluefin population in the Atlantic or several. ICCAT, the U.S. National Academy of Sciences, the National Audubon Society, and industry groups disagree over how many bluefin migrate across the Atlantic, and whether or not they are all part of the same breeding stock. What's the big deal? If there are two (or more) stocks, as ICCAT maintains, then onservation efforts can can vary from one side of the Atlantic to the other.

When ICCAT registered a dramatic decline in bluefin catches off North America, it imposed stringent quotas on North America's mainly small-scale fishing outfits. On the European side of the Atlantic, however, industrial-strength fishing efforts continued. American fishers, not surprisingly, point to evidence of cross-Atlantic migration and genetic studies of intermingling to argue that Europeans need to conserve bluefin more strenuously as well. ICCAT's regulations, they argue, protect bluefin at America's expense only, and ultimately, fishers from other countries pocket Japanese yen.

—T.C.B.

In 1929, the *Ladies' Home Journal* introduced Japanese cooking to North American women, but discreetly skirted the subject of raw fish: "There have been purposely omitted... any recipes using the delicate and raw tuna fish which is sliced wafer thin and served iced with attractive garnishes. [These]...might not sound so entirely delicious as they are in reality." Little mention of any Japanese food appeared in U.S. media until well after World War II. By the 1960s, articles on sushi began to show up in lifestyle magazines like *Holiday* and *Sunset*. But the recipes they suggested were canapés like cooked shrimp on caraway rye bread, rather than raw fish on rice.

A decade later, however, sushi was growing in popularity throughout North America, turning into a sign of class and educational standing. In 1972, the *New York Times* covered the opening of a sushi bar in the elite sanctum of New York's Harvard Club. *Esquire* explained the fare in an article titled "Wake up Little Sushi!" Restaurant reviewers guided readers to Manhattan's sushi scene, including innovators like Shalom Sushi, a kosher sushi bar in SoHo.

Japan's emergence on the global economic scene in the 1970s as the business destination du jour, coupled with a rejection of hearty red-meat American fare in favor of healthy cuisine like rice, fish, and vegetables, and the appeal of the high-concept aesthetics of Japanese design all prepared the world for a sushi fad. And so, from an exotic, almost unpalatable ethnic specialty, then to haute cuisine of the most rarefied sort, sushi has become not just cool, but popular. The painted window of a Cambridge, Massachusetts, coffee shop advertises "espresso, cappuccino, carrot juice, lasagna, and sushi." Mashed potatoes with wasabi (horseradish), sushi-ginger relish, and seared sashimi-grade tuna steaks show Japan's growing cultural influence on upscale nouvelle cuisine throughout North America, Europe, and Latin America. Sushi has even become the stuff of fashion, from "sushi" lip gloss, colored the deep red of raw tuna, to "wasabi" nail polish, a soft avocado green.

ANGLING FOR NEW CONSUMERS

Japan remains the world's primary market for fresh tuna for sushi and sashimi; demand in other countries is a product of Japanese influence and the creation of new markets by domestic producers looking to expand their reach. Perhaps not surprisingly, sushi's global popularity as an emblem of a sophisticated, cosmopolitan consumer class more or less coincided with a profound transformation in the international role of the Japanese fishing industry. From the 1970s onward, the expansion of 200-mile fishing limits around the world excluded foreign fleets from the prime fishing grounds of many coastal nations. And international environmental campaigns forced many countries, Japan among them, to scale back their distant water fleets. With their fishing operations curtailed and their yen for sushi still growing, Japanese had to turn to foreign suppliers.

Jumbo jets brought New England's bluefin tuna into easy reach of Tokyo, just as Japan's consumer economy—a byproduct of the now disparaged "bubble" years—went into hyperdrive. The sushi business boomed. During the 1980s, total Japanese imports of fresh bluefin tuna worldwide increased from 957 metric tons (531 from the United States) in 1984 to 5,235 metric tons (854 from the United States) in 1993. The average wholesale price peaked in 1990 at 4,00 yen (U.S. $34) per kilogram, bones and all, which trimmed out to approximately U.S. $33 wholesale per edible pound.

Not surprisingly, Japanese demand for prime bluefin tuna—which yields a firm red meat, lightly marbled with veins of fat, highly prized (and priced) in Japanese cuisine—

created a gold-rush mentality on fishing grounds across the globe wherever bluefin tuna could be found. But in the early 1990s, as the US. bluefin industry was taking off, the Japanese economy went into a stall, then a slump, then a dive. U.S. producers suffered as their high-end export market collapsed. Fortunately for them, the North American sushi craze took up the slack. U.S. businesses may have written off Japan, but Americans' taste for sushi stuck. An industry founded exclusively on Japanese demand survived because of Americans' newly trained palates and a booming U.S. economy.

A TRANSATLANTIC TUSSLE

Atlantic bluefin tuna ("ABT" in the trade) are a highly migratory species that ranges from the equator to Newfoundland, from Turkey to the Gulf of Mexico. Bluefin can be huge fish; the record is 1,496 pounds. In more normal ranges, 600-pound tuna, 10 feet in length, are not extraordinary, and 250- to 300-pound bluefin, six feet long, are commercial mainstays.

Before bluefin became a commercial species in New England, before Japanese buyers discovered the stock, before the 747, bluefin were primarily sports fish, caught with fighting tackle by trophy hunters out of harbors like Montauk, Hyannis, and Kennebunkport. Commercial fishers, if they caught bluefin at all, sold them for cat food when they could and trucked them to town dumps when they couldn't. Japanese buyers changed all of that. Since the 1970s, commercial Atlantic bluefin tuna fisheries have been almost exclusively focused on Japanese markets like Tsukiji.

In New England waters, most bluefin are taken one fish at a time, by rod and reel, by hand line, or by harpoon—techniques of a small-scale fisher, not of a factory fleet. On the European side of the Atlantic, the industry operates under entirely different conditions. Rather than rod and reel or harpooning, the typical gear is industrial—the purse seiner (a fishing vessel closing a large net around a school of fish) or the long line (which catches fish on baited hooks strung along lines played out for many miles behind a swift vessel). The techniques may differ from boat to boat and from country to country, but these fishers are all angling for a share of the same Tsukiji yen—and in many cases, some biologists argue, a share of the same tuna stock. Fishing communities often think of themselves as close-knit and proudly parochial; but the sudden globalization of this industry has brought fishers into contact—and often into conflict—with customers, governments, regulators, and environmentalists around the world.

Two miles off the beach in Barbate, Spain, a huge maze of nets snakes several miles out into Spanish waters near the Strait of Gibraltar. A high-speed, Japanese-made workboat heads out to the nets. On board are five Spanish hands, a Japanese supervisor, 2,500 kilograms of frozen herring and mackerel imported from Norway and Holland, and two American researchers. The boat is making one of its twice-daily trips to Spanish nets, which contain captured Mediterranean tuna being raised under Japanese supervision for harvest and export to Tsukiji.

Behind the guard boats that stand watch over the nets 24 hours a day, the headlands of Morocco are a hazy purple in the distance. Just off Barbate's white cliffs to the northwest, the light at the Cape of Trafalgar blinks on and off. For 20 minutes, the men toss herring and mackerel over the gunwales of the workboat while tuna the size (and speed) of Harley-Davidsons dash under the boat, barely visible until, with a flash of silver and blue, they wheel around to snatch a drifting morsel.

The nets, lines, and buoys are part of an *almadraba*, a huge fish trap used in Spain as well as Sicily, Tunisia, and Morocco. The *almadraba* consists of miles of nets anchored to the channel floor suspended from thousands of buoys, all laid out to cut across the migration routes of bluefin tuna leaving the strait. This *almadraba* remains in place for about six weeks in June and July to intercept tuna leaving the Mediterranean after their spawning season is over. Those tuna that lose themselves in the maze end up in a huge pen, roughly the size of a football field. By the end of the tuna run through the strait, about 200 bluefin are in the pen.

Two hundred fish may not sound like a lot, but if the fish survive the next six months, if the fish hit their target weights, if the fish hit the market at the target price, these 200 bluefin may be worth $1.6 million dollars. In November and December, after the bluefin season in New England and Canada is well over, the tuna are harvested and shipped by air to Tokyo in time for the end-of-the-year holiday spike in seafood consumption.

The pens, huge feed lots for tuna, are relatively new, but *almadraba* are not. A couple of miles down the coast from Barbate is the evocatively named settlement of Zahara de los Atunes (Zahara of the Tunas), where Cervantes lived briefly in the late 16th century. The centerpiece of the village is a huge stone compound that housed the men and nets of Zahara's *almadraba* in Cervantes's day, when the port was only a seasonally occupied tuna outpost (occupied by scoundrels, according to Cervantes). Along the Costa de la Luz, the three or four *almadraba* that remain still operate under the control of local fishing bosses who hold the customary fishing rights, the nets, the workers, the boats, and the locally embedded cultural capital to make the *almadraba* work—albeit for distant markets and in collaboration with small-scale Japanese fishing firms.

Inside the Strait of Gibraltar, off the coast of Cartagena, another series of tuna farms operates under entirely different auspices, utilizing neither local skills nor traditional technology. The Cartagena farms rely on French purse seiners to tow captured tuna to their pens, where joint ventures between Japanese trading firms and large-scale Spanish fishing companies have set up farms using the latest in Japanese fishing technology. The waters and the workers are Spanish, but almost everything else is part of a global flow of techniques and capital: financing from major Japanese trading companies; Japanese vessels to tend the nets; aquacultural techniques developed in Australia; vitamin supplements from European pharmaceutical giants packed into frozen herring from Holland to be heaved over the gunwales for the tuna; plus computer models of feeding schedules, weight gains, and target market prices developed by Japanese technicians and fishery scientists.

These "Spanish" farms compete with operations throughout the Mediterranean that rely on similar high-tech, high-capital approaches to the fish business. In the Adriatic Sea, for example, Croatia is emerging as a formidable tuna producer. In Croatia's case, the technology and the capital were transplanted by émigré Croatians who returned to the country from Australia after Croatia achieved independence from Yugoslavia in 1991. Australia, for its part, has developed a major aquacultural industry for southern bluefin tuna, a species closely related to the Atlantic bluefin of the North Atlantic and Mediterranean and almost equally desired in Japanese markets.

GLOBALIZATION AND CULTURE CHANGE

PROFILE 12.2: TOKYO'S PANTRY

Tsukiji, Tokyo's massive wholesale seafood market, is the center of the global trade in tuna. Here, 60,000 traders come each day to buy and sell seafood for Tokyo's 27 million mouths, moving more than 2.4 million kilograms of it in less than 12 hours. Boosters encourage the homey view that Tsukiji is *Tokyo no daidokoro*—Tokyo's pantry—but it is a pantry where almost $6 billion worth of fish change hands each year. New York City's Fulton Fish Market, the largest market in North America, handles only about $1 billion worth, and only about 13 percent of the tonnage of Tsukiji's catch.

Tuna are sold at a "moving auction." The auctioneer, flanked by assistants who record prices and fill out invoice slips at lightning speed, strides across the floor just above rows and rows of fish, moving quickly from one footstool to the next without missing a beat, or a bid. In little more than half an hour, teams of auctioneers from five auction houses sell several hundred (some days several thousand) tuna. Successful buyers whip out their cellphones, calling chefs to tell them what they've got. Meanwhile, faxes with critical information on prices and other market conditions alert fishers in distant ports to the results of Tsukiji's morning auctions. In return, Tsukiji is fed a constant supply of information on tuna conditions off Montauk, Cape Cod, Cartagena, Barbate, and scores of other fishing grounds around the world.

Tsukiji is the command post for a global seafood trade. In value, foreign seafood far exceeds domestic Japanese products on the auction block. (Tsukiji traders joke that Japan's leading fishing port is Tokyo's Narita International Airport.) On Tsukiji's slippery auction floor, tuna from Massachusetts may sell at auction for over $30,000 apiece, near octopus from Senegal, eel from Guangzhou, crab from Sakhalin, salmon from British Columbia and Hokkaido, snapper from Kyushu, and abalone from California.

Given the sheer volume of global trade, Tsukiji effectively sets the world's tuna prices. Last time I checked, the record price was over $200,000 for a particularly spectacular fish from Turkey—a sale noteworthy enough to make the front pages of Tokyo's daily papers. But spectacular prices are just the tip of Tsukiji's influence. The auction system and the commodity chains that flow in and out of the market integrate fishers, firms, and restaurants worldwide in a complex network of local and translocal economies.

As an undisputed hub of the fishing world, Tsukiji creates and deploys enormous amounts of Japanese cultural capital around the world. Its control of information, its enormous role in orchestrating and responding to Japanese culinary tastes, and its almost hegemonic definitions of supply and demand allow it the unassailable privilege of imposing its own standards of quality standards that producers worldwide must heed.

— T.C.B.

CULTURE SPLASH

Just because sushi is available, in some form or another, in exclusive Fifth Avenue restaurants, in baseball stadiums in Los Angeles, at airport snack carts in Amsterdam, at an apartment in Madrid (delivered by motorcycle), or in Buenos Aires, Tel Aviv, or Moscow, doesn't mean that sushi has lost its status as Japanese cultural property. Globalization doesn't necessarily homogenize cultural differences nor erase the salience of cultural labels. Quite the contrary, it grows the franchise. In the global economy of consump-tion, the brand equity of sushi as Japanese cultural property adds to the cachet of both the country and the cuisine. A Texan Chinese-American restauranteur told me, for example, that he had converted his chain of restaurants from Chinese to Japanese cuisine because the prestige factor of the latter meant he could charge a premium; his clients couldn't distinguish between Chinese and Japanese employees (and often failed to notice that some of the chefs behind his sushi bars were Latinos).

The brand equity is sustained by complicated flows of labor and ethnic biases. Outside of Japan, having Japanese hands (or a reasonable facsimile) is sufficient warrant for sushi competence. Guidebooks for the current generation of Japanese global *wandervogel* sometimes advise young Japanese looking for a job in a distant city to work as a sushi chef; U.S. consular offices in Japan grant more than 1,000 visas a year to sushi chefs, tuna buyers, and other workers in the global sushi business. A trade school in Tokyo, operating under the name Sushi Daigaku (Sushi University) offers short courses in sushi preparation so "students" can impress prospective employers with an imposing certificate. Even without papers, however, sushi remains firmly linked in the minds of Japanese and foreigners alike with Japanese cultural identity. Throughout the world, sushi restaurants operated by Koreans, Chinese, or Vietnamese maintain Japanese identities. In sushi bars from Boston to Valencia, a customer's simple greeting in Japanese can throw chefs into a panic (or drive them to the far end of the counter).

On the docks, too, Japanese cultural control of sushi remains unquestioned. Japanese buyers and "tuna techs" sent from Tsukiji to work seasonally on the docks of New England laboriously instruct foreign fishers on the proper techniques for catching, handling, and packing tuna for export. A bluefin tuna must approximate the appropriate *kata*, or "ideal form," of color, texture, fat content, body shape, and so forth, all prescribed by Japanese specifications. Processing requires proper attention as well. Special paper is sent from Japan for wrapping the fish before burying them in crushed ice. Despite high shipping costs and the fact that 50 percent of the gross weight of a tuna is unusable, tuna is sent to Japan whole, not sliced into salable portions. Spoilage is one reason for this, but form is another. Everyone in the trade agrees that Japanese workers are much more skilled in cutting and trimming tuna than Americans, and no one would want to risk sending botched cuts to Japan.

Not to impugn the quality of the fish sold in the United States, but on the New England docks, the first determination of tuna buyers is whether they are looking at a "domestic" fish or an "export" fish. On that judgment hangs several dollars a pound for the fisher, and the supply of sashimi-grade tuna for fishmongers, sushi bars, and seafood restaurants up and down the Eastern seaboard. Some of the best tuna from New England may make it to New York or Los Angeles, but by way of Tokyo—validated as top quality (and top price) by the decision to ship it to Japan by air for sale at Tsukiji, where it may be purchased by one of the handful of Tsukiji sushi exporters who supply premier expatriate sushi chefs in the world's leading cities.

PLAYING THE MARKET

The tuna auction at Yankee Co-op in Seabrook, New Hampshire is about to begin on the second-to-last day of the 1999 season. The weather is stormy, few boats are out. Only three bluefin, none of them terribly good, are up for sale today, and the half-dozen buyers at the auction, three Americans and three Japanese, gloomily discuss the impending end of a lousy season.

In July, the bluefin market collapsed just as the U.S. fishing season was starting. In a stunning miscalculation, Japanese purse seiners operating out of Kesennuma in northern Japan managed to land their entire year's quota from that fishery in only three days. The oversupply sent tuna prices at Tsukiji through the floor, and they never really recovered.

Today, the news from Spain is not good. The day before, faxes and e-mails from Tokyo brought word that a Spanish fish farm had suffered a disaster. Odd tidal conditions near Cartagena led to a sudden and unexpected depletion of oxygen in the inlet where one of the great tuna nets was anchored. Overnight, 800 fish suffocated. Divers hauled out the tuna. The fish were quickly processed, several months before their expected prime, and shipped off to Tokyo. For the Japanese corporation and its Spanish partners, a harvest potentially worth $6.5 million would yield only a tiny fraction of that. The buyers at the morning's auctions in New Hampshire know they will suffer as well. Whatever fish turn up today and tomorrow, they will arrive at Tsukiji in the wake of an enormous glut of hastily exported Spanish tuna.

Fishing is rooted in local communities and local economies—even for fishers dipping their lines (or nets) in the same body of water, a couple hundred miles can be worlds away. Now, a Massachusetts fisher's livelihood can be transformed in a matter of hours by a spike in market prices halfway around the globe or by a disaster at a fish farm across the Atlantic. Giant fishing conglomerates in one part of the world sell their catch alongside family outfits from another. Environmental organizations on one continent rail against distant industry regulations implemented an ocean away. Such instances of convergence are common in a globalizing world. What is surprising, and perhaps more profound, in the case of today's tuna fishers, is the complex interplay between industry and culture, as an esoteric cuisine from an insular part of the world has become a global fad in the span of a generation, driving, and driven by, a new kind of fishing business.

Many New England fishers, whose traditional livelihood now depends on unfamiliar tastes and distant markets, turn to a kind of armchair anthropology to explain Japan's ability to transform tuna from trash into treasure around the world. For some, the quick answer is simply national symbolism. The deep red of tuna served as sashimi or sushi contrasts with the stark white rice, evoking the red and white of the Japanese national flag. Others know that red and white is an auspicious color combination in Japanese ritual life (lobster tails are popular at Japanese weddings for just this reason). Still others think the cultural prize is a fighting spirit, pure machismo, both their own and the tuna's. Taken by rod and reel, a tuna may battle the fisher for four or five hours. Some tuna literally fight to the death. For some fishers, the meaning of tuna—the equation of tuna with Japanese identity—is simple: Tuna is nothing less than the samurai fish!

Of course, such mystification of a distant market's motivations for desiring a local commodity is not unique. For decades, anthropologists have written of "cargo cults" and "commodity fetishism" from New Guinea to Bolivia. But the ability of fishers today to visualize Japanese culture and the place of tuna within its demanding culinary tradition is constantly shaped and reshaped by the flow of cultural images that now travel around the globe in all directions simultaneously, bumping into each other in airports, fishing ports, bistros, bodegas, and markets everywhere. In the newly rewired circuitry of global cultural and economic affairs, Japan is the core, and the Atlantic seaboard, the Adriatic, and the Australian coast are all distant peripheries. Topsy-turvy as Gilbert and Sullivan never imagined it.

Japan is plugged into the popular North American imagination as the sometimes inscrutable superpower, precise and delicate in its culinary tastes, feudal in its cultural symbolism, and insatiable in its appetites. Were Japan not a prominent player in so much of the daily life of North Americans, the fishers outside of Bath or in Seabrook would have less to think about in constructing their Japan. As it is, they struggle with unfamiliar exchange rates for cultural capital that compounds in a foreign currency.

And they get next season.

Theodore Be w Sushi Went Global," *Foreign Policy*, Novem ber 2000, pp. 54–63. Reprint by permission opyright Clearance Center.

Chinese Table Manners: You Are *How* You Eat— *Eugene Cooper*

I had been looking forward to this dinner with an important client for over a week. We were going to close the biggest deal of my career. He arrived on time, and I ordered a bit of wine. It was a fancy restaurant and I was trying to behave appropriately; I tucked my napkin neatly on my lap and lifted my wine glass carefully with my little finger extended in the way I had always seen it done. But what began well began to go awry. I looked on in horror as my client ladled a number of different dishes together into a soup bowl, lifted it to his mouth and began to shovel it in. I was so embarrassed by this display of bad manners that I hoped no one I knew would happen by. My face must have betrayed my thoughts, but my client did not let on. He simply asked if I was not enjoying my food because I had left the dishes flat on the table. This took me by surprise, because I realized for the first time that he was looking at me and finding *my* behavior odd. Our smiles became realizations and turned into laughter. Luckily, we had a good sense of humor about our ethnocentrism. Somebody should have warned us; this could have been a real disaster.

Consider yourself warned. Table manners, like a great many everyday events, are heavily laden with cultural meaning. Understanding culturally prescribed behaviors is of practical importance, not merely interesting. More anthropologists need to be involved in cross-cultural training for situations where there is likely to be interaction between people from different cultures or ethnic groups.

"Etiquette of this kind (not putting half eaten meat back in the bowl, [not] wiping one's nose on one's sleeve) is not superficial, a matter for the surface rather than the depths; refined ways of acting are so internalized as to make alternative behavior truly 'disgusting,' 'revolting,' 'nauseous,' turning them into some of the most highly charged and deeply felt of intra-social differences, so that 'rustic' behavior is not merely quaint but barbarous" (Goody 1982:140).

"Probably no common practice is more diversified than the familiar one of eating in company, for what Europeans consider as correct and decent may by other races be looked upon as wrong or indelicate. Similarly, few social observances provide more opportunities for offending the stranger than the etiquette of the table" (Hammerton 1936:23).

Our shrinking world makes encounters with people of other cultures increasingly common in our life experiences. Whether in the conduct of business, in interactions with our "ethnic" neighbors, or as visitors to other countries, we are frequently called on to communicate with others whose assumptions about what constitutes appropriate behavior are widely different from our own.

In such contexts, it is often difficult to know whether habits and customs one takes for granted in one's own home may be creating unfavorable impressions in one's host's home. No less an authority than Confucius, writing more than two thousand years ago, was aware of the potential difficulties involved in intercultural communication, and provided the following advice: "When entering a country inquire of its customs. When crossing a border, inquire of the prohibitions" (Li Chi 1971:17).

Among such customs and prohibitions, those associated with behavior at the table can make an enormous difference in the way one is perceived by a foreign host.

As regards the Chinese in particular, the way one handles oneself at the table gives off signals of the clearest type as to what kind of a person one is, and it is all too easy to offend, as I hope to show. At the same time, however, it is easy enough to equip oneself with a few simple points to bear in mind that will not only pleasantly surprise one's Chinese host, but also convince him or her that one is a sensitive, cultivated, courteous, respectful, and considerate individual.

Surprisingly, for a civilization which has generated so many handbooks of its various cuisines, China has not produced any popular guidebooks for table manners of the Emily Post variety. The field, of course, has for the most part been preempted by the *Li Chi*—records of etiquette and ceremonial—most of which is said to date from the early Han. Indeed, many of the themes which characterize contemporary Chinese table manners are present in the minute descriptions of behaviors appropriate to people of various stations in all the gradations of Han social structure, such as the prescription to yield or defer. However, one is hard pressed to find a general rough and ready guide to contemporary Chinese table manners of anything more than the most superficial kind, usually present in popular Chinese cookbooks for Western audiences.

The absence of attention to table manners may be the result of the fact that table manners are among those habits most taken for granted—rules no grown up needs instruction in. A Chinese culinary enthusiast of my acquaintance assures me that table manners are not important in Chinese history, being far outweighed by the scarcity of food generally as the major issue. Nevertheless, an examination of Chinese table manners provides sufficient contrast with Western table habits in terms of structure and performance, as to make significant features of Chinese etiquette emerge in comparison—features taken for granted by the native.

Those few who have written on the subject (Chang 1977; Hsü and Hsü 1977) generally qualify as bi-cultural individuals with sufficient experience of both Chinese and Western rules to tease out the areas of contrastive significance. My five years of field research (and eating) in Hong Kong, and eight years of marriage to a Chinese woman who taught me Chinese table manners as to a child, also qualify me for the assignment, although my former European colleagues at the University of Hong Kong might question my credentials as an expert on Western etiquette, to be sure.

BASIC STRUCTURES AND PARAPHERNALIA

To begin with, it is useful to consider K. C. Chang's (1977) broad outline of the important distinctions in Chinese food between food (*shih*) and drink (*yin*), and then within the category food, between *fan* (grain/rice) and *ts'ai* (dishes). Chang establishes a hierarchy with grain as the base, vegetables and fruit as next least expendable, and meat as most expendable in the preparation of a meal. Fish would probably fall between vegetables and meat at least as far as contemporary Hong Kong is concerned, particularly if one includes the enormous variety of preserved fish available.

In any event, it is fair to say that a Chinese meal is not a meal without *fan*. The morning food event, at which rice is not normally taken, or if so is taken as gruel, is not thought of as a meal. When Chinese speak of a full day's eating fare, it is two square meals per day rather than three. Thus rice (or grain) defines a meal, and its treatment and consumption are circumscribed in a number of ways.

It will be helpful, however, to lay out the general paraphernalia with which the diner is equipped, and the structure in which it is deployed before returning to the rules governing rice. On this subject, Hsü and Hsü (1977:304) have written:

> The typical Chinese dining table is round or square, the *ts'ai* dishes are laid in the center, and each participant in the meal is equipped with a bowl for *fan*, a pair of chopsticks, a saucer, and a spoon. All at the table take from the *ts'ai* dishes as they proceed with the meal.

The *ts'ai* dishes are typically shared by all, and must be treated much as common property, whereas one's bowl is a private place which comes directly in touch with the mouth. The chopsticks are of both the mouth and the table, and mediate between. They are thin, and when employed appropriately only touch the one piece or small quantity a person touches first. Many Westerners find the habit of sharing from a common plate potentially unhygienic, and one might be tempted to dismiss this as a bit of ethnocentricity. However, the point has recently been made by no less an authority than Communist party secretary Hu Yaobang, who called attention to the unsanitary character of traditional Chinese eating habits and urged change.

One employs the chopsticks to take from the common plate and place food in one's bowl, then one raises the bowl to the mouth and pushes food into the mouth with the chopsticks. Hsü and Hsü state, "The diner who lets his *fan* bowl stay on the table and eats by picking up lumps of *fan* from the bowl is expressing disinterest in or dissatisfaction with the food. If he or she is a guest in someone's house, that is seen as an open insult to the host" (1977:304). Since one's bowl is a private place, "good manners do not

preclude resting a piece of meat (or other items) in one's bowl between bites" (1977:304). However, one never puts a partially chewed piece of anything back into one of the common plates (I would not have thought this necessary to mention; however, an otherwise culturally sensitive person I know had the audacity to do so recently so it may bear mentioning.) Also, it is extremely poor manners to suck or bite your chopsticks.

In some cases the bowl may be substituted for by a spoon, as, for example, when one goes out to lunch with one's workmates, and each diner is supplied with a flat plate piled high with rice topped with roast pork, chicken, duck and/or *lap cheong* (Chinese sausage), or with a helping of a single *ts'ai* dish (the latter known as *hui fan*).

Eating rice off a flat plate with chopsticks alone is not an easy task. Westerners exasperated with the use of chopsticks often feel their most intense frustration when trying to accomplish this task, and are often reduced to picking up small bits of rice with the ends of their chopsticks and placing them in the mouth. Seeming to pick at one's food in this way is not good manners and marks one as an incompetent foreign devil, confirming in most Chinese minds all of their previous prejudices about *guailos*.

No self-respecting Chinese would attempt to eat rice directly from a flat plate without first piling the rice onto, or scooping the rice into, a spoon. One eats the *ts'ai* or meat with one's chopsticks, but rice is most often carried to the mouth in a spoon. The spoon stands in for the bowl in the mini-context of an individual serving, and one can also think of the bowl itself as serving in the capacity of an enlarged spoon in the context of regular dining as well.

Rice is usually doled out from a common pot by the host or hostess. When someone has filled your rice bowl for you, it is accepted with two hands. To accept rice with one hand suggests disinterest, disrespect, and carelessness. One places the full bowl in front of oneself and waits until everyone has been served. It is very impolite to begin eating before everyone at the table has had his bowl filled with rice. When one has finished the rice in one's bowl, one does not continue to eat of the common *ts'ai* dishes. To eat *ts'ai* without rice in one's bowl is to appear a glutton interested only in *ts'ai*, of which one must consume a great deal to get full without rice. Depending on the degree of intimacy of a relationship, one may, when eating at the home of a friend or acquaintance, rise from the table to refill one's bowl with rice from the rice pot in the kitchen. However, at formal occasions one's host will usually be alert enough to notice when one's rice bowl is empty and move to fill it before one might be forced to request more rice. When one rises to get more rice, the host will usually insist on taking one's bowl and filling it. One may decline such assistance if the host is a close friend by simply saying "I'll serve myself."

At banquets one is expected to fill up on *ts'ai*, and consumption of too much rice may be a sign of disrespect to the quality of the *ts'ai* dishes. No rice should ever be left over in one's bowl at the end of the meal.

> As children we were always taught to leave not a single grain of *fan* in our bowl when we finished. Our elders strongly impressed on us that each single grain of rice or corn was obtained through the drops of sweat of the tillers of the soil (Hsü and Hsü 1977:308).

A corollary of this rule is never to take so much rice, or anything else for that matter, in your bowl as to be unable to finish it. It is also extremely disrespectful of the meal and of one's host to leave bits of rice on the table around one's bowl, and Chinese children are often told that each of these grains will materialize as a pockmark on the face of their future spouse.

As regards the *ts'ai*, it is important to note again that it is arrayed for all to share. Generally speaking, especially on formal occasions, one does not serve oneself without first offering to others, at least those seated immediately to either side. This applies also to the taking of tea, and one generally fills a neighbor's cup before taking tea for oneself. When tea is poured for you, it is customary to tap the table with your fingers to convey your thanks.

The overriding rule of Chinese table customs is deference. Defer to others in everything. Be conscious of the need to share what is placed in common. This means don't eat only from those dishes that you like.

> One very common point of instruction from parents to children is that the best mannered person does not allow co-diners to be aware of what his or her favorite dishes are by his or her eating pattern (Hsü and Hsü 1977:304).

When taking from the common dishes one should also only take in such proportions that everyone else will be left with a roughly equivalent amount. It is polite to take the remains of a common *ts'ai* dish after a new dish has been brought out. The desirability of the remains is diminished by the introduction of a new dish, and the remains of the old become fair game. However, it is rather poor manners to incline a common plate toward oneself and scrape the remains into one's bowl. This "looking in the mirror" evokes the idea of narcissistic concern with oneself.

In general, young should defer to old in order of eating, and on formal occasions when guests are present children may even be excluded from the dining table until the adults are finished, or seated at a table separate from the adults. In the household of the boss of the factory where I did my fieldwork, apprentices commonly sat with the boss at the family table, but were relegated to the children's table at the New Year's feast.

A host will usually signal that it is appropriate to begin eating, after each person at the table has taken rice, by picking up his chopsticks and saying "*sik fan*." When a guest has eaten his fill, he indicates that he is finished by putting down his chopsticks and encouraging others still eating to take their time. They in turn will inquire if the guest is full, and if he is he should say so. Upon finishing one may either remain at the table or leave. A guest of honor is expected to remain until all are finished.

In addition, one should be careful not to take large mouthfuls, to refrain from making noise while chewing, and to try to maintain the same pace of eating as others at the table. In contrast to Western etiquette in which "toothpicks are never used outside the privacy of one's room" (McLean 1941:63), toothpicks are provided at most Chinese tables and it is not impolite to give one's teeth a thorough picking at the table, provided one covers one's mouth with the opposite hand.

Spitting is not good manners at a Chinese table, although this is a rule often honored more in the breach. Spittoons are often provided in Chinese restaurants, both as a repository for waste water and tea used to sterilize one's utensils, and for expectorations of various sorts. Often the contents of the spittoons threaten to get up and walk away, so vile are the contents. The floor is fair game in many restaurants for just about anything remaining in one's mouth not swallowable, such as small bits of bone or gristle. Hong Kong has improved considerably in this regard in recent years, but in working-class restaurants and *daipaidongs*, spitting is still quite common.

INFLECTIONS OF GENERAL PRINCIPLES

Having laid out these basic ground rules, it remains to explore how these rules are inflected in the various contexts in which food events occur in contemporary Hong Kong. These contexts are many and varied, ranging from informal and intimate occasions when the family is together at home for a meal, to the more formal occasions involving elaborate feasts usually held in restaurants. Somewhat intermediate between these are the meals eaten out, but in somewhat less formal contexts—from breakfast taken at *dim saam* houses, lunches taken at foodstalls with workmates, to evening meals prepared in restaurants for individual diners (*hak fan*), and midnight snacks. Expectations as to appropriate comportment at the table will also vary with region of origin, age, and class position.

For example, for Cantonese a full meal usually includes soup, and many Cantonese feel uncomfortable leaving the table without having partaken of soup. The minimal structure of the Cantonese meal includes not just *fan* (grain) and *ts'ai* (dishes), but also soup. This minimal structure is served up in what is known as *hak fan*, a specialty of some restaurants (usually Shanghainese) in which one may choose from a daily set menu of *hak* dishes, served with an extra large bowl of rice and the soup of the day. *Hak fan* is designed for people who must eat alone for some reason, not considered the most desirable circumstances. Two Chinese who knew each other would not sit down at the same table and order two individual dishes of *hak fan*. They would surely grasp the opportunity of sharing the greater variety available to each through social eating.

Jack Goody has likened eating alone to defecating in public (1982:306) because of the absence of the social in meeting essentially biological needs. *Hak fan* assures that even taken alone, the minimum structural entity of a Cantonese meal is available to be consumed. This basic structure is also revealed in a variety of thermos containers used for carrying lunch to work which are equipped with compartments for rice, *ts'ai* and soup. Since the contexts in which food events occur in Hong Kong are so varied, soup is not always the focus of attention. Proceeding through

the ordinary day's food events from morning to evening will give us occasion to note context-linked inflections of our general principles.

As mentioned previously, the morning food event does not pass muster as a meal, largely due to the absence of rice. Still, there are a variety of contexts in which this event may take place. At home, the morning food event usually involves rice from the evening before boiled down to congee with a variety of pickles and condiments tossed in or served on the side. This is usually grabbed quickly in the kitchen on the way out to work, if it is eaten at all, and seldom involves the entire family seated at a single table.

Eaten out, the morning food event may take several forms. Consistent with the quick and superficial character of the event at home is the food event taken at a food stall or *daipaidong*, of which several different types serve suitable breakfast fare—congee (most commonly with preserved egg and pork), *yautiu* (unsweetened fried dough strips), hot *dao-jeung* (soy bean milk), *jucheung fen* (rolled rice noodles), all served with tea, usually in a glass.

Eating at a *daipaidong*, and even in some restaurants, one assumes the probability that the chopsticks, stuffed together in a can and set at the center of the table for individual diners to take, as well as one's cup, bowl, and spoon, will not have been properly washed. A brief ritualized washing usually precedes the meal in which one pours a glass of boiling hot tea into one's glass, stirring the ends of the chopsticks in the water to sterilize them, pouring the still hot water into one's bowl where one's cup and spoon are immersed and sterilized. The wash water is then thrown out, usually on the street in the case of a *daipaidong*, or in a spittoon at a restaurant, and one is prepared to commence eating. Occasionally, one is even provided with a separate bowl for washing one's eating implements, filled by one's waiter with boiling water from a huge kettle.

At a *daipaidong* for breakfast, one usually shares a table with a stranger, or perhaps a neighbor or workmate, depending on whether one eats near home or near work. In any case, one's portion is usually one's own, and the rules of formal dining apply only in the most general terms. Food is usually taken with dispatch, as one is usually rushing to work or to school, and the idea is just to put something in one's stomach to suppress hunger till the first meal of the day—*ng fan* (lunch).

The slightly more formal morning food event is *dim saam*, referred to most often as *yam ch'a* (drink tea). "Drinking tea" again refers to something less than a "meal," although on weekends, taken with one's family at a large table, *dim saam* often involves the consumption of large quantities of buns, dumplings, rice noodles in various shapes, a variety of innards, and the like. One sits down, is approached by one's waiter, or in fancier restaurants by a host or hostess, who will inquire what kind of tea one will be drinking—*sao mei, bo lei, soy sin*, and that old perceived favorite of *guailos*—*heung pien* (jasmine). When the tea arrives the host will fill everyone's cup and the meal may begin.

One acquires food from carts pushed around by young children and/or aged women, and less frequently by older men. One may find oneself sharing a table with strangers, or with regular customers who eat at the same restaurant at the same time every morning. Going to *yam ch'a* on a regular schedule assures one of continuous contact with the usual crowd, and it is common to find oneself seated at the same table with many of the same people each morning. While polite conversation is the general rule, more juicy gossip is not inappropriate as the relationship between morning diners becomes more familiar.

Generally, each diner is aware of what he has consumed, and the position of the plates may be adjusted where they have been ambiguously placed so the waiter can figure the tab. One eats from one's own plates under such circumstances, and pays for one's own plates; however, it is polite to fill the teacup of one's neighbor from one's own pot if one is acquainted with him or her. There are still some restaurants in Hong Kong which serve tea in a covered bowl, quite literally stuffed with tea, and poured into a cup to be drunk, extremely dark, but the standard tea pot has replaced the bowl as a tea vessel in most restaurants.

A table shared with strangers or neighbors is usually an informal arrangement in which one eats one's own food. However, taking *dim saam* may also be a more formal occasion, especially on weekends, or when one has been *cheng*-ed (asked out). In such circumstances many of the rules of formal dining apply, i.e., the food on the table is common and should only be taken in such proportions that enough is left for others. One may order dishes one likes from the passing wagons, but one should always offer to others before taking from the dish for oneself.

The dishes accumulate somewhat at random due to the vagaries of the itinerary of the carts, so there is no formal order to the dishes' arrival, although sweeter dishes are usually taken last.

Dim saam often trails off into lunch on formal or informal occasions, and by noon after the diners have warmed up with a few *dim saam* dishes, it is polite to inquire of one's fellow diners whether a plate of noodles or rice (a real meal) is in order, and if so, to order such dishes from the kitchen from one's waiter. Varieties of *dim saam* are also available from *daipaidong* as well, sometimes served up in individual portions to go.

The midday food event in Hong Kong includes rice or a reasonable substitute (rice noodles, bean noodles, wheat noodles), and is most often taken during a lunch hour break from factory or office labor. A variety of choices confront the Hong Kong worker eating out for lunch. Food stalls serve a variety of dishes, usually in individual portions on flat plates heaped high with rice, and covered with a single *ts'ai* dish. A glass of tea is usually served, and doubles again as a vessel for sterilizing one's chopsticks and spoon. Blue collar workers I knew in Hong Kong would, often consume a full-to-the-brim tea tumbler of high octane spirits with such meals, and trundle back to work with the warm glow and slightly glazed look of a two-martini-lunch executive.

A plate of noodles may also be ordered from stalls specializing in such things. These may be served in individual portions, but given the easy divisibility of noodle dishes it is common for workmates to order a variety of noodle dishes and share them in common. A portion is lifted from the plate to one's bowl; with chopsticks initially, when the noodles are easily grasped in quantity; with help from the spoon as the plate gets progressively emptied. The setting of shared common dishes makes the general rules of the table outlined above once again applicable.

Co-workers will often go out to lunch at large *dim saam* restaurants, catch the tail end of the morning *dim saam* and order a variety of more substantial noodle or rice dishes. Where eating has taken place in common, and occasionally even where individual portions have been served, it is unusual for the check to be divided. Someone usually pays the whole tab. Among workmates, or those who often eat together, there is an implicit assumption that in the long run reciprocity will be achieved. It is not impolite among status equals to grab the check and pay for one's fellow diner, but this is not polite if the status difference is too great. Fights over the check occasionally occur in a way which evokes the potlatches of Northwest Coast Indians in which a status hierarchy is confirmed. Paying the check validates one's status superiority over one's fellow diners. Of course, the wider social setting must also be taken into account. One may be desirous of seeking a favor of an important person, in which case paying the check may serve as a mild form of pressure in which the obligation of reciprocity is finessed, enjoining one's fellow diner to comply with one's request. Food events are first and foremost social events.

The evening meal taken at home usually includes some warmed-over *ts'ai* from the previous day's meal plus an increment of newly prepared dishes. It is not good manners to ignore the leftovers, despite the fact that they may not be quite as attractive as when served the day before. The general rules of the table apply, although the intimate setting of the family at home makes their application somewhat less formal. Still and all, parents will most commonly instruct children as to the appropriate forms of behavior at the table in this setting, and the children must show that they understand and are learning. In many working-class homes in Hong Kong it is still common for the men to eat first, with the women joining later and/or hovering over the meal without ever formally sitting down.

At more formal dinners or at banquets or feasts associated with weddings, New Year's, funerals or festivals, the primacy of the *fan* and the secondary character of the *ts'ai* dishes is reversed, with attention devoted to the quality of the *ts'ai* dishes (Hsü and Hsü 1977:307), and rice not served till last. Thus at a banquet one may eat *ts'ai* without rice in one's bowl, and one is expected to fill up on *ts'ai* such that when the rice is finally served, one can only take a token portion, which is to say, this has been a real feast.

> During festivals and especially when acting as hosts all Chinese seem to ignore their sense of frugality and indulge in extravagance. *Ts'ai* dishes are served in abundance. The host or hostess will heap the guests' saucers with piece after piece of meat, fish, chicken and so on, in spite of repeated excuses or even protests on the guests'

part. When fan is finally served, most around the table are full and can at best nibble a few grains (Hsü and Hsü 1977:307).

By the time the rice has been served at a banquet the diner has already had a share of cold appetizer, several stir fry dishes, or whole chickens, ducks, fish, soup, and a sweet/salty dessert. The emphasis on whole items (with head and tail attached) symbolizes completeness and fullness, and evokes these meanings at the table. One tries to serve fish, *yü*, a homophone for surplus, *yü*, to sympathetically bring about that condition in one's guests.

It is not polite to turn over a fish at the table. Rather, when the side facing up has been finished, the skeleton is lifted off to leave the meat underneath exposed. Apparently, turning over the fish is **taboo** among boat people, since the fish symbolizes the boat which will capsize sympathetically if a fish is turned over. Waiters in Hong Kong are never sure which of their customers are boat folk and might take offense, so they generally refrain from turning over any fish and apparently the practice has now become general.

A variety of prestige foods, such as shark's fin soup and the various eight precious dishes, are served at banquets more for the social recognition they confer than for the pleasure derived from their consumption (see de Garine 1976:150).

Conceptually, whiskey belongs with grain from which it is distilled and may be taken with food as a rice substitute. On formal occasions in Hong Kong scotch or VSOP Cognac is the rule, served straight in water tumblers, and often diluted with Seven-Up.

Another food event of note in Hong Kong is *siu yeh*—loosely translated as snacks. Usually taken late in the evening, they may include anything from congee, noodles and won ton, to roast pork, duck or chicken, to *hung dao sa* (sweet red bean soup—hot or iced) and *daofufa* (sweet bean curd usually flavored with almond). *Siu yeh* is usually served in individual portions. If you go out for won ton mein, everyone gets his own bowl. If you order duck's neck soup with rice, you are served an individual helping of soup, and an individual bowl of rice. Depending on the class of restaurant you take your *siu yeh* in, you may or may not find it advisable to wash your utensils with tea.

Itinerant street vendors with wheeled carts dispense a variety of prepared *siu yeh* in some residential neighborhoods, calling housewives and amahs to the street clutching their large porcelain bowls, or doling out cuttlefish parts to schoolchildren on street corners.

In all these contexts the general pattern that emerges is one that centers on deference, in thinking first of the other, in suppressing one's inclination to satiate oneself before the other has had a chance to begin, in humility. One yields to the other before satisfying one's own urges. At the macro level of China's great tradition, one finds such behavior characteristic of the *chün-tzu*, the individual skilled in the *li* (etiquette, rites, and ceremonies). He is one also skilled in the art of *jang*—of yielding, of accomplishing without activity, of boundless generosity, of cleaving to the *li*. There is even something of a Taoist resonance in all this, getting at things indirectly, without obvious instrumental effort.

Generally, it can be stated that the degree to which a Chinese practices the rules of etiquette marks his class position with respect to his fellow Chinese; although the degree to which the behavior of lower-class people at the table is informed by these rules should not be underestimated. Disregard of the rules on the part of a Chinese is regarded with as much distaste by their fellows as the *faux pas* normally committed by Westerners, except that the latter can be excused by their hopeless, if expected, ignorance.

It does not take much study for a Westerner to perform well enough at the table to impress most Chinese, since their expectations are exceedingly low. Keeping in mind a few simple things without slavishly parading one's knowledge, one can usually avoid provoking disgust and revulsion, and convince one's fellow diners that one is sensitive to others on their own terms, as well as to the world at large. Among the most basic of cultural patterns, learned early in life, the degree to which one observes these patterns has a lot to do with the way one is perceived as a person in Chinese terms.

Simple knowledge of the structural contexts, behavioral expectations, and symbolic associations of food events can provide access across social boundaries that would otherwise be less easily breached, and make it possible to more easily achieve one's goals. Table manners are part of an inventory of symbolic behaviors that may be manipulated, finessed, and encoded to communicate messages about oneself. For the Chinese, as for almost everyone else, you are *how* you eat.

REFERENCES

Chang, K. C. (ed.), 1977, Introduction. In *Food in Chinese Culture*. New Haven; Yale University Press.

de Garine, I., 1976, Food, Tradition and Prestige. In *Food, Man and Society*. D. Walcher, N. Kretchmer, and H. L. Barnett, eds. New York: Plenum Press.

Goody, J., 1982, *Cooking, Cuisine and Class*. Cambridge: Cambridge University Press.

Hammerton, J. A., 1936, *Manners and Customs of Mankind*, Vol. I. New York: W. M. A. Wise.

Hsü, F. L. K., and V. Y. N. Hsü, 1977 Modern China: North. In *Food in Chinese Culture*. K. C. Chang, ed. New Haven: Yale University Press.

Li Chi 1971, *Chü Li, Part I*. Taipei: World Publishing.

McLean, N. B., 1941, *The Table Graces: Setting, Service and Manners for the American House without Servants*. Peoria, IL: Manual Arts Press.

From Eugene Cooper, 1986, "Chinese Table Manners: You are *How* You Eat," *Human Organization*, Vol. 45, No. 2, pp. 179–184. Reprinted by permission.

GLOBALIZATION AND CULTURE CHANGE

Playing Indian at Halftime: The Controversy over American Indian Mascots, Logos, and Nicknames in School-related Events—
Cornel D. Pewewardy

Every school year, classroom teachers face the reality and challenge of educating diverse children in a multicultural society. Teaching multiculturally requires educators to examine sensitive, diverse topics and cultural issues. It means looking at historical and contemporary events from various perspectives, rather than a single one. Teachers and administrators whose knowledge of history and current events is monocultural in scope and who are unaware of their own prejudices are likely to hinder the academic success and personal development of many students, however unintentional this may be (Bennett 1999). Multicultural teaching encourages students to investigate the institutional racism, classism, and sexism that have served different populations in discriminatory ways. Educators can help monocultural classes and schools examine their own biases and stereotypes related to different cultural groups. Although one's ethnic group is just one of a number of possible identity sources, ethnicity is at the heart of the equity problem in American society. Therefore, discussions about achieving educational excellence should address those ethnic groups that have been consistently cut off from equal access to a quality education.

Educators have a professional responsibility to eliminate racism in all aspects of school life. Accordingly, educators should not ignore multicultural issues in school. Instead, these issues should become teachable moments in which these concerns are confronted and discussed. Accurate information can begin to displace the myths that many students hold about others. Today, one teachable moment is the controversy over using American Indian mascots, logos, and nicknames in school-related events. Supporters of such mascots claim they honor American Indian people, embody institutional traditions, foster a shared identity, and intensify the pleasures of sports and athletics. According to those who oppose them, however, the mascots give life to racial stereotypes, as well as revivify historical patterns of appropriation and oppression. These results often foster discomfort and pain among American Indian people (Springwood and King 2001).

Non-Indian people may not be culturally aware that some American Indian symbols used by cheerleaders and cheering fans—war chants, peace pipes, eagle feathers, war bonnets, and dances—are highly revered or even sacred in many American Indian tribal communities. Many mascots, logos, and nicknames represent stereotypical and racist images that relegate American Indian people to a colonial representation history. The exploitation of Indian mascots, logos, and nicknames in schools is, in reality, an issue of decolonization and educational equity.[1]

This article discusses the creation of stereotypical Indian mascots, how our society reinforces and accepts those stereotypes, how negative stereotypes have affected the relationship between American Indians and the rest of society, and it suggests solutions educators might use to eliminate these mascots from school-related events. In writing this article, I hope not to demean schools but to provide a rationale and approach by which ethnocentrism, elitism, sexism, and racism effectively can be eradicated in schools.

COUNTERING THE ASSAULT OF AMERICAN INDIAN MASCOTS, LOGOS, AND NICKNAMES

Using the word *countering*, which means to confront defensive or retaliatory attacks or arguments, to describe certain behaviors and thinking in our society is a strong indictment of the existing social fabric of the United States. Many educators in this country are serious players when it comes to countering racism, thereby protecting the mental health of school children today. However, many more teachers are unresponsive to or unaware of the issues of racism in schools today. Like these teachers, parents, educators, and liberals who deny being racists but remain silent when confronted with the issue also allow institutional racism to continue.

This issue has turned into a debate and torn schools and communities apart. Administrators spend months fending off angry alumni on both sides of the issue, calming students, and dealing with mainstream news media that oversimplify these issues. After it is all over, school districts often must spend additional time and energy healing the wounds and community ruptures left in the wake of efforts to counter institutional racism by eradicating American Indian mascots, logos, and nicknames in schools (Riede 2001).

STILL "PLAYING INDIAN" IN SCHOOL

Many schools around the country "play Indian" by exhibiting American Indian mascots, logos, and nicknames at sporting events: school bands play so-called "Indian" fight songs (for example, "One-little-two-little-three-little Indians....") during both pregame and halftime entertainment; mascots dress in stereotypical cartoon character-like costumes and beat hand drums and/or carry foam tomahawks; and fans do the "tomahawk chop"[2] in unison. These all are inauthentic representations of American Indian cultures. Many school officials claim they are honoring American Indians and insist that the activities are not offensive. I argue otherwise and contend that these racist activities are forms of cultural violence in schools (Pewewardy 1999; 2001).

After studying this issue for fifteen years, I found that groups outside the American Indian community imposed most Indian mascots, logos, and nicknames on athletic teams. Even in the earliest U.S. government boarding schools, Indian children had no involvement in choosing their schools' mascots, logos, and nicknames. For example, the first recorded instance of an "Indian" nickname for a sports team was in 1894 at the Carlisle Indian School, an off-reservation U.S. government boarding school for American Indian students, located in Carlisle, Pennsylvania. Mainstream sports journalists praised the team's football performance in the early years of their program. From 1894 until 1917, the Carlisle football team defeated the major power football team of the day (Adams 1995). Subsequently, opposing college football teams and sports media nicknamed team members the Carlisle "Indians." Ironically, most American Indians have always opposed the use of "Indian" mascots, logos, and nicknames for sports teams. Yet, these traditions of doing so are enthusiastically supported by most European Americans (Muir 1999).

Although images of Indians in mainstream sports culture have become as American as apple pie and baseball, educators should be aware that American Indians never would have associated sacred practices with the hoopla of high school pep rallies and halftime entertainments.

HOW AMERICAN INDIAN MASCOTS, LOGOS, AND NICKNAMES BECOME RACIST

The unfortunate portrayal of Indian mascots in sports today takes many forms. Some teams use generic Indian names—such as Indians, Braves, Warriors, or Chiefs—while others adopt specific tribal names—such as Seminoles, Comanches, or Apaches. Indian mascots exhibit either idealized or comical facial features and native dress,

ranging from body-length feathered (usually turkey) headdresses to fake buckskin attire or skimpy loincloths. Some teams and supporters display counterfeit Indian paraphernalia, including foam tomahawks, feathers, face paints, drums, and pipes. They also use mock "Indian" behaviors, such as the tomahawk chop, dances, war chants (for example, at Florida State University), drum beating, war-whooping, and symbolic scalping. Many European Americans rely on these manufactured images to anchor them to the land and verify a false account of a shared history. These "Indians," however, exist only in the imagination: they provide a self-serving historical connection that leaves actual American Indian people untethered and rootless in or erased from the historical accounts of European Americans (Spindel 2000).

Many school officials are all too familiar with the current legal and educational battles toward eliminating Indian mascots, logos, and nicknames from school-related events. The U.S. Commission of Civil Rights (CCR), the highest official governmental body of its kind, issued a strong statement in 2001 condemning their use and recommending that schools eliminate Indian images and nicknames as sports symbols (U.S. Department of Justice 2001). Grassroots efforts of thousands of American Indian parents nationwide prompted this decision among CCR members. Moreover, the critical mass of American Indian educational organizations and professionals supported the CCR statement. American Indian educators showed school officials that negative images, symbols, and behaviors play a crucial role in distorting and warping American Indian children's cultural perceptions of themselves, as well as non-Indian children's attitudes toward and simplistic understanding of American Indian culture. Hollywood scriptwriters originally manufactured most of these stereotypes. Over time, they have evolved into contemporary racist images that prevent millions of school-age students from understanding American Indians' past and present experiences.

HOW STEREOTYPICAL IMAGES IMPACT YOUNG CHILDREN'S SELF-ESTEEM

Children begin to develop racial awareness at an early age, perhaps as early as three or four years old. Clinical psychologists have established that negative stereotypes and derogatory images engender and perpetuate undemocratic and unhealthy attitudes in children, plaguing them for years to come. Many non-Indian children exposed to these Hollywood stereotypes at early ages grow into adults who may unwittingly or unknowingly discriminate against American Indians. These children have been prevented from developing authentic, healthy attitudes about Indians. Moreover, Indian children who constantly see themselves being stereotyped and their cultures belittled grow into adults who feel and act inferior to other people. These racial and inauthentic behaviors mock Indian culture and cause many Indian youngsters to have low self-esteem and feel shame about their cultural identity. School environments should be places where students unlearn negative stereotypes that such mascots represent and promote. However, athletic events where Indian mascots are frequently used teach children the exact opposite.

Perhaps some people at these sporting events do not hear the foul language shouted out in the stands and seating arenas associated with the usage of Indian mascots, logos, and nicknames. The most obvious offense is the usage of the terms *redskins* (lady redskins) and *squaws*. According to one explanation, the word *redskin* originated in early colonial times when European colonists paid bounties for Indians' red skins—thereby coining the term *redskin*. The word *squaw* is a French corruption of the Iroquois word *otsiskwa*, meaning female properties. Both words are almost always used in a derogatory fashion in sporting events. Although these terms may be facing increasing social disdain, they certainly are far from dead. These words accentuate the differences in appearance, culture, gender, nationality, or sexual orientation of people and underplay—if not to deny—the similarities between people.

Given this background, no one, especially those associated with schools, should allow students to adopt a cartoon version of American Indian cultures as a mascot or logo. Educators and students need to be more educated about the negative effects of racist Indian mascots and logos on American Indian people. Many students do not recognize that the Indian mascot issue is as important in the American Indian community as alcoholism, substance abuse, and poverty. Some people excuse their ambivalence on the issue by saying there is "too much fuss over team names," "we're just having fun," "we're not harming anybody," or "what's the point?" They miss the connection because they are removed from the issues of American Indian education. It is hard to take American Indians seriously or to empathize with them when they are always portrayed as

speaking in old, broken, stoic Indian clichés, such as "many moons ago"; dressing up in Halloween or Thanksgiving costumes; or acting crazy like a "bunch of wild Indians." These make-believe Indians are prohibited from changing over time to be like real people. On athletic fields and in gymnasiums, they are denied the dignity of their tribal histories, the validity of their major contributions to modern American society, the distinctiveness of their multitribal identities.

In 1998, Children Now initiated a study of children's perceptions of race and class in the media, focusing on images of American Indians presented in national news and entertainment. The Children Now study revealed similar results to the perceptions survey conducted by the League of Women Voters in 1975: most children in America view American Indians far removed from their own way of life.[3] Not only do these studies have to be conducted and their results disseminated, but the misconceptions and stereotypes about American Indian people, which bombard the child from outside of the classroom, need to be counteracted.

MAKING RACISM VISIBLE IN SCHOOL-RELATED EVENTS

Despite years of cultural diversity teacher training and integration of multicultural education lesson plans into the school curricula, children still play "cowboys and Indians" at some schools. Most teachers, undoubtedly, have seen (or perhaps even supported) children running around in turkey feathers and cardboard headbands, carrying homemade bows and arrows, patting a hand against their mouth and yelling "woo-woo-woo," or raising their hands over their shoulder and saying "how." The perpetuation of these invented Indian behaviors reflects the influence of peer socialization, schooling, and mainstream movies. They mock American Indian cultural practices, demean actual human beings, and treat American Indian people as subhumans incapable of verbal communication. This manufactured image of the Indian as something wild and inferior implies white superiority, a value judgment made namely by Hollywood scriptwriters. (Rollins and O'Connor 1998).

Another popular character born of the racist images of American Indian people is the clown. Traditional clown societies of many tribes (for example, Apaches, Pueblos) attempt to make their people laugh during celebrations and ceremonies. On the other hand, the contemporary clown, born of American popular culture, is more like the jester or the fool, the inferior one responsible for making his superiors laugh. The use of clowns has always been a major way to assert dominance over a particular person or a certain group of people. During ballgames, the exaggerated images of Indians become clown-like, serving to manipulate and keep in place negative images during school-related events.

However, I hypothesize that the use of American Indian mascots in sporting events was influenced by the philosophical views of the Enlightenment and the developing Romantic movement. During those periods, American Indians were seen either as amusing exotics or as Noble Savages, excellent types for representing ideas in literature, in film, or on the stage. But the reality was that these figures were never more than white characters with cliché comic or noble personalities, thinly disguised in red skins and feathered costumes. American Indian people were never considered real human beings whose existence might be dramatically interesting (Jones 1988).

DEFENSIVE TACTICS AND ATTRIBUTES

Who should decide what is demeaning and racist? Clearly, the affected party determines what is offensive. Unaffected members of society should not dictate how the affected party should feel. Moreover, efforts to retire Indian mascots, logos, and nicknames should not be met with ugly alumni and student backlashes that label grassroots complainants as troublemakers, activist, militant, gadflies, or practitioners of political correctness. Therefore, educators who advocate and affirm cultural diversity must be ready for a challenge. Only a concerted effort to debunk Hollywood's mythology can alter the distorted image of the American Indian people for the better.

Educators should examine the biases and stereotypes their students hold. These stereotypes, caused by ignorance, hard times, and folk wisdom socialization, can be countered by accurate and culturally responsive information. Education can become a tool for liberation from bigotry—rather than a facilitator of racism (Corntassel n.d.).

LARGE SCHOOL DISTRICTS AND ORGANIZATIONS AS TRAILBLAZERS

Hope for change can be found in two large school districts in the United States. Both Dallas Public Schools and Los Angeles Public Schools have already eliminated Indian mascots from their school districts as the result of active parent and education advocacy groups working [together] with school officials. The states of Wisconsin and Minnesota also have recommended that publicly funded schools eliminate the use of Indian mascots, logos, and nicknames deemed offensive to American Indians.

Professional organizations dedicated to the unique problems of American Indians must take forthright positions on this issue as well. As a teacher educator, I show future teachers why Indian mascots are one cause of low self-esteem among American Indian children in schools. Throughout my practical experience working in K-8 schools, I have learned that self-esteem fuels academic performance. Educators must realize that this issue is detrimental to the academic achievement of all students. As such, negative Indian mascots, logos, and nicknames are harmful to both Indian and non-Indian students. American Indian students endure the psychological damage and dehumanizing effects of seeing caricatures of themselves embodied in school mascots, logos, and nicknames. It is no coincidence that American Indians have the highest suicide, school dropout, and unemployment rates of any ethnic group in the U.S. (Rider 1999). To illustrate my point, I refer to the mental health organizations that have rushed to support the elimination of negative Indian mascots used in schools (for example, the American Indian Mental Health Association of Minnesota in 1992 and the Society of Indian Psychologists of the Americas in 1999). They drafted statements condemning the presence of ethnic images as psychologically destructive to the minds of American Indian children. Other professional organizations that have passed resolutions in support of eliminating negative Indian mascots used in school-related activities and events include the National Indian Education Association, United Indian Nations of Oklahoma, Governors' Interstate Indian Council, Great Lakes Inter Tribal Council, National Congress of American Indians, National Association for the Advancement of Colored People, and National College Athletic Association.

Although such resolutions exist today, political and cultural leaders in many states (such as Oklahoma) have hundreds of Indian mascots and logos in use in school-related events but remain unconcerned with this national issue. They are uneducated about the issues or have little educational leadership to initiate transformational change toward truly honoring American Indians. Consequently, there is a critical need for experts to monitor more carefully these destructive influences in our shared physical, mental, social, and spiritual environments. Educators, parents, and community leaders must build coalitions to preserve the reality of our shared history. Educators must develop educational materials, artistic productions, economic structures, fashions, and concepts that counteract these damaging stereotypes.

WHAT MUST BE DONE

The recognition of embedded racism in the English language is an important first step. Consciousness of the influence of language on our perceptions can help negate much of that influence. But it is not enough to simply be aware of the effects of racist language in conditioning attitudes. Although society may not be able to change the entire language, educators can help students change their use of many unkind words. Educators should not use degrading and dehumanizing words and should make a conscious effort to use terminology that reflects a progressive, rather than distorting, perspective. Most important, educators should provide students with opportunities to increase their cultural awareness by exploring racism in language and also should teach terminology that is culturally responsive and does not perpetuate negative human values and experiences.

To correct these negative stereotypes, concerned individuals or groups should consult the local school Title IX Indian Education Program coordinator, curriculum specialist, cultural resource librarian, university professor, or the National Indian Education Association to assist in the elimination of negative ethnic images and materials from the academic curriculum and school-related events. Some complainants of Indian mascots and logos have also filed complaints with the U.S. Department of Education, Office of Civil Rights. Every public school district is required to have a complaint procedure adopted by the school board for residents to use.

One of the finest award-winning reference books on this topic is *American Indian Stereotypes in the World of Children* by Arlene Hirschfelder, Paulette Fairbanks Molin, and Yvonne Wakim (1999). Robert Eurich also maintains a comprehensive website on American Indian sports teams mascots at http://earnestman.tripod.com/fr.2001.retrospective.htm. This website tracks all schools that have Indian names as well as those schools that have been changed to a non-Indian mascot.[4]

Every school year, American Indian students, parents, educators, and other allies must continue the hard work to educate our young people and us about how Indian mascots are used in school-related events. We must find every opportunity to celebrate ourselves, challenging the fear that causes us to hesitate in taking control of our own ethnic images. We must work together and have faith that our struggle will be successful, regardless of the opposition.

CONCLUSION

The ongoing use of Indian mascots in school-sponsored events is an issue of educational equity. Therefore, my professional challenge is to educators. As long as such mascots remain within the arena of school activities, both Indian and non-Indian children are learning to tolerate racism in schools. By tolerating the use of demeaning stereotypes in our public schools, we further desensitize entire generations of children (Milner 1991, 67). As a result, schools reinforce the stereotypical negative images projected in the broader mainstream American cultural imagination. Sport teams with Indian mascots, logos, and nicknames teach them that it is acceptable to demean a race or group of people through American sports culture. Educators must turn the use of these mascots, logos, and nicknames into powerful teaching moments that could help counter the fabricated images and manufactured pictures of Indians that most school-age children have ingrained in their psyche by one hundred years of mass media. Finally, I challenge administrators and policymakers to provide the intellectual school leadership that truly embraces multicultural education, helping to eliminate the cultural violence associated with and triggered by the use of American Indian mascots in school-related events.

As a former kindergarten teacher and principal, I have a profound respect and admiration for teachers and administrators. The work they do is honorable, although rarely cherished. At the same time, I recognize that many teachers and administrators have not been given the time or support to help them teach in the most culturally responsive way. I hope this explanation of why educators should not ignore Indian mascots is a tool both teachers and administrators can use to help children think critically about multicultural issues in another school year.

NOTES

1. Many of the contemporary Indian mascots, logos, and nicknames of today originated at the turn of the twenty-first century. However, crude stereotyping of these ethnic characters became more and more obvious as the first half of the century progressed, even surviving the social reconstruction of the Civil Rights Era.

2. The tomahawk chop is a social phenomenon created by those sports fans who perceive the need for a supportive physical display of action to cheer on the favored athletic team. It is the extension of a single arm out in front on an individual—swinging the hand and forearm in an up and down motion. The act of the tomahawk chop usually takes place in large crowds in sport stadiums accompanied by a so-called Indian war chant. The tomahawk perpetuates the negative stereotype of the Noble Savage that falsely represents American Indians, and it certainly is not reflective of modern America.

3. See Children Now: Native American children's perceptions of race and class in the media. http://www.childrennow.org/media/nativeam/report.html.

4. See Robert Eurich's website dedicated to educating individuals about Indian mascots. http://members.tripod.com/earnestman/getinvolved.htm.

REFERENCES

Adams, D. W. 1995. *Education for extinction: American Indians and the boarding school experience, 1875–1928*. Lawrence, KS: University Press of Kansas.

Bennett, C. I. 1999. Comprehensive multicultural education: Theory and practice. Boston: Allyn and Bacon.

Comtassel, J. J. n.d. *Let's teach respect, not racism: Ethnic mascots demean American Indians*. http://members.tripod.com/~earnestman/jeff_j_corntassel_essay.htm (accessed August 1, 2003; site discontinued).

Hirschfelder, A., P. Fairbanks Molin, and Y. Wakim. 1999. *American Indian stereotypes in the world of children: A reader and bibliography*. Lanham, MA: Scarecrow Press.

Jones, E. H. *Native Americans as shown on the stage, 1753–1916*. Metuchen, NJ: The Scarecrow Press.

Miner, B. 1991. The Danger of Harmless School Mascots. In *Rethinking Columbus: A special issue of Rethinking Schools*: 67.

Muir, S. P. 1999. Native Americans as Sports Mascots. *Social Education* 63 (1):56–57.

Pewewardy, C. 1999. From enemy to mascot: The deculturation of Indian mascots in sport culture. *Canadian Journal of Native Education* 23 (2):176–89.

——, 2001. Educators and mascots: Challenging contradictions. In *Team spirits: The Native American mascots controversy*. Eds. C. R. King and C. F. Springwood. Lincoln, NE: University of Nebraska Press, 257–78.

Rider, D. P. 1999. *Stereotypes/Discrimination/Identity*. http://www.aics.org/mascot/david.html (accessed August 1, 2003).

Riede, P. 2001. More Than a Mascot. *The School Administrator* 58(8): 27–33.

Rollins, P. C., and J. E. O'Connor. 1998. *Hollywood's Indian: The portrayal of the Native American in film*. Lexington, KY: University Press of Kentucky.

Spindel, C. *Dancing at halftime: Sports and the controversy over American Indian mascots*. New York: New York University Press.

Springwood, C. F., and C. R. King. Playing Indian: Why Native American Mascots Must End. *The Chronicle of Higher Education: The Chronicle Review*, November 19, 2001.

US Department of Justice. *Racism Report by US Department of Justice*. http://www.aics.org/mascots/racism.html.

Excerpt from Cornel D. Pewewardy, "Playing Indian at Halftime," *The Clearing House*, May/June 2004, pp. 180–185. Reprinted by permission.

EXERCISE

Name

Section

Date

EXERCISE 12.2: WRITING AN ETHNOGRAPHY

Helpful Hints to Writing an Ethnography

Here are some sample headlines students chose from newspapers: "Amish Community Copes with Rare Murder," "Black Astronaut Carries Navajo Flag," "Korean University Professor Develops Education Program in Finland," "Art Teacher Saves Drowning Child in Treacherous River Dam," "Small Business Grant Slashed in Favor of Community Fireworks Display," "Kiwanis Club Donates Funds toward Little Juanita's New Kidney." Note that the headlines are specific, full of cultural details. Our students' analyses were twice as long as the news articles they chose. They asked more questions than they were able to answer as they peeled back layers of information to find out "Where is the culture?" An example follows.

1. Choose an article like the one that follows from a local news source:

Black Astronaut Carries Navajo Flag

Cape Canaveral, Fla. (AP)—Before Bernard Harris Jr. was allowed to take a Navajo flag aboard Discovery, tribal medicine men had to bless it with corn pollen and make sure the space shuttle's path fit with their beliefs: it had to orbit clockwise.

When the Navajo decided that from their viewpoint, Discovery's orbit met the requirement, all signals were go for Harris to carry the first Navajo item to fly in space. NASA allows astronauts to carry up a few small belongings.

"I'm flying this flag for them because being there I could see their plight as the original Americans," said Harris, a 38-year-old black physician who lived on a Navajo reservation from ages 7 to 15. His mother taught at boarding schools run by the U.S. Bureau of Indian Affairs.

Harris, who today will become the first black to spacewalk, approached the Navajo in December about taking some tribal item with him on the mission.

Navajo Nation President Albert Hale decided on a flag after consulting with medicine men to make sure no spiritual traditions would be violated. The flag was blessed last month by Navajo medicine man Ross Nez.

GLOBALIZATION AND CULTURE CHANGE

Through a ceremony Nez "was told by the Creator and the Holy People that it would strengthen the Navajo Nation for this flag to go around Mother Earth," Navajo spokeswoman Valerie Taliman said Wednesday.

"The flag is a symbol of our nation and reminds us of how we must live in balance with our Mother Earth to survive," Hale said.

Nez blessed the flag by sprinkling it with corn pollen, which has an importance for the Navajo roughly similar to holy water in the Catholic church.

Hale sent the blessed flag to NASA. A few days later, he said, a NASA official called: "We have the flag, but we have a question. What is this yellow stuff on it?"

Hale assured NASA the powder was sacred pollen used in prayers.

The Navajo flag depicts the four mountains that delineate traditional Navajo territory.

"Black Astronaut Carries Navajo Flag," *Cedar Rapids Gazette*, February 10, 1995. Copyright © 1995 The Associated Press. Reprinted by permission.

Preparing a Student Essay: Using the Ethnographic Perspective:
"Black Astronaut Carries Navajo Flag," *Cedar Rapids Gazette*, February 10, 1995

The article discusses Bernard Harris Jr.'s choice to carry a Navajo flag on board the NASA shuttle plane, *Discovery*. Harris is an African American who spent 8 years of his youth on a Navajo reservation. The article reveals general details about the circumstances and the way in which the decision was approved by Navajo tribal leaders.

Regarding the cultural issues, there are several things the article doesn't include. Why does Harris consider the Navajo the "first Americans," as he is quoted as saying? What daily interaction did Harris have with the Navajo during his youth, and what specific influence did they have on him? Why did he leave when he was 15? Did he maintain contact with the Navajo after he left the reservation? How much does he know about his African-American heritage compared to the Navajo culture? Did he also take an artifact from his African-American heritage? Why or why not? If so, what was it, and is there any connection to the Navajo flag?

Other questions worth pursuing might be knowing how Navajo officials and tribal leaders felt about Harris's choice for an artifact. Perhaps one could interview childhood friends of Harris's from the reservation to hear their reflections and opinions. Do they have the same opinion of him now that they did then? Why or why not? Did Harris actively participate in the Navajo culture and rituals as a young person? To what extent does his choice to carry their flag represent a sincere and genuine belief in their culture?

EXERCISE

I would think tribal elders and the medicine man referred to in the article would be good sources for more insight into the cultural implications and details of this event. Another curiosity is the writer's choice to compare the use of corn pollen in Navajo rituals to the use of holy water in the Catholic church. This could be an example of a "mixed" metaphor since the frame of reference of the writer is the Christian church, and although there are some obvious general similarities (i.e., creation stories and the hereafter), there are many contradictions between the two, especially if one starts to pursue the concept of land ownership and its relationship to Christianity.

Obviously, an ethnographer could find numerous trails and sources to pursue.

2. Now choose your own article, published in the last two years. Complete a one-page student essay. Be sure to include a list of potential questions that you feel would enhance the readers' understanding of related cultural issues.

GLOBALIZATION AND CULTURE CHANGE

Ownership and Control of Ethnographic Materials—
Sjoerd R. Jaarsma
U of Nijmegen/Papua Heritage Foundation

What has changed most about ethnographic research in the present age of globalization is not the way academic anthropologists deal with the communities they study, but how members of those communities deal with their anthropologists. A few years ago, I met with a group of anthropologists, ethnomusicologists, archivists and librarians to consider the problems relating to the disposition of ethnographic field materials. We concluded that basic questions like "Who owns the information?" and "Should everything be accessible?" should be reconsidered not only by academic anthropologists, but also by the communities being studied.

Ever since fieldwork became the preferred approach to gathering ethnographic information, the quality and quantity of research data being gathered has increased radically. Present-day students have both the training and equipment to make the most of their temporary stay in the field. Yet, the way we relate to the people we study has changed little since the first anthropologists left for the field in colonial days. Most fieldwork still follows the same general pattern. Anthropologists go into the field and gather their material, usually explaining that it will be used to write a book. Having gathered the material needed, they leave their careers on the merits of the research done. While these days a copy of the thesis written is sent back to local informants, research data will remain under the anthropologists' care and control. Access to raw field materials rarely is granted to others, including members of the study community, during an anthropologist's lifetime.

INDIGENOUS ACCESS AND CONTROL
Until recently, people in the field rarely were able to follow up on any of the issues dealt with in the published research results, let alone seek access to the data gathered by the researcher. Equally, they were unable to point out the lack of balance in "services rendered" that surrounds this pattern of research. Even today, with more rules and regulations in place, local grip on field research remains limited. Unless the local community sponsors the research being done, it has few means for managing the flow of research information.

Two issues that academic anthropologists can no longer ignore stand out. First, the flow of information going in and out of any fieldwork location is, as a rule, hugely unbalanced. Second, very little thought has been given so far to control over and access to the data gathered while in the field.

A world growing ever smaller makes it easier for anthropologists to visit the field and keep in contact. Likewise, informants may keep in touch with the anthropologists via phone, email, visits, or communication through family or friends. The Internet allows people to access materials even from the field. The ease with which information can be shared makes the control over data gathered by individual anthropologists an ever more relevant issue.

VALUE OF INFORMATION
Ethnographic information, like all information, has a market value, even if anthropologists are not used to thinking in such terms. Although ethnobiologists appreciate the need to establish an equitable tradeoff based on the value placed on indigenous knowledge concerning plants and medicines, the opposite is well-known too. First World musicians still harvest indigenous songs written down by ethnomusicologists to include in their compositions. Sampled compositions sell millions of CDs without revenues flowing to the original indigenous artists or mention being made of their contributions.

Ethnography affects the nature of indigenous knowledge itself. Anthropologists' published materials place indigenous knowledge, previously protected by individual ownership, in the public domain. For example, written records of land ownership differ from "traditional" oral discourse on such matters. Access to the written records by anthropologists shifts the power balance inherent in the use of knowledge. Here, too, the disposition of control over and access to indigenous knowledge is of paramount importance.

EFFECTS ON ANTHROPOLOGY
Recently indigenous peoples have become aware that they have a right to exercise control over their own cultural resources. Conferences like the 1993 First International Conference on the Cultural and Intellectual Property Rights of Indigenous Peoples sponsored by the UN provide a forum on these rights. Similarly, the 1991 Native

American Graves Protection Act [NAGPRA] has established indigenous control over ethnographic artifacts in museums and the disposition of burial sites. Such rights will only expand further.

What does this mean for anthropological fieldwork? With anthropologists studying ever more critically aware and emancipated communities, they will be held accountable for their responsibilities concerning the data gathered. Laws will circumscribe rights to the data gathered. Though not written with anthropologists in mind, these laws apply to the anthropologists' research. Similarly, a foreseeable increase in sponsoring of research by indigenous communities themselves will affect the way anthropologists deal with data.

NEEDED ACTION

The field data presently in the possession of anthropologists and stored by them in archives and libraries should be made more readily accessible. Implicitly, this means sorting out and protecting ownership rights to knowledge recorded in the field notes, sifting out potentially harmful and damaging information and safeguarding future research interests. This is best done by the original researcher, as archivists and librarians, or even fellow anthropologists, rarely share the knowledge necessary to do this properly.

It is better to plan all this at the start of fieldwork than put it in place afterward. Therefore not only the setup of fieldwork, but also training for fieldwork, should be reviewed in such a way that safeguarding the informant's interests in the data becomes second nature to anthropologists.

Anthropologists are entrusted to use and work with other people's knowledge, but "ownership" remains limited to what they add as interpretation. They have to acknowledge that the communities being studied have equal if not greater legitimate rights to the ethnographic materials gathered. These rights are only mitigated by an obligation to prevent damage deriving from any access provided to the material. If the academic community does not make itself and the data anthropologists gather accessible and accountable, it may eventually be forced to do so.

ANTHROPOLOGISTS AT WORK TODAY:
Will Tribal Knowledge Survive the Millennium?—
Paul Alan Cox

As we begin a new millennium and contemplate how our current understandings might be evaluated in 1000 years, it may be useful to look backward. What pieces of knowledge do we treasure that come from 1000 years ago? Accounts from the end of the last millennium herald innovations like the metal plow, but were imbued with folk knowledge from an era when trolls, fairies, and personifications of the elements, such as Jack Frost, were thought to play important roles in determining the course of human life.

A bit broader glance at the past might unearth the mathematical work of Leonardo Pisano Fibonacci, who introduced Western culture to the concept of zero, a decimal positional system of numerals far different from the Roman numerals then in use, and the beginnings of linear algebra. Fibonacci's work underlies nearly all modern engineering calculations, stock market transactions, and computer manipulations. Credit for these innovations, however, does not belong to the west: Fibonacci spent his youth in Northern Africa and learned his arithmetic from Indian and Arabian merchants. Is it possible that knowledge systems outside of our current Western canon may be esteemed 1000 years from now?

When I first met Epenesa Mauigoa, she seemed unremarkable—a diminutive 73-year-old who tended her infirm husband in their modest *fale* or hut on the outskirts of Apia, Western Samoa. True, some of the plants growing in her garden were unusual, but I did not expect anything extraordinary during my first interview. "Do you know anything about herbal medicine?" I asked respectfully. "I know a little," Epenesa quietly replied. Then for the next 3 hours, as I rapidly typed on my laptop computer, Epenesa related the most detailed account of Samoan herbal medicine that I have ever recorded. By the end of our sessions several weeks later, Epenesa had taught me the details of 121 different herbal remedies she carefully mixed from 90 different species of flowering plants and ferns. The 37th remedy Epenesa told me caught my attention: Epenesa claimed to be able to treat *five samasama*, a term used to describe hepatitis. "*E fasi ogala' au o le mamala moni*," she said in her quiet, but dignified Samoan: "Take the stem of the true *mamala* tree (which botanists call *Homalanthus nutans*). Boil it, and pour off the water. The person who is ill should drink it twice a day.

Other healers confirmed Epenesa Mauigoa's report. Soon a team at the U.S. National Cancer Institute found healer preparations of *Homalanthus* to be active against a very different virus—human immunodeficiency virus—type 1—and discovered an antiviral drug called prostratin.* The U.S. government has guaranteed that half of all royalty income from prostratin will go back to the people of Samoa, which is one of the first formal legal recognitions of indigenous intellectual property rights. Unfortunately, despite its promise, prostratin still languishes as one of several interesting lead compounds that have not been picked up by pharmaceutical firms for clinical testing. However, the significance is clear: an indigenous claim of efficacy of a plant used in traditional medicine had been corroborated by a laboratory finding. **Ethnobotany** is the study of the uses of plants by indigenous people. When I began my ethnobotanical research on Samoan medicine in the mid-1980s, some colleagues warned that my interest in traditional plant lore might blight an otherwise promising scientific career in evolutionary ecology. In our modern era, when science has largely superseded superstition in explaining the causes of disease, the nature of meteorological events and the source of astronomical phenomena, why should ethnobotanists, anthropologists, and linguists struggle to record folk knowledge in remote parts of the world?

On one point there is agreement: traditional knowledge systems are rapidly falling away. Linguist Michael Krauss suggests that half of the 6000 or so languages spoken at the beginning of the 20th century have now vanished, along with the cultures they once kept alive. Of those languages that remain, 80% are spoken only by small groups of elders.†

Consider, for example, the Gosiutes, an American Indian tribe of several hundred people clustered in two small reservations in Utah and Nevada. Fluent speakers of this language number fewer than 20. When those last 20 Gosiute speakers die, the language and much of their culture will disappear forever. Why, on the cusp of a new millennium, should we care?

Among the 20 are elders whose experience as little children is extraordinary: they were raised as hunter-gatherers in the deserts of the Great Basin. The desert life they described from their childhoods is not, however, one of deprivation. They were taught to demarcate seasons by the flowering times of different plant species. By racking a diverse palette of edible roots and tubers, a desert habitat that might otherwise appear foreboding was transformed for them into a moveable feast. Unlike agricultural peoples dependent on a few crops, the Gosiutes could rely on many plant and insect species for nourishment. Gosiute children, though, have scant interest in learning this wisdom. As one aged Gosiute matriarch sadly told me, her grandchildren would rather watch television than listen to stories of a now-forgotten way of life. Whether the cause is considered to be the touted superiority of Western technology, the introduction of foreign money and goods, or the siren call of a new culture to young people, few indigenous societies have been able to withstand the onslaught of Western culture.

Yet, clearly, it is in the interests of Western societies to help protect **indigenous cultures**. By 1994, pharmacologist Norman Farnsworth had identified over 119 plant-derived substances that are used globally as drugs.‡ Many of the prescription drugs sold in the United States contain molecules derived from, or modeled after, naturally occurring molecules in plants§, and many of these (including reserpine, digitalis, and vincristine) come from plants used in traditional medicine.

Once, ethnobotany was the major source of new pharmaceuticals. In the 20th century, however, antibiotics derived from soil cultures, and advances in molecular pharmacology led to a precipitous decline in the importance of pharmacognosy and ethnobotany in drug discovery programs. The pendulum is slowly swinging back, however. Interest in natural product research has been rekindled by discoveries of novel molecules from marine organisms (such as bryostatin) and potent new chemotherapeutic agents from plants (such as taxol). Research has been facilitated by new rapid-throughput bioessays, in which robotic arms and computer-controlled cameras test exceedingly small quantities of plant samples for the presence of compounds active against a multiplicity of disease targets. It is possible to accomplish in a few minutes what once took months to analyze in the lab. Even with new technology, it appears that one of the best sources for finding plant species to test is still the healer's pouch, because such plants have often been tested by generations of indigenous people.

Issues other than merely scientific ones complicate ethno-botanical drug discovery programs, however. Soon after the discovery of prostratin, loggers arrived in Falealupo and began to clear-cut the rain forest where I first collected *H. nutans*. Required by the government to pay for a new school, the village had no recourse but to accept the logger's offer of $1.83 per acre for their 30,000 acre rain forest. Fortunately, with the courageous leadership of village chiefs and assistance from outside donors, funds were raised to pay for the school and to protect the forest.

Too often, though, forests disappear without any notice. Currently, 12.5% of all plant species are threatened with immediate extinction. Most botanists regard this estimate by the International Union for the Conservation of Nature (IUCN) as conservative, because it considers only species known to science: numerous undiscovered species pass from the world unrecorded and unmourned.

The extinction crisis is so acute that, within my short career, the conservation stance of the academic community has changed from detached solipsism to widespread activism. No longer can the problem be ignored. In Hawaii (where I write these words) fully one-half of the indigenous flora are threatened with immediate extinction. If, as some argue, the current loss of biodiversity might be misinterpreted by future observers as the aftermath of an asteroid strike, then the impact crater might be sought in the vicinity of the Hawaiian archipelago. Here at the National Tropical Botanical Garden, I have joined a team of young energetic botanists who rappel down cliffs, dangle from helicopters, and face nearly any challenge to collect seeds from endangered Hawaiian plant species (89 at last count) that have fewer than 20 known representatives remaining alive. The other 174 endangered plant species are separated from extinction by fewer than 100 known survivors. Unfortunately, Hawaii is not unique among oceanic islands in its devastating loss of native species. Yet only a single conservation organization, Seacology (in Berkeley, California), is solely focused on island preservation.

In our endeavor to discover new medicines from the diverse life around us, we enter the next millennium with significant advances, but also significant challenges. At this moment, when we have never been better poised technologically to evaluate natural products, the plant species themselves are disappearing. Similarly, ease of air travel, better linguistic sophistication on the part of investigators (an increasing number of whom are citizens of developing countries), and renewed respect for the intellectual property rights and dignity of indigenous peoples have positioned ethnobotany for significant advances as never before. College courses and international conferences in ethnobotany are multiplying throughout the world, yet at this crescendo of enthusiasm, an increasing number of aged healers are dying, with their knowledge left unrecorded.

Is there hope? The 1992 Convention on Biological Diversity, which for the first time established international protocols for protection and sharing of national biological resources, specifically addresses issues of traditional knowledge. It binds the signatory nations to three laudatory goals: (i) to respect, preserve, and maintain traditional knowledge; (ii) to promote wide application of traditional knowledge, and (iii) to encourage equitable sharing of benefits from traditional knowledge. This international advocacy of indigenous rights is mirrored by advancement of indigenous causes in Western media. Indigenous peoples are no longer feared as the savages once portrayed by Hollywood, indigenous religious concepts are no longer reviled as pagan, and indigenous healers—once denigrated as witch doctors—are no longer ridiculed.

Equally important, conservation biology is now seen as a science in its own right, and advocates for plant conservation are no longer dismissed as dilettantes. To me it seems that conservation science, politics, and advocacy of indigenous issues are moving in the right direction. The question for the new millennium is whether these advances will occur fast enough to overtake the current rates of plant extinction and indigenous culture loss. Will tribal knowledge survive this millennium? If it doesn't, the world will be far poorer for its loss.

NOTES

*K. R. Gustafson et.al., J. *Med. Chem.* 35, 1978 (1992).

† M. Krauss, *Language* 68, 1(1992).

‡ N R. Farnsworth, *Ciba Found. Symp.* 185, 42–5 1 (1994): F. Grifo, D. Newman, A. S. Fairfield, B. Bhattacharya, J. T. Grupenhoff, in *Biodiversity and Human Health*, F. Grifo and J. Rosenthal, Eds. (Island Press, Washington, DC, 1997), pp. 131–163.

ˢDuke, in *New Crops*, J. Janick and J. F. Simon, Eds. (Wiley, NewYork, 1993).

GLOBALIZATION AND CULTURE CHANGE

E X E R C I S E

Name

Section

Date

EXERCISE 12.3: PERPETUATING INDIGENOUS CULTURES

Compile your list of "Top 10" ways to keep indigenous cultures alive.

10.

9.

8.

7.

6.

5.

4.

3.

2.

1.

The loss of cultural diversity is a loss to us all.

GLOBALIZATION AND CULTURE CHANGE

KEY TERMS

Name _____

Section _____

Date _____

CITES (Convention on International Trade and Endangered Species):

Countering:

Customs:

Ethnobotany:

Ethnology:

Globalization:

Indigenous:

Informants:

Regional economy:

Symbols:

GLOSSARY

Acculturation. The process of acceptance resulting for the contact between two cultures, or an individual interacting in at least two cultures.

Achieved status. Position in a social structure dependent upon personal qualifications and individual ability.

Adaptation. The process in which a population or society alters its culture to better succeed in its total environment This increases an individual's ability to reproduce and survive.

Affinal links. Connections between kin groups established by marriage.

African American Vernacular English (AAVE). A form of English commonly spoken among rural and urban African Americans of working-class background.

Age grades. Categories of individuals of the same age that are recognized by being given a name and that crosscut an entire society.

Age sets. A group of individuals of the same age that moves as a unit through successive age grades.

Alliance. A linkage between kin groups established through marriage for the mutual benefit of the two groups.

Ancestor-oriented group. A social unit that traces kin relationships back to a common ancestor.

Animism. A belief in the spiritual or noncorporeal counterparts of human beings.

Anthropological linguistics. The subdiscipline of cultural anthropology that specializes in the study of human languages.

Applied anthropology. The organized interaction between professional anthropologists and policy making bodies; the application of anthropology to the solution of human problems.

Arranged marriage. The process by which senior family members exercise a great degree of control over the choice of their children's spouses.

Ascribed status. An inherited position in the social structure.

Authority. An institutionalized position of power.

Avunculocal residence. A form of postmarital residence in which the bride goes to live with her husband after he has moved to live with his mother's brother.

Balanced reciprocity. An exchange of goods of nearly equal value, with a clear obligation to return them within a specified time limit.

Band organization. A type of social group with a fixed membership that comes together annually for a period to carry out joint ritual and economic activities.

GLOSSARY

Barter. An immediate exchange of unlike objects, which may involve bargaining.

Big Man structure. An achieved position of leadership in which the group is defined as the Big Man and his followers.

Bilateral cross cousins. Cross cousins through both the mother's and father's side.

Bilateral societies. Societies with kindreds but without unilineal descent groups.

Bilocal residence. A form of postmarital residence in which husband and wife alternate between living with the husband's relatives for a period of time and then with the wife's relatives.

Black English Vernacular (BEV). See African American Vernacular English.

Boundary maintenance mechanisms. The ways in which a social group maintains its individual identity by separating itself from the dominant society.

Bride service. A custom whereby the groom works for the bride's family before marriage.

Bridewealth payments. Payments made by the groom's family to the family of the bride.

Capital. Productive resources that are used with the primary goal of increasing their owner's financial wealth.

Capitalism. An economic system in which people work for wages, land and capital goods are privately owned, and capital is invested for individual profit.

Caste system. Grouping of economically specialized, hierarchically organized, endogamous social units.

Chiefdom. A type of political organization in which fixed positions of centralized leadership are present along with a method for succession to those positions.

Clan. A social group based on common descent of over ten generations.

Clan totem. An animal from which members of a clan believe themselves descended and with whom they have a special relationship that may prohibit the eating of that animal.

Class system. A form of social stratification in which the different strata form a continuum and in which social mobility is possible.

Collateral relative. A relative not in the direct line of descent.

Community. A naturally bounded social unit.

Components. The criteria used to characterize and differentiate any kind of category.

Composite (or compound) family. An aggregate of nuclear families linked by a common spouse.

Conflict theory. A theory of social stratification that holds that the natural condition of society is constant change and conflict. The inequality in systems of social stratification is considered evidence of this conflict.

Corporate descent group. A social group based upon common descent that owns property in common and extends beyond the lifetime of any one individual.

Cosmology. A system of beliefs that deals with fundamental questions in the cosmic and social order.

Cross cousins. Children of one's mother's brother or one's father's sister.

Cultural anthropology. The study of human behavior that is learned rather than genetically transmitted, and that is typical of a particular human group.

Cultural relativism. The emphasis on the unique aspects of each culture, without judgments or categories based on our culture.

Cultural rules. Internalized rules of behavior covering all aspects of life.

Culture. The way of life of a people, including their behavior, the things they make, and their ideas.

Descent. The culturally established affiliation between a child and one or both parents.

Developing world. The approximately 110 nations with per capita GNP less than $10,000 per year.

Dialects. Variations within a single language between one speech community and another.

Diffusion. The process by means of which a culture trait that originates in one society spreads to another.

Direct reciprocal exchange. A continuing exchange of like for like between two parties.

Distribution. The manner in which products circulatethrough a society.

Double descent. The presence of matrilineal and patrilineal descent rules in a single society.

Dowry goods. that are given by the bride's family to the groom's family at marriage.

Economic system. The norms governing production, distribution, and consumption of goods and services within a society.

Egalitarian society. A society in which no individual or group has more privileged access to resources, power, or prestige than any other.

Ego. The kinship status from which a kinship diagram is constructed.

Ego-oriented group. A kinship unit defined in terms of a particular individual.

Emic (perspective). A form of analysis that uses concepts, categories, and distinctions that are meaningful to participants in a culture.

Enculturation. The process by which culture is learned and acquired by particular individuals. How young children learn to become productive adults within their society.

Endogamy. A rule requiring group members to marry within their own group.

Ethnic groups. Distinctive groups within a state who preserve cultural items from their past.

Ethnic identity. The subjective experience of oneself as a member of an ethnic group.

Ethnocentrism. The idea that what is present in your own culture represents the natural and best way to do things.

Etic (perspective). A form of analysis using concepts, categories, and rules derived from science; an outsider's perspective, which may not be meaningful to native participants in a culture.

Exogamy. A rule requiring group members to marry outside their own social group.

Extended family. Several related nuclear families living together in a single household.

Fieldwork. The firsthand, systematic exploration of a society. It involves living with a group of people and participating in and observing their behavior.

Fourth World peoples. Oppressed tribal peoples living in Third World nations.

Fraternal polyandry. A form of marriage in which a woman is simultaneously married to several brothers.

Function. The way a particular unit or structure operates and what it does.

Functionalism. The anthropological theory that specific cultural institutions function to support the structure of society or serve the needs of individuals in society.

Gender. The social classification of masculine and feminine.

Government. The process by which those in office make and implement decisions on behalf of an entire group in order to carry out commonly held goals.

Grammar. The complete description of a language, including phonology, morphology, and syntax.

Holistic/holism. The philosophical proposition that the whole is greater than the sum of its parts.

GLOSSARY

Horticulture. A form of cultivation in which crops are grown in gardens without the use of a plow.

Human Relations Area File. An ethnographic data base including cultural descriptions of over 300 cultures.

Hunting and gathering. A food-getting strategy that does not involve food production or domestication of animals (also called foraging).

Industrialization. The process of the mechanization of production.

Incest taboo. Prohibition on sexual relations between certain categories of close relatives.

Influence. The ability to persuade others to follow one's lead when one lacks the authority to command them.

Informant. A person particularly knowledgeable about his or her own culture who is a major source of the anthropologist's information.

Initiation rite. A ritual that marks the passage from childhood to adult status.

Innovation. The process of bringing about cultural change through the recombination of existing ideas into creative new forms.

Invention. New combinations of existing cultural elements.

Joint family. A type of extended family in which married brothers and their families remain together after the death of their parents.

Joint stock company. A firm that is managed by a centralized board of directors but owned by shareholders. A joint stock company has shares that may be transferred from own owner to another. It differs from a modern corporation because a joint stock company's shareholders are directly responsible for the firm's debts.

Kindred. A kin group oriented in terms of a particular individual.

Kinship terminology. A set of terms used to refer to relatives.

Law. Social norms whose neglect or violation is regularly met by the application of force by those in a society who have the socially recognized authority to do so.

Levirate. A rule whereby the widow of a deceased man must marry his brother.

Lineages. Unilineal descent groups in which descent is demonstrated.

Lineal relative. A relative in the direct line of descent.

Linguistics. A field of cultural anthropology that specializes in the study of human languages.

Marriage. The customs, rules, and obligations that establish a special relationship between a sexually cohabitating adult male and female, between them and any children they produce, and between the kin of the bride and groom.

Matrilineal rule of descent. A rule stating that a child belongs to his or her mother's group.

Matrilocal residence rule. System under which a husband lives with his wife's family after marriage.

Metaphor. An analytical concept in which one idea stands for another because of some similarity they are seen to share.

Moieties. A grouping based upon descent in which the entire society is divided into two halves.

Monogamy. Marriage with only one spouse at a time.

Morpheme. The smallest unit of language conveying meaning.

Myth. A sacred narrative recounting the creation of the universe or historical events.

Nation. A sovereign political state with a single national culture.

Nation-state. See *nation*.

Native anthropologist. An anthropologist who does fieldwork in his or her own culture.

Nativistic movements. Religious cults that develop in periods of drastic cultural change and synthesize traditional cultural elements with newly introduced ones.

Negative reciprocity. Exchange conducted for the purpose of material advantage and the desire to get something for nothing.

Neolocal residence. A rule of postmarital residence in which the newly married couple forms an independent household.

Nomadic pastoralists. Societies completely, or almost completely, dependent upon herds of domesticated animals.

Nomadism. The constant mobility of human groups in pursuit of food (as in foraging) or a form of pastoralism in which the whole social group (men, women, children, and animals) moves in search of pasture.

Norm. An ideal cultural pattern that influences behavior in a particular society.

Nuclear family. A family consisting of husband, wife, and their unmarried children.

Office. A recognized political position.

Parallel cousins. The children of two brothers or of two sisters.

Participant observation. The anthropological method of collecting data by living with another people, learning their language, and understanding their culture.

Pastoralism. A food-getting strategy that depends on the care of domesticated herd animals. It occurs in areas where large human populations cannot be supported through agriculture.

Patrilineal rule of descent. A rule stating that a child belongs to his or her father's group.

Patrilocal residence rule. System under which a bride lives with her husband's family after marriage.

Peasants. Food-producing populations that are incorporated politically, economically, and culturally into nation states.

Phratry. A unilineal descent group composed of a number of clans whose members feel themselves to be closely related.

Political economy. The interpretation of politics and economy.

Politics. The competition for political positions for power.

Polyandry. Marriage in which one woman has several husbands at one time.

Polygamy. Marriage with plural spouses, either husbands or wives.

Polygyny. Marriage in which one man has several wives at one time.

Postmarital residence rule. A rule that states where a couple should live after marriage.

Potlatch. A large-scale ceremonial distribution of goods found among the indigenous peoples of the Northwest Coast of North America.

Power. The ability to command others to do certain things and get compliance from them.

Primogeniture. A rule of inheritance of property or office by the firstborn child.

Production. The process whereby a society uses the tools and energy sources at its disposal and its own people's labor to create the goods necessary for supplying itself.

Proto-language ancestral. Form of a language arrived at by reconstruction.

Psychological anthropology. A theoretical perspective that focuses on culture as the principal force in shaping the typical personality of a society as well as on the role of personality in the maintainance of cultural institutions.

GLOSSARY

Religion. The process among members of a society that helps to order their society and provides them with meaning, unity, peace of mind, and the degree of control over events they believe is possible.

Rites of passage. Communal rituals held to mark changes in status as individuals progress through the life cycle.

Serial monogamy. The practice of marrying a series of spouses, one after the other.

Sex. The biological difference between male and female.

Shaman. A ritual specialist whose primary function is to cure illness.

Shifting cultivation. A type of horticulture in which new gardens are made every few years, when the soil is exhausted.

Social role. The behavior associated with a particular social status in a society.

Social status. The position an individual occupies in a society.

Social structure. The pattern of social relationships that characterize a society.

Society. A social grouping characterizing humans and other social animals, differentiated by age and sex.

Sociolinguistics. The study of that aspect of language which deals with status and class differences.

Sorcery. The learned practice of evil magic.

Sororate. The custom whereby a widower marries his deceased wife's sister.

State. A hierarchical, centralized form of political organization in which a central government had the legal monopoly over the use of force.

Status. A social position within a social structure; a role is the behavioral norms associated with a social status.

Stipulated descent. A social unit, such as a clan, in which all members consider themselves to be related though they cannot actually trace the geneological relationship.

Stratified society. A society with formal, permanent social and economic inequality in which some people are denied access to basic resources.

Structure. A description of parts or elements in relationship to one another.

Subcultural variation. Cultural differences between communities within a single society.

Swidden. See *shifting cultivation*.

Technology. That part of culture by means of which people directly exploit their environment.

Total social phenomena. Large-scale rituals that integrate all aspects of society—economic, political, kinship, religion, art, etc.

Tribe. A unit used by colonial powers to refer to groups with a common language and culture.

Unilineal descent group. A kin group, such as a clan, in which membership is based on either matrilineal or patrilineal descent.

Vision quest. The search for a protective supernatural spirit through starvation and deprivation.

Wealth. The accumulation of material resources or access to the means of producing these resources.

Wiccan. A member of a new religion that claims descent from pre-Christian Europe and the Middle East.

Witchcraft. A form of magic practiced by individuals born with this ability.

Zietgeist. Spirit of the times; what it is that a society holds as important during a given period of time.